7.92

D0396874

DISCARD

CFD 663 (48)

Italian Hours

Henry James

Italian Hours

Edited by
John Auchard

The Pennsylvania State University Press
University Park, Pennsylvania

This publication has been supported by the National Endowment for the Humanities, a federal agency which supports the study of such fields as history, philosophy, literature, and languages.

Library of Congress Cataloging-in-Publication Data

James, Henry, 1843–1916.
   Italian hours : Henry James ; edited by John Auchard.

       p.   cm.
   Includes bibliographical references and index.
   ISBN 0-271-00726-5 (alk. paper)
   1. Italy—Description and travel—1861–1900.   2. James, Henry,
1843–1916—Journeys—Italy.   3. Authors, American—19th century
—Journeys—Italy.   I. Auchard, John.   II. Title.
DG427.J35 1991
914.504'84—dc20   90-43218
                                                                   CIP

It is the policy of The Pennsylvania State University Press to use acid-free paper for the first printing of all clothbound books. Publications on uncoated stock satisfy the minimum requirements of American National Standard for Information Sciences—Permanence of Paper for Printed Library Materials, ANSI Z39.48–1984. ∞

Contents

———

Acknowledgments   vii

Introduction   ix

Suggestions for Further Reading   xxxi

A Note on the Text   xxxiii

Italian Hours:

New York and Boston: Houghton Mifflin Company, 1909   1

Appendix I: Textual Variants   321

Appendix II: Henry James on Italian Travel Books
(Reviews of W. D. Howells, Hippolyte Taine, Nathaniel
Hawthorne, Auguste Laugel, and Augustus J. C.
Hare)   325

General Bibliography   345

Bibliography of Period Photography   355

Index   359

Acknowledgments

═══

As I left to take a post as a Fulbright Lecturer in American Literature at the Università degli Studi di Milano, Charles Caramello, a fellow Jamesian and my colleague at the University of Maryland, suggested that I pack my dog-eared copy of *Italian Hours* and see if I could do something with it. I am in his debt for the all-important *donnée* of a project that I regret to see end. Also at Maryland, I wish to thank Elizabeth Loizeaux and Deirdre David for comments on some problems in the text. The University of Maryland Graduate Research Board provided support that allowed me to complete this edition. In Washington, considerable assistance was offered by Luciana Iacono, Sylvie Bouvier, Glenn Moumau, Ruth Stolk, and Karen Faul. Bonney MacDonald shared warm interest, as did Alfred Bendixen. Steven Auchard really helped out in a pinch, as did Anne Hall and Phil Read.

Professor Robert Gale, one of the first Italian Fulbrights and a Jamesian who has kept the sacred flame for the Italy for over thirty years, reviewed this edition with astonishing care, expertise, and generosity. No one could possibly have given my work more encouragement or a more helpful reading. I also sincerely thank Professor Leon Edel for reading the manuscript of this edition and for providing many helpful suggestions. Philip Winsor and Cherene Holland at Penn State have been ideal editors, and Keith Monley an outstanding proofreader.

Henry James called Milan the last of the prose cities, if not the first of the poetic. I griped over this remark for some time, but now I suspect that he just did not meet the kind of people I met there. At the University of Milan, I thank Mario Corona, Mario Maffi, Roberta Mazzanti, Caroline Patey, and Margaret Rose, who were the finest colleagues. John and Christine Keller, of USIS Milan, provided support at every stage of my work. And I would particularly like to thank Margherita Uras and Margherita De Amici of the USIS Library. The staffs of the Biblioteca Sormani in Milan and especially of the Bibliotheca Hertziana in Rome offered great assistance. Margherita Rossi gave sound advice on *cose romane*. Alessandra Angelini helped discover the *pino* at Monte Mario and much more. At the Vatican, David Gibson took on this project as if it were his own, and he almost never complained. Also at the Vatican I would like to thank Veronica Scarisbrick; and in London, the Contessa Alessandra Rabossi-Motta Freeman, Rob Freeman, and particularly Keton Motta-Freeman, who has an auspicious birthday. Finally, and not least by any means, deep thanks to Dorotea Gastone— of Naples and forgotten Foligno—who missed trains but almost nothing else.

A few hours before I began to write these acknowledgments, I received news of the death of Lewis Leary, my distinguished colleague and a friend of many years. It was said of Henry Fielding that it was a pity he could not live forever: he was so formed for happiness. I feel that way about Lewis. Let me persist in thanking him, and as always in thanking Mary Warren Leary, for their spirit, for their wit, for knowing what is important, and for letting me in on the secret.

Introduction

From midday to dusk I have been roaming the streets. Que vous
en dirai-je? *At last—for the first time—I live! It beats everything:
it leaves the Rome of your fancy—your education—nowhere. It
makes Venice—Florence—Oxford—London—seem like little cities
of pasteboard. I went reeling and moaning thro' the streets, in a
fever of enjoyment.*
—Letter to William James, 1869

*But the abatements and changes and modernisms and vulgarities, the
crowd and the struggle and the frustration (of real communion with
what one wanted) are quite dreadful—and I really quite revel in the
thought that I shall never come to Italy at all* again.
—Letter to William "Billy" James, Jr., 1907

*The charm was, as always in Italy, in the tone and the air and the
happy hazard of things, which made any positive pretension or
claimed importance a comparatively trifling question. We slid, in the
steep little place, more or less down hill. . . . We stayed no long time,
and "went to see" nothing; yet we communicated to intensity, we lay
at our ease in the bosom of the past, we practised intimacy, in short,
an intimacy so much greater than the mere accidental and ostensible:
the difficulty for the right and grateful expression of which makes the
old, the familiar tax on the luxury of loving Italy.*
—Conclusion of Italian Hours, 1909

Henry James first arrived in Italy at a critical moment, when for dramatic
political and social reasons the country was rapidly changing. Although over
the next forty years the promise of Italy would remain for him a constant
force, subtle and occasionally violent changes would sometimes cloud
James's impressions and leave him uneasy concerning what might lie ahead.
Italian Hours is unquestionably a celebration, but part of the volume's
interest derives from the ambiguity of the tribute, from the ebb and flow of
approval and disgust concerning the transformations in progress. In a sense,
the loosely shaped *Italian Hours* is unified by an awareness of how inexorably Italy is sliding into the twentieth century. But aside from providing
James's complex reaction to major social and cultural evolutions, *Italian*

Hours serves as a primary document of what, to one highly acute observer, Italy *was* from 1870 to 1908. For Henry James, Italy provided a more complex and sometimes more surprising metaphor than that which is generally understood by the modern-day traveler and reader.

To begin with, a title suggesting "Italian hours" provides a more complex orientation than at first might be expected. There is a long tradition of various "hours," the matin and vesper prayers of old Catholic ritual, the secular or sacred vignettes of fourteenth- and fifteenth-century illuminated manuscripts, and even James's own *English Hours* of 1905. And yet the experienced nineteenth-century traveler would have associated this title with at least one more persistent, and often troubling, tradition.

As early as 1815, guidebooks to Italy (see Coxe, *Picture of Italy,* xxxv–xxxvi) supplied a "Table of Italian Hours" for those who normally would be disoriented by the fact that the "manner of reckoning time in some parts of Italy is peculiar to.themselves." Italy was to be unified by 1870, but the fierce independence and chauvinism of its various regions did not die easily, and it took many years before standard Greenwich mean time, proposed in 1884, was widely adopted. Throughout most of the nineteenth century, and even into the twentieth, time in Italy was considered a local phenomenon, varying approximately four minutes for every degree of longitude. In Turin, Parma, and Florence, the hour was calculated as it was in much of Europe, but the tables show that noon, as defined in Milan, Venice, Genoa, Florence, Rome, and Naples, arrived at many different moments, up to sixteen minutes apart in winter and fourteen minutes apart in summer. Without the "Table of Italian Hours," the punctual foreigner might be stunned by a train's apparently early departure from a Roman or Neapolitan railroad station.

The title "Italian Hours" provides a broad context for consideration—slightly sacred, partly artistic and impressionistic, and partly, and literally, anachronistic—made especially uneasy by the relentless and erratic ticking off of hours and years.[1] The suggestion of confounded time and of resolute temporal progression may help explain a troublesome feature of these articles, the fact that when they were collated in the 1909 first edition they were arranged without respect to the chronology of their original publication. Perhaps James intended to communicate a sense of time out of joint, and therefore the book begins in the Venice in 1882, moves to 1892, back to 1872, up to 1899, and so on throughout. The effect allows some correlative

---

1. On the cloth cover of the 1909 English edition of *Italian Hours* there is a gold medallion and in that medallion there is an hourglass; the sand falling through the waist of the glass has passed the halfway point. (The cover of the American edition, as beautifully produced as that of the English edition, provides an entirely different decoration; the words "Italian Hours" are reproduced in simulation of cosmati mosaic work.)

of the traveler's experience in Italy, lost in the fourteenth century, thrust into the twentieth upon entering the piazza, allowed to reclaim some nostalgia while walking down an avenue of ilexes, but increasingly disoriented along the way.

The modern reader should recall how different the Italy of 1869 was from that of 1872—after the success of the Risorgimento and the unification of the various regions of the peninsula under one government, and, more or less, under one tongue. Since the publication of *Italian Hours* the country has continued to experience changes that probably would have shocked the nineteenth century: artistic reputations have soared and plummeted, the tourist has conquered everywhere, the turbulent ceiling of the Sistine Chapel has been taken out of the shadows and discovered to be pastel, decaying towns have been refurbished as medieval showplaces hosting jazz festivals, the Italians have grown rich and their hotels very expensive, and generally the country has made a very complacent peace with the modern world. *Italian Hours* shows a lost face of Italy, as well as a rare view of the singular privilege of the fortunate, and wary, nineteenth-century English or American traveler who came to Europe expecting, knowing, and fearing different things.

The twentieth-century high season, for example, was soon to refer to another world, and not simply because travel is now a far more catholic privilege. Modern readers of *Italian Hours* learn in "The After-Season in Rome" that the foreigners begin to *depart* at the end of May: "The place has passed so completely for the winter months into the hands of the barbarians that that estimable character the passionate pilgrim finds it constantly harder to keep his passion clear." An occasional hardy northern European on the Grand Tour stayed on into early summer, but few travelers remained in Italy in July and August. Part of the metamorphosis of the twentieth-century tourist industry—and the vulgarization that, in the Venice essays, James begins to bemoan—derives from realities of middle-class holidays and waves of college students on long vacations. But an equally important revolution was scientific.

In "Daisy Miller" it is acknowledged that "if nocturnal meditations on the Colosseum are recommended by the poets, they are deprecated by the doctors. The historic atmosphere was there, certainly; but the historic atmosphere, scientifically considered, was no better than a villainous miasma."[2] Even as late as 1913, Norman Douglas spoke of the Roman air as "the withering blast whose hot and clammy touch hastens death and putrefaction."[3] The amorphous threat of death in Venice, Rome, Siena, Naples, Ravenna, on Ischia, or in the Maremma, because of something vague and

2. *Complete Tales,* IV, 201.
3. Douglas, *South Wind,* 3.

bad in the air, was a suggestive metaphor for many writers, but it was also a genuine danger that was never completely forgotten by the tourist. "The Roman air," writes James in 1873, "however, is not a tonic medicine, and it seldom suffers exercise to be all exhilarating. It has always seemed to me indeed part of the charm of the latter that your keenest consciousness is haunted with a vague languor. Occasionally when the sirocco blows that sensation becomes strange and exquisite. . . . This quality in the Roman element may now and then 'relax' you almost to ecstasy; but a season of sirocco would be an overdose of morbid pleasure."

By the turn of the century researchers understood that malaria was caused not by a romantically evil African wind, but by the anopheles mosquito. Disinfectants, drainage, and bottles of quinine water transfigured the disease-ridden countryside and eventually gave three extra months to all the passionate pilgrims. Yet throughout these essays there are still the numerous aside references to malaria, swamps, pestilence, disease, and ague.

Fully aware of the menace of summer, tourists generally experienced Italy in autumn, winter, and early spring, and even then they spent much time indoors, but June, July, and August were forbidden lands. Therefore, the lush landscape under a blinding sun—the particularly sensuous Italy that today many of us know best—was not generally known to these Americans and these British. Just before World War I, seduction and death do not come to Gustav von Aschenbach in August. He is considered mad to stay on as long as he does, and he dies in mid-June. During the 1870s Daisy Miller longs to see the Colosseum at midnight, just as the season begins to grow dangerous, and, virtually as predicted, she dies—in April. All this has changed, and with it so has the metaphor of Italy. Today the people of Lombardia and the Veneto seem to use the delicious Arabic word *scirocco* less frequently when they speak of the pernicious air, but they do rather often talk of the *föhn,* a warm, dry Teutonic wind that makes its way over the Alps in late winter to blanket Lombardia and the Po valley. The Germanic *föhn,* unromantically enough, is what Italians also call an electric hair-dryer.

If the Italy of *Italian Hours* is rarely smoldering or sensuous, the explanation may in part derive from the perspective of an idiosyncratic author, but also that fact reflects the face of the land the vast majority of nineteenth-century tourists knew best. It is regrettable that James never fulfilled an early wish to tour Sicily, as Goethe ("To have seen Italy without having seen Sicily is not to have seen Italy at all, for Sicily is the clue to everything")[4] had done before him. If the youthful Henry James felt an outsider to the turbulence of the Lenten carnival, one wonders what the deep south, the more intensely Mediterranean land, would have communicated to him—during almost any

4. Goethe, *Italian Journey,* 240.

season. Until the late essays written after 1900, nothing in *Italian Hours* vibrates with *meridionale* energy, but neither does much else in any nineteenth-century English or American literature. Although James would complain that Hawthorne's notebooks showed the great novelist to be "excessively detached" from Italy, "touching it throughout mistrustfully, shrinkingly,"[5] among all nineteenth-century American tales perhaps only "Rappaccini's Daughter" approaches the force of the particularly pungent and overripe landscape. Nonetheless, not even mysterious Hawthorne comprehends the magnificently disturbing sensuality of Prince Fabrizio Salinas's garden in di Lampedusa's masterpiece, *The Leopard*.

> It was a garden for the blind: a constant offense to the eyes, a pleasure strong if somewhat crude to the nose. The Paul Neyron roses, whose cuttings he had himself bought in Paris, had degenerated; first stimulated and then enfeebled by the strong if languid pull of Sicilian earth, burned by apocalyptic Julys, they had changed into things like flesh-colored cabbages, obscene and distilling a dense, almost indecent, scent which no French horticulturist would have dared hope for. The prince put one under his nose and seemed to be sniffing the thigh of a dancer from the Opera.[6]

Despite the assertion of many clichés concerning Henry James, he was not immune to the force of passion. In a 1904 review of Gabriele D'Annunzio, he warily but enthusiastically discusses the eroticism of *The Triumph of Death* and recalls the tremendous final moment when "the delirious protagonist beguiles his vaguely but not fully suspicious companion into coming out with him toward the edge of a dizzy place over the sea, where he suddenly grasps her for her doom and the sense of his awful intention, flashing a light back as into their monstrous past, makes her shriek for her life. She dodges him at the first betrayal, panting and trembling." In *Italian Hours* D'Annunzio is mentioned in relation to a particularly sensual Italian landscape, and, in the review, his work is called "a queer high-flavoured fruit from overseas, grown under another sun than ours, passed round and solemnly partaken of at banquets organised to try it, but not found on the whole really to agree with us, not proving thoroughly digestible. It brought with it no repose, brought with it only agitation."[7] In James's greatest fiction the Italian meta-

5. "Review of *Passages from the French and Italian Note-Books of Nathaniel Hawthorne*," reprinted in *Literary Criticism: Essays on Literature*, 309.

6. di Lampedusa, *The Leopard*, 20–21.

7. "Review of Gabriele D'Annunzio, *The Triumph of Death, The Virgins of the Rocks, The Flame of Life*, and *Francesca da Rimini*," reprinted in *Literary Criticism: French Writers*, 907–43.

phor often retains a fundamentally indoor character; Tita Bordereau, Gilbert Osmond, and Milly Theale hardly ever leave their various palazzi. But late in his life, in the final travel essays and the reviews after 1900, the energy of that metaphor finds less claustrophobic expression.

When considering *Italian Hours* against a background of a century of such changes, it is important to remember that the modern tourist views a remarkably different country and yet is offered a better—and different—consideration of many things. For one, lighting has been improved dramatically. For another, Victorian prudery has diminished. Julian Klaczko's 1903 *Rome and the Renaissance* provides photographs of both Michelangelo's David and the Apollo Belvedere—with the fig leaves one seems to remember from grammar-school days.[8] The photographs look obscene. And restoration has done more than anything else to revitalize works of art and centers of art, and at the same time to annihilate the pervasive sense of romantic decay that James observes all up and down the Italian peninsula. He saw and admired Siena "cracking, peeling, fading, crumbling, rotting . . . battered and befouled," an accumulation of "shabbiness upon shabbiness"; except for an occasional back street, the modern tourist's impression is that of a well-preserved and rather wealthy town. As an aside it is interesting to note that James considered the San Benedetto frescoes at the nearby Monastero di Monte Oliveto Maggiore to be in "admirable condition," when modern estimates frequently note the poor preservation of the surfaces. Either the past century has been particularly hard on the works by Signorelli—and there is no evidence of especially rapid deterioration—or, in 1873, James's standard of admirable preservation was considerably lower than that of the modern tourist accustomed to the restorer's intervening hand—an intervention that James suspected would obliterate "the work of the quiet centuries."

All the cities have changed, and yet the experience of Rome has undergone the greatest transformation over the past 120 years. Today, at times and at least from a distance, it appears more imperial than it has at any time since the age of Constantine—with the great monuments of the Forum more completely excavated, with the Colosseum less entwined with capricious weeds, with the postfascist Via della Conciliazione slicing a bombastic boulevard up to San Pietro, and with the immense monument to Vittorio Emanuele II looming heartlessly above everything. It is startling to learn that the magnificent Piazza Navona was an unpaved, dirt-filled square until the mid-nineteenth century, and amazing to read, in Alberto Moravia's early tales, that only forty years ago apartments that faced onto it were sometimes very cheap. But the metamorphosis that came to Rome in the momentous year of

8. Klaczko, *Rome and the Renaissance: The Pontificate of Julius II*, 79, 89.

1870—the year after James's first visit to the city—must be singled out. It was almost as great as anything that Gibbon had recorded.

The modern tourist scarcely can imagine the social world that welcomed the privileged nineteenth-century sojourner in Rome. Leon Edel's five-volume biography provides a complete record of the magnificent expatriate homes that James knew in almost every Italian city—the rented, or bought-up, palazzi and villas of Isabella Stewart Gardner, F. Marion Crawford, Axel Munthe, Constance Fenimore Woolson, of the Bronsons, the Curtises, the Terrys, the Storys, the Bootts, and many others. Venice, Rome, Naples, Capri, Siena, Milan, and Florence continue to offer splendid treasures, but as with much of the rest of Europe, they now provide far more public beneficence—more museums and admission fees—than the daily domestic splendor and charm that was known to our fortunate ancestors.

Readers of Stendhal's *The Charterhouse of Parma* follow the passionate Duchessa Sanseverina through fearful consideration of refuge in many cities: Como, Grianta, Piacenza, Florence, Bologna, Milan, and ultimately the promise of happiness in distant Naples. Eventually she retires to Vignano, in the Austrian states, where she holds her court in self-imposed exile. In France, the Abbé Prévost's Manon Lescaut would come to Amien to become a nun, but eventually all that changes, and of course, inevitably, she must reach Paris. It may seem strange that in the early years of nineteenth-century Italy the heroine of Stendhal's narrative—alluded to in *Italian Hours* as "one of the novels of 'immoral' tendency"—hardly even mentions Rome, much less seriously considers it as a possible place to live. Rome, before it fell to the Italian troops on 20 September 1870, remained a world apart for many people. It belonged to the pope, and, as capital of the Papal States, it continued the tradition of offering tremendous ecclesiastical grandeur and rigid moral pressure, with little emphasis on the rococo pursuit of pleasure that was the mark, to Stendhal and to others, of the brilliant café and court societies of Milan or Naples.

When in 1873 James went to Rome for a second time, the pope was already held virtual captive in his palace. He would remain so until the Lateran Pacts of 1929 resolved the conflict with the Republic of Italy, established his official status and that of Vatican City, and thereby allowed him, for the first time in almost sixty years, freely to leave the walls of his magnificent prison. The secularization of Rome dates from 1870, and the changes, many of which are recorded here by James, were tremendous. The carnival degenerated, the state took over ecclesiastical properties, monuments began to be neglected, the moral stance of the city began to shift, commercialism began to move in, villas suddenly were sold off, and, of course, a new kind of liberty was felt in the air. For the first time in centuries, or so it seemed, Rome was heaving on its foundations and stretching its limbs, and like many others, at first James seemed eager for the change. In 1869 he had written to Alice about his first wary sight of Pius IX.

> I made no attempt to enter the church: but I saw tolerably well the arrival of the cardinals and ambassadors etc and finally of the Grand Llama in person. . . . When you have seen that flaccid old woman waving his ridiculous fingers over the prostrate multitude and have duly felt the picturesqueness of the scene—and then turned away sickened by its absolute *obscenity*—you may climb the steps of the Capitol and contemplate the equestrian statue of Marcus Aurelius. . . . As you revert to that poor sexless old Pope enthroned upon his cushion—and then glance at those imperial legs swinging in their immortal bronze, you cry out that here at least was a *man!*[9]

Over the next forty years James's sympathies would evolve, as would his nostalgia for papal Rome. Already in 1873 the first Roman articles refer back to this same pope with a tender diminutive, "papalino," and the sarcasm aimed at the Church begins to subside. Occasionally a moderate discourse on Catholicism, motivated by "sentimental allowances," provides a sense of genuine yearning for the abandoned religious world—if not so surely for religion. James eventually finds himself overwhelmed by the splendor of Santa Maria Maggiore: "I sat for half an hour on the edge of the base of one of the marble columns of the beautiful nave and enjoyed a perfect revel of—what shall I call it?—taste, intelligence, fancy, perceptive emotion?" In 1907 a "musing mature visitor" finds that "the current Rome affects him as a world governed by new conditions altogether and ruefully pleading that sorry fact in the ear of the antique wanderer wherever he may yet mournfully turn for some re-capture of what he misses"; so he journeys as a pilgrim to Monte Cassino and Subiaco, "the miraculous home of St. Benedict," with Alphonse Dantier's *Monastères Bénédictins d'Italie* in hand. In 1909 he revised all the early essays and made numerous subtle changes, but when recalling a singularly fine Roman spring day, he added one completely new line that had nothing to do with his early impressions: "It's almost as if the old all-papal paradise had come back."[10]

They still tell the tourist, "Roma, non basta una vita" (one life is not enough for her), and it is still true. Nonetheless, for profound social reasons, as well as for more pedestrian ones, that insufficient life has been dramatically different for each generation of travelers going at least as far back as

9. *Letters*, I, 164, 165.
10. See A Note on the Text for further indications of differences among the various printings of the essays in *Italian Hours*.

Montaigne. In 1873 James reports that one may visit a different villa for every day in the week, and he offers an impressive roll call of more than seven: "The Doria, the Ludovisi, the Medici, the Albani, the Wolkonski, the Chigi, the Mellini, the Massimo." Today none offers general access to the tourist. At the Villa Doria Pamphili, the park has recently been reopened to the public after having been closed for decades, but entrance to its main house, the Casino di Allegrezza, at present a state property and used for state functions, is allowed only after written application and for impressive reasons. At the end of the nineteenth century the Villa Ludovisi ("There is nothing so blissfully *right* in Rome") was sold to investors by the Principe Boncompagni and was cut up into building lots; nothing remains of it but one structure, the Casino dell'Aurora—closed to the public and oddly isolated in its high-walled yard amidst blocks of twentieth-century urban development. At the Villa Medici the French Academy now denies public access to all rooms but the exhibit gallery, and, except for two hours on Wednesday mornings, the surrounding park also remains closed. The Albani (now the Villa Torlonia) admits scholars by previous written permission. The British Embassy at the Wolkonski fears the threat of terrorism and receives only official visitors. (The French Embassy at the Palazzo Farnese has recently made a similar decision to end its exceedingly slim tradition of allowing tourist access to its courtyard, for two hours only, on the first Sunday of each month.) The Villa Chigi, closed and abandoned for decades, emptied of furniture, its gardens grown wild, and generally in decrepit condition, was bought up by land developers in 1987. The Villa Mellini, brutally disfigured by observation domes in 1938, is now an astronomical observatory and does not admit the public. The Villa Massimo Rignano, sold to speculators in 1888, was completely demolished in 1923.

If Rome's transformation was sudden and drastic for the priest, for the citizen, and for the tourist, Venice's metaphor knew a far more gradual transmutation. It was the city's peculiar decline that was to preoccupy many imaginations, although its physical decay was not particularly dramatic. Little there so sadly struck the note of oblivion as did the Florentine houses James saw backing onto the Arno: "Anything more battered and befouled, more cracked and disjointed, dirtier, drearier, poorer, it would be impossible to conceive. They look as if fifty years ago the liquid mud had risen over their chimneys and then subsided again and left them coated for ever with its unsightly slime." Florence had not known preeminence since the Renaissance, but its physical decline, infinitely more dreary than that of Venice, rarely worked as a metaphor and rarely called up many mournful associations. Over the centuries, time and the Florentine river had caused as much pervasive destruction as had the Venetian lagoon, but tradition has been that death rarely comes, to foreigners at least, in Florence. The reason was partly because travelers to Florence anticipated art, much of it religious art, and some salon society. Throughout the eighteenth century, however, visitors to Venice had expected a more energetic program, one of beauty, of vibrant pleasure, and of an intense carnival, which, as James reports from the Président de Brosses, lasted six months.

Nowhere better than in the exceedingly charming social paintings of Pietro Longhi, works filled with loveliness, with bursts of irony and gaiety, and with delightful animals, is the vitality of eighteenth-century Venice better expressed. In James's time the city still dimly remembered its joyful golden age—and was beginning to bemoan its loss. If in the corner of an occasional Longhi a shadow is cast by a shocking black oval mask, the sinister masker has little to do with anything moribund, but merely the sinful. Death in Venice may seem an immemorial cliché to the twentieth century, but the decay of the city—physical, artistic, spiritual, political, and particularly social—was to the nineteenth-century traveler a recent phenomenon. Certainly Venice offered nothing like the threat, in Melville's words, of "Rome's accursed Campagna." The decline may be dated from the abdication of the last Doge, the collapse into Austrian rule in 1797, and into the Napoleonic "Regno Italico" in 1805. By 1866, when Venice was annexed by the newly formed Kingdom of Italy, its days as a world power were over and, after a thousand years of growth and independence, it shifted toward eternity, linked itself to the mainland with the railroad from Mestre, and began to linger on as the expensive jewel of tourism that it remains today.

Wordsworth's 1805 "On the Extinction of the Venetian Republic"— "Venice, the eldest Child of Liberty / She was a maiden City, bright and free"—seems to be one of the earliest markers of the loss, but the poem is clearly more a dirge to liberty than to life. Although a genuine reconsideration began with Robert Browning, his "A Toccata of Galuppi's" calls up exquisite deathly inevitabilities more as the dominant fact of the human condition than as a feature of the idiosyncratic city of Saint Mark's. The *Italian Hours* essays, however, along with *The Aspern Papers* and *The Wings of the Dove,* did much to transform the tradition of a city which, before James, was not often seen as being particularly moribund. Other writers still managed to rejoice in the energy of the city.

"Read Théophile Gautier's *Italia,*" James wrote to his brother William in 1869,[11] and in his *Italian Hours* "Venice" of 1882 he reiterates that advice. No nineteenth-century travel writer wrote longer, more deeply felt, more allusive or suggestive Venetian essays than Gautier. In his 365-page reminiscences of a voyage in Italy, 232 pages are dedicated to Venice alone.

11. *Letters,* I, 141–42.

Gautier's treatment of the city was famous, and his influence may help explain why, although *Italian Hours* explores almost twenty cities, the Venice chapters take up one-fourth of the book's length. For Gautier, however, the dream city still brimmed with vitality, with the noise outside one's window. It is rare for him to break the song of celebration and upon occasion of bacchanalia; in an 1873 review James praised Gautier on Venice, reporting that his "unfaltering robustness of vision—of appetite, one may say—made him not only strong but enviable."[12] When for a single uncharacteristic page the French traveler describes a funeral barge and a specific death in Venice, he soon declares, "Let us leave these melancholy subjects here. The wake of the red bark is closed over: let us think no more about it. Let us forget as do the waves, which preserve no trace of anything; it is of life and not of death that we must dream."[13] A far more representative scene is when the gondoliers

> seated on a marble step or on the poop of their gondolas . . . eat shell-fish, drink Friulian wine, and sup gaily by the light of the stars and the little lamps at the street corners lighted in front of the niches of the Madonnas. Certain of their friends, voluptuous vagabonds who have church porticoes for alcoves and for mattresses the big flagstones warmed by the day's sun, come to join them and increase the tumult. Add to these some pretty servant-girls, taking advantage of the slumbers of their mistresses to go to meet some big fellow with bronzed skin, shaggy cap, and jacket of Persian cotton, dragging around on his breast more amulets than an American savage has of colored glass beads, and whose contralto voices, by turns shrill and deep, flow on in waves of inexhaustible chatter with that sonorousness peculiar to the languages of the South, and you have a very clear idea of the silence of Venice.[14]

James's appreciation of the city demonstrated little robustness but tremendous aesthetic allure. When he published his first Venetian essay (the third in the collection, but written in 1872), he felt that the "mere use of one's eyes in Venice is happiness enough."

> To be a young American painter unperplexed by the mocking, elusive soul of things and satisfied with their wholesome light-bathed surface

12. "Review of *Théatre de Théophile Gautier: Mystères, Comédies, et Ballets*," reprinted in *Literary Criticism: French Writers*, 374–75.

13. Gautier, *Journeys in Italy*, 165.

14. Ibid., 195.

and shape; keen of eye; fond of colour, of sea and sky and anything
that may chance between them; of old lace and old brocade and old
furniture (even when made to order); of time-mellowed harmonies
on nameless canvases and happy contours in cheap old engravings;
to spend one's mornings in still, productive analysis of the clustered
shadows of the Basilica . . . this, I consider, is to be as happy as is
consistent with the preservation of reason.

The intense visual celebration is broken only during the side trip to Torcello,
once the mother city of Venice, now "a mere mouldering vestige." By 1882
the impressions have changed; Venice resembles "a nervous woman . . .
always interesting, and almost always sad," but it is once again at Torcello
that the note of darkness is struck, where the cathedral has "been restored
and made cheerful, and the charm of the place, its strange and suggestive
desolation, has well-nigh departed." In the 1880s the old-world reserve was
fading and the jolt of tourism that James notes was well under way, but
famous deaths in Venice began to do much more to help influence the
metaphor of the city. In February 1883 the composer Richard Wagner died
at the Palazzo Vendramin, shortly after finishing the score of *Parsifal;* Robert Browning's end came at the Ca' Rezzonico, where he had been visiting
his son "Pen" in 1889. The image of Venice was recast during the next
several decades, by history as well as by literature. A shift of tone is evident
in James's 1892 essay: ". . . the essential present character of the most melancholy of cities resides simply in its being the most beautiful of tombs. Nowhere else has the past been laid to rest with such tenderness, such a sadness
of resignation and remembrance. Nowhere else is the present so alien, so
discontinuous, so like a crowd in a cemetery without garlands for the
graves."

 Among nineteenth-century writers James did much to darken and deepen
the peculiarly resilient beauty of Venice—"the whole scene profits by the
general law that renders decadence and ruin in Venice more brilliant than
any prosperity. Decay is in this extraordinary place golden in tint and misery
couleur de rose." By the time James wrote in 1899, Venice had lost some of
its enchantment as the gorgeous site of the expiration of poets. It had
become a place of particularly sinister death. On 24 January 1894, James's
friend Constance Fenimore Woolson leaped or fell to the pavement from an
upper story of her Venetian palazzo. The shock of the news of her death was
tremendous, and thereafter, for James, the aspect of the city becomes darker,
less shimmering, less reminiscent of pastel. In 1899 he writes that "one
clings, even in the face of the colder stare, to one's prized Venetian privilege
of making the sense of doom and decay part of every impression." For many
years Venice had provided a sufficiently prolific and happy inspiration, for

Mandeville, for Roger Ascham, for Thomas Nashe, for Shakespeare, for Ben Jonson, for Otway, in Addison, in Defoe, for Lady Mary Wortley Montagu, Voltaire, Monk Lewis, Byron, Gautier, George Sand, and Pater, and for many others before Henry James. Wordsworth's brief republican tribute had recognized an end, and some of Browning's verse suspects the luxurious atmosphere of decline, but nowhere before Henry James does the fragrance of Venetian aestheticism blend so persistently with the odor of the tomb. Proust and Thomas Mann were to come afterward.

> It comes to you there with longer knowledge, and with all deference to what flushes and shimmers, that the night is the real time. . . . This is certainly true for the form of progression that is most characteristic, for every question of departure and arrival by gondola. The little closed cabin of this perfect vehicle, the movement, the darkness and the plash, the indistinguishable swerves and twists, all the things you don't see and all the things you do feel—each dim recognition and obscure arrest is a possible throb of your sense of being floated to your doom. . . .

Venice, more than Florence or even Rome, was the goal of the Grand Tour during the nineteenth century, and most travelers did something to prepare themselves for its wonders. James studied his Gautier, and so did some other tourists, but everyone knew John Ruskin. In 1873 James learned from a friend that the great man had admired his early published responses to Venice, and in particular the passages on Tintoretto in "From Venice to Strassburg" ("Venice: An Early Impression" in *Italian Hours*). He had been eager, according to Charles Eliot Norton, that Cambridge University might offer the young novelist the post of Slade Professor of Fine Arts; the position went to Sidney Colvin, but an immense compliment had been extended to a young writer who was not yet thirty.[15] For better or for worse, James never forgot Ruskin, and it is a mark of intellectual courage and some arrogance that he soon rebelled. The essay that had won approval had already been tempered by a certain degree of independence—"Mr. Ruskin, whose eloquence in dealing with the great Venetians sometimes outruns his discretion"—but something surprising and slightly unappealing emerges in the eventual treatment of the author of *The Stones of Venice*. Ruskin lived until 1900, and, if he read James's later travel essays, he surely must have felt some resentment toward the young man he had recommended forcefully. He had in fact rarely written with more seriousness of purpose or more suppressed—and expressed—rage than he had in

---

15. Edel, *Henry James: The Conquest of London,* 128. Edel relates the particulars of the compliment and discusses James's misgivings concerning the value of art criticism.

Mornings in Florence; he believed, as later James eventually would believe (in an 1894 letter he would refer to Venice as the "vomitorium of Boston"),[16] that Italy was being destroyed by the vulgarization of the modern world and the rush of the tourist. And yet in 1877, James, with considerable condescension, refers to "these amusing little books" and reports that while waiting for a friend:

> . . . I had an hour with Mr. Ruskin, whom I called just now a light *littérateur,* because in these little Mornings in Florence he is for ever making his readers laugh. I remembered of course where I was, and in spite of my latent hilarity felt I had rarely got such a snubbing. . . . Nothing in fact is more comical than the familiar asperity of the author's style and the pedagogic fashion in which he pushes and pulls his unhappy pupils about, jerking their heads toward this, rapping their knuckles for that. . . . Instead of a place in which human responsibilities are lightened and suspended, he finds a region governed by a kind of Draconic legislation.

Yet despite such uncharacteristic insolence, James continued to carry copies of Ruskin along on his tours, as many people did, and the influence on *Italian Hours* is clear: both men grew more and more pessimistically aware of pervasive loss. James may have scorned the Ruskin who subtitled the 1872 *Mornings in Florence,* "Written for the Help of the Few Travellers Who Still Care for Her Monuments," but James in his own 1909 preface asks the modern observer to remember that here is presented "the interesting face of things as it mainly *used* to be." The commercialization of Italy becomes an increasing issue, particularly in the essays on Rome and Venice—driven home with excessive reiteration of this or that monument appearing as "a big bazaar," as "the biggest booth," as "the peep show," as one of the "most flourishing booths," as one of "the biggest booths at the fair," as "booths of the bazaar." Ruskinian rage is rarely apparent, but there is considerable scorn: "Everything else," he wrote to Clare Benedict in 1907, "now is too profaned and vulgarized—swimming in a sauce that might have been cooked (it often seems to one) at Oshkosh."[17]

Modern tourists seeking background material on any artist face an embarrassment of riches—and lots of color reproductions. But aside from Ruskin, at least until Bernard Berenson, the literature of art criticism was spare and largely impressionistic. In 1868, James published an unsigned article entitled,

16. An unpublished letter to W. Morton Fullerton, quoted by Edel in *Henry James: The Middle Years,* 375.

17. *Letters,* IV, 461.

curiously, "An English Critic of French Painting,"[18] where he complained of the dearth of good books available on the principles of art. He cites Vasari's *Lives,* Sir Joshua Reynolds's *Discourses on Art,* the immense and still valuable survey of Crowe and Cavalcaselle, Anna Brownell Jameson's efforts to relate the *Acta Sanctorum* and the *Golden Legend* to the iconography of Christian art, and finally the broadly theoretical and not very interesting *Handbook for Young Painters* by Charles Leslie. And yet, despite these impressive recommendations, their influence is not obvious throughout *Italian Hours;* perhaps the twenty-five-year-old "English critic" was unsure of himself and used bibliography to help establish authority. Years later he would write to John Addington Symonds, expressing admiration for the first few volumes of his influential *Renaissance in Italy,*[19] and upon occasion he would carry a volume of Ruskin or Stendhal or Goethe on his journey, but the author of at least the early articles often relied on more pedestrian *ciceroni.*

Despite scorn expressed (in two early tales, "Travelling Companions" and "At Isella") for the routine Murray handbook traveler, James knew both his Murray and his Baedeker, two excellent stock guidebooks that deliver up all the art and history, along with discussions of every aspect of the grinding chore of travel—from the question of hotels, to restaurants, to *poste restante* stops, to foreign tailors and caterers and clergymen and barbers and dentists, to agents where one might commission a *valet-de-place,* a rowboat, or a Renaissance palace. One overriding aim was to reduce terror, and both Murray and Baedeker made fortunes. But mediating between such practical efficiency and the sometimes furious impressionism of Ruskin was Augustus J. C. Hare, who, although never mentioned in *Italian Hours,* provided James with an impressive model. Hare's approach was a pleasing one and his guides are still rewarding; he generally compiled memorable reactions to places rather than provide reactions of his own. "On the whole," wrote James in a review of Hare's *Days Near Rome,* "we have not been disappointed. . . . It was noticeable in the 'Walks' that almost every one who had written with any conspicuity about anything else in the world, had also written something about Rome that could be made to pass muster as an 'extract.'"[20] Unlike Hare, who addresses a reasonably sophisticated traveler (the many French, German, and Latin passages are rarely translated) but a somewhat less universally well-read audience (passages are rarely alluded to without direct quotation), James often provides reference or allusion with-

18. "An English Critic of French Painting," [unsigned] in *North American Review* (April 1868); reprinted in *The Painter's Eye,* 34–5.

19. *Letters,* III, 29–32.

20. "Review of *Days Near Rome.* By Augustus J. C. Hare," reprinted in *Literary Criticism: Essays on Literature,* 1049.

out direct quotation. He writes to a particularly rarefied voyager—one who, for example, might catch the allusion to the Latin of Horace on page 319, or fully appreciate the reference to "les délicats" of Ernest Renan on page 277, or remember the somewhat lurid specifics of an untranslated minor novel by George Sand, mentioned on page 167.

A final model for the *Italian Hours* articles, one that assumes such a hypersophisticated reader, is once again Gautier—whose nonfictional *Italia, Constantinople, Voyage en Espagne,* and *Voyage en Russie* were considered by James "his most substantial literary titles." With an appreciation of allusion that anticipates T. S. Eliot, James wrote:

> Buried authors and actors are packed away in Gautier's pages as on the shelves of an immense mausoleum; and if, here and there, they exhibit the vivifying touch of the embalmer, the spectacle is on the whole little less lugubrious. It takes away one's breath to think of the immense consumption of witticisms involved in the development of civilization. Gautier's volumes seem an enormous monument to the shadowy swarm of jokes extinct and plots defunct—dim-featured ghosts, still haunting the lawless circumference of literature in pious confidence that the transmigration of souls will introduce them to the foot-lights again.[21]

Henry James might be standing breathless before the encrustation of civilization evident at the Theater of Marcellus or the church of San Nicola in Carcere. Despite an initially delighted and often casual tone, James's conception of travel literature grows serious and subtly demanding, as again and again, in the midst of wonder, the shadowy images of a ghostly and dimly retrievable past assert themselves. James might have agreed with Eliot's dictum that tradition is a matter of deep significance, one that cannot be inherited but must be obtained by great labor. The pleasure may come easily enough in reading *Italian Hours,* but these essays ask things of the reader that few nineteenth-century travel writers were in the habit of asking and that none do today.

James was providing more than a pleasant travelogue. He was posing questions about the durability of civilization itself. The knotty irony of Rome with all its past—and in this one aspect the city may stand for all of Italy—is that it seems there is little eternal about it. Virtually nothing in the Eternal City, except on first glance the Pantheon, has been immune to the accumulations of many centuries, to the constant detritus of invaders, princes, restorers, investors, and popes. But even the Pantheon had been

---

21. "Théâtre de Théophile Gautier," reprinted in *Literary Criticism: French Writers,* 372.

tampered with by Bernini, and it was not until 1883, ten years after James's first Roman essays, that the great architect's unfortunate church towers were removed and the structure was returned to its apparent original integrity. The progress of Italian hours may be ticked off inexorably in a thousand palimpsests on every piazza, and each may serve to record the death of a vision that had come before. But somehow Rome remains Rome. Today, as twenty years ago, as in Ruskin's time, as probably in Gibbon's, as perhaps in Constantine's, Romans say with grim resignation that only twenty years ago it was all a paradise. James was not above echoing this refrain: "the enormous crowds, the new streets, the horse-cars (you might think yourself in Brattle Street!) the ruination of the Coliseum, the hideous iron bridge over the Tiber, the wholesale desecration of the Pincio, etc., are all so many death blows to the picturesque."[22]

Auden judged a civilization by the degree of diversity attained and the degree of unity retained. The same standard might be applied to more personal genius—all of Picasso looks different, and yet all of it looks unmistakably like Picasso—or the genius of a place. Despite the fears expressed about loss of "the picturesque" and about the distance recognized from any golden age, James offers a similar standard, and the total effect of these various articles is to celebrate diversity and energy. In spite of the changes and the roar of jarring elements, the Italy of *Italian Hours* remains resiliently Italy. It is essential that any belief in civilization must presuppose such a faith—the confidence that a culture will not collapse because a hero dies, foreigners settle in, or a palazzo is converted into a fast-food restaurant. James perceives Venice as an exquisitely serene and undiversified city, the eternal *morceau de musée,* but eventually he understands that, for all its seduction, he views a delicious but disturbingly moribund scene—where, except for incremental decay, time had virtually stood still.

During an age of particularly intense social turmoil, many other parts of Italy provided far more movement, threat, and contradiction, and the capital in particular is seen as consistently vital and sometimes fearsome. Implicit questions involve James's attempt to grasp both civilization and beauty and keep them somehow yoked to vitality. Near the end of *Italian Hours,* just south of Naples, James enters a church where old women are knitting, gossiping, yawning, and shuffling about. Children romp and "lark," and in another chapel someone is cooking. It might normally be considered a decidedly un-Jamesian scene, but he approves of it all:

> The odd thing is that it all appears to interfere so little with that special civilised note—the note of manners—which is so constantly

22. *Letters,* II, 283.

touched. It is barbarous to expectorate in the temple of your faith, but that doubtless is an extreme case. Is civilization really measured by the number of things people do respect? There would seem to be much evidence against it.

In the fifteenth century Pope Julius II tore down Old Saint Peter's, one of the largest and most important churches in the world, and, dating from the year 326, one of the most ancient. His was an act of daring that might still shock us today, but it was also a gesture of unsurpassed confidence in the direction of Western civilization and in culture itself. The result was the stupendous new basilica of Saint Peter's, the collaboration of great and varied artistic genius, but Julius II deserves credit for a vital conception of progress that no true Ruskinian would have risked. Although James himself might have shuddered before such arrogant obliteration of precious past, he was neither the cultural nor the aesthetic conservative that Ruskin was. In fact at moments his general quarrel with Ruskin seems subtly political, as, in an 1876 review, it was with Hare:

> We differ, however, from Mr. Hare in the estimation in which we hold Italian unity, and the triumph of what he never alludes to but as the "Sardinian Government." He deplores the departure of the little ducal courts, thinks Italy had no need to be united, and never mentions the new order of things without a sneer. His tone strikes us as very childish. Certainly the "Sardinians" have destroyed the picturesque old walls of Florence, and increased—very heavily—the taxes, but it is a very petty view of matters that cannot perceive that these are but regrettable incidents in a great general gain. It is certainly something that Italy has been made a nation, with a voice in the affairs of Europe (to say nothing of her own, for the first time), and able to offer her admirable people (if they will choose to take it) an opportunity to practise some of those responsible civic virtues which it can do no harm even to the gifted Italians to know something about. But on this subject Mr. Hare is really rabid; in a writer who loves Italy as much as he does, his state of mind is an incongruity.[23]

Hare viewed Italy largely as accumulated literary response or magnificent vista, and even the title of Ruskin's *The Stones of Venice* turned its back on the pulse of life in the streets. Too much should not be made of the arrange-

---

23. "Review of *Cities of Northern and Central Italy.* By Augustus J. C. Hare," reprinted in *Literary Criticism: Essays on Literature,* 1054–55.

ment of essays in *Italian Hours,* but it is curious that James's record ends in, of all places, Naples.

James began *Italian Hours* with the tribute to Venice, an exquisite, other-worldly, aesthetic capital where, however, it would seem that vitality was on the wane. If over time the allure of Venice became slightly *louche* to Henry James, it is perhaps not an accident that he closed the volume with the 1901 and 1909 sections on the Bay of Naples. In the final and last-written section of *Italian Hours,* James admits that "the Bay of Naples in June" struck him "as the last word; and it is the last word that comes back to me, after a short interval, in a green, gray northern nook." The distance traveled is tremen-dous, from preoccupation with the tenebrous *couleur de rose* on the Grand Canal to the surprising appreciation, in "The Saint's Afternoon," of brass bands and "bare-bodied babies," the tarantella, "all purple wine," and the "wonder how so many men, women and children could cram themselves into so much smell." In maturity James found Naples vital and congenial—and few other travelers did. Decades before, he had written to his brother William that "I conceived at Naples a tenfold deeper loathing than ever of the hideous heritage of the past—and felt for a moment as if I should like to devote my life to laying rail-roads and erecting long blocks of stores on the most classic and romantic sites."[24] Toward the end of the nineteenth cen-tury, disdain for Naples was the habit of the day. It might be noted that, in his discussion of Neapolitan customs, Augustus Hare even mocked the fact that "that horrible condiment called *Pizza* (made of dough baked with garlic, rancid bacon, and strong cheese) is esteemed a feast."[25]

Yet in order to appreciate how alien the cultivated Anglo-American tour-ist could find the impoverished and volatile landscape around Naples, one might recall the impression that the bay had made on Arthur Symons in 1897. This vicious prose is not easy to read. Nonetheless, its vehemence expresses a reaction among visitors which was not uncommon.

> A Christian ascetic, wishing to meditate on the disgust of the flesh, might well visit these quays. There he will see the flaccid yellowness of old women, like the skin of a rotten apple; wrinkles eaten in with grime, until they broaden into ruts; feet and ankles that have been caked and roasted and soaked into iridescent reds, smoky violets, shot purples; the horror of decayed eyes, deformed limbs, hair crawl-ing with lice, and about these dishonored bodies flutters a medley of blackened and yellowing linen, tattered trousers without buttons, tattered dresses without strings, torn shawls, still loud in colour, but

24. *Letters,* I, 182.
25. Hare, *Cities of Southern Italy and Sicily,* 85.

purple where they had been red, and lavender where they had been blue. And all this malodorous medley is a-swarm, hoarse voices crying, hands in continual movement, the clatter of heelless shoes on the pavement, the splash of emptied vessels, laughter, the harsh notes of a song, rising out of their midst like the bubble of steam escaping out of a boiling pot.[26]

Symons's aesthete sensibilities are revolted by the whole lot—by the poverty, smell, and degradation, but also by the laughter, the expressiveness, and the bursts of song—the incontrovertible pulses of life. James's late impressions are deeply more humane and far better reconciled to the landscape's carnal assertiveness. "The place," he writes, "is at the best wild and weird and sinister, and yet seemed on this occasion to be seated more at her ease in her immense natural dignity." More than ever he is struck with the "merciless June beauty of Naples Bay at sunset hour" and by the "splendid human plant by the wayside." James never finds Naples or its people vulgar. In fact in the final essay he wonders that civilization reveals itself so clearly in the cadences of such vigorous common life.

James's sympathy with the prospect of Naples in summer is not completely surprising when one considers that in the three great works of the major phase, sexuality and passion were at the heart of the matter. One wishes all the more that this mature artist and traveler might have produced another complicated masterpiece during his final years. Yet although the pull of the land's sensuality continued to fascinate and disturb him until the end of his life, James knew all along that his true home could be neither Italy, nor Rome, hardly even the rarefied dream of Venice, and much less the true *meridionale*. When in 1894 Bonaparte Count Giuseppe Primoli introduced him to Matilde Serao, the celebrated Neapolitan novelist and founder of the great newspaper *Il Mattino,* he judged her to be spirited, "robust and wonderful."[27] In 1901, however, when he would return to her "evocation of the absolute ravage of Venus," he would note his continued admiration of her "poetry of *passione,*" but would close his essay with a particularly charming and telling passage. James admits that after reading Serao's Roman and Neapolitan tales with genuine pleasure, inevitably a "feeling revives at last, after a timed intermission, that we may not immediately be quite able, quite assured enough, to name, but which, gradually clearing up, soon defines

26. Symons, *Cities of Italy,* 117–18; the 1907 volume contains an 1897 impression of Naples.
27. In a letter to Grace Norton: "Did you ever hear of the Serao—the she-Zola of Italy?— or read any of her really 'talented' fictions? She is a wonderful little burly Balzac in petticoats— full of Neapolitan life and sound and familiarity" (*Letters,* III, 474).

itself almost as a yearning. We turn round in obedience to it—unmistakably we turn round again to the opposite pole, and there before we know it have positively laid a clinging hand on dear old Jane Austen."[28]

Among travel books *Italian Hours* is unusual in providing observations that unfold over the long expanse of forty years. Movement over terrain is secondary to the sense of a fascinated temporal journey, which, upon occasion, becomes a grumbling ride past fading beauties, political shifts, and inevitable desecrations in the modern world. But of equal interest are the developments in the voice and in the perceptions of the author himself, for although in 1909 all these essays were amended, "expressively," as the preface states it, the earlier ones clearly present the style of a younger man, while the later provide the matchless cadence and vocabulary of the mature Henry James. Riding in the Campagna in 1873, he would spot a tavern, "reign up and demand a bottle of their best." In 1907, motoring through the same Campagna, he reports that he and his companions had "wished, stomachically, we had rather addressed ourselves to a tea-basket." The reader who feels a sly fondness for Henry James feels it in part for such an inimitable locution. But some of the enigma of travel has to do with just such changes as these. Here, as elsewhere, each reader and each traveler must decide where the greater changes have occurred, in the turbulence of the external or of the internal landscape.

A fruitful reading of *Italian Hours* benefits from an awareness both of the quiet revolutions that James suggests and of those that came after him, since each generation of travelers comprehends different features of Roderick Hudson's Rome or of Milly Theale's Venice. These essays provide a sense of such differences as well as a surer context for the complex moral dramas that James sets on Italian soil. Benedetto Croce, who like James himself united a profoundly serious aesthetic with a deep concern for morality, was "comforted," to use the phrase of Luigi Barzini, "by the knowledge that history has but one meaning, the slow, bloody, meandering progress of human liberty."[29] There is charged ambiguity in any such statement of comfort, as there is throughout these essays, for the encounter of any aesthetic with human vitality and human liberty necessarily must be perplexing. In *Italian Hours* Henry James considers these difficult questions and many others, but looking south and into the sun he also evokes the rich seduction and the delicious impulses of an extraordinary land that stirred "the whole adventure of one's sensibility." He was prophetic in 1873 when he admitted that the task of summing up, "for tribute and homage, one's experience, one's gain," was one that baffled him:

28. James, "Matilde Serao," reprinted in *Literary Criticism: French Writers*, 967.
29. Barzini, *The Europeans*, 14–15.

What is simply clear is the sense of an acquired passion for the place and of an incalculable number of gathered impressions. Many of these have been intense and momentous, but one has trodden on the other—there are always the big fish that swallow up the little—and one can hardly say what has become of them. They store themselves noiselessly away, I suppose, in the dim but safe places of memory and "taste," and we live in quiet faith that they will emerge into vivid relief if life or art should demand them.

Suggestions for Further Reading

Henry James made fourteen visits to Italy, his first in 1869, his last in 1907. Leon Edel's five-volume *Henry James* (1952–73) provides a detailed account of almost all aspects of these journeys; a one-volume condensation of the biography, *Henry James: A Life* (1985), offers a fine overview of the Italian experience and, in the index, a handy chronological listing of the travels. Edel's four-volume edition of *Henry James: Letters* (1974–84) is another essential resource. In his early letters to his family, James provided rich accounts of his travels; particularly interesting—and lengthy—are the initial impressions of Italy in the 1869 letters to Alice, to William, to his mother, and to his father.

Bonney MacDonald's recent phenomenological study, *Henry James's "Italian Hours": Revelatory and Resistant Impressions* (1990), illuminates the reconstruction and revision of the early Italian travels and explores their influence on the later career. Apart from MacDonald, relatively little work has focused on the *Italian Hours* essays, but several critical studies have examined the more general metaphor of Italy. Notable are Robert L. Gale's seminal article, "Henry James and Italy," *Studi Americani* 3 (1957): 189–204, and Carl Maves's *Sensuous Pessimism: Italy in the Work of Henry James* (1973). Nathalia Wright's *American Novelists in Italy: The Discoverers, Allston to James* (1965) offers the most comprehensive survey of Italian references in the fiction. William Vance's *America's Rome* (1989) is essential reading. A 1988 symposium held at New York University is collected in James W. Tuttleton and Agostino Lombardo, eds., *The Sweetest Impression of Life: The James Family and Italy* (New York: New York University Press, and Rome: Istituto della Enciclopedia Italiana, 1990). Readers who read Italian will benefit from Cristina Giorcelli's *Henry James e l'Italia* (1968) and Marilla Battilana's *Venezia: Sfondo e simbolo nella narrativa di Henry James* (1987). Battilana's 182-page study of James's relationship to a single Italian city offers a startlingly specific and particularly worthwhile emphasis; there are two sections on *Ore Italiane*.

James's statements on the visual arts, in Italy and elsewhere, merit consideration in their own right. John L. Sweeney, ed., *Henry James: The Painter's Eye: Notes and Essays on the Pictorial Arts* (1956), provides a selection and commentary, and Viola Hopkins Winner, *Henry James and the Visual Arts* (1970), examines both James's theoretical formulations and his specific appreciations. Adeline R. Tintner's *The Museum World of Henry James* (1986) is the essential sourcebook of virtually all the specifically named works of art in the fiction.

For general background on American writers in Italy, especially helpful are Van Wyck Brooks, *The Dream of Arcadia: American Writers and Artists in Italy, 1760–1915* (1958), again Nathalia Wright, *American Novelists in Italy*, and William Vance, *America's Rome*.

The bibliographies at the end of this volume are selective and have the particular, although not the exclusive, aim of facilitating research on the Italy James knew.

Salon of the Doges, Hotel Royal Danieli, Venice, c. 1890. (Alinari/Art Resource, New York)
"Madame Sand's famous Venetian year has been of late immensely in the air. . . . the present
Hotel Danieli had been the scene of its first remarkable stages."

**The Margherita di Savoia, wife of Umberto I,
and first queen of the united Italy, 1880.**
(Alinari/Art Resource, New York) "I would
have waited half an hour any day to see the
Princess Margaret hold a dove on her forefinger."

Two views of the Piazza San Marco, Venice, 1902. (Alinari/Art Resource, New York) In 1902 the campanile of San Marco collapsed and a reconstruction replaced it. The incident, unnoted in *Italian Hours*, was nonetheless an emphatic example of James's view that the "old softness and mellowness of colour—the work of the quiet centuries and of the breath of the salt sea— is giving way to large crude patches of new material . . ."

The Duomo at Milan, seen from the Corso Vittorio Emanuele, c. 1890. (Alinari/Art Resource, New York) ". . . the far-shining mass of the bigger prodigy at Milan, of which your first glimpse as you leave your hotel is generally through another such dark avenue." Most of the buildings leading to the duomo were destroyed by bombing in the Corso Vittorio Emanuele during World War II.

Saint Peter's, Rome, 1929. (Alinari/Art Resource, New York) This photograph, taken before Mussolini's architects cut the Via della Conciliazione to the Tiber, shows the dramatically different approach to the basilica that Henry James knew. "We kept on and on into the great dim rather sordidly papal streets that approach the quarter of St. Peter's."

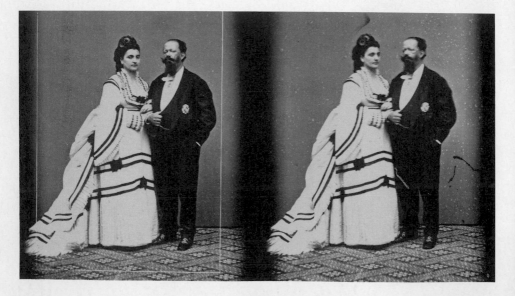

Victor Emmanuel II, with "Rosina," the Contessa di Mirafiori, 1870. (Alinari/Art Resource, New York) "Villa Ludovisi has been all winter the residence of the lady familiarly known in Roman society as 'Rosina,' Victor Emmanuel's morganatic wife."

Saint Peter's, Rome, seen from the Tiber before the embankments were built, c. 1870. (Alinari/ Art Resource, New York) ". . . the sad-looking, more than sad-looking, evil-looking, Tiber." In 1888 the river was uniformly walled to prevent flooding; thereafter it assumed a less sinister aspect (as can be seen in the 1929 aerial photograph of Saint Peter's).

Torcello, the Duomo, the church of Santa Fosca, and the Museo dell'Estuario, 1890. (Alinari/ Art Resource, New York) "Yet all youthful things at Torcello were not cheerful, for the poor lad who brought us the key of the cathedral was shaking with an ague, and his melancholy presence seemed to point the moral of forsaken nave and choir."

The Duomo at Florence, with the old facade, c. 1853. (Alinari/Art Resource, New York) This rare photograph shows, behind the baptistry, the unfinished duomo that James knew. Emilio De Fabris's neo-gothic facade was not unveiled until 1887.

Piazza Vittorio Emanuele II, Turin, c. 1890. (Alinari/Art Resource, New York) "But if the place is less bravely peninsular than Florence and Rome, at least it is more in the scenic tradition than New York and Paris."

Florence, the Cascine Park, 1870. (Alinari/Art Resource, New York) "There is no crush along the Cascine, as on the sunny days of winter. . . ."

The Marchesa Corsini di Lojatico and the Marchesa Corsini di Giovegallo in allegorical costume, 1868. (Alinari/Art Resource, New York) "I went the other morning to the Corsini Palace. . . . In places that have been lived in so long and so much and in such a fine old way, as my friend said—that is under social conditions so multifold and to a comparatively starved and democratic sense so curious—the past seems to have left a sensible deposit, an aroma, and atmosphere."

A Note on the Text

Four of these essays were written expressly for *Italian Hours* ("A Few Other Roman Neighbourhoods," the second part of "Siena Early and Late," "Other Tuscan Cities," and parts VI and VII of "The Saint's Afternoon and Others"); all others had appeared previously in magazines or as contributions to books, and several had appeared first in magazines and later were reprinted in either *Transatlantic Sketches* (1875) or *Portraits of Places* (1883). (The details of the publication history of each essay are provided among the notes.) Although with every successive printing some degree of revision is evident, in 1909 James was involved in the major task of revising his earlier fiction for the New York Edition of his works; the editorial pencil also fell heavily on the *Italian Hours* essays, particularly on those written in 1872, 1873, and 1874. In his 1909 preface James reports that "I have not hesitated to amend my text, expressively, wherever it seemed urgently to ask for this." The final revisions are numerous and substantial, although in the opinion of this editor they do not merit the judgment that their product constitutes a distinctly different work.

Changes made between the early magazine publications and initial book publications in *Transatlantic Sketches* and *Portraits of Places* are minimal when compared with those made in the editions of 1909; these early changes generally provide corrections rather than emendations, but already there are occasional signs of more serious reconsideration. Since James was on tour in Europe when he sent his earliest manuscripts to the *Nation, Galaxy,* and the *Atlantic,* it was virtually impossible for him to review any proofs, and therefore a significant number of errors crept in. Very obvious errors, particularly obvious to any traveler familiar with Italy or Italian spellings, were printed in the magazine articles and corrected in their first reprintings.

From the 1873 *Atlantic* publication to the inclusion in the 1875 *Transatlantic Sketches,* for example, the changes in "Roman Rides" are, relative to other changes among editions in James, minor. On the first two pages of the magazine article an occasional long paragraph is broken down, the word *contadino* is taken out of italics, an occasional word receives a varied spelling, and the city of Veii, erroneously given as if a German city, Veü, with an umlaut, is corrected. Other examples of representative changes are less subtle. In "A Roman Holiday" a somewhat extended passage on the Basilica Julia is omitted in all reprintings. In "The After-Season in Rome," there is a single change in the long first paragraph: "*Eh,* this is nothing! Come back in May," in the *Nation,* becomes "*Ah,* this is nothing! Come back in May" in *Transatlantic Sketches.* The shift may seem to be a correction of a typographical error, but the overall tone of the later essays, as well as of the late revisions, is that of increased nostalgia and tenderness, and therefore such a small shift may indicate an intentional development of sensibility. Perhaps the most significant difference between texts comes in the last line: the magazine article reports that "everything has an amiable side, even *émeutes,*" while the reprinted version provides the translation of "popular uprisings." A particular aspect of interest among the printings relates to different attitudes toward the use—the frequent use—of foreign words and expressions.

Although a prefatory remark by James in the 1883 Continental edition of *Foreign Parts* reports that "the sketches have been revised," there is little evidence of revision, and those revisions seem directed at printing errors, except in the case "From a Roman Note-Book," where the arbitrarily anonymous designations of James's companions—X, Z, I, a blank space—are made more specific. In the 1909 *Italian Hours* revision, the designations often are changed and do not match the denotations of *Foreign Parts.* The *Foreign Parts* "Mrs. W." [Sarah Butler Wistler] is designated as "L" [Lizzie Boott] in *Italian Hours;* "L. B." [Lizzie Boott] becomes "F" [Frank Boott] in 1909.

Later essays, for example the "Venice" of the *Portraits of Places* reprinting, generally show few changes when compared to the magazine publications. The final revisions, however, are often very extensive, as may be seen from the representative parallel texts—those of the third paragraph of "The After-Season in Rome"—printed below.

1873 Text

It is the same good-nature that leads me to violate the instinct of monopoly, and proclaim that Rome in May is worth waiting. I have just been so gratified at finding myself in undisturbed possession for a couple of hours of the Museum of the Lateran that I can afford to be magnanimous. And yet I keep within the bounds of reason when I say that it would be hard as a traveller or student to pass pleasanter days than these. The weather for a month has been perfect, the sky magnificently blue, the air lively enough, the nights cool, too cool, and the whole gray old city illumined with the most irresistible smile. Rome, which in some moods, especially to new-comers, seems a terribly gloomy place, gives on the whole, and as one knows it better, an indefinable impression of gaiety. This contagious influence lurks in all its darkness and dirt and decay—a something more careless and hopeless than our thrifty Northern cheerfulness, and yet more genial, more urbane, than mere indifference. The Roman temper is a healthy and happy one, and you feel it abroad in the streets even when the *scirocco* blows, and the goal of man's life assumes a horrible identity with the mouth of a furnace. But

1909 Text

Practically I violate thus the instinct of monopoly, since it's a shame not to publish that Rome in May is exquisitely worth your patience. I have just been so gratified at finding myself in undisturbed possession for a couple of hours of the Museum of the Lateran that I can afford to be magnanimous. It's almost as if the old all-papal paradise had come back. The weather for a month has been perfect, the sky an extravagance of blue, the air lively enough, the nights cool, nippingly cool, and the whole ancient greyness lighted with an irresistible smile. Rome, which in some moods, especially to new-comers, seems a place of almost sinister gloom, has an occasional art, as one knows her better, of brushing away care by the grand gesture with which some splendid impatient mourning matron—just the Niobe of Nations, surviving, emerging and looking about her again—might pull off and cast aside an oppression of muffling crape. This admirable power still temperamentally to react and take notice lurks in all her darkness and dirt and decay—a something more careless and hopeless than our thrifty northern cheer, and yet more genial and urbane than the Parisian spirit of *blague*. The

who can analyze even the simplest Roman impression? It is compounded of so many things, it says so much, it suggests so much, it so quickens the intellect and so flatters the heart, that before we are fairly conscious of it the imagination has marked it for her own, and exposed us to a perilous likelihood of talking nonsense about it.

collective Roman nature is a healthy and hearty one, and you feel it abroad in the streets even when the sirocco blows and the medium of life seems to proceed more or less from the mouth of a furnace. But who shall analyse even the simplest Roman impression? It is compounded of so many things, it says so much, it involves so much, it so quickens the intelligence and so flatters the heart, that before we fairly grasp the case the imagination has marked it for her own and exposed us to a perilous likelihood of talking nonsense about it.

These passages indicate a degree of revision—at least of an early essay—not uncommon in *Italian Hours*. Notable is the addition of two entirely new passages. One remembers the "old all-papal paradise," suggesting a sympathy that was not obvious in the earlier versions of the articles. Another personifies the city as Niobe and extends the metaphor (in his introduction to *The American Scene*, Auden noted the characteristic of the late prose that "outside of fairy tales, I know of no book in which things so often and so naturally become persons. . . . [S]ince *The Fairie Queene*, what book has been more hospitable to allegorical figures?").[1] The late prose of Henry James is generally delivered with a more extended sense of rhythm and a more complex syntax. Some readers may prefer the earlier prose, and a few may feel, for example, that the force of "the goal of man's life assumes a horrible identity with the mouth of a furnace" is slightly diminished in the revision.

No variorum collation of the several versions of the essays would be easily decipherable or very helpful—and since the magazine printings of these articles are available in most American research libraries, such extensive collation is not necessary; the serious students of James will wish to examine those printed texts—often replete with engraved illustrations (the *Century* magazine printing of "Venice," for example, is illustrated by A. Whitney Blum, T. Suseler, H. Davidson, Frank French, D. Martin Rico, Clara Montalba, and the unspecified A.C.C.). An incremental shift of tone and intention sometimes will be apparent, but James rarely controverts the fun-

1. Henry James, *The American Scene*, xi–xii.

damental sense of his early prose. It is, for example, interesting to note that none of James's early, sarcastic, and harsh references to Ruskin is at all modified by the mature novelist.

The first edition of *Italian Hours* was published in London by William Heinemann on 28 October 1909. At first it seems that particular care was taken with the production of this first edition: it contains an index, and an "errata" page faces the first page of text and indicates two relatively minor corrections of comma placement. Yet upon occasion more serious errors in the text go unnoted—for example, misspelled Italian and French words and proper names, errors in page headings, and omitted accent marks for foreign words.

The index is a strange feature of this volume. Perhaps it was part of a William Heinemann marketing strategy to make *Italian Hours* more attractive to a traveler who might consult it while on a journey—although the large format of the volume ($10\frac{3}{8}$ by 8 inches) would have made it a much more clumsy companion than Ruskin's "Traveller's Edition" of *The Stones of Venice*. In any case, the index surely was not the work of Henry James. On first glance it seems surprisingly complete, and reasonably lengthy, but it is often wrong-headed and insecure. One index entry, for example, reads, "Barca, signore!" On page 53 in the first edition the text reads that, in Venice, "the keynote of the great medley of voices borne back from the exit is not 'Cab, sir!' but 'Barca, signore!' " Notations such as these ("Campi" is indexed for page 70, although as an ordinary and general word for field or square it appears numerous other times throughout), and citations such as "Pink, the colour in Venice," "Lark, the advent of the," "Olive, the," "Arme d'Inghilterra, Siena"—an exotic enough sounding designation, but merely the name of a defunct hotel—indicate that the index was compiled by an assistant with little knowledge of Italy and an insufficient understanding of the text that he or she was indexing. This inadequate understanding is especially clear when one considers that no note is given in the index of the more important conceptual issues of *Italian Hours*—"civilization," "commercialization," "restoration," "Roman Catholicism," or "Risorgimento."

It would seem surprising that James did not pay more attention to all aspects of production of such a handsomely bound and attractively illustrated book on a subject that was dear to him; it does seem unlikely, however, that he corrected proofs of the index. Since in the fall of 1909 he was involved in work on the prefaces and texts of the New York Edition of the novels and tales, *Italian Hours,* with its very small printing, may not have been a priority. Furthermore, the few references to the project in James's correspondence indicate rather considerable ambivalence concerning the published book. He thanks Mrs. William Darwin for her "so sweet and generous tribute to the poor old *Italian Hours.*—Tricked out in their abandoned ancientry, and their great out-of-printness, to make—or to see— some sort of fresh little fortune. I delight to think that they bear at all the test of being read again in the so dangerous presence of the unutterable scenes they tried to give their rude reflection of!"[2] The note of slight rapacity in James's response seems playful; there were only one thousand copies in the first and only English printing. In his edition of the Henry James–Edmund Gosse letters, Rayburn S. Moore explains James's November 1909 reference to the "lumpish & not intrinsically very successful (I fear) piece of catch-penny bookmaking entitled 'English Hours,'" as "a slip of the pen for *Italian Hours.*" In another letter to Gosse, James notes that "isn't it a grievous pity that the fortune of my poor old Italian book might have made for me as pornographic has been dashed from my hands by the appearance that the soft impeachment was made by mistake." Moore reports that, for a short time, the Circulating Libraries' Association misjudged *Italian Hours* as unacceptable for its organization. One of its members had read it and, in a 15 December 1909 letter to the *Times,* reported that it was not an example of "thoroughly wholesome literature."[3]

The text for this edition is that of the first American edition, published in Boston and New York by Houghton Mifflin on 20 November 1909; 1,500 copies were struck. Although it included all thirty-two color plates that Joseph Pennell had provided for the English edition, it lacked the additional thirty-two sepia plates by Pennell that were tipped into that edition. Further-more, it lacked the index of the Heinemann *Italian Hours.* Nonetheless, the errata noted in the Heinemann text were corrected and amended in the American edition, and several of the more glaring spelling errors—for exam-ple, "Botticieli" and "Manilla"—were corrected, as were errors in page headings. On page 100 in the Heinemann *Italian Hours* James notes that the Monte Rosa is five miles high; the eighteen-thousand-foot peak is corrected to "three miles high" in the Houghton Mifflin edition. Other errors, how-ever, for example, the misspelling of Goldoni's *I Quattro Rusteghi,* as well as of one French and several Italian words, are not corrected. An exception-ally clean edition otherwise reproduces the Heinemann text, and it main-tains the British spellings that James preferred, although adopting the print-ing practice of breaking contractions of two words into two pieces (for example, *isn't* becomes *is n't, can't* becomes *ca n't,* and *wasn't* becomes *was n't*).

Where the errata listing noted errors in the Heinemann text, the Houghton Mifflin edition corrects those errors; in the place of the error noted on page 72 of the Heinemann text, the Houghton Mifflin *Italian Hours* provides a sub-

2. *Letters,* IV, 550.
3. Moore, ed., *Selected Letters of Henry James to Edmund Gosse,* 245–49.

stantially different—and less ambiguous—reading.[4] Such changes indicate, in the judgment of this editor, that the American edition was closer to James's final intention.

Very few of James's nonfictional manuscripts have been preserved. The holograph of the *Century* "Venice" is held by the Berg Collection at the New York Public Library. In 1954 Richard C. Harrier presented for the first time " 'Very Modern Rome'—An Unpublished Essay of Henry James"; Harrier's article introduces a transcript of the holograph and photographically reproduces two pages, pages clearly in the process of composition. Given to the year 1873, "Very Modern Rome" reiterates both specific and general features of several of the 1873 Roman essays and repeats some of their concerns. Other features would surface elsewhere; a commentary, for example, on "the suppressed transitions that unite all contrasts,"[5] from George Eliot's *Middlemarch,* later would be reiterated in the 1874 "Florentine Notes."

4. English edition, 1909:
  . . . and why the fond observer of the footprints of genius is likely so to continue, attentive to an altercation neither in itself and in its day . . . [the errata page noted that the comma between "continue, attentive" should be eliminated]

American edition, 1909:
  . . . and why the fond observer of the footprints of genius is likely so to continue, with a body of discussion, neither in itself and in its day . . .
5. Harrier, "Very Modern Rome," 137.

Italian Hours: New York and Boston: Houghton Mifflin Company, 1909

Italian Hours

Preface

The chapters of which this volume is composed have with few exceptions already been collected, and were then associated with others commemorative of other impressions of (no very extensive) excursions and wanderings. The notes on various visits to Italy are here for the first time exclusively placed together, and as they largely refer to quite other days than these—the date affixed to each paper sufficiently indicating this—I have introduced a few passages that speak for a later and in some cases a frequently repeated vision of the places and scenes in question. I have not hesitated to amend my text, expressively, wherever it seemed urgently to ask for this, though I have not pretended to add the element of information or the weight of curious and critical insistence to a brief record of light inquiries and conclusions. The fond appeal of the observer concerned is all to aspects and appearances—above all to the interesting face of things as it mainly *used* to be.

H.J.

Contents

VENICE	7
THE GRAND CANAL	32
VENICE: AN EARLY IMPRESSION	51
TWO OLD HOUSES AND THREE YOUNG WOMEN	61
CASA ALVISI	72
FROM CHAMBÉRY TO MILAN	77
THE OLD SAINT-GOTHARD	88
ITALY REVISITED	99
A ROMAN HOLIDAY	122
ROMAN RIDES	139
ROMAN NEIGHBOURHOODS	152
THE AFTER-SEASON IN ROME	168
FROM A ROMAN NOTE-BOOK	176
A FEW OTHER ROMAN NEIGHBOURHOODS	194
A CHAIN OF CITIES	205
SIENA EARLY AND LATE	220
THE AUTUMN IN FLORENCE	238
FLORENTINE NOTES	247
TUSCAN CITIES	272
OTHER TUSCAN CITIES	280
RAVENNA	293
THE SAINT'S AFTERNOON AND OTHERS	303

Editorial Preface

All annotations, except those unmarked in the text and relegated to the hinterlands of a distant appendix, distract the reader. Nonetheless, since James's intention was to convey information as well as impressions, the editorial decision here has been to provide notation on the most relevant textual page. In an attempt to present the text of Italian Hours *with as much integrity as possible, the editor provides neither supralinear numbers nor marginal apparatus which might further break the flow of the prose. The reader with questions about a particular passage may wish to come to the end of a page—or essay—before consulting, or ignoring, any notations. The footnotes sometimes provide comment on subsequent related, and often rather discursive, Jamesian points.*

These notes make no attempt to replicate the task of general guidebooks. They are provided when, for example, identification or clarification is judged to be important to James's meaning, or when a foreign word or expression seems particularly remote from American English. The editor is aware that his choices have been difficult calls. Sometimes their aim is merely to help the scholar, or traveler, locate what is being described, or to recognize the more significant changes in the Italian scene since James wrote on Italy.

Venice

It is a great pleasure to write the word; but I am not sure there is not a certain impudence in pretending to add anything to it. Venice has been painted and described many thousands of times, and of all the cities of the world is the easiest to visit without going there. Open the first book and you will find a rhapsody about it; step into the first picture-dealer's and you will find three or four high-coloured "views" of it. There is notoriously nothing more to be said on the subject. Every one has been there, and every one has brought back a collection of photographs. There is as little mystery about the Grand Canal as about our local thoroughfare, and the name of St. Mark is as familiar as the postman's ring. It is not forbidden, however, to speak of familiar things, and I hold that for the true Venice-lover Venice is always in order. There is nothing new to be said about her certainly, but the old is better than any novelty. It would be a sad day indeed when there should be something new to say. I write these lines with the full consciousness of having no information whatever to offer. I do not pretend to enlighten the reader; I pretend only to give a fillip to his memory; and I hold any writer sufficiently justified who is himself in love with his theme.

[Originally published in the *Century Magazine*, xxv (November 1882), 3–23; reprinted in *Portraits of Places*, 1883.]

I

MR. RUSKIN has given it up, that is very true; but only after extracting half a lifetime of pleasure and an immeasurable quantity of fame from it. We all may do the same, after it has served our turn, which it probably will not cease to do for many a year to come. Meantime it is Mr. Ruskin who beyond any one helps us to enjoy. He has indeed lately produced several aids to depression in the shape of certain little humorous—ill-humorous—pamphlets (the series of *St. Mark's Rest*) which embody his latest reflections on the subject of our city and describe the latest atrocities perpetrated there. These latter are numerous and deeply to be deplored; but to admit that they have spoiled Venice would be to admit that Venice may be spoiled—an admission pregnant, as it seems to us, with disloyalty. Fortunately one reacts against the Ruskinian contagion, and one hour of the lagoon is worth a hundred pages of demoralised prose. This queer late-coming prose of Mr. Ruskin (including the revised and condensed issue of the *Stones of Venice,* only one little volume of which has been published, or perhaps ever will be) is all to be read, though much of it appears addressed to children of tender age. It is pitched in the nursery-key, and might be supposed to emanate from an angry governess. It is, however, all suggestive, and much of it is delightfully just. There is an inconceivable want of form in it, though the author has spent his life in laying down the principles of form and scolding people for departing from them; but it throbs and flashes with the love of his subject—a love disconcerted and abjured, but which has still much of the force of inspiration. Among the many strange things that have befallen Venice, she has had the good fortune to become the object of a passion to a man of splendid genius, who has made her his own and in doing so has made her the world's. There is no better reading at Venice therefore, as I say, than Ruskin, for every true Venice-lover can separate the wheat from the chaff. The narrow theological spirit, the moralism *à tout propos,* the queer provincialities and pruderies, are mere wild weeds in a mountain of flowers. One may doubtless be very happy in Venice without reading at all—without criticising or analysing or thinking a strenuous thought. It is a city in which, I suspect, there is very little strenuous thinking, and yet it is a city in which there

---

Mr. Ruskin . . . *St. Mark's Rest* . . . revised and condensed issue of the *Stones of Venice* . . . angry governess. In 1879 Ruskin published the first volume of a "Traveller's Edition" of his lengthy *The Stones of Venice* (1851; 1853). The second and final volume had actually been issued in 1881, the year before James voiced skepticism concerning the project's completion. The angry emotional tone—sometimes called evidence of "pathological fury" (Rosenberg, 181)—of *St. Mark's Rest* (1877–84) and *Mornings in Florence* (1875–77) partly is suggested by the qualifying subtitle of the pamphlet: "Written for the Help of the Few Travellers Who Still Care for Her Monuments" (see pages 113–17 below, for more pointed impatience with Ruskin).

must be almost as much happiness as misery. The misery of Venice stands
there for all the world to see; it is part of the spectacle—a thoroughgoing devotee of local colour might consistently say it is part of the pleasure. The Venetian people have little to call their own—little more than the bare privilege of
leading their lives in the most beautiful of towns. Their habitations are decayed; their taxes heavy; their pockets light; their opportunities few. One receives an impression, however, that life presents itself to them with attractions
not accounted for in this meagre train of advantages, and that they are on
better terms with it than many people who have made a better bargain. They
lie in the sunshine; they dabble in the sea; they wear bright rags; they fall into
attitudes and harmonies; they assist at an eternal *conversazione*. It is not easy
to say that one would have them other than they are, and it certainly would
make an immense difference should they be better fed. The number of persons
in Venice who evidently never have enough to eat is painfully large; but it
would be more painful if we did not equally perceive that the rich Venetian
temperament may bloom upon a dog's allowance. Nature has been kind to it,
and sunshine and leisure and conversation and beautiful views form the
greater part of its sustenance. It takes a great deal to make a successful American, but to make a happy Venetian takes only a handful of quick sensibility.
The Italian people have at once the good and the evil fortune to be conscious
of few wants; so that if the civilisation of a society is measured by the number
of its needs, as seems to be the common opinion to-day, it is to be feared that
the children of the lagoon would make but a poor figure in a set of comparative tables. Not their misery, doubtless, but the way they elude their misery, is
what pleases the sentimental tourist, who is gratified by the sight of a beautiful race that lives by the aid of its imagination. The way to enjoy Venice is to
follow the example of these people and make the most of simple pleasures.
Almost all the pleasures of the place are simple; this may be maintained even
under the imputation of ingenious paradox. There is no simpler pleasure than
looking at a fine Titian, unless it be looking at a fine Tintoret or strolling into
St. Mark's,—abominable the way one falls into the habit,—and resting one's
light-wearied eyes upon the windowless gloom; or than floating in a gondola
or than hanging over a balcony or than taking one's coffee at Florian's. It is of
such superficial pastimes that a Venetian day is composed, and the pleasure of
the matter is in the emotions to which they minister. These are fortunately of
the finest—otherwise Venice would be insufferably dull. Reading Ruskin is
good; reading the old records is perhaps better; but the best thing of all is

---

eternal *conversazione*. Suggesting the Renaissance tradition of the "sacra conversazione," a
particularly harmonious pictorial composition representing the Madonna and Child with saints
who are united in a sort of genial discussion.

simply staying on. The only way to care for Venice as she deserves it is to give her a chance to touch you often—to linger and remain and return.

II

THE danger is that you will not linger enough—a danger of which the author of these lines had known something. It is possible to dislike Venice, and to entertain the sentiment in a responsible and intelligent manner. There are travellers who think the place odious, and those who are not of this opinion often find themselves wishing that the others were only more numerous. The sentimental tourist's sole quarrel with his Venice is that he has too many competitors there. He likes to be alone; to be original; to have (to himself, at least) the air of making discoveries. The Venice of to-day is a vast museum where the little wicket that admits you is perpetually turning and creaking, and you march through the institution with a herd of fellow-gazers. There is nothing left to discover or describe and originality of attitude is completely impossible. This is often very annoying; you can only turn your back on your impertinent playfellow and curse his want of delicacy. But this is not the fault of Venice; it is the fault of the rest of the world. The fault of Venice is that, though she is easy to admire, she is not so easy to live with as you count living in other places. After you have stayed a week and the bloom of novelty has rubbed off you wonder if you can accommodate yourself to the peculiar conditions. Your old habits become impracticable and you find yourself obliged to form new ones of an undesirable and unprofitable character. You are tired of your gondola (or you think you are) and you have seen all the principal pictures and heard the names of the palaces announced a dozen times by your gondolier, who brings them out almost as impressively as if he were an English butler bawling titles into a drawing-room. You have walked several hundred times round the Piazza and bought several bushels of photographs. You have visited the antiquity mongers whose horrible sign-boards dishonour some of the grandest vistas in the Grand Canal; you have tried the opera and found it very bad; you have bathed at the Lido and found the water flat. You have begun to have a shipboard-feeling—to regard the Piazza as an enormous saloon and the Riva degli Schiavoni as a promenade-deck. You are obstructed and encaged;

Lido. See page 29 and note.

Riva degli Schiavoni. In the spring of 1881, on the fourth floor of number 4161 Riva degli Schiavoni, James "finished, or virtually finished" (*Complete Notebooks,* 221) work on *The*

your desire for space is unsatisfied; you miss your usual exercise. You try to take a walk and you fail, and meantime, as I say, you have come to regard your gondola as a sort of magnified baby's cradle. You have no desire to be rocked to sleep, though you are sufficiently kept awake by the irritation produced, as you gaze across the shallow lagoon, by the attitude of the perpetual gondolier, with his turned-out toes, his protruded chin, his absurdly unscientific stroke. The canals have a horrible smell, and the everlasting Piazza, where you have looked repeatedly at every article in every shopwindow and found them all rubbish, where the young Venetians who sell bead bracelets and "panoramas" are perpetually thrusting their wares at you, where the same tightly-buttoned officers are for ever sucking the same black weeds, at the same empty tables, in front of the same cafés—the Piazza, as I say, has resolved itself into a magnificent tread-mill. This is the state of mind of those shallow inquirers who find Venice all very well for a week; and if in such a state of mind you take your departure you act with fatal rashness. The loss is your own, moreover; it is not—with all deference to your personal attractions—that of your companions who remain behind; for though there are some disagreeable things in Venice there is nothing so disagreeable as the visitors. The conditions are peculiar, but your intolerance of them evaporates before it has had time to become a prejudice. When you have called for the bill to go, pay it and remain, and you will find on the morrow that you are deeply attached to Venice. It is by living there from day to day that you feel the fulness of her charm; that you invite her exquisite influence to sink into your spirit. The creature varies like a nervous woman, whom you know only when you know all the aspects of her beauty. She has high spirits or low, she is pale or red, grey or pink, cold or warm, fresh or wan, according to the weather or the hour. She is always interesting and almost always sad; but she has a thousand occasional graces and is always liable to happy accidents. You become extraordinarily fond of these things; you count upon them; they make part of your life. Tenderly fond you become; there is something indefinable in those depths of personal acquaintance that gradually establish themselves. The place seems to personify itself, to become human and sentient and conscious of your affection. You desire

---

Portrait of a Lady, a novel he had begun—"that is, I took up, and worked over, an old beginning"—at the Hotel de l'Arno in Florence during the spring of 1879 (219). A somewhat more evocative reminiscence of the Riva degli Schiavoni as the site of the completion of *Portrait* is developed in the novel's New York Edition preface: "I seem to myself to have been constantly driven, in the fruitless fidget of composition, as if to see whether, out in the blue channel, the ship of some right suggestion, of some better phrase, of the next happy twist of my subject, the next true touch for my canvas, might n't come into sight" (*Literary Criticism: French Writers,* 1070).

to embrace it, to caress it, to possess it; and finally a soft sense of possession grows up and your visit becomes a perpetual love-affair. It is very true
that if you go, as the author of these lines on a certain occasion went,
about the middle of March, a certain amount of disappointment is possible. He had paid no visit for several years, and in the interval the beautiful
and helpless city had suffered an increase of injury. The barbarians are in
full possession and you tremble for what they may do. You are reminded
from the moment of your arrival that Venice scarcely exists any more as a
city at all; that she exists only as a battered peep-show and bazaar. There
was a horde of savage Germans encamped in the Piazza, and they filled the
Ducal Palace and the Academy with their uproar. The English and Americans came a little later. They came in good time, with a great many French,
who were discreet enough to make very long repasts at the Caffè Quadri,
during which they were out of the way. The months of April and May of
the year 1881 were not, as a general thing, a favourable season for visiting
the Ducal Palace and the Academy. The *valet-de-place* had marked them
for his own and held triumphant possession of them. He celebrates his
triumphs in a terrible brassy voice, which resounds all over the place, and
has, whatever language he be speaking, the accent of some other idiom.
During all the spring months in Venice these gentry abound in the great
resorts, and they lead their helpless captives through churches and galleries
in dense irresponsible groups. They infest the Piazza; they pursue you
along the Riva; they hang about the bridges and the doors of the cafés. In
saying just now that I was disappointed at first, I had chiefly in mind the
impression that assails me to-day in the whole precinct of St. Mark's. The
condition of this ancient sanctuary is surely a great scandal. The pedlars
and commissioners ply their trade—often a very unclean one—at the very
door of the temple; they follow you across the threshold, into the sacred
dusk, and pull your sleeve, and hiss into your ear, scuffling with each other
for customers. There is a great deal of dishonour about St. Mark's altogether, and if Venice, as I say, has become a great bazaar, this exquisite
edifice is now the biggest booth.

III

IT is treated as a booth in all ways, and if it had not somehow a great spirit of
solemnity within it the traveller would soon have little warrant for regarding

---

valet-de-place. A servant available for hire to travelers.

it as a religious affair. The restoration of the outer walls, which has lately been so much attacked and defended, is certainly a great shock. Of the necessity of the work only an expert is, I suppose, in a position to judge; but there is no doubt that, if a necessity it be, it is one that is deeply to be regretted. To no more distressing necessity have people of taste lately had to resign themselves. Wherever the hand of the restorer has been laid all semblance of beauty has vanished; which is a sad fact, considering that the external loveliness of St. Mark's has been for ages less impressive only than that of the still comparatively uninjured interior. I know not what is the measure of necessity in such a case, and it appears indeed to be a very delicate question. To-day, at any rate, that admirable harmony of faded mosaic and marble which, to the eye of the traveller emerging from the narrow streets that lead to the Piazza, filled all the further end of it with a sort of dazzling silver presence—to-day this lovely vision is in a way to be completely reformed and indeed well-nigh abolished. The old softness and mellowness of colour—the work of the quiet centuries and of the breath of the salt sea—is giving way to large crude patches of new material which have the effect of a monstrous malady rather than of a restoration to health. They look like blotches of red and white paint and dishonourable smears of chalk on the cheeks of a noble matron. The face toward the Piazzetta is in especial the newest-looking thing conceivable—as new as a new pair of boots or as the morning's paper. We do not profess, however, to undertake a scientific quarrel with these changes; we admit that our complaint is a purely sentimental one. The march of industry in united Italy must doubtless be looked at as a whole, and one must endeavour to believe that it is through innumerable lapses of taste that this deeply interesting country is groping her way to her place among the nations. For the present, it is not to be denied, certain odd phases of the process are more visible than the result, to arrive at which it seems necessary that, as she was of old a passionate votary of the beautiful, she should to-day burn everything that she has adored. It is

---

restoration of the outer walls... so much attacked and defended. In England a violent polemic blew up when restoration efforts to stabilize the walls of St. Mark's obliterated some picturesque qualities. Brief articles appeared in the London *Times* (13 November 1879, 5; 17 December 1879, 5; 25 March 1880, 5), but the *New York Times*, beginning with an article entitled "Venetian Outrages," featured the English debate. The correspondent argued that Venice was so precious that "Europe should take it out of the possession of the Italian Government, and place it under the protection of a European commission." Critics who castigated the "blind and blasphemous stupidity" of the city's municipal authorities advocated Venice's return to Austrian rule and foresaw an imminent destruction "far worse than the burning of the Alexandrian library." William Morris fueled fears when he reported, erroneously, that in restructuring the walls of St. Mark's, "the entire front of the building, with its ancient mosaics and wonderful carvings, is to be pulled down immediately." (*New York Times,* 18 November 1879, 4; 25 November 1879, 4. The defenses followed: 12 December 1879, 3, and 25 January 1880, 8.)

doubtless too soon to judge her, and there are moments when one is willing to forgive her even the restoration of St. Mark's. Inside as well there has been a considerable attempt to make the place more tidy; but the general effect, as yet, has not seriously suffered. What I chiefly remember is the straightening out of that dark and rugged old pavement—those deep undulations of primitive mosaic in which the fond spectator was thought to perceive an intended resemblance to the waves of the ocean. Whether intended or not the analogy was an image the more in a treasure-house of images; but from a considerable portion of the church it has now disappeared. Throughout the greater part indeed the pavement remains as recent generations have known it—dark, rich, cracked, uneven, spotted with porphyry and time-blackened malachite, polished by the knees of innumerable worshippers; but in other large stretches the idea imitated by the restorers is that of the ocean in a dead calm, and the model they have taken the floor of a London club-house or of a New York hotel. I think no Venetian and scarcely any Italian cares much for such differences; and when, a year ago, people in England were writing to the *Times* about the whole business and holding meetings to protest against it the dear children of the lagoon—so far as they heard or heeded the rumour—thought them partly busy-bodies and partly asses. Busy-bodies they doubtless were, but they took a good deal of disinterested trouble. It never occurs to the Venetian mind of to-day that such trouble may be worth taking; the Venetian mind vainly endeavours to conceive a state of existence in which personal questions are so insipid that people have to look for grievances in the wrongs of brick and marble. I must not, however, speak of St. Mark's as if I had the pretension of giving a description of it or as if the reader desired one. The reader has been too well served already. It is surely the best-described building in the world. Open the *Stones of Venice,* open Théophile Gautier's *Italia,* and you will see. These writers take it very seriously, and it is only because there is another way of taking it that I venture to speak of it; the way that offers itself after you have been in Venice a couple of months, and the light is hot in the

---

the best-described building in the world . . . Théophile Gautier's *Italia.* Cf. pages 55, 81, and notes. See Gautier, *Italia,* chapter 8, "Saint-Marc," 96–109, and chapter 9, "Saint-Marc," 110–28. In an 1872 review James calls Gautier "the apostle of visual observation—the poet of the look of things," but decries the fact that there "is the oddest contrast between his descriptive *brio* and grace and the feeble note of reflection which from time to time crops up through it" (*Literary Criticism: French Writers,* 353, 355). See also *Letters,* I, 138, where he recommends to William James that he read Gautier's *Italia* and states that "if I weren't a base Anglo-Saxon and a coward slave, I should ask nothing better than his [Veronese's] *Rape of Europa* in the Doge's Palace where a great rosy blond, gorgeous with brocade and pearls and bouncing with salubrity and with a great mellow splendor of sea and sky and nymphs and flowers do their best to demoralize the world into a herd of Théophile Gautiers."

great Square, and you pass in under the pictured porticoes with a feeling of habit and friendliness and a desire for something cool and dark. There are moments, after all, when the church is comparatively quiet and empty, and when you may sit there with an easy consciousness of its beauty. From the moment, of course, that you go into any Italian church for any purpose but to say your prayers or look at the ladies, you rank yourself among the trooping barbarians I just spoke of; you treat the place as an orifice in the peep-show. Still, it is almost a spiritual function—or, at the worst, an amorous one—to feed one's eyes on the molten colour that drops from the hollow vaults and thickens the air with its richness. It is all so quiet and sad and faded and yet all so brilliant and living. The strange figures in the mosaic pictures, bending with the curve of niche and vault, stare down through the glowing dimness; the burnished gold that stands behind them catches the light on its little uneven cubes. St. Mark's owes nothing of its character to the beauty of proportion or perspective; there is nothing grandly balanced or far-arching; there are no long lines nor triumphs of the perpendicular. The church arches indeed, but arches like a dusky cavern. Beauty of surface, of tone, of detail, of things near enough to touch and kneel upon and lean against—it is from this the effect proceeds. In this sort of beauty the place is incredibly rich, and you may go there every day and find afresh some lurking pictorial nook. It is a treasury of bits, as the painters say; and there are usually three or four of the fraternity with their easels set up in uncertain equilibrium on the undulating floor. It is not easy to catch the real complexion of St. Mark's, and these laudable attempts at portraiture are apt to look either lurid or livid. But if you cannot paint the old loose-looking marble slabs, the great panels of basalt and jasper, the crucifixes of which the lonely anguish looks deeper in the vertical light, the tabernacles whose open doors disclose a dark Byzantine image spotted with dull, crooked gems—if you cannot paint these things you can at least grow fond of them. You grow fond even of the old benches of red marble, partly worn away by the breeches of many generations and attached to the base of those wide pilasters of which the precious plating, delightful in its faded brownness, with a faint grey bloom upon it, bulges and yawns a little with honourable age.

IV

EVEN at first, when the vexatious sense of the city of the Doges reduced to earning its living as a curiosity-shop was in its keenness, there was a great deal of entertainment to be got from lodging on Riva Schiavoni and looking out at the far-shimmering lagoon. There was entertainment indeed in simply getting into the place and observing the queer incidents of a Venetian installation. A great many persons contribute indirectly to this undertaking, and it is surprising how they spring out at you during your novitiate to remind you that they are bound up in some mysterious manner with the constitution of your little establishment. It was an interesting problem for instance to trace the subtle connection existing between the niece of the landlady and the occupancy of the fourth floor. Superficially it was none too visible, as the young lady in question was a dancer at the Fenice theatre—or when that was closed at the Rossini—and might have been supposed absorbed by her professional duties. It proved necessary, however, that she should hover about the premises in a velvet jacket and a pair of black kid gloves with one little white button; as also, that she should apply a thick coating of powder to her face, which had a charming oval and a sweet weak expression, like that of most of the Venetian maidens, who, as a general thing—it was not a peculiarity of the landlady's niece—are fond of besmearing themselves with flour. You soon recognise that it is not only the many-twinkling lagoon you behold from a habitation on the Riva; you see a little of everything Venetian. Straight across, before my windows, rose the great pink mass of San Giorgio Maggiore, which has for an ugly Palladian church a success beyond all reason. It is a success of position, of colour, of the immense detached Campanile, tipped with a tall gold angel. I know not whether it is because San Giorgio is so grandly conspicuous, with a great deal of worn, faded-looking brickwork; but for many persons the whole place has a kind of suffusion of rosiness. Asked what may be the leading colour in the Venetian concert, we should inveterately say Pink, and yet without remembering after all that this elegant hue occurs very often. It is a faint, shimmering, airy, watery pink; the bright sea-light seems to flush with it and the pale whiteish-green of lagoon and canal to drink it in. There is indeed a great deal of very evident brickwork, which is never fresh or loud in colour, but always burnt out, as it were, always exquisitely mild.

Certain little mental pictures rise before the collector of memories at the simple mention, written or spoken, of the places he has loved. When I hear, when I see, the magical name I have written above these pages, it is not of the great Square that I think, with its strange basilica and its high arcades, nor of the wide mouth of the Grand Canal, with the stately steps and the well-poised dome of the Salute; it is not of the low lagoon, nor the sweet Piazzetta, nor the dark chambers of St. Mark's. I simply see a narrow canal

---

San Giorgio Maggiore . . . worn, faded-looking brickwork. The church was extensively restored from 1951 to 1956; Forlati, *S. Giorgio Maggiore: Il complesso monumentale e i suoi restauri* provides photographs of the neglected structure James saw.

in the heart of the city—a patch of green water and a surface of pink wall. The gondola moves slowly; it gives a great smooth swerve, passes under a bridge, and the gondolier's cry, carried over the quiet water, makes a kind of splash in the stillness. A girl crosses the little bridge, which has an arch like a camel's back, with an old shawl on her head, which makes her characteristic and charming; you see her against the sky as you float beneath. The pink of the old wall seems to fill the whole place; it sinks even into the opaque water. Behind the wall is a garden, out of which the long arm of a white June rose—the roses of Venice are splendid—has flung itself by way of spontaneous ornament. On the other side of this small water-way is a great shabby façade of Gothic windows and balconies—balconies on which dirty clothes are hung and under which a cavernous-looking doorway opens from a low flight of slimy water-steps. It is very hot and still, the canal has a queer smell, and the whole place is enchanting.

It is poor work, however, talking about the colour of things in Venice. The fond spectator is perpetually looking at it from his window, when he is not floating about with that delightful sense of being for the moment a part of it, which any gentleman in a gondola is free to entertain. Venetian windows and balconies are a dreadful lure, and while you rest your elbows on these cushioned ledges the precious hours fly away. But in truth Venice is n't in fair weather a place for concentration of mind. The effort required for sitting down to a writing-table is heroic, and the brightest page of MS. looks dull beside the brilliancy of your *milieu*. All nature beckons you forth and murmurs to you sophistically that such hours should be devoted to collecting impressions. Afterwards, in ugly places, at unprivileged times, you can convert your impressions into prose. Fortunately for the present proser the weather was n't always fine; the first month was wet and windy, and it was better to judge of the matter from an open casement than to respond to the advances of persuasive gondoliers. Even then however there was a constant entertainment in the view. It was all cold colour, and the steel-grey floor of the lagoon was stroked the wrong way by the wind. Then there were charming cool intervals, when the churches, the houses, the anchored fishing-boats, the whole gently-curving line of the Riva, seemed to be washed with a pearly white. Later it all turned warm—warm to the eye as well as to other senses. After the middle of May the whole place was in a glow. The sea took on a thousand shades, but they were only infinite variations of blue, and those rosy walls I just spoke of began to flush in the thick sunshine. Every patch of colour, every yard of weather-stained stucco, every glimpse of nestling garden or daub of sky above a *calle*, began to shine and sparkle—

---

calle. A narrow Venetian lane.

began, as the painters say, to "compose." The lagoon was streaked with odd currents, which played across it like huge smooth finger-marks. The gondolas multiplied and spotted it all over; every gondola and gondolier looking, at a distance, precisely like every other.

There is something strange and fascinating in this mysterious impersonality of the gondola. It has an identity when you are in it, but, thanks to their all being of the same size, shape and colour, and of the same deportment and gait, it has none, or as little as possible, as you see it pass before you. From my windows on the Riva there was always the same silhouette—the long, black, slender skiff, lifting its head and throwing it back a little, moving yet seeming not to move, with the grotesquely-graceful figure on the poop. This figure inclines, as may be, more to the graceful or to the grotesque— standing in the "second position" of the dancing-master, but indulging from the waist upward in a freedom of movement which that functionary would deprecate. One may say as a general thing that there is something rather awkward in the movement even of the most graceful gondolier, and something graceful in the movement of the most awkward. In the graceful men of course the grace predominates, and nothing can be finer than the large, firm way in which, from their point of vantage, they throw themselves over their tremendous oar. It has the boldness of a plunging bird and the regularity of a pendulum. Sometimes, as you see this movement in profile, in a gondola that passes you—see, as you recline on your own low cushions, the arching body of the gondolier lifted up against the sky—it has a kind of nobleness which suggests an image on a Greek frieze. The gondolier at Venice is your very good friend—if you choose him happily—and on the quality of the personage depends a good deal that of your impressions. He is a part of your daily life, your double, your shadow, your complement. Most people, I think, either like their gondolier or hate him; and if they like him, like him very much. In this case they take an interest in him after his departure; wish him to be sure of employment, speak of him as the gem of gondoliers and tell their friends to be certain to "secure" him. There is usually no difficulty in securing him; there is nothing elusive or reluctant about a gondolier. Nothing would induce me not to believe them for the most part excellent fellows, and the sentimental tourist must always have a kindness for them. More than the rest of the population, of course, they are the children of Venice; they are associated with its idiosyncrasy, with its essence, with its silence, with its melancholy.

When I say they are associated with its silence I should immediately add that they are associated also with its sound. Among themselves they are an extraordinarily talkative company. They chatter at the *traghetti*, where they

---

traghetti. Ferries.

always have some sharp point under discussion; they bawl across the canals; they bespeak your commands as you approach; they defy each other from afar. If you happen to have a *traghetto* under your window, you are well aware that they are a vocal race. I should go even further than I went just now, and say that the voice of the gondolier is in fact for audibility the dominant or rather the only note of Venice. There is scarcely another heard sound, and that indeed is part of the interest of the place. There is no noise there save distinctly human noise; no rumbling, no vague uproar, nor rattle of wheels and hoofs. It is all articulate and vocal and personal. One may say indeed that Venice is emphatically the city of conversation; people talk all over the place because there is nothing to interfere with its being caught by the ear. Among the populace it is a general family party. The still water carries the voice, and good Venetians exchange confidences at a distance of half a mile. It saves a world of trouble, and they don't like trouble. Their delightful garrulous language helps them to make Venetian life a long *conversazione*. This language, with its soft elisions, its odd transpositions, its kindly contempt for consonants and other disagreeables, has in it something peculiarly human and accommodating. If your gondolier had no other merit he would have the merit that he speaks Venetian. This may rank as a merit even—some people perhaps would say especially—when you don't understand what he says. But he adds to it other graces which make him an agreeable feature in your life. The price he sets on his services is touchingly small, and he has a happy art of being obsequious without being, or at least without seeming, abject. For occasional liberalities he evinces an almost lyrical gratitude. In short he has delightfully good manners, a merit which he shares for the most part with the Venetians at large. One grows very fond of these people, and the reason of one's fondness is the frankness and sweetness of their address. That of the Italian family at large has much to recommend it; but in the Venetian manner there is something peculiarly ingratiating. One feels that the race is old, that it has a long and rich civilisation in its blood, and that if it has n't been blessed by fortune it has at least been polished by time. It has n't a genius for stiff morality, and indeed makes few pretensions in that direction. It scruples but scantly to represent the false as the true, and has been accused of cultivating the occasion to grasp and to overreach, and of steering a crooked course—not to your and my advantage—amid the sanctities of property. It has been accused further of loving if not too well at least too often, of being in fine as little austere as possible. I am not sure it is very brave, nor struck with its being very industrious. But it has an unfailing sense of the amenities of life; the poorest Venetian is a natural man of the world. He is better company than persons of his class are apt to be among the nations of industry and virtue—where people are also sometimes perceived to lie and steal and otherwise misconduct themselves. He has a great desire to please and to be pleased.

V

IN that matter at least the cold-blooded stranger begins at last to imitate him; begins to lead a life that shall be before all things easy; unless indeed he allow himself, like Mr. Ruskin, to be put out of humour by Titian and Tiepolo. The hours he spends among the pictures are his best hours in Venice, and I am ashamed to have written so much of common things when I might have been making festoons of the names of the masters. Only, when we have covered our page with such festoons what more is left to say? When one has said Carpaccio and Bellini, the Tintoret and the Veronese, one has struck a note that must be left to resound at will. Everything has been said about the mighty painters, and it is of little importance that a pilgrim the more has found them to his taste. "Went this morning to the Academy; was very much pleased with Titian's 'Assumption.' " That honest phrase has doubtless been written in many a traveller's diary, and was not indiscreet on the part of its author. But it appeals little to the general reader, and we must moreover notoriously not expose our deepest feelings. Since I have mentioned Titian's "Assumption" I must say that there are some people who have been less pleased with it than the observer we have just imagined. It is one of the possible disappointments of Venice, and you may if you like take

---

like Mr. Ruskin, to be put out of humour by Titian and Tiepolo. Irritation with Titian, whom Ruskin consistently praises and on one occasion calls the "greatest painter who ever lived" (*Works,* XVI, 314) is, on the contrary, unrepresentative; yet in the "Guide to the Academy" Ruskin finds Titian's *Presentation of the Virgin* the "most stupid and uninteresting picture ever painted by him" (*Works,* XXIV, 157–58). The sole reference to Tiepolo in Ruskin's thirty-nine volumes comes in *St. Mark's Rest* when he claims that two pictures by Tiepolo "are exactly like what a first-rate Parisian Academy student would do, settling himself to conceive the sentiment of Christ's flagellation, after having read unlimited quantities of George Sand and Dumas" (*Works,* XXIV, 357–58).

Titian's "Assumption." . . . two or three other works. James's 25 September 1869 letter to William James provides his earlier reaction, twelve years before the publication of this essay: "For the present I give up Titian altogether. He is not adequately represented here. His *Assumption* strikes me as a magnificent second-rate picture"; his 1882 reaction seems to echo Ruskin: "The traveller is generally too much struck by Titian's great picture of 'The Assumption' to be able to pay proper attention to the other works in the gallery. . . . [L]et him be assured that the picture is in reality not one whit the better either for being large or gaudy in colour, and he will then be better disposed to give the pains necessary to discover the merit of the more profound work of Bellini and Tintoret" ("Guide to the Academy of Venice," *Works,* XXIV, 152).

In 1518 the painting was placed as an altarpiece for the Frari, but later was moved to the Accademia, where James saw it. The 1882 Baedeker *Italien,* 233–34, lists more than twenty-five pictures in the *sala,* but elsewhere James singles out the Bellini (see 26 and note); seven Tintorettos, including "St. Mark Freeing a Slave," also were displayed in the room, as were two works by Veronese. Today the *Assumption* is back at the Frari.

advantage of your privilege of not caring for it. It imparts a look of great richness to the side of the beautiful room of the Academy on which it hangs; but the same room contains two or three works less known to fame which are equally capable of inspiring a passion. "The 'Annunciation' struck me as coarse and superficial": that note was once made in a simple-minded tourist's book. At Venice, strange to say, Titian is altogether a disappointment; the city of his adoption is far from containing the best of him. Madrid, Paris, London, Florence, Dresden, Munich—these are the homes of his greatness.

There are other painters who have but a single home, and the greatest of these is the Tintoret. Close beside him sit Carpaccio and Bellini, who make with him the dazzling Venetian trio. The Veronese may be seen and measured in other places; he is most splendid in Venice, but he shines in Paris and in Dresden. You may walk out of the noon-day dusk of Trafalgar Square in November, and in one of the chambers of the National Gallery see the family of Darius rustling and pleading and weeping at the feet of Alexander. Alexander is a beautiful young Venetian in crimson pantaloons, and the picture sends a glow into the cold London twilight. You may sit before it for an hour and dream you are floating to the water-gate of the Ducal Palace, where a certain old beggar who has one of the handsomest heads in the world—he has sat to a hundred painters for Doges and for personages more sacred—has a prescriptive right to pretend to pull your gondola to the steps and to hold out a greasy immemorial cap. But you must go to Venice in very fact to see the other masters, who form part of your life while you are there, who illuminate your view of the universe. It is difficult to express one's relation to them; the whole Venetian art-world is so near, so familiar, so much an extension and adjunct of the spreading actual, that it seems almost invidious to say one owes more to one of them than to the other. Nowhere, not even in Holland, where the correspondence between the real aspects and the little polished canvases is so constant and so exquisite, do art and life seem so interfused and, as it were, so consanguineous. All the splendour of light and colour, all the Venetian air and the Venetian history are on the walls and ceilings of the palaces; and all the genius of the masters, all the images and visions they have left upon canvas, seem to tremble in the sunbeams and dance upon the waves. That is the perpetual interest of the place—that you live in a certain sort of knowledge as in a rosy cloud. You don't go into the churches and galleries by way of a change from the streets; you go into them because they offer you an exquisite reproduction of the things that surround you. All Venice was both model and painter, and life

---

Veronese . . . Darius. *The Family of Darius before Alexander* in the National Gallery in London.

was so pictorial that art could n't help becoming so. With all diminutions life is pictorial still, and this fact gives an extraordinary freshness to one's perception of the great Venetian works. You judge of them not as a connoisseur, but as a man of the world, and you enjoy them because they are so social and so true. Perhaps of all works of art that are equally great they demand least reflection on the part of the spectator—they make least of a mystery of being enjoyed. Reflection only confirms your admiration, yet is almost ashamed to show its head. These things speak so frankly and benignantly to the sense that even when they arrive at the highest style—as in the Tintoret's "Presentation of the little Virgin at the Temple"—they are still more familiar.

But it is hard, as I say, to express all this, and it is painful as well to attempt it—painful because in the memory of vanished hours so filled with beauty the consciousness of present loss oppresses. Exquisite hours, enveloped in light and silence, to have known them once is to have always a terrible standard of enjoyment. Certain lovely mornings of May and June come back with an ineffaceable fairness. Venice is n't smothered in flowers at this season, in the manner of Florence and Rome; but the sea and sky themselves seem to blossom and rustle. The gondola waits at the wavewashed steps, and if you are wise you will take your place beside a discriminating companion. Such a companion in Venice should of course be of the sex that discriminates most finely. An intelligent woman who knows her Venice seems doubly intelligent, and it makes no woman's perceptions less keen to be aware that she can't help looking graceful as she is borne over the waves. The handsome Pasquale, with uplifted oar, awaits your command, knowing, in a general way, from observation of your habits, that your intention is to go to see a picture or two. It perhaps does n't immensely matter what picture you choose: the whole affair is so charming. It is charming to wander through the light and shade of intricate canals, with perpetual architecture above you and perpetual fluidity beneath. It is charming to disembark at the polished steps of a little empty *campo*—a sunny shabby square with an old well in the middle, an old church on one side and tall Venetian windows looking down. Sometimes the windows are tenantless; sometimes a lady in a faded dressing-gown leans vaguely on the sill. There is always an old man holding out his hat for coppers; there are always three or four small boys dodging possible umbrella-pokes while they precede you, in the manner of custodians, to the door of the church.

Tintoret's "Presentation." In Santa Maria dell'Orto.

campo. Literally, and perhaps in the past, a field, but generally taken to be a piazza.

VI

THE churches of Venice are rich in pictures, and many a masterpiece lurks in the unaccommodating gloom of side-chapels and sacristies. Many a noble work is perched behind the dusty candles and muslin roses of a scantily-visited altar; some of them indeed, hidden behind the altar, suffer in a darkness that can never be explored. The facilities offered you for approaching the picture in such cases are a mockery of your irritated wish. You stand at tip-toe on a three-legged stool, you climb a rickety ladder, you almost mount upon the shoulders of the *custode*. You do everything but see the picture. You see just enough to be sure it's beautiful. You catch a glimpse of a divine head, of a fig-tree against a mellow sky, but the rest is impenetrable mystery. You renounce all hope, for instance, of approaching the magnificent Cima da Conegliano in San Giovanni in Bragora; and bethinking yourself of the immaculate purity that shines in the spirit of this master, you renounce it with chagrin and pain. Behind the high altar in that church hangs a Baptism of Christ by Cima which I believe has been more or less repainted. You make the thing out in spots, you see it has a fulness of perfection. But you turn away from it with a stiff neck and promise yourself consolation in the Academy and at the Madonna dell'Orto, where two noble works by the same hand—pictures as clear as a summer twilight—present themselves in better circumstances. It may be said as a general thing that you never see the Tintoret. You admire him, you adore him, you think him the greatest of painters, but in the great majority of cases your eyes fail to deal with him. This is partly his own fault; so many of his works have turned to blackness and are positively rotting in their frames. At the Scuola di San Rocco, where there are acres of him, there is scarcely anything at all ade-

---

Cima da Conegliano . . . Baptism . . . more or less repainted. The work is now well illuminated and far better viewed behind a less obstructive altar, but it remains extremely high, in an architectural niche, on the church wall. Menegazzi (99–100) speaks of a particularly brutal sixteenth-century restoration that was partly recovered in 1832.

in the Academy . . . at the Madonna dell'Orto . . . two noble works. In 1876 Hare notes two holdings by Cima in the Accademia, a Virgin and Child, and, particularly, a Virgin and Child with Saints John and Paul. Humfrey lists nine works, six of which were part of the collection in 1882; an additional painting of Saint Mark was attributed to Cima in 1882, but is now given to Andrea Busati. *Saint John the Baptist with Saints Peter, Mark, Jerome, and Paul* (c. 1493) was considered a supremely successful work at the time James viewed it. For several decades the original was displayed at the Accademia and a copy was exhibited at the church, but later the original was brought back to the Madonna dell'Orto.

Scuola di San Rocco . . . scarcely anything at all adequately visible. See page 57 and note.

quately visible save the immense "Crucifixion" in the upper story. It is true that in looking at this huge composition you look at many pictures; it has not only a multitude of figures but a wealth of episodes; and you pass from one of these to the other as if you were "doing" a gallery. Surely no single picture in the world contains more of human life; there is everything in it, including the most exquisite beauty. It is one of the greatest things of art; it is always interesting. There are works of the artist which contain touches more exquisite, revelations of beauty more radiant, but there is no other vision of so intense a reality, an execution so splendid. The interest, the impressiveness, of that whole corner of Venice, however melancholy the effect of its gorgeous and ill-lighted chambers, gives a strange importance to a visit to the Scuola. Nothing that all travellers go to see appears to suffer less from the incursions of travellers. It is one of the loneliest booths of the bazaar, and the author of these lines has always had the good fortune, which he wishes to every other traveller, of having it to himself. I think most visitors find the place rather alarming and wicked-looking. They walk about a while among the fitful figures that gleam here and there out of the great tapestry (as it were) with which the painter has hung all the walls, and then, depressed and bewildered by the portentous solemnity of these objects, by strange glimpses of unnatural scenes, by the echo of their lonely footsteps on the vast stone floors, they take a hasty departure, finding themselves again, with a sense of release from danger, a sense that the *genius loci* was a sort of mad white-washer who worked with a bad mixture, in the bright light of the *campo,* among the beggars, the orange-vendors and the passing gondolas. Solemn indeed is the place, solemn and strangely suggestive, for the simple reason that we shall scarcely find four walls elsewhere that inclose within a like area an equal quantity of genius. The air is thick with it and dense and difficult to breathe; for it was genius that was not happy, inasmuch as it lacked the art to fix itself for ever. It is not immortality that we breathe at the Scuola di San Rocco, but conscious, reluctant mortality.

Fortunately, however, we can turn to the Ducal Palace, where everything is so brilliant and splendid that the poor dusky Tintoret is lifted in spite of himself into the concert. This deeply original building is of course the loveli-

---

"Crucifixion." . . . **wealth of episodes.** In the preface to *The Tragic Muse* James defends Tintoretto's running the risk of "too ample a canvas": "A story was a story, a picture a picture, and I had a mortal horror of two stories, two pictures, in one. . . . It was a fact, apparently, that one *had* on occasion seen two pictures in one; were there not for instance certain sublime Tintorettos at Venice, a measureless Crucifixion in especial, which showed without loss of authority half a dozen actions separately taking place?" (*Literary Criticism: French Writers,* 1107). In *Letters,* 1, 137–41, he discusses Tintoretto and states, "[B]ut if Shakespeare is the greatest of poets Tintoretto is assuredly the greatest of painters."

est thing in Venice, and a morning's stroll there is a wonderful illumination. Cunningly select your hour—half the enjoyment of Venice is a question of dodging—and enter at about one o'clock, when the tourists have flocked off to lunch and the echoes of the charming chambers have gone to sleep among the sunbeams. There is no brighter place in Venice—by which I mean that on the whole there is none half so bright. The reflected sunshine plays up through the great windows from the glittering lagoon and shimmers and twinkles over gilded walls and ceilings. All the history of Venice, all its splendid stately past, glows around you in a strong sea-light. Every one here is magnificent, but the great Veronese is the most magnificent of all. He swims before you in a silver cloud; he thrones in an eternal morning. The deep blue sky burns behind him, streaked across with milky bars; the white colonnades sustain the richest canopies, under which the first gentlemen and ladies in the world both render homage and receive it. Their glorious garments rustle in the air of the sea and their sun-lighted faces are the very complexion of Venice. The mixture of pride and piety, of politics and religion, of art and patriotism, gives a splendid dignity to every scene. Never was a painter more nobly joyous, never did an artist take a greater delight in life, seeing it all as a kind of breezy festival and feeling it through the medium of perpetual success. He revels in the gold-framed ovals of the ceilings, multiplies himself there with the fluttering movement of an embroidered banner that tosses itself into the blue. He was the happiest of painters and produced the happiest picture in the world. "The Rape of Europa" surely deserves this title; it is impossible to look at it without aching with envy. Nowhere else in art is such a temperament revealed; never did inclination and opportunity combine to express such enjoyment. The mixture of flowers and gems and brocade, of blooming flesh and shining sea and waving groves, of youth, health, movement, desire—all this is the brightest vision that ever descended upon the soul of a painter. Happy the artist who could entertain such a vision; happy the artist who could paint it as the masterpiece I here recall is painted.

---

happiest picture in the world. "The Rape of Europa." James's view suggests the influence of Gautier: "quel sourire d'éternelle jeunesse dans cette toile merveilleuse, où Paul Véronèse semble avoir dit son dernier mot! . . . rien de malsain dans cette rayonnante allég esse" ["What a smile of eternal youth in this marvelous canvas in which Paul Veronese seems t ɔ have uttered his final word! . . . nothing unhealthy in this radiant joyousness"] (*Italia,* 143; trans. Vermilye, 139). In an 1869 letter to his brother William, Henry James described the painting (see note to page 14, on Gautier). John Addington Symonds was later to observe that Veronese "uses the tale of Europa, for example, as the motive for rich toilettes and delightful landscape, choosing the moment that has least in it of pathos" (*Renaissance in Italy,* III, 274). See also pages 55–56 and note to "deep spiritual intentions."

The Tintoret's visions were not so bright as that; but he had several that
were radiant enough. In the room that contains the work just cited are
several smaller canvases by the greatly more complex genius of the Scuola di
San Rocco, which are almost simple in their loveliness, almost happy in their
simplicity. They have kept their brightness through the centuries, and they
shine with their neighbours in those golden rooms. There is a piece of
painting in one of them which is one of the sweetest things in Venice and
which reminds one afresh of those wild flowers of execution that bloom so
profusely and so unheeded in the dark corners of all of the Tintoret's work.
"Pallas chasing away Mars" is, I believe, the name that is given to the
picture; and it represents in fact a young woman of noble appearance admin-
istering a gentle push to a fine young man in armour, as if to tell him to keep
his distance. It is of the gentleness of this push that I speak, the charming
way in which she puts out her arm, with a single bracelet on it, and rests her
young hand, its rosy fingers parted, on his dark breastplate. She bends her
enchanting head with the effort—a head which has all the strange fairness
that the Tintoret always sees in women—and the soft, living, flesh-like glow
of all these members, over which the brush has scarcely paused in its course,
is as pretty an example of genius as all Venice can show. But why speak of
the Tintoret when I can say nothing of the great "Paradise," which unfolds
its somewhat smoky splendour and the wonder of its multitudinous circles
in one of the other chambers? If it were not one of the first pictures in the
world it would be about the biggest, and we must confess that the spectator
gets from it at first chiefly an impression of quantity. Then he sees that this
quantity is really wealth; that the dim confusion of faces is a magnificent
composition, and that some of the details of this composition are extremely
beautiful. It is impossible however in a retrospect of Venice to specify one's
happiest hours, though as one looks backward certain ineffaceable moments
start here and there into vividness. How is it possible to forget one's visits to
the sacristy of the Frari, however frequent they may have been, and the great
work of John Bellini which forms the treasure of that apartment?

VII

NOTHING in Venice is more perfect than this, and we know of no work of art
more complete. The picture is in three compartments; the Virgin sits in the

---

"Paradise." . . . about the biggest. Often identified as the largest oil painting in existence,
measuring 7 by 22 meters.

sacristy of the Frari . . . John Bellini. Giovanni Bellini's triptych *Madonna Enthroned, with
Child and Saints* (1488), at the church of Santa Maria Gloriosa dei Frari.

central division with her child; two venerable saints, standing close together, occupy each of the others. It is impossible to imagine anything more finished or more ripe. It is one of those things that sum up the genius of a painter, the experience of a life, the teaching of a school. It seems painted with molten gems, which have only been clarified by time, and it is as solemn as it is gorgeous and as simple as it is deep. Giovanni Bellini is more or less everywhere in Venice, and, wherever he is, almost certain to be first—first, I mean, in his own line: he paints little else than the Madonna and the saints; he has not Carpaccio's care for human life at large, nor the Tintoret's nor that of the Veronese. Some of his greater pictures, however, where several figures are clustered together, have a richness of sanctity that is almost profane. There is one of them on the dark side of the room at the Academy that contains Titian's "Assumption," which if we could only see it—its position is an inconceivable scandal—would evidently be one of the mightiest of so-called sacred pictures. So too is the Madonna of San Zaccaria, hung in a cold, dim, dreary place, ever so much too high, but so mild and serene, and so grandly disposed and accompanied, that the proper attitude for even the most critical amateur, as he looks at it, strikes one as the bended knee. There is another noble John Bellini, one of the very few in which there is no Virgin, at San Giovanni Crisostomo—a St. Jerome, in a red dress, sitting aloft upon the rocks and with a landscape of extraordinary purity behind him. The absence of the peculiarly erect Madonna makes it an interesting surprise among the works of the painter and gives it a somewhat less strenuous air. But it has brilliant beauty and the St. Jerome is a delightful old personage.

The same church contains another great picture for which the haunter of these places must find a shrine apart in his memory; one of the most interesting things he will have seen, if not the most brilliant. Nothing appeals more to him than three figures of Venetian ladies which occupy the foreground of a smallish canvas of Sebastian del Piombo, placed above the high altar of San Giovanni Crisostomo. Sebastian was a Venetian by birth, but few of his productions are to be seen in his native place; few indeed are to be seen

---

one of them . . . at the Academy. No longer in the same room in the Accademia, the *Madonna Enthroned, with Child, and Saints Francis, John the Baptist, Sebastian, Dominic, and with Job,* after whom the canvas generally is called *La Pala di San Giobbe.*

Madonna of San Zaccaria. Bellini's *Virgin Enthroned, with Child, and Saints Peter, Catherine, Lucy, and Jerome,* called *La Pala di San Zaccaria.*

Bellini . . . St. Jerome. *Saint Jerome with Saint Christopher and Saint Augustine* (1513).

at San Giovanni Crisostomo . . . Sebastian del Piombo. The celebrated *Saint John Crisostomo, with Saints Augustine, John the Baptist, Liberale, Catherine, Agnes, and the Magdalene* (1509); the painting was particularly recommended to James by Constance Fenimore Woolson (*Letters,* III, 561–62).

anywhere. The picture represents the patron-saint of the church, accompanied by other saints and by the worldly votaries I have mentioned. These ladies stand together on the left, holding in their hands little white caskets; two of them are in profile, but the foremost turns her face to the spectator. This face and figure are almost unique among the beautiful things of Venice, and they leave the susceptible observer with the impression of having made, or rather having missed, a strange, a dangerous, but a most valuable, acquaintance. The lady, who is superbly handsome, is the typical Venetian of the sixteenth century, and she remains for the mind the perfect flower of that society. Never was there a greater air of breeding, a deeper expression of tranquil superiority. She walks a goddess—as if she trod without sinking the waves of the Adriatic. It is impossible to conceive a more perfect expression of the aristocratic spirit either in its pride or in its benignity. This magnificent creature is so strong and secure that she is gentle, and so quiet that in comparison all minor assumptions of calmness suggest only a vulgar alarm. But for all this there are depths of possible disorder in her light-coloured eye.

I had meant however to say nothing about her, for it's not right to speak of Sebastian when one has n't found room for Carpaccio. These visions come to one, and one can neither hold them nor brush them aside. Memories of Carpaccio, the magnificent, the delightful—it's not for want of such visitations, but only for want of space, that I have n't said of him what I would. There is little enough need of it for Carpaccio's sake, his fame being brighter to-day—thanks to the generous lamp Mr. Ruskin has held up to it—than it has ever been. Yet there is something ridiculous in talking of Venice without making him almost the refrain. He and the Tintoret are the two great realists, and it is hard to say which is the more human, the more various. The Tintoret had the mightier temperament, but Carpaccio, who had the advantage of more newness and more responsibility, sailed nearer to perfection. Here and there he quite touches it, as in the enchanting picture, at the Academy, of St. Ursula asleep in her little white bed, in her high clean room, where the angel visits her at dawn; or in the noble St. Jerome in his study at S. Giorgio Schiavoni. This latter work is a pearl of sentiment, and I

St. Ursula asleep. Vittore Carpaccio's *Dream of Saint Ursula* (1495), depicting the crucial moment in the life of a legendary British princess of the third (or, according to some sources, the fifth) century; an angel appeared to her in a dream and told her to postpone her marriage to a pagan prince until after she—and 11,000 other virgins—might spend three years visiting the world's most important sanctuaries. After a trip down the Rhine, and a journey on foot to Rome, they were slaughtered by the Huns.

S. Giorgio Schiavoni. The Scuola di San Giorgio Schiavoni holds a series on Saint George and Saint Jerome.

may add without being fantastic a ruby of colour. It unites the most masterly finish with a kind of universal largeness of feeling, and he who has it well in his memory will never hear the name of Carpaccio without a throb of almost personal affection. Such indeed is the feeling that descends upon you in that wonderful little chapel of St. George of the Slaves, where this most personal and sociable of artists has expressed all the sweetness of his imagination. The place is small and incommodious, the pictures are out of sight and ill-lighted, the custodian is rapacious, the visitors are mutually intolerable, but the shabby little chapel is a palace of art. Mr. Ruskin has written a pamphlet about it which is a real aid to enjoyment, though I can't but think the generous artist, with his keen senses and his just feeling, would have suffered to hear his eulogist declare that one of his other productions—in the Museo Civico of Palazzo Correr, a delightful portrait of two Venetian ladies with pet animals—is the "finest picture in the world." It has no need of that to be thought admirable; and what more can a painter desire?

VIII

MAY in Venice is better than April, but June is best of all. Then the days are hot, but not too hot, and the nights are more beautiful than the days. Then Venice is rosier than ever in the morning and more golden than ever as the day descends. She seems to expand and evaporate, to multiply all her reflections and iridescences. Then the life of her people and the strangeness of her constitution become a perpetual comedy, or at least a perpetual drama. Then the gondola is your sole habitation, and you spend days between sea and sky. You go to the Lido, though the Lido has been spoiled. When I first

---

Ruskin has written a pamphlet . . . "finest picture in the world." Ruskin's "The Shrine of the Slaves, Being a Guide to the Principal Pictures by Victor Carpaccio in Venice," a supplement to *St. Mark's Rest,* where he speaks on the damaged picture generally known as *The Courtesans,* but called by him *Two Venetian Ladies with their Pets;* discussing the painting in relation to two other Correr gallery paintings, Ruskin writes that "I rank this Carpaccio above either of them, and therefore, in these respects, the best picture in the world. I know no other which unites every nameable quality of painter's art in so intense a degree—breadth with minuteness, brillancy with quietness, decision with tenderness, colour with light and shade: all that is faithfullest in Holland, fancifullest in Venice, severest in Florence, naturallest in England. . . . I know no other painting in the world which can be compared with it" (*St. Mark's Rest, Works,* XXIV, 363–64).

Lido . . . part of united Italy . . . Santa Elisabetta . . . bitumen walks . . . *teatro diurno.* Approximately two miles southeast of Venice, the Lido beach was rapidly becoming one of

saw it, in 1869, it was a very natural place, and there was but a rough lane across the little island from the landing-place to the beach. There was a bathing-place in those days, and a restaurant, which was very bad, but where in the warm evenings your dinner did n't much matter as you sat letting it cool on the wooden terrace that stretched out into the sea. To-day the Lido is a part of united Italy and has been made the victim of villainous improvements. A little cockney village has sprung up on its rural bosom and a third-rate boulevard leads from Santa Elisabetta to the Adriatic. There are bitumen walks and gas-lamps, lodging-houses, shops and a *teatro diurno*. The bathing-establishment is bigger than before, and the restaurant as well; but it is a compensation perhaps that the cuisine is no better. Such as it is, however, you won't scorn occasionally to partake of it on the breezy platform under which bathers dart and splash, and which looks out to where the fishing-boats, with sails of orange and crimson, wander along the darkening horizon. The beach at the Lido is still lonely and beautiful, and you can easily walk away from the cockney village. The return to Venice in the sunset is classical and indispensable, and those who at that glowing hour have floated toward the towers that rise out of the lagoon will not easily part with the impression. But you indulge in larger excursions—you go to Burano and Torcello, to Malamocco and Chioggia. Torcello, like the Lido, has been improved; the deeply interesting little cathedral of the eighth century, which stood there on the edge of the sea, as touching in its ruin, with its grassy threshold and its primitive mosaics, as the bleached bones of a human skeleton washed ashore by the tide, has now been restored and made cheerful, and the charm of the place, its strange and suggestive desolation, has well-nigh departed.

It will still serve you as a pretext, however, for a day on the lagoon, especially as you will disembark at Burano and admire the wonderful fisherfolk, whose good looks—and bad manners, I am sorry to say—can scarcely be exaggerated. Burano is celebrated for the beauty of its women and the

---

Europe's fashionable late nineteenth-century resorts; Santa Elisabetta was the first, and primary, bathing establishment. James here prefers "bitumen," a word somewhat unusual in English but more common in Latin, to describe the unaesthetic material generally known as asphalt. The emphasis, on the generally ruinous effect of the unification of Italy—at least in terms of the beauty, the mystery, and the grace of Italian life—is a more reiterated theme in the Roman chapters. A *teatro diurno* was a matinee theater.

Burano... Torcello... Malamocco... Chioggia... celebrated for the beauty of its women. Outlying towns. Chioggia was once the second city of the Venetian state; for Torcello, see pages 52–53 and note; in part the distinction of the women of the small town of Burano was due to its having been the site of a large royally endowed school of lacemaking that trained, and then employed, hundreds of young women.

rapacity of its children, and it is a fact that though some of the ladies are rather bold about it every one of them shows you a handsome face. The children assail you for coppers, and in their desire to be satisfied pursue your gondola into the sea. Chioggia is a larger Burano, and you carry away from either place a half-sad, half-cynical, but altogether pictorial impression; the impression of bright-coloured hovels, of bathing in stagnant canals, of young girls with faces of a delicate shape and a susceptible expression, with splendid heads of hair and complexions smeared with powder, faded yellow shawls that hang like old Greek draperies, and little wooden shoes that click as they go up and down the steps of the convex bridges; of brown-cheeked matrons with lustrous tresses and high tempers, massive throats encased with gold beads, and eyes that meet your own with a certain traditional defiance. The men throughout the islands of Venice are almost as handsome as the women; I have never seen so many good-looking rascals. At Burano and Chioggia they sit mending their nets, or lounge at the street corners, where conversation is always high-pitched, or clamour to you to take a boat; and everywhere they decorate the scene with their splendid colour— cheeks and throats as richly brown as the sails of their fishing-smacks— their sea-faded tatters which are always a "costume," their soft Venetian jargon, and the gallantry with which they wear their hats, an article that nowhere sits so well as on a mass of dense Venetian curls. If you are happy you will find yourself, after a June day in Venice (about ten o'clock), on a balcony that overhangs the Grand Canal, with your elbows on the broad ledge, a cigarette in your teeth and a little good company beside you. The gondolas pass beneath, the watery surface gleams here and there from their lamps, some of which are coloured lanterns that move mysteriously in the darkness. There are some evenings in June when there are too many gondo- las, too many lanterns, too many serenades in front of the hotels. The serenading in particular is overdone; but on such a balcony as I speak of you need n't suffer from it, for in the apartment behind you—an accessible refuge—there is more good company, there are more cigarettes. If you are wise you will step back there presently.

1882.

The Grand Canal

The honour of representing the plan and the place at their best might perhaps appear, in the City of St. Mark, properly to belong to the splendid square which bears the patron's name and which is the centre of Venetian life so far (this is pretty well all the way indeed) as Venetian life is a matter of strolling and chaffering, of gossiping and gaping, of circulating without a purpose, and of staring—too often with a foolish one—through the shop-windows of dealers whose hospitality makes their doorsteps dramatic, at the very vulgarest rubbish in all the modern market. If the Grand Canal, however, is not quite technically a "street," the perverted Piazza is perhaps even less normal; and I hasten to add that I am glad not to find myself studying my subject under the international arcades, or yet (I will go the length of saying) in the solemn presence of the church. For indeed in that case I forsee I should become still more confoundingly conscious of the stumbling-block that inevitably, even with his first few words, crops up in the path of the lover of Venice who rashly addresses himself to expression. "Venetian life" is a mere literary convention, though it be an indispensable figure. The words have played an effective part in the literature of sensibility; they constituted thirty years ago the title of Mr. Howells's delightful volume of impressions; but in using them

[Originally published in *Scribner's Magazine*, XII (November 1892), 531–50; reprinted in Richard Harding Davis et al., *The Great Streets of the World*, 1892.]

"Venetian life" is a mere literary convention. . . Mr. Howells. In an 1868 review of William Dean Howells's *Italian Journeys*, James praises Howells's 1866 *Venetian Life* and calls its author "a descriptive writer in a sense and with a perfection that, in our view, can be claimed for no American writer except Hawthorne." See Appendix II.

to-day one owes some frank amends to one's own lucidity. Let me carefully premise therefore that so often as they shall again drop from my pen, so often shall I beg to be regarded as systematically superficial.

Venetian life, in the large old sense, has long since come to an end, and the essential present character of the most melancholy of cities resides simply in its being the most beautiful of tombs. Nowhere else has the past been laid to rest with such tenderness, such a sadness of resignation and remembrance. Nowhere else is the present so alien, so discontinuous, so like a crowd in a cemetery without garlands for the graves. It has no flowers in its hands, but, as a compensation perhaps—and the thing is doubtless more to the point— it has money and little red books. The everlasting shuffle of these irresponsible visitors in the Piazza is contemporary Venetian life. Everything else is only a reverberation of that. The vast mausoleum has a turnstile at the door, and a functionary in a shabby uniform lets you in, as per tariff, to see how dead it is. From this *constatation,* this cold curiosity, proceed all the industry, the prosperity, the vitality of the place. The shopkeepers and gondoliers, the beggars and the models, depend upon it for a living; they are the custodians and the ushers of the great museum—they are even themselves to a certain extent the objects of exhibition. It is in the wide vestibule of the square that the polyglot pilgrims gather most densely; Piazza San Marco is the lobby of the opera in the intervals of the performance. The present fortune of Venice, the lamentable difference, is most easily measured there, and that is why, in the effort to resist our pessimism, we must turn away both from the purchasers and from the vendors of *ricordi.* The *ricordi* that we prefer are gathered best where the gondola glides—best of all on the noble waterway that begins in its glory at the Salute and ends in its abasement at the railway station. It is, however, the cockneyfied Piazzetta (forgive me, shade of St. Theodore—has not a brand new café begun to glare there, electrically, this very year?) that introduces us most directly to the great picture by which the Grand Canal works its first spell, and to which a thousand artists, not always with a talent apiece, have paid their tribute. We pass into the Piazzetta to look down the great throat, as it were, of Venice, and the vision must console us for turning our back on St. Mark's.

---

constatation. Certified establishment of facts.

ricordi. Souvenirs, but also memories.

shade of St. Theodore. The original patron of Venice, to whom the first Venetian church, near the site of the present Saint Mark's, was dedicated; his identity among several Saint Theodores is unsure; in the Piazzetta San Marco, near the Doge's Palace, stands a large marble column topped by a statue, erected in 1172, of a warrior San Teodoro, under whose feet stretches a curiously docile and not surely dead crocodile-like creature.

We have been treated to it again and again, of course, even if we have never stirred from home; but that is only a reason the more for catching at any freshness that may be left in the world of photography. It is in Venice above all that we hear the small buzz of this vulgarising voice of the familiar; yet perhaps it is in Venice too that the picturesque fact has best mastered the pious secret of how to wait for us. Even the classic Salute waits like some great lady on the threshold of her saloon. She is more ample and serene, more seated at her door, than all the copyists have told us, with her domes and scrolls, her scolloped buttresses and statues forming a pompous crown, and her wide steps disposed on the ground like the train of a robe. This fine air of the woman of the world is carried out by the well-bred assurance with which she looks in the direction of her old-fashioned Byzantine neighbour; and the juxtaposition of two churches so distinguished and so different, each splendid in its sort, is a sufficient mark of the scale and range of Venice. However, we ourselves are looking away from St. Mark's—we must blind our eyes to that dazzle; without it indeed there are brightnesses and fascinations enough. We see them in abundance even while we look away from the shady steps of the Salute. These steps are cool in the morning, yet I don't know that I can justify my excessive fondness for them any better than I can explain a hundred of the other vague infatuations with which Venice sophisticates the spirit. Under such an influence fortunately one need n't explain— it keeps account of nothing but perceptions and affections. It is from the Salute steps perhaps, of a summer morning, that this view of the open mouth of the city is most brilliantly amusing. The whole thing composes as if composition were the chief end of human institutions. The charming architectural promontory of the Dogana stretches out the most graceful of arms, balancing in its hand the gilded globe on which revolves the delightful satirical figure of a little weathercock of a woman. This Fortune, this Navigation, or whatever she is called—she surely needs no name—catches the wind in the bit of drapery of which she has divested her rotary bronze loveliness. On the other side of the Canal twinkles and glitters the long row of the happy palaces which are mainly expensive hotels. There is a little of everything everywhere, in the bright Venetian air, but to these houses belongs especially the appearance of sitting, across the water, at the receipt of custom, of watching in their hypocritical loveliness for the stranger and the victim. I call them happy, because even their sordid uses and their vulgar signs melt somehow, with their vague sea-stained pinks and drabs, into that

---

Salute . . . Dogana. Both the church of Santa Maria della Salute and the seventeenth-century Dogana da Mar, the former customhouse, stand on the point of land across the Grand Canal from San Marco.

strange gaiety of light and colour which is made up of the reflection of superannuated things. The atmosphere plays over them like a laugh, they are of the essence of the sad old joke. They are almost as charming from other places as they are from their own balconies, and share fully in that universal privilege of Venetian objects which consists of being both the picture and the point of view.

This double character, which is particularly strong in the Grand Canal, adds a difficulty to any control of one's notes. The Grand Canal may be practically, as in impression, the cushioned balcony of a high and well-loved palace—the memory of irresistible evenings, of the sociable elbow, of endless lingering and looking; or it may evoke the restlessness of a fresh curiosity, of methodical inquiry, in a gondola piled with references. There are no references, I ought to mention, in the present remarks, which sacrifice to accident, not to completeness. A rhapsody of Venice is always in order, but I think the catalogues are finished. I should not attempt to write here the names of all the palaces, even if the number of those I find myself able to remember in the immense array were less insignificant. There are many I delight in that I don't know, or at least don't keep, apart. Then there are the bad reasons for preference that are better than the good, and all the sweet bribery of association and recollection. These things, as one stands on the Salute steps, are so many delicate fingers to pick straight out of the row a dear little featureless house which, with its pale green shutters, looks straight across at the great door and through the very keyhole, as it were, of the church, and which I need n't call by a name—a pleasant American name— that every one in Venice, these many years, has had on grateful lips. It is the very friendliest house in all the wide world, and it has, as it deserves to have, the most beautiful position. It is a real *porto di mare,* as the gondoliers say— a port within a port; it sees everything that comes and goes, and takes it all in with practised eyes. Not a tint or a hint of the immense iridescence is lost upon it, and there are days of exquisite colour on which it may fancy itself the heart of the wonderful prism. We wave to it from the Salute steps, which we must decidedly leave if we wish to get on, a grateful hand across the water, and turn into the big white church of Longhena—an empty shaft

the very friendliest house in all the wide world . . . *porto di mare.* The Casa Alvisi, home of Mrs. Arthur Bronson (see page 72 and note). Literally meaning "seaport," *porto di mare* figuratively suggests the sense of an "open house."

Longhena . . . great Tintoretto. Baldassare Longhena (1604–82), architect of Santa Maria della Salute. Tintoretto's *The Marriage Feast of Cana;* for other and earlier reactions to the artist—James does not always arrange the essays in *Italian Hours* in the order in which they were written or first published—see pages 54–58 below.

beneath a perfunctory dome—where an American family and a German party, huddled in a corner upon a pair of benches, are gazing, with a conscientiousness worthy of a better cause, at nothing in particular.

For there is nothing particular in this cold and conventional temple to gaze at save the great Tintoretto of the sacristy, to which we quickly pay our respects, and which we are glad to have for ten minutes to ourselves. The picture, though full of beauty, is not the finest of the master's; but it serves again as well as another to transport—there is no other word—those of his lovers for whom, in far-away days when Venice was an early rapture, this strange and mystifying painter was almost the supreme revelation. The plastic arts may have less to say to us than in the hungry years of youth, and the celebrated picture in general be more of a blank; but more than the others any fine Tintoret still carries us back, calling up not only the rich particular vision but the freshness of the old wonder. Many things come and go, but this great artist remains for us in Venice a part of the company of the mind. The others are there in their obvious glory, but he is the only one for whom the imagination, in our expressive modern phrase, sits up. "The Marriage in Cana," at the Salute, has all his characteristic and fascinating unexpectedness—the sacrifice of the figure of our Lord, who is reduced to the mere final point of a clever perspective, and the free, joyous presentation of all the other elements of the feast. Why, in spite of this queer one-sidedness, does the picture give us no impression of a lack of what the critics call reverence? For no other reason that I can think of than because it happens to be the work of its author, in whose very mistakes there is a singular wisdom. Mr. Ruskin has spoken with sufficient eloquence of the serious loveliness of the row of heads of the women on the right, who talk to each other as they sit at the foreshortened banquet. There could be no better example of the roving independence of the painter's vision, a real spirit of adventure for which his subject was always a cluster of accidents; not an obvious order, but a sort of peopled and agitated chapter of life, in which the figures are submissive pictorial notes. These notes are all there in their beauty and heterogeneity, and if the abundance is of a kind to make the principle of selection seem in comparison timid, yet the sense of "composition" in the spectator—if it happen to exist—reaches out to the painter in peculiar sympathy. Dull must be the spirit of the worker tormented in any

---

Mr. Ruskin has spoken with sufficient eloquence. *The Stones of Venice,* "Venetian Index," "Salute, Church of Sta. Maria della" (*Works,* IX, 430), ". . . on one side men, on the other women; the men are set with their backs to the light, which, passing over their heads and glancing slightly on the tablecloth, falls in full length along the line of young Venetian women, who thus fill the whole centre of the picture with one broad sunbeam, made up of fair faces and golden hair."

field of art with that particular question who is not moved to recognise in the eternal problem the high fellowship of Tintoretto.

If the long reach from this point to the deplorable iron bridge which discharges the pedestrian at the Academy—or, more comprehensively, to the painted and gilded Gothic of the noble Palazzo Foscari—is too much of a curve to be seen at any one point as a whole, it represents the better the arched neck, as it were, of the undulating serpent of which the Canalazzo has the likeness. We pass a dozen historic houses, we note in our passage a hundred component "bits," with the baffled sketcher's sense, and with what would doubtless be, save for our intensely Venetian fatalism, the baffled sketcher's temper. It is the early palaces, of course, and also, to be fair, some of the late, if we could take them one by one, that give the Canal the best of its grand air. The fairest are often cheek-by-jowl with the foulest, and there are few, alas, so fair as to have been completely protected by their beauty. The ages and the generations have worked their will on them, and the wind and the weather have had much to say; but disfigured and dishonoured as they are, with the bruises of their marbles and the patience of their ruin, there is nothing like them in the world, and the long succession of their faded, conscious faces makes of the quiet waterway they overhang a *promenade historique* of which the lesson, however often we read it, gives, in the depth of its interest, an incomparable dignity to Venice. We read it in the Romanesque arches, crooked to-day in their very curves, of the early middle-age, in the exquisite individual Gothic of the splendid time, and in the cornices and columns of a decadence almost as proud. These things at present are almost equally touching in their good faith; they have each in their degree so effectually parted with their pride. They have lived on as they could and lasted as they might, and we hold them to no account of their infirmities, for even those of them whose blank eyes to-day meet criticism with most submission are far less vulgar than the uses we have mainly managed to put them to. We have botched them and patched them and covered them with sordid signs; we have restored and improved them with a merciless taste, and the best of them we have made over to the pedlars. Some of the most striking objects in the finest vistas at present are the huge advertisements of the curiosity-shops.

The antiquity-mongers in Venice have all the courage of their opinion, and it is easy to see how well they know they can confound you with an unanswerable question. What is the whole place but a curiosity-shop, and

---

deplorable iron bridge. Considered (by nearly everyone) aesthetically inappropriate to its setting, the 1854 iron bridge was reconstructed in wood in 1932.

Canalazzo. The popular name for the Grand Canal.

what are you here for yourself but to pick up odds and ends? "We pick them up *for* you," say these honest Jews, whose prices are marked in dollars, "and who shall blame us if, the flowers being pretty well plucked, we add an artificial rose or two to the composition of the bouquet?" They take care, in a word, that there be plenty of relics, and their establishments are huge and active. They administer the antidote to pedantry, and you can complain of them only if you never cross their thresholds. If you take this step you are lost, for you have parted with the correctness of your attitude. Venice becomes frankly from such a moment the big depressing dazzling joke in which after all our sense of her contradictions sinks to rest—the grimace of an over-strained philosophy. It's rather a comfort, for the curiosity-shops are amusing. You have bad moments indeed as you stand in their halls of humbug and, in the intervals of haggling, hear through the high windows the soft plash of the sea on the old water-steps, for you think with anger of the noble homes that are laid waste in such scenes, of the delicate lives that must have been, that might still be, led there. You reconstruct the admirable house according to your own needs; leaning on a back balcony, you drop your eyes into one of the little green gardens with which, for the most part, such establishments are exasperatingly blessed, and end by feeling it a shame that you yourself are not in possession. (I take for granted, of course, that as you go and come you are, in imagination, perpetually lodging yourself and setting up your gods; for if this innocent pastime, this borrowing of the mind, be not your favourite sport there is a flaw in the appeal that Venice makes to you.) There may be happy cases in which your envy is tempered, or perhaps I should rather say intensified, by real participation. If you have had the good fortune to enjoy the hospitality of an old Venetian home and to lead your life a little in the painted chambers that still echo with one of the historic names, you have entered by the shortest step into the inner spirit of the place. If it did n't savour of treachery to private kindness I should like to speak frankly of one of these delightful, even though alienated, structures, to refer to it as a splendid example of the old palatial type. But I can only do so in passing, with a hundred precautions, and, lifting the curtain at the edge, drop a commemorative word on the success with which, in this particularly happy instance, the cosmopolite habit, the modern sympathy, the intelligent, flexible attitude, the latest fruit of time, adjust themselves to the great gilded, relinquished shell and try to fill it out. A Venetian palace that has not too grossly suffered and that is not overwhelming by its mass makes almost any life graceful that may be led in it. With cultivated and generous contempo-

---

private kindness ... the old palatial type. James was the guest of Mrs. and Mrs. Daniel Curtis, at the Palazzo Barbaro (see pages 63–64 and notes).

rary ways it reveals a pre-established harmony. As you live in it day after day its beauty and its interest sink more deeply into your spirit; it has its moods and its hours and its mystic voices and its shifting expressions. If in the absence of its masters you have happened to have it to yourself for twenty-four hours you will never forget the charm of its haunted stillness, late on the summer afternoon for instance, when the call of playing children comes in behind from the campo, nor the way the old ghosts seemed to pass on tip-toe on the marble floors. It gives you practically the essence of the matter that we are considering, for beneath the high balconies Venice comes and goes, and the particular stretch you command contains all the characteristics. Everything has its turn, from the heavy barges of merchandise, pushed by long poles and the patient shoulder, to the floating pavilions of the great serenades, and you may study at your leisure the admirable Venetian arts of managing a boat and organising a spectacle. Of the beautiful free stroke with which the gondola, especially when there are two oars, is impelled, you never, in the Venetian scene, grow weary; it is always in the picture, and the large profiled action that lets the standing rowers throw themselves forward to a constant recovery has the double value of being, at the fag-end of greatness, the only energetic note. The people from the hotels are always afloat, and, at the hotel pace, the solitary gondolier (like the solitary horse-man of the old-fashioned novel) is, I confess, a somewhat melancholy figure. Perched on his poop without a mate, he re-enacts perpetually, in high relief, with his toes turned out, the comedy of his odd and charming movement. He always has a little the look of an absent-minded nursery-maid pushing her small charges in a perambulator.

But why should I risk too free a comparison, where this picturesque and amiable class are concerned? I delight in their sun-burnt complexions and their childish dialect; I know them only by their merits, and I am grossly prejudiced in their favour. They are interesting and touching, and alike in their virtues and their defects human nature is simplified as with a big effective brush. Affecting above all is their dependence on the stranger, the whimsical stranger who swims out of their ken, yet whom Providence some-times restores. The best of them at any rate are in their line great artists. On the swarming feast-days, on the strange feast-night of the Redentore, their

---

strange feast-night of the Redentore . . . Vauxhall. In thanksgiving for the end of the plague of 1576, the Venetian senate ordered the construction, on the island of the Giudecca, of a great Palladian church dedicated to the Redeemer. The feast of the Redentore, still held on the third Sunday in July, is the direct descendant of the initial celebratory visit made by Doge Sebastiano Vernier, on foot—across the water—to the church's proposed site; in full pomp he traversed the considerable distance on a bridge constructed of rafts, or "zattere," which generally were used to load and unload coal. James's sense of the extraordinarily festive nature of this religious

steering is a miracle of ease. The master-hands, the celebrities and winners of prizes—you may see them on the private gondolas in spotless white, with brilliant sashes and ribbons, and often with very handsome persons—take the right of way with a pardonable insolence. They penetrate the crush of boats with an authority of their own. The crush of boats, the universal sociable bumping and squeezing, is great when, on the summer nights, the ladies shriek with alarm, the city pays the fiddlers, and the illuminated barges, scattering music and song, lead a long train down the Canal. The barges used to be rowed in rhythmic strokes, but now they are towed by the steamer. The coloured lamps, the vocalists before the hotels, are not to my sense the greatest seduction of Venice; but it would be an uncandid sketch of the Canalazzo that should n't touch them with indulgence. Taking one nuisance with another, they are probably the prettiest in the world, and if they have in general more magic for the new arrival than for the old Venice-lover, they in any case, at their best, keep up the immemorial tradition. The Venetians have had from the beginning of time the pride of their processions and spectacles, and it's a wonder how with empty pockets they still make a clever show. The Carnival is dead, but these are the scraps of its inheritance. Vauxhall on the water is of course more Vauxhall than ever, with the good fortune of home-made music and of a mirror that reduplicates and multiplies. The feast of the Redeemer—the great popular feast of the year—is a wonderful Venetian Vauxhall. All Venice on this occasion takes to the boats for the night and loads them with lamps and provisions. Wedged together in a mass it sups and sings; every boat is a floating arbour, a private *café-concert*. Of all Christian commemorations it is the most ingenuously and harmlessly pagan. Toward morning the passengers repair to the Lido, where, as the sun rises, they plunge, still sociably, into the sea. The night of the Redentore has been described, but it would be interesting to have an account, from the domestic point of view, of its usual morrow. It is mainly an

---

ceremony is emphasized by the reference to Vauxhall Bridge and Vauxhall Gardens on the Thames (the Foxhall of Pepys's diaries, where he and many others drank, sang, and generally did what they wished).

The Carnival is dead. After the unification of Italy, and the defeat of papist Rome in 1870, the newly formed Kingdom of Italy worked actively and passively ("The King this year, however, has had as little to do with the Carnival as the Pope," 124) to suppress the influence of the church; therefore the pre-Lenten carnival—which was celebrated with greatest force in papal Rome—lost much of its life (see below, "A Roman Holiday," particularly pages 122–24 and notes). The feast of the Redentore was, however, more a Venetian tradition than a papal recollection and was maintained. Recently the carnival has been given new life in Venice, but purely as a secular and tourist-oriented event.

affair of the Giudecca, however, which is bridged over from the Zattere to the great church. The pontoons are laid together during the day—it is all done with extraordinary celerity and art—and the bridge is prolonged across the Canalazzo (to Santa Maria Zobenigo), which is my only warrant for glancing at the occasion. We glance at it from our palace windows; lengthening our necks a little, as we look up toward the Salute, we see all Venice, on the July afternoon, so serried as to move slowly, pour across the temporary footway. It is a flock of very good children, and the bridged Canal is their toy. All Venice on such occasions is gentle and friendly; not even all Venice pushes any one into the water.

But from the same high windows we catch without any stretching of the neck a still more indispensable note in the picture, a famous pretender eating the bread of bitterness. This repast is served in the open air, on a neat little terrace, by attendants in livery, and there is no indiscretion in our seeing that the pretender dines. Ever since the table d'hôte in "Candide" Venice has been the refuge of monarchs in want of thrones—she would n't know herself without her *rois en exil*. The exile is agreeable and soothing, the gondola lets them down gently. Its movement is an anodyne, its silence a philtre, and little by little it rocks all ambitions to sleep. The proscript has plenty of leisure to write his proclamations and even his memoirs, and I believe he has organs in which they are published; but the only noise he makes in the world is the harmless splash of his oars. He comes and goes along the Canalazzo, and he might be much worse employed. He is but one of the interesting objects it presents, however, and I am by no means sure that he is the most striking. He has a rival, if not in the iron bridge, which, alas, is within our range, at least—to take an immediate example—in the Montecuculi Palace. Far-descended and weary, but beautiful in its crooked old age, with its lovely proportions, its delicate round arches, its carvings and its disks of marble, is the haunted Montecuculi. Those who have a

---

"Candide." . . . the refuge of monarchs . . . *rois in exil.* In chapter 26 of *Candide,* Voltaire's hero sups with six strangers, all revealed to be errant monarchs in exile, in Venice for the carnival: dethroned Sultan Achmet III (1673–1736), Ivan IV (1740–64) of Russia, Bonnie Prince Charlie (1720–88), dethroned King Augustus III (1696–1763) of Poland, Stanislas Lechzinski (1677–1766), who abdicated the Polish throne in 1736, and Theodore von Neuhof (c. 1690–1756), elected King of Corsica and later exiled. In Shelley's "Julian and Maddalo," the setting of a great conversation is Venice, and part of the discussion is of "Thou Paradise of exiles, Italy!" See also page 49 and note on "Comte de Chambord."

Montecuculi Palace. Far-descended. Also known by the many other names that indicate its long descent: Palazzo Contarini S. Vito, and Contarini dal Zaffo, and Ruzzini, and Menzoni, and Angarem, and Polignac-Decazes.

kindness for Venetian gossip like to remember that it was once for a few months the property of Robert Browning, who, however, never lived in it, and who died in the splendid Rezzonico, the residence of his son and a wonderful cosmopolite "document," which, as it presents itself, in an admirable position, but a short way farther down the Canal, we can almost see, in spite of the curve, from the window at which we stand. This great seventeenth century pile, throwing itself upon the water with a peculiar florid assurance, a certain upward toss of its cornice which gives it the air of a rearing sea-horse, decorates immensely—and within, as well as without—the wide angle that it commands.

There is a more formal greatness in the high square Gothic Foscari, just below it, one of the noblest creations of the fifteenth century, a masterpiece of symmetry and majesty. Dedicated to-day to official uses—it is the property of the State—it looks conscious of the consideration it enjoys, and is one of the few great houses within our range whose old age strikes us as robust and painless. It is visibly "kept up"; perhaps it is kept up too much; perhaps I am wrong in thinking so well of it. These doubts and fears course rapidly through my mind—I am easily their victim when it is a question of architecture—as they are apt to do to-day, in Italy, almost anywhere, in the presence of the beautiful, of the desecrated or the neglected. We feel at such moments as if the eye of Mr. Ruskin were upon us; we grow nervous and lose our confidence. This makes me inevitably, in talking of Venice, seek a pusillanimous safety in the trivial and the obvious. I am on firm ground in rejoicing in the little garden directly opposite our windows—it is another proof that they really show us everything—and in feeling that the gardens of Venice would deserve a page to themselves. They are infinitely more numerous than the arriving stranger can suppose; they nestle with a charm all their own in the complications of most back-views. Some of them are exquisite, many are large, and even the scrappiest have an artful understanding, in the interest of colour, with the waterways that edge their foundations. On the

---

Robert Browning . . . Rezzonico . . . cosmopolite "document." In 1889 the poet died here, while staying with his son Robert "Pen" Browning, one of the many foreigners who were to rent the palazzo after the last member of the Rezzonico family died in 1810 (see Lauritzen, 205–10). Begun in the 1660s, the Ca' Rezzonico was considered particularly well preserved even during the nineteenth century; since 1936, as the city's museum of eighteenth-century decorative arts (the "settecento" of its Italian designation translates as eighteenth century in English), it has existed as a more literal document of baroque furnishings and general splendor.

the eye of Mr. Ruskin. *The Stones of Venice,* "Venetian Index," III, 309—"but lately restored and spoiled, all but the stone-work of the main windows" (*Works,* XI, 378); Ruskin also notes that the Venetian municipality had given the palazzo over to the Austrians to be used as barracks. Today the Ca' Foscari is the seat of the University of Venice.

small canals, in the hunt for amusement, they are the prettiest surprises of all. The tangle of plants and flowers crowds over the battered walls, the greenness makes an arrangement with the rosy sordid brick. Of all the reflected and liquefied things in Venice, and the number of these is countless, I think the lapping water loves them most. They are numerous on the Canalazzo, but wherever they occur they give a brush to the picture and in particular, it is easy to guess, give a sweetness to the house. Then the elements are complete—the trio of air and water and of things that grow. Venice without them would be too much a matter of the tides and the stones. Even the little trellises of the *traghetti* count charmingly as reminders, amid so much artifice, of the woodland nature of man. The vine-leaves, trained on horizontal poles, make a roof of chequered shade for the gondoliers and ferrymen, who doze there according to opportunity, or chatter or hail the approaching "fare." There is no "hum" in Venice, so that their voices travel far; they enter your windows and mingle even with your dreams. I beg the reader to believe that if I had time to go into everything, I would go into the *traghetti,* which have their manners and their morals, and which used to have their piety. This piety was always a *madonnina,* the protectress of the passage—a quaint figure of the Virgin with the red spark of a lamp at her feet. The lamps appear for the most part to have gone out, and the images doubtless have been sold for *bric-a-brac.* The ferrymen, for aught I know, are converted to Nihilism—a faith consistent happily with a good stroke of business. One of the figures has been left, however—the Madonnetta which gives its name to a *traghetto* near the Rialto. But this sweet survivor is a carven stone inserted ages ago in the corner of an old palace and doubtless difficult of removal. *Pazienza,* the day will come when so marketable a relic will also be extracted from its socket and purchased by the devouring American. I leave that expression, on second thought, standing; but I repent of it when I remember that it is a devouring American—a lady long resident in Venice and whose kindnesses all Venetians, as well as her country-people,

---

madonnina . . . Madonnetta *. . .* a devouring American—a lady long resident *. . . palo.* The diminutive "madonnina" generally refers to a small sculptural representation of the Madonna. The particular figure called the "Madoneta" (in the orthography of the Veneto), between the Ponte della Madoneta and the Campo S. Polo, dated from the 1500s. James's prediction was fulfilled; Tassini notes that in 1887 the figure was mutilated by vandals. Although in 1927 a new image of the Madonna was replaced in its tabernacle, by 1970 the tabernacle was again empty; in 1988 an uninspired low-relief image was found to have been restored. This "custodian" of some of the neglected treasures of Venice is Mrs. Bronson (see page 72 and note, and page 75). Gautier speaks of the tradition of patronage—in his day perpetuated by the Duchess de Berry—which maintained the tutelary figures for the gondoliers (*Journeys in Italy,* 89). Palo refers here to the famous striped mooring post for gondolas.

know, who has rekindled some of the extinguished tapers, setting up especially the big brave Gothic shrine, of painted and gilded wood, which, on the top of its stout *palo,* sheds its influence on the place of passage opposite the Salute.

If I may not go into those of the palaces this devious discourse has left behind, much less may I enter the great galleries of the Academy, which rears its blank wall, surmounted by the lion of St. Mark, well within sight of the windows at which we are still lingering. This wondrous temple of Venetian art—for all it promises little from without—overhangs, in a manner, the Grand Canal, but if we were so much as to cross its threshold we should wander beyond recall. It contains, in some of the most magnificent halls—where the ceilings have all the glory with which the imagination of Venice alone could over-arch a room—some of the noblest pictures in the world; and whether or not we go back to them on any particular occasion for another look, it is always a comfort to know that they are there, as the sense of them on the spot is a part of the furniture of the mind—the sense of them close at hand, behind every wall and under every cover, like the inevitable reverse of a medal, of the side exposed to the air that reflects, intensifies, completes the scene. In other words, as it was the inevitable destiny of Venice to be painted, and painted with passion, so the wide world of picture becomes, as we live there, and however much we go about our affairs, the constant habitation of our thoughts. The truth is, we are in it so uninterruptedly, at home and abroad, that there is scarcely a pressure upon us to seek it in one place more than in another. Choose your standpoint at random and trust the picture to come to you. This is manifestly why I have not, I find myself conscious, said more about the features of the Canalazzo which occupy the reach between the Salute and the position we have so obstinately taken up. It is still there before us, however, and the delightful little Palazzo Dario, intimately familiar to English and American travellers, picks itself out in the foreshortened brightness. The Dario is covered with the loveliest little marble plates and sculptured circles; it is made up of exquisite pieces—as if there had been only enough to make it small—so that it looks, in its extreme antiquity, a good deal like a house of cards that hold together by a tenure it would be fatal to touch. An old Venetian house dies hard indeed, and I should add that this delicate thing,

---

Palazzo Dario, intimately familiar to English and American travellers. From 1838 to 1842 the home of Rawdon Brown, who came to Venice to find the tomb of the "banish'd Norfolk" of Richard II and stayed for the rest of his life; he transcribed documents in the Archivio and provided a meeting place for many English-speaking travelers. Ruskin was one of his distinguished guests.

with submission in every feature, continues to resist the contact of generations of lodgers. It is let out in floors (it used to be let as a whole) and in how many eager hands—for it is in great requisition—under how many fleeting dispensations have we not known and loved it? People are always writing in advance to secure it, as they are to secure the Jenkins's gondolier, and as the gondola passes we see strange faces at the windows—though it's ten to one we recognise them—and the millionth artist coming forth with his traps at the water-gate. The poor little patient Dario is one of the most flourishing booths at the fair.

The faces at the window look out at the great Sansovino—the splendid pile that is now occupied by the Prefect. I feel decidedly that I don't object as I ought to the palaces of the sixteenth and seventeenth centuries. Their pretensions impose upon me, and the imagination peoples them more freely than it can people the interiors of the prime. Was not moreover this masterpiece of Sansovino once occupied by the Venetian post-office, and thereby intimately connected with an ineffaceable first impression of the author of these remarks? He had arrived, wondering, palpitating, twenty-three years ago, after nightfall, and, the first thing on the morrow, had repaired to the post-office for his letters. They had been waiting a long time and were full of delayed interest, and he returned with them to the gondola and floated slowly down the Canal. The mixture, the rapture, the wonderful temple of the *poste restante,* the beautiful strangeness, all humanised by good news—the memory of this abides with him still, so that there always proceeds from the splendid water-front I speak of a certain secret appeal, something that seems to have been uttered first in the sonorous chambers of youth. Of course this association falls to the ground—or rather splashes into the water—if I am the victim of a confusion. *Was* the edifice in question twenty-three years ago the post-office, which has occupied since, for many a day, very much humbler quarters? I am afraid to take the proper steps for finding out, lest I should learn that during these years I have misdirected my emotion. A better reason for the sentiment, at any rate, is that such a great house has surely, in the high beauty of its tiers, a refinement of its own. They make one think of colosseums and aqueducts and bridges, and they constitute doubtless, in Venice, the most pardonable specimen of the imitative. I have even a timid kindness for the

---

great Sansovino . . . Prefect. The Palazzo della Prefettura was designed by Jacopo Tatti, called Il Sansovino. It is more commonly known as the Palazzo Corner della Ca' Grande (not to be confused with the Palazzo Corner-Spinelli) or the Palazzo Cornaro a San Maurizio.

Was the edifice in question . . . the post-office . . . ? It was not as James remembered it; from 1805 until 1872 the post office was located in the Palazzo Grimani a San Luca, and after that it moved to the Palazzo Facanon, Merceria del Salvatore.

huge Pesaro, far down the Canal, whose main reproach, more even than the coarseness of its forms, is its swaggering size, its want of consideration for the general picture, which the early examples so reverently respect. The Pesaro is as far out of the frame as a modern hotel, and the Cornaro, close to it, oversteps almost equally the modesty of art. One more thing they and their kindred do, I must add, for which, unfortunately, we can patronise them less. They make even the most elaborate material civilisation of the present day seem woefully shrunken and *bourgeois,* for they simply—I allude to the biggest palaces—can't be lived in as they were intended to be. The modern tenant may take in all the magazines, but he bends not the bow of Achilles. He occupies the place, but he does n't fill it, and he has guests from the neighbouring inns with ulsters and Baedekers. We are far at the Pesaro, by the way, from our attaching window, and we take advantage of it to go in rather a melancholy mood to the end. The long straight vista from the Foscari to the Rialto, the great middle stretch of the Canal, contains, as the phrase is, a hundred objects of interest, but it contains most the bright oddity of its general Deluge air. In all these centuries it has never got over its resemblance to a flooded city; for some reason or other it is the only part of Venice in which the houses look as if the waters had overtaken them. Everywhere else they reckon with them—have chosen them; here alone the lapping seaway seems to confess itself an accident.

There are persons who hold this long, gay, shabby, spotty perspective, in which, with its immense field of confused reflection, the houses have infinite variety, the dullest expanse in Venice. It was not dull, we imagine, for Lord Byron, who lived in the midmost of the three Mocenigo palaces, where the writing-table is still shown at which he gave the rein to his passions. For other observers it is sufficiently enlivened by so delightful a creation as the Palazzo Loredan, once a masterpiece and at present the Municipio, not to speak of a variety of other immemorial bits whose beauty still has a degree of freshness. Some of the most touching relics of early Venice are here—for it was here she precariously clustered—peeping out of a submersion more pitiless than the sea. As we approach the Rialto indeed the picture falls off

---

Pesaro ... far out of the frame ... Cornaro. Palazzo Pesaro a Sant'Eustachio (c. 1621); "The most powerful and impressive in effect of all the palaces of the Grotesque Renaissance"; Ruskin, *The Stones of Venice,* "Venetian Index," "Pesaro" (*Works,* XI, 398). The Palazzo Cornaro della Ca' Grande.

Lord Byron ... three Mocenigo palaces. Here is where Byron settled with Teresa Guiccioli; actually a complex of four palaces, with two middle structures nearly identical. Of the seven distinct Mocenigo palaces in Venice, James refers to the Palazzo Mocenigo a San Samuele, also called the Case dei Mocenigo.

and a comparative commonness suffuses it. There is a wide paved walk on either side of the Canal, on which the waterman—and who in Venice is not a waterman?—is prone to seek repose. I speak of the summer days—it is the summer Venice that is the visible Venice. The big tarry barges are drawn up at the *fondamenta,* and the bare-legged boatmen, in faded blue cotton, lie asleep on the hot stones. If there were no colour anywhere else there would be enough in their tanned personalities. Half the low doorways open into the warm interior of waterside drinking-shops, and here and there, on the quay, beneath the bush that overhangs the door, there are rickety tables and chairs. Where in Venice is there not the amusement of character and of detail? The tone in this part is very vivid, and is largely that of the brown plebeian faces looking out of the patchy miscellaneous houses—the faces of fat undressed women and of other simple folk who are not aware that they enjoy, from balconies once doubtless patrician, a view the knowing ones of the earth come thousands of miles to envy them. The effect is enhanced by the tattered clothes hung to dry in the windows, by the sun-faded rags that flutter from the polished balustrades—these are ivory-smooth with time; and the whole scene profits by the general law that renders decadence and ruin in Venice more brilliant than any prosperity. Decay is in this extraordinary place golden in tint and misery *couleur de rose.* The gondolas of the correct people are unmitigated sable, but the poor market-boats from the islands are kaleidoscopic.

The Bridge of the Rialto is a name to conjure with, but, honestly speaking, it is scarcely the gem of the composition. There are of course two ways of taking it—from the water or from the upper passage, where its small shops and booths abound in Venetian character; but it mainly counts as a feature of the Canal when seen from the gondola or even from the awful *vaporetto.* The great curve of its single arch is much to be commended, especially when, coming from the direction of the railway-station, you see it frame with its sharp compass-line the perfect picture, the reach of the Canal on the other side. But the backs of the little shops make from the water a graceless collective hump, and the inside view is the diverting one. The big arch of the bridge—like the arches of all the bridges—is the waterman's friend in wet weather. The gondolas, when it rains, huddle beside the peopled barges, and the young ladies from the hotels, vaguely fidgeting, complain of the communication of insect life. Here indeed is a little of everything, and the jewellers of

---

fondamenta. The stone foundations that support the city, particularly those exposed to the water.

vaporetto. A recent invention in James's time, the *vaporetti* motorboats still speed along the canals.

this celebrated precinct—they have their immemorial row—make almost as fine a show as the fruiterers. It is a universal market, and a fine place to study Venetian types. The produce of the islands is discharged there, and the fishmongers announce their presence. All one's senses indeed are vigorously attacked; the whole place is violently hot and bright, all odorous and noisy. The churning of the screw of the *vaporetto* mingles with the other sounds— not indeed that this offensive note is confined to one part of the Canal. But just here the little piers of the resented steamer are particularly near together, and it seems somehow to be always kicking up the water. As we go further down we see it stopping exactly beneath the glorious windows of the Ca' d'Oro. It has chosen its position well, and who shall gainsay it for having put itself under the protection of the most romantic façade in Europe? The companionship of these objects is a symbol; it expresses supremely the present and the future of Venice. Perfect, in its prime, was the marble Ca' d'Oro, with the noble recesses of its *loggie,* but even then it probably never "met a want," like the successful *vaporetto.* If, however, we are not to go into the Museo Civico—the old Museo Correr, which rears a staring renovated front far down on the left, near the station, so also we must keep out of the great vexed question of steam on the Canalazzo, just as a while since we prudently kept out of the Accademia. These are expensive and complicated excursions. It is obvious that if the *vaporetti* have contributed to the ruin of the gondoliers, already hard pressed by fate, and to that of the palaces, whose foundations their waves undermine, and that if they have robbed the Grand Canal of the supreme distinction of its tranquillity, so on the other hand they have placed "rapid transit," in the New York phrase, in everybody's reach, and enabled everybody—save indeed those who would n't for the world—to rush about Venice as furiously as people rush about New York. The suitability of this consummation need n't be pointed out.

Even we ourselves, in the irresistible contagion, are going so fast now that we have only time to note in how clever and costly a fashion the Museo Civico, the old Fondaco dei Turchi, has been reconstructed and restored. It is a glare of white marble without, and a series of showy majestic halls within, where a thousand curious mementos and relics of old Venice are gathered and classified. Of its miscellaneous treasures I fear I may perhaps frivolously prefer the series of its remarkable living Longhis, an illustration of manners

---

Museo Civico—the old Museo Correr. In 1922 the Civico Museo Correr moved from the contiguous Casa Correr/Fondaco dei Turchi on the right bank of the Grand Canal.

Longhis . . . Carpaccio. In 1892 the museum held twenty-three of its present forty paintings by Pietro Longhi (1702–85) and four less interesting works by Alessandro Longhi (1733– 1813) (Pignatti, 145–215). See James's, and Ruskin's, remarks on the Carpaccio, pages 28–29 and notes.

more copious than the celebrated Carpaccio, the two ladies with their little animals and their long sticks. Wonderful indeed to-day are the museums of Italy, where the renovations and the *belle ordonnance* speak of funds apparently unlimited, in spite of the fact that the numerous custodians frankly look starved. What is the pecuniary source of all this civic magnificence—it is shown in a hundred other ways—and how do the Italian cities manage to acquit themselves of expenses that would be formidable to communities richer and doubtless less æsthetic? Who pays the bills for the expressive statues alone, the general exuberance of sculpture, with which every *piazzetta* of almost every village is patriotically decorated? Let us not seek an answer to the puzzling question, but observe instead that we are passing the mouth of the populous Canareggio, next widest of the waterways, where the race of Shylock abides, and at the corner of which the big colourless church of San Geremia stands gracefully enough on guard. The Canareggio, with its wide lateral footways and humpbacked bridges, makes on the feast of St. John an admirable noisy, tawdry theatre for one of the prettiest and the most infantile of the Venetian processions.

The rest of the course is a reduced magnificence, in spite of interesting bits, of the battered pomp of the Pesaro and the Cornaro, of the recurrent memories of royalty in exile which cluster about the Palazzo Vendramin Calergi, once the residence of the Comte de Chambord and still that of his

---

Canareggio . . . race of Shylock. The canal of the Cannareggio or Canareggio, named for the cane bamboo that once proliferated here, forms a general border of the northern section of the city, the famous Jewish quarter that gave the word *ghetto* to the English vocabulary; *ghetto* derives from the Venetian dialect, *gettare,* to cast in metal. Here, originally, the foundries were located and, when the quarter was set aside for the Jews in about 1132, the sector's name retained its old association. A closed ghetto only after the fifteenth century, it was opened by Napoleon in 1797.

feast of Saint John. Commemorating the victory of the battle of Negroponte, which fell on the feast day of San Giovanni Decollato.

Palazzo Vendramin Calergi . . . Comte de Chambord. Also known as the Palazzo Loredan-Vendramin-Calergi. At one time the home and splendid court of Henry Charles Ferdinand, Duc de Bordeaux, Comte de Chambord (1820–83), son of Duc de Berry, grandson of Charles X, last male heir of the Bourbon line and, consequently, the exiled Henri V of the French royalists. For a time there were hopes that the count would regain his throne, but his extreme opposition to the tricolor of the Republic won the movement strong opposition (see also page 99 and note); a significant group of legitimist exiles settled near him during his Venice exile.

Eventually the house went to the heirs of his mother's morganatic husband, Sicilian Count Enrico Lucchesi-Palli, who in September 1882 let fifteen rooms of the garden wing to Richard Wagner; Wagner died there on 13 February 1883. Writing in 1892, James makes no mention of this last fact. See *Letters,* II, 283, and Edel, *Henry James: The Conquest of London,* 404–7, for James's decision to decline an invitation in 1880 to meet Wagner, "the musician of the future."

half-brother, in spite too of the big Papadopoli gardens, opposite the station, the largest private grounds in Venice, but of which Venice in general mainly gets the benefit in the usual form of irrepressible greenery climbing over walls and nodding at water. The rococo church of the Scalzi is here, all marble and malachite, all a cold, hard glitter and a costly, curly ugliness, and here too, opposite, on the top of its high steps, is San Simeone Profeta, I won't say immortalised, but unblushingly misrepresented, by the perfidious Canaletto. I shall not stay to unravel the mystery of this prosaic painter's malpractices; he falsified without fancy, and as he apparently transposed at will the objects he reproduced, one is never sure of the particular view that may have constituted his subject. It would look exactly like such and such a place if almost everything were not different. San Simeone Profeta appears to hang there upon the wall; but it is on the wrong side of the Canal and the other elements quite fail to correspond. One's confusion is the greater because one does n't know that everything may not really have changed, even beyond all probability—though it's only in America that churches cross the street or the river—and the mixture of the recognisable and the different makes the ambiguity maddening, all the more that the painter is almost as attaching as he is bad. Thanks at any rate to the white church, domed and porticoed, on the top of its steps, the traveller emerging for the first time upon the terrace of the railway-station seems to have a Canaletto before him. He speedily discovers indeed even in the presence of this scene of the final accents of the Canalazzo—there is a charm in the old pink warehouses on the hot *fondamenta*—that he has something much better. He looks up and down at the gathered gondolas; he has his surprise after all, his little first Venetian thrill; and as the terrace of the station ushers in these things we shall say no harm of it, though it is not lovely. It is the beginning of his experience, but it is the end of the Grand Canal.

1892.

Papadopoli gardens. At present the Giardino Communale.

Scalzi. The church of Santa Maria di Nazareth, generally known as the church of gli Scalzi.

San Simeone Profeta . . . perfidious Canaletto. Across the canal from gli Scalzi is the church of S. Simeone piccolo e Giuda, atop a high stair, near the wall. The church of S. Simeone Profeta, or S. Simeone Grande, is found nearby, down the Rio Marin, but does not face onto the Grand Canal and appears to hang onto no wall. Apparently James confused a picture of S. Simeone Profeta with the view of S. Simeone Piccolo, yet the catalogues of Canaletto's work indicate no views of S. Simeone Profeta, and the views of S. Simeone piccolo (Constable, *Canaletto,* 2:316–19) offer no significant distortion; in some cases, in fact, they accurately provide unusual detail. Barcham on the "capricci" in Canaletto discusses the more surely inventive or "perfidious" paintings.

Venice:
An Early Impression

There would be much to say about that golden chain of historic cities which stretches from Milan to Venice, in which the very names—Brescia, Verona, Mantua, Padua—are an ornament to one's phrase; but I should have to draw upon recollections now three years old and to make my short story a long one. Of Verona and Venice only have I recent impressions, and even to these must I do hasty justice. I came into Venice, just as I had done before, toward the end of a summer's day, when the shadows begin to lengthen and the light to glow, and found that the attendant sensations bore repetition remarkably well. There was the same last intolerable delay at Mestre, just before your first glimpse of the lagoon confirms the already distinct sea-smell which has added speed to the precursive flight of your imagination; then the liquid level, edged afar off by its band of undiscriminated domes and spires, soon distinguished and proclaimed, however, as excited and contentious heads multiply at the windows of the train; then your long rumble on the immense white railway-bridge, which, in spite of the invidious contrast drawn, and very properly, by Mr.

[Originally published (unsigned) as "From Venice to Strassburg." Although James notes the date 1872 after this essay in *Italian Hours*, the original essay was published in the *Nation*, XVI (March 1873), 163–64; reprinted in *Transatlantic Sketches*, 1875; reprinted in *Foreign Parts*, 1883.]

the invidious contrast drawn, and very properly, by Mr. Ruskin. *The Stones of Venice*, vol. I, "The Vestibule" (*Works*, IX, 415)—"on the right, but a few years back, we might have seen the lagoon stretching to the horizon, and the warm southern sky bending over Malamocco to the sea. Now we can see nothing but what seems a low and monotonous deck-yard wall, with flat arches to let the tide through it; this is the railroad bridge, conspicuous above all things." The

Ruskin between the old and the new approach, does truly, in a manner, shine across the green lap of the lagoon like a mighty causeway of marble; then the plunge into the station, which would be exactly similar to every other plunge save for one little fact—that the keynote of the great medley of voices borne back from the exit is not "Cab, sir!" but "Barca, signore!"

I do not mean, however, to follow the traveller through every phase of his initiation, at the risk of stamping poor Venice beyond repair as the supreme bugbear of literature; though for my own part I hold that to a fine healthy romantic appetite the subject can't be too diffusely treated. Meeting in the Piazza on the evening of my arrival a young American painter who told me that he had been spending the summer just where i found him, I could have assaulted him for very envy. He was painting forsooth the interior of St. Mark's. To be a young American painter unperplexed by the mocking, elusive soul of things and satisfied with their wholesome light-bathed surface and shape; keen of eye; fond of colour, of sea and sky and anything that may chance between them; of old lace and old brocade and old furniture (even when made to order); of time-mellowed harmonies on nameless canvases and happy contours in cheap old engravings; to spend one's mornings in still, productive analysis of the clustered shadows of the Basilica, one's afternoons anywhere, in church or campo, on canal or lagoon, and one's evenings in star-light gossip at Florian's, feeling the sea-breeze throb languidly between the two great pillars of the Piazzetta and over the low black domes of the church—this, I consider, is to be as happy as is consistent with the preservation of reason.

The mere use of one's eyes in Venice is happiness enough, and generous observers find it hard to keep an account of their profits in this line. Everything the attention touches holds it, keeps playing with it—thanks to some inscrutable flattery of the atmosphere. Your brown-skinned, white-shirted gondolier, twisting himself in the light, seems to you, as you lie at contemplation beneath your awning, a perpetual symbol of Venetian "effect." The light here is in fact a mighty magician and, with all respect to Titian, Veronese and Tintoret, the greatest artist of them all. You should see in places the material with which it deals—slimy brick, marble battered and befouled, rags, dirt, decay. Sea and sky seem to meet half-way, to blend their tones into a soft iridescence, a lustrous compound of wave and cloud and a hundred nameless

---

railway station and rail bridge were constructed between 1841 and 1846. The Porto di Malamocco is one of the southern entrances to the lagoon from the sea.

Florian's. Founded in 1720, the world-famous café figures in *The Wings of the Dove* and in several tales.

local reflections, and then to fling the clear tissue against every object of vision. You may see these elements at work everywhere, but to see them in their intensity you should choose the finest day in the month and have yourself rowed far away across the lagoon to Torcello. Without making this excursion you can hardly pretend to know Venice or to sympathise with that longing for pure radiance which animated her great colourists. It is a perfect bath of light, and I could n't get rid of a fancy that we were cleaving the upper atmosphere on some hurrying cloud-skiff. At Torcello there is nothing but the light to see—nothing at least but a sort of blooming sand-bar intersected by a single narrow creek which does duty as a canal and occupied by a meagre cluster of huts, the dwellings apparently of market-gardeners and fishermen, and by a ruinous church of the eleventh century. It is impossible to imagine a more penetrating case of unheeded collapse. Torcello was the mother-city of Venice, and she lies there now, a mere mouldering vestige, like a group of weather-bleached parental bones left impiously unburied. I stopped my gondola at the mouth of the shallow inlet and walked along the grass beside a hedge to the low-browed, crumbling cathedral. The charm of certain vacant grassy spaces, in Italy, overfrowned by masses of brickwork that are honeycombed by the suns of centuries, is something that I hereby renounce once for all the attempt to express; but you may be sure that whenever I mention such a spot enchantment lurks in it.

A delicious stillness covered the little campo at Torcello; I remember none so subtly audible save that of the Roman Campagna. There was no life but the visible tremor of the brilliant air and the cries of half-a-dozen young children who dogged our steps and clamoured for coppers. These children, by the way, were the handsomest little brats in the world, and each was furnished with a pair of eyes that could only have signified the protest of nature against the meanness of fortune. They were very nearly as naked as savages, and their little bellies protruded like those of infant cannibals in the illustrations of books of travel; but as they scampered and sprawled in the soft, thick grass, grinning like suddenly-translated cherubs and showing their hungry little teeth, they suggested forcibly that the best assurance of happiness in this world is to be found in the maximum of innocence and the minimum of wealth. One small urchin—framed, if ever a child was, to be the joy of an

---

Torcello was the mother-city of Venice. "Mother and daughter, you behold them both in their widowhood,—Torcello and Venice"; Ruskin, *The Stones of Venice*, vol. II, "Torcello" (*Works*, x, 18). The Hun invasion under Attila caused the eventual settlers of Venice to move from the dry land into the estuary around 452, first to Torcello and later to the islands that now form Venice.

aristocratic mamma—was the most expressively beautiful creature I had ever looked upon. He had a smile to make Correggio sigh in his grave; and yet here he was running wild among the sea-stunted bushes, on the lonely margin of a decaying world, in prelude to how blank or to how dark a destiny? Verily nature is still at odds with propriety; though indeed if they ever really pull together I fear nature will quite lose her distinction. An infant citizen of our own republic, straight-haired, pale-eyed and freckled, duly darned and catechised, marching into a New England schoolhouse, is an object often seen and soon forgotten; but I think I shall always remember with infinite tender conjecture, as the years roll by, this little unlettered Eros of the Adriatic strand. Yet all youthful things at Torcello were not cheerful, for the poor lad who brought us the key of the cathedral was shaking with an ague, and his melancholy presence seemed to point the moral of forsaken nave and choir. The church, admirably primitive and curious, reminded me of the two or three oldest churches of Rome—St. Clement and St. Agnes. The interior is rich in grimly mystical mosaics of the twelfth century and the patchwork of precious fragments in the pavement not inferior to that of St. Mark's. But the terribly distinct Apostles are ranged against their dead gold backgrounds as stiffly as grenadiers presenting arms—intensely personal sentinels of a personal Deity. Their stony stare seems to wait for ever vainly for some visible revival of primitive orthodoxy, and one may well wonder whether it finds much beguilement in idly-gazing troops of Western heretics—passionless even in their heresy.

I had been curious to see whether in the galleries and temples of Venice I should be disposed to transpose my old estimates—to burn what I had adored and adore what I had burned. It is a sad truth that one can stand in the Ducal Palace for the first time but once, with the deliciously ponderous sense of that particular half-hour's being an era in one's mental history; but I had the satisfaction of finding at least—a great comfort in a short stay— that none of my early memories were likely to change places and that I could take up my admirations where I had left them. I still found Carpaccio delightful, Veronese magnificent, Titian supremely beautiful and Tintoret scarce to be appraised. I repaired immediately to the little church of San

---

shaking with an ague ... to point the moral of forsaken nave and choir. For centuries malaria devastated and depopulated Torcello, but in the 1880s land reclamation brought new life back to the island.

the church ... mystical mosaics. At the cathedral of Santa Maria Assunta, founded 639, modified in 864, partially reconstructed 1008, the mosaics, noted by Ruskin, *The Stones of Venice*, vol. II, "Torcello" (*Works*, x, 21), depict the Last Judgment.

Cassano, which contains the smaller of Tintoret's two great Crucifixions; and when I had looked at it a while I drew a long breath and felt I could now face any other picture in Venice with proper self-possession. It seemed to me I had advanced to the uttermost limit of painting; that beyond this another art—inspired poetry—begins, and that Bellini, Veronese, Giorgione, and Titian, all joining hands and straining every muscle of their genius, reach forward not so far but that they leave a visible space in which Tintoret alone is master. I well remember the exaltations to which he lifted me when first I learned to know him; but the glow of that comparatively youthful amazement is dead, and with it, I fear, that confident vivacity of phrase of which, in trying to utter my impressions, I felt less the magniloquence than the impotence. In his power there are many weak spots, mysterious lapses and fitful intermissions; but when the list of his faults is complete he still remains to me the most *interesting* of painters. His reputation rests chiefly on a more superficial sort of merit—his energy, his unsurpassed productivity, his being, as Théophile Gautier says, *le roi des fougueux*. These qualities are immense, but the great source of his impressiveness is that his indefatigable hand never drew a line that was not, as one may say, a moral line. No painter ever had such breadth and such depth; and even Titian, beside him, scarce figures as more than a great decorative artist. Mr. Ruskin, whose eloquence in dealing

---

San Cassano. Or San Cassiano. Tintoretto's 1568 Crucifixion (see page 24 for James on Tintoretto's more famous San Rocco Crucifixion). Ruskin recommends a long look at the painting (infrequently noted in the guidebooks) and calls it one of the "finest Tintorettos in Europe" (*Stones of Venice*, "Venetian Index," III, 297–98). In "Travelling Companions" (1870) the narrator provides a lengthy appreciation of the work, ending with the statement that "it is hard to say which is more impressive, the naked horror of the fact represented, or the sensible power of the artist. You breathe a silent prayer of thanks that you, for your part, are without the terrible clairvoyance of genius" (*Complete Tales*, II, 205–6).

Théophile Gautier . . . *le roi des fougueux*. The king of the hot-blooded or ardent. "Un des côtés de la salle, celui de la porte d'entrée, est occupé tout entier par un gigantesque paradis de Tintoret, qui contient tout un monde de figures. L'esquisse d'un sujet analogue, que l'on voit au Musée du Louvre, à Paris, peut donner l'idée de cette composition, dont le genre plaisait au génie fougueux et tumultueux de ce mâle artiste qui remplit si bien le programme de son nom, Jacopo Robusti (Gautier, 136). ["One of the sides of the hall, that of the door of the entrance, is entirely occupied by a gigantic paradise by Tintoretto, which contains a whole world of figures. The sketch of an analogous subject, which may be seen in the Museum of the Louvre, in Paris, furnished an idea of their composition, the genre of which pleased the fiery and tumultuous genius of this virile artist, who fitted so well his name, Jacopo Robusti," trans. Daniel B. Vermilye, 132.]

Ruskin . . . Veronese . . . deep spiritual intentions. Even in his own lifetime Paolo Veronese faced the criticism that the details of his worldly canvases—the costumes, the characters, the architectural details, the splendor—were patently unsuitable to their serious spiritual subjects.

with the great Venetians sometimes outruns his discretion, is fond of speaking even of Veronese as a painter of deep spiritual intentions. This, it seems to me, is pushing matters too far, and the author of "The Rape of Europa" is, pictorially speaking, no greater casuist than any other genius of supreme good taste. Titian was assuredly a mighty poet, but Tintoret—well, Tintoret was almost a prophet. Before his greatest works you are conscious of a sudden evaporation of old doubts and dilemmas, and the eternal problem of the conflict between idealism and realism dies the most natural of deaths. In his genius the problem is practically solved; the alternatives are so harmoniously interfused that I defy the keenest critic to say where one begins and the other ends. The homeliest prose melts into the most ethereal poetry—the literal and the imaginative fairly confound their identity.

This, however, is vague praise. Tintoret's great merit, to my mind, was his unequalled distinctness of vision. When once he had conceived the germ of a scene it defined itself to his imagination with an intensity, an amplitude, an individuality of expression, which makes one's observation of his pictures seem less an operation of the mind than a kind of supplementary experience

---

In 1573, after completing an immense Last Supper for the convent of SS. Giovanni e Paoli, he was brought before the Inquisition and ordered to defend his inclusion of drunks, buffoons, dwarfs, and Germans in the representation of such a holy scene. Partly to escape condemnation he eventually changed the title to *Feast in the House of Levi,* but initially he defended his latitude and argued that Michelangelo was not condemned for the nudity of Christ and of the saints in his Sistine Chapel *Last Judgment.* In a famous reply the chief inquisitor asked Veronese if he did not realize that in Michelangelo, in each figure and in every detail, there was nothing which was not spiritual—"non vi è cosa se non de spirito?"

During the nineteenth century Ruskin attempted something of a defense:

> But I perceive a tendency among some of the more thoughtful critics of the day to forget the business of a painter is to *paint,* and so altogether to despise those men, Veronese and Rubens for instance, who were painters, par excellence, and in whom the expressional qualities are subordinate. Now it is well, when we have strong moral or political feeling manifested in painting, to mark this as the best part of the work; but it is not well to consider as a thing of small account, the painter's language in which that feeling is conveyed; for if that language be not good and lovely, the man may indeed be a just moralist or a great poet, but he is not a *painter,* and it was wrong of him to paint. . . . On the other hand, if the man be a painter indeed, and have the gift of colours and lines, what is in him will come from his hand freely and faithfully; and the language itself is so difficult and vast, that the mere possession of it argues that the man is great, and that his works are worth reading. So that I have never yet seen the case in which this true artistical excellence, visible by eye-glance, was not the index of some true expressional worth in the work. (*The Stones of Venice,* vol. I, "Appendix" [*Works,* IX, 448–49])

Henry James and John Addington Symonds, among others, would remain unconvinced; Symonds later wrote: "All the equipage of wealth and worldliness, the lust of the eye, and the pride of life—such a vision as the fiend offered to Christ on the mountain of temptation; this is Veronese's realm" (*Renaissance in Italy,* III, 273).

of life. Veronese and Titian are content with a much looser specification, as their treatment of any subject that the author of the Crucifixion at San Cassano has also treated abundantly proves. There are few more suggestive contrasts than that between the absence of a total character at all commensurate with its scattered variety and brilliancy in Veronese's "Marriage of Cana," at the Louvre, and the poignant, almost startling, completeness of Tintoret's illustration of the theme at the Salute church. To compare his "Presentation of the Virgin," at the Madonna dell' Orto, with Titian's at the Academy, or his "Annunciation" with Titian's close at hand, is to measure the essential difference between observation and imagination. One has certainly not said all that there is to say for Titian when one has called him an observer. *Il y mettait du sien,* and I use the term to designate roughly the artist whose apprehension, infinitely deep and strong when applied to the single figure or to easily balanced groups, spends itself vainly on great dramatic combinations—or rather leaves them ungauged. It was the whole scene that Tintoret seemed to have beheld in a flash of inspiration intense enough to stamp it ineffaceably on his perception; and it was the whole scene, complete, peculiar, individual, unprecedented, that he committed to canvas with all the vehemence of his talent. Compare his "Last Supper," at San Giorgio—its long, diagonally placed table, its dusky spaciousness, its scattered lamp-light and halo-light, its startled, gesticulating figures, its richly realistic foreground—with the customary formal, almost mathematical rendering of the subject, in which impressiveness seems to have been sought in elimination rather than comprehension. You get from Tintoret's work the impression that he *felt,* pictorially, the great, beautiful, terrible spectacle of human life very much as Shakespeare felt it poetically—with a heart that never ceased to beat a passionate accompaniment to every stroke of his brush. Thanks to this fact his works are signally grave, and their almost universal and rapidly increasing decay does n't relieve their gloom. Nothing indeed can well be sadder than the great collection of Tintorets at San Rocco. Incurable blackness is settling fast upon all of them, and they frown at you across the sombre splendour of their great chambers like gaunt twilight phantoms of pictures. To our children's children Tintoret, as things are going, can be hardly more than a name; and such of them as shall miss the tragic beauty, already so dimmed and stained, of the great "Bearing of the Cross" in that temple of his spirit will live and die without knowing the

---

Il y mettait du sien. He makes a real contribution.

San Rocco . . . children's children . . . shall miss the tragic beauty. In 1971–72 a major restoration took place at San Rocco (Pallucchini and Rossi, I, 224–27). Today the works appear brilliant and are well-lit.

largest eloquence of art. If you wish to add the last touch of solemnity to the place recall as vividly as possible while you linger at San Rocco the painter's singularly interesting portrait of himself, at the Louvre. The old man looks out of the canvas from beneath a brow as sad as a sunless twilight, with just such a stoical hopelessness as you might fancy him to wear if he stood at your side gazing at his rotting canvases. It is n't whimsical to read it as the face of a man who felt that he had given the world more than the world was likely to repay. Indeed before every picture of Tintoret you may remember this tremendous portrait with profit. On one side the power, the passion, the illusion of his art; on the other the mortal fatigue of his spirit. The world's knowledge of him is so small that the portrait throws a doubly precious light on his personality; and when we wonder vainly what manner of man he was, and what were his purpose, his faith and his method, we may find forcible assurance there that they were at any rate his life—one of the most intellectually passionate ever led.

Verona, which was my last Italian stopping-place, is in any conditions a delightfully interesting city; but the kindness of my own memory of it is deepened by a subsequent ten days' experience of Germany. I rose one morning at Verona, and went to bed at night at Botzen! The statement needs no comment, and the two places, though but fifty miles apart, are as painfully dissimilar as their names. I had prepared myself for your delectation with a copious tirade on German manners, German scenery, German art and the German stage—on the lights and shadows of Innsbrück, Munich, Nüremberg and Heidelberg; but just as I was about to put pen to paper I glanced into a little volume on these very topics lately published by that famous novelist and moralist, M. Ernest Feydeau, the fruit of a summer's observation at Homburg. This work produced a reaction; and if I chose to follow M. Feydeau's own example when he wishes to qualify his approbation I might call his treatise by any vile name known to the speech of man. But I content myself with pronouncing it superficial. I then reflect that my own opportunities for seeing and judging were extremely limited, and I suppress my tirade, lest some more enlightened critic should come and hang me with the same rope. Its sum and substance was to have been that—

Botzen! A Hapsburg city since the fourteenth century, but annexed from Austria to Italy—as Bolzano—at the end of World War I; the city continues to retain decidedly Teutonic features in the midst of the Trentino Alto–Adige region of Italy.

M. Ernest Feydeau. Most famous for his novel *Fanny* (1858), in 1872 French writer Ernest-Aimé Feydeau published *L'Allemagne en 1871*, a satirical portrait of German manners; upon occasion James found his fiction "repulsive" ("Charles Augustin Sainte-Beuve," in *Literary Criticism: French Authors*, 694).

superficially—Germany is ugly; that Munich is a nightmare, Heidelberg a disappointment (in spite of its charming castle) and even Nüremberg not a joy for ever. But comparisons are odious, and if Munich is ugly Verona is beautiful enough. You may laugh at my logic, but will probably assent to my meaning. I carried away from Verona a precious mental picture upon which I cast an introspective glance whenever between Botzen and Strassburg the oppression of external circumstance became painful. It was a lovely August afternoon in the Roman arena—a ruin in which repair and restoration have been so watchfully and plausibly practised that it seems all of one harmonious antiquity. The vast stony oval rose high against the sky in a single clear, continuous line, broken here and there only by strolling and reclining loungers. The massive tiers inclined in solid monotony to the central circle, in which a small open-air theatre was in active operation. A small quarter of the great slope of masonry facing the stage was roped off into an auditorium, in which the narrow level space between the foot-lights and the lowest step figured as the pit. Foot-lights are a figure of speech, for the performance was going on in the broad glow of the afternoon, with a delightful and apparently by no means misplaced confidence in the good-will of the spectators. What the piece was that was deemed so superbly able to shift for itself I know not—very possibly the same drama that I remember seeing advertised during my former visit to Verona; nothing less than *La Tremenda Giustizia di Dio*. If titles are worth anything this product of the melodramatist's art might surely stand upon its own legs. Along the tiers above the little group of regular spectators was gathered a free-list of unauthorised observers, who, although beyond ear-shot, must have been enabled by the generous breadth of Italian gesture to follow the tangled thread of the piece. It was all deliciously Italian—the mixture of old life and new, the mountebank's booth (it was hardly more) grafted on the antique circus, the dominant presence of a mighty architecture, the loungers and idlers beneath the kindly sky and upon the sun-warmed stones. I never felt more keenly the difference between the background to life in very old and very new civilisations. There are other things in Verona to make it a liberal education to be born there,

---

the Roman arena . . . repair and restoration . . . plausibly practised. James would complain that after centuries of romanticizing neglect the Colosseum in Rome had been ruined by drastic restoration (see pages 129–30 and note), but he appreciated the manner in which the Verona arena had, incrementally, been kept up. Battered by an earthquake in the twelfth century, the first-century arena, which holds 22,000 spectators, was soon restored, and then restored again and again over the centuries. In the sixteenth century it was used for tournaments, in the seventeenth century for the running of bulls, in the eighteenth century for horse races, in the nineteenth for theater, and since 1913 it has been the site of the famous Verona summer opera festival.

though that it *is* one for the contemporary Veronese I don't pretend to say. The Tombs of the Scaligers, with their soaring pinnacles, their high-poised canopies, their exquisite refinement and concentration of the Gothic idea, I can't profess, even after much worshipful gazing, to have fully comprehended and enjoyed. They seemed to me full of deep architectural meanings, such as must drop gently into the mind one by one, after infinite tranquil contemplation. But even to the hurried and preoccupied traveller the solemn little chapel-yard in the city's heart, in which they stand girdled by their great swaying curtain of linked and twisted iron, is one of the most impressive spots in Italy. Nowhere else is such a wealth of artistic achievement crowded into so narrow a space; nowhere else are the daily comings and goings of men blessed by the presence of *manlier* art. Verona is rich furthermore in beautiful churches—several with beautiful names: San Fermo, Santa Anastasia, San Zenone. This last is a structure of high antiquity and of the most impressive loveliness. The nave terminates in a double choir, that is a sub-choir or crypt into which you descend and where you wander among primitive columns whose variously grotesque capitals rise hardly higher than your head, and an upper choral plane reached by broad stairways of the bravest effect. I shall never forget the impression of majestic chastity that I received from the great nave of the building on my former visit. I then decided to my satisfaction that every church is from the devotional point of view a solecism that has not something of a similar absolute felicity of proportion; for strictly formal beauty seems best to express our conception of spiritual beauty. The nobly serious character of San Zenone is deepened by its single picture—a masterpiece of the most serious of painters, the severe and exquisite Mantegna.

1872.

Mantegna. Behind the high altar, the Madonna and Child, enthroned.

Two Old Houses
and Three Young Women

There are times and places that come back yet again, but that, when the brooding tourist puts out his hand to them, meet it a little slowly, or even seem to recede a step, as if in slight fear of some liberty he may take. Surely they should know by this time that he is capable of taking none. He has his own way—he makes it all right. It now becomes just a part of the charming solicitation that it presents precisely a problem—that of *giving* the particular thing as much as possible without at the same time giving it, as we say, away. There are considerations, proprieties, a necessary indirectness—he must use, in short, a little art. No necessity, however, more than this, makes him warm to his work, and thus it is that, after all, he hangs his three pictures.

I

THE evening that was to give me the first of them was by no means the first occasion of my asking myself if that inveterate "style" of which we talk so much be absolutely conditioned—in dear old Venice and elsewhere—on decrepitude. Is it the style that has brought about the decrepitude, or the decrepitude that has, as it were, intensified and consecrated the style? There is an ambiguity about it all that constantly haunts and beguiles. Dear old Venice

[Originally published in the *Independent,* LI (September 1899), 2406–12.]

has lost her complexion, her figure, her reputation, her self-respect; and yet, with it all, has so puzzlingly not lost a shred of her distinction. Perhaps indeed the case is simpler than it seems, for the poetry of misfortune is familiar to us all, whereas, in spite of a stroke here and there of some happy justice that charms, we scarce find ourselves anywhere arrested by the poetry of a run of luck. The misfortune of Venice being, accordingly, at every point, what we most touch, feel and see, we end by assuming it to be of the essence of her dignity; a consequence, we become aware, by the way, sufficiently discouraging to the general application or pretension of style, and all the more that, to make the final felicity deep, the original greatness must have been something tremendous. If it be the ruins that are noble we have known plenty that were not, and moreover there are degrees and varieties: certain monuments, solid survivals, hold up their heads and decline to ask for a grain of your pity. Well, one knows of course when to keep one's pity to oneself; yet one clings, even in the face of the colder stare, to one's prized Venetian privilege of making the sense of doom and decay a part of every impression. Cheerful work, it may be said of course; and it is doubtless only in Venice that you gain more by such a trick than you lose. What was most beautiful is gone; what was next most beautiful is, thank goodness, going—that, I think, is the monstrous description of the better part of your thought. Is it really your fault if the place makes you want so desperately to read history into everything?

You do that wherever you turn and wherever you look, and you do it, I should say, most of all at night. It comes to you there with longer knowledge, and with all deference to what flushes and shimmers, that the night is the real time. It perhaps even would n't take much to make you award the palm to the nights of winter. This is certainly true for the form of progression that is most characteristic, for every question of departure and arrival by gondola. The little closed cabin of this perfect vehicle, the movement, the darkness and the plash, the indistinguishable swerves and twists, all the things you don't see and all the things you do feel—each dim recognition and obscure arrest is a possible throb of your sense of being floated to your doom, even when the truth is simply and sociably that you are going out to tea. Nowhere else is anything as innocent so mysterious, nor anything as mysterious so pleasantly deterrent to protest. These are the moments when you are most daringly Venetian, most content to leave cheap trippers and other aliens the high light of the mid-lagoon and the pursuit of pink and gold. The splendid day is good enough for *them;* what is best for you is to stop at last, as you are now stopping, among clustered *pali* and softly-shifting poops and prows, at a great flight of water-steps that play their admirable part in the general effect of a great entrance. The high doors stand open from them to the paved chamber of a basement tremendously tall and not vulgarly lighted, from which, in turn, mounts the slow stone staircase that draws you further on. The great point is, that if you are worthy of this impression at all, there is n't a single item of it of which the association is n't noble. Hold to it fast that there is no other such dignity of arrival as arrival by water. Hold to it that to float and slacken and gently bump, to creep out of the low, dark *felze* and make the few guided movements and find the strong crooked and offered arm, and then, beneath lighted palace-windows, pass up the few damp steps on the precautionary carpet—hold to it that these things constitute a preparation of which the only defect is that it may sometimes perhaps really prepare too much. It's so stately that what can come after?—it's so good in itself that what, upstairs, as we comparative vulgarians say, can be better? Hold to it, at any rate, that if a lady, in especial, scrambles out of a carriage, tumbles out of a cab, flops out of a tram-car, and hurtles, projectile-like, out of a "lightning-elevator," she alights from the Venetian conveyance as Cleopatra may have stepped from her barge. Upstairs—whatever may be yet in store for her—her entrance shall still advantageously enjoy the support most opposed to the "momentum" acquired. The beauty of the matter has been in the absence of all momentum—elsewhere so scientifically applied to us, from behind, by the terrible life of our day—and in the fact that, as the elements of slowness, the felicities of deliberation, doubtless thus all hang together, the last of calculable dangers is to enter a great Venetian room with a rush.

Not the least happy note, therefore, of the picture I am trying to frame is that there was absolutely no rushing; not only in the sense of a scramble over marble floors, but, by reason of something dissuasive and distributive in the very air of the place, a suggestion, under the fine old ceilings and among types of face and figure abounding in the unexpected, that here were many things to consider. Perhaps the simplest rendering of a scene into the depths of which there are good grounds of discretion for not sinking would be just this emphasis on the value of the unexpected for such occasions— with due qualification, naturally, of its degree. Unexpectedness pure and simple, it is needless to say, may easily endanger any social gathering, and I hasten to add moreover that the figures and faces I speak of were probably not in the least unexpected to each other. The stage they occupied was a stage of variety—Venice has ever been a garden of strange social flowers. It is only as reflected in the consciousness of the visitior from afar—brooding tourist even call him, or sharp-eyed bird on the branch—that I attempt to give you the little drama; beginning with the felicity that most appealed to him, the visible, unmistakable fact that he was the only representative of his class. The whole of the rest of the business was but what he saw and felt and

---

felze. The cabin of a gondola.

fancied—what he was to remember and what he was to forget. Through it all, I may say distinctly, he clung to his great Venetian clue—the explanation of everything by the historic idea. It was a high historic house, with such a quantity of recorded past twinkling in the multitudinous candles that one grasped at the idea of something waning and displaced, and might even fondly and secretly nurse the conceit that what one was having was just the very last. Was n't it certainly, for instance, no mere illusion that there is no appreciable future left for such manners—an urbanity so comprehensive, a form so transmitted, as those of such a hostess and such a host? The future is for a different conception of the graceful altogether—so far as it's for a conception of the graceful at all. Into that computation I shall not attempt to enter; but these representative products of an antique culture, at least, and one of which the secret seems more likely than not to be lost, were not common, nor indeed was any one else—in the circle to which the picture most insisted on restricting itself.

Neither, on the other hand, was any one either very beautiful or very fresh: which was again, exactly, a precious "value" on an occasion that was to shine most, to the imagination, by the complexity of its references. Such old, old women with such old, old jewels; such ugly, ugly ones with such handsome, becoming names; such battered, fatigued gentlemen with such inscrutable decorations; such an absence of youth, for the most part, in either sex—of the pink and white, the "bud" of new worlds; such a general personal air, in fine, of being the worse for a good deal of wear in various old ones. It was not a society—that was clear—in which little girls and boys set the tune; and there was that about it all that might well have cast a shadow on the path of even the most successful little girl. Yet also—let me not be rudely inexact—it was in honour of youth and freshness that we had all been convened. The *fiançailles*

It was a high historic house. The magnificent Palazzo Barbaro, owned by Mr. and Mrs. Daniel Curtis, with whom James stayed in 1887 and again in 1907; generally considered the model for the Palazzo Leporelli, Milly Theale's Venetian residence in *The Wings of the Dove*. Upon occasion the Barbaro was rented from the Curtises by another of James's hostesses, Isabella Stewart Gardner, whom it provided with the inspiration for her Boston townhouse Fenway Court, today the Isabella Stewart Gardner Museum (Lauritzen, 106; photographs in Battilana, *Venezia*).

Such old, old women with such old, old jewels; such ugly, ugly ones with such handsome, becoming names. Edel identifies the occasion when the Curtises were hosts to the dowager Empress Victoria—known as the Empress Frederick—widow of German Emperor and King of Prussia, Frederick III (*Henry James: The Treacherous Years*, 286). Battilana identifies the young women as the Duchessa Maria Carolina di Berry and Maria Carolina Lucchesi-Palli, and the decorated Austrian gentleman as Conte Rodolfo d'Enzemberg, the fiancé of Signorina Lucchesi-Palli ("Sei personaggi," 217–30).

of the last—unless it were the last but one—unmarried daughter of the house had just been brought to a proper climax; the contract had been signed, the betrothal rounded off—I'm not sure that the civil marriage had n't, that day, taken place. The occasion then had in fact the most charming of heroines and the most ingenuous of heroes, a young man, the latter, all happily suffused with a fair Austrian blush. The young lady had had, besides other more or less shining recent ancestors, a very famous paternal grandmother, who had played a great part in the political history of her time and whose portrait, in the taste and dress of 1830, was conspicuous in one of the rooms. The granddaughter of this celebrity, of royal race, was strikingly like her and, by a fortunate stroke, had been habited, combed, curled in a manner exactly to reproduce the portrait. These things were charming and amusing, as indeed were several other things besides. The great Venetian beauty of our period was there, and nature had equipped the great Venetian beauty for her part with the properest sense of the suitable, or in any case with a splendid generosity—since on the ideally suitable *character* of so brave a human symbol who shall have the last word? This responsible agent was at all events the beauty in the world about whom probably, most, the absence of question (an absence never wholly propitious) would a little smugly and monotonously flourish: the one thing wanting to the interest she inspired was thus the possibility of ever discussing it. There were plenty of suggestive subjects round about, on the other hand, as to which the exchange of ideas would by no means necessarily have dropped. You profit to the full at such times by all the old voices, echoes, images—by that element of the history of Venice which represents all Europe as having at one time and another revelled or rested, asked for pleasure or for patience there; which gives you the place supremely as the refuge of endless strange secrets, broken fortunes and wounded hearts.

II

THERE had been, on lines of further or different speculation, a young Englishman to luncheon, and the young Englishman had proved "sympathetic"; so that when it was a question afterwards of some of the more hidden treasures, the browner depths of the old churches, the case became one for mutual guidance and gratitude—for a small afternoon tour and the wait of a pair of friends in the warm little *campi,* at locked doors for which the nearest urchin had scurried off to fetch the keeper of the key. There are few brown depths to-day into which the light of the hotels does n't shine, and few hidden treasures about which pages enough, doubtless, have n't already been printed: my business, accordingly, let me hasten to say, is not now with the fond renewal of any discovery—at least in the order of impressions most usual. Your discovery may be, for that matter, renewed every week; the only essential is the good luck—which a fair amount of practice has taught you to count upon—of not finding, for the particular occasion, other discoverers in the field. Then, in the quiet corner, with the closed door—then in the presence of the picture and of your companion's sensible emotion—not only the original happy moment, but everything else, is renewed. Yet once again it can all come back. The old custode, shuffling about in the dimness, jerks away, to make sure of his tip, the old curtain that is n't much more modern than the wonderful work itself. He does his best to create light where light can never be; but you have your practised groping gaze, and in guiding the young eyes of your less confident associate, moreover, you feel you possess the treasure. These are the refined pleasures that Venice has still to give, these odd happy passages of communication and response.

But the point of my reminiscence is that there were other communications that day, as there were certainly other reponses. I have forgotten exactly what it was we were looking for—without much success—when we met the three Sisters. Nothing requires more care, as a long knowledge of Venice works in, than not to lose the useful faculty of getting lost. I had so successfully done my best to preserve it that I could at that moment conscientiously profess an absence of any suspicion of where we might be. It proved enough that, wherever we were, we were where the three sisters found us. This was on a little bridge near a big campo, and a part of the charm of the matter was the theory that it was very much out of the way. They took us promptly in hand—they were only walking over to San Marco to match some coloured wool for the manufacture of such belated cushions as still bloom with purple and green in the long leisures of old palaces; and that mild errand could easily open a parenthesis. The obscure church we had feebly imagined we were looking for proved, if I am not mistaken, that of the sisters' parish; as to which I have but a confused recollection of a large grey void and of admiring for the first time a fine work of art of which I have now quite lost the identity. This was the effect of the charming beneficence of the three sisters, who presently were to give our adventure a turn in the emotion of

---

three Sisters. James's capitalization of "Sisters," in reference to three women wandering in search of wool, and into whose blighted *sala* one entered "almost soft enough for a death-chamber" (68), may suggest the three Moerae of Greek mythology—Clotho, Lachesis, and Atropos—daughters of Night and Darkness who spun, drew, and severed the thread of life. Battilani recognizes a specific reference to Maria, Bianca, and Moceniga Mocenigo, of the S. Stae branch of the Mocenigo line (Battilana, *Venezia*, 125).

which everything that had preceded seemed as nothing. It actually strikes me even as a little dim to have been told by them, as we all fared together, that a certain low, wide house, in a small square as to which I found myself without particular association, had been in the far-off time the residence of George Sand. And yet this was a fact that, though I could then only feel it must be for another day, would in a different connection have set me richly reconstructing.

Madame Sand's famous Venetian year has been of late immensely in the air—a tub of soiled linen which the muse of history, rolling her sleeves well up, has not even yet quite ceased energetically and publicly to wash. The house in question must have been the house to which the wonderful lady betook herself when, in 1834, after the dramatic exit of Alfred de Musset, she enjoyed that remarkable period of rest and refreshment with the so long silent, the but recently rediscovered, reported, extinguished, Doctor Pagello. As an old Sandist—not exactly indeed of the *première heure,* but of the fine high noon and golden afternoon of the great career—I had been, though I confess too inactively, curious as to a few points in the topography of the eminent adventure to which I here allude; but had never got beyond the little public fact, in itself always a bit of a thrill to the Sandist, that the present Hotel Danieli had been the scene of its first remarkable stages. I am not sure indeed that the curiosity I speak of has not at last, in my breast, yielded to another form of wonderment—truly to the rather rueful question of why we have so continued to concern ourselves, and why the fond observer of the footprints of genius is likely so to continue, with a body of discussion, neither in itself and in its day, nor in its preserved and attested records, at all positively edifying. The answer to such an inquiry would doubtless reward

---

George Sand . . . Alfred de Musset . . . recently rediscovered, reported, extinguished, Doctor Pagello. The Sand-Musset love affair had been much in the news. In a January 1897 essay on George Sand for *The Yellow Book,* James refers to an "admirable short biography" (Arvède Barine, *Alfred de Musset,* 1893) that examined Sand's relationships with Pietro Pagello, her lover during and after Musset's serious 1834 illness (Henry James, "She and He: Recent Documents," *The Yellow Book,* XII, January 1897, 15–38; reprinted in *Literary Criticism: French Writers,* 736–55). Two years before James's essay, Paul Mariéton had published *Une Histoire d'Amour: Les Amants de Venise, George Sand et Musset,* a documented account of the tempestuous affair. In 1898 Pagello died.

present Hotel Danieli. On the Riva degli Schiavoni, a fourteenth-century palace, formerly the Palazzo Dandolo, since 1822 the Albergo Danieli, the "most famous hotel in the world" according to its reputation in Venice. Sand and Musset stayed there for a time during 1833 and 1834, but the hotel has been the temporary residence of many other distinguished guests, among them King William of Prussia, Balzac, Dickens, Robert Browning, Ruskin, Wagner, and Proust.

patience, but I fear we can now glance at its possibilities only long enough to say that interesting persons—so they be of a sufficiently approved and established interest—render in some degree interesting whatever happens to them, and give it an importance even when very little else (as in the case I refer to) may have operated to give it a dignity. Which is where I leave the issue of further identifications.

For the three sisters, in the kindest way in the world, had asked us if we already knew their sequestered home and whether, in case we did n't, we should be at all amused to see it. My own acquaintance with them, though not of recent origin, had hitherto lacked this enhancement, at which we both now grasped with the full instinct, indescribable enough, of what it was likely to give. But how, for that matter, either, can I find the right expression of what was to remain with us of this episode? It is the fault of the sad-eyed old witch of Venice that she so easily puts more into things that can pass under the common names that do for them elsewhere. Too much for a rough sketch was to be seen and felt in the home of the three sisters, and in the delightful and slightly pathetic deviation of their doing us so simply and freely the honours of it. What was most immediately marked was their resigned cosmopolite state, the effacement of old conventional lines by foreign contact and example; by the action, too, of causes full of a special interest, but not to be emphasised perhaps—granted indeed they be named at all—without a certain sadness of sympathy. If "style," in Venice, sits among ruins, let us always lighten our tread when we pay her a visit.

Our steps were in fact, I am happy to think, almost soft enough for a death-chamber as we stood in the big, vague *sala* of the three sisters, spectators of their simplified state and their beautiful blighted rooms, the memories, the portraits, the shrunken relics of nine Doges. If I wanted a first chapter it was here made to my hand; the painter of life and manners, as he glanced about, could only sigh—as he so frequently has to—over the vision of so much more truth than he can use. What on earth is the need to "invent," in the midst of tragedy and comedy that never cease? Why, with the subject itself, all round, so inimitable, condemn the picture to the silliness of trying not to be aware of it? The charming lonely girls, carrying so simply their great name and fallen fortunes, the despoiled *decaduta* house, the unfailing Italian grace, the space so out of scale with actual needs, the absence of books, the presence of ennui, the sense of the length of the hours and the shortness of everything else—all this was a matter not only for a second chapter and a third, but for a whole volume, a *dénoûment* and a sequel.

This time, unmistakably, it *was* the last—Wordsworth's stately "shade of that which once was great"; and it was almost as if our distinguished young friends had consented to pass away slowly in order to treat us to the vision. Ends are only ends in truth, for the painter of pictures, when they are more or less conscious and prolonged. One of the sisters had been to London, whence she had brought back the impression of having seen at the British Museum a room exclusively filled with books and documents devoted to the commemoration of her family. She must also then have encountered at the National Gallery the exquisite specimen of an early Venetian master in which one of her ancestors, then head of the State, kneels with so sweet a dignity before the Virgin and Child. She was perhaps old enough, none the less, to have seen this precious work taken down from the wall of the room in which we sat and—on terms so far too easy—carried away for ever; and not too young, at all events, to have been present, now and then, when her candid elders, enlightened too late as to what their sacrifice might really have done for them, looked at each other with the pale hush of the irreparable. We let ourselves note that these were matters to put a great deal of old, old history into sweet young Venetian faces.

III

IN Italy, if we come to that, this particular appearance is far from being only in the streets, where we are apt most to observe it—in countenances caught as we pass and in the objects marked by the guide-books with their respective stellar allowances. It is behind the walls of the houses that old, old history is thick and that the multiplied stars of Baedeker might often best find their application. The feast of St. John the Baptist is the feast of the year in Florence, and it seemed to me on that night that I could have scattered about me a handful of these signs. I had the pleasure of spending a couple of

---

Wordsworth's stately "shade of that which once was great." Wordsworth's "On the Extinction of the Venetian Republic" (1807): "Men are we, and must grieve when even the Shade / Of that which once was great is passed away."

Venetian master. Vincenzo Catena's *Warrior Adoring the Infant Christ and the Virgin*, until 1898 attributed to the Venetian "School of Giovanni Bellini"; both the Mocenigo and Contarini families have associations with the picture.

feast of St. John the Baptist . . . Ponte Carraja. The feast day of the patron saint of the city falls on 24 June. Today there continue a *palio* horse race, soccer matches, and, in the Piazza Signoria and still on the Ponte alla Carraia, fireworks.

hours on a signal high terrace that overlooks the Arno, as well as in the
galleries that open out to it, where I met more than ever the pleasant curious
question of the disparity between the old conditions and the new manners.
Make our manners, we moderns, as good as we can, there is still no getting
over it that they are not good enough for many of the great places. This was
one of those scenes, and its greatness came out to the full into the hot
Florentine evening, in which the pink and golden fires of the pyrotechnics
arranged on Ponte Carraja—the occasion of our assembly—lighted up the
large issue. The "good people" beneath were a huge, hot, gentle, happy
family; the fireworks on the bridge, kindling river as well as sky, were
delicate and charming; the terrace connnected the two wings that give bravery to the front of the palace, and the close-hung pictures in the rooms, open
in a long series, offered to a lover of quiet perambulation an alternative hard
to resist.

Wherever he stood—on the broad loggia, in the cluster of company,
among bland ejaculations and liquefied ices, or in the presence of the mixed
masters that led him from wall to wall—such a seeker for the spirit of each
occasion could only turn it over that in the first place this was an intenser,
finer little Florence than ever, and that in the second the testimony was again
wonderful to former fashions and ideas. What did they do, in the other time,
the time of so much smaller a society, smaller and fewer fortunes, more taste
perhaps as to some particulars, but fewer tastes, at any rate, and fewer
habits and wants—what did they do with chambers so multitudinous and so
vast? Put their "state" at its highest—and we know of many ways in which
it must have broken down—how did they live in them without the aid of
variety? How did they, in minor communities in which every one knew every
one, and every one's impression and effect had been long, as we say, dis-
counted, find representation and emulation sufficiently amusing? Much of
the charm of thinking of it, however, is doubtless that we are not able to say.
This leaves us with the conviction that does them most honour: the old
generations built and arranged greatly for the simple reason that they liked
it, and they could bore themselves—to say nothing of each other, when it
came to that—better in noble conditions than in mean ones.

It was not, I must add, of the far-away Florentine age that I most thought,
but of periods more recent and of which the sound and beautiful house more
directly spoke. If one had always been homesick for the Arno-side of the
seventeenth and eighteenth centuries, here was a chance, and a better one
than ever, to taste again of the cup. Many of the pictures—there was a
charming quarter of an hour when I had them to myself—were bad enough
to have passed for good in those delightful years. Shades of Grand-Dukes
encompassed me—Dukes of the pleasant later sort who were n't really
grand. There was still the sense of having come too late—yet not too late,

after all, for this glimpse and this dream. My business was to people the place—its own business had never been to save us the trouble of understanding it. And then the deepest spell of all was perhaps that just here I was supremely out of the way of the so terribly actual Florentine question. This, as all the world knows, is a battle-ground, to-day, in many journals, with all Italy practically pulling on one side and all England, America and Germany pulling on the other: I speak of course of the more or less articulate opinion. The "improvement," the rectification of Florence is in the air, and the problem of the particular ways in which, given such desperately delicate cases, these matters should be understood. The little treasure-city is, if there ever was one, a delicate case—more delicate perhaps than any other in the world save that of our taking on ourselves to persuade the Italians that they may n't do as they like with their own. They so absolutely may that I profess I see no happy issue from the fight. It will take more tact than our combined tactful genius may at all probably muster to convince them that their own is, by an ingenious logic, much rather *ours*. It will take more subtlety still to muster for them that truly dazzling show of examples from which they may learn that what in general is "ours" shall appear to them as a rule a sacrifice to beauty and a triumph of taste. The situation, to the truly analytic mind, offers in short, to perfection, all the elements of despair; and I am afraid that if I hung back, at the Corsini palace, to woo illusions and invoke the irrelevant, it was because I could think, in the conditions, of no better way to meet the acute responsibility of the critic than just to shirk it.

1899.

---

actual Florentine question. At the end of the nineteenth century, partly in emulation of the modernization—and imperialization by Napoleon III and Baron Haussmann—of aspects of Paris, many European cities began to lay thoroughfares through ancient quarters that were considered sacred, at least by many foreigners; Rome, and particularly Florence, was at the heart of the controversies that developed. See James's earlier remarks (1873) on the new boulevards and new squares of Florence; page 240 and note.

Corsini palace . . . invoke the irrelevant. The Corsini (see pages 262–63), the finest private art collection in the city and "the only grandiose piece of secular Baroquery in Florence" (Borsook, 169), appears as an anachronism in its Renaissance setting.

Casa Alvisi

Invited to "introduce" certain pages of cordial and faithful reminiscence from another hand,[1] in which a frankly predominant presence seems to live again, I undertook that office with an interest inevitably somewhat sad—so passed and gone to-day is so much of the life suggested. Those who fortunately knew Mrs. Bronson will read into her notes still more of it—more of her subject, more of herself too, and of many things—than she gives, and some may well even feel tempted to do for her what she has done here for her distinguished friend. In Venice, during a long period, for many pilgrims, Mrs. Arthur Bronson, originally of New York, was, so far as society, hospitality, a charming personal welcome were concerned, almost in sole possession; she had become there, with time, quite the prime representative of those private amenities which the Anglo-Saxon abroad is apt to miss just in proportion as the place visited is publicly wonderful, and in which he therefore finds a value twice as great as at home. Mrs. Bronson really earned in this way the gratitude of mingled generations and races. She sat for twenty years at the wide mouth, as it were, of the Grand Canal, holding out her hand, with endless good-nature, patience,

---

[Originally published as a prefatory note to Mrs. Katharine De Kay Bronson's "Browning in Venice," in the *Cornhill Magazine,* February 1902; the preface appeared separately, under the title "The Late Mrs. Arthur Bronson," in the *Critic,* XL (February 1902), 162–64.]

[1] "Browning in Venice," being Recollections of the late Katharine De Kay Bronson, with a Prefatory Note by H. J. (*Cornhill Magazine,* February, 1902). [James's note.]

Casa Alvisi . . . Mrs. Arthur Bronson. The Palazzino Alvisi, today forming part of the luxurious Hotel Europa-Regina, the former residence of Katharine De Kay Bronson, who entertained many illustrious guests in Venice, among them Robert Browning and Henry James.

charity, to all decently accredited petitioners, the incessant troop of those either bewilderedly making or fondly renewing acquaintance with the dazzling city.

Casa Alvisi is directly opposite the high, broad-based florid church of S. Maria della Salute—so directly that from the balcony over the water-entrance your eye, crossing the canal, seems to find the key-hole of the great door right in a line with it; and there was something in this position that for the time made all Venice-lovers think of the genial *padrona* as thus levying in the most convenient way the toll of curiosity and sympathy. Every one passed, every one was seen to pass, and few were those not seen to stop and to return. The most generous of hostesses died a year ago at Florence; her house knows her no more—it had ceased to do so for some time before her death; and the long, pleased procession—the charmed arrivals, the happy sojourns at anchor, the reluctant departures that made Ca' Alvisi, as was currently said, a social *porto di mare*—is, for remembrance and regret, already a possession of ghosts; so that, on the spot, at present, the attention ruefully averts itself from the dear little old faded but once familiarly bright façade, overtaken at last by the comparatively vulgar uses that are doing their best to "paint out" in Venice, right and left, by staring signs and other vulgarities, the immemorial note of distinction. The house, in a city of palaces, was small, but the tenant clung to her perfect, her inclusive position—the one right place that gave her a better command, as it were, than a better house obtained by a harder compromise; not being fond, moreover, of spacious halls and massive treasures, but of compact and familiar rooms, in which her remarkable accumulation of minute and delicate Venetian objects could show. She adored—in the way of the Venetian, to which all her taste addressed itself—the small, the domestic and the exquisite; so that she would have given a Tintoretto or two, I think, without difficulty, for a cabinet of tiny gilded glasses or a dinner-service of the right old silver.

The general receptacle of these multiplied treasures played at any rate, through the years, the part of a friendly private-box at the constant operatic show, a box at the best point of the best tier, with the cushioned ledge of its front raking the whole scene and with its withdrawing rooms behind for more detached conversation; for easy—when not indeed slightly difficult—polyglot talk, artful *bibite,* artful cigarettes too, straight from the hand of the hostess, who could do all that belonged to a hostess, place people in relation and keep them so, take up and put down the topic, cause delicate tobacco and little gilded glasses to circulate, without ever leaving her sofa-

---

bibite. Soft drinks.

cushions or intermitting her good-nature. She exercised in these conditions, with never a block, as we say in London, in the traffic, with never an admission, an acceptance of the least social complication, her positive genius for easy interest, easy sympathy, easy friendship. It was as if, at last, she had taken the human race at large, quite irrespective of geography, for her neighbours, with neighbourly relations as a matter of course. These things, on her part, had at all events the greater appearance of ease from their having found to their purpose—and as if the very air of Venice produced them—a cluster of forms so light and immediate, so pre-established by picturesque custom. The old bright tradition, the wonderful Venetian legend had appealed to her from the first, closing round her house and her well-plashed water-steps, where the waiting gondolas were thick, quite as if, actually, the ghost of the defunct Carnival—since I have spoken of ghosts—still played some haunting part.

Let me add, at the same time, that Mrs. Bronson's social facility, which was really her great refuge from importunity, a defence with serious thought and serious feeling quietly cherished behind it, had its discriminations as well as its inveteracies, and that the most marked of all these, perhaps, was her attachment to Robert Browning. Nothing in all her beneficent life had probably made her happier than to have found herself able to minister, each year, with the returning autumn, to his pleasure and comfort. Attached to Ca' Alvisi, on the land side, is a somewhat melancholy old section of a Giustiniani palace, which she had annexed to her own premises mainly for the purpose of placing it, in comfortable guise, at the service of her friends. She liked, as she professed, when they were the real thing, to have them under her hand; and here succeeded each other, through the years, the company of the privileged and the more closely domesticated, who liked, harmlessly, to distinguish between themselves and outsiders. Among visitors partaking of this pleasant provision Mr. Browning was of course easily first. But I must leave her own pen to show him as her best years knew him. The point was, meanwhile, that if her charity was great even for the outsider, this was by reason of the inner essence of it—her perfect tenderness for Venice, which she always recognised as a link. That was the true principle of fusion, the key to communication. She communicated in proportion—little or much, measuring it as she felt people more responsive or less so; and she expressed herself, or in other words her full affection for the place, only to those who had most of the same sentiment. The rich and interesting form in which she found it in Browning may well be imagined—together with the quite independent quantity of the genial at large that she also found; but I am not sure that his favour was not primarily based on his paid tribute of such things as "Two in a Gondola" and "A Toccata of Galuppi." He had more ineffaceably than any one recorded his initiation from of old.

She was thus, all round, supremely faithful; yet it was perhaps after all with the very small folk, those to the manner born, that she made the easiest terms. She loved, she had from the first enthusiastically adopted, the engaging Venetian people, whose virtues she found touching and their infirmities but such as appeal mainly to the sense of humour and the love of anecdote; and she befriended and admired, she studied and spoiled them. There must have been a multitude of whom it would scarce be too much to say that her long residence among them was their settled golden age. When I consider that they have lost her now I fairly wonder to what shifts they have been put and how long they may not have to wait for such another messenger of Providence. She cultivated their dialect, she renewed their boats, she piously relighted—at the top of the tide-washed *pali* of traghetto or lagoon—the neglected lamp of the tutelary Madonnetta; she took cognisance of the wives, the children, the accidents, the troubles, as to which she became, perceptibly, the most prompt, the established remedy. On lines where the amusement was happily less one-sided she put together in dialect many short comedies, dramatic proverbs, which, with one of her drawing-rooms permanently arranged as a charming diminutive theatre, she caused to be performed by the young persons of her circle—often, when the case lent itself, by the wonderful small offspring of humbler friends, children of the Venetian lower class, whose aptitude, teachability, drollery, were her constant delight. It was certainly true that an impression of Venice as humanly sweet might easily found itself on the frankness and quickness and amiability of these little people. They were at least so much to the good; for the philosophy of their patroness was as Venetian as everything else; helping her to accept experience without bitterness and to remain fresh, even in the fatigue which finally overtook her, for pleasant surprises and proved sincerities. She was herself sincere to the last for the place of her predilection; inasmuch as though she had arranged herself, in the later time—and largely for the love of "Pippa Passes"—an alternative refuge at Asolo, she absented herself from Venice with continuity only under coercion of illness.

---

piously relighted . . . tutelary Madonnetta. See page 43 and note.

Asolo . . . Browning. In 1838 Browning spent four days in this medieval town near Treviso and began gathering impressions and details for the settings of both *Sordello* (1840) and *Pippa Passes* (1841). Part of the romance of Asolo was associated with the fact that in 1489 it had become the home of the exiled—and last—queen of Cyprus, Caterina Cornaro. As the town's first great hostess, she established a distinguished court, and there humanist Cardinal Pietro Bembo, a noble defender of platonic love in both Castiglione's *Cortegiano* (1528) and in his own *Gli Asolani* (1505), was her guest from 1489 to 1513. Toward the end of his life Browning came to Asolo and visited Mrs. Bronson, who sometimes signed her letters "Caterina"; his last collection of poems, *Asolando: Fancies and Facts* (1889), made reference to aspects of these romantic historical matters.

At Asolo, periodically, the link with Browning was more confirmed than weakened, and there, in old Venetian territory, and with the invasion of visitors comparatively checked, her preferentially small house became again a setting for the pleasure of talk and the sense of Italy. It contained again its own small treasures, all in the pleasant key of the homelier Venetian spirit. The plain beneath it stretched away like a purple sea from the lower cliffs of the hills, and the white *campanili* of the villages, as one was perpetually saying, showed on the expanse like scattered sails of ships. The rumbling carriage, the old-time, rattling, red-velveted carriage of provincial, rural Italy, delightful and quaint, did the office of the gondola; to Bassano, to Treviso, to high-walled Castelfranco, all pink and gold, the home of the great Giorgione. Here also memories cluster; but it is in Venice again that her vanished presence is most felt, for there, in the real, or certainly the finer, the more sifted Cosmopolis, it falls into its place among the others evoked, those of the past seekers of poetry and dispensers of romance. It is a fact that almost every one interesting, appealing, melancholy, memorable, odd, seems at one time or another, after many days and much life, to have gravitated to Venice by a happy instinct, settling in it and treating it, cherishing it, as a sort of repository of consolations; all of which to-day, for the conscious mind, is mixed with its air and constitutes its unwritten history. The deposed, the defeated, the disenchanted, the wounded, or even only the bored, have seemed to find there something that no other place could give. But such people came for themselves, as we seem to see them—only with the egotism of their grievances and the vanity of their hopes. Mrs. Bronson's case was beautifully different—she had come altogether for others.

[1902.]

From Chambéry to Milan

Your truly sentimental tourist will never take it from any occasion that there is absolutely nothing for him, and it was at Chambéry—but four hours from Geneva—that I accepted the situation and decided there might be mysterious delights in entering Italy by a whizz through an eight-mile tunnel, even as a bullet through the bore of a gun. I found my reward in the Savoyard landscape, which greets you betimes with the smile of anticipation. If it is not so Italian as Italy it is at least more Italian than anything *but* Italy—more Italian, too, I should think, than can seem natural and proper to the swarming red-legged soldiery who so publicly proclaim it of the empire of M. Thiers. The light and the complexion of things had to my eyes not a little of that mollified depth last loved by them rather further on. It was simply perhaps that the weather was hot and the mountains drowsing in that iridescent haze that I have seen nearer home than at Chambéry. But the vegetation, assuredly, had an all but Transalpine twist and curl, and the classic wayside tangle of corn and vines left nothing to be desired in the line of careless grace. Chambéry as a town, however, constitutes no foretaste of the monumental cities. There is shabbiness and shabbiness, the fond critic of such things will tell you; and that of the ancient

---

[Originally published (unsigned) in the *Nation,* xv (21 November 1872), 332–34; reprinted in *Transatlantic Sketches,* 1875; reprinted in *Foreign Parts,* 1883.]

the empire of M. Thiers. Louis Adolphe Thiers (1797–1877), the French statesman whose attempts to stir French pride and regain French prestige had helped bring on the 1870 war with Germany, a war that he opposed. Chosen in 1871 as president of the yet-unformed French Republic, his support of the Third Republic soon motivated the monarchist opposition in the National Assembly to attack him and to bring about his resignation.

capital of Savoy lacks style. I found a better pastime, however, than strolling through the dark dull streets in quest of effects that were not forthcoming. The first urchin you meet will show you the way to Les Charmettes and the Maison Jean-Jacques. A very pleasant way it becomes as soon as it leaves the town—a winding, climbing by-road, bordered with such a tall and sturdy hedge as to give it the air of an English lane—if you can fancy an English lane introducing you to the haunts of a Madame de Warens.

The house that formerly sheltered this lady's singular ménage stands on a hillside above the road, which a rapid path connects with the little grass-grown terrace before it. It is a small shabby, homely dwelling, with a certain reputable solidity, however, and more of internal spaciousness than of outside promise. The place is shown by an elderly competent dame who points out the very few surviving objects which you may touch with the reflection—complacent in whatsoever degree suits you—that they have known the familiarity of Rousseau's hand. It was presumably a meagrely-appointed house, and I wondered that on such scanty features so much expression should linger. But the structure has an ancient ponderosity, and the dust of the eighteenth century seems to lie on its worm-eaten floors, to cling to the faded old *papiers à ramages* on the walls and to lodge in the crevices of the brown wooden ceilings. Madame de Warens's bed remains, with the narrow couch of Jean-Jacques as well, his little warped and cracked yellow spinet, and a battered, turnip-shaped silver timepiece, engraved with its master's name—its primitive tick as extinct as his passionate heart-beats. It cost me, I confess, a somewhat pitying acceleration of my own to see this intimately personal relic of the *genius loci*—for it had dwelt in his waistcoat-pocket, than which there is hardly a material point in space nearer to a man's consciousness—tossed so irreverently upon the table on which you deposit your fee, beside the dog's-eared visitors' record or *livre de cuisine* recently denounced by Madame George Sand. In fact the place generally, in so far as some faint ghostly presence of its famous inmates seems to linger there, is by no means exhilarat-

---

Les Charmettes. In March 1728, at Annency, sixteen-year-old Jean Jacques Rousseau was introduced to Françoise-Louise de la Tour, Baronne de Warens, a young widow almost fifteen years his senior. A year later, embittered by experience and outcast both by his father and his family, he took refuge with this woman, who at first became his protector and guide, and later, at the Chambéry estate of Les Charmettes, his lover—a relationship that lasted sporadically from 1733 to 1747. Nineteenth-century guidebooks tended to establish the geography of their affair at Chambéry (Monmarché, 295), as did Rousseau's posthumous *Les Confessions* (1781–88).

papiers à ramages. Flowered wallpaper.

livre de cuisine **recently denounced by Madame George Sand.** The editor is unable to locate the reference.

ing. Coppet and Ferney tell, if not of pure happiness, at least of prosperity and honour, wealth and success. But Les Charmettes is haunted by ghosts unclean and forlorn. The place tells of poverty, perversity, distress. A good deal of clever modern talent in France has been employed in touching up the episode of which it was the scene and tricking it out in idyllic love-knots. But as I stood on the charming terrace I have mentioned—a little jewel of a terrace, with grassy flags and a mossy parapet, and an admirable view of great swelling violet hills—stood there reminded how much sweeter Nature is than man, the story looked rather wan and unlovely beneath these literary decorations, and I could pay it no livelier homage than is implied in perfect pity. Hero and heroine have become too much creatures of history to take up attitudes as part of any poetry. But, not to moralise too sternly for a tourist between trains, I should add that, as an illustration to be inserted mentally in the text of the "Confessions," a glimpse of Les Charmettes is pleasant enough. It completes the rare charm of good autobiography to behold with one's eyes the faded and battered background of the story; and Rousseau's narrative is so incomparably vivid and forcible that the sordid little house at Chambéry seems of a hardly deeper shade of reality than so many other passages of his projected truth.

If I spent an hour at Les Charmettes, fumbling thus helplessly with the past, I recognised on the morrow how strongly the Mont Cenis Tunnel smells of the time to come. As I passed along the Saint-Gothard highway a couple of months since, I perceived, half up the Swiss ascent, a group of navvies at work in a gorge beneath the road. They had laid bare a broad surface of granite and had punched in the centre of it a round black cavity, of about the dimensions, as it seemed to me, of a soup-plate. This was to attain its perfect development some eight years hence. The Mont Cenis may therefore be held to have set a fashion which will be followed till the highest Himalaya is but the ornamental apex or snow-capped gable-tip of some resounding fuliginous corridor. The tunnel differs but in length from other tunnels; you spend half an hour in it. But you whirl out into the blest peninsula, and as you look back seem to see the mighty mass shrug its

---

Coppet and Ferney . . . prosperity and honour, wealth and success. Coppet, a small town on the shore of Lac Léman with a fine château that was the home of Jacques Necker (1732–1808), finance minister for Louis XVI and, later, of his daughter, Madame de Staël. Ferney, a village in the canton l'Ain, where Marie-Louise Mignot, the widow of Nicolas-Charles Denis, bought a château for Voltaire, who lived here from 1759 to 1777; his presence helped change an extremely tiny hamlet into a memorable town.

Mont Cenis Tunnel smells of the time to come. Opened in 1870, at a length of 13,636 meters, and considered a miracle of modern engineering.

shoulders over the line, the mere turn of a dreaming giant in his sleep. The tunnel is certainly not a poetic object, but there is no perfection without its beauty; and as you measure the long rugged outline of the pyramid of which it forms the base you accept it as the perfection of a short cut. Twenty-four hours from Paris to Turin is speed for the times—speed which may content us, at any rate, until expansive Berlin has succeeded in placing itself at thirty-six from Milan.

To enter Turin then of a lovely August afternoon was to find a city of arcades, of pink and yellow stucco, of innumerable cafés, of blue-legged officers, of ladies draped in the North-Italian mantilla. An old friend of Italy coming back to her finds an easy waking for dormant memories. Every object is a reminder and every reminder a thrill. Half an hour after my arrival, as I stood at my window, which overhung the great square, I found the scene, within and without, a rough epitome of every pleasure and every impression I had formerly gathered from Italy: the balcony and the Venetian-blind, the cool floor of speckled concrete, the lavish delusions of frescoed wall and ceiling, the broad divan framed for the noonday siesta, the massive mediæval Castello in mid-piazza, with its shabby rear and its pompous Palladian front, the brick campaniles beyond, the milder, yellower light, the range of colour, the suggestion of sound. Later, beneath the arcades, I found many an old acquaintance: beautiful officers, resplendent, slow-strolling, contemplative of female beauty; civil and peaceful dandies, hardly less gorgeous, with that religious faith in moustache and shirt-front which distinguishes the *belle jeunesse* of Italy; ladies with heads artfully shawled in Spanish-looking lace, but with too little art—or too much nature at least—in the region of the bodice; well-conditioned young *abbati* with neatly drawn stockings. These indeed are not objects of first-rate interest, and with such Turin is rather meagrely furnished. It has no architecture, no churches, no monuments, no romantic street-scenery. It has the great votive temple of the Superga, which stands on a high hilltop above the city, gazing across at Monte Rosa and lifting its own fine dome against the sky with no contemptible art. But when you have seen the Superga from the quay beside the Po, a skein of a few yellow threads in August, despite its frequent habit of rising high and running wild, and said to yourself that in architecture position is half the battle, you have nothing left to visit but the Museum of pictures. The Turin Gallery, which is large and well arranged, is the fortunate owner of three or four masterpieces:

---

mediæval Castello . . . pompous Palladian front. Actually built in the fifteenth century, the Palazzo Madama's facade, by Filippo Juvarra, was constructed in the eighteenth century and is somewhat reminiscent of Palladio's Palazzo Chiericata in Vicenza.

abbati. Priests.

Turin Gallery. Today the Galleria Sabauda.

a couple of magnificent Vandycks and a couple of Paul Veroneses; the latter a Queen of Sheba and a Feast of the House of Levi—the usual splendid combination of brocades, grandees and marble colonnades dividing those skies *de turquoise malade* to which Théophile Gautier is fond of alluding. The Veroneses are fine, but with Venice in prospect the traveller feels at liberty to keep his best attention in reserve. If, however, he has the proper relish for Vandyck, let him linger long and fondly here; for that admiration will never be more potently stirred than by the adorable group of the three little royal highnesses, sons and the daughter of Charles I. All the purity of childhood is here, and all its soft solidity of structure, rounded tenderly beneath the spangled satin and contrasted charmingly with the pompous rigidity. Clad respectively in crimson, white and blue, these small scions stand up in their ruffs and fardingales in dimpled serenity, squaring their infantine stomachers at the spectator with an innocence, a dignity, a delightful grotesqueness, which make the picture a thing of close truth as well as of fine decorum. You might kiss their hands, but you certainly would think twice before pinching their cheeks—provocative as they are of this tribute of admiration—and would altogether lack presumption to lift them off the ground or the higher level or dais on which they stand so sturdily planted by right of birth. There is something inimitable in the paternal gallantry with which the painter has touched off the young lady. She was a princess, yet she was a baby, and he has contrived, we let ourselves fancy, to interweave an intimation that she was a creature whom, in her teens, the lucklessly smitten—even as he was prematurely—must vainly sigh for. Though the work is a masterpiece of execution its merits under this head may be emulated, at a distance; the lovely modulations of colour in the three contrasted and harmonised little satin petticoats, the solidity of the little heads, in spite of all their prettiness, the happy, unexaggerated squareness and maturity of *pose,* are, severally, points to study, to imitate, and to reproduce with profit. But the taste of such a consummate thing is its great secret as well as its great merit—a taste which seems one of the lost instincts of mankind. Go and enjoy this supreme expression of Vandyck's fine sense, and admit that never was a politer production.

Milan speaks to us of a burden of felt life of which Turin is innocent, but in its general aspect still lingers a northern reserve which makes the place

---

de turquoise malade . . . Gautier. "Le ciel, peint sans doute avec cette cendre bleue d'Egypte qui a joué de si mauvais tours aux artistes de ce temps-là, a des tons faux et louches désagréables à l'oeil qu'il ne devait pas offrir avant la carbonisation de cette couleur trompeuse, qui a si bizarrement noirci les fonds des *Pèlerins d'Emmaüs,* de Paul Véronèse" (Gautier, *Italia,* 309): "The sky, doubtless painted with the blue ash from Egypt which played such unpleasant tricks upon the artists of that period, has false and ambiguous tones, disagreeable to the eye, which were not present before the carbonization of that deceitful color, which has so oddly blackened the background of the 'Pilgrims of Emmaus' of Paul Veronese" (trans. Vermilye, 286).

rather perhaps the last of the prose capitals than the first of the poetic. The long Austrian occupation perhaps did something to Germanise its physiognomy; though indeed this is an indifferent explanation when one remembers how well, temperamentally speaking, Italy held her own in Venetia. Milan, at any rate, if not bristling with the æsthetic impulse, opens to us frankly enough the thick volume of her past. Of that volume the Cathedral is the fairest and fullest page—a structure not supremely interesting, not logical, not even, to some minds, commandingly beautiful, but grandly curious and superbly rich. I hope, for my own part, never to grow too particular to admire it. If it had no other distinction it would still have that of impressive, immeasurable achievement. As I strolled beside its vast indented base one evening, and felt it, above me, rear its grey mysteries into the starlight while the restless human tide on which I floated rose no higher than the first few layers of street-soiled marble, I was tempted to believe that beauty in great architecture is almost a secondary merit, and that the main point is mass— such mass as may make it a supreme embodiment of vigorous effort. Viewed in this way a great building is the greatest conceivable work of art. More than any other it represents difficulties mastered, resources combined, labour, courage and patience. And there are people who tell us that art has nothing to do with morality! Little enough, doubtless, when it is concerned, even ever so little, in painting the roof of Milan Cathedral within to represent carved stone-work. Of this famous roof every one has heard—how

<hr />

long Austrian occupation. From 1535, the year in which Francesco Sforza died, until the 1714 War of Spanish Succession, Milan was occupied by Spanish troops. At the close of the war the city was given to Austria, and it remained in Austrian hands until the 1796 Napoleonic capture, which Stendhal celebrates memorably at the beginning of *The Charterhouse of Parma;* when Napoleon abdicated in 1814, Milan turned against the French and reestablished Austrian ties.

tempted to believe that beauty in great architecture . . . mass. Tempted to agree with one of the opinions of Ruskin, whose *Mornings in Florence,* in consideration of the Duomo in Florence and Saint Peter's in Rome, debated the issue of mass: "Vastness *has* its value. But the glory of architecture is to be—whatever you wish it to be,—lovely, or grand, or comfortable,—on such terms as it can easily obtain" (*Works,* XXIII, 363–68; see also *The Seven Lamps of Architecture, Works,* VIII, 103ff.).

people who tell us that art has nothing to do with morality! James writes in 1873, the year of Walter Pater's *Studies in the History of the Renaissance.* Pater's conclusion provided the Aesthetic movement with a touchstone, for as many "pulsations as possible" from life, and proposed the "love of art for art's sake."

Of this famous roof every one has heard—how good it is, how bad, how perfect a delusion. In his well-known architectural study, *Brick and Marble in the Middle Ages* (1855), Edmund Street had written, "The solitary blot upon this otherwise noble work is one for which its architect is in no way responsible—the cells of the groining are all filled with painted imitations of elaborate traceries in brown colour, an abominable device" (100–101). The problematic traceries have been obliterated.

good it is, how bad, how perfect a delusion, how transparent an artifice. It is the first thing you cicerone shows you on entering the church. The occasionally accommodating art-lover may accept it philosophically, I think; for the interior, though admirably effective as a whole, has no great sublimity, nor even purity, of pitch. It is splendidly vast and dim; the altar-lamps twinkle afar through the incense-thickened air like fog-lights at sea, and the great columns rise straight to the roof, which hardly curves to meet them, with the girth and altitude of oaks of a thousand years; but there is little refinement of design—few of those felicities of proportion which the eye caresses, when it finds them, very much as the memory retains and repeats some happy lines of poetry or some haunting musical phrase. Consistently brave, none the less, is the result produced, and nothing braver than a certain exhibition that I privately enjoyed of the relics of St. Charles Borromeus. This holy man lies at his eternal rest in a small but gorgeous sepulchral chapel, beneath the boundless pavement and before the high altar; and for the modest sum of five francs you may have his shrivelled mortality unveiled and gaze at it with whatever reserves occur to you. The Catholic Church never renounces a chance of the sublime for fear of a chance of the ridiculous—especially when the chance of the sublime may be the very excellent chance of five francs. The performance in question, of which the good San Carlo paid in the first instance the cost, was impressive certainly, but as a monstrous matter or a grim comedy may still be. The little sacristan, having secured his audience, whipped on a white tunic over his frock, lighted a couple of extra candles and proceeded to remove from above the altar, by means of a crank, a sort of sliding shutter, just as you may see a shop-boy do of a morning at his master's window. In this case too a large sheet of plate-glass was uncovered, and to form an idea of the *étalage* you must imagine that a jeweller, for reasons of his own, has struck an unnatural partnership with an undertaker.

St. Charles Borromeus. This holy man. A leader of the Counter-Reformation, Carlo Borromeo (1538–84) is remembered for helping implement the reforms at the Council of Trent, as well as for his fearless behavior in Milan during the plague years—an episode central to Alessandro Manzoni's *I Promessi Sposi* (1825–27). His mother was the sister of Pius IV, who soon made him archbishop and then cardinal of Milan; as "cardinal-nephew," his official designation, he held power that was second only to that of the pope.

chance of the sublime . . . chance of the ridiculous. Thomas Paine, *The Age of Reason* (1795): "One step above the sublime, makes the ridiculous; one step above the ridiculous, makes the sublime again."

five francs. James persists in referring to the French currency rather than the Italian lira. The Latin Monetary Union (1865) had made the lira exactly equivalent to the French, Belgian, and Swiss francs.

étalage. Shop-window display.

The black mummified corpse of the saint is stretched out in a glass coffin, clad in his mouldering canonicals, mitred, crosiered and gloved, glittering with votive jewels. It is an extraordinary mixture of death and life; the desiccated clay, the ashen rags, the hideous little black mask and skull, and the living, glowing, twinkling splendour of diamonds, emeralds and sapphires. The collection is really fine, and many great historic names are attached to the different offerings. Whatever may be the better opinion as to the future of the Church, I can't help thinking she will make a figure in the world so long as she retains this great fund of precious "properties," this prodigious capital decoratively invested and scintillating throughout Christendom at effectively-scattered points. You see I am forced to agree after all, in spite of the sliding shutter and the profane swagger of the sacristan, that a certain pastoral majesty saved the situation, or at least made irony gape. Yet it was from a natural desire to breathe a sweeter air that I immediately afterwards undertook the interminable climb to the roof of the cathedral. This is another world of wonders, and one which enjoys due renown, every square inch of wall on the winding stairways being bescribbled with a traveller's name. There is a great glare from the far-stretching slopes of marble, a confusion (like the masts of a navy or the spears of any army) of image-capped pinnacles, biting the impalpable blue, and, better than either, the goodliest view of level Lombardy sleeping in its rich transalpine light and resembling, with its white-walled dwellings and the spires on its horizon, a vast green sea spotted with ships. After two months of Switzerland the Lombard plain is a rich rest to the eye, and the yellow, liquid, free-flowing light—as if on favoured Italy the vessels of heaven were more widely opened—had for mine a charm which made me think of a great opaque mountain as a blasphemous invasion of the atmospheric spaces.

I have mentioned the cathedral first, but the prime treasure of Milan at the present hour is the beautiful, tragical Leonardo. The cathedral is good for

---

Leonardo . . . **most luckless of frescoes . . . the irony of fate.** The Cenacolo, or *Last Supper* (1494–97), technically not a fresco, had begun to deteriorate during Leonardo's lifetime, and Vasari, viewing it in 1566, discovered that of the work "nothing was visible but a mass of blots." Partly it was the humidity in the hall that caused the deterioration, but in larger part the artist's ingenious attempts to circumvent the limitations of the fresco technique worked the doom. Leonardo had experimented with a method which allowed for modification and rethinking, a method, however, which produced an extremely unstable painted surface which soon began to detach from the refectory wall. A major restoration, carried out according to strict scientific principles, at present is in progress under the direction of Pinin Brambilla Barcilon and is revealing what remains of the actual work by the hand of Leonardo, not the overpainted accumulations of centuries. David Alan Brown's *Leonardo's "Last Supper": The Restoration* provides details of the method, the method's consequences, and the attempts at restoration.

another thousand years, but we ask whether our children will find in the most majestic and most luckless of frescoes much more than the shadow of a shadow. Its fame has been for a century or two that, as one may say, of an illustrious invalid whom people visit to see how he lasts, with leave-taking sighs and almost death-bed or tiptoe precautions. The picture needs not another scar or stain, now, to be the saddest work of art in the world; and battered, defaced, ruined as it is, it remains one of the greatest. We may really compare its anguish of decay to the slow conscious ebb of life in a human organism. The production of the prodigy was a breath from the infinite, and the painter's conception not immeasurably less complex than the scheme, say, of his own mortal constitution. There has been much talk lately of the irony of fate, but I suspect fate was never more ironical than when she led the most scientific, the most calculating of all painters to spend fifteen long years in building his goodly house upon the sand. And yet, after all, may not the playing of that trick represent but a deeper wisdom, since if the thing enjoyed the immortal health and bloom of a first-rate Titian we should have lost one of the most pertinent lessons in the history of art? We know it as hearsay, but here is the plain proof, that there is no limit to the amount of "stuff" an artist may put into his work. Every painter ought once in his life to stand before the Cenacolo and decipher its moral. Mix with your colours and mess on your palette every particle of the very substance of your soul, and this lest perchance your "prepared surface" shall play you a

---

In James's "Travelling Companions" (1870), *The Last Supper* merits an enraptured description:

> Since that day, I have seen all the great art treasures of Italy: I have seen Tintoretto at Venice, Michael Angelo at Florence and Rome, Correggio at Parma; but I have looked at no other picture with an emotion equal to that which rose within me as this great creation of Leonardo slowly began to dawn upon my intelligence from the tragical twilight of its ruin. A work so nobly conceived can never utterly die, so long as the half-dozen main lines of its design remain. Neglect and malice are less cunning than the genius of the great painter. It has stored away with masterly skill such a wealth of beauty as only perfect love and sympathy can fully detect. So, under my eyes, the restless ghost of the dead fresco returned to its mortal abode. From the beautiful central image of Christ I perceived its radiation right and left along the sadly broken line of the disciples. One by one, out of the depths of their grim dismemberment, the figures trembled into meaning and life, and the vast, serious beauty of the work stood revealed. What is the ruling force of this magnificent design? Is it art? is it science? is it sentiment? is it knowledge? I am sure I can't say; but in moments of doubt and depression I find it of excellent use to recall the great picture with all possible distinctness. Of all the works of man's hand it is the least superficial. (*Complete Tales*, II, 172)

"prepared surface." James's emphasis here—James alludes to the intonaco plaster stage of fresco painting rather than to the idiosyncratic mural method of Leonardo—borrows vocabulary from the visual artist to make the literary reference. James himself frequently reiterated

trick! Then, and then only, it will fight to the last—it will resist even in death. Raphael was a happier genius; you look at his lovely "Marriage of the Virgin" at the Brera, beautiful as some first deep smile of conscious inspiration, but to feel that he foresaw no complaint against fate, and that he knew the world he wanted to know and charmed it into never giving him away. But I have left no space to speak of the Brera, nor of that paradise of bookworms with an eye for their background—if such creatures exist—the Ambrosian Library; nor of that mighty basilica of St. Ambrose, with its spacious atrium and its crudely solemn mosaics, in which it is surely your own fault if you don't forget Dr. Strauss and M. Renan and worship as grimly as a Christian of the ninth century.

It is part of the sordid prose of the Mont Cenis road that, unlike those fine old unimproved passes, the Simplon, the Splügen and—yet awhile longer—the Saint-Gothard, it denies you a glimpse of that paradise adorned by the four lakes even as that of uncommented Scripture by the rivers of Eden. I made, however, an excursion to the Lake of Como, which, though brief, lasted long enough to suggest to me that I too was a hero of romance with leisure for a love-affair, and not a hurrying tourist with a Bradshaw in his

---

such terminology, notably in the New York Edition preface to *Roderick Hudson:* "The subject of 'Roderick' figured to me vividly this employment of canvas. . . . All of which will perhaps pass but for a supersubtle way of pointing the plain moral that a young embroiderer of the canvas of life soon began to work in terror, fairly, of the vast expanse of that surface" (*Literary Criticism: French Writers,* 1040–41)—when addressing the conceptual problems facing the artist.

Dr. Strauss and M. Renan. David Friedrich Strauss (1808–74), German theologian and philosopher, whose *Das Leben Jesu* (1835), using a somewhat deconstructive methodology to deny the historical validity of many Christian beliefs, suggested the probability of a myth. His controversial *Der Alte und der Neue Glaube* (1873), recently published when James wrote this essay, had demonstrated a more sure and more extreme skepticism.

Ernest Renan (1823–92), French philologist and historical writer whose seminary education, especially his philological study of Hebrew, Arabic, and Syriac, helped strain his faith in the historical Jesus. He finally left the seminary in 1845, but his *Vie de Jésus* (1843), influenced in part by Strauss, had already demonstrated a growing scientific perspective and a skeptical temper. The book became an international success. Upon occasion James reviewed Renan's later works with deep appreciation of genius and saw each new publication as "an intellectual feast." Reviews reprinted in *Literary Criticism: French Writers,* 628–45; see particularly James on Renan's *Souvenirs d'Enfance et de Jeunesse* (1883), and the fact that Renan, who could not be a good Catholic, claimed instead, "I was a good scholar; I can never be damned for that."

Bradshaw. George Bradshaw (1801–53), engraver and cartographer, produced a well-known series of railroad guides and city maps for the British Isles and for the European continent.

pocket. The Lake of Como has figured largely in novels of "immoral" tendency—being commonly the spot to which inflamed young gentlemen invite the wives of other gentlemen to fly with them and ignore the restrictions of public opinion. But even the Lake of Como has been revised and improved; the fondest prejudices yield to time; it gives one somehow a sense of an aspiringly high tone. I should pay a poor compliment at least to the swarming inmates of the hotels which now alternate attractively by the water-side with villas old and new were I to read the appearances more cynically. But if it is lost to florid fiction it still presents its blue bosom to most other refined uses, and the unsophisticated tourist, the American at least, may do any amount of private romancing there. The pretty hotel at Cadenabbia offers him, for instance, in the most elegant and assured form, the so often precarious adventure of what he calls at home summer board. It is all so unreal, so fictitious, so elegant and idle, so framed to undermine a rigid sense of the chief end of man not being to float for ever in an ornamental boat, beneath an awning tasselled like a circus-horse, impelled by an affable Giovanni or Antonio from one stately stretch of lake-laved villa steps to another, that departure seems as harsh and unnatural as the dream-dispelling note of some punctual voice at your bedside on a dusky winter morning. Yet I wondered, for my own part, where I had seen it all before— the pink-walled villas gleaming through their shrubberies of orange and oleander, the mountains shimmering in the hazy light like so many breasts of doves, the constant presence of the melodious Italian voice. Where indeed but at the Opera when the manager has been more than usually regardless of expense? Here in the foreground was the palace of the nefarious barytone, with its banqueting-hall opening as freely on the stage as a railway buffet on the platform; beyond, the delightful back scene, with its operatic gamut of colouring; in the middle the scarlet-sashed *barcaiuoli,* grouped like a chorus, hat in hand, awaiting the conductor's signal. It was better even than being in a novel—this being, this fairly wallowing, in a libretto.

[1872.]

Lake of Como . . . novels of "immoral" tendency. Notably Stendhal's novel set in part on the shores of the Lago di Como, "The 'Chartreuse de Parme,' where every one is grossly immoral"—as judged in James's review of *Henry Beyle (otherwise De Stendahl* [sic]*): A Critical and Biographical Study,* by Andrew Archibald Paton," *Nation,* xix (17 September 1874); reprinted in *Literary Criticism: French Writers,* 812–18. In James's early tale "Travelling Companions," the narrator reports that he tours northern Italy "with a volume of Stendhal in my pocket" and asks, "Have you read Stendhal's *Chartreuse de Parme?*" (*Complete Tales,* ii, 185).

barcaiuoli. Boatmen or ferrymen.

The Old Saint-Gothard

Leaves from a Note-Book

Berne, *September,* 1873.—In Berne again, some eleven weeks after having left it in July. I have never been in Switzerland so late, and I came hither innocently supposing the last Cook's tourist to have paid out his last coupon and departed. But I was lucky, it seems, to discover an empty cot in an attic and a very tight place at a table d'hôte. People are all flocking out of Switzerland, as in July they were flocking in, and the main channels of egress are terribly choked. I have been here several days, watching them come and go; it is like the march-past of an

[Here dated by James 1873; originally published as "An Autumn Journey," in *Galaxy,* XVII (April 1874), 536–44; reprinted in *Transatlantic Sketches,* 1875, as "The St. Gothard"; reprinted in *Foreign Parts,* 1883, as "The St. Gotthard."]

Cook's tourist to have paid out his last coupon. Thomas Cook's pioneering British travel firm provided members of tours with coupon booklets that covered payment of rail fares, hotels, and selected meals, thereby minimizing the difficulties and expense that travelers might face when making transactions that required currency exchange and consequent commissions. In the unsigned 1872 "Swiss Notes," James had written that

> though . . . we laugh at Mr. Cook, the great *entrepreneur* of travel, with his *coupons* and his caravans of 'personally-conducted' sight-seers, we have all pretty well come to belong to his party. . . . I have even fancied that it is a sadly ineffectual pride that prevents us from buying one of Mr. Cook's little bundles of tickets, and saving our percentage, whatever it is, of money and trouble, for I am sure that the poor bewildered and superannuated genius of the Grand Tour, as it was taken forty years ago, wherever she may have buried her classic head, beyond hearing of the eternal telegraphic click bespeaking 'rooms' on mountain tops, confounds us alike in a sweeping reprobation.

army. It gives one, for an occasional change from darker thoughts, a lively impression of the numbers of people now living, and above all now moving, at extreme ease in the world. Here is little Switzerland disgorging its tens of thousands of honest folk, chiefly English, and rarely, to judge by their faces and talk, children of light in any eminent degree; for whom snow-peaks and glaciers and passes and lakes and chalets and sunsets and a *café complet,* "including honey," as the coupon says, have become prime necessities for six weeks every year. It's not so long ago that lords and nabobs monopolised these pleasures; but nowadays a month's tour in Switzerland is no more a *jeu de prince* than a Sunday excursion. To watch this huge Anglo-Saxon wave ebbing through Berne suggests, no doubt most fallaciously, that the common lot of mankind is n't after all so very hard and that the masses have reached a high standard of comfort. The view of the Oberland chain, as you see it from the garden of the hotel, really butters one's bread most handsomely; and here are I don't know how many hundred Cook's tourists a day looking at it through the smoke of their pipes. Is it really the "masses," however, that I see every day at the table d'hôte? They have rather too few h's to the dozen, but their good-nature is great. Some people complain that they "vulgarise" Switzerland; but as far as I am concerned I freely give it up to them and offer them a personal welcome and take a peculiar satisfaction in seeing them here. Switzerland is a "show country"—I am more and more struck with the bearings of that truth; and its use in the world is to reassure persons of a benevolent imagination when they begin to wish for the drudging millions a greater supply of elevating amusement. Here is amusement for a thousand years, and as elevating certainly as mountains three miles high can make it. I expect to live to see the summit of Monte Rosa heated by steam-tubes and adorned with a hotel setting three tables d'hôte a day.

I have been walking about the arcades, which used to bestow a grateful shade in July, but which seem rather dusky and chilly in these shortening autumn days. I am struck with the way the English always speak of them— with a shudder, as gloomy, as dirty, as evil-smelling, as suffocating, as freezing, as anything and everything but admirably picturesque. I take us Americans for the only people who, in travelling, judge things on the first impulse—when we do judge them at all—not from the standpoint of simple comfort. Most of us, strolling forth into these bustling basements, are, I imagine, too much amused, too much diverted from the sense of an alienable right to public ease, to be conscious of heat or cold, of thick air, or even of the universal smell of strong *charcuterie*. If the visible romantic were ban-

---

café complet. A small breakfast.

ished from the face of the earth I am sure the idea of it would still survive in some typical American heart. . . .

Lucerne, September.—Berne, I find, has been filling with tourists at the expense of Lucerne, which I have been having almost to myself. There are six people at the table d'hôte; the excellent dinner denotes on the part of the *chef* the easy leisure in which true artists love to work. The waiters have nothing to do but lounge about the hall and chink in their pockets the fees of the past season. The day has been lovely in itself, and pervaded, to my sense, by the gentle glow of a natural satisfaction at my finding myself again on the threshold of Italy. I am lodged *en prince,* in a room with a balcony hanging over the lake—a balcony on which I spent a long time this morning at dawn, thanking the mountain-tops, from the depths of a landscape-lover's heart, for their promise of superbly fair weather. There were a great many mountain-tops to thank, for the crags and peaks and pinnacles tumbled away through the morning mist in an endless confusion of grandeur. I have been all day in better humour with Lucerne than ever before—a forecast reflection of Italian moods. If Switzerland, as I wrote the other day, is so furiously a show-place, Lucerne is certainly one of the biggest booths at the fair. The little quay, under the trees, squeezed in between the decks of the steamboats and the doors of the hotels, is a terrible medley of Saxon dialects—a jumble of pilgrims in all the phases of devotion, equipped with book and staff, alpenstock and Baedeker. There are so many hotels and trinket-shops, so many omnibuses and steamers, so many Saint-Gothard *vetturini,* so many ragged urchins poking photographs, minerals and Lucernese English at you, that you feel as if lake and mountains themselves, in all their loveliness, were but a part of the "enterprise" of landlords and pedlars, and half expect to see the Righi and Pilatus and the fine weather figure as items on your hotel-bill between the *bougie* and the *siphon.* Nature herself assists you to this conceit; there is something so operatic and suggestive of footlights and scene-shifters in the

---

Baedeker. Karl Baedeker's series of guidebooks for the German tourist (1801–59)—based largely on Murray's revolutionary model of accuracy and completeness (see page 132 and note)—eventually would become the authority on travel throughout much of what was termed the civilized world; their immense success in part derived from Baedeker's decision to translate his guides into French and English. A species of "Baedeker Guide," profusely illustrated with color photographs but providing barely an echo of the textual thoroughness that was the rule in the nineteenth century, is still published today.

vetturini. Cab men; the currency of the Italian word indicates the Italian heritage of the Saint-Gothard/San Gottardo region of Switzerland.

Righi and Pilatus. Two neighboring alpine peaks.

bougie and the *siphon.* Candle and seltzer water.

view on which Lucerne looks out. You are one of five thousand—fifty thousand—"accommodated" spectators; you have taken your season-ticket and there is a responsible impresario somewhere behind the scenes. There is such a luxury of beauty in the prospect—such a redundancy of composition and effect—so many more peaks and pinnacles than are needed to make one heart happy or regale the vision of one quiet observer, that you finally accept the little Babel on the quay and the looming masses in the clouds as equal parts of a perfect system, and feel as if the mountains had been waiting so many ages for the hotels to come and balance the colossal group, that they show a right, after all, to have them big and numerous. The scene-shifters have been at work all day long, composing and discomposing the beautiful background of the prospect—massing the clouds and scattering the light, effacing and reviving, making play with their wonderful machinery of mist and haze. The mountains rise, one behind the other, in an enchanting gradation of distances and of melting blues and greys; you think each successive tone the loveliest and haziest possible till you see another loom dimly behind it. I could n't enjoy even *The Swiss Times,* over my breakfast, till I had marched forth to the office of the Saint-Gothard service of coaches and demanded the banquette for to-morrow. The one place at the disposal of the office was taken, but I might possibly *m'entendre* with the conductor for his own seat—the conductor being generally visible, in the intervals of business, at the post-office. To the post-office, after breakfast, I repaired, over the fine new bridge which now spans the green Reuss and gives such a woeful air of country-cousinship to the crooked old wooden structure which did sole service when I was here four years ago. The old bridge is covered with a running hood of shingles and adorned with a series of very quaint and vivid little paintings of the "Dance of Death," quite in the Holbein manner; the new sends up a painful glare from its white limestone, and is ornamented with candelabra in a meretricious imitation of platinum. As an almost professional cherisher of the quaint I ought to have chosen to return at least by the dark and narrow way; but mark how luxury unmans us. I was already demoralised. I crossed the threshold of the timbered portal, took a few steps, and retreated. It *smelt badly!* So I marched back, counting the lamps in their fine falsity. But the other, the

---

m'entendre. Come to an understanding.

Reuss . . . old bridge . . . "Dance of Death," . . . Holbein. Lucerne is positioned at the mouth of the Reuss River, where it feeds into the Lake of Lucerne. The sixteenth-century painter Caspar Melinger was the artist of the scenes of the "Dance of Death" on the Spreuer-Brücke, or the Mill-bridge, the "mystical paintings in the manner of Holbein" of James's 1871 tale "At Isella" (*Complete Tales,* ii, 307); Hans Holbein, the younger (c. 1497–1543), noted primarily for his portraits, was also famous for his forty-one woodcut illustrations of the dance of death.

crooked and covered way, smelt very badly indeed; and no good American is without a fund of accumulated sensibility to the odour of stale timber.

Meanwhile I had spent an hour in the great yard of the post-office, waiting for my conductor to turn up and seeing the yellow malles-postes pushed to and fro. At last, being told my man was at my service, I was brought to speech of a huge, jovial, bearded, delightful Italian, clad in the blue coat and waistcoat, with close, round silver buttons, which are a heritage of the old postilions. No, it was not he; it was a friend of his; and finally the friend was produced, *en costume de ville,* but equally jovial, and Italian enough—a brave Lucernese, who had spent half of his life between Bellinzona and Camerlata. For ten francs this worthy man's perch behind the luggage was made mine as far as Bellinzona, and we separated with reciprocal wishes for good weather on the morrow. To-morrow is so manifestly determined to be as fine as any other 30th of September since the weather became on this planet a topic of conversation that I have had nothing to do but stroll about Lucerne, staring, loafing and vaguely intent on regarding the fact that, whatever happens, my place is paid to Milan. I loafed into the immense new Hôtel National and read the *New York Tribune* on a blue satin divan; after which I was rather surprised, on coming out, to find myself staring at a green Swiss lake and not at the Broadway omnibuses. The Hôtel National is adorned with a perfectly appointed Broadway bar—one of the "prohibited" ones seeking hospitality in foreign lands after the manner of an old-fashioned French or Italian refugee.

Milan, October.—My journey hither was such a pleasant piece of traveller's luck that I feel a delicacy for taking it to pieces to see what it was made of. Do what we will, however, there remains in all deeply agreeable impressions a charming something we can't analyse. I found it agreeable even, given the rest of my case, to turn out of bed, at Lucerne, by four o'clock, into the chilly autumn darkness. The thick-starred sky was cloudless, and there was as yet no flush of dawn; but the lake was wrapped in a ghostly white mist which crept halfway up the mountains and made them look as if they too had been lying down for the night and were casting away the vaporous tissues of their bedclothes. Into this fantastic fog the little steamer went creaking away, and I hung about the deck with the two or three travellers

---

Broadway bar . . . "prohibited." The distilled liquor industry in the United States had grown tremendously after the Civil War, and although temperance groups had been active since the early years of the nineteenth century, James writes at the beginning of a movement that would eventually bring about the Eighteenth Amendment to the Constitution and the Volstead Act. In 1868 the Prohibition Party was established, and the Woman's Christian Temperance Union was organized in 1874; both worked to restrict licensing of the rapidly burgeoning "saloons" (see also page 314 and note) in many American cities.

who had known better than to believe it would save them francs or midnight sighs—over those debts you "pay with your person"—to go and wait for the diligence at the Poste at Flüelen, or yet at the Guillaume Tell. The dawn came sailing up over the mountain-tops, flushed but unperturbed, and blew out the little stars and then the big ones, as a thrifty matron after a party blows out her candles and lamps; the mist went melting and wandering away into the duskier hollows and recesses of the mountains, and the summits defined their profiles against the cool soft light.

At Flüelen, before the landing, the big yellow coaches were actively making themselves bigger, and piling up boxes and bags on their roofs in a way to turn nervous people's thoughts to the sharp corners of the downward twists of the great road. I climbed into my own banquette, and stood eating peaches—half-a-dozen women were hawking them about under the horses' legs—with an air of security that might have been offensive to the people scrambling and protesting below between coupé and intérieur. They were all English and all had false alarms about the claim of somebody else to their place, the place for which they produced their ticket, with a declaration in three or four different tongues of the inalienable right to it given them by the expenditure of British gold. They were all serenely confuted by the stout, purple-faced, many-buttoned conductors, patted on the backs, assured that their bath-tubs had every advantage of position on the top, and stowed away according to their dues. When once one has fairly started on a journey and has but to go and go by the impetus received, it is surprising what entertainment one finds in very small things. We surrender to the gaping traveller's mood, which surely is n't the unwisest the heart knows. I don't envy people, at any rate, who have outlived or outworn the simple sweetness of feeling settled to go somewhere with bag and umbrella. If we are settled on the top of a coach, and the "somewhere" contains an element of the new and strange, the case is at its best. In this matter wise people are content to become children again. We don't turn about on our knees to look out of the omnibus-window, but we indulge in very much the same round-eyed contemplation of accessible objects. Responsibility is left at home or at the worst packed away in the valise, relegated to quite another part of the diligence with the clean shirts and the writing-case. I sucked in the gladness of gaping, for this occasion, with the somewhat acrid juice of my indifferent peaches; it made me think them very good. This was the first of a series of kindly services it rendered me. It made me agree next, as we started, that the gentleman at the booking-office at Lucerne had but played a harmless joke when he told me the regular seat in the banquette was taken. No one

---

diligence. A stagecoach.

appeared to claim it; so the conductor and I reversed positions, and I found him quite as conversible as the usual Anglo-Saxon.

He was trolling snatches of melody and showing his great yellow teeth in a jovial grin all the way to Bellinzona—and this in face of the sombre fact that the Saint-Gothard tunnel is scraping away into the mountain, all the while, under his nose, and numbering the days of the many-buttoned brotherhood. But he hopes, for long service's sake, to be taken into the employ of the railway; *he* at least is no cherisher of quaintness and has no romantic perversity. I found the railway coming on, however, in a manner very shocking to mine. About an hour short of Andermatt they have pierced a huge black cavity in the mountain, around which has grown up a swarming, digging, hammering, smoke-compelling colony. There are great barracks, with tall chimneys, down in the gorge that bristled the other day but with natural graces, and a wonderful increase of wine-shops in the little village of Göschenen above. Along the breast of the mountain, beside the road, come wandering several miles of very handsome iron pipes, of a stupendous girth—a conduit for the water-power with which some of the machinery is worked. It lies at its mighty length among the rocks like an immense black serpent, and serves, as a mere detail, to give one the measure of the central enterprise. When at the end of our long day's journey, well down in warm Italy, we came upon the other aperture of the tunnel, I could but uncap with a grim reverence. Truly Nature is great, but she seems to me to stand in very much the shoes of my poor friend the conductor. She is being superseded at her strongest points, successively, and nothing remains but for her to take humble service with her master. If she can hear herself think amid that din of blasting and hammering she must be reckoning up the years to elapse before the cleverest of Ober-Ingénieurs decides that mountains are mere obstructive matter and has the Jungfrau melted down and the residuum carried away in balloons and dumped upon another planet.

The Devil's Bridge, with the same failing apparently as the good Homer, was decidedly nodding. The volume of water in the torrent was shrunken, and I missed the thunderous uproar and far-leaping spray that have kept up a miniature tempest in the neighbourhood on my other passages. It suddenly occurs to me that the fault is not in the good Homer's inspiration, but simply in the big black pipes above-mentioned. They dip into the rushing stream higher up, presumably, and pervert its fine frenzy to their prosaic uses. There

---

Devil's Bridge . . . Homer, was decidedly nodding. The Teufelsbrüvkr, about two miles from Göschen, crossed the Reuss above a magnificent cascade and was the eighth bridge in this particularly stressful site. James alludes to Horace, *Ars Poetica,* "Indignor quandoque bonus dormitat Homerus" [But if Homer, usually good, nods for a moment, I think it shame].

could hardly be a more vivid reminder of the standing quarrel between use and beauty, and of the hard time poor beauty is having. I looked wistfully, as we rattled into dreary Andermatt, at the great white zigzags of the Oberalp road, which climbed away to the left. Even on one's way to Italy one may spare a throb of desire for the beautiful vision of the castled Grisons. Dear to me the memory of my day's drive last summer through that long blue avenue of mountains, to queer little mouldering Ilanz, visited before supper in the ghostly dusk. At Andermatt a sign over a little black doorway flanked by two dung-hills seemed to me tolerably comical: *Minéraux, Quadrupèdes, Oiseaux, Œufs, Tableaux Antiques.* We bundled in to dinner and the American gentleman in the banquette made the acquaintance of the Irish lady in the coupé, who talked of the weather as *foine* and wore a Persian scarf twisted about her head. At the other end of the table sat an Englishman, out of the intérieur, who bore an extraordinary resemblance to the portraits of Edward VI's and Mary's reigns. He was a walking, a convincing Holbein. The impression was of value to a cherisher of quaintness, and he must have wondered—not knowing me for such a character—why I stared at him. It was n't him I was staring at, but some handsome Seymour or Dudley or Digby with a ruff and a round cap and plume.

From Andermatt, through its high, cold, sunny valley, we passed into rugged little Hospenthal, and then up the last stages of the ascent. From here the road was all new to me. Among the summits of the various Alpine passes there is little to choose. You wind and double slowly into keener cold and deeper stillness; you put on your overcoat and turn up the collar; you count the nestling snow-patches and then you cease to count them; you pause, as you trudge before the lumbering coach, and listen to the last-heard cow-bell tinkling away below you in kindlier herbage. The sky was tremendously blue, and the little stunted bushes on the snow-streaked slopes were all dyed with autumnal purples and crimsons. It was a great display of colour. Purple and crimson too, though not so fine, were the faces thrust out at us from the greasy little double casements of a barrack beside the road, where the horses paused before the last pull. There was one little girl in particular, beginning to *lisser* her hair, as civilisation approached, in a manner not to be described, with her poor little blue-black hands. At the summit are the two usual grim little stone taverns, the steel-blue tarn, the snow-white peaks, the pause in the cold sunshine. Then we begin to rattle down with two horses. In five minutes we are swinging along the famous zigzags. Engineer, driver, horses—it's very handsomely done by all of them. The road curves and curls and twists and plunges like the tail of a kite; sitting perched in the banquette,

---

lisser. Smooth down.

you see it making below you and in mid-air certain bold gyrations which bring you as near as possible, short of the actual experience, to the philosophy of that immortal Irishman who wished that his fall from the house-top would only last. But the zigzags last no more than Paddy's fall, and in due time we were all coming to our senses over *café au lait* in the little inn at Faido. After Faido the valley, plunging deeper, began to take thick afternoon shadows from the hills, and at Airolo we were fairly in the twilight. But the pink and yellow houses shimmered through the gentle gloom, and Italy began in broken syllables to whisper that she was at hand. For the rest of the way to Bellinzona her voice was muffled in the grey of evening, and I was half vexed to lose the charming sight of the changing vegetation. But only half vexed, for the moon was climbing all the while nearer the edge of the crags that overshadowed us, and a thin magical light came trickling down into the winding, murmuring gorges. It was a most enchanting business. The chestnut-trees loomed up with double their daylight stature; the vines began to swing their low festoons like nets to trip up the fairies. At last the ruined towers of Bellinzona stood gleaming in the moonshine, and we rattled into the great post-yard. It was eleven o'clock and I had risen at four; moonshine apart I was n't sorry.

All that was very well; but the drive next day from Bellinzona to Como is to my mind what gives its supreme beauty to this great pass. One can't describe the beauty of the Italian lakes, nor would one try if one could; the floweriest rhetoric can recall it only as a picture on a fireboard recalls a Claude. But it lay spread before me for a whole perfect day: in the long gleam of the Major, from whose head the diligence swerves away and begins to climb the bosky hills that divide it from Lugano; in the shimmering, melting azure of the southern slopes and masses; in the luxurious tangle of nature and the familiar amenity of man; in the lawn-like inclinations, where the great grouped chestnuts make so cool a shadow in so warm a light; in the rusty vineyards, the littered cornfields and the tawdry wayside shrines. But most of all it's the deep yellow light that enchants you and tells you where you are. See it come filtering down through a vine-covered trellis on the red handkerchief with which a ragged contadina has bound her hair, and all the magic of Italy, to the eye, makes an aureole about the poor girl's head. Look at a brown-breasted reaper eating his chunk of black bread under a spreading chestnut; nowhere is shadow so charming, nowhere is colour so

---

picture on a fireboard . . . Claude. Paintings sometimes decorated the boards that were used during the warm months to close up fireplaces. Claude Gellée, called Claude Lorraine (1600–1682), eminently influential painter of graceful, idealized Italian landscapes; see pages 149–50, 198, and notes.

charged, nowhere has accident such grace. The whole drive to Lugano was one long loveliness, and the town itself is admirably Italian. There was a great unlading of the coach, during which I wandered under certain brown old arcades and bought for six sous, from a young woman in a gold necklace, a hatful of peaches and figs. When I came back I found the young man holding open the door of the second diligence, which had lately come up, and beckoning to me with a despairing smile. The young man, I must note, was the most amiable of Ticinese; though he wore no buttons he was attached to the diligence in some amateurish capacity, and had an eye to the mail-bags and other valuables in the boot. I grumbled at Berne over the want of soft curves in the Swiss temperament; but the children of the tangled Tessin are cast in the Italian mould. My friend had as many quips and cranks as a Neapolitan; we walked together for an hour under the chestnuts, while the coach was plodding up from Bellinzona, and he never stopped singing till we reached a little wine-house where he got his mouth full of bread and cheese. I looked into his open door, à la Sterne, and saw the young woman sitting rigid and grim, staring over his head and with a great pile of bread and butter in her lap. He had only informed her most politely that she was to be transferred to another diligence and must do him the favour to descend; but she evidently knew of but one way for a respectable young insulary of her sex to receive the politeness of a foreign adventurer guilty of an eye betraying latent pleasantry. Heaven only knew what he was saying! I told her, and she gathered up her parcels and emerged. A part of the day's great pleasure perhaps was my grave sense of being an instrument in the hands of the powers toward the safe consignment of this young woman and her boxes. When once you have really bent to the helpless you are caught; there is no such steel trap, and it holds you fast. My rather grim Abigail was a neophyte in foreign travel, though doubtless cunning enough at her trade, which I inferred to be that of making up those prodigious chignons worn mainly by English ladies. Her mistress had gone on a mule over the mountains to Cadenabbia, and she herself was coming up with the wardrobe, two big boxes and a bath-tub. I had played my part, under the powers, at

tangled Tessin are cast in the Italian mould. James refers to the German name of the winding Ticino river, the natural border defining the Italian-speaking ("the dreadful Ticinese French," 98) Ticino canton, part of the Duchy of Milan until it was conquered by the Swiss in 1803.

à la Sterne. Laurence Sterne, *A Sentimental Journey through France and Italy* (1767), particularly the chapters grouped under the heading "The Remise Door."

Abigail. A colloquial term (for the "waiting gentlewoman" in Beaumont and Fletcher's *The Scornful Lady,* and frequently for Mrs. Honour, Sophia Western's servant in Fielding's *Tom Jones*) for a lady's maid.

Bellinzona, and had interposed between the poor girl's frightened English and the dreadful Ticinese French of the functionaries in the post-yard. At the custom-house on the Italian frontier I was of peculiar service; there was a kind of fateful fascination in it. The wardrobe was voluminous; I exchanged a paternal glance with my charge as the *douanier* plunged his brown fists into it. Who was the lady at Cadenabbia? What was she to me or I to her? She would n't know, when she rustled down to dinner next day, that it was I who had guided the frail skiff of her public basis of vanity to port. So unseen but not unfelt do we cross each other's orbits. The skiff however may have foundered that evening in sight of land. I disengaged the young woman from among her fellow-travellers and placed her boxes on a hand-cart in the picturesque streets of Como, within a stone's throw of that lovely striped and toned cathedral which has the façade of cameo medallions. I could only make the *facchino* swear to take her to the steamboat. He too was a jovial dog, but I hope he was polite with precautions.

                                                                    1873.

---

facchino. A porter.

Italy Revisited

I

I waited in Paris until after the elections for the new Chamber (they took place on the 14th of October); as only after one had learned that the famous attempt of Marshal MacMahon and his ministers to drive the French nation to the polls like a flock of huddling sheep, each with the white ticket of an official candidate round his neck, had not achieved the success which the energy of the process might have promised— only then it was possible to draw a long breath and deprive the republican party of such support as might have been conveyed in one's sympathetic presence. Seriously speaking too, the weather had been enchanting—there were Italian fancies to be gathered without leaving the banks of the Seine. Day

---

[Originally published as two separate essays, "Italy Revisited" in the *Atlantic Monthly,* XLI (April 1878), 437–44, and "Recent Florence" in the *Atlantic Monthly,* XLI (May 1878), 586–93; reprinted as one essay in *Portraits of Places,* 1883.]

Marshal MacMahon. Marie Edmé Patrice Maurice De MacMahon (Le Maréchal Mac-Mahon—1808–93), president of the French Republic after Thier's resignation (see page 77 and note), elected by almost unanimous vote. Aligned with the Monarchists, his government was frequently thwarted by the Republicans. James was in Paris for the October elections, before which MacMahon had promised to resign if his party did not win strong support for its attempt to form a stable monarchical government with "Henri V," the Comte de Chambord, on the throne (see page 49 and note). The Republicans won 335 seats, the MacMahonists only 30, but President MacMahon failed to keep his promise and in fact continued many reactionary policies. Finally, after the Union des Gauches won the election, he resigned in 1879.

after day the air was filled with golden light, and even those chalkish vistas of the Parisian *beaux quartiers* assumed the iridescent tints of autumn. Autumn weather in Europe is often such a very sorry affair that a fair-minded American will have it on his conscience to call attention to a rainless and radiant October.

The echoes of the electoral strife kept me company for a while after starting upon that abbreviated journey to Turin which, as you leave Paris at night, in a train unprovided with encouragements to slumber, is a singular mixture of the odious and the charming. The charming indeed I think prevails; for the dark half of the journey is the least interesting. The morning light ushers you into the romantic gorges of the Jura, and after a big bowl of *café au lait* at Culoz you may compose yourself comfortably for the climax of your spectacle. The day before leaving Paris I met a French friend who had just returned from a visit to a Tuscan country-seat where he had been watching the vintage. "Italy," he said, "is more lovely than words can tell, and France, steeped in this electoral turmoil, seems no better than a bear-garden." The part of the bear-garden through which you travel as you approach the Mont Cenis seemed to me that day very beautiful. The autumn colouring, thanks to the absence of rain, had been vivid and crisp, and the vines that swung their low garlands between the mulberries round about Chambéry looked like long festoons of coral and amber. The frontier station of Modane, on the further side of the Mont Cenis Tunnel, is a very ill-regulated place; but even the most irritable of tourists, meeting it on his way southward, will be disposed to consider it good-naturedly. There is far too much bustling and scrambling, and the facilities afforded you for the obligatory process of ripping open your luggage before the officers of the Italian custom-house are much scantier than should be; but for myself there is something that deprecates irritation in the shabby green and grey uniforms of all the Italian officials who stand loafing about and watching the northern invaders scramble back into marching order. Wearing an administrative uniform does n't necessarily spoil a man's temper, as in France one is sometimes led to believe; for these excellent under-paid Italians carry theirs as lightly as possible, and their answers to your inquiries don't in the least bristle with rapiers, buttons and cockades. After leaving Modane you slide straight downhill into the Italy of your desire; from which point the road edges, after the grand manner, along those great precipices that stand shoulder to shoulder, in a prodigious perpendicular file, till they finally admit you to a distant glimpse of the ancient capital of Piedmont.

Turin is no city of a name to conjure with, and I pay an extravagant tribute to subjective emotion in speaking of it as ancient. But if the place is less bravely peninsular than Florence and Rome, at least it is more in the

scenic tradition than New York and Paris; and while I paced the great
arcades and looked at the fourth-rate shop windows I did n't scruple to
cultivate a shameless optimism. Relatively speaking, Turin touches a chord;
but there is after all no reason in a large collection of shabbily-stuccoed
houses, disposed in a rigidly rectangular manner, for passing a day of deep,
still gaiety. The only reason, I am afraid, is the old superstition of Italy—that
property in the very look of the written word, the evocation of a myriad
images, that makes any lover of the arts take Italian satisfactions on easier
terms than any others. The written word stands for something that eternally
tricks us; we juggle to our credulity even with such inferior apparatus as is
offered to our hand at Turin. I roamed all the morning under the tall porticoes, thinking it sufficient joy to take note of the soft, warm air, of that local
colour of things that is at once so broken and so harmonious, and of the
comings and goings, the physiognomy and manners, of the excellent Tu-
rinese. I had opened the old book again; the old charm was in the style; I
was in a more delightful world. I saw nothing surpassingly beautiful or
curious; but your true taster of the most seasoned of dishes finds well-nigh
the whole mixture in any mouthful. Above all on the threshold of Italy he
knows again the solid and perfectly definable pleasure of finding himself
among the traditions of the grand style in architecture. It must be said that
we have still to go there to recover the sense of the domiciliary mass. In
northern cities there are beautiful houses, picturesque and curious houses;
sculptured gables that hang over the street, charming bay-windows, hooded
doorways, elegant proportions, a profusion of delicate ornament; but a
good specimen of an old Italian palazzo has a nobleness that is all its own.
We laugh at Italian "palaces," at their peeling paint, their nudity, their
dreariness; but they have the great palatial quality—elevation and extent.
They make of smaller things the apparent abode of pigmies; they round their
great arches and interspace their huge windows with a proud indifference to
the cost of materials. These grand proportions—the colossal basements, the
doorways that seem meant for cathedrals, the far away cornices—impart by
contrast a humble and *bourgeois* expression to interiors founded on the

---

more in the scenic tradition than New York and Paris. The New York of James's recollection
still knew no skyscrapers, and in 1877 Paris was in the process of undergoing great transformation. The grand boulevards, Saint-Germain, de l'Opéra, Raspail, and Haussmann, had not yet
been completed. New quarters, particularly those around the Champs-Elysées, the Trocadéro,
and the Champs de Mars, were being created. Work on the Basilica of Sacré-Coeur had just
been begun, the Eiffel Tower was still ten years off, the Palais de Chaillot fifty, the Louvre still to
be enlarged. James viewed a dramatically different city from that of the twentieth-century
tourist.

sacrifice of the whole to the part, and in which the air of grandeur depends largely on the help of the upholsterer. At Turin my first feeling was really one of renewed shame for our meaner architectural manners. If the Italians at bottom despise the rest of mankind and regard them as barbarians, disinherited of the tradition of form, the idea proceeds largely, no doubt, from our living in comparative mole-hills. They alone were really to build their civilisation.

An impression which on coming back to Italy I find even stronger than when it was first received is that of the contrast between the fecundity of the great artistic period and the vulgarity there of the genius of to-day. The first few hours spent on Italian soil are sufficient to renew it, and the question I allude to is, historically speaking, one of the oddest. That the people who but three hundred years ago had the best taste in the world should now have the worst; that having produced the noblest, loveliest, costliest works, they should now be given up to the manufacture of objects at once ugly and paltry; that the race of which Michael Angelo and Raphael, Leonardo and Titian were characteristic should have no other title to distinction than third-rate *genre* pictures and catchpenny statues—all this is a frequent perplexity to the observer of actual Italian life. The flower of "great" art in these latter years ceased to bloom very powerfully anywhere; but nowhere does it seem so drooping and withered as in the shadow of the immortal embodiments of the old Italian genius. You go into a church or a gallery and feast your fancy upon a splendid picture or an exquisite piece of sculpture, and on issuing from the door that has admitted you to the beautiful past are confronted with something that has the effect of a very bad joke. The aspect of your lodging—the carpets, the curtains, the upholstery in general, with their crude and violent colouring and their vulgar material—the trumpery things in the shops, the extreme bad taste of the dress of the women, the cheapness and baseness of every attempt at decoration in the cafés and railway-stations, the hopeless frivolity of everything that pretends to be a work of art—all this modern crudity runs riot over the relics of the great period.

We can do a thing for the first time but once; it is but once for all that we can have a pleasure in its freshness. This is a law not on the whole, I think, to be regretted, for we sometimes learn to know things better by not enjoying them too much. It is certain, however, at the same time, that a visitor who has worked off the immediate ferment for this inexhaustibly interesting country has by no means entirely drained the cup. After thinking of Italy as historical and artistic it will do him no great harm to think of her for a while as panting both for a future and for a balance at the bank; aspirations supposedly much at variance with the Byronic, the Ruskinian, the artistic, poetic, æsthetic manner of considering our eternally attaching peninsula. He may grant—I don't say it is absolutely necessary—that its actual aspects and economics are ugly, prosaic, provokingly out of relation to the diary and the album; it is nevertheless true that, at the point things have come to, modern Italy in a manner imposes herself. I had n't been many hours in the country before that truth assailed me; and I may add that, the first irritation past, I found myself able to accept it. For, if we think, nothing is more easy to understand than an honest ire on the part of the young Italy of to-day at being looked at by all the world as a kind of soluble pigment. Young Italy, preoccupied with its economical and political future, must be heartily tired of being admired for its eyelashes and its pose. In one of Thackeray's novels occurs a mention of a young artist who sent to the Royal Academy a picture representing "A Contadino dancing with a Trasteverina at the door of a Locanda, to the music of a Pifferaro." It is in this attitude and with these conventional accessories that the world has hitherto seen fit to represent young Italy, and one does n't wonder that if the youth has any spirit he should at last begin to resent our insufferable æsthetic patronage. He has established a line of tram-cars in Rome, from the Porta del Popolo to the Ponte Molle, and it is on one of these democratic vehicles that I seem to see him taking his triumphant course down the vista of the future. I won't pretend to rejoice with him any more than I really do; I won't pretend, as the sentimental tourists say about it all, as if it were the setting of an intaglio or the border of a Roman scarf, to "like" it. Like it or not, as we may, it is evidently destined to be; I see a new Italy in the future which in many important respects will equal, if not surpass, the most enterprising sections of our native land. Perhaps by that time Chicago and San Francisco will have acquired a pose, and their sons and daughters will dance at the doors of *locande.*

However this may be, the accomplished schism between the old order and the new is the promptest moral of a fresh visit to this ever-suggestive part of the world. The old has become more and more a museum, preserved and perpetuated in the midst of the new, but without any further relation to it— it must be admitted indeed that such a relation is considerable—than that of the stock on his shelves to the shopkeeper, or of the Siren of the South to the showman who stands before his booth. More than once, as we move about

---

Thackeray's novels . . . "A Contadino dancing . . ." In William Makepeace Thackeray's *The Newcomes* (1855), chapter 22, the young artist is Mr. O'Gogstay; such a clichéd picture would offer a scene where, in the doorway of an inn, to the music of a piper, a peasant dances with a woman from the picturesque Trastevere section of Rome. A common sight in nineteenth-century papal Rome was that of the characteristically dressed *pifferari,* shawm players who wandered the streets playing tunes, gathering coins, and, at least in the opinion of Stendhal, disturbing sleep with their musical wails.

nowadays in the Italian cities, there seems to pass before our eyes a vision of the coming years. It represents to our satisfaction an Italy united and prosperous, but altogether scientific and commercial. The Italy indeed that we sentimentalise and romance about was an ardently mercantile country; though I suppose it loved not its ledgers less, but its frescoes and altar-pieces more. Scattered through this paradise regained of trade—this country of a thousand ports—we see a large number of beautiful buildings in which an endless series of dusky pictures are darkening, dampening, fading, failing, through the years. By the doors of the beautiful buildings are little turnstiles at which there sit a great many uniformed men to whom the visitor pays a tenpenny fee. Inside, in the vaulted and frescoed chambers, the art of Italy lies buried as in a thousand mausoleums. It is well taken care of; it is constantly copied; sometimes it is "restored"—as in the case of that beautiful boy-figure of Andrea del Sarto at Florence, which may be seen at the gallery of the Uffizi with its honourable duskiness quite peeled off and heaven knows what raw, bleeding cuticle laid bare. One evening lately, near the same Florence, in the soft twilight, I took a stroll among those encircling hills on which the massive villas are mingled with the vaporous olives. Presently I arrived where three roads met at a wayside shrine, in which, before some pious daub of an old-time Madonna, a little votive lamp glimmered through the evening air. The hour, the atmosphere, the place, the twinkling taper, the sentiment of the observer, the thought that some one had been rescued here from an assassin or from some other peril and had set up a little grateful altar in consequence, against the yellow-plastered wall of a tangled *podere;* all this led me to approach the shrine with a reverent, an emotional step. I drew near it, but after a few steps I paused. I became aware of an incongruous odour; it seemed to me that the evening air was charged with a perfume which, although to a certain extent familiar, had not hitherto associated itself with rustic frescoes and wayside altars. I wondered, I gently sniffed, and the question so put left me no doubt. The odour was that of petroleum; the votive taper was nourished with the essence of Pennsylvania. I confess that I burst out laughing, and a picturesque contadino, wending his homeward way in the dusk, stared at me as if I were an iconoclast. He noticed the petroleum only, I imagine, to snuff it fondly up; but to me the

---

sometimes it is "restored" . . . **boy-figure.** Perhaps James recalls Andrea del Sarto's *John the Baptist as a Boy* in the Pitti Palace, noted in the Pitti catalogue as particularly damaged by restoration—"the present blotchy appearance seems to be due to incomplete removal of bituminous overpainting . . . in a restoration late in the last century" (Shearman, 259); the Uffizi catalogues indicate no picture of this description.

podere. Estate or farm.

thing served as a symbol of the Italy of the future. There is a horse-car from the Porta del Popolo to the Ponte Molle, and the Tuscan shrines are fed with kerosene.

II

IF it's very well meanwhile to come to Turin first it's better still to go to Genoa afterwards. Genoa is the tightest topographic tangle in the world, which even a second visit helps you little to straighten out. In the wonderful crooked, twisting, climbing, soaring, burrowing Genoese alleys the traveller is really up to his neck in the old Italian sketchability. The pride of the place, I believe, is a port of great capacity, and the bequest of the late Duke of Galliera, who left four millions of dollars for the purpose of improving and enlarging it, will doubtless do much toward converting it into one of the great commercial stations of Europe. But as, after leaving my hotel the afternoon I arrived, I wandered for a long time at hazard through the tortuous byways of the city, I said to myself, not without an accent of private triumph, that here at last was something it would be almost impossible to modernise. I had found my hotel, in the first place, extremely entertaining—the Croce di Malta, as it is called, established in a gigantic palace on the edge of the swarming and not over-clean harbour. It was the biggest house I had ever entered—the basement alone would have contained a dozen American caravansaries. I met an American gentleman in the vestibule who (as he had indeed a perfect right to be) was annoyed by its troublesome dimensions—one was a quarter of an hour ascending out of the basement—and desired to know if it were a "fair sample" of the Genoese inns. It appeared an excellent specimen of Genoese architecture generally; so far as I observed there were few houses perceptibly smaller than this Titanic tavern. I lunched in a dusky ballroom whose ceiling was vaulted, frescoed and gilded with the fatal facility of a couple of centuries ago, and which looked out upon another ancient house-front, equally huge and equally battered, separated from it only by a little wedge of dusky space—one of the principal streets, I believe, of Genoa—whence out of dim abysses the population sent up to the windows (I had to crane out very far to see it) a perpetual clattering, shuffling, chaffering sound. Issuing forth presently into this crevice of a street I found myself up to my neck in that element of the rich and strange—as to visible and reproducible "effect," I mean—for the love of which one revisits Italy. It offered itself indeed in a variety of colours, some of which were not remarkable for their freshness or purity. But their combined charm was not to be resisted, and the picture glowed with the rankly human side of southern low-life.

Genoa, as I have hinted, is the crookedest and most incoherent of cities; tossed about on the sides and crests of a dozen hills, it is seamed with gullies and ravines that bristle with those innumerable palaces for which we have heard from our earliest years that the place is celebrated. These great structures, with their mottled and faded complexions, lift their big ornamental cornices to a tremendous height in the air, where, in a certain indescribably forlorn and desolate fashion, overtopping each other, they seem to reflect the twinkle and glitter of the warm Mediterranean. Down about the basements, in the close crepuscular alleys, the people are for ever moving to and fro or standing in their cavernous doorways and their dusky, crowded shops, calling, chattering, laughing, lamenting, living their lives in the conversational Italian fashion. I had for a long time had no such vision of possible social pressure. I had n't for a long time seen people elbowing each other so closely or swarming so thickly out of populous hives. A traveller is often moved to ask himself whether it has been worth while to leave his home—whatever his home may have been—only to encounter new forms of human suffering, only to be reminded that toil and privation, hunger and sorrow and sordid effort, are the portion of the mass of mankind. To travel is, as it were, to go to the play, to attend a spectacle; and there is something heartless in stepping forth into foreign streets to feast on "character" when character consists simply of the slightly different costume in which labour and want present themselves. These reflections were forced upon me as I strolled as through a twilight patched with colour and charged with stale smells; but after a time they ceased to bear me company. The reason of this, I think, is because—at least to foreign eyes—the sum of Italian misery is, on the whole, less than the sum of the Italian knowledge of life. That people should thank you, with a smile of striking sweetness, for the gift of twopence, is a proof, certainly, of extreme and constant destitution; but (keeping in mind the sweetness) it also attests an enviable ability not to be depressed by circumstances. I know that this may possibly be great nonsense; that half the time we are acclaiming the fine quality of the Italian smile the creature so constituted for physiognomic radiance may be in a sullen frenzy of impatience and pain. Our observation in any foreign land is extremely superficial, and our remarks are happily not addressed to the inhabitants themselves, who would be sure to exclaim upon the impudence of the fancy-picture.

The other day I visited a very picturesque old city upon a mountain-top, where, in the course of my wanderings, I arrived at an old disused gate in the ancient town-wall. The gate had n't been absolutely forfeited; but the recent completion of a modern road down the mountain led most vehicles away to another egress. The grass-grown pavement, which wound into the plain by a hundred graceful twists and plunges, was now given up to ragged contadini and their donkeys, and to such wayfarers as were not alarmed at the disrepair into which it had fallen. I stood in the shadow of the tall old gateway admiring the scene, looking to right and left at the wonderful walls of the little town, perched on the edge of a shaggy precipice; at the circling mountains over against them; at the road dipping downward among the chestnuts and olives. There was no one within sight but a young man who slowly trudged upward with his coat slung over his shoulder and his hat upon his ear in the manner of a cavalier in an opera. Like an operatic performer too he sang as he came; the spectacle, generally, was operatic, and as his vocal flourishes reached my ear I said to myself that in Italy accident was always romantic and that such a figure had been exactly what was wanted to set off the landscape. It suggested in a high degree that knowledge of life for which I just now commended the Italians. I was turning back under the old gateway when the young man overtook me and, suspending his song, asked me if I could favour him with a match to light the hoarded remnant of a cigar. This request led, as I took my way again to the inn, to my falling into talk with him. He was a native of the ancient city, and answered freely all my inquiries as to its manners and customs and its note of public opinion. But the point of my anecdote is that he presently acknowledged himself a brooding young radical and communist, filled with hatred of the present Italian government, raging with discontent and crude political passion, professing a ridiculous hope that Italy would soon have, as France had had, her " '89," and declaring that he for his part would willingly lend a hand to chop off the heads of the king and the royal family. He was an unhappy, underfed, unemployed young man, who took a hard, grim view of everything and was operatic only quite in spite of himself. This made it very absurd of me to have looked at him simply as a graceful ornament to the prospect, an harmonious little figure in the middle distance. "Damn the prospect, damn the middle distance!" would have been all *his* philosophy. Yet but for the accident of my having gossipped with him I should have made him do service, in memory, as an example of sensuous optimism!

I am bound to say however that I believe a great deal of the sensuous optimism observable in the Genoese alleys and beneath the low, crowded arcades along the port was very real. Here every one was magnificently sunburnt, and there were plenty of those queer types, mahogany-coloured,

---

young radical and communist, filled with hatred of the present Italian government. The political right had consistently held power since 1849, but the elections of 1876 shifted control to the left. Agostino Depretis was entrusted by the king with the formation of the liberal government, but his ministers, most of whom had held claim to some previous revolutionary associations, soon settled into the status quo of the old right; they quarreled among themselves, voted a sizable pension increase to a king who had willingly reduced his own income, and generally became known for their inefficiency.

bare-chested mariners with earrings and crimson girdles, that seem to people a southern seaport with the chorus of "Masaniello." But it is not fair to speak as if at Genoa there were nothing but low-life to be seen, for the place is the residence of some of the grandest people in the world. Nor are all the palaces ranged upon dusky alleys; the handsomest and most impressive form a splendid series on each side of a couple of very proper streets, in which there is plenty of room for a coach-and-four to approach the big doorways. Many of these doorways are open, revealing great marble staircases with couchant lions for balustrades and ceremonious courts surrounded by walls of sun-softened yellow. One of the great piles in the array is coloured a goodly red and contains in particular the grand people I just now spoke of. They live indeed on the third floor; but here they have suites of wonderful painted and gilded chambers, in which foreshortened frescoes also cover the vaulted ceilings and florid mouldings emboss the ample walls. These distinguished tenants bear the name of Vandyck, though they are members of the noble family of Brignole-Sale, one of whose children—the Duchess of Galliera—has lately given proof of nobleness in presenting the gallery of the red palace to the city of Genoa.

III

ON leaving Genoa I repaired to Spezia, chiefly with a view of accomplishing a sentimental pilgrimage, which I in fact achieved in the most agreeable conditions. The Gulf of Spezia is now the headquarters of the Italian fleet, and there were several big iron-plated frigates riding at anchor in front of the town. The streets were filled with lads in blue flannel, who were receiving instruction at a schoolship in the harbour, and in the evening—there was a brilliant moon—the little breakwater which stretched out into the Mediterranean offered a scene of recreation to innumerable such persons. But this fact is from the point of view of the cherisher of quaintness of little account,

---

"Masaniello." On 7 July 1647, Tommaso Aniello Masaniello (1620–47) successfully stirred the Neapolitan populace to revolt against Spanish control. Daniel Auber's 1828 opera *La Muette de Portici,* better known as *Masaniello,* enjoyed wide popularity throughout Europe, with one of its duets, "Amour sacré de la patrie," becoming, like the "Marseillaise," a signal for revolution.

One of the great piles . . . the Duchess of Galliera. In 1874 Maria Brignole-Sale, Duchess of Galliera, donated the Palazzo Rosso to the city of Genoa; although it retains its original external aspect, after the World War II bombing its interior was radically altered and today has the disposition of a modern museum.

for since it has become prosperous Spezia has grown ugly. The place is filled with long, dull stretches of dead wall and great raw expanses of artificial land. It wears that look of monstrous, of more than far-western newness which distinguishes all the creations of the young Italian State. Nor did I find any great compensation in an immense inn of recent birth, an establishment seated on the edge of the sea in anticipation of a *passeggiata* which is to come that way some five years hence, the region being in the meantime of the most primitive formation. The inn was filled with grave English people who looked respectable and bored, and there was of course a Church of England service in the gaudily-frescoed parlour. Neither was it the drive to Porto Venere that chiefly pleased me—a drive among vines and olives, over the hills and beside the Mediterranean, to a queer little crumbling village on a headland, as sweetly desolate and superannuated as the name it bears. There is a ruined church near the village, which occupies the site (according to tradition) of an ancient temple of Venus; and if Venus ever revisits her desecrated shrines she must sometimes pause a moment in that sunny stillness and listen to the murmur of the tideless sea at the base of the narrow promontory. If Venus sometimes comes there Apollo surely does as much; for close to the temple is a gateway surmounted by an inscription in Italian and English, which admits you to a curious, and it must be confessed rather cockneyfied, cave among the rocks. It was here, says the inscription, that the great Byron, swimmer and poet, "defied the waves of the Ligurian sea." The fact is interesting, though not supremely so; for Byron was always defying something, and if a slab had been put up wherever this performance came off these commemorative tablets would be in many parts of Europe as thick as milestones.

No; the great merit of Spezia, to my eye, is that I engaged a boat there of a lovely October afternoon and had myself rowed across the gulf—it took about an hour and a half—to the little bay of Lerici, which opens out of it. This bay of Lerici is charming; the bosky grey-green hills close it in, and on either side of the entrance, perched on a bold headland, a wonderful old crumbling castle keeps ineffectual guard. The place is classic to all English travellers, for in the middle of the curving shore is the now desolate little

---

passeggiata. The common word for the evening walk, here used to refer to a type, in Italy, of a stone boardwalk frequently found at seaside resorts.

Byron ... Lerici ... Shelley. Porto Venere is identified with the ancient Roman Portus Veneris, near where, in 1822, Byron swam across the gulf to visit Shelley at the Casa Magni in Lerici. Beneath the church of San Pietro, James read the inscription in "Byron's Grotto" (la grotta Arpaja), where much of the "Corsair" is said to have been written. The grotto collapsed in 1932; Lerici has evolved into a fully modern resort town.

villa in which Shelley spent the last months of his short life. He was living at Lerici when he started on that short southern cruise from which he never returned. The house he occupied is strangely shabby and as sad as you may choose to find it. It stands directly upon the beach, with scarred and battered walls and a loggia of several arches opening to a little terrace with a rugged parapet, which, when the wind blows, must be drenched with the salt spray. The place is very lonely—all overwearied with sun and breeze and brine— very close to nature, as it was Shelley's passion to be. I can fancy a great lyric poet sitting on the terrace of a warm evening and feeling very far from England in the early years of the century. In that place, and with his genius, he would as a matter of course have heard in the voice of nature a sweetness which only the lyric movement could translate. It is a place where an English-speaking pilgrim himself may very honestly think thoughts and feel moved to lyric utterance. But I must content myself with saying in halting prose that I remember few episodes of Italian travel more sympathetic, as they have it here, than that perfect autumn afternoon; the half-hour's station on the little battered terrace of the villa; the climb to the singularly felicitous old castle that hangs above Lerici; the meditative lounge, in the fading light, on the vine-decked platform that looked out toward the sunset and the darkening mountains and, far below, upon the quiet sea, beyond which the pale-faced tragic villa stared up at the brightening moon.

IV

I HAD never known Florence more herself, or in other words more attaching, than I found her for a week in that brilliant October. She sat in the sunshine beside her yellow river like the little treasure-city she has always seemed, without commerce, without other industry than the manufacture of mosaic paper-weights and alabaster Cupids, without actuality or energy or earnest-ness or any of those rugged virtues which in most cases are deemed indispens-able for civic cohesion; with nothing but the little unaugmented stock of her mediæval memories, her tender-coloured mountains, her churches and pal-aces, pictures and statues. There were very few strangers; one's detested fellow-pilgrim was infrequent; the native population itself seemed scanty; the sound of wheels in the streets was but occasional; by eight o'clock at night, apparently, every one had gone to bed, and the musing wanderer, still wandering and still musing, had the place to himself—had the thick shadow-masses of the great palaces, and the shafts of moonlight striking the polygonal paving-stones, and the empty bridges, and the silvered yellow of the Arno, and the stillness broken only by a homeward step, a step accompanied by a snatch of song from a warm Italian voice. My room at the inn looked out on the river and was flooded all day with sunshine. There was an absurd orange-coloured paper on the walls; the Arno, of a hue not altogether different, flowed beneath; and on the other side of it rose a line of sallow houses, of extreme antiquity, crumbling and mouldering, bulging and protruding over the stream. (I seem to speak of their fronts; but what I saw was their shabby backs, which were exposed to the cheerful flicker of the river, while the fronts stood for ever in the deep damp shadow of a narrow mediæval street.) All this brightness and yellowness was a perpetual delight; it was a part of that indefinably charming colour which Florence always seems to wear as you look up and down at it from the river, and from the bridges and quays. This is a kind of grave radiance—a harmony of high tints—which I scarce know how to describe. There are yellow walls and green blinds and red roofs, there are intervals of brilliant brown and natural-looking blue; but the picture is not spotty nor gaudy, thanks to the distribution of the colours in large and comfortable masses, and to the washing-over of the scene by some happy softness of sunshine. The river-front of Florence is in short a delightful composition. Part of its charm comes of course from the generous aspect of those high-based Tuscan palaces which a renewal of acquaintance with them has again commended to me as the most dignified dwellings in the world. Nothing can be finer than that look of giving up the whole immense ground-floor to simple purposes of vestibule and staircase, of court and high-arched entrance; as if this were all but a massive pedestal for the real habitation and people were n't properly housed unless, to begin with, they should be lifted fifty feet above the pavement. The great blocks of the basement; the great intervals, horizontally and vertically, from window to window (telling of the height and breadth of the rooms within); the armorial shield hung forward at one of the angles; the wide-brimmed roof, overshadowing the narrow street; the rich old browns and yellows of the walls: these definite elements put themselves together with admirable art.

Take a Tuscan pile of this type out of its oblique situation in the town; call it no longer a palace, but a villa; set it down by a terrace on one of the hills that encircle Florence, place a row of high-waisted cypresses beside it, give it a grassy courtyard and a view of the Florentine towers and the valley of the

---

a Tuscan pile . . . a villa. In the fall of 1877 James was the guest of Frank Boott and his daughter Lizzie, who were to supply some of the inspiration for Gilbert and Pansy Osmond, at the Villa Castellani on the Bellosguardo hill outside Florence (see page 177 and note).

Arno, and you will think it perhaps even more worthy of your esteem. It was a Sunday noon, and brilliantly warm, when I again arrived; and after I had looked from my windows a while at that quietly-basking river-front I have spoken of I took my way across one of the bridges and then out of one of the gates—that immensely tall Roman Gate in which the space from the top of the arch to the cornice (except that there is scarcely a cornice, it is all a plain massive piece of wall) is as great, or seems to be, as that from the ground to the former point. Then I climbed a steep and winding way—much of it a little dull if one likes, being bounded by mottled, mossy garden-walls—to a villa on a hill-top, where I found various things that touched me with almost too fine a point. Seeing them again, often, for a week, both by sunlight and moonshine, I never quite learned not to covet them; not to feel that not being a part of them was somehow to miss an exquisite chance. What a tranquil, contented life it seemed, with romantic beauty as a part of its daily texture!—the sunny terrace, with its tangled *podere* beneath it; the bright grey olives against the bright blue sky; the long, serene, horizontal lines of other villas, flanked by their upward cypresses, disposed upon the neighbouring hills; the richest little city in the world in a softly-scooped hollow at one's feet, and beyond it the most appealing of views, the most majestic, yet the most familiar. Within the villa was a great love of art and a painting-room full of felicitous work, so that if human life there confessed to quietness, the quietness was mostly but that of the intent act. A beautiful occupation in that beautiful position, what could possibly be better? That is what I spoke just now of envying—a way of life that does n't wince at such refinements of peace and ease. When labour self-charmed presents itself in a dull or an ugly place we esteem it, we admire it, but we scarce feel it to be the ideal of good fortune. When, however, its votaries move as figures in an ancient, noble landscape, and their walks and contemplations are like a turning of the leaves of history, we seem to have before us an admirable case of virtue made easy; meaning here by virtue contentment and concentration, a real appreciation of the rare, the exquisite though composite, medium of life. You need n't want a rush or a crush when the scene itself, the mere scene, shares with you such a wealth of consciousness.

It is true indeed that I might after a certain time grow weary of a regular afternoon stroll among the Florentine lanes; of sitting on low parapets, in intervals of flower-topped wall, and looking across at Fiesole or down the rich-hued valley of the Arno; of pausing at the open gates of villas and wondering at the height of cypresses and the depth of loggias; of walking home in the fading light and noting on a dozen westward-looking surfaces the glow of the opposite sunset. But for a week or so all this was delightful. The villas are innumerable, and if you're an aching alien half the talk is about villas. This one has a story; that one has another; they all look as if

they had stories—none in truth predominantly gay. Most of them are offered to rent (many of them for sale) at prices unnaturally low; you may
have a tower and a garden, a chapel and an expanse of thirty windows, for
five hundred dollars a year. In imagination you hire three or four; you take
possession and settle and stay. Your sense of the fineness of the finest is of
something very grave and stately; your sense of the bravery of two or three
of the best something quite tragic and sinister. From what does this latter
impression come? You gather it as you stand there in the early dusk, with
your eyes on the long, pale-brown façade, the enormous windows, the iron
cages fastened to the lower ones. Part of the brooding expression of these
great houses comes, even when they have not fallen into decay, from their
look of having outlived their original use. Their extraordinary largeness and
massiveness are a satire on their present fate. They were n't built with such a
thickness of wall and depth of embrasure, such a solidity of staircase and
superfluity of stone, simply to afford an economical winter residence to
English and American families. I don't know whether it was the appearance
of these stony old villas, which seemed so dumbly conscious of a change of
manners, that threw a tinge of melancholy over the general prospect; certain
it is that, having always found this note as of a myriad old sadnesses in
solution in the view of Florence, it seemed to me now particularly strong.
"Lovely, lovely, but it makes me 'blue,' " the sensitive stranger could n't but
murmur to himself as, in the late afternoon, he looked at the landscape from
over one of the low parapets, and then, with his hands in his pockets, turned
away indoors to candles and dinner.

V

BELOW, in the city, through all frequentation of streets and churches and
museums, it was impossible not to have a good deal of the same feeling; but
here the impression was more easy to analyse. It came from a sense of the
perfect separateness of all the great productions of the Renaissance from the
present and the future of the place, from the actual life and manners, the
native ideal. I have already spoken of the way in which the vast aggregation
of beautiful works of art in the Italian cities strikes the visitor nowadays—so
far as present Italy is concerned—as the mere stock-in-trade of an impecunious but thrifty people. It is this spiritual solitude, this conscious disconnec-
tion of the great works of architecture and sculpture that deposits a certain
weight upon the heart; when we see a great tradition broken we feel something of the pain with which we hear a stifled cry. But regret is one thing and
resentment is another. Seeing one morning, in a shop-window, the series of

Mornings in Florence published a few years since by Mr. Ruskin, I made haste to enter and purchase these amusing little books, some passages of which I remembered formerly to have read. I could n't turn over many pages without observing that the "separateness" of the new and old which I just mentioned had produced in their author the liveliest irritation. With the more acute phases of this condition it was difficult to sympathise, for the simple reason, it seems to me, that it savours of arrogance to demand of any people, as a right of one's own, that they shall be artistic. "Be artistic yourselves!" is the very natural reply that young Italy has at hand for English critics and censors. When a people produces beautiful statues and pictures it gives us something more than is set down in the bond, and we must thank it for its generosity; and when it stops producing them or caring for them we may cease thanking, but we hardly have a right to begin and rail. The wreck of Florence, says Mr. Ruskin, "is now too ghastly and heart-breaking to any human soul that remembers the days of old"; and these desperate words are an allusion to the fact that the little square in front of the cathedral, at the foot of Giotto's Tower, with the grand Baptistery on the other side, is now the resort of a number of hackney-coaches and omni-buses. This fact is doubtless lamentable, and it would be a hundred times more agreeable to see among people who have been made the heirs of so priceless a work of art as the sublime campanile some such feeling about it as would keep it free even from the danger of defilement. A cab-stand is a very ugly and dirty thing, and Giotto's Tower should have nothing in common with such conveniences. But there is more than one way of taking such things, and the sensitive stranger who has been walking about for a week with his mind full of the sweetness and suggestiveness of a hundred Florentine places may feel at last in looking into Mr. Ruskin's little tracts that, discord for discord, there is n't much to choose between the importunity of the author's personal ill-humour and the incongruity of horse-pails and

---

Mornings in Florence . . . Ruskin . . . amusing little books. James exercises heavy irony in these passages; Ruskin's tone is furious, perhaps "pathological," and anything but amusing (see page 8 and note). Ruskin discusses Domenico Ghirlandaio and Giotto di Bondone, to whom he mistakenly attributes the frescoes at the Chiostrino dei Morti—"you are never likely to see a more true piece of Giotto's work in the world" (*Works*, XXIII, 314). Despite such conviction, these frescoes, illustrating scenes from the life of the Virgin, are now attributed either to Giottino, a follower of Giotto, or to Nardo di Cione.

"separateness" of the new and old . . . "ghastly and heart-breaking." James, without much Ruskinian irony, closely echoes Ruskin's sense of how dramatically Florence had changed: "the hackney coaches, with their more or less farmyard-like manure, are yet in more permissible harmony with the place than the ordinary populace of a fashionable promenade would be, with its cigars, spitting, and harlot planned fineries" (*Works*, XXIII, 213).

bundles of hay. And one may say this without being at all a partisan of the doctrine of the inevitableness of new desecrations. For my own part, I believe there are few things in this line that the new Italian spirit is n't capable of, and not many indeed that we are n't destined to see. Pictures and buildings won't be completely destroyed, because in that case the *forestieri*, scatterers of cash, would cease to arrive and the turn-stiles at the doors of the old palaces and convents, with the little patented slit for absorbing your half-franc, would grow quite rusty, would stiffen with disuse. But it's safe to say that the new Italy growing into an old Italy again will continue to take her elbow-room wherever she may find it.

I am almost ashamed to say what I did with Mr. Ruskin's little books. I put them into my pocket and betook myself to Santa Maria Novella. There I sat down and, after I had looked about for a while at the beautiful church, drew them forth one by one and read the greater part of them. Occupying one's self with light literature in a great religious edifice is perhaps as bad a piece of profanation as any of those rude dealings which Mr. Ruskin justly deplores; but a traveller has to make the most of odd moments, and I was waiting for a friend in whose company I was to go and look at Giotto's beautiful frescoes in the cloister of the church. My friend was a long time coming, so that I had an hour with Mr. Ruskin, whom I called just now a light *littérateur* because in these little Mornings in Florence he is for ever making his readers laugh. I remembered of course where I was, and in spite of my latent hilarity felt I had rarely got such a snubbing. I had really been enjoying the good old city of Florence, but I now learned from Mr. Ruskin that this was a scandalous waste of charity. I should have gone about with an imprecation on my lips, I should have worn a face three yards long. I had taken great pleasure in certain frescoes by Ghirlandaio in the choir of that very church; but it appeared from one of the little books that these frescoes were as naught. I had much admired Santa Croce and had thought the Duomo a very noble affair; but I had now the most positive assurance I knew nothing about them. After a while, if it was only ill-humour that was needed for doing honour to the city of the Medici, I felt that I had risen to a proper level; only now it was Mr. Ruskin himself I had lost patience with, not the stupid Brunelleschi, not the vulgar Ghirlandaio. Indeed I lost patience altogether, and asked myself by what right this informal votary of form pretended to run riot through a poor charmed *flâneur's* quiet contemplations, his attachment to the noblest of pleasures, his enjoyment of the loveliest of cities. The little books seemed invidious and insane, and it was

---

forestieri. Foreigners.

flâneur. An idle stroller.

only when I remembered that I had been under no obligation to buy them that I checked myself in repenting of having done so.

Then at last my friend arrived and we passed together out of the church, and, through the first cloister beside it, into a smaller enclosure where we stood a while to look at the tomb of the Marchesa Strozzi-Ridolfi, upon which the great Giotto has painted four superb little pictures. It was easy to see the pictures were superb; but I drew forth one of my little books again, for I had observed that Mr. Ruskin spoke of them. Hereupon I recovered my tolerance; for what could be better in this case, I asked myself, than Mr. Ruskin's remarks? They are in fact excellent and charming—full of appreciation of the deep and simple beauty of the great painter's work. I read them aloud to my companion; but my companion was rather, as the phrase is, "put off" by them. One of the frescoes—it is a picture of the birth of the Virgin—contains a figure coming through a door. "Of ornament," I quote, "there is only the entirely simple outline of the vase which the servant carries; of colour two or three masses of sober red and pure white, with brown and grey. That is all," Mr. Ruskin continues. "And if you are pleased with this you can see Florence. But if not, by all means amuse yourself there, if you find it amusing, as long as you like; you can never see it." *You can never see it.* This seemed to my friend insufferable, and I had to shuffle away the book again, so that we might look at the fresco with the unruffled geniality it deserves. We agreed afterwards, when in a more convenient place I read aloud a good many more passages from the precious tracts, that there are a great many ways of seeing Florence, as there are of seeing most beautiful and interesting things, and that it is very dry and pedantic to say that the happy vision depends upon our squaring our toes with a certain particular chalk-mark. We see Florence wherever and whenever we enjoy it, and for enjoying it we find a great many more pretexts than Mr. Ruskin seems inclined to allow. My friend and I convinced ourselves also, however, that the little books were an excellent purchase, on account of the great charm and felicity of much of their incidental criticism; to say nothing, as I hinted just now, of their being extremely amusing. Nothing in fact is more comical than the familiar asperity of the author's style and the pedagogic fashion in which he pushes and pulls his unhappy pupils about, jerking their heads toward this, rapping their knuckles for that, sending them to stand in corners and giving them Scripture texts to copy. But it is neither the felicities nor the aberrations of detail, in Mr. Ruskin's writings, that are the main affair for most readers; it is the general tone that, as I have said, puts them off or draws them on. For many persons he will never bear the test of being read in this rich old Italy, where art, so long as it really lived at all, was spontaneous, joyous, irresponsible. If the reader is in daily contact with those beautiful Florentine works which do still, in a way, force themselves into notice through the vulgarity and cruelty of modern profanation, it will seem to him that this commentator's comment is pitched in the strangest falsetto key. "One may read a hundred pages of this sort of thing," said my friend, "without ever dreaming that he is talking about *art*. You can say nothing worse about him than that." Which is perfectly true. Art is the one corner of human life in which we may take our ease. To justify our presence there the only thing demanded of us is that we shall have felt the representational impulse. In other connections our impulses are conditioned and embarrassed; we are allowed to have only so many as are consistent with those of our neighbours; with their convenience and well-being, with their convictions and prejudices, their rules and regulations. Art means an escape from all this. Wherever her shining standard floats the need for apology and compromise is over; there it is enough simply that we please or are pleased. There the tree is judged only by its fruits. If these are sweet the tree is justified—and not less so the consumer.

One may read a great many pages of Mr. Ruskin without getting a hint of this delightful truth; a hint of the not unimportant fact that art after all is made for us and not we for art. This idea that the value of a work is in the amount of illusion it yields is conspicuous by its absence. And as for Mr. Ruskin's world's being a place—his world of art—where we may take life easily, woe to the luckless mortal who enters it with any such disposition. Instead of a garden of delight, he finds a sort of assize court in perpetual session. Instead of a place in which human responsibilities are lightened and suspended, he finds a region governed by a kind of Draconic legislation. His responsibilities indeed are tenfold increased; the gulf between truth and error is for ever yawning at his feet; the pains and penalties of this same error are advertised, in apocalyptic terminology, upon a thousand signposts; and the rash intruder soon begins to look back with infinite longing to the lost paradise of the artless. There can be no greater want of tact in dealing with those things with which men attempt to ornament life than to be perpetually talking about "error." A truce to all rigidities is the law of the place; the only thing absolute there is that some force and some charm have worked. The grim old bearer of the scales excuses herself; she feels this not to be her province. Differences here are not iniquity and righteousness; they are simply variations of temperament, kinds of curiosity. We are not under theological government.

VI

IT was very charming, in the bright, warm days, to wander from one corner of Florence to another, paying one's respects again to remembered masterpieces. It was pleasant also to find that memory had played no tricks and

that the rarest things of an earlier year were as rare as ever. To enumerate
these felicities would take a great deal of space; for I never had been more
struck with the mere quantity of brilliant Florentine work. Even giving up
the Duomo and Santa Croce to Mr. Ruskin as very ill-arranged edifices, the
list of the Florentine treasures is almost inexhaustible. Those long outer
galleries of the Uffizi had never beguiled me more; sometimes there were not
more than two or three figures standing there, Baedeker in hand, to break
the charming perspective. One side of this upstairs portico, it will be remembered, is entirely composed of glass; a continuity of old-fashioned windows,
draped with white curtains of rather primitive fashion, which hang there till
they acquire a perceptible tone. The light, passing through them, is softly
filtered and diffused; it rests mildly upon the old marbles—chiefly antique
Roman busts—which stand in the narrow intervals of the casements. It is
projected upon the numerous pictures that cover the opposite wall and that
are not by any means, as a general thing, the gems of the great collection; it
imparts a faded brightness to the old ornamental arabesques upon the
painted wooden ceiling, and it makes a great soft shining upon the marble

---

Even giving up the Duomo and Santa Croce to Mr. Ruskin as very ill-arranged edifices.
Doubts voiced about the Duomo of Santa Maria del Fiore in Florence are perhaps difficult for
the modern tourist to appreciate; the magnificent, unifying, multicolored facade facing the
Baptistry was not, however, what Ruskin had viewed and what James viewed in 1877. As was
common with many great Italian churches, the complex facade of the cathedral of Florence, a
church that had been under construction since the thirteenth century, was only attempted after
most of the work had been completed on the other parts of the structure. Up until the nineteenth century the facade remained largely incomplete (old engravings in fact show a relatively
uncomplicated—and jarring—baroque front that had been meant to serve for a time). In 1862
and 1865 design competitions were held and eventually Emilio De Fabris's neo-gothic conception, following the lines of Giotto's campanile and the flanks of the cathedral, was chosen. The
final result, gratifying to many visitors and residents in Florence but scorned by some as a
northern-Gothic transplant, was not unveiled until 1887 (James mentions the event in *Letters*,
III, 182), almost ten years after this essay was published. The nineteenth-century neo-gothic
facade of Santa Croce was constructed from 1853 to 1863, and although successful, had
already raised many questions concerning the appropriateness of such historical fakes.
    In *Mornings in Florence* Ruskin writes at length concerning the relationship between the
proportion and scale of both structures; although he casts doubts—"Grand by proportion, I
said; but ought to have said by *dis*proportion"—his more characteristic tone is that of someone
who "will begin to wonder that human daring ever achieved anything so magnificent" (*Works*,
XXIII, 363–404). His fundamentally positive description of Santa Croce's interior begins with
the impression that it is, "somehow, the ugliest Gothic church you ever were in. . . . There are
two features, on which, more than on any others, the grace and delight of a fine Gothic building
depends; one's the springing of its vaultings, the other the proportion of fantasy of its traceries.
This church of Santa Croce has no vaultings at all, but the roof of a farm-house barn. And its
windows are all the same pattern. . . . Can this clumsy and ungraceful arrangement be indeed
the design of the renowned Arnolfo?" (*Works*, XXIII, 302–3).

floor, in which, as you look up and down, you see the strolling tourists and the motionless copyists almost reflected. I don't know why I should find all this very pleasant, but in fact, I have seldom gone into the Uffizi without walking the length of this third-story cloister, between the (for the most part) third-rate canvases and panels and the faded cotton curtains. Why is it that in Italy we see a charm in things in regard to which in other countries we always take vulgarity for granted? If in the city of New York a great museum of the arts were to be provided, by way of decoration, with a species of verandah enclosed on one side by a series of small-paned windows draped in dirty linen, and furnished on the other with an array of pictorial feebleness, the place being surmounted by a thinly-painted wooden roof, strongly suggestive of summer heat, of winter cold, of frequent leakage, those amateurs who had had the advantage of foreign travel would be at small pains to conceal their contempt.

Contemptible or respectable, to the judicial mind, this quaint old loggia of the Uffizi admitted me into twenty chambers where I found as great a number of ancient favourites. I don't know that I had a warmer greeting for any old friend than for Andrea del Sarto, that most touching of painters who is not one of the first. But it was on the other side of the Arno that I found him in force, in those dusky drawing-rooms of the Pitti Palace to which you take your way along the tortuous tunnel that wanders through the houses of Florence and is supported by the little goldsmiths' booths on the Ponte Vecchio. In the rich insufficient light of these beautiful rooms, where, to look at the pictures, you sit in damask chairs and rest your elbows on tables of malachite, the elegant Andrea becomes deeply effective. Before long he has drawn you close. But the great pleasure, after all, was to revisit the earlier masters, in those specimens of them chiefly that bloom so unfadingly on the big plain walls of the Academy. Fra Angelico and Filippo Lippi, Botticelli and Lorenzo di Credi are the clearest, the sweetest and best of all painters; as I sat for an hour in their company, in the cold great hall of the institution I have mentioned—there are shabby rafters above and an immense expanse of brick tiles below, and many bad pictures as well as good— it seemed to me more than ever that if one really had to choose one could n't do better than choose here. You may rest at your ease at the Academy, in this big first room—at the upper end especially, on the left—because more than many other places it savours of old Florence. More for instance, in reality, than the Bargello, though the Bargello makes great pretensions. Beautiful and masterful though the Bargello is, it smells too strongly of restoration, and, much of old Italy as still lurks in its furbished and renovated chambers, it speaks even more distinctly of the ill-mannered young kingdom that has— as "unavoidably" as you please—lifted down a hundred delicate works of sculpture from the convent-walls where their pious authors placed them. If the early Tuscan painters are exquisite I can think of no praise pure enough for the sculptors of the same period, Donatello and Luca della Robbia, Matteo Civitale and Mina da Fiesole, who, as I refreshed my memory of them, seemed to me to leave absolutely nothing to be desired in the way of straightness of inspiration and grace of invention. The Bargello is full of early Tuscan sculpture, most of the pieces of which have come from suppressed religious houses; and even if the visitor be an ardent liberal he is uncomfortably conscious of the rather brutal process by which it has been collected. One can hardly envy young Italy the number of odious things she has had to do.

The railway journey from Florence to Rome has been altered both for the better and for the worse; for the better in that it has been shortened by a couple of hours; for the worse inasmuch as when about half the distance has been traversed the train deflects to the west and leaves the beautiful old cities of Assisi, Perugia, Terni, Narni, unvisited. Of old it was possible to call at these places, in a manner, from the window of the train; even if you did n't stop, as you probably could n't, every time you passed, the immensely interesting way in which, like a loosened belt on an aged and shrunken person, their ample walls held them easily together was something well worth noting. Now, however, for compensation, the express train to Rome stops at Orvieto, and in consequence . . . In consequence what? What is the result of the stop of an express train at Orvieto? As I glibly wrote that sentence I suddenly paused, aware of the queer stuff I was uttering. That an express train would graze the base of the horrid purple mountain from the apex of which this dark old Catholic city uplifts the glittering front of its cathedral—that might have been foretold by a keen observer of contemporary manners. But that it would really have the grossness to hang about is a fact over which, as he records it, an inveterate, a perverse cherisher of the sense of the past order, the order still largely prevailing at the time of his first visit to Italy, may well make what is vulgarly called an ado. The train does stop at Orvieto, not very long, it is true, but long enough to let you out. The same phenomenon takes place on the following day, when, having visited the city, you get in again. I availed myself without scruple of both of these occasions, having formerly neglected to drive to the place in a post-chaise. But frankly, the railway-station being in the plain and the town on the summit of an extraordinary hill, you have time to forget the puffing indiscretion while you wind upwards to the city-gate. The position of Orvieto is

---

this dark old Catholic city. An ancient Etruscan settlement, "Catholic" Orvieto offered refuge to many besieged popes, including Clement VII, who fled the Sack of Rome by Emperor Charles V in May 1527.

superb—worthy of the "middle distance" of an eighteenth-century land-scape. But, as every one knows, the splendid Cathedral is the proper attraction of the spot, which, indeed, save for this fine monument and for its craggy and crumbling ramparts, is a meanly arranged and, as Italian cities go, not particularly impressive little town. I spent a beautiful Sunday there and took in the charming church. I gave it my best attention, though on the whole I fear I found it inferior to its fame. A high concert of colour, however, is the densely carved front, richly covered with radiant mosaics. The old white marble of the sculptured portions is as softly yellow as ancient ivory; the large exceedingly bright pictures above them flashed and twinkled in the glorious weather. Very striking and interesting the theological frescoes of Luca Signorelli, though I have seen compositions of this general order that appealed to me more. Characteristically fresh, finally, the clear-faced saints and seraphs, in robes of pink and azure, whom Fra Angelico has painted upon the ceiling of the great chapel, along with a noble sitting figure—more expressive of movement than most of the creations of this pictorial peace-maker—of Christ in judgment. Yet the interest of the cathedral of Orvieto is mainly not the visible result, but the historical process that lies behind it; those three hundred years of the applied devotion of a people of which an American scholar has written an admirable account.[1]

1877.

---

[1]   Charles Eliot Norton, *Notes of Travel and Study in Italy*. [James's note.]

theological frescoes of Luca Signorelli. In the Cappella della Madonna di San Brizio. The frescoes, completed by Signorelli, actually begun by Fra Angelico, are "theological" in their complex depiction of the rarely treated subject of the Antichrist, as well as in their more ordinary representations of the saved and the damned.

Charles Eliot Norton. In 1864 James had met Norton (1827–1908), Harvard fine-arts professor, Italophile, friend of Ruskin, and founder of *The Nation* (1865), in Boston. Norton's *Notes of Travel and Study in Italy* (1859) provides an interesting if idiosyncratic account; mostly on Rome, with fewer than twenty pages on Venice and fifteen on Florence, the study provides more than sixty on the building of the cathedral at Orvieto—"No city in Italy boasts a more perfect monument of the past munificence and spirit of its people" (105). Norton's preface claims personal affection for some Catholics, but he admits that he has not "hesitated in the following pages to express myself strongly in regard to some of the corrupt doctrines of the Roman Church and methods of the Papal government." (James's notation also appeared in the two previous publications of this essay.)

A Roman Holiday

It is certainly sweet to be merry at the right moment; but the right moment hardly seems to me the ten days of the Roman Carnival. It was my rather cynical suspicion perhaps that they would n't keep to my imagination the brilliant promise of legend; but I have been justified by the event and have been decidedly less conscious of the festal influences of the season than of the inalienable gravity of the place. There was a time when the Carnival was a serious matter—that is a heartily joyous one; but, thanks to the seven-league boots the kingdom of Italy has lately donned for the march of progress in quite other directions, the fashion of public revelry has fallen woefully out of step. The state of mind and manners under which the Carnival was kept in generous good faith I doubt if an American can exactly conceive: he can only say to himself that for a month in the year there must have been things—things considerably of

[Originally published in the *Atlantic Monthly*, xxxii (July 1873), 1–11; reprinted in *Transatlantic Sketches*, 1875; reprinted in *Foreign Parts*, 1883.]

Roman Carnival . . . September, 1870. After papal Rome was annexed to the newly formed kingdom of Italy on 20 September 1870, the carnival, held from the second Saturday before Ash Wednesday to Shrove Tuesday, gradually declined and grew brutish and coarse. Eventually, according to the 1909 Baedeker, it was marked only by a greater throng than usual in the Corso and by a few organized festivities at a few specific locations such as the Villa Borghese; "Ladies," reports Baedeker in 1909, "are advised to eschew the Corso on the chief days of the carnival." Goethe, in the record of his visit to Rome in 1788, provides a full report of the crush of festivities during the eighteenth-century carnival—"everyone has leave to be as mad and foolish as he likes, and almost everything, except fisticuffs and stabbing, is permissible"; the celebrations were so intense that "On Wednesday I thanked God and the Church for Lent" (*Italian Journey*, 445–76).

humiliation—it was comfortable to forget. But now that Italy is made the Carnival is unmade; and we are not especially tempted to envy the attitude of a population who have lost their relish for play and not yet acquired to any striking extent an enthusiasm for work. The spectacle on the Corso has seemed to me, on the whole, an illustration of that great breach with the past of which Catholic Christendom felt the somewhat muffled shock in September, 1870. A traveller acquainted with the fully papal Rome, coming back any time during the past winter, must have immediately noticed that something momentous had happened—something hostile to the elements of picture and colour and "style." My first warning was that ten minutes after my arrival I found myself face to face with a newspaper stand. The impossibility in the other days of having anything in the journalistic line but the *Osservatore Romano* and the *Voce della Verità* used to seem to me much connected with the extraordinary leisure of thought and stillness of mind to which the place admitted you. But now the slender piping of the Voice of Truth is stifled by the raucous note of eventide vendors of the *Capitale*, the *Libertà* and the *Fanfulla;* and Rome reading unexpurgated news is another Rome indeed. For every subscriber to the *Libertà* there may well be an antique masker and reveller less. As striking a sign of the new régime is the extraordinary increase of population. The Corso was always a well-filled street, but now it's a perpetual crush. I never cease to wonder where the new-comers are lodged, and how such spotless flowers of fashion as the gentlemen who stare at the carriages can bloom in the atmosphere of those *camere mobiliate* of which I have had glimpses. This, however, is their own question, and bravely enough they meet it. They proclaimed somehow, to the first freshness of my wonder, as I say, that by force of numbers Rome

---

Osservatore Romano . . . Voce della Verità . . . Capitale . . . Libertà . . . Fanfulla. In Rome alone more than ninety newspapers were founded during the politically fertile period between 1848 and 1933. The *Osservatore Romano* became the official Vatican daily newspaper after the 1929 Lateran Treaty between the Kingdom of Italy and the papacy established the autonomous state of Vatican City; it had begun publication, however, eighty years before, in 1849. Founded in 1871, the *Voce della Verità* was one of the more staunchly conservative Catholic newspapers. *La Capitale: Gazzetta di Roma,* known for strong radical ideas, was founded in 1870 by the violently anticlerical Raffaele Sonzogno, who was murdered by one of his own editors in 1875; for more on *La Capitale,* see page 137 and note. Having begun publication as *La Gazzetta del Popolo,* only two days after the Porta Pia was breached and Rome taken by Italian troops, this moderate newspaper took the name *La Libertà* in November. *Il Fanfulla,* issuing from Rome after 21 October 1871, had begun publication in Florence a year before and was considered more lively than most newspapers, bearing the mark of a particularly cultivated editorial consciousness and the trademark of vigorous articles, aggressively written under pseudonyms.

camere mobiliate. Furnished rooms.

had been secularised. An Italian dandy is a figure visually to reckon with, but these goodly throngs of them scarce offered compensation for the absent monsignori, treading the streets in their purple stockings and followed by the solemn servants who returned on their behalf the bows of the meaner sort; for the mourning gear of the cardinals' coaches that formerly glittered with scarlet and swung with the weight of the footmen clinging behind; for the certainty that you'll not, by the best of traveller's luck, meet the Pope sitting deep in the shadow of his great chariot with uplifted fingers like some inaccessible idol in his shrine. You may meet the King indeed, who is as ugly, as imposingly ugly, as some idols, though not so inaccessible. The other day as I passed the Quirinal he drove up in a low carriage with a single attendant; and a group of men and women who had been waiting near the gate rushed at him with a number of folded papers. The carriage slackened pace and he pocketed their offerings with a business-like air—that of a good-natured man accepting handbills at a street-corner. Here was a monarch at his palace gate receiving petitions from his subjects—being adjured to right their wrongs. The scene ought to have thrilled me, but somehow it had no more intensity than a woodcut in an illustrated newspaper. Homely I should call it at most; admirably so, certainly, for there were lately few sovereigns standing, I believe, with whom their people enjoyed these filial hand-to-hand relations. The King this year, however, has had as little to do with the Carnival as the Pope, and the innkeepers and Americans have marked it for their own.

It was advertised to begin at half-past two o'clock of a certain Saturday, and punctually at the stroke of the hour, from my room across a wide court, I heard a sudden multiplication of sounds and confusion of tongues in the Corso. I was writing to a friend for whom I cared more than for any mere romp; but as the minutes elapsed and the hubbub deepened curiosity got the better of affection, and I remembered that I was really within eye-shot of an affair the fame of which had ministered to the day-dreams of my infancy. I used to have a scrap-book with a coloured print of the starting of the bedizened wild horses, and the use of a library rich in keepsakes and annuals with a frontispiece commonly of a masked lady in a balcony, the heroine of a delightful tale further on. Agitated by these tender memories I descended into the street; but I confess I looked in vain for a masked lady who might serve as a frontispiece, in vain for any object whatever that might adorn a tale. Masked and muffled ladies there were in abundance; but their masks were of ugly wire, perfectly resembling the little covers placed upon strong cheese in German hotels, and their drapery was a shabby water-proof with the hood pulled over their chignons. They were armed with great tin scoops

---

the King. Victor Emmanuel II of Sardinia (1820–78), first king of the united Italy.

or funnels, with which they solemnly shovelled lime and flour out of bushel-baskets and down on the heads of the people in the street. They were packed into balconies all the way along the straight vista of the Corso, in which their calcareous shower maintained a dense, gritty, unpalatable fog. The crowd was compact in the street, and the Americans in it were tossing back confetti out of great satchels hung round their necks. It was quite the "you're another" sort of repartee, and less seasoned than I had hoped with the airy mockery tradition hangs about this festival. The scene was striking, in a word; but somehow not as I had dreamed of its being. I stood regardful, I suppose, but with a peculiarly tempting blankness of visage, for in a moment I received half a bushel of flour on my too-philosophic head. Decidedly it was an ignoble form of humour. I shook my ears like an emergent diver, and had a sudden vision of how still and sunny and solemn, how peculiarly and undisturbedly themselves, how secure from any intrusion less sympathetic than one's own, certain outlying parts of Rome must just then be. The Carnival had received its death-blow in my imagination; and it has been ever since but a thin and dusky ghost of pleasure that has flitted at intervals in and out of my consciousness.

I turned my back accordingly on the Corso and wandered away to the grass-grown quarters delightfully free even from the possibility of a fellow-countryman. And so having set myself an example I have been keeping Carnival by strolling perversely along the silent circumference of Rome. I have doubtless lost a great deal. The Princess Margaret has occupied a balcony opposite the open space which leads into Via Condotti and, I believe, like the discreet princess she is, has dealt in no missiles but bonbons, bouquets and white doves. I would have waited half an hour any day to see the Princess Margaret hold a dove on her forefinger; but I never chanced to notice any preparation for that effect. And yet do what you will you can't really elude the Carnival. As the days elapse it filters down into the manners of the common people, and before the week is over the very beggars at the church-doors seem to have gone to the expense of a domino. When you meet these specimens of dingy drollery capering about in dusky back-streets at all hours of the day and night, meet them flitting out of black doorways between the greasy groups that cluster about Roman thresholds, you feel that a love of "pranks," the more vivid the better, must from far back have been

---

Princess Margaret. Margherita di Savoia (1851–1926), wife of Humbert I (Umberto I), who succeeded his father Victor Emmanuel II on 9 January 1878. Victor Emmanuel II had married his mistress, known as his morganatic wife, in 1869; Margherita was therefore the first queen of the united Italy. See reference to the morganatic marriage on page 171 and related note.

domino. A masquerade costume, generally with a black half-mask.

implanted in the Roman temperament with a strong hand. An unsophisticated American is wonderstruck at the number of persons, of every age and various conditions, whom it costs nothing in the nature of an ingenuous blush to walk up and down the streets in the costume of a theatrical supernumerary. Fathers of families do it at the head of an admiring progeniture; aunts and uncles and grandmothers do it; all the family does it, with varying splendour but with the same good conscience. "A pack of babies!" the doubtless too self-conscious alien pronounces it for its pains, and tries to imagine himself strutting along Broadway in a battered tin helmet and a pair of yellow tights. Our vices are certainly different; it takes those of the innocent sort to be so ridiculous. A self-consciousness lapsing so easily, in fine, strikes me as so near a relation to amenity, urbanity and general gracefulness that, for myself, I should be sorry to lay a tax on it, lest these other commodities should also cease to come to market.

I was rewarded, when I had turned away with my ears full of flour, by a glimpse of an intenser life than the dingy foolery of the Corso. I walked down by the back streets to the steps mounting to the Capitol—that long inclined plane, rather, broken at every two paces, which is the unfailing disappointment, I believe, of tourists primed for retrospective raptures. Certainly the Capitol seen from this side is n't commanding. The hill is so low, the ascent so narrow, Michael Angelo's architecture in the quadrangle at the top so meagre, the whole place somehow so much more of a mole-hill than a mountain, that for the first ten minutes of your standing there Roman history seems suddenly to have sunk through a trap-door. It emerges however on the other side, in the Forum; and here meanwhile, if you get no sense of the sublime, you get gradually a sense of exquisite composition. Nowhere in Rome is more colour, more charm, more sport for the eye. The mild

---

Capitol . . . Michael Angelo's architecture . . . at the top so meagre . . . Hawthorne. James's disparagement of Michelangelo is by no means unique in the nineteenth century. He may be recalling Hawthorne's opinion of the Campidoglio: "The architecture that surrounds the piazza is very ineffective; and so, in my opinion, are the other architectural works of Michel Angelo, including St. Peter's itself of which he has made as little as could possibly be made of such a pile of material. He balances everything in such a way that it seems but half of itself" (Hawthorne, *The French and Italian Note-books,* 183–84). Michelangelo's original pavement design, a unique design that dramatically sets off his architectural plan of the piazza, was not fulfilled until 1940; photographs of the former piazza, with the design of spokes radiating from a center, indicate that both Hawthorne and James saw a much less impressive setting for Michelangelo's buildings.

Nowhere in Rome . . . more charm . . . Ara Cœli . . . no latent *risorgimenti.* Ironically, the charming prospect that James notes was virtually obliterated by the unyieldingly white *risorgimento* monument to Vittorio Emanuele II, an immense, some say monstrous, structure (1885– 1911) that rose up beside the ancient church of Santa Maria in Ara Cœli to dwarf the Capitol and transform the aspect of the city.

incline, during the winter months, is always covered with lounging sun-seekers, and especially with those more constantly obvious members of the Roman population—beggars, soldiers, monks and tourists. The beggars and peasants lie kicking their heels along that grandest of loafing-places the great steps of the Ara Cœli. The dwarfish look of the Capitol is intensified, I think, by the neighbourhood of this huge blank staircase, mouldering away in disuse, the weeds thick in its crevices, and climbing to the rudely solemn façade of the church. The sunshine glares on this great unfinished wall only to light up its featureless despair, its expression of conscious, irremediable incompleteness. Sometimes, massing its rusty screen against the deep blue sky, with the little cross and the sculptured porch casting a clear-cut shadow on the bricks, it seems to have even more than a Roman desolation, it confusedly suggests Spain and Africa—lands with no latent *risorgimenti,* with absolutely nothing but a fatal past. The legendary wolf of Rome has lately been accommodated with a little artificial grotto, among the cacti and the palms, in the fantastic triangular garden squeezed between the steps of the church and the ascent to the Capitol, where she holds a perpetual levee and "draws" apparently as powerfully as the Pope himself. Above, in the piazzetta before the stuccoed palace which rises so jauntily on a basement of thrice its magnitude, are more loungers and knitters in the sun, seated round the massively inscribed base of the statue of Marcus Aurelius. Hawthorne has perfectly expressed the attitude of this admirable figure in saying that it extends its arm with "a command which is in itself a benediction." I doubt if any statue of king or captain in the public places of the world has more to commend it to the general heart. Irrecoverable simplicity—residing so in irrecoverable Style—has no sturdier representative. Here is an impression that the sculptors of the last three hundred years have been laboriously trying to reproduce; but contrasted with this mild old monarch their prancing horsemen suggest a succession of riding-masters taking out young ladies' schools. The admirably human character of the figure survives the rusty decomposition of the bronze and the slight "debasement" of the art; and one may call it singular that in the

---

legendary wolf of Rome. Now in the Palazzo dei Conservatori of the Capitoline Museum.

Hawthorne ... "a command which is in itself a benediction." "It is the most majestic representation of the kingly character that ever the world has seen. A sight of this old heathen Emperor is enough to create an evanescent sentiment of loyalty even in a democratic bosom; so august does he look, so fit to rule, so worthy of man's profoundest homage and obedience, so inevitably attractive of his love. He stretches forth his hand, with an air of grand beneficence and unlimited authority, as if uttering a decree from which no appeal was permissible, but in which the obedient subject would find his highest interests consulted; a command, that was in itself a benediction" (Hawthorne, *The Marble Faun,* 165–66).

capital of Christendom the portrait most suggestive of a Christian conscience is that of a pagan emperor.

You recover in some degree your stifled hopes of sublimity as you pass
beyond the palace and take your choice of either curving slope to descend
into the Forum. Then you see that the little stuccoed edifice is but a modern
excrescence on the mighty cliff of a primitive construction, whose great
squares of porous tufa, as they underlie each other, seem to resolve themselves back into the colossal cohesion of unhewn rock. There are prodigious
strangenesses in the union of this airy and comparatively fresh-faced super-
structure and these deep-plunging, hoary foundations; and few things in
Rome are more entertaining to the eye than to measure the long plumb-line
which drops from the inhabited windows of the palace, with their little over-
peeping balconies, their muslin curtains and their bird-cages, down to the
rugged constructional work of the Republic. In the Forum proper the sublime is eclipsed again, though the late extension of the excavations gives a
chance for it.

Nothing in Rome helps your fancy to a more vigorous backward flight
than to lounge on a sunny day over the railing which guards the great central
researches. It "says" more things to you than you can repeat to see the past,
the ancient world, as you stand there, bodily turned up with the spade and
transformed from an immaterial, inaccessible fact of time into a matter of
soils and surfaces. The pleasure is the same—in kind—as what you enjoy of
Pompeii, and the pain the same. It was n't here, however, that I found my
compensation for forfeiting the spectacle on the Corso, but in a little church
at the end of the narrow byway which diverges up the Palatine from just
beside the Arch of Titus. This byway leads you between high walls, then
takes a bend and introduces you to a long row of rusty, dusty little pictures
of the stations of the cross. Beyond these stands a small church with a front
so modest that you hardly recognise it till you see the leather curtain. I never
see a leather curtain without lifting it; it is sure to cover a constituted *scene*
of some sort—good, bad or indifferent. The scene this time was meagre—
whitewash and tarnished candlesticks and mouldy muslin flowers being its
principal features. I should n't have remained if I had n't been struck with
the attitude of the single worshipper—a young priest kneeling before one of
the side-altars, who, as I entered, lifted his head and gave me a sidelong look
so charged with the languor of devotion that he immediately became an

---

portrait most suggestive of a Christian conscience. James alludes to the fact that during the
Middle Ages the statue was thought to represent the Christian emperor Constantine. This confusion helped save it from the destruction that met other bronze figures of Roman emperors.

a small church. The church of S. Bonaventura.

object of interest. He was visiting each of the altars in turn and kissing the balustrade beneath them. He was alone in the church, and indeed in the whole region. There were no beggars even at the door; they were plying their trade on the skirts of the Carnival. In the entirely deserted place he alone knelt for religion, and as I sat respectfully by it seemed to me I could hear in the perfect silence the far-away uproar of the maskers. It was my late impression of these frivolous people, I suppose, joined with the extraordinary gravity of the young priest's face—his pious fatigue, his droning prayer and his isolation—that gave me just then and there a supreme vision of the religious passion, its privations and resignations and exhaustions and its terribly small share of amusement. He was young and strong and evidently of not too refined a fibre to enjoy the Carnival; but, planted there with his face pale with fasting and his knees stiff with praying, he seemed so stern a satire on it and on the crazy thousands who were preferring it to *his* way, that I half expected to see some heavenly portent out of a monastic legend come down and confirm his choice. Yet I confess that though I was n't enamoured of the Carnival myself, his seemed a grim preference and this forswearing of the world a terrible game—a gaining one only if your zeal never falters; a hard fight when it does. In such an hour, to a stout young fellow like the hero of my anecdote, the smell of incense must seem horribly stale and the muslin flowers and gilt candlesticks to figure no great bribe. And it would n't have helped him much to think that not so very far away, just beyond the Forum, in the Corso, there was sport for the million, and for nothing. I doubt on the other hand whether my young priest had thought of this. He had made himself a temple out of the very elements of his innocence, and his prayers followed each other too fast for the tempter to slip in a whisper. And so, as I say, I found a solider fact of human nature than the love of *coriandoli*.

One of course never passes the Colosseum without paying it one's

---

coriandoli. Sugared candies, also known as carnival confetti. "Now and then, a masked fair lady mischievously flings some sugar-coated almonds at her passing friend to attract his attention and, naturally enough, he turns round to see who has thrown the missile. But real sugared confetti is expensive, so a cheaper substitute must be provided for this kind of petty warfare, and there are traders who specialize in plaster bonbons. . . . No one is safe from attack, everyone is on the defensive, so now and then, from high spirits or necessity, a duel, a skirmish or a battle ensues" (Goethe, *Italian Journey*, 458).

Colosseum . . . Alpine valley. This description will be recalled in *Roderick Hudson* (1876), chapter 7, "Saint Cecilia's": "There are chance anfractuosities of ruin in the upper portions of the Coliseum which offer a very fair imitation of the rugged face of an Alpine cliff." In the 1870s and 1880s excavation removed the plant growth and the destructive root systems, and, in James's consideration, spoiled one of the most romantic sights in Italy (*Letters*, II, 283). In

respects—without going in under one of the hundred portals and crossing the long oval and sitting down a while, generally at the foot of the cross in the centre. I always feel, as I do so, as if I were seated in the depths of some Alpine valley. The upper portions of the side toward the Esquiline look as remote and lonely as an Alpine ridge, and you raise your eyes to their rugged sky-line, drinking in the sun and silvered by the blue air, with much the same feeling with which you would take in a grey cliff on which an eagle might lodge. This roughly mountainous quality of the great ruin is its chief interest; beauty of detail has pretty well vanished, especially since the high-growing wild-flowers have been plucked away by the new government, whose functionaries, surely, at certain points of their task, must have felt as if they shared the dreadful trade of those who gather samphire. Even if you are on your way to the Lateran you won't grudge the twenty minutes it will take you, on leaving the Colosseum, to turn away under the Arch of Constantine, whose noble battered bas-reliefs, with the chain of tragic statues—fettered, drooping barbarians—round its summit, I assume you to have profoundly admired, toward the piazzetta of the church of San Giovanni e Paolo, on the slope of Cælian. No spot in Rome can show a cluster of more charming accidents. The ancient brick apse of the church peeps down into the trees of the little wooded walk before the neighbouring church of San Gregorio, intensely venerable beneath its excessive modernisation; and a series of heavy brick buttresses, flying across to an opposite wall, overarches the short, steep, paved passage which leads into the small square. This is flanked on one side by the long mediæval portico of the church of the two saints, sustained by eight time-blackened columns of granite and marble. On another rise the great scarce-windowed walls of a Passionist convent, and on the third the portals of a grand villa, whose

---

1893 further excavation fully uncovered the interior compartments of the arena, and in the 1930s some final restoration scraped away the last vestiges of weedy overgrowth.

samphire. An herb traditionally gathered on treacherous British cliffs—"Halfe way downe / Hangs one that gathers samphire; dreadful trade!" (*King Lear,* IV.vi.55).

chain of tragic statues. James refers to the sculptural frieze that shows the Dacians being subdued by Trajan's armies and beseeching the emperor for mercy.

San Gregorio, intensely venerable. San Gregorio Magno, also called San Gregorio al Celio, built in 575 by Pope Gregory the Great on the site of his own father's house. It is from this church that Saint Augustine set out, on Gregory's bidding, with forty monks to preach Christianity in England. Radical modernization transformed the facade in 1642 and the interior between 1725 and 1734.

Passionist convent. Founded in 1720 by Paul Francis Danei (Saint Paul of the Cross, whose body rests in the Church of SS. Giovanni e Paolo), the Passionist order was an austere congrega-

tall porter, with his cockade and silver-topped staff, standing sublime behind his grating, seems a kind of mundane St. Peter, I suppose, to the beggars who sit at the church door or lie in the sun along the farther slope which leads to the gate of the convent. The place always seems to me the perfection of an out-of-the-way corner—a place you would think twice before telling people about, lest you should find them there the next time you were to go. It is such a group of objects, singly and in their happy combination, as one must come to Rome to find at one's house door; but what makes it peculiarly a picture is the beautiful dark red campanile of the church, which stands embedded in the mass of the convent. It begins, as so many things in Rome begin, with a stout foundation of antique travertine, and rises high, in delicately quaint mediæval brickwork—little tiers and apertures sustained on miniature columns and adorned with small cracked slabs of green and yellow marble, inserted almost at random. When there are three or four brown-breasted contadini sleeping in the sun before the convent doors, and a departing monk leading his shadow down over them, I think you will not find anything in Rome more *sketchable*.

If you stop, however, to observe everything worthy of your water-colours you will never reach St. John Lateran. My business was much less with the interior of that vast and empty, that cold clean temple, which I have never found peculiarly interesting, than with certain charming features of its surrounding precinct—the crooked old court beside it, which admits you to the Baptistery and to a delightful rear-view of the queer architectural odds and ends that may in Rome compose a florid ecclesiastical façade. There are more of these, a stranger jumble of chance detail, of lurking recesses and wanton projections and inexplicable windows, than I have memory or phrase for; but the gem of the collection is the oddly perched peaked turret, with its yellow travertine welded upon the rusty brickwork, which was not meant to be suspected, and the brickwork retreating beneath and leaving it in the odd position of a tower *under* which you may see the sky. As to the great front of the church overlooking the Porta San Giovanni, you are not admitted behind the scenes; the term is quite in keeping, for the architecture has a vastly theatrical air. It is extremely imposing—that of St. Peter's alone is more so; and when from far off on the Campagna you see the colossal images of the mitred saints along the top standing distinct against the sky, you forget their coarse construction and their inflated draperies. The view from the great space which stretches from the church steps to the city wall is the very prince of views. Just beside you, beyond the great alcove of mosaic,

---

tion of religious men who worked to foster devotion to the passion of Christ in an age of declining fervor.

is the Scala Santa, the marble staircase which (says the legend) Christ descended under the weight of Pilate's judgment, and which all Christians must for ever ascend on their knees; before you is the city gate which opens upon the Via Appia Nuova, the long gaunt file of arches of the Claudian aqueduct, their jagged ridge stretching away like the vertebral column of some monstrous mouldering skeleton, and upon the blooming brown and purple flats and dells of the Campagna and the glowing blue of the Alban Mountains, spotted with their white, high-nestling towns; while to your left is the great grassy space, lined with dwarfish mulberry-trees, which stretches across to the damp little sister-basilica of Santa Croce in Gerusalemme. During a former visit to Rome I lost my heart to this idle tract,[1] and wasted much time in sitting on the steps of the church and watching certain white-cowled friars who were sure to be passing there for the delight of my eyes. There are fewer friars now, and there are a great many of the king's recruits, who inhabit the ex-conventual barracks adjoining Santa Croce and are led forward to practise their goose-step on the sunny turf. Here too the poor old cardinals who are no longer to be seen on the Pincio descend from their mourning-coaches and relax their venerable knees. These members alone still testify to the traditional splendour of the princes of the Church; for as they advance the lifted black petticoat reveals a flash of scarlet stockings and makes you groan at the victory of civilisation over colour.

If St. John Lateran disappoints you internally, you have an easy compensation in pacing the long lane which connects it with Santa Maria Maggiore and entering the singularly perfect nave of that most delightful of churches. The first day of my stay in Rome under the old dispensation I spent in wandering at random through the city, with accident for my *valet-de-place*. It served me to perfection and introduced me to the best things; among others to an immediate happy relation with Santa Maria Maggiore. First impressions, memorable impressions, are generally irrecoverable; they often leave one the wiser, but they rarely return in the same form. I remember, of my coming uninformed and unprepared into the place of worship and of curiosity that I have named, only that I sat for half an hour on the edge of the base of one of the marble columns of the beautiful nave and enjoyed a perfect revel of—what shall I call it?—taste, intelligence, fancy, perceptive emotion? The place proved so endlessly suggestive that perception became a throbbing confusion of images, and I departed with a sense of knowing a good deal that is not set down in Murray. I have seated myself more than

---

[1] Utterly overbuilt and gone—1909. [James's note.]

Murray. The famous guidebooks of the firm of John Murray, one of the most successful London publishing houses of the nineteenth century. The firm was founded in 1768 by the first

once again at the base of the same column; but you live your life only once, the parts as well as the whole. The obvious charm of the church is the elegant grandeur of the nave—its perfect shapeliness and its rich simplicity, its long double row of white marble columns and its high flat roof, embossed with intricate gildings and mouldings. It opens into a choir of an extraordinary splendour of effect, which I recommend you to look out for of a fine afternoon. At such a time the glowing western light, entering the high windows of the tribune, kindles the scattered masses of colour into sombre brightness, scintillates on the great solemn mosaic of the vault, touches the porphyry columns of the superb baldachino with ruby lights, and buries its shining shafts in the deep-toned shadows that hang about frescoes and sculptures and mouldings. The deeper charm even than in such things, however, is the social or historic note or tone or atmosphere of the church— I fumble, you see, for my right expression; the sense it gives you, in common with most of the Roman churches, and more than any of them, of having been prayed in for several centuries by an endlessly curious and complex society. It takes no great attention to let it come to you that the authority of Italian Catholicism has lapsed not a little in these days; not less also perhaps than to feel that, as they stand, these deserted temples were the fruit of a society leavened through and through by ecclesiastical manners, and that they formed for ages the constant background of the human drama. They are, as one may say, the *churchiest* churches in Europe—the fullest of gathered memories, of the experience of their office. There's not a figure one has read of in old-world annals that is n't to be imagined on proper occasion kneeling before the lamp-decked Confession beneath the altar of Santa Maria Maggiore. One sees after all, however, even among the most palpable realities, very much what the play of one's imagination projects there; and I present my remarks simply as a reminder that one's constant excursions into these places are not the least interesting episodes of one's walks in Rome.

I had meant to give a simple illustration of the church-habit, so to speak, but I have given it at such a length as leaves scant space to touch on the innumerable topics brushed by the pen that begins to take Roman notes. It is by the aimless *flânerie* which leaves you free to follow capriciously every hint

---

John Murray (1745–93); brought to celebrity by the second John Murray (1778–1843), who published Byron and won from him the nickname "the Anak of publishers"; and advanced to great financial success by the third John Murray (1808–92), who developed the extensive and very popular travel-guide series. A fourth John Murray (1852–1928) continued the tradition as editor. *A Handbook of Rome and Its Environs* was in its eleventh edition when James published his first Roman essays in 1873, and in its nineteenth edition when he published his 1909 views.

flânerie. Strolling.

of entertainment that you get to know Rome. The greater part of the life about you goes on in the streets; and for an observer fresh from a country in which town scenery is at the least monotonous incident and character and picture seem to abound. I become conscious with compunction, let me hasten to add, that I have launched myself thus on the subject of Roman churches and Roman walks without so much as a preliminary allusion to St. Peter's. One is apt to proceed thither on rainy days with intentions of exercise—to put the case only at that—and to carry these out body and mind. Taken as a walk not less than as a church, St. Peter's of course reigns alone. Even for the profane "constitutional" it serves where the Boulevards, where Piccadilly and Broadway, fall short, and if it did n't offer to our use the grandest area in the world it would still offer the most diverting. Few great works of art last longer to the curiosity, to the perpetually transcended attention. You think you have taken the whole thing in, but it expands, it rises sublime again, and leaves your measure itself poor. You never let the ponderous leather curtain bang down behind you—your weak lift of a scant edge of whose padded vastness resembles the liberty taken in folding back the parchment corner of some mighty folio page—without feeling all former visits to have been but missed attempts at apprehension and the actual to achieve your first real possession. The conventional question is ever as to whether one has n't been "disappointed in the size," but a few honest folk here and there, I hope, will never cease to say no. The place struck me from the first as the hugest thing conceivable—a real exaltation of one's idea of space; so that one's entrance, even from the great empty square which either glares beneath the deep blue sky or makes of the cool far-cast shadow of the immense front something that resembles a big slate-coloured country on a map, seems not so much a going in somewhere as a going out. The mere man of pleasure in quest of new sensations might well not know where to better his encounter there of the sublime shock that brings him, within the threshold, to an immediate gasping pause. There are days when the vast nave looks mysteriously vaster than on others and the gorgeous baldachino a longer journey beyond the far-spreading tessellated plain of the pavement, and when the light has yet a quality which lets things loom their largest, while the scattered figures—I mean the human, for there are plenty of others—mark happily the scale of items and parts. Then you have only to stroll and stroll and gaze and gaze; to watch the glorious altar-canopy lift its bronze architecture, its colossal embroidered contortions, like a temple within a temple, and feel yourself, at the bottom of the abysmal shaft of the dome, dwindle to a crawling dot.

Much of the constituted beauty resides in the fact that it is all general beauty, that you are appealed to by no specific details, or that these at least, practically never importunate, are as taken for granted as the lieutenants and captains are taken for granted in a great standing army—among whom

indeed individual aspects may figure here the rather shifting range of decorative dignity in which details, when observed, often prove poor (though never not massive and substantially precious) and sometimes prove ridiculous. The sculptures, with the sole exception of Michael Angelo's ineffable "Pietà," which lurks obscurely in a side-chapel—this indeed to my sense the rarest artistic *combination* of the greatest things the hand of man has produced—are either bad or indifferent; and the universal incrustation of marble, though sumptuous enough, has a less brilliant effect than much later work of the same sort, that for instance of St. Paul's without the Walls. The supreme beauty is the splendidly sustained simplicity of the whole. The thing represents a prodigious imagination extraordinarily strained, yet strained; at its happiest pitch, without breaking. Its happiest pitch I say, because this is the only creation of its strenuous author in presence of which you are in presence of serenity. You may invoke the idea of ease at St. Peter's without a sense of sacrilege—which you can hardly do, if you are at all spiritually nervous, in Westminster Abbey or Notre Dame. The vast enclosed clearness has much to do with the idea. There are no shadows to speak of, no marked effects of shade; only effects of light innumerable—points at which this element seems to mass itself in airy density and scatter itself in enchanting gradations and cadences. It performs the office of gloom or of mystery in Gothic churches; hangs like a rolling mist along the gilded vault of the nave, melts into bright interfusion the mosaic scintillations of the dome, clings and clusters and lingers, animates the whole huge and otherwise empty shell. A good Catholic, I suppose, is the same Catholic anywhere, before the grandest as well as the humblest altars; but to a visitor not formally enrolled St. Peter's speaks less of aspiration than of full and convenient assurance. The soul infinitely expands there, if one will, but all on its quite human level. It marvels at the reach of our dream and the immensity of our resources. To be so impressed and put in our place, we say, is to be sufficiently "saved"; we can't be more than that in heaven itself; and what specifically celestial beauty such a show or such a substitute may lack it makes up for in certainty and tangibility. And yet if one's hours on the scene are not actually spent in praying, the spirit seeks it again as for the finer comfort, for the blessing, exactly, of its example, its protection and its exclusion. When you are weary of the swarming democracy of your fellow-tourists, of the unremunerative

---

much later work . . . St. Paul's without the Walls. Although the first oratorio of San Paolo fuori le Mura was built by the Roman woman Lucina over the place where she buried Saint Paul, and although a basilica was begun in the year 386, James refers to "much later work" because the basilica was splendidly rebuilt by Leo XII after a fire almost totally destroyed it in 1823.

aspects of human nature on Corso and Pincio, of the oppressively frequent combination of coronets on carriage panels and stupid faces in carriages, of addled brains and lacquered boots, of ruin and dirt and decay, of priests and beggars and takers of advantage, of the myriad tokens of a halting civilisation, the image of the great temple depresses the balance of your doubts, seems to rise above even the highest tide of vulgarity and make you still believe in the heroic will and the heroic act. It's a relief, in other words, to feel that there's nothing but a cab-fare between your pessimism and one of the greatest of human achievements.

This might serve as a Lenten peroration to these remarks of mine which have strayed so woefully from their jovial text, save that I ought fairly to confess that my last impression of the Carnival was altogether Carnivalesque. The merry-making of Shrove Tuesday had life and felicity; the dead letter of tradition broke out into nature and grace. I pocketed my scepticism and spent a long afternoon on the Corso. Almost every one was a masker, but you had no need to conform; the pelting rain of confetti effectually disguised you. I can't say I found it all very exhilarating; but here and there I noticed a brighter episode—a capering clown inflamed with contagious jollity, some finer humourist forming a circle every thirty yards to crow at his indefatigable sallies. One clever performer so especially pleased me that I should have been glad to catch a glimpse of the natural man. You imagined for him that he was taking a prodigious intellectual holiday and that his gaiety was in inverse ratio to his daily mood. Dressed as a needy scholar, in an ancient evening-coat and with a rusty black hat and gloves fantastically patched, he carried a little volume carefully under his arm. His humours were in excellent taste, his whole manner the perfection of genteel comedy. The crowd seemed to relish him vastly, and he at once commanded a gleefully attentive audience. Many of his sallies I lost; those I caught were excellent. His trick was often to begin by taking some one urbanely and caressingly by the chin and complimenting him on the *intelligenza della sua fisionomia*. I kept near him as long as I could; for he struck me as a real ironic artist, cherishing a disinterested, and yet at the same time a motived and a moral, passion for the grotesque. I should have liked, however—if indeed I should n't have feared—to see him the next morning, or when he unmasked that night over his hard-earned supper in a smoky *trattoria*. As the evening went on the crowd thickened and became a motley press of shouting, pushing, scrambling, everything but squabbling, revellers. The rain of missiles ceased at dusk, but the universal deposit of chalk and flour was trampled into a cloud made lurid by flaring pyramids of the gas-lamps

---

intelligenza della sua fisionomia. The intelligent look of his face.

that replaced for the occasion the stingy Roman luminaries. Early in the evening came off the classic exhibition of the *moccoletti,* which I but half saw, like a languid reporter resigned beforehand to be cashiered for want of enterprise. From the mouth of a side-street, over a thousand heads, I caught a huge slow-moving illuminated car, from which blue-lights and rockets and Roman candles were in course of discharge, meeting all in a dim fuliginous glare far above the house-tops. It was like a glimpse of some public orgy in ancient Babylon. In the small hours of the morning, walking homeward from a private entertainment, I found Ash Wednesday still kept at bay. The Corso, flaring with light, smelt like a circus. Every one was taking friendly liberties with every one else and using up the dregs of his festive energy in convulsive hootings and gymnastics. Here and there certain indefatigable spirits, clad all in red after the manner of devils and leaping furiously about with torches, were supposed to affright you. But they shared the universal geniality and bequeathed me no midnight fears as a pretext for keeping Lent, the *carnevale dei preti,* as I read in that profanely radical sheet the *Capitale.*

---

moccoletti . . . slow-moving illuminated car . . . orgy in ancient Babylon. From *moccolo,* or a piece of a candle. "The balconies are decorated with transparent paper lanterns, everyone holds a candle, all the windows, all the stands are illuminated, and it is a pleasure to look into the interiors of the carriages, which often have small crystal chandeliers hanging from the ceiling, while in others the ladies sit with coloured candles in their hands as if inviting one to admire their beauty. . . . It becomes everyone's duty to carry a lighted candle in his hand, and the favourite imprecation of the Romans, 'Sia ammazzato,' is heard repeatedly on all sides. 'Sia ammazzato chi non porta moccolo': 'Death to anyone who is not carrying a candle.' This is what you say to others, while at the same time you try to blow out their candles. No matter who it belongs to, a friend or a stranger, you try to blow out the nearest candle, or light your own from it first and then blow it out. The louder the cries of *Sia ammazzato,* the more these words lose their sinister meaning, and you forget that you are in Rome, where, at any other time but Carnival, and for a trifling reason, the wish expressed by these words might be literally fulfilled" (Goethe, *Italian Journey,* 467).

the *carnevale dei preti* . . . profanely radical sheet the *Capitale.* During most of 1873 *La Capitale* was printed as a simple four-page sheet mixing political diatribes and anticlerical editorials, occasionally supplemented by serial novels. On 26 February 1873 a column noted the beginning of "il carnevale dei preti," the priests' carnival, and went on to deride the event as a "baccanale" and to remind the priests of the humility of the Nazarene; the editors promised to offer their own series on the "Vita di Gesù Cristo," in an attempt to provide a worthy reminder of Christ's sublime teachings—and not the negation of those teachings, which was the carnival itself.

The attack that James notes was a strong one and met resistance. *La Capitale* had also claimed that, in a speech before Italian nobility, Pope Pius IX had committed the final debasement by arguing the aristocratic heritage of Jesus Christ. Eventually copies of the newspaper were sequestered by the authorities, but when the paper reappeared, it announced the unlawful confiscation and claimed that such action proved beyond a shadow of a doubt that the new government and the Vatican were collaborators. See also page 123 and note.

Of this too I have been having glimpses. Going lately into Santa Francesca Romana, the picturesque church near the Temple of Peace, I found a feast for the eyes—a dim crimson-toned light through curtained windows, a great festoon of tapers round the altar, a bulging girdle of lamps before the sunken shrine beneath, and a dozen white-robed Dominicans scattered in the happiest composition on the pavement. It was better than the *moccoletti*.

1873.

Santa Francesca Romana. Also known as Santa Maria Nova. Several items here are confused. The reference to the sunken shrine suggests Santa Francesca Romana, but it is the church of SS. Cosma e Damiano, which adjoins the Templum et Forum Pacis, or the "Temple of Peace" (more commonly called the Forum of Peace). Santa Francesca Romana was built from the ruins of the Temple of Venus and Rome. James may have witnessed a particular Dominican ceremony, but SS. Cosma e Damiano has been linked to the Franciscans since the sixteenth century; S. Francesca Romana is a Benedictine church.

Roman Rides

I shall always remember the first I took: out of the Porta del Popolo, to where the Ponte Molle, whose single arch sustains a weight of historic tradition, compels the sallow Tiber to flow between its four great-mannered ecclesiastical statues, over the crest of the hill and along the old posting-road to Florence. It was mild midwinter, the season peculiarly of colour on the Roman Campagna; and the light was full of that mellow purple glow, that tempered intensity, which haunts the after-visions of those who have known Rome like the memory of some supremely irresponsible pleasure. An hour away I pulled up and at the edge of a meadow gazed away for some time into remoter distances. Then and there, it seemed to me, I measured the deep delight of knowing the Campagna. But I saw more things in it than I can easily tell. The country rolled away around me into slopes and dells of long-drawn grace, chequered with purple and blue and blooming brown. The lights and shadows were at play on the Sabine Mountains—an alternation of tones so exquisite as to be conveyed only by some fantastic comparison to sapphire and amber. In the foreground a contadino in his cloak and peaked hat jogged solitary on his ass; and here and there in the distance, among blue undulations, some white village, some grey tower, helped deliciously to make the picture the typical "Italian landscape" of old-fashioned

[Originally published in the *Atlantic Monthly,* XXXII (August 1873), 190–98; reprinted in *Transatlantic Sketches,* 1875; reprinted in *Foreign Parts,* 1883.]

Ponte Molle . . . historic tradition. Better known as the Ponte Milvio (Pons Milvius), the bridge was built in 109 B.C. and has long been honored as the oldest bridge in Rome. Remodeled in the fifteenth century, it was reconstructed under Pius VII in 1805, blown up in 1849 in an attempt by Garibaldi to halt French troops, and restored by Pius IX in 1850.

art. It was so bright and yet so sad, so still and yet so charged, to the su-
persensuous ear, with the murmur of an extinguished life, that you could only
say it was intensely and adorably strange, could only impute to the whole
overarched scene an unsurpassed secret for bringing tears of appreciation to
no matter how ignorant—archæologically ignorant—eyes. To ride once, in
these conditions, is of course to ride again and to allot to the Campagna a
generous share of the time one spends in Rome.

It is a pleasure that doubles one's horizon, and one can scarcely say
whether it enlarges or limits one's impression of the city proper. It certainly
makes St. Peter's seem a trifle smaller and blunts the edge of one's curiosity
in the Forum. It must be the effect of the experience, at all extended, that
when you think of Rome afterwards you will think still respectfully and
regretfully enough of the Vatican and the Pincio, the streets and the picture-
making street life; but will even more wonder, with an irrepressible contraction of the heart, when again you shall feel yourself bounding over the
flower-smothered turf, or pass from one framed picture to another beside
the open arches of the crumbling aqueducts. You look back at the City so
often from some grassy hill-top—hugely compact within its walls, with St.
Peter's overtopping all things and yet seeming small, and the vast girdle of
marsh and meadow receding on all sides to the mountains and the sea—that
you come to remember it at last as hardly more than a respectable parenthesis in a great sweep of generalisation. Within the walls, on the other hand,
you think of your intended ride as the most romantic of all your possibilities; of the Campagna generally as an illimitable experience. One's rides
certainly give Rome an inordinate scope for the reflective—by which I
suppose I mean after all the æsthetic and the "esoteric"—life. To dwell in a
city which, much as you grumble at it, is after all very fairly a modern city;
with crowds and shops and theatres and cafés and balls and receptions and
dinner-parties, and all the modern confusion of social pleasures and pains;
to have at your door the good and evil of it all; and yet to be able in half an
hour to gallop away and leave it a hundred miles, a hundred years, behind,
and to look at the tufted broom glowing on a lonely tower-top in the still
blue air, and the pale pink asphodels trembling none the less for the stillness,
and the shaggy-legged shepherds leaning on their sticks in motionless brotherhood with the heaps of ruin, and the scrambling goats and staggering little
kids treading out wild desert smells from the top of hollow-sounding
mounds; and then to come back through one of the great gates and a couple
of hours later find yourself in the "world," dressed, introduced, entertained,
inquiring, talking about "Middlemarch" to a young English lady or listening

---

"Middlemarch." George Eliot's *Middlemarch: A Study of Provincial Life* (1872) had recently been published; it had been reviewed by James in *Galaxy* (*Literary Criticism: Essays on*

to Neapolitan songs from a gentleman in a very low-cut shirt—all this is to lead in a manner a double life and to gather from the hurrying hours more impressions than a mind of modest capacity quite knows how to dispose of.

I touched lately upon this theme with a friend who, I fancied, would understand me, and who immediately assured me that he had just spent a day that this mingled diversity of sensation made to the days one spends elsewhere what an uncommonly good novel may be to the daily paper. "There was an air of idleness about it, if you will," he said, "and it was certainly pleasant enough to have been wrong. Perhaps, being after all un-used to long stretches of dissipation, this was why I had a half-feeling that I was reading an odd chapter in the history of a person very much more of a *héros de roman* than myself." Then he proceeded to relate how he had taken a long ride with a lady whom he extremely admired. "We turned off from the Tor di Quinto Road to that castellated farm-house you know of—once a Ghibelline fortress—whither Claude Lorraine used to come to paint pictures of which the surrounding landscape is still so artistically, so compositionally, suggestive. We went into the inner court, a cloister almost, with the carven capitals of its loggia columns, and looked at a handsome child swinging shyly against the half-opened door of a room whose impenetrable shadow, behind her, made her, as it were, a sketch in bituminous water-colours. We talked with the farmer, a handsome, pale, fever-tainted fellow with a well-to-do air that did n't in the least deter his affability from a turn compatible with the acceptance of small coin; and then we galloped away and away over the meadows which stretch with hardly a break to Veii. The day was strangely delicious, with a cool grey sky and just a touch of moisture in the air stirred by our rapid motion. The Campagna, in the colourless even light, was more solemn and romantic than ever; and a ragged shepherd, driving a meagre straggling flock, whom we stopped to ask our way of, was a perfect type of pastoral, weather-beaten misery. He was precisely the shepherd for the foreground of a scratchy etching. There were faint odours of spring in

---

Literature, 958–66) three months before the publication of "Roman Rides."

Tor di Quinto Road . . . castellated farm-house. The virtually forgotten Castello Farnese, the center of the tiny hamlet, the Isola Farnese, located about twenty kilometers from the center of Rome, and today most easily reached from the Via Cassia. The impressive medieval structure, restored in 1930, has been owned by the Church, the Orsinis, the Colonnas, the Rospigliosis, and the Farnese family. At times used as residence, as prison, and as school, today the castello is subdivided into four condominium apartments and offers no public access.

Veii. Extremely popular with nineteenth-century tourists and the subject of an entire chapter in Hare (*Days Near Rome*, I, 131–42), Veii, or Veio, the extensive site of the ruins of one of the most famous Etruscan cities, still being excavated, is ignored or virtually ignored by most modern English-language guidebooks; as in James's time, Veii is under partial cultivation and is best seen with a hired guide; see Amina Andreola, *Veio*, 1966.

the air, and the grass here and there was streaked with great patches of daisies; but it was spring with a foreknowledge of autumn, a day to be enjoyed with a substrain of sadness, the foreboding of regret, a day somehow to make one feel as if one had seen and felt a great deal—quite, as I say, like a *héros de roman*. Touching such characters, it was the illustrious Pelham, I think, who, on being asked if he rode, replied that he left those violent exercises to the ladies. But under such a sky, in such an air, over acres of daisied turf, a long, long gallop is certainly a supersubtle joy. The elastic bound of your horse is the poetry of motion; and if you are so happy as to add to it not the prose of companionship riding comes almost to affect you as a spiritual exercise. My gallop, at any rate," said my friend, "threw me into a mood which gave an extraordinary zest to the rest of the day." He was to go to a dinner-party at a villa on the edge of Rome, and Madam X——, who was also going, called for him in her carriage. "It was a long drive," he went on, "through the Forum, past the Colosseum. She told me a long story about a most interesting person. Toward the end my eyes caught through the carriage window a slab of rugged sculptures. We were passing under the Arch of Constantine. In the hall pavement of the villa is a rare antique mosaic—one of the largest and most perfect; the ladies on their way to the drawing-room trail over it the flounces of Worth. We drove home late, and there's my day."

On your exit from most of the gates of Rome you have generally half-an-hour's progress through winding lanes, many of which are hardly less charming than the open meadows. On foot the walls and high hedges would vex you and spoil your walk; but in the saddle you generally overtop them, to an endless peopling of the minor vision. Yet a Roman wall in the springtime is for that matter almost as interesting as anything it conceals. Crumbling grain by grain, coloured and mottled to a hundred tones by sun and storm, with its rugged structure of brick extruding through its coarse complexion of peeling stucco, its creeping lacework of wandering ivy starred with miniature violets, and its wild fringe of stouter flowers against the sky—it is as little as possible a blank partition; it is practically a luxury of landscape. At the moment at which I write, in mid-April, all the ledges and cornices are wreathed with flaming poppies, nodding there as if they knew so well what faded greys and yellows are an offset to their scarlet. But the best point in a

---

Pelham. Henry Pelham (1695?–1754), a prime minister of England not at all famous for strong character, although, as a supporter of Walpole, he had a remarkably successful career.

Worth. Worth of Paris, the famous couturier, founded by Charles Frederick Worth in 1858, soon patronized by the Empress Eugénie and subsequently by much of Parisian society, and then by that of America.

dilapidated enclosing surface of vineyard or villa is of course the gateway, lifting its great arch of cheap rococo scroll-work, its balls and shields and mossy dish-covers—as they always perversely figure to me—and flanked with its dusky cypresses. I never pass one without taking out my mental sketch-book and jotting it down as a vignette in the insubstantial record of my ride. They are as sad and dreary as if they led to the moated grange where Mariana waited in desperation for something to happen; and it's easy to take the usual inscription over the porch as a recommendation to those who enter to renounce all hope of anything but a glass of more or less agreeably acrid *vino romano*. For what you chiefly see over the walls and at the end of the straight short avenue of rusty cypresses are the appurtenances of a *vigna*—a couple of acres of little upright sticks blackening in the sun, and a vast sallow-faced, scantily windowed mansion, whose expression denotes little of the life of the mind beyond what goes to the driving of a hard bargain over the tasted hogsheads. If Mariana is there she certainly has no pile of old magazines to beguile her leisure. The life of the mind, if the term be in any application here not ridiculous, appears to any asker of curious questions, as he wanders about Rome, the very thinnest deposit of the past. Within the rococo gateway, which itself has a vaguely æsthetic self-consciousness, at the end of the cypress walk, you will probably see a mythological group in rusty marble—a Cupid and Psyche, a Venus and Paris, an Apollo and Daphne—the relic of an age when a Roman proprietor thought it fine to patronise the arts. But I imagine you are safe in supposing it to constitute the only allusion savouring of culture that has been made on the premises for three or four generations.

There is a franker cheerfulness—though certainly a proper amount of that forlornness which lurks about every object to which the Campagna forms a background—in the primitive little taverns where, on the homeward stretch, in the waning light, you are often glad to rein up and demand a bottle of their best. Their best and their worst are indeed the same, though with a shifting price, and plain *vino bianco* or *vino rosso* (rarely both) is the sole article of refreshment in which they deal. There is a ragged bush over the door, and within, under a dusky vault, on crooked cobble-stones, sit half-a-dozen contadini in their indigo jackets and goatskin breeches and with their elbows on the table. There is generally a rabble of infantile beggars at the door, pretty enough in their dusty rags, with their fine eyes and intense Italian smile, to make you forget your private vow of doing your individual

---

moated grange where Mariana. Shakespeare's *Measure for Measure*—"there, at this moated grange, resides this dejected Mariana" (III.i.264)—had inspired Tennyson's "Mariana" (1830) and "Mariana in the South" (1832).

best to make these people, whom you like so much, unlearn their old vices. Was Porta Pia bombarded three years ago that Peppino should still grow up to whine for a copper? But the Italian shells had no direct message for Peppino's stomach—and you are going to a dinner-party at a villa. So Peppino "points" an instant for the copper in the dust and grows up a Roman beggar. The whole little place represents the most primitive form of hostelry; but along any of the roads leading out of the city you may find establishments of a higher type, with Garibaldi, superbly mounted and fore-shortened, painted on the wall, or a lady in a low-necked dress opening a fictive lattice with irresistible hospitality, and a yard with the classic vine-wreathed arbour casting thin shadows upon benches and tables draped and cushioned with the white dust from which the highways from the gates borrow most of their local colour. None the less, I say, you avoid the highroads, and, if you are a person of taste, don't grumble at the occasional need of following the walls of the city. City walls, to a properly constituted American, can never be an object of indifference; and it is emphatically "no end of a sensation" to pace in the shadow of this massive cincture of Rome. I have found myself, as I skirted its base, talking of trivial things, but never without a sudden reflection on the deplorable impermanence of first impressions. A twelvemonth ago the raw plank fences of a Boston suburb, inscribed with the virtues of healing drugs, bristled along my horizon: now I glance with idle eyes at a compacted antiquity in which a more learned sense may read portentous dates and signs—Servius, Aurelius, Honorius. But even to idle eyes the prodigious, the continuous thing bristles with eloquent passages. In some places, where the huge brickwork is black with time and certain strange square towers look down at you with still blue eyes, the Roman sky peering through lidless loopholes, and there is nothing but white dust in the road and solitude in the air, I might take myself for a wandering Tartar touching on the confines of the Celestial Empire. The wall of China must have very much such a gaunt robustness. The colour of the Roman ramparts is everywhere fine, and their rugged patchwork has been subdued by time and weather into a mellow harmony that the brush only asks to catch up. On the northern side of the city, behind the Vatican, St. Peter's and the Trastevere, I have seen them glowing in the late afternoon with the tones

---

Porta Pia bombarded. On 20 September 1870 the city gate of the Porta Pia was breached by the troops of General Mazé de la Roche and the papal city fell to the Kingdom of Italy.

Servius, Aurelius, Honorius. Servius Tullus (reign 578–534 B.C.), sixth king of Rome; organized Latin alliance uniting Rome with other cities of Latium. Marcus Aurelius Antoninus (A.D. 121–80), emperor and author of the *Meditations*. Flavius Honorius, the "Emperor of the West" (A.D. 384–423); see page 293 and note.

of ancient bronze and rusty gold. Here at various points they are embossed with the Papal insignia, the tiara with its flying bands and crossed keys; to the high style of which the grace that attaches to almost any lost cause— even if not quite the "tender" grace of a day that is dead—considerably adds a style. With the dome of St. Peter's resting on their cornice and the hugely clustered architecture of the Vatican rising from them as from a terrace, they seem indeed the valid bulwark of an ecclesiastical city. Vain bulwark, alas! sighs the sentimental tourist, fresh from the meagre entertainment of this latter Holy Week. But he may find monumental consolation in this neighbourhood at a source where, as I pass, I never fail to apply for it. At half-anhour's walk beyond Porta San Pancrazio, beneath the wall of the Villa Doria, is a delightfully pompous ecclesiastical gateway of the seventeenth century, erected by Paul V to commemorate his restoration of the aqueducts through which the stream bearing his name flows towards the fine florid portico protecting its clear-sheeted outgush on the crest of the Janiculan. It arches across the road in the most ornamental manner of the period, and one can hardly pause before it without seeming to assist at a ten minutes' revival of old Italy—without feeling as if one were in a cocked hat and sword and were coming up to Rome, in another mood than Luther's, with a letter of recommendation to the mistress of a cardinal.

The Campagna differs greatly on the two sides of the Tiber; and it is hard to say which, for the rider, has the greater charm. The half-dozen rides you may take from Porta San Giovanni possess the perfection of traditional Roman interest and lead you through a far-strewn wilderness of ruins—a scattered maze of tombs and towers and nameless fragments of antique masonry. The landscape here has two great features; close before you on one side is the long, gentle swell of the Alban Hills, deeply, fantastically blue in most weathers, and marbled with the vague white masses of their scattered towns and villas. It would be difficult to draw the hard figure to a softer curve than that with which the heights sweep from Albano to the plain; this a perfect example of the classic beauty of line in the Italian landscape—that beauty which, when it fills the background of a picture, makes us look in the foreground for a broken column couched upon flowers and a shepherd

---

delightfully pompous ecclesiastical gateway . . . stream bearing his name . . . florid portico . . . revival of old Italy. The so-called Arco dell'Acqua Paola, on the Via Aurelia Antica, leading the waters of Trajan's restored aqueduct to the edge of the city, where it emerges on the Gianicolo at the splendid Fontana Paola (1612) and then proceeds down to Trastevere as the Acqua Paola. The spectacle remains exceptionally dynamic today and motivates many who view it to think, along with James and Goethe ("The columns, arches, cornices and pediments reminded us of those sumptuous arches through which, in times past, returning conquerors used to enter in triumph," *Italian Journey*, 431), of Rome at the apotheosis of its glory.

piping to dancing nymphs. At your side, constantly, you have the broken
line of the Claudian Aqueduct, carrying its broad arches far away into the
plain. The meadows along which it lies are not the smoothest in the world
for a gallop, but there is no pleasure greater than to wander near it. It stands
knee-deep in the flower-strewn grass, and its rugged piers are hung with ivy
as the columns of a church are draped for a festa. Every archway is a picture,
massively framed, of the distance beyond—of the snow-tipped Sabines and
lonely Soracte. As the spring advances the whole Campagna smiles and
waves with flowers; but I think they are nowhere more rank and lovely than
in the shifting shadow of the aqueducts, where they muffle the feet of the
columns and smother the half-dozen brooks which wander in and out like
silver meshes between the legs of a file of giants. They make a niche for
themselves too in every crevice and tremble on the vault of the empty
conduits. The ivy hereabouts in the springtime is peculiarly brilliant and
delicate; and though it cloaks and muffles these Roman fragments far less
closely than the castles and abbeys of England it hangs with the light elegance of all Italian vegetation. It is partly doubtless because their mighty
outlines are still unsoftened that the aqueducts are so impressive. They seem
the very source of the solitude in which they stand; they look like architectural spectres and loom through the light mists of their grassy desert, as you
recede along the line, with the same insubstantial vastness as if they rose out
of Egyptian sands. It is a great neighbourhood of ruins, many of which, it
must be confessed, you have applauded in many an album. But station a
peasant with sheepskin coat and bandaged legs in the shadow of a tomb or
tower best known to drawing-room art, and scatter a dozen goats on the
mound above him, and the picture has a charm which has not yet been
sketched away.

The other quarter of the Campagna has wider fields and smoother turf
and perhaps a greater number of delightful rides; the earth is sounder, and
there are fewer pitfalls and ditches. The land for the most part lies higher
and catches more wind, and the grass is here and there for great stretches as
smooth and level as a carpet. You have no Alban Mountains before you, but
you have in the distance the waving ridge of the nearer Apennines, and west
of them, along the course of the Tiber, the long seaward level of deep-

---

Sabines and lonely Soracte. See pages 148–50. "Once more upon the woody Apennine, /
The infant Alps. . . . / These hills seem things of lesser dignity, / All, save the lone Soracte's
height" (Byron, *Childe Harold's Pilgrimage,* canto IV, lxxiii–lxxiv). Part of the chain that
borders the Roman plain as the Sabine mountains, Soracte, also known as Soratte, is unnoted
or sparely noted by many modern guidebooks, although nineteenth-century travelers compared
it to Gibraltar and made it a popular outing (Hare, *Days Near Rome,* II, 42–52). See also the
following note.

coloured fields, deepening as they recede to the blue and purple of the sea itself. Beyond them, of a very clear day, you may see the glitter of the Mediterranean. These are the occasions perhaps to remember most fondly, for they lead you to enchanting nooks, and the landscape has details of the highest refinement. Indeed when my sense reverts to the lingering impressions of so blest a time, it seems a fool's errand to have attempted to express them, and a waste of words to do more than recommend the reader to go citywards at twilight of the end of March, making for Porta Cavalleggieri, and note what he sees. At this hour the Campagna is to the last point its melancholy self, and I remember roadside "effects" of a strange and intense suggestiveness. Certain mean, mouldering villas behind grass-grown courts have an indefinably sinister look; there was one in especial of which it was impossible not to argue that a despairing creature must have once committed suicide there, behind bolted door and barred window, and that no one has since had the pluck to go in and see why he never came out. Every wayside mark of manners, of history, every stamp of the past in the country about Rome, touches my sense to a thrill, and I may thus exaggerate the appeal of very common things. This is the more likely because the appeal seems ever to rise out of heaven knows what depths of ancient trouble. To delight in the aspects of *sentient* ruin might appear a heartless pastime, and the pleasure, I confess, shows the note of perversity. The sombre and the hard are as common an influence from southern things as the soft and the bright, I think; sadness rarely fails to assault a northern observer when he misses what he takes for comfort. Beauty is no compensation for the loss, only making it more poignant. Enough beauty of climate hangs over these Roman cottages and farm-houses—beauty of light, of atmosphere and of vegetation; but their charm for the maker-out of the stories in things is the way the golden air shows off their desolation. Man lives more with Nature in Italy than in New or than in Old England; she does more work for him and gives him more holidays than in our short-summered climes, and his home is therefore much more bare of devices for helping him to do without her, forget her and forgive her. These reflections are perhaps the source of the character you find in a moss-coated stone stairway climbing outside of a wall; in a queer inner court, befouled with rubbish and drearily bare of convenience; in an ancient quaintly carven well, worked with infinite labour from an overhanging window; in an arbour of time-twisted vines under which you may sit with your feet in the dirt and remember as a dim fable that there are races for which the type of domestic allurement is the parlour hearth-rug. For reasons apparent or otherwise these things amuse me beyond expression, and I am never weary of staring into gateways, of lingering by dreary, shabby, half-barbaric farm-yards, of feasting a foolish gaze on sun-cracked plaster and unctuous indoor shadows.

I must n't forget, however, that it's not for wayside effects that one rides away behind St. Peter's, but for the strong sense of wandering over boundless space, of seeing great classic lines of landscape, of watching them dispose themselves into pictures so full of "style" that you can think of no painter who deserves to have you admit that they suggest him—hardly knowing whether it is better pleasure to gallop far and drink deep of air and grassy distance and the whole delicious opportunity, or to walk and pause and linger, and try and grasp some ineffaceable memory of sky and colour and outline. Your pace can hardly help falling into a contemplative measure at the time, everywhere so wonderful, but in Rome so persuasively divine, when the winter begins palpably to soften and quicken. Far out on the Campagna, early in February, you feel the first vague earthly emanations, which in a few weeks come wandering into the heart of the city and throbbing through the close, dark streets. Springtime in Rome is an immensely poetic affair; but you must stand often far out in the ancient waste, between grass and sky, to measure its deep, full, steadily accelerated rhythm. The winter has an incontestable beauty, and is pre-eminently the time of colour—the time when it is no affectation, but homely verity, to talk about the "purple" tone of the atmosphere. As February comes and goes your purple is streaked with green and the rich, dark bloom of the distance begins to lose its intensity. But your loss is made up by other gains; none more precious than that inestimable gain to the ear—the disembodied voice of the lark. It comes with the early flowers, the white narcissus and the cyclamen, the half-buried violets and the pale anemones, and makes the whole atmosphere ring like a vault of tinkling glass. You never see the source of the sound, and are utterly unable to localise his note, which seems to come from everywhere at once, to be some hundred-throated voice of the air. Sometimes you fancy you just catch him, a mere vague spot against the blue, an intenser throb in the universal pulsation of light. As the weeks go on the flowers multiply and the deep blues and purples of the hills, turning to azure and violet, creep higher toward the narrowing snow-line of the Sabines. The temperature rises, the first hour of your ride you feel the heat, but you beguile it with brushing the hawthorn-blossoms as you pass along the hedges, and catching at the wild rose and honeysuckle; and when you get into the meadows there is stir enough in the air to lighten the dead weight of the sun. The Roman air, however, is not a tonic medicine, and it seldom suffers exercise to be all exhilarating. It has always seemed to me indeed part of the charm of the latter that your keenest consciousness is haunted with a vague languor. Occasionally when the sirocco blows that sensation becomes strange and exquisite. Then, under the grey sky, before the dim distances which the south-wind mostly brings with it, you seem to ride forth into a world from which all hope has departed and in which, in spite of the flowers that make your horse's footfalls soundless, nothing is left save some queer probability that your imagination is unable to measure, but from which it hardly shrinks. This quality in the Roman element may now and then "relax" you almost to ecstasy; but a season of sirocco would be an overdose of morbid pleasure. You may at any rate best feel the peculiar beauty of the Campagna on those mild days of winter when the mere quality and temper of the sunshine suffice to move the landscape to joy, and you pause on the brown grass in the sunny stillness and, by listening long enough, almost fancy you hear the shrill of the midsummer cricket. It is detail and ornament that vary from month to month, from week to week even, and make your returns to the same places a constant feast of unexpectedness; but the great essential features of the prospect preserve throughout the year the same impressive serenity. Soracte, be it January or May, rises from its blue horizon like an island from the sea and with an elegance of contour which no mood of the year can deepen or diminish. You know it well; you have seen it often in the mellow backgrounds of Claude; and it has such an irresistibly classic, academic air that while you look at it you begin to take your saddle for a faded old arm-chair in a palace gallery. A month's rides in different directions will show you a dozen prime Claudes. After I had seen them all I went piously to the Doria gallery to refresh my memory of its two famous specimens and to enjoy to the utmost their delightful air of reference to something that had become a part of my personal experience. Delightful it certainly is to feel the common element in one's own sensibility and those of a genius whom that element has helped to do great things. Claude must have haunted the very places of one's personal preference and adjusted their divine undulations to his splendid scheme of romance, his view of the poetry of life. He was familiar with aspects in which there was n't a single uncompromising line. I saw a few days ago a small finished sketch from his hand, in the possession of an American artist, which was almost startling in its clear reflection of forms unaltered by the two centuries that have dimmed and cracked the paint and canvas.

This unbroken continuity of the impressions I have tried to indicate is an excellent example of the intellectual background of all enjoyment in Rome. It effectually prevents pleasure from becoming vulgar, for your sensation rarely begins and ends with itself; it reverberates—it recalls, commemorates, resuscitates something else. At least half the merit of everything you enjoy

---

Doria gallery . . . two famous specimens. The Palazzo Doria Pamphilj gallery (not to be confused with the collection, which James previously noted, at the villa of the same name) holds five Claude Lorraines; two suggest Soracte—*Landscape with Cephalus and Procris Reunited by Diana* and, particularly, *Landscape with Dancing Figures.*

must be that it suits you absolutely; but the larger half here is generally that it has suited some one else and that you can never flatter yourself you have discovered it. It has been addressed to some use a million miles out of your range, and has had great adventures before ever condescending to please you. It was in admission of this truth that my discriminating friend who showed me the Claudes found it impossible to designate a certain delightful region which you enter at the end of an hour's riding from Porta Cavalleggieri as anything but Arcadia. The exquisite correspondence of the term in this case altogether revived its faded bloom; here veritably the oaten pipe must have stirred the windless air and the satyrs have laughed among the brookside reeds. Three or four long grassy dells stretch away in a chain between low hills over which delicate trees are so discreetly scattered that each one is a resting place for a shepherd. The elements of the scene are simple enough, but the composition has extraordinary refinement. By one of those happy chances which keep observation in Italy always in her best humour a shepherd had thrown himself down under one of the trees in the very attitude of Meliboeus. He had been washing his feet, I suppose, in the neighbouring brook, and had found it pleasant afterwards to roll his short breeches well up on his thighs. Lying thus in the shade, on his elbow, with his naked legs stretched out on the turf and his soft peaked hat over his long hair crushed back like the veritable bonnet of Arcady, he was exactly the figure of the background of this happy valley. The poor fellow, lying there in rustic weariness and ignorance, little fancied that he was a symbol of old-world meanings to new-world eyes.

Such eyes may find as great a store of picturesque meanings in the cork-woods of Monte Mario, tenderly loved of all equestrians. These are less severely pastoral than our Arcadia, and you might more properly lodge there a damosel of Ariosto than a nymph of Theocritus. Among them is strewn a lovely wilderness of flowers and shrubs, and the whole place has such a charming woodland air, that, casting about me the other day for a compliment, I declared that it reminded me of New Hampshire. My compliment had a double edge, and I had no sooner uttered it than I smiled—or sighed—to perceive in all the undiscriminated botany about me the wealth of detail, the idle elegance and grace of Italy alone, the natural stamp of the land which has the singular privilege of making one love her unsanctified

---

Meliboeus. One of the two interlocutors in Virgil's first *Eclogue*.

damosel of Ariosto than a nymph of Theocritus. The beautiful adventure-prone Angelica of Aristo's romantic epic *Orlando Furioso* (1532); she marries Medoro the Moor, thereby causing the raging madness of the knight Orlando. The passions inspired by the nymphs in Theocritus's pastoral poetry are considerably gentler.

beauty all but as well as those features of one's own country toward which nature's small allowance doubles that of one's own affection. For this effect of casting a spell no rides have more value than those you take in Villa Doria or Villa Borghese; or don't take, possibly, if you prefer to reserve these particular regions—the latter in especial—for your walking hours. People do ride, however, in both villas, which deserve honourable mention in this regard. Villa Doria, with its noble site, its splendid views, its great groups of stone-pines, so clustered and yet so individual, its lawns and flowers and fountains, its altogether princely disposition, is a place where one may pace, well mounted, of a brilliant day, with an agreeable sense of its being rather a more elegant pastime to balance in one's stirrups than to trudge on even the smoothest gravel. But at Villa Borghese the walkers have the best of it; for they are free of those adorable outlying corners and bosky byways which the rumble of barouches never reaches. In March the place becomes a perfect epitome of the spring. You cease to care much for the melancholy greenness of the disfeatured statues which has been your chief winter's intimation of verdure; and before you are quite conscious of the tender streaks and patches in the great quaint grassy arena round which the Propaganda students, in their long skirts, wander slowly, like dusky seraphs revolving the gossip of Paradise, you spy the brave little violets uncapping their azure brows beneath the high-stemmed pines. One's walks here would take us too far, and one's pauses detain us too long, when in the quiet parts under the wall one comes across a group of charming small school-boys in full-dress suits and white cravats, shouting over their play in clear Italian, while a grave young priest, beneath a tree, watches them over the top of his book. It sounds like nothing, but the force behind it and the frame round it, the setting, the air, the chord struck, make it a hundred wonderful things.

1873.

Propaganda students. From the nearby Collegio di Propaganda Fide, off the Piazza di Spagna. Since the time of Gregory XV the school has been responsible for missionary activities.

Roman Neighbourhoods

I made a note after my first stroll at Albano to the effect that I had been talking of the "picturesque" all my life, but that now for a change I beheld it. I had been looking all winter across the Campagna at the free-flowing outline of the Alban Mount, with its half-dozen towns shining on its purple side even as vague sun-spots in the shadow of a cloud, and thinking it simply an agreeable incident in the varied background of Rome. But now that during the last few days I have been treating it as a foreground, have been suffering St. Peter's to play the part of a small mountain on the horizon, with the Campagna swimming mistily through the ambiguous lights and shadows of the interval, I find the interest as great as in the best of the by-play of Rome. The walk I speak of was just out of the village, to the south, toward the neighbouring town of L' Ariccia, neighbouring these twenty years, since the Pope (the late Pope, I was on the point of calling him) threw his superb viaduct across the deep ravine which divides it from Albano. At the risk of seeming to fantasticate I confess that the Pope's having built the viaduct—in this very recent antiquity—made me linger there in a pensive posture and marvel at the march of history and at Pius the Ninth's beginning already to profit by the sentimental allowances

[Originally published in the *Atlantic Monthly*, XXXII (December 1873), 671–80; reprinted in *Transatlantic Sketches*, 1875; reprinted in *Foreign Parts*, 1883.]

L'Ariccia . . . viaduct. The viaduct was blown up by the Germans in 1944; poorly reconstructed, it collapsed in 1967 and finally was replaced by a firm new structure. (*Guida ai Misteri e Segreti del Lazio*, 157, reproduces an engraving that offers the view James saw.)

we make to vanished powers. An ardent *nero* then would have had his own way with me and obtained a frank admission that the Pope was indeed a father to his people. Far down into the charming valley which slopes out of the ancestral woods of the Chigis into the level Campagna winds the steep stone-paved road at the bottom of which, in the good old days, tourists in no great hurry saw the mules and oxen tackled to their carriage for the opposite ascent. And indeed even an impatient tourist might have been content to lounge back in his jolting chaise and look out at the mouldy foundations of the little city plunging into the verdurous flank of the gorge. Questioned, as a cherisher of quaintness, as to the best "bit" hereabouts, I should certainly name the way in which the crumbling black houses of these ponderous villages plant their weary feet on the flowery edges of all the steepest chasms. Before you enter one of them you invariably find yourself lingering outside its pretentious old gateway to see it clutched and stitched to the stony hillside by this rank embroidery of the wildest and bravest things that grow. Just at this moment nothing is prettier than the contrast between their dusky ruggedness and the tender, the yellow and pink and violet fringe of that mantle. All this you may observe from the viaduct at the Ariccia; but you must wander below to feel the full force of the eloquence of our imaginary *papalino*. The pillars and arches of pale grey peperino arise in huge tiers with a magnificent spring and solidity. The older Romans built no better; and the work has a deceptive air of being one of their sturdy bequests which help one to drop another sigh over the antecedents the Italians of to-day are so eager to repudiate. Will those *they* give their descendants be as good?

At the Ariccia, in any case, I found a little square with a couple of mossy fountains, occupied on one side by a vast dusky-faced Palazzo Chigi and on the other by a goodly church with an imposing dome. The dome, within, covers the whole edifice and is adorned with some extremely elegant stucco-work of the seventeenth century. It gave a great value to this fine old decoration that preparations were going forward for a local festival and that the village carpenter was hanging certain mouldy strips of crimson damask against the piers of the vaults. The damask might have been of the seventeenth century too, and a group of peasant-women were seeing it unfurled

---

nero. Literally, "black," but with a long history of reference to reactionary or strongly conservative forces, especially those backing the clerics; in the twentieth century *nero* came to refer to fascist sympathizers.

papalino. Literally "little pope," a diminutive of some tenderness.

Palazzo Chigi . . . a goodly church. In Arriccia, Bernini amplified the palace and built the church of Santa Maria dell'Assunzione. During the 1870s palace apartments were let during the summer (Hare, *Days Near Rome*, I, 63). Today there is virtually no admission.

with evident awe. I regarded it myself with interest—it seemed so the tattered remnant of a fashion that had gone out for ever. I thought again of the poor disinherited Pope, wondering whether, when such venerable frippery will no longer bear the carpenter's nails, any more will be provided. It was hard to fancy anything but shreds and patches in that musty tabernacle. Wherever you go in Italy you receive some such intimation as this of the shrunken proportions of Catholicism, and every church I have glanced into on my walks hereabouts has given me an almost pitying sense of it. One finds one's self at last—without fatuity, I hope—feeling sorry for the solitude of the remaining faithful. It's as if the churches had been made so for the world, in its social sense, and the world had so irrevocably moved away. They are in size out of all modern proportion to the local needs, and the only thing at all alive in the melancholy waste they collectively form is the smell of stale incense. There are pictures on all the altars by respectable third-rate painters; pictures which I suppose once were ordered and paid for and criticised by worshippers who united taste with piety. At Genzano, beyond the Ariccia, rises on the grey village street a pompous Renaissance temple whose imposing nave and aisles would contain the population of a capital. But where is the *taste* of the Ariccia and Genzano? Where are the choice spirits for whom Antonio Raggi modelled the garlands of his dome and a hundred clever craftsmen imitated Guido and Caravaggio? Here and there, from the pavement, as you pass, a dusky crone interlards her devotions with more profane importunities, or a grizzled peasant on rusty-jointed knees, tilted forward with his elbows on a bench, reveals the dimensions of the patch in his blue breeches. But where is the connecting link between Guido and Caravaggio and those poor souls for whom an undoubted original is only a something behind a row of candlesticks, of no very clear meaning save that you must bow to it? You find a vague memory of it at best in the useless grandeurs about you, and you seem to be looking at a structure of which the stubborn earth-scented foundations alone remain, with the carved and painted shell that bends above them, while the central substance has utterly crumbled away.

I shall seem to have adopted a more meditative pace than befits a brisk constitutional if I say that I also fell a-thinking before the shabby façade of the old Chigi Palace. But it seemed somehow in its grey forlornness to respond to the sadly superannuated expression of the opposite church; and indeed in any condition what self-respecting cherisher of quaintness can

---

Genzano . . . **pompous Renaissance temple** . . . **Antonio Raggi.** The church of San Tommaso da Villanova, by Giuseppe Camporese (1763–1822). Antonio Raggi (1624–86) painted Bernini's dome in Santa Maria dell'Assunzione.

forbear to do a little romancing in the shadow of a provincial palazzo? On the face of the matter, I know, there is often no very salient peg to hang a romance on. A sort of dusky blankness invests the establishment, which has often a rather imbecile old age. But a hundred brooding secrets lurk in this inexpressive mask, and the Chigi Palace did duty for me in the suggestive twilight as the most haunted of houses. Its basement walls sloped outward like the beginning of a pyramid, and its lower windows were covered with massive iron cages. Within the doorway, across the court, I saw the pale glimmer of flowers on a terrace, and I made much, for the effect of the roof, of a great covered loggia or belvedere with a dozen window-panes missing or mended with paper. Nothing gives one a stronger impression of old manners than an ancestral palace towering in this haughty fashion over a shabby little town; you hardly stretch a point when you call it an impression of feudalism. The scene may pass for feudal to American eyes, for which a hundred windows on a façade mean nothing more exclusive than a hotel kept (at the most invidious) on the European plan. The mouldy grey houses on the steep crooked street, with their black cavernous archways pervaded by bad smells, by the braying of asses and by human intonations hardly more musical, the haggard and tattered peasantry staring at you with hungry-heavy eyes, the brutish-looking monks (there are still enough to point a moral), the soldiers, the mounted constables, the dirt, the dreariness, the misery, and the dark over-grown palace frowning over it all from barred window and guarded gateway—what more than all this do we dimly descry in a mental image of the dark ages? For all his desire to keep the peace with the vivid image of things if it be only vivid enough, the votary of this ideal may well occasionally turn over such values with the wonder of what one takes them as paying for. They pay sometimes for such sorry "facts of life." At Genzano, out of the very midst of the village squalor, rises the Palazzo Cesarini, separated from its gardens by a dirty lane. Between peasant and prince the contact is unbroken, and one would suppose Italian good-nature sorely taxed by their mutual allowances; that the prince in especial must

---

Palazzo Cesarini . . . Between peasant and prince the contact is unbroken. The palace is a relatively uninteresting nineteenth-century structure, but James seems to allude to a curious but supposedly factual story concerning the palace. The Duchess of Cesarini dreamed that she would give birth to twin sons, one of whom would endanger the other's life. When twin boys were in fact born, she bribed the midwife to take one child away and raise him in secret, as a shepherd. When, however, duke, duchess, and the young duke all died, and no heirs were to be found, the midwife informed her supposed peasant son of his true princely birthright, and she supplied absolute proof to him and to the authorities involved. The young man took possession of the inheritance and became the Duke of Cesarini, linking peasant and prince (Hare, *Days Near Rome,* I, 91–93).

cultivate a firm impervious shell. There are no comfortable townsfolk about him to remind him of the blessings of a happy mediocrity of fortune. When he looks out of his window he sees a battered old peasant against a sunny wall sawing off his dinner from a hunch of black bread.

I must confess, however, that "feudal" as it amused me to find the little piazza of the Ariccia, it appeared to threaten in no manner an exasperated rising. On the contrary, the afternoon being cool, many of the villagers were contentedly muffled in those ancient cloaks, lined with green baize, which, when tossed over the shoulder and surmounted with a peaked hat, form one of the few lingering remnants of "costume" in Italy; others were tossing wooden balls light-heartedly enough on the grass outside the town. The egress on this side is under a great stone archway thrown out from the palace and surmounted with the family arms. Nothing could better confirm your theory that the townsfolk are groaning serfs. The road leads away through the woods, like many of the roads hereabouts, among trees less remarkable for their size than for their picturesque contortions and posturings. The woods, at the moment at which I write, are full of the raw green light of early spring, a *jour* vastly becoming to the various complexions of the wild flowers that cover the waysides. I have never seen these untended parterres in such lovely exuberance; the sturdiest pedestrian becomes a lingering idler if he allows them to catch his eye. The pale purple cyclamen, with its hood thrown back, stands up in masses as dense as tulip-beds; and here and there in the duskier places great sheets of forget-me-not seem to exhale a faint blue mist. These are the commonest plants; there are dozens more I know no name for—a rich profusion in especial of a beautiful five-petalled flower whose white texture is pencilled with hair-strokes certain fair copyists I know of would have to hold their breath to imitate. An Italian oak has neither the girth nor the height of its English brothers, but it contrives in proportion to be perhaps even more effective. It crooks its back and twists its arms and clinches its hundred fists with the queerest extravagance, and wrinkles its bark into strange rugosities from which its first scattered sprouts of yellow green seem to break out like a morbid fungus. But the tree which has the greatest charm to northern eyes is the cold grey-green ilex, whose clear crepuscular shade drops against a Roman sun a veil impenetrable, yet not oppressive. The ilex has even less colour than the cypress, but it is much less funereal, and a landscape in which it is frequent may still be said to smile faintly, though by no means to laugh. It abounds in old Italian gardens, where the boughs are trimmed and interlocked into vaulted corridors in which, from point to point, as in the niches of some dimly frescoed hall, you see mildewed busts stare at you with a solemnity which the even grey light makes strangely intense. A humbler relative of the ilex, though it does better things than help broken-nosed emperors to look dignified, is the olive, which covers many of the neighbouring hillsides with its little smoky puffs of foliage. A stroke of composition I never weary of is that long blue stretch of the Campagna which makes a high horizon and rests on this vaporous base of olive-tops. A reporter intent upon a simile might liken it to the ocean seen above the smoke of watch-fires kindled on the strand.

To do perfect justice to the wood-walk away from the Ariccia I ought to touch upon the birds that were singing vespers as I passed. But the reader would find my rhapsody as poor entertainment as the programme of a concert he had been unable to attend. I have no more learning about bird-music than would help me to guess that a dull dissyllabic refrain in the heart of the wood came from the cuckoo; and when at moments I heard a twitter of fuller tone, with a more suggestive modulation, I could only *hope* it was the nightingale. I have listened for the nightingale more than once in places so charming that his song would have seemed but the articulate expression of their beauty, and have never heard much beyond a provoking snatch or two—a prelude that came to nothing. In spite of a natural grudge, however, I generously believe him a great artist or at least a great genius—a creature who despises any prompting short of absolute inspiration. For the rich, the multitudinous melody around me seemed but the offering to my ear of the prodigal spirit of tradition. The wood was ringing with sound because it was twilight, spring and Italy. It was also because of these good things and various others besides that I relished so keenly my visit to the Capuchin convent upon which I emerged after half-an-hour in the wood. It stands above the town on the slope of the Alban Mount, and its wild garden climbs away behind it and extends its melancholy influence. Before it is a small stiff avenue of trimmed live-oaks which conducts you to a grotesque little shrine beneath the staircase ascending to the church. Just here, if you are apt to grow timorous at twilight, you may take a very pretty fright; for as you draw near you catch behind the grating of the shrine the startling semblance of a gaunt and livid monk. A sickly lamplight plays down upon his face, and he stares at you from cavernous eyes with a dreadful air of death in life. Horrors of horrors, you murmur, is this a Capuchin penance? You discover of course in a moment that it is only a Capuchin joke, that the monk is a pious dummy and his spectral visage a matter of the paint-brush. You resent his intrusion on the surrounding loveliness; and as you proceed to demand entertainment at their convent you pronounce the Capuchins very foolish fellows. This declaration, as I made it, was supported by the conduct of the simple brother who opened the door of the cloister in obedience to my knock and, on learning my errand, demurred about admitting me at so late

---

Capuchin convent. Il Santuario di Santa Maria di Galloro.

an hour. If I would return on the morrow morning he'd be most happy. He broke into a blank grin when I assured him that this was the very hour of my desire and that the garish morning light would do no justice to the view. These were mysteries beyond his ken, and it was only his good-nature (of which he had plenty) and not his imagination that was moved. So that when, passing through the narrow cloister and out upon the grassy terrace, I saw another cowled brother standing with folded hands profiled against the sky, in admirable harmony with the scene, I questioned his knowing the uses for which he is still most precious. This, however, was surely too much to ask of him, and it was cause enough for gratitude that, though he was there before me, he was not a fellow-tourist with an opera-glass slung over his shoulder. There was support to my idea of the convent in the expiring light, for the scene was in its way unsurpassable. Directly below the terrace lay the deep-set circle of the Alban Lake, shining softly through the light mists of evening. This beautiful pool—it is hardly more—occupies the crater of a prehistoric volcano, a perfect cup, shaped and smelted by furnace-fires. The rim of the cup, rising high and densely wooded round the placid stone-blue water, has a sort of natural artificiality. The sweep and contour of the long circle are admirable; never was a lake so charmingly lodged. It is said to be of extraordinary depth; and though stone-blue water seems at first a very innocent substitute for boiling lava, it has a sinister look which betrays its dangerous antecedents. The winds never reach it and its surface is never ruffled; but its deep-bosomed placidity seems to cover guilty secrets, and you fancy it in communication with the capricious and treacherous forces of nature. Its very colour is of a joyless beauty, a blue as cold and opaque as a solidified sheet of lava. Streaked and wrinkled by a mysterious motion of its own, it affects the very type of a legendary pool, and I could easily have believed that I had only to sit long enough into the evening to see the ghosts of classic nymphs and naiads cleave its sullen flood and beckon me with irresistible arms. Is it because its shores are haunted with these vague Pagan influences

---

legendary pool. Legends proliferated concerning the Lake of Albano, but Niebuhr and Hare offer the most interesting. Hare reports a story related by a nineteenth-century peasant boy: " 'Where the lake now lies, there once stood a great city. Here, when Jesus Christ came to Italy, he begged alms. None took compassion on him, but an old woman who gave him two handfuls of meal. He bade her to leave the city: she obeyed: the city instantly sank, and the lake rose in its place.' " The peasant boy told Hare, "Sta scritto nei libri"—it is written in the books (Hare, *Days Near Rome*, I, 67). Neibuhr speaks of the siege against Veii, whose destiny soothsayers linked to the prodigy of the Alban lake; in the middle of dogday summer, for no apparent reason, the lake began to overflow its shores and flood the neighboring countryside. It was said that if the lake kept overflowing, Veii could not be taken, but if the waters reached the sea, Rome would perish (Niebuhr, II, 475–76).

that two convents have risen there to purge the atmosphere? From the Capuchin terrace you look across at the grey Franciscan monastery of Palazzuola, which is not less romantic certainly than the most obstinate myth it may have exorcised. The Capuchin garden is a wild tangle of great trees and shrubs and clinging, trembling vines which in these hard days are left to take care of themselves; a weedy garden, if there ever was one, but none the less charming for that, in the deepening dusk, with its steep grassy vistas struggling away into impenetrable shadow. I braved the shadow for the sake of climbing upon certain little flat-roofed crumbling pavilions that rise from the corners of the further wall and give you a wider and lovelier view of lake and hills and sky.

I have perhaps justified to the reader the mild proposition with which I started—convinced him, that is, that Albano is worth a walk. It may be a different walk each day, moreover, and not resemble its predecessors save by its keeping in the shade. "Galleries" the roads are prettily called, and with the justice that they are vaulted and draped overhead and hung with an immense succession of pictures. As you follow the few miles from Genzano to Frascati you have perpetual views of the Campagna framed by clusters of trees; the vast iridescent expanse of which completes the charm and comfort of your verdurous dusk. I compared it just now to the sea, and with a good deal of truth, for it has the same incalculable lights and shades, the same confusion of glitter and gloom. But I have seen it at moments—chiefly in the misty twilight—when it resembled less the waste of waters than something more portentous, the land itself in fatal dissolution. I could believe the fields to be dimly surging and tossing and melting away into quicksands, and that one's very last chance of an impression was taking place. A view, however, which has the merit of being really as interesting as it seems, is that of the Lake of Nemi; which the enterprising traveller hastens to compare with its sister sheet of Albano. Comparison in this case is particularly odious, for in order to prefer one lake to the other you have to discover faults where there are none. Nemi is a smaller circle, but lies in a deeper cup, and if with no grey Franciscan pile to guard its woody shores, at least, in the same position, the little high-perched black town to which it gives its name and which looks across at Genzano on the opposite shore as Palazzuola regards Castel Gandolfo. The walk from the Ariccia to Genzano is charming, most of all when it reaches a certain grassy piazza from which three public avenues stretch away under a double row of stunted and twisted elms. The Duke Cesarini has a villa at Genzano—I mentioned it just now—whose gardens overhang the lake; but he has also a porter in a faded rakish-looking livery

---

Castel Gandolfo. Since 1624 the primary summer residence of almost all the popes.

who shakes his head at your proffered franc unless you can reinforce it with a permit countersigned at Rome. For this annoying complication of dignities he is justly to be denounced; but I forgive him for the sake of that ancestor who in the seventeenth century planted this shady walk. Never was a prettier approach to a town than by these low-roofed light-chequered corridors. Their only defect is that they prepare you for a town of rather more rustic coquetry than Genzano exhibits. It has quite the usual allowance, the common cynicism, of accepted decay, and looks dismally as if its best families had all fallen into penury together and lost the means of keeping anything better than donkeys in their great dark, vaulted basements and mending their broken window-panes with anything better than paper. It was on the occasion of this drear Genzano that I had a difference of opinion with a friend who maintained that there was nothing in the same line so pretty in Europe as a pretty New England village. The proposition seemed to a cherisher of quaintness on the face of it inacceptable; but calmly considered it has a measure of truth. I am not fond of chalk-white painted planks, certainly; I vastly prefer the dusky tones of ancient stucco and peperino; but I succumb on occasion to the charms of a vine-shaded porch, of tulips and dahlias glowing in the shade of high-arching elms, of heavy-scented lilacs bending over a white paling to brush your cheek.

"I prefer Siena to Lowell," said my friend; "but I prefer Farmington to such a thing as this." In fact an Italian village is simply a miniature Italian city, and its various parts imply a town of fifty times the size. At Genzano are neither dahlias nor lilacs, and no odours but foul ones. Flowers and other graces are all confined to the high-walled precincts of Duke Cesarini, to which you must obtain admission twenty miles away. The houses on the other hand would generally lodge a New England cottage, porch and garden and high-arching elms included, in one of their cavernous basements. These vast grey dwellings are all of a fashion denoting more generous social needs than any they serve nowadays. They speak of better days and of a fabulous time when Italy was either not shabby or could at least "carry off" her shabbiness. For what follies are they doing penance? Through what melancholy stages have their fortunes ebbed? You ask these questions as you choose the shady side of the long blank street and watch the hot sun glare upon the dust-coloured walls and pause before the fetid gloom of open doors.

I should like to spare a word for mouldy little Nemi, perched upon a cliff high above the lake, at the opposite side; but after all, when I had climbed up into it from the water-side, passing beneath a great arch which I suppose once topped a gateway, and counted its twenty or thirty apparent inhabitants peeping at me from black doorways, and looked at the old round tower at whose base the village clusters, and declared that it was all queer, queer, desperately queer, I had said all that is worth saying about it. Nemi has a much better appreciation of its lovely position than Genzano, where your only view of the lake is from a dunghill behind one of the houses. At the foot of the round tower is an overhanging terrace, from which you may feast your eyes on the only freshness they find in these dusky human hives—the blooming seam, as one may call it, of strong wild flowers which binds the crumbling walls to the face of the cliff. Of Rocca di Papa I must say as little. It consorted generally with the bravery of its name; but the only object I made a note of as I passed through it on my way to Monte Cavo, which rises directly above it, was a little black house with a tablet in its face setting forth that Massimo d' Azeglio had dwelt there. The story of his sojourn is not the least attaching episode in his delightful *Ricordi*. From the summit of Monte Cavo is a prodigious view, which you may enjoy with whatever good-nature is left you by the reflection that the modern Passionist convent occupying this admirable site was erected by the Cardinal of York (grandson of James II) on the demolished ruins of an immemorial temple of Jupiter: the last foolish act of a foolish race. For me I confess this folly spoiled the convent, and the convent all but spoiled the view; for I kept thinking how fine it would have been to emerge upon the old pillars and sculptures from the lava pavement of the Via Triumphalis, which wanders grass-grown and untrodden through the woods. A convent, however, which nothing spoils is that of Palazzuola, to which I paid my respects on this same occasion. It rises on a

---

Rocca di Papa ... Massimo d'Azeglio ... *Ricordi.* In 1190 the antipope John resided here, and it was the stronghold of the Colonna family for over two centuries before it passed into the hands of the Orsinis. Although later in the nineteenth century the Rocca di Papa became famous as an English summer residence, the artist and statesman Massimo d'Azeglio—for a time head of Victor Emmanuel II's ministers—lived here in 1821 and wrote about the site in his famous memoirs (*Ricordi*, II, 13–73).

Passionist convent ... Cardinal of York ... immemorial temple of Jupiter: the last foolish act. On the Passionist order, see page 130 and note. Born in Rome, Henry Stuart (1725–1807), created Duke of York by his father, James, and created Cardinal York by Pope Benedict, was the last prince of the royal house of Stuart. From 1783 to 1788 he built a Passionist convent— which eventually was to become a hotel. Murray reports that Roman antiquarians who viewed the cardinal's destruction of the temple of Jupiter Latialis, erected by Tarquinius Superbus as the meeting place of the Feriae Latinae, "justly denounced this proceeding of the last of the Stuarts" (Murray, 1873, 402). The accomplishment of the "last" foolish act came soon after York had had struck a portrait medal declaring himself "Hen. IX. Mag. Brit. Fr. et Hib. Rex. Fid. Def. Card. Ep. Tusc," Henry the Ninth of Great Britain, France, and Ireland, King, Defender of the Faith, Cardinal, Bishop of Frascati.

Palazzuola ... antiquarians are still quarrelling. Also, Palazzolo and Palazzuolo, a Franciscan monastery that Hare (*Days Near Rome*, I, 82) describes as deriving from a consular tomb cut into the rock overhanging the convent garden and resembling the ancient tombs of Etruria. Disagreement arose concerning the evidence, not convincing, that the tomb might be

lower spur of Monte Cavo, on the edge, as we have seen, of the Alban Lake, and though it occupies a classic site, that of early Alba Longa, it displaced nothing more precious than memories and legends so dim that the antiquarians are still quarrelling about them. It has a meagre little church and the usual sham Perugino with a couple of tinsel crowns for the Madonna and the Infant inserted into the canvas; and it has also a musty old room hung about with faded portraits and charts and queer ecclesiastical knick-knacks, which borrowed a mysterious interest from the sudden assurance of the simple Franciscan brother who accompanied me that it was the room of the Son of the King of Portugal. But my peculiar pleasure was the little thick-shaded garden which adjoins the convent and commands from its massive artificial foundations an enchanting view of the lake. Part of it is laid out in cabbages and lettuce, over which a rubicund brother, with his frock tucked up, was bending with a solicitude which he interrupted to remove his skull-cap and greet me with the unsophisticated sweet-humoured smile that every now and then in Italy does so much to make you forget the ambiguities of monachism. The rest is occupied by cypresses and other funereal umbrage, making a dank circle round an old cracked fountain black with water-moss. The parapet of the terrace is furnished with good stone seats where you may lean on your elbows to gaze away a sunny half-hour and, feeling the general charm of the scene, declare that the best mission of such a country in the world has been simply to produce, in the way of prospect and picture, these masterpieces of mildness. Mild here as a dream the whole attained effect, mild as resignation, mild as one's thoughts of another life. Such a session was n't surely an experience of the irritable flesh; it was the deep degustation, on a summer's day, of something immortally expressed by a man of genius.

From Albano you may take your way through several ancient little cities to Frascati, a rival centre of *villeggiatura,* the road following the hillside for a long morning's walk and passing through alternations of denser and clearer shade—the dark vaulted alleys of ilex and the brilliant corridors of fresh-sprouting oak. The Campagna is beneath you continually, with the sea

---

that of Caius Cornelius Scioppio Hispallus—unique as both consul and pontifex-maximus—who died at Cumae in 176 B.C. while on a pilgrimage to the temple of the Alban Mount.

usual sham Perugino. *The Madonna with Child,* in the church of Santa Maria, is now attributed to Roman-born Umbrian painter Antoniazzo Romano (active 1461–1508), who at times collaborated with Perugino. Attribution of Italian paintings was casual and unscholarly during much of the nineteenth century; after Bernard Berenson's more rigorous work on connoisseurship began in the 1890s, sham Peruginos became less frequent.

villeggiatura. Vacation.

beyond Ostia receiving the silver arrows of the sun upon its chased and burnished shield, and mighty Rome, to the north, lying at no great length in the idle immensity around it. The highway passes below Castel Gandolfo, which stands perched on an eminence behind a couple of gateways surmounted with the Papal tiara and twisted cordon; and I have more than once chosen the roundabout road for the sake of passing beneath these pompous insignia. Castel Gandolfo is indeed an ecclesiastical village and under the peculiar protection of the Popes, whose huge summer-palace rises in the midst of it like a rural Vatican. In speaking of the road to Frascati I necessarily revert to my first impressions, gathered on the occasion of the feast of the Annunziata, which falls on the 25th of March and is celebrated by a peasants' fair. As Murray strongly recommends you to visit this spectacle, at which you are promised a brilliant exhibition of all the costumes of modern Latium, I took an early train to Frascati and measured, in company with a prodigious stream of humble pedestrians, the half-hour's interval to Grotta Ferrata, where the fair is held. The road winds along the hillside, among the silver-sprinkled olives and through a charming wood where the ivy seemed tacked upon the oaks by women's fingers and the birds were singing to the late anemones. It was covered with a very jolly crowd of vulgar pleasure-takers, and the only creatures not in a state of manifest hilarity were the pitiful little overladen, overbeaten donkeys (who surely deserve a chapter to themselves in any description of these neighbourhoods) and the horrible beggars who were thrusting their sores and stumps at you from under every tree. Every one was shouting, singing, scrambling, making light of dust and distance and filling the air with that childlike jollity which the blessed Italian temperament never goes roundabout to conceal. There is no crowd surely at once so jovial and so gentle as an Italian crowd, and I doubt if in any other country the tightly packed third-class car in which I went out from Rome would have introduced me to so much smiling and so little swearing. Grotta Ferrata is a very dirty little village, with a number of raw new houses baking on the hot hillside and nothing to charm the fond gazer but its situation and its old fortified abbey. After pushing about among

---

peasants' fair . . . Murray strongly recommends. "Travellers should endeavor to attend the Fair held here on the 25th of March, to see the varied costumes of the peasantry of the environs" (Murray, 8th edition, 1867, 386); the fair, called "la fiera di Carne suina," or Pork Fair, has continued to be held in recent years.

Grotta Ferrata . . . grey ecclesiastical stronghold. In the only Basilian monastery in the former Papal States, monks performed the service in Greek according to the Greek ritual. The monastery was founded by Saint Nilo in 1004 and fortified by Giuliano da Sangallo at the end of the sixteenth century.

the shabby little booths and declining a number of fabulous bargains in
tinware, shoes and pork, I was glad to retire to a comparatively uninvaded
corner of the abbey and divert myself with the view. This grey ecclesiastical
stronghold is a thoroughly scenic affair, hanging over the hillside on plunging foundations which bury themselves among the dense olives. It has massive round towers at the corners and a grass-grown moat, enclosing a church
and a monastery. The fore-court, within the abbatial gateway, now serves as
the public square of the village and in fair-time of course witnesses the best
of the fun. The best of the fun was to be found in certain great vaults and
cellars of the abbey, where wine was in free flow from gigantic hogsheads.
At the exit of these trickling grottos shady trellises of bamboo and gathered
twigs had been improvised, and under them a grand guzzling proceeded. All
of which was so in the fine old style that I was roughly reminded of the
wedding-feast of Gamacho. The banquet was far less substantial of course,
but it had a note as of immemorial manners that could n't fail to suggest
romantic analogies to a pilgrim from the land of no cooks. There was a feast
of reason close at hand, however, and I was careful to visit the famous
frescoes of Domenichino in the adjoining church. It sounds rather brutal
perhaps to say that, when I came back into the clamorous little piazza, the
sight of the peasants swilling down their sour wine appealed to me more
than the masterpieces—Murray calls them so—of the famous Bolognese. It
amounts after all to saying that I prefer Teniers to Domenichino; which I am
willing to let pass for the truth. The scene under the rickety trellises was the
more suggestive of Teniers that there were no costumes to make it too
Italian. Murray's attractive statement on this point was, like many of his
statements, much truer twenty years ago than to-day. Costume is gone or
fast going; I saw among the women not a single crimson bodice and not a
couple of classic head-cloths. The poorer sort, dressed in vulgar rags of no
fashion and colour, and the smarter ones in calico gowns and printed shawls
of the vilest modern fabric, had honoured their dusky tresses but with rich
applications of grease. The men are still in jackets and breeches, and, with

---

Gamacho. In Cervantes' *Don Quixote,* Gamacho or Camacho "the rich," whose lavish
wedding to the fair Quiteria was thwarted when the poor Basilio stole away the prospective
bride. Gamacho decided to continue the splendid feast without her.

I prefer Teniers to Domenichino. Work by the Belgian artist David Teniers (1610–90),
notable for his landscapes and peasant scenes, may be found in Rome at the Vatican Pinacoteca,
at the Galleria Spada, and at the Galleria Borghese. In "The Metropolitan Museum 1871
Purchase" James praises "every merit which we commonly attribute to those vivid portrayals of
rustic conviviality. . . . To drink and to dance, to dance and drink again, was for the imagination of Teniers the great formula of human life" (reprinted in *Painter's Eye,* 59). Domenico
Zampieri, called Domenichino (see following note), lived from 1581 to 1641.

their slouched and pointed hats and open-breasted shirts and rattling leather leggings, may remind one sufficiently of the Italian peasant as he figured in the woodcuts familiar to our infancy. After coming out of the church I found a delightful nook—a queer little terrace before a more retired and tranquil drinking-shop—where I called for a bottle of wine to help me to guess why I "drew the line" at Domenichino.

This little terrace was a capricious excrescence at the end of the piazza, itself simply a greater terrace; and one reached it, picturesquely, by ascending a short inclined plane of grass-grown cobble-stones and passing across a little dusky kitchen through whose narrow windows the light of the mighty landscape beyond touched up old earthen pots. The terrace was oblong and so narrow that it held but a single small table, placed lengthwise; yet nothing could be pleasanter than to place one's bottle on the polished parapet. Here you seemed by the time you had emptied it to be swinging forward into immensity—hanging poised above the Campagna. A beautiful gorge with a twinkling stream wandered down the hill far below you, beyond which Marino and Castel Gandolfo peeped above the trees. In front you could count the towers of Rome and the tombs of the Appian Way. I don't know that I came to any very distinct conclusion about Domenichino; but it was perhaps because the view was perfection that he struck me as more than ever mediocrity. And yet I don't think it was one's bottle of wine, either, that made one after all maudlin about him; it was the sense of the foolishly usurped in his tenure of fame, of the derisive in his ever having been put forward. To say so indeed savours of flogging a dead horse, but it is surely an unkind stroke of fate for him that Murray assures ten thousand Britons every winter in the most emphatic manner that his Communion of St. Jerome is the "second finest picture in the world." If this were so one would certainly here in Rome, where such institutions are convenient, retire into the very nearest convent; with such a world one would have a standing quarrel. And yet this sport of destiny is an interesting case, in default of being an interesting painter, and I would take a moderate walk, in most moods, to see one of his pictures. He is so supremely good an example of effort detached from inspiration and school-merit divorced from spontane-

---

"second finest picture" . . . David or the Chase of Diana or the red-nosed Persian Sibyl. Adjoining the abbey of Grottaferrata is the church of Santa Maria, where frescoes by Domenichino depict the lives of Saints Nilo and Bartolomeo. In 1884 Murray writes of the Vatican's *Communion of Saint Jerome,* "This magnificent work, the undoubted masterpiece of Domenichino, is generally considered second only to the Transfiguration of Raphael, opposite which it stands" (285). The *Triumph of David* is in the Museo Civico e Pinacoteca in the Palazzo Malatesta at Fano, near Pesaro; the other two works are found at the Villa Borghese in Rome.

ity, that one of his fine frigid performances ought to hang in a conspicuous place in every academy of design. Few things of the sort contain more urgent lessons or point a more precious moral; and I would have the head-master in the drawing-school take each ingenuous pupil by the hand and lead him up to the Triumph of David or the Chase of Diana or the red-nosed Persian Sibyl and make him some such little speech as the following: "This great picture, my son, was hung here to show you how you must *never* paint; to give you a perfect specimen of what in its boundless generosity the providence of nature created for our fuller knowledge—an artist whose development was a negation. The great thing in art is charm, and the great thing in charm is spontaneity. Domenichino, having talent, is here and there an excellent model—he was devoted, conscientious, observant, industrious; but now that we've seen pretty well what can simply be learned do its best, these things help him little with us, because his imagination was cold. It loved nothing, it lost itself in nothing, its efforts never gave it the heart-ache. It went about trying this and that, concocting cold pictures after cold receipts, dealing in the second-hand, in the ready-made, and putting into its performances a little of everything but itself. When you see so many things in a composition you might suppose that among them all some charm might be born; yet they're really but the hundred mouths through which you may hear the unhappy thing murmur 'I'm dead!' It's by the simplest thing it has that a picture lives—by its temper. Look at all the great talents, Domenichino as well as at Titian; but think less of dogma than of plain nature, and I can almost promise you that yours will remain true." This is very little to what the æsthetic sage I have imagined *might* say; and we are after all unwilling to let our last verdict be an unkind one on any great bequest of human effort. The faded frescoes in the chapel at Grotta Ferrata leave us a memory the more of man's effort to dream beautifully; and they thus mingle harmoniously enough with our multifold impressions of Italy, where dreams and realities have both kept such pace and so strangely diverged. It was absurd—that was the truth—to be critical at all among the appealing old Italianisms round me and to treat the poor exploded Bolognese more harshly than, when I walked back to Frascati, I treated the charming old water-works of the Villa Aldobrandini. I confound these various products of antiquated art in a genial absolution, and should like especially to tell how fine it was to watch this prodigious fountain come tumbling down its channel of mouldy rock-work, through its magnificent vista of ilex, to the fantas-

---

water-works of the Villa Aldobrandini. The Villa Belvedere Aldobrandini, at Frascati, where magnificent fountains proliferate and where elaborate water systems turned mechanical organs to create a sort of music; in recent years the fountains have been dry and in need of repair.

tic old hemicycle where a dozen tritons and naiads sit posturing to receive it. The sky above the ilexes was incredibly blue and the ilexes themselves incredibly black; and to see the young white moon peeping above the trees you could easily have fancied it was midnight. I should like furthermore to expatiate on Villa Mondragone, the most grandly impressive hereabouts, of all such domestic monuments. The great Casino in the midst is as big as the Vatican, which it strikingly resembles, and it stands perched on a terrace as vast as the parvise of St. Peter's, looking straight away over black cypress-tops into the shining vastness of the Campagna. Everything somehow seemed immense and solemn; there was nothing small but certain little nestling blue shadows on the Sabine Mountains, to which the terrace seems to carry you wonderfully near. The place has been for some time lost to private uses, since it figures fantastically in a novel of George Sand—*La Daniella*—and now, in quite another way, as a Jesuit college for boys. The afternoon was perfect, and as it waned it filled the dark alleys with a wonderful golden haze. Into this came leaping and shouting a herd of little collegians with a couple of long-skirted Jesuits striding at their heels. We all know—I make the point for my antithesis—the monstrous practices of these people; yet as I watched the group I verily believe I declared that if I had a little son he should go to Mondragone and receive their crooked teachings for the sake of the other memories, the avenues of cypress and ilex, the view of the Campagna, the atmosphere of antiquity. But doubtless when a sense of "mere character," shameless incomparable character, has brought one to this it is time one should pause.

[1873.]

Villa Mondragone . . . a novel of George Sand—*La Daniella*— . . . in quite another way. At Frascati, the villa, which had belonged to the Borghese family, was a Jesuit seminary when James wrote. George Sand, however, used it as part of the setting for *La Daniella*, superficially the tale of a Frascati laundress and a French artist, but more memorable for its strident antipapist voice. The sense of the Villa Mondragone in the novel is indeed somewhat fantastic: "Imaginez-vous un château qui a trois cent soixante quatorze fenêtres, un château compliqué comme ceux d'Ann Radcliffe, un monde d'énigmes à débrouiller, un enchaînement de surprises, un rêve de Piranèse" (George Sand, *La Daniella*, I, 271–72) [Imagine here a castle with 374 windows, a castle intricate as any in Ann Radcliffe, a world of enigmas waiting to be unfolded, a chain of surprises, a dream out of Piranesi.] In James's 1889 "The Solution," an important meeting takes place at the Villa Mondragone (*Tales*, VII, 389).

Jesuit college . . . monstrous practices of these people. Although there was great anti-Jesuit sentiment during the nineteenth century, the intention here seems ironic; in reviews of Francis Parkman's *The Jesuits in North America in the Seventeenth Century* (1867) and *The Old Régime in Canada* (1874), James speaks highly both of the Jesuits' moral firmness and of their work: "When one can boast of such miracles as these, what is the use of insisting on disease cured by the touch of saintly bones" (*Literary Criticism: Essays on Literature*, 568–79).

The After-Season in Rome

One may at the blest end of May say without injustice to any-body that the state of mind of many a *forestiero* in Rome is one of intense impatience for the moment when all other *forestieri* shall have taken themselves off. One may confess to this state of mind and be no misanthrope. The place has passed so completely for the winter months into the hands of the barbarians that that estimable character the passionate pilgrim finds it constantly harder to keep his passion clear. He has a rueful sense of impressions perverted and adulterated; the all-venerable visage disconcerts us by a vain eagerness to see itself mirrored in English, American, German eyes. It is n't simply that you are never first or never alone at the classic or historic spots where you have dreamt of persuad-ing the shy *genius loci* into confidential utterance; it is n't simply that St. Peter's, the Vatican, the Palatine, are for ever ringing with the false note of the languages without style: it is the general oppressive feeling that the city of the soul has become for the time a monstrous mixture of watering-place and curiosity-shop and that its most ardent life is that of the tourists who haggle over false intaglios and yawn through palaces and temples. But you are told of a happy time when these abuses begin to pass away, when Rome becomes Rome again and you may have her all to yourself. "You may like her more or less now," I was assured at the height of the season; "but you must wait till the month of May, when she'll give you *all* she has, to love her. Then the foreigners, or the excess of them, are gone; the galleries and ruins

[Originally published (unsigned) in the *Nation*, XVI (12 June 1873), 399–400; reprinted in *Transatlantic Sketches*, 1875.]

are empty, and the place," said my informant, who was a happy Frenchman of the Académie de France, "*renaît à elle-même.*" Indeed I was haunted all winter by an irresistible prevision of what Rome *must* be in declared spring. Certain charming places seemed to murmur: "Ah, this is nothing! Come back at the right weeks and see the sky above us almost black with its excess of blue, and the new grass already deep, but still vivid, and the white roses tumble in odorous spray and the warm radiant air distil gold for the smelting-pot that the *genius loci* then dips his brush into before making play with it, in his inimitable way, for the general effect of complexion."

A month ago I spent a week in the country, and on my return, the first time I approached the Corso, became conscious of a change. Something delightful had happened, to which at first I could n't give a name, but which presently shone out as the fact that there were but half as many people present and that these were chiefly the natural or the naturalised. We had been docked of half our irrelevance, our motley excess, and now physically, morally, æsthetically there was elbow-room. In the afternoon I went to the Pincio, and the Pincio was almost dull. The band was playing to a dozen ladies who lay in landaus poising their lace-fringed parasols; but they had scarce more than a light-gloved dandy apiece hanging over their carriage doors. By the parapet to the great terrace that sweeps the city stood but three or four interlopers looking at the sunset and with their Baedekers only just showing in their pockets—the sunsets not being down among the tariffed articles in these precious volumes. I went so far as to hope for them that, like myself, they were, under every precaution, taking some amorous intellectual liberty with the scene.

Practically I violate thus the instinct of monopoly, since it's a shame not to publish that Rome in May is indeed exquisitely worth your patience. I have just been so gratified at finding myself in undisturbed possession for a couple of hours of the Museum of the Lateran that I can afford to be magnanimous. It's almost as if the old all-papal paradise had come back. The weather for a month has been perfect, the sky an extravagance of blue, the air lively enough, the nights cool, nippingly cool, and the whole ancient greyness lighted with an irresistible smile. Rome, which in some moods, especially to new-comers, seems a place of almost sinister gloom, has an occasional art, as one knows her better, of brushing away care by the grand

---

happy Frenchman . . . Académie de France, "*renaît à elle-même.*" This remark—that Rome returns to herself again—and the identification of M. Hébert (see page 185 and note below) is given in a letter of 10 February 1873 to Alice James (*Letters*, I, 337–39).

Museum of the Lateran. In 1970 the Lateran collections were moved to the newly built Museo Paolino at the Vatican.

gesture with which some splendid impatient mourning matron—just the Niobe of Nations, surviving, emerging and looking about her again—might pull off and cast aside an oppression of muffling crape. This admirable power still temperamentally to react and take notice lurks in all her darkness and dirt and decay—a something more careless and hopeless than our thrifty northern cheer, and yet more genial and urbane than the Parisian spirit of *blague*. The collective Roman nature is a healthy and hearty one, and you feel it abroad in the streets even when the sirocco blows and the medium of life seems to proceed more or less from the mouth of a furnace. But who shall analyse even the simplest Roman impression? It is compounded of so many things, it says so much, it involves so much, it so quickens the intelligence and so flatters the heart, that before we fairly grasp the case the imagination has marked it for her own and exposed us to a perilous likelihood of talking nonsense about it.

The smile of Rome, as I have called it, and its insidious message to those who incline to ramble irresponsibly and take things as they come, is ushered in with the first breath of spring, and then grows and grows with the advancing season till it wraps the whole place in its tenfold charm. As the process develops you can do few better things than go often to Villa Borghese and sit on the grass—on a stout bit of drapery—and watch its exquisite stages. It has a frankness and a sweetness beyond any relenting of *our* clumsy climates even when ours leave off their damnable faces and begin. Nature departs from every reserve with a confidence that leaves one at a loss where, as it were, to look—leaves one, as I say, nothing to do but to lay one's head among the anemones at the base of a high-stemmed pine and gaze up crestward and skyward along its slanting silvery column. You may watch the whole business from a dozen of these choice standpoints and have a different villa for it every day in the week. The Doria, the Ludovisi, the Medici, the Albani, the Wolkonski, the Chigi, the Mellini, the Massimo—there are more of them, with all their sights and sounds and odours and memories, than you have senses for. But I prefer none of them to the Borghese, which is free to all the world at all times and yet never crowded; for when the whirl of carriages is great in the middle regions you may find a hundred untrodden spots and silent corners, tenanted at the worst by a

---

The Doria, the Ludovisi, the Medici, the Albani, the Wolkonski, the Chigi, the Mellini, the Massimo, . . . the Borghese. See the Introduction, page xvii, for the status of the first eight villas James names. The Villa Borghese has been preserved. It now belongs to the Comune of Rome and since 1902 has been known as the greatest Roman public park; the Casino Borghese houses the famous Galleria Borghese, closed for major restoration early in 1984 but gradually reopening to the public.

group of those long-skirted young Propagandists who stalk about with solemn angularity, each with a book under his arm, like silhouettes from a mediæval missal, and "compose" so extremely well with the still more processional cypresses and with stretches of golden-russet wall overtopped by ultramarine. And yet if the Borghese is good the Medici is strangely charming, and you may stand in the little belvedere which rises with such surpassing oddity out of the dusky heart of the Boschetto at the latter establishment—a miniature presentation of the wood of the Sleeping Beauty—and look across at the Ludovisi pines lifting their crooked parasols into a sky of what a painter would call the most morbid blue, and declare that the place where *they* grow is the most delightful in the world. Villa Ludovisi has been all winter the residence of the lady familiarly known in Roman society as "Rosina," Victor Emmanuel's morganatic wife, the only familiarity, it would seem, that she allows, for the grounds were rigidly closed, to the inconsolable regret of old Roman sojourners. Just as the nightingales began to sing, however, the quasi-august *padrona* departed, and the public, with certain restrictions, have been admitted to hear them. The place takes, where it lies, a princely ease, and there could be no better example of the expansive tendencies of ancient privilege than the fact that its whole vast extent is contained by the city walls. It has in this respect very much the same enviable air of having got up early that marks the great intramural demesne of Magdalen College at Oxford. The stern old ramparts of Rome form the outer enclosure of the villa, and hence a series of "striking scenic effects" which it would be unscrupulous flattery to say you can imagine. The grounds are laid out in the formal last-century manner; but nowhere do the straight black cypresses lead off the gaze into vistas of a melancholy more charged with associations—poetic, romantic, historic; nowhere are there grander, smoother walls of laurel and myrtle.

---

what a painter would call the most morbid blue. See "de turquoise malade," page 81 and note.

"Rosina," Victor Emmanuel's morganatic wife. Hapsburg archduchess Adelaide, first wife of Sardinian King Vittorio Emanuele (1820–78), died in 1855, after bearing eight children. In 1861 Victor Emmanuel became the first king of the united Italy, and in 1869 he married his mistress, Rosa Vercellone, after creating her the Contessa Mirafiori e Fontanafredda. This detail concerning a king's mistress may reflect on the degree of suspicion raised, in *The Europeans* (1878), by the revelation of the "morganatic" marriage between the Baroness Eugenia-Camilla-Delores Young Münster and the Prince Adolf of Silberstadt-Schreckenstein. Although fully recognized by the Church, a morganatic marriage, one between parties of unequal rank, conferred hereditary rights neither of title nor of property; strictly referring to a form of German marriage, it is used with precision in *The Europeans* and with latitude in *Italian Hours*.

I recently spent an afternoon hour at the little Protestant cemetery close to St. Paul's Gate, where the ancient and the modern world are insidiously contrasted. They make between them one of the solemn places of Rome—although indeed when funereal things are so interfused it seems ungrateful to call them sad. Here is a mixture of tears and smiles, of stones and flowers, of mourning cypresses and radiant sky, which gives us the impression of our looking back at death from the brighter side of the grave. The cemetery nestles in an angle of the city wall, and the older graves are sheltered by a mass of ancient brickwork, through whose narrow loopholes you peep at the wide purple of the Campagna. Shelley's grave is here, buried in roses—a happy grave every way for the very type and figure of the Poet. Nothing could be more impenetrably tranquil than this little corner in the bend of the protecting rampart, where a cluster of modern ashes is held tenderly in the rugged hand of the Past. The past is tremendously embodied in the hoary pyramid of Caius Cestius, which rises hard by, half within the wall and half without, cutting solidly into the solid blue of the sky and casting its pagan shadow upon the grass of English graves—that of Keats, among them—with an effect of poetic justice. It is a wonderful confusion of mortality and a grim enough admonition of our helpless promiscuity in the crucible of time. But the most touching element of all is the appeal of the pious English inscriptions among all these Roman memories; touching because of their universal expression of that trouble within trouble, misfortune in a foreign land. Something special stirs the heart through the fine Scriptural language in which everything is recorded. The echoes of massive Latinity with which the atmosphere is charged suggest nothing more majestic and monumental. I may seem unduly to refine, but the injunction to the reader in the monument

---

little Protestant cemetery . . . Shelley's grave . . . Keats. Near the Porta San Paolo, beside the twelfth-century B.C. pyramid tomb of the praetorian Caius Cestius, the so-called Protestant Cemetery—although in fact founded in 1738 for any non-Catholics—is made up of an old and a new graveyard. Keats died in Rome in September 1821 and his remains were buried in the old cemetery—beneath the bitter inscription he had written for himself: "Here lies One / Whose Name was writ in water." In 1822 Shelley drowned in the gulf of La Spezia; his body was cremated and his heart removed by Leigh Hunt. Although it was Shelley's ashes that found rest at the Protestant Cemetery (his heart was taken to England), the stone over his remains bears the inscription "Cor Cordium," heart of hearts.

In 1878 James interred his heroine Daisy Miller at the Protestant Cemetery; in 1894, in Venice, his close friend Constance Fenimore Woolson apparently committed suicide, and, according to her request, her remains were brought here. During his final visit to Rome in 1907, James found the site of Miss Woolson's grave "the most beautiful thing in Italy. . . . [T]he exquisite summer luxuriance and perfect tendance of that spot—I mean of course that very particular spot—below the great grey wall, the cypresses and the time-silvered Pyramid. It is tremendously, inexhaustibly touching—its effect never fails to overwhelm" (*Letters*, IV, 460).

to Miss Bathurst, drowned in the Tiber in 1824, "If thou art young and lovely, build not thereon, for she who lies beneath thy feet in death was the loveliest flower ever cropt in its bloom," affects us irresistibly as a case for tears on the spot. The whole elaborate inscription indeed says something over and beyond all it does say. The English have the reputation of being the most reticent people in the world, and as there is no smoke without fire I suppose they have done something to deserve it; yet who can say that one does n't constantly meet the most startling examples of the insular faculty to "gush"? In this instance the mother of the deceased takes the public into her confidence with surprising frankness and omits no detail, seizing the opportunity to mention by the way that she had already lost her husband by a most mysterious visitation. The appeal to one's attention and the confidence in it are withal most moving. The whole record has an old-fashioned gentility that makes its frankness tragic. You seem to hear the garrulity of passionate grief.

To be choosing these positive commonplaces of the Roman tone for a theme when there are matters of modern moment going on may seem none the less to require an apology. But I make no claim to your special correspondent's faculty for getting an "inside" view of things, and I have hardly more than a pictorial impression of the Pope's illness and of the discussion of the

---

monument to Miss Bathurst. James slightly misquotes—and improves upon—the inscription. In 1909 he chooses not to add to the original 1873 passage any mention of the fact that the tomb of Rosa Bathurst is located a few feet to the right of Constance Fenimore Woolson's grave, near Shelley's remains. The visitor to the Bathurst monument, which was well known during the nineteenth century, can still read the lengthy inscription that was composed by the young girl's mother, in both English and Italian:

Beneath this stone are interred the remains of ROSA BATHURST who was accidently drowned in the Tiber on the 11 of March 1824, whilst on a riding party, owing to the swollen state of the river and her spirited horse taking flight. She was the daughter of BENJAMIN BATHURST whose disappearance when on a special mission to Vienna some years since was as tragical as unaccountable: no positive account of his death ever having been received by his distracted wife. He was lost at twenty-six years of age. His daughter who inherited her father's perfections, both personal and mental[,] had completed her sixteenth year when she perished by as disastrous a fate.

Reader

whosoever thou art, who may pause to peruse this tale of sorrows, let this awful lesson of the instability of human happiness sink deep in thy mind. If thou art young and lovely, build not thereon, for she who sleeps in death under thy feet was the loveliest flower ever cropt in its bloom. She was everything that the fondest heart could desire or the eye covet, the joy, the hope of her widowed mother who erects this poor memorial of her irreparable loss. "Early, bright, transient, chaste, as morning dew." "She sparkled, was exhaled, and went to heaven."

Pope's illness. Pius IX was to live for five more years, but in 1873, first during April and then during May, he was struck down by two bouts of rheumatic disorder so severe that the hostile

Law of the Convents. Indeed I am afraid to speak of the Pope's illness at all, lest I should say something egregiously heartless about it, recalling too forcibly that unnatural husband who was heard to wish that his wife would "either" get well——! He had his reasons, and Roman tourists have theirs in the shape of a vague longing for something spectacular at St. Peter's. If it takes the sacrifice of somebody to produce it let somebody then be sacrificed. Meanwhile we have been having a glimpse of the spectacular side of the Religious Corporations Bill. Hearing one morning a great hubbub in the Corso I stepped forth upon my balcony. A couple of hundred men were strolling slowly down the street with their hands in their pockets, shouting in unison "Abbasso il ministero!" and huzzaing in chorus. Just beneath my window they stopped and began to murmur "Al Quirinale, al Quirinale!"

---

government reported he was dying and even dead. Church officials, intensely aware of the high level of animosity felt by the people of Rome, began making plans for a conclave outside Italy (Halperin, 307ff.).

Law of the Convents . . . Religious Corporations Bill. When in 1848 Pope Pius IX withdrew support of the crusade against the occupying Austrians, he roused much resentment against the Church. A republican uprising drove him from Rome, but he was restored by French troops under Napoleon III, and until 1859 his power—and his territories—remained virtually undisturbed. Thereafter, however, revolutions and military occupations caused the loss of many papal holdings in central Italy, most of which passed into the hands of the House of Savoy; in 1866 and 1867, bills were enacted that reduced the autonomy of the convents, the monasteries, the schools, and most other church institutions.

The provisions of these bills, generally referred to as the seizure of the States of the Church (1870)—James seems to derive his unofficial designation from a 24 January 1873 article in *La Capitale*, "Le Vendite dei Beni delle corporazioni religiose"—were more or less ignored until 1872, when moves were made to suppress recalcitrant religious organizations and to eliminate university chairs of theology. In his Roman journals the German historian Ferdinand Gregorovius recognized the pivotal nature of this turn of events. The vocal crowds that James observed were ecclesiastical supporters who strongly opposed the government's attempt to divest religious corporations of their juridical personality; the protests were, however, largely unsuccessful and the government soon put civil administrators in charge of the formerly religious schools, hospitals, and orphanages, and then moved to suppress convents and monasteries, selling them or converting them to prisons or schools. Eventually pensions were initiated for nuns and monks, and at one point the pope himself was offered a yearly stipend—one that he rejected (Massé, 149–55). *La Capitale* (see pages 123, 137, and notes), the "profanely radical sheet," actually felt the state's actions were insufficient and made the extreme and erroneous claim that the hateful church was systematically sending abroad its most precious artistic treasures and financial holdings, leaving behind denuded ecclesiastical buildings and emptied coffers.

"Al Quirinale, al Quirinale!" The Palazzo del Quirinale was a symbol of discord between church and state toward the end of the nineteenth century. Since 1585 it had been a papal summer home, its nature distinct from that of the two other Roman papal residences in that the Quirinale was identified with the pope's temporal or political authority, while the residences at

The crowd surged a moment gently and then drifted to the Quirinal, where it scuffled harmlessly with half-a-dozen of the king's soldiers. It ought to have been impressive, for what was it, strictly, unless the seeds of revolution? But its carriage was too gentle and its cries too musical to send the most timorous tourist to packing his trunk. As I began with saying: in Rome, in May, everything has an amiable side, even popular uprisings.

[1873.]

---

the Lateran and the Vatican called up fundamentally religious associations. In 1870, during the critical struggle between the Church and the Italian government, the palazzo was given over— in spite of considerable opposition voiced by parties loyal to the papacy—to the first king of the united Italy, Victor Emmanuel II, as his official residence; since 1947 it has been the state residence of the President of the Republic.

From a Roman Note-Book

December 28, 1872.—In Rome again for the last three days— that second visit which, when the first is n't followed by a fatal illness in Florence, the story goes that one is doomed to pay. I did n't drink of the Fountain of Trevi on the eve of departure the other time; but I feel as if I had drunk of the Tiber itself. Nevertheless as I drove from the station in the evening I wondered what I should think of it at this first glimpse had n't I already known it. All manner of evil perhaps. Paris, as I passed along the Boulevards three evenings before to take the train, was swarming and glittering as befits a great capital. Here, in the black, narrow, crooked, empty streets, I saw nothing I would fain regard as eternal. But there were new gas-lamps round the spouting Triton in Piazza Barberini and a newspaper stall on the corner of the Condotti and the Corso—salient signs of the emancipated state. An hour later I walked up to Via Gregoriana by Piazza di Spagna. It was all silent and deserted, and the great flight of steps looked surprisingly small. Everything seemed meagre, dusky, provincial. Could Rome after all really *be* a world-city? That queer old rococo garden gateway at the top of the Gregoriana stirred a dormant memory; it awoke

[Originally published in the *Galaxy,* XVI (November 1873), 679–86; reprinted in *Transatlantic Sketches,* 1875; reprinted in *Foreign Parts,* 1883.]

queer old rococo garden gateway . . . dormant memory . . . crimson drawing-room. In 1872, on Christmas morning, James wrote to his father from the "little crimson drawing room" of Aunt Mary and Edward Tweedy's apartment at 33, Via Gregoriana (*Letters,* I, 315–16). The adjacent Palazzetto Zuccari, called the "casa dei mostri," with a central portal and windows in the form of the mouths of monsters, is part of the present-day Bibliotheca Hertziana, the preeminent Roman library for the study of Italian art and travel, as is the Tweedy dwelling. It

into a consciousness of the delicious mildness of the air, and very soon, in a little crimson drawing-room, I was reconciled and re-initiated. . . . Everything is dear (in the way of lodgings), but it hardly matters, as everything is taken and some one else paying for it. I must make up my mind to a bare perch. But it seems poorly perverse here to aspire to an "interior" or to be conscious of the economic side of life. The æsthetic is so intense that you feel you should live on the taste of it, should extract the nutritive essence of the atmosphere. For positively it's *such* an atmosphere! The weather is perfect, the sky as blue as the most exploded tradition fames it, the whole air glowing and throbbing with lovely colour. . . . The glitter of Paris is now all gaslight. And oh the monotonous miles of rain-washed asphalte!

December 30th.—I have had nothing to do with the "ceremonies." In fact I believe there have hardly been any—no midnight mass at the Sistine chapel, no silver trumpets at St. Peter's. Everything is remorselessly clipped and curtailed—the Vatican in deepest mourning. But I saw it in its superbest scarlet in '69. . . . I went yesterday with L. to the Colonna gardens—an adventure that would have reconverted me to Rome if the thing were n't already done. It's a rare old place—rising in mouldy bosky terraces and

---

has been the residence of many distinguished visitors, among them Sir Joshua Reynolds, Raphael Meng, and Winckelmann, and it is named as the residence of D'Annunzio's protagonist in *Il Piacere*.

Everything is remorselessly clipped and curtailed . . . in '69. James had visited Rome in 1869, a year before the papacy lost Rome to the kingdom of Italy. See Introduction, pages xiv–xvii.

I went yesterday with L. Lizzie Boott, remembered in the 1914 *Notes of a Son and Brother* as the "markedly *produced* Lizzie. This delightful girl, educated, accomplished, toned above all, as from steeping in a rich old medium, to a degree of the rarest among her coevals 'on our side,' " was the daughter of the old family friend and Florentine expatriate Francis Boott; these late recollections—after Lizzie's tragic death in 1888 ("quenched in the void")—do not suggest his impression of her in 1880, when, in a letter to his father, he reports that "Lizzie is if possible even more mouselike" (*Letters*, II, 277). James often expressed genuine fondness for the Bootts, yet in *Notes* he recalls that when he sought a model for Gilbert Osmond, an "Italianate bereft American with a little moulded daughter in the setting of a massive old Tuscan residence," he "shouldn't have had the Gilbert Osmonds at all without the early 'form' of the Frank Bootts" (reprinted in *Henry James Autobiography*, 519–22).

James's use of initials (L., H., L. B., S., R. W. E., etc.) to indicate the identities of his acquaintants is a unique feature of this essay as reprinted in 1909. In the original 1873 *Galaxy* publication, and in the reprinted version of *Transatlantic Sketches*, greater anonymity was maintained: references were made to "X.," to "Z.," to "my companion," to "Mr. E." for Ralph Waldo Emerson (R. W. E.), and upon occasion a blank space was left in the place of a specific name. See A Note on the Text.

Colonna gardens. Now closed to the public.

mossy stairways and winding walks from the back of the palace to the top of the Quirinal. It's the grand style of gardening, and resembles the present natural manner as a chapter of Johnsonian rhetoric resembles a piece of clever contemporary journalism. But it's a better style in horticulture than in literature; I prefer one of the long-drawn blue-green Colonna vistas, with a maimed and mossy-coated garden goddess at the end, to the finest possible quotation from a last-century classic. Perhaps the best thing there is the old orangery with its trees in fantastic terra-cotta tubs. The late afternoon light was gilding the monstrous jars and suspending golden chequers among the golden-fruited leaves. Or perhaps the best thing is the broad terrace with its mossy balustrade and its benches; also its view of the great naked Torre di Nerone (I think), which might look stupid if the rosy brickwork did n't take such a colour in the blue air. Delightful, at any rate, to stroll and talk there in the afternoon sunshine.

January 2nd, 1873.—Two or three drives with A.—one to St. Paul's without the Walls and back by a couple of old churches on the Aventine. I was freshly struck with the rare distinction of the little Protestant cemetery at the Gate, lying in the shadow of the black sepulchral Pyramid and the thick-growing black cypresses. Bathed in the clear Roman light the place is heart-breaking for what it asks you—in such a world as *this*—to renounce. If it should "make one in love with death to lie there," that's only if death should be conscious. As the case stands, the weight of a tremendous past presses upon the flowery sod, and the sleeper's mortality feels the contact of all the mortality with which the brilliant air is tainted. . . . The restored Basilica is incredibly splendid. It seems a last pompous effort of formal Catholicism, and there are few more striking emblems of later Rome—the Rome foredoomed to see Victor Emmanuel in the Quirinal, the Rome of

---

Torre di Nerone . . . might look stupid. The Torre delle Milizie, odd looking because it leans and only claims two-thirds of its original height, was built by Gregory IX in the thirteenth century; nonetheless, popular belief held that this was the tower from which Nero watched Rome burn.

Two or three drives with A. Aunt Mary Tweedy, mentioned in a letter of 8 January 1873 as generously providing a coach for excursions near Rome (*Letters,* I, 321).

black sepulchral Pyramid . . . "make one in love with death to lie there." Shelley, in the preface to "Adonais," describes the grave of Keats in the old section of the Protestant Cemetery: "It might make one in love with death, to think that one should be buried in so sweet a place"; Shelley's own remains would be brought to the same cemetery in 1822; see also page 173 and note. The soot-blackened tomb of Caius Cestius has been restored to its original whiteness.

restored Basilica. San Paolo fuori le Mura; see page 135 and note.

abortive councils and unheeded anathemas. It rises there, gorgeous and useless, on its miasmatic site, with an air of conscious bravado—a florid advertisement of the superabundance of faith. Within it's magnificent, and its magnificence has no shabby spots—a rare thing in Rome. Marble and mosaic, alabaster and malachite, lapis and porphyry, incrust it from pavement to cornice and flash back their polished lights at each other with such a splendour of effect that you seem to stand at the heart of some immense prismatic crystal. One has to come to Italy to know marbles and love them. I remember the fascination of the first great show of them I met in Venice—at the Scalzi and Gesuiti. Colour has in no other form so cool and unfading a purity and lustre. Softness of tone and hardness of substance—is n't that the sum of the artist's desire? G., with his beautiful caressing, open-lipped Roman utterance, so easy to understand and, to my ear, so finely suggestive of genuine Latin, not our horrible Anglo-Saxon and Protestant kind, urged upon us the charms of a return by the Aventine and the sight of a couple of old churches. The best is Santa Sabina, a very fine old structure of the fifth century, mouldering in its dusky solitude and consuming its own antiquity. What a massive heritage Christianity and Catholicism are leaving here! What a substantial fact, in all its decay, this memorial Christian temple outliving its uses among the sunny gardens and vineyards! It has a noble nave, filled with a stale smell which (like that of the onion) brought tears to my eyes, and bordered with twenty-four fluted marble columns of Pagan origin. The crudely primitive little mosaics along the entablature are ex-

---

G., with his beautiful caressing, open-lipped Roman utterance . . . genuine Latin. Aunt Mary's "most affable coachman"—perhaps a Giovanni, a Giuseppe, or a Giovanelli—"who talks, not Italian, but Roman—delicious stately full-lipped *Latin*" (*Letters*, I, 321). *Romanesco*, the Roman dialect, was widely spoken in Latium throughout the nineteenth century, and it has not disappeared entirely today; sometimes *romanesco* was translated as "old Roman" (*Encyclopedia Britannica,* 11th edition, XIV, 897, "Italian Language"; bibliographic item, "Notes on old Roman," by E. Monaci), the term ambiguously used in *The Golden Bowl* to describe the peculiar Italian spoken by Charlotte and Amerigo in the Bloomsbury antique shop: "They had had between them often in talk the refrain, jocosely, descriptively applied, of 'old Roman' " (book I, chapter VI).

Santa Sabina . . . massive heritage . . . columns of Pagan origin. On the Aventine hill, site of the house of Sabina, a noble Roman matron martyred under Hadrian, the church was built from 422 to 432. Gregory the Great preached here, as did Saint Dominic, and when Saint Hyacinth heard him, he became a missionary. Saint Thomas Aquinas came here to begin the monastic life, and Michele Ghislieri, later Pius V, stayed for years when he came as a pilgrim. Saint Francis is said to have spent many nights here, conversing with Saint Dominic. In 1287, during a conclave at Santa Sabina to elect Pope Honorius IV, six cardinals were stricken and died of malaria. The pagan columns that James notes were thought to have come from the neighboring Temple of Juno or Isis.

tremely curious. A Dominican monk, still young, who showed us the church, seemed a creature generated from its musty shadows and odours. His physiognomy was wonderfully *de l'emploi,* and his voice, most agreeable, had the strangest jaded humility. His lugubrious salute and sanctimonious impersonal appropriation of my departing franc would have been a master-touch on the stage. While we were still in the church a bell rang that he had to go and answer, and as he came back and approached us along the nave he made with his white gown and hood and his cadaverous face, against the dark church background, one of those pictures which, thank the Muses, have not yet been reformed out of Italy. It was the exact illustration, for insertion in a text, of heaven knows how many old romantic and conventional literary Italianisms—plays, poems, mysteries of Udolpho. We got back into the carriage and talked of profane things and went home to dinner—drifting recklessly, it seemed to me, from æsthetic luxury to social.

On the 31st we went to the musical vesper-service at the Gesù—hitherto done so splendidly before the Pope and the cardinals. The manner of it was eloquent of change—no Pope, no cardinals, and indifferent music; but a great *mise-en-scène* nevertheless. The church is gorgeous; late Renaissance, of great proportions, and full, like so many others, but in a pre-eminent degree, of seventeenth and eighteenth century Romanism. It does n't impress the imagination, but richly feeds the curiosity, by which I mean one's sense of the curious; suggests no legends, but innumerable anecdotes à la Stendhal. There is a vast dome, filled with a florid concave fresco of tumbling foreshortened angels, and all over the ceilings and cornices a wonderful outlay of dusky gildings and mouldings. There are various Bernini saints and seraphs in stucco-sculpture, astride of the tablets and door-tops, backing against their rusty machinery of coppery *nimbi* and egg-shaped cloudlets. Marble, damask and tapers in gorgeous profusion. The high altar a great

---

mysteries of Udolpho. The title of the gothic novel (1794) by Ann Radcliffe.

vesper-service . . . the Gesù . . . no Pope. Although the pope's participation in the service—outside the walls of the Vatican—was suspended after 1870, the Lateran Treaty of 1929 permitted him once again to enter Rome freely and lead the New Year's Eve Te Deum at the church of Il Gesù.

anecdotes à la Stendhal. Referring to the French novelist's belief that the "petit fait significatif" was of crucial importance. In his review of Paton's *Henry Beyle* (see note, page 87 above), James cites one of Stendhal's letters to his sister: "I like *examples,* and not, like Montesquieu, Buffon, and Rousseau, systems. . . . I need examples and facts. Write quickly, without seeking fine phrases. . . . Contribute to my knowledge of women, facts, facts!" (813). Stendhal's travel writing provided examples of particularly memorable anecdotal richness (for his remarks on Il Gesù, see *Promenades dans Rome,* VI, 200–201).

screen of twinkling chandeliers. The choir perched in a little loft high up in
the right transept, like a balcony in a side-scene at the opera, and indulging
in surprising roulades and flourishes. . . . Near me sat a handsome, opulent-
looking nun—possibly an abbess or prioress of noble lineage. Can a holy
woman of such a complexion listen to a fine operatic barytone in a sumptuous temple and receive none but ascetic impressions? What a cross-fire of
influences does Catholicism provide!

January 4th.—A drive with A. out of Porta San Giovanni and along Via
Appia Nuova. More and more beautiful as you get well away from the walls
and the great view opens out before you—the rolling green-brown dells and
flats of the Campagna, the long, disjointed arcade of the aqueducts, the
deep-shadowed blue of the Alban Hills, touched into pale lights by their
scattered towns. We stopped at the ruined basilica of San Stefano, an affair
of the fifth century, rather meaningless without a learned companion. But
the perfect little sepulchral chambers of the Pancratii, disinterred beneath
the church, tell their own tale—in their hardly dimmed frescoes, their beautiful sculptured coffin and great sepulchral slab. Better still the tomb of the
Valerii adjoining it—a single chamber with an arched roof, covered with
stucco mouldings perfectly intact, exquisite figures and arabesques as sharp
and delicate as if the plasterer's scaffold had just been taken from under
them. Strange enough to think of these things—so many of them as there
are—surviving their immemorial eclipse in this perfect shape and coming up
like long-lost divers from the sea of time.

January 16th.—A delightful walk last Sunday with F. to Monte Mario.
We drove to Porta Angelica, the little gate hidden behind the right wing of

---

ruined basilica of San Stefano. Often confused with the also-ancient San Stefano Rotondo,
undergoing extensive restoration during the 1980s, the rarely noted basilica of San Stefano, on
the Via Latina, remains in ruins.

Pancratii . . . Valerii. The Pancratii were one of the Roman burial societies commonly
formed during the third and fourth centuries to assure that the members of a guild would
receive a proper funeral, often with a requisite amount of pomp. The tomb of the Valerii was
founded, as its dedicatory inscription reports, by a certain Gaius Valerius Herma, for himself,
for his family, for his freedmen, freedwomen, and for all their descendants (photographs in
Andreae, 422–26).

In 1874 James published "The Last of the Valerii" (*Complete Tales*, III, 89–122); when a
mysterious and ancient statue of Juno is excavated from the grounds of Count Marco Valerio's
Roman estate, he becomes obsessive and begins to worship the "implacably grave" Juno, to the
deep distress of his wife, until finally she reburies the statue and regains her husband.

delightful walk last Sunday with F. Francis Boott and his daughter Lizzie had been among
James's hosts during the Christmas season in Rome; see page 177 and note.

Bernini's colonnade, and strolled thence up the winding road to the Villa Mellini, where one of the greasy peasants huddled under the wall in the sun admits you for half a franc into the finest old ilex-walk in Italy. It is all vaulted grey-green shade with blue Campagna stretches in the interstices. The day was perfect; the still sunshine, as we sat at the twisted base of the old trees, seemed to have the drowsy hum of midsummer—with that charm of Italian vegetation that comes to us as its confession of having scenically served, to weariness at last, for some pastoral these many centuries a classic. In a certain cheapness and thinness of substance—as compared with the English stoutness, never left athirst—it reminds me of our own, and it is relatively dry enough and pale enough to explain the contempt of many unimaginative Britons. But it has an idle abundance and wantonness, a romantic shabbiness and dishevelment. At the Villa Mellini is the famous lonely pine which "tells" so in the landscape from other points, bought off from the axe by (I believe) Sir George Beaumont, commemorated in a like connection in Wordsworth's great sonnet. He at least was not an unimaginative Briton. As you stand under it, its far-away shallow dome, supported on a single column almost white enough to be marble, seems to dwell in the dizziest depths of the blue. Its pale grey-blue boughs and its silvery stem make a wonderful harmony with the ambient air. The Villa Mellini is full of the elder Italy of one's imagination—the Italy of Boccaccio and Ariosto. There are twenty places where the Florentine story-tellers might have sat round on the grass. Outside the villa walls, beneath the overcrowding orange-boughs, straggled old Italy as well—but not in Boccaccio's velvet: a row of ragged and livid contadini, some simply stupid in their squalor, but some downright brigands of romance, or of reality, with matted locks and terribly sullen eyes.

A couple of days later I walked for old acquaintance' sake over to San Onofrio on the Janiculan. The approach is one of the dirtiest adventures in

　　Villa Mellini . . . famous lonely pine . . . Sir George Beaumont . . . Wordsworth's great sonnet. See pages xvii and 170 on the general disfigurement of the villa. The lone pine, today neither as magnificent nor as lonely as in Beaumont's or James's time, still stands, braced up by cables, next to a bar, and overlooks the city. English painter, collector, and patron Sir George Beaumont was a friend of Sir Joshua Reynolds, Constable, Coleridge, and Benjamin Haydon; in 1828 his bequeathal of sixteen important paintings was to form the core of the National Gallery in London. Beaumont bought the pine when he heard of its imminent destruction; Wordsworth, who, according to the dedication of his 1815 poems, wrote several pieces at Beaumont's Coleorton Hall, commemorated the action in the sonnet "The Pine of Monte Mario at Rome."

　　San Onofrio . . . Tasso . . . Leonardo. Tasso died here on 25 April 1595 (his death mask is in the Museo Tassiano). The attribution to Leonardo da Vinci has not held, and the fresco in the

Rome, and though the view is fine from the little terrace, the church and convent are of a meagre and musty pattern. Yet here—almost like pearls in a dunghill—are hidden mementos of two of the most exquisite of Italian minds. Torquato Tasso spent the last months of his life here, and you may visit his room and various warped and faded relics. The most interesting is a cast of his face taken after death—looking, like all such casts, almost more than mortally gallant and distinguished. But who should look all ideally so if not he? In a little shabby, chilly corridor adjoining is a fresco of Leonardo, a Virgin and Child with the *donatorio*. It is very small, simple and faded, but it has all the artist's magic, that mocking, illusive refinement and hint of a vague *arrière-pensée* which mark every stroke of Leonardo's brush. Is it the perfection of irony or the perfection of tenderness? What does he mean, what does he affirm, what does he deny? Magic would n't be magic, nor the author of such things stand so absolutely alone, if we were ready with an explanation. As I glanced from the picture to the poor stupid little red-faced brother at my side I wondered if the thing might n't pass for an elegant epigram on monasticism. Certainly, at any rate, there is more intellect in it than under all the monkish tonsures it has seen coming and going these three hundred years.

January 21st.—The last three or four days I have regularly spent a couple of hours from noon baking myself in the sun of the Pincio to get rid of a cold. The weather perfect and the crowd (especially to-day) amazing. Such a staring, lounging, dandified, amiable crowd! Who does the vulgar stay-at-home work of Rome? All the grandees and half the foreigners are there in their carriages, the *bourgeoisie* on foot staring at them and the beggars lining all the approaches. The great difference between public places in America and Europe is in the number of unoccupied people of every age and condition sitting about early and late on benches and gazing at you, from your hat to your boots, as you pass. Europe is certainly the continent of the practised stare. The ladies on the Pincio have to run the gauntlet; but they seem to do so complacently enough. The European woman is brought up to the sense of having a definite part in the way of manners or manner to play in public. To lie back in a barouche alone, balancing a parasol and seeming to ignore the extremely immediate gaze of two serried ranks of male creatures on each side of her path, save here and there to recognise one of them

---

monastery is now judged to be the work of one of his greatest pupils, Giovanni Boltraffio (c. 1466–1516).

donatorio. James misspells *donatario* and mistakes its meaning; the word refers to the recipient of a gift, not the *donatore,* or giver.

arrière-pensée. Mental reservation.

with an imperceptible nod, is one of her daily duties. The number of young men here who, like the cœnobites of old, lead the purely contemplative life is enormous. They muster in especial force on the Pincio, but the Corso all day is thronged with them. They are well-dressed, good-humoured, good-looking, polite; but they seem never to do a harder stroke of work than to stroll from the Piazza Colonna to the Hôtel de Rome or *vice versâ*. Some of them don't even stroll, but stand leaning by the hour against the doorways, sucking the knobs of their canes, feeling their back hair and settling their shirt-cuffs. At my café in the morning several stroll in already (at nine o'clock) in light, in "evening" gloves. But they order nothing, turn on their heels, glance at the mirrors and stroll out again. When it rains they herd under the *portes-cochères* and in the smaller cafés. . . . Yesterday Prince Humbert's little *primogenito* was on the Pincio in an open landau with his governess. He's a sturdy blond little man and the image of the King. They had stopped to listen to the music, and the crowd was planted about the carriage-wheels, staring and criticising under the child's snub little nose. It appeared bold cynical curiosity, without the slightest manifestation of "loyalty," and it gave me a singular sense of the vulgarisation of Rome under the new régime. When the Pope drove abroad it was a solemn spectacle; even if you neither kneeled nor uncovered you were irresistibly impressed. But the Pope never stopped to listen to opera tunes, and he had no little popelings, under the charge of superior nurse-maids, whom you might take liberties with. The family at the Quirinal make something of a merit, I believe, of their modest and inexpensive way of life. The merit is great; yet, representationally, what a change for the worse from an order which proclaimed stateliness a part of its essence! The divinity that doth hedge a king must be pretty well on the wane. But how many more fine old traditions will the extremely sentimental traveller miss in the Italians over whom that little jostled prince in the landau will have come into his kinghood? . . . The Pincio continues to beguile; it's a great resource. I am for ever being reminded of the "æsthetic luxury," as I called it above, of living in Rome. To be able to choose of an afternoon for a lounge (respectfully speaking) between St. Peter's and the high precinct you approach by the gate just beyond Villa Medici—counting nothing else—is a proof that if in Rome you may suffer from ennui, at least your ennui has a throbbing soul in it. It is something to say for the Pincio that you don't always choose St. Peter's. Sometimes I lose patience with its parade of eternal idleness, but at others this

---

family at the Quirinal . . . inexpensive way of life. See note, page 107; the king had willingly reduced the income that the new government had promised to provide for him and for his family.

very idleness is balm to one's conscience. Life on just these terms seems so easy, so monotonously sweet, that you feel it would be unwise, would be really unsafe, to change. The Roman air is charged with an elixir, the Roman cup seasoned with some insidious drop, of which the action is fatally, yet none the less agreeably, "lowering."

January 26th.—With S. to the Villa Medici—perhaps on the whole the most enchanting place in Rome. The part of the garden called the Boschetto has an incredible, impossible charm; an upper terrace, behind locked gates, covered with a little dusky forest of evergreen oaks. Such a dim light as of a fabled, haunted place, such a soft suffusion of tender grey-green tones, such a company of gnarled and twisted little miniature trunks—dwarfs playing with each other at being giants—and such a shower of golden sparkles drifting in from the vivid west! At the end of the wood is a steep, circular mound, up which the short trees scramble amain, with a long mossy staircase climbing up to a belvedere. This staircase, rising suddenly out of the leafy dusk to you don't see where, is delightfully fantastic. You expect to see an old woman in a crimson petticoat and with a distaff come hobbling down and turn into a fairy and offer you three wishes. I should name for my own first wish that one did n't have to be a Frenchman to come and live and dream and work at the Académie de France. Can there be for a while a happier destiny than that of a young artist conscious of talent and of no errand but to educate, polish and perfect it, transplanted to these sacred shades? One has fancied Plato's Academy—his gleaming colonnades, his blooming gardens and Athenian sky; but was it as good as this one, where Monsieur Hébert does the Platonic? The blessing in Rome is not that this or that or the other isolated object is so very unsurpassable; but that the general air so contributes to interest, to impressions that are not as any other impressions anywhere in the world. And from this general air the Villa Medici has distilled an essence of its own— walled it in and made it delightfully private. The great façade on the gardens is like an enormous rococo clock-face all incrusted with images and arabesques and tablets. What mornings and afternoons one might spend there, brush in hand, unpreoccupied, untormented, pensioned, satisfied—either persuading

---

With S. to the Villa Medici . . . Boschetto . . . Académie de France. The S. W. of later references, Sarah Butler Wister—daughter of actress Fanny Kemble and mother of American novelist Owen Wister—called a "beautiful Bore" by James (*Letters,* I, 331). Students who win the Prix de Rome at the Paris École des Beaux Arts spend three years here; the garden, or *boschetto,* still offers some public access.

Monsieur Hébert. Ernest Hébert (1817–1908), French painter and director of the Académie from 1867 to 1873, called "my intimate friend" in a letter to Alice James (*Letters,* I, 337); see page 169.

one's self that one would be "doing something" in consequence or not caring if one should n't be.

At a later date—middle of March.—A ride with S. W. out of the Porta Pia to the meadows beyond the Ponte Nomentana—close to the site of Phaon's villa where Nero in hiding had himself stabbed. It all spoke as things here only speak, touching more chords than one can *now* really know or say. For these are predestined memories and the stuff that regrets are made of; the mild divine efflorescence of spring, the wonderful landscape, the talk suspended for another gallop. . . . Returning, we dismounted at the gate of the Villa Medici and walked through the twilight of the vaguely perfumed, bird-haunted alleys to H.'s studio, hidden in the wood like a cottage in a fairy tale. I spent there a charming half-hour in the fading light, looking at the pictures while my companion discoursed of her errand. The studio is small and more like a little salon; the painting refined, imaginative, somewhat morbid, full of consummate French ability. A portrait, idealised and ethe-realised, but a likeness of Mme. de——(from last year's Salon) in white satin, quantities of lace, a coronet, diamonds and pearls; a striking combination of brilliant silvery tones. A "Femme Sauvage," a naked dusky girl in a wood, with a wonderfully clever pair of shy, passionate eyes. The author is different enough from any of the numerous American artists. They may be producers, but he's a product as well—a product of influences of a sort of which we have as yet no general command. One of them is his charmed lapse of life in that unprofessional-looking little studio, with his enchanted wood on one side and the plunging wall of Rome on the other.

January 30th.—A drive the other day with a friend to Villa Madama, on the side of Monte Mario; a place like a page out of one of Browning's richest evocations of this clime and civilisation. Wondrous in its haunting melancholy, it might have inspired half "The Ring and the Book" at a stroke.

Phaon's villa. Near the end of his short reign, Nero escaped the rebelling praetorian guards and fled to the villa of his freeman Phaon, where he heard of the senators' decree of death "in the ancient fashion," whereby the accused was "stripped, his head placed in a fork, and his body smitten with a stick till death." Nero had a slave stab him. (Hare, *Days Near Rome*, I, 170–71).

H.'s studio. That of Ernest Hébert.

Villa Madama . . . haunting melancholy. Begun by Giulio Romano on Raphael's plans; today viewed by special permission of the Ministro degli Affari Esteri. James saw near-ruins, but after over a century of virtual abandonment, the villa was purchased by Maurice Bèrges in 1913 and restoration began. There is virtually no public access today.

"The Ring and the Book." Robert Browning's poem in twelve books, published in installments from 1868 to 1869, offers the complex and partly factual story of a seventeenth-century

What a grim commentary on history such a scene—what an irony of the past! The road up to it through the outer enclosure is almost impassable with mud and stones. At the end, on a terrace, rises the once elegant Casino, with hardly a whole pane of glass in its façade, reduced to its sallow stucco and degraded ornaments. The front away from Rome has in the basement a great loggia, now walled in from the weather, preceded by a grassy belittered platform with an immense sweeping view of the Campagna; the sad-looking, more than sad-looking, evil-looking, Tiber beneath (the colour of gold, the sentimentalists say, the colour of mustard, the realists); a great vague stretch beyond, of various complexions and uses; and on the horizon the ever-iridescent mountains. The place has become the shabbiest farm-house, with muddy water in the old *pièces d'eau* and dunghills on the old parterres. The "feature" is the contents of the loggia: a vaulted roof and walls decorated by Giulio Romano; exquisite stucco-work and still brilliant frescoes; arabesques and figurini, nymphs and fauns, animals and flowers—gracefully lavish designs of every sort. Much of the colour—especially the blues—still almost vivid, and all the work wonderfully ingenious, elegant and charming. Apartments so decorated can have been meant only for the recreation of people greater than any we know, people for whom life was impudent ease and success. Margaret Farnese was the lady of the house, but where she trailed her cloth of gold the chickens now scamper between your legs over rotten straw. It is all inexpressibly dreary. A stupid peasant scratching his head, a couple of critical Americans picking their steps, the walls tattered and befouled breast-high, dampness and decay striking in on your heart, and the scene overbowed by these heavenly frescoes, mouldering there in their airy artistry! It's poignant; it provokes tears; it tells so of the waste of effort. Something human seems to pant beneath the grey pall of time and to implore you to rescue it, to pity it, to stand by it somehow. But you leave it to its lingering death without compunction, almost with pleasure; for the place seems vaguely crime-haunted—paying at least the penalty of some hard immorality. The end of a Renaissance pleasure-house. Endless for the didactic observer the moral, abysmal for the story-seeker the tale.

Italian murder trial. In 1912 James delivered a lecture entitled "The Novel in *The Ring and the Book*" before the Academic Committee of the Royal Society of Literature (*Literary Criticism: Essays on Literature*, 791–811).

pièces d'eau. Artificial lakes.

Margaret Farnese. "Madama" Margherita di Parma (1522–86), the natural child of Charles V. A woman of particularly distinguished ability and training, she married Ottavio Farnese, Duke of Parma, and for a time served as the regent of the Netherlands.

February 12th.—Yesterday to the Villa Albani. Over-formal and (as my companion says) too much like a tea-garden; but with beautiful stairs and splendid geometrical lines of immense box-hedge, intersected with high pedestals supporting little antique busts. The light to-day magnificent; the Alban Hills of an intenser broken purple than I had yet seen them—their white towns blooming upon it like vague projected lights. It was like a piece of very modern painting, and a good example of how Nature has at times a sort of mannerism which ought to make us careful how we condemn out of hand the more refined and affected artists. The collection of marbles in the Casino (Winckelmann's) admirable and to be seen again. The famous Antinous crowned with lotus a strangely beautiful and impressive thing. The "Greek manner," on the showing of something now and again encountered here, moves one to feel that even for purely romantic and imaginative effects it surpasses any since invented. If there be not imagination, even in our comparatively modern sense of the word, in the baleful beauty of that perfect young profile there is none in "Hamlet" or in "Lycidas." There is five hundred times as much as in "The Transfiguration." With this at any rate to point to it's not for sculpture not professedly to produce any emotion producible by painting. There are numbers of small and delicate fragments of bas-reliefs of exquisite grace, and a huge piece (two combatants—one, on horseback, beating down another—murder made eternal and beautiful) attributed to the Parthenon and certainly as grandly impressive as anything in the Elgin marbles. S. W. suggested again the Roman villas as a "subject." Excellent if one could find a feast of facts à la Stendhal. A lot of vague ecstatic descriptions and anecdotes would n't at all pay. There have been too many already. Enough facts are recorded, I suppose; one should discover them and soak in them for a twelvemonth. And yet a Roman villa, in spite of statues, ideas and atmosphere, affects me as of a scanter human and social *portée,* a shorter, thinner reverberation, than an old English country-house, round which experience seems piled so thick. But this perhaps is either hair-splitting or "racial" prejudice.

March 9th.—The Vatican is still deadly cold; a couple of hours there

---

Villa Albani ... Winckelmann's ... Antinous. Johann Joachim Winckelmann (1717–68), German archaeologist, friend and adviser to Cardinal Alessandro Albani, helped build the great collection of antique sculpture at the Villa Albani, now the Villa Torlonia (see pages xvii and 170). The Antinous, considered by Winckelmann the pearl of the collection, had come from the excavations of Hadrian's villa at Tivoli (in *History of Ancient Art,* IV, 335–37, he examines the Antinous and discusses the lotus crown that James notes).

The Transfiguration. In the Vatican Museum, Raphael's final work. Incomplete at his death, the painting was finished by other hands. See also page 245 and note.

yesterday with R. W. E. Yet he, illustrious and enviable man, fresh from the East, had no overcoat and wanted none. Perfect bliss, I think, would be to live in Rome without thinking of overcoats. The Vatican seems very familiar, but strangely smaller than of old. I never lost the sense before of confusing vastness. *Sancta simplicitas!* All my old friends however stand there in un-dimmed radiance, keeping most of them their old pledges. I am perhaps more struck now with the enormous amount of padding—the number of third-rate, fourth-rate things that weary the eye desirous to approach freshly the twenty and thirty best. In spite of the padding there are dozens of treasures that one passes regretfully; but the impression of the whole place is the great thing—the feeling that through these solemn vistas flows the source of an incalculable part of our present conception of Beauty.

April 10th.—Last night, in the rain, to the Teatro Valle to see a comedy of Goldoni in Venetian dialect—"I Quattro Rustighi." I could but half follow it; enough, however, to be sure that, for all its humanity of irony, it was n't so good as Molière. The acting was capital—broad, free and natural; the play of talk easier even than life itself; but, like all the Italian acting I have seen, it was wanting in *finesse,* that shade of the shade by which, and by which alone, one really knows art. I contrasted the affair with the evening in December last that I walked over (also in the rain) to the Odéon and saw the "Plaideurs" and the "Malade Imaginaire." There, too, was hardly more than a handful of spectators; but what rich, ripe, fully representational and above all intellectual comedy, and what polished, educated playing! These Venetians in particular, however, have a marvellous *entrain* of their own; they seem even less than the French to recite. In some of the women—ugly, with red hands and shabby dresses—an extraordinary gift of natural utter-ance, of seeming to invent joyously as they go.

R. W. E. Ralph Waldo Emerson. The original essay in the *Galaxy* kept more indefinite the identity of the visitor, simply referring to a vist with "Mr. E" (see note on "L.," page 177, for comment on James's use of initials).

"I Quattro Rustighi." I could but half follow it. Non-native Italian speakers who have attended a performance of Carlo Goldoni's *I Quattro Rusteghi* (The Four Rustics), in the Venetian dialect in which it was written, will appreciate that to "half follow it" suggests an unusually strong ear for Italian and related dialects; native Italians from outside the Veneto often admit to great difficulty understanding the spoken dialogue of Goldoni. Nonetheless, as on other occasions in *Italian Hours,* James misspells, with *rusteghi,* an Italian word.

"Plaideurs" . . . "Malade Imaginaire." James's unsigned article, "The Parisian Stage," ap-peared in the *Nation* on 9 January 1873 and reviewed the city's theatrical season up through December; in the article he discusses Molière but makes reference neither to *Le Malade Imaginaire* nor to Racine's sole comedy, *Les Plaideurs* (*The Scenic Art,* 3–12).

Later.—Last evening in H.'s box at the Apollo to hear Ernesto Rossi in "Othello." He shares supremacy with Salvini in Italian tragedy. Beautiful great theatre with boxes you can walk about in; brilliant audience. The Princess Margaret was there—I have never been to the theatre that she was not—and a number of other princesses in neighbouring boxes. G. G. came in and instructed us that they were the M., the L., the P., &c. Rossi is both very bad and very fine; bad where anything like taste and discretion is required, but "all there," and more than there, in violent passion. The last act reduced too much, however, to mere exhibitional sensibility. The interesting thing to me was to observe the Italian conception of the part—to see how crude it was, how little it expressed the hero's moral side, his depth, his dignity—anything more than his being a creature terrible in mere tantrums. The great point was his seizing Iago's head and whacking it half-a-dozen times on the floor, and then flinging him twenty yards away. It was wonderfully done, but in the doing of it and in the evident relish for it in the house there was I scarce knew what force of easy and thereby rather cheap expression.

April 27th.—A morning with L. B. at Villa Ludovisi, which we agreed

---

the Apollo. The theater was demolished in 1888, when plans to wall the Tiber were carried out (photographs in Raviaglioi, I, 77, 182–83). Today a small plaque on the Lungotevere degli Altoviti marks the theater's location, history, and importance.

Ernesto Rossi . . . Salvini. Both were considered among the greatest actors of their day; Rossi (1827–96), who helped introduce Shakespeare to the Italian public, made successful tours throughout Europe, South America, the United States, and Russia. Tommaso Salvini (1829–1915) was acclaimed as one of the greatest Shakespearean actors of his time after a run of thirty consecutive nights of *Othello* before enthusiastic London audiences.

In an 1875 review James wrote that Rossi's Paris performance as Macbeth "was so ludicrously Italian—I am sorry to associate so disrespectful an adverb with so glorious an adjective"; in another anonymous 1884 review written for the *Atlantic* James highly praised Salvini's "very great triumph" in a Boston performance, saying that "no other artist today begins to be capable of giving us such an exhibition of tragic power" (*The Scenic Art*, 45ff., 168–91).

Princess Margaret . . . morganatic wife. Cf. page 125 and note. Later, as Queen Margaret, she continued to shine in international society. "Nothing can exceed the exquisite courtesy of the Queen, and her perfect knowledge of French, English, and German enables her to converse fluently in their own language with foreigners who have the honor of being presented to Her Majesty. The King is also extremely affable" (Murray, 1881, 31). Cf. page 171 and note on the morganatic status of the wife of King Victor Emmanuel II.

G. G. . . . the M., the L., the P., &c. The editor is unable to identify G. G., or the families of the Roman princesses, who, it would seem, are here offered as representatives of a class.

Villa Ludovisi . . . the beautiful sitting Mars . . . the great Juno. Also see pages xvii and 170. The most important villa in Rome was sold to land speculators in 1886 and divided into lots. The main casino was demolished and in 1901 the famous Ludovisi collection of sculpture was moved to the Museo Nazionale (the Mars, or Ares Ludovisi, inventory no. 8602; the Juno,

that we should n't soon forget. The villa now belongs to the King, who has lodged his morganatic wife there. There is nothing so blissfully *right* in Rome, nothing more consummately consecrated to style. The grounds and gardens are immense, and the great rusty-red city wall stretches away behind them and makes the burden of the seven hills seem vast without making *them* seem small. There is everything—dusky avenues trimmed by the clippings of centuries, groves and dells and glades and glowing pastures and reedy fountains and great flowering meadows studded with enormous slanting pines. The day was delicious, the trees all one melody, the whole place a revelation of what Italy and hereditary pomp can do together. Nothing could be more in the grand manner than this garden view of the city ramparts, lifting their fantastic battlements above the trees and flowers. They are all tapestried with vines and made to serve as sunny fruit-walls—grim old defence as they once were; now giving nothing but a splendid buttressed privacy. The sculptures in the little Casino are few, but there are two great ones—the beautiful sitting Mars and the head of the great Juno, the latter thrust into a corner behind a shutter. These things it's almost impossible to praise; we can only mark them well and keep them clear, as we insist on silence to hear great music. . . . If I don't praise Guercino's Aurora in the greater Casino, it's for another reason; this is certainly a very muddy masterpiece. It figures on the ceiling of a small low hall; the painting is coarse and the ceiling too near. Besides, it's unfair to pass straight from the Greek mythology to the Bolognese. We were left to roam at will through the house; the custode shut us in and went to walk in the park. The apartments were all open, and I had an opportunity to reconstruct, from its *milieu* at least, the character of a morganatic queen. I saw nothing to indicate that it was not amiable; but I should have thought more highly of the lady's discrimination if she had had the Juno removed from behind her shutter. In such a house, girdled about with such a park, methinks I could be amiable—and perhaps discriminating too. The Ludovisi Casino is small, but the perfection of the

---

inventory no. 8631; photographs of both in Giuliano, 119–20, 135–36)—where, since World War II, it has been seen infrequently by the public. Goethe said that the Juno was like a song from Homer and kept a plaster copy, but now the Juno is believed to be a first-century Roman copy. The Casino dell'Aurora, with the Guercino frescoes, survives as a relic of the old villa, but access is limited. Several of the details of this passage on the Villa Ludovisi relate to the beginning of *Roderick Hudson*, chapter 3, "Rome," where the young sculptor and his friend sit "among the high stemmed pines of the Villa Ludovisi. They had been spending an hour in the mouldy little garden-house, where the colossal mask of the famous Juno looks out with blank eyes from that dusky corner which must seem to her the last possible stage of a lapse from Olympus. . . . Roderick declared that he would go nowhere else; that, after the Juno, it was profanation to look at anything but sky and trees. There was a fresco of Guercino, to which Rowland, though he had seen it on his former visit to Rome, went dutifully to pay his respects."

life of ease might surely be led there. There are English houses enough in wondrous parks, but they expose you to too many small needs and observances—to say nothing of a red-faced butler dropping his h's. You are oppressed with the detail of accommodation. Here the billiard-table is old-fashioned, perhaps a trifle crooked; but you have Guercino above your head, and Guercino, after all, is almost as good as Guido. The rooms, I noticed, all pleased by their shape, by a lovely proportion, by a mass of delicate ornamentation on the high concave ceilings. One might live over again in them some deliciously benighted life of a forgotten type—with graceful old *sale,* and immensely thick walls, and a winding stone staircase, and a view from the loggia at the top; a view of twisted parasol-pines balanced, high above a wooden horizon, against a sky of faded sapphire.

May 17th.—It was wonderful yesterday at St. John Lateran. The spring now has turned to perfect summer; there are cascades of verdure over all the walls; the early flowers are a fading memory, and the new grass knee-deep in the Villa Borghese. The winter aspect of the region about the Lateran is one of the best things in Rome; the sunshine is nowhere so golden and the lean shadows nowhere so purple as on the long grassy walk to Santa Croce. But yesterday I seemed to see nothing but green and blue. The expanse before Santa Croce was vivid green; the Campagna rolled away in great green billows, which seemed to break high about the gaunt aqueducts; and the Alban Hills, which in January and February keep shifting and melting along the whole scale of azure, were almost monotonously fresh, and had lost some of their finer modelling. But the sky was ultramarine and everything radiant with light and warmth—warmth which a soft steady breeze kept from excess. I strolled some time about the church, which has a grand air enough, though I don't seize the point of view of Miss——, who told me the other day how vastly finer she thought it than St. Peter's. But on Miss——'s lips this seemed a very pretty paradox. The choir and transepts have a sombre splendour, and I like the old vaulted passage with its slabs and monuments behind the choir. The charm of charms at St. John Lateran is the admirable twelfth-century cloister, which was never more charming than yesterday. The shrubs and flowers about the ancient well were blooming away in the intense light, and the twisted pillars and chiselled capitals of the perfect little colonnade seemed to enclose them like the sculptured rim of a precious vase. Standing out among the flowers you may look up and see a section of the summit of the great façade of the church. The robed and mitred apostles, bleached and rain-washed by the ages, rose into the blue air like huge snow figures. I spent at the incorporated museum a subsequent hour of fond vague attention, having it quite to myself. It is rather scantily stocked, but the great cool halls open out impressively one after the other, and the wide spaces between the statues seem to suggest at first that each is a masterpiece. I was in the loving mood of one's last days in Rome, and when I had nothing else to admire I admired the magnificent thickness of the embrasures of the doors and windows. If there were no objects of interest at all in the Lateran the palace would be worth walking through every now and then, to keep up one's idea of solid architecture. I went over to the Scala Santa, where was no one but a very shabby priest sitting like a ticket-taker at the door. But he let me pass, and I ascended one of the profane lateral stairways and treated myself to a glimpse of the Sanctum Sanctorum. Its threshold is crossed but once or twice a year, I believe, by three or four of the most exalted divines, but you may look into it freely enough through a couple of gilded lattices. It is very sombre and splendid, and conveys the impression of a very holy place. And yet somehow it suggested irreverent thoughts; it had to my fancy—perhaps on account of the lattice—an Oriental, a Mahometan note. I expected every moment to see a sultana appear in a silver veil and silken trousers and sit down on the crimson carpet.

Farewell, packing, the sharp pang of going. One would like to be able after five months in Rome to sum up for tribute and homage, one's experience, one's gains, the whole adventure of one's sensibility. But one has really vibrated too much—the addition of so many items is n't easy. What is simply clear is the sense of an acquired passion for the place and of an incalculable number of gathered impressions. Many of these have been intense and momentous, but one has trodden on the other—there are always the big fish that swallow up the little—and one can hardly say what has become of them. They store themselves noiselessly away, I suppose, in the dim but safe places of memory and "taste," and we live in a quiet faith that they will emerge into vivid relief if life or art should demand them. As for the passion we need n't perhaps trouble ourselves about that. Fifty swallowed palmfuls of the Fountain of Trevi could n't make us more ardently sure that we shall at any cost come back.

1873.

Scala Santa . . . the profane lateral stairways. See page 132. James ascended the "profane" side steps that had been especially constructed to allow the free descent of believers who had performed their devotions by climbing the Scala Santa—the staircase believed to have been that which Christ himself ascended at Pilate's house—on their knees.

A Few Other Roman
Neighbourhoods

If I find my old notes, in all these Roman connections, inevitably bristle with the spirit of the postscript, so I give way to this prompting to the extent of my scant space and with the sense of other occasions awaiting me on which I shall have to do no less. The impression of Rome was repeatedly to renew itself for the author of these now rather antique and artless accents; was to overlay itself again and again with almost heavy thicknesses of experience, the last of which is, as I write, quite fresh to memory; and he has thus felt almost ashamed to drop his subject (though it be one that tends so easily to turn to the infinite) as if the law of change had in all the years had nothing to say to his case. It's of course but of his case alone that he speaks—wondering little what he may make of it for the profit of others by an attempt, however brief, to point the moral of the matter, or in other words compare the musing *mature* visitor's "feeling about Rome" with that of the extremely agitated, even if though extremely inexpert, consciousness reflected in the previous pages. The actual, the current Rome affects him as a world governed by new conditions altogether and ruefully pleading that sorry fact in the ear of the antique wanderer wherever he may yet mournfully turn for some re-capture of what he misses. The city of his first unpremeditated rapture shines to memory, on the other hand, in the manner of a lost paradise the rustle of whose gardens is still just audible enough in the air to make him wonder if some sudden turn, some recovered vista, may n't lead him back to the thing itself. My genial, my helpful tag, at this point, would doubtless properly resolve itself,

---

[First publication in *Italian Hours*.]

for the reader, into a clue toward some such successful ingenuity of quest; a remark I make, I may add, even while reflecting that the Paradise is n't apparently at all "lost" to visitors not of my generation. It is the seekers of *that* remote and romantic tradition who have seen it, from one period of ten, or even of five, years to another, systematically and remorselessly built out from their view. Their helpless plaint, their sense of the generally irrecoverable and unspeakable, is not, however, what I desire here most to express; I should like, on the contrary, with ampler opportunity, positively to enumerate the cases, the cases of contact, impression, experience, in which the cold ashes of a long-chilled passion may fairly feel themselves made to glow again. No one who has ever loved Rome as Rome could be loved in youth and before her poised basketful of the finer appeals to fond fancy was actually upset, wants to stop loving her; so that our bleeding and wounded, though perhaps not wholly moribund, loyalty attends us as a hovering admonitory, anticipatory ghost, one of those magnanimous life-companions who before complete extinction designate to the other member of the union their approved successor. So it is at any rate that I conceive the pilgrim old enough to have become aware in all these later years of what he misses to be counselled and pacified in the interest of recognitions that shall a little make up for it.

It was this wisdom I was putting into practice, no doubt, for instance, when I lately resigned myself to motoring of a splendid June day "out to" Subiaco; as a substitute for a resignation that had anciently taken, alas, but the form of my never getting there at all. Everything that day, moreover, seemed right, surely; everything on certain other days that were like it through their large indebtedness, at this, that and the other point, to the last new thing, seemed so right that they come back to me now, after a moderate interval, in the full light of that unchallenged felicity. I could n't at all gloriously recall, for instance, as I floated to Subiaco on vast brave wings, how on the occasion of my first visit to Rome, thirty-eight years before, I had devoted certain evenings, evenings of artless "preparation" in my room at the inn, to the perusal of Alphonse Dantier's admirable *Monastères Béné-*

Subiaco. On the slope of Monte Livata, Subiaco was the retreat of Saint Benedict (Benedetto da Norcia, c. 480–c. 550), called the "Patriarch of Western Monasticism." The original monastery was soon followed by twelve neighboring monasteries, and the rule of Saint Benedict was under way.

Alphonse Dantier's admirable *Monastères Bénédictins d'Italie.* Dantier's 1866 study devotes almost a thousand pages to the early days of the Benedictine monasteries, with half its length reviewing the histories of Subiaco and Monte Cassino; the work provides literary recollections of many secular travelers, among them Goethe, Montaigne, and Chateaubriand, as well as of Francis of Assisi, Augustine, and Thomas Aquinas.

dictins d'Italie, taking piously for granted that I should get myself somehow conveyed to Monte Cassino and to Subiaco at least: such an affront to the passion of curiosity, the generally infatuated state then kindled, would any suspicion of my foredoomed, my all but interminable, privation during visits to come have seemed to me. Fortune, in the event, had never favoured my going, but I was to give myself up at last to the sense of her quite taking me by the hand, and that is how I now think of our splendid June day at Subiaco. The note of the wondrous place itself is conventional "wild" Italy raised to the highest intensity, the ideally, the sublimely conventional and wild, complete and supreme in itself, without a disparity or a flaw; which character of perfect picturesque orthodoxy seemed more particularly to begin for me, I remember, as we passed, on our way, through that indescribable and indestructible Tivoli, where the jumble of the elements of the familiarly and exploitedly, the all too notoriously fair and queer, was more violent and vociferous than ever—so the whole spectacle there seemed at once to rejoice in cockneyfication and to resist it. There at least I had old memories to renew—including that in especial, from a few years back, of one of the longest, hottest, dustiest return-drives to Rome that the Campagna on a sirocco day was ever to have treated me to.

That was to be more than made up on this later occasion by an hour of early evening, snatched on the run back to Rome, that remains with me as one of those felicities we are wise to leave for ever, just as they are, just, that is, where they fell, never attempting to renew or improve them. So happy a chance was it that ensured me at the afternoon's end a solitary stroll through the Villa d'Este, where the day's invasion, whatever it might have been, had left no traces and where I met nobody in the great rococo passages and chambers, and in the prodigious alleys and on the repeated flights of tortuous steps, but the haunting Genius of Style, into whose noble battered old face, as if it had come out clearer in the golden twilight and on recognition of response so deeply moved, I seemed to exhale my sympathy. This was

---

Monte Cassino. Founded by Saint Benedict after he left Subiaco to escape local jealousies, Monte Cassino became the principal monastery of the Benedictine order. The great complex of buildings was almost totally destroyed by bombings during World War II; considerable efforts at restoration have since been made.

Villa d'Este . . . The ruined fountains. In 1803, with the extinction of the last d'Este family heir, the villa passed into the hands of the Archduchess of Austria and faced more than a century of sporadic Hapsburg neglect. After 1896 it became the property of Archduke Franz Ferdinand, and, at the close of World War I, the Villa d'Este was given to the Italian government as part of the peace settlement; only then did serious repair and a magnificent restoration begin.

truly, amid a conception and order of things all mossed over from disuse, but still without a form abandoned or a principle disowned, one of the hours that one does n't forget. The ruined fountains seemed strangely to *wait,* in the stillness and under cover of the approaching dusk, not to begin ever again to play, also, but just only to be tenderly imagined to do so; quite as everything held its breath, at the mystic moment, for the drop of the cruel and garish exposure, for the Spirit of the place to steal forth and go his round. The vistas of the innumerable mighty cypresses ranged themselves, in their files and companies, like beaten heroes for their captain's review; the great artificial "works" of every description, cascades, hemicycles, all graded and grassed and stone-seated as for floral games, mazes and bowers and alcoves and grottos, brave indissoluble unions of the planted and the builded symmetry, with the terraces and staircases that overhang and the arcades and cloisters that underspread, made common cause together as for one's taking up a little, in kindly lingering wonder, the "feeling" out of which they have sprung. One did n't see it, under the actual influence, one would n't for the world have seen it, as that they longed to be justified, during a few minutes in the twenty-four hours, of their absurdity of pomp and circumstance—but only that they asked for company, once in a way, as they were so splendidly formed to give it, and that the best company, in a changed world, at the end of time, what could they hope it to be but just the lone, the dawdling person of taste, the visitor with a flicker of fancy, not to speak of a pang of pity, to spare for them? It was in the flicker of fancy, no doubt, that as I hung about the great top-most terrace in especial, and then again took my way through the high gaunt corridors and the square and bare alcoved and recessed saloons, all overscored with such a dim waste of those painted, those delicate and capricious decorations which the loggie of the Vatican promptly borrowed from the ruins of the Palatine, or from whatever other revealed and inspiring ancientries, and which make ghostly confession here of that descent, I gave the rein to my sense of the sinister too, of that vague after-taste as of evil things that lurks so often, for a suspicious sensibility, wherever the terrible game of the life of the Renaissance was played as the Italians played it; wherever the huge tessellated chessboard seems to stretch about us, swept bare, almost always violently swept bare, of its chiselled and shifting figures, of every value and degree, but with this echoing desolation itself representing the long gasp, as it were, of over-strained time, the great after-hush that follows on things too wonderful or dreadful.

I am putting here, however, my cart before my horse, for the hour just glanced at was but a final tag to a day of much brighter curiosity, and which seemed to take its baptism, as we passed through prodigious perched and huddled, adorably scattered and animated and even crowded Tivoli, from the universal happy spray of the drumming Anio waterfalls, all set in their permanent rainbows and Sibylline temples and classic allusions and Byronic quotations; a wondrous romantic jumble of such things and quite others— heterogeneous inns and clamorous *guinguettes* and factories grabbing at the torrent, to say nothing of innumerable guides and donkeys and white-tied, swallow-tailed waiters dashing out of grottos and from under cataracts, and of the air, on the part of the whole population, of standing about, in the most characteristic *contadino* manner, to pounce on you and take you some-where, snatch you from somebody else, shout something at you, the aqueous and other uproar permitting, and then charge you for it, your innocence aiding. I'm afraid our run the rest of the way to Subiaco remains with me but as an after-sense of that exhilaration, in spite of our rising admirably higher, all the while, and plunging constantly deeper into splendid solitary gravities, supreme romantic solemnities and sublimities, of landscape. The Benedic-tine convent, which clings to certain more or less vertiginous ledges and slopes of a vast precipitous gorge, constitutes, with the whole perfection of its setting, the very ideal of the tradition of that *extraordinary in the roman-tic* handed down to us, as the most attaching and inviting spell of Italy, by all the old academic literature of travel and art of the Salvator Rosas and Claudes. This is the main tribute I may pay in a few words to an impression of which a sort of divine rightness of oddity, a pictorial felicity that was almost not of this world, but of a higher degree of distinction altogether, affected me as the leading note; yet about the whole exquisite complexity of which I can't pretend to be informing.

Anio waterfalls . . . Sibylline temples and classic allusions and Byronic quotations. Byron, *Childe Harold's Pilgrimage,* canto IV, lxvii–lxxi: "And on thy happy shore a Temple still," identified for a time with Pliny's *templum priscum,* and "The roar of waters!—from the headlong height / Velino cleaves the wave-worn precipice / . . . The Hell of Waters! where they howl and hiss." But Byron refers to the falls at Terni, not Tivoli; the Great Cascade at the Villa Gregoriana cleaves the Anio or Aniene river, not the Velino (see notes to Byron, *Works,* II, 380–81). Hare comments (*Days Near Rome,* I, 194–96) on the ancient Temple of Sibyl and the classical allusions in Statius; his comparison of the Anio falls to that at Terni may have contributed to James's Byronic confusion, as may have the fact that both cascades were artifi-cially constructed. Since James's times the Anio has been redirected and the Grande Cascata now precipitates at some distance from where it did from the seventeenth through the nine-teenth centuries.

guinguettes. Suburban cafés. **contadino.** Peasant.

Salvator Rosas and Claudes. Like Claude Lorraine (see page 96 and note), Neapolitan painter Salvator Rosa (1615–73) worked mainly at Rome; his landscapes were perhaps less idealized and more romantically wild than Claude Lorraine's.

All the elements of the scene melted for me together; even from the pause for luncheon on a grassy wayside knoll, over heaven knows what admirable preparatory headlong slopes and ravines and iridescent distances, under spreading chestnuts and in the high air that was cool and sweet, to the final pedestrian climb of sinuous mountain-paths that the shining limestone and the strong green of shrub and herbage made as white as silver. There the miraculous home of St. Benedict awaited us in the form of a builded and pictured-over maze of chapels and shrines, cells and corridors, stupefying rock-chambers and caves, places all at an extraordinary variety of different levels and with labyrinthine intercommunications; there the spirit of the centuries sat like some invisible icy presence that only permits you to stare and wonder. I stared, I wondered, I went up and down and in and out and lost myself in the fantastic fable of the innumerable hard facts themselves; and whenever I could, above all, I peeped out of small windows and hung over chance terraces for the love of the general outer picture, the splendid fashion in which the fretted mountains of marble, as they might have been, round about, seemed to inlay themselves, for the effect of the "distinction" I speak of, with vegetations of dark emerald. There above all—or at least in what such aspects did further for the prodigy of the Convent, whatever that prodigy might do for *them*—was, to a life-long victim of Italy, almost verily as never before, the operation of the old love-philtre; there were the inexhaustible sources of interest and charm.

These mystic fountains broke out for me elsewhere, again and again, I rejoice to say—and perhaps more particularly, to be frank about it, where the ground about them was pressed with due emphasis of appeal by the firm wheels of the great winged car. I motored, under invitation and protection, repeatedly back into the sense of the other years, that sense of the "old" and comparatively idle Rome of my particular infatuated prime which I was living to see superseded, and this even when the fond vista bristled with innumerable "signs of the times," unmistakable features of the new era, that, by I scarce know what perverse law, succeeded in ministering to a happy effect. Some of these false notes proceed simply from the immense growth of every sort of facilitation—so that people are much more free than of old to come and go and do, to inquire and explore, to pervade and generally "infest"; with a consequent loss, for the fastidious individual, of

---

fantastic fable of the innumerable hard facts. Repeatedly destroyed and rebuilt, the convent of Santa Scolastica, successor of the first Benedictine monastery at Subiaco, was founded in the fifth century by Abbott Honoratus, Benedict's successor. It is said that in the rose garden Benedict rolled on a bed of thorns to extinguish his passion; Torquemada was abbot here, as was Rodrigo Borgia—later Pope Alexander VI—and his daughter Lucrezia Borgia was born at Subiaco. Bombed during World War II, Santa Scolastica has been rebuilt.

his blest earlier sense, not infrequent, of having the occasion and the impression, as he used complacently to say, all to himself. We none of us had anything quite all to ourselves during an afternoon at Ostia, on a beautiful June Sunday; it was a different affair, rather, from the long, the comparatively slow and quite unpeopled drive that I was to remember having last taken early in the autumn thirty years before, and which occupied the day—with the aid of a hamper from once supreme old Spillman, the provider for picnics to a vanished world (since I suspect the antique ideal of "a picnic in the Campagna," the fondest conception of a happy day, has lost generally much of its glamour). Our idyllic afternoon, at any rate, left no chord of sensibility that could possibly have been in question untouched—not even that of tea on the shore at Fiumincino, after we had spent an hour among the ruins of Ostia and seen our car ferried across the Tiber, almost saffron-coloured here and swirling towards its mouth, on a boat that was little more than a big rustic raft and that yet bravely resisted the prodigious weight. What shall I say, in the way of the particular, of the general felicity before me, for the sweetness of the hour to which the incident just named, with its strange and amusing juxtapositions of the patriarchally primitive and the insolently supersubtle, the earliest and the latest efforts of restless science, were almost immediately to succeed?

We had but skirted the old gold-and-brown walls of Castel Fusano, where the massive Chigi tower and the immemorial stone-pines and the afternoon sky and the desolate sweetness and concentrated rarity of the picture all kept their appointment, to fond memory, with that especial form of Roman faith, the fine æsthetic conscience in things, that is never, never broken. We had wound through tangled lanes and met handsome sallow country-folk lounging at leisure, as became the Sunday, and ever so pleasantly and garishly clothed, if not quite consistently costumed, as just on purpose to feed our wanton optimism; and then we had addressed ourselves with a soft superficiality to the open, the exquisite little Ostian reliquary, an exhibition of stony vaguenesses half straightened out. The ruins of the ancient port of Rome, the still recoverable identity of streets and habitations and other forms of civil life, are a not inconsiderable handful, though making of the place at best a

---

Spillman. Spillman Frères, 10 and 12 Via Condotti, was the standard for catering in Rome throughout the second half of the nineteenth century.

Ostia . . . Castel Fusano. Although serious excavation at Pompeii had been under way since soon after 1800, rigorous work at the presently extensive Ostia Antica, a large city of perhaps 100,000 in Roman times compared to Pompeii's 25,000, began only in 1907. On the grounds of the walled pine forest, which is itself named Castel Fusano, stands the four-towered Palazzo Chigi, near the Lido di Ostia.

very small sister to Pompeii; but a soft superficiality is ever the refuge of my shy sense before any ghost of informed reconstitution, and I plead my surrender to it with the less shame that I believe I "enjoy" such scenes even on such futile pretexts as much as it can be appointed them by the invidious spirit of History to *be* enjoyed. It may be said, of course, that enjoyment, question-begging term at best, is n't in these austere connections designated—but rather some principle of appreciation that can at least give a coherent account of itself. On that basis then—as I could, I profess, *but* revel in the looseness of my apprehension, so wide it seemed to fling the gates of vision and divination—I won't pretend to dot, as it were, too many of the i's of my incompetence. I was competent only to have been abjectly interested. On reflection, moreover, I see that no impression of over-much company invaded the picture till the point was exactly reached for its contributing thoroughly to character and amusement; across at Fiumincino, which the age of the bicycle has made, in a small way, the handy Gravesend or Coney Island of Rome, the cafés and *birrerie* were at high pressure, and the bustle all motley and friendly beside the melancholy river, where the water-side life itself had twenty quaint and vivid notes and where a few upstanding objects, ancient or modern, looked eminent and interesting against the delicate Roman sky that dropped down and down to the far-spreading marshes of malaria. Besides which "company" is ever intensely gregarious, hanging heavily together and easily outwitted; so that we had but to proceed a scant distance further and meet the tideless Mediterranean, where it tumbled in a trifle breezily on the sands, to be all to ourselves with our tea-basket, quite as in the good old fashion—only in truth with the advantage that the contemporary tea-basket is so much improved.

I jumble my memories as a tribute to the whole idyll—I give the golden light in which they come back to me for what it is worth; worth, I mean, as allowing that the possibilities of charm of the Witch of the Seven Hills, as we used to call her in magazines, have n't all been vulgarised away. It was precisely there, on such an occasion and in such a place, that this might seem

---

Fiumincino . . . the handy Gravesend or Coney Island. Or Fiumicino, now better known as the site of the Leonardo da Vinci Airport; the amusement park of James's reference existed up until 1988, although it had been transformed into a safari park. Gravesend, in Kent, has had a long history as a favorite resort for Londoners; the famous Steeplechase Park (opened in 1897), ten miles from Manhattan at Coney Island, Brooklyn, was closed down in 1964.

birrerie. Beer halls.

marshes of malaria. ". . . and they have also constantly recurring malaria to struggle against, borne up every night by the poisonous vapours of the marsh, which renders Ostia almost uninhabitable even to the natives in the summer, and death to the stranger who attempts to pass the night there" (Hare, *Days Near Rome*, I, 47).

signally to have happened; whereas in fact the mild suburban riot, in which the so gay but so light potations before the array of little houses of entertainment were what struck one as really making most for mildness, was brushed over with a fabled grace, was harmonious, felicitous, distinguished, quite after the fashion of some thoroughly trained chorus or phalanx of opera or ballet. Bicycles were stacked up by the hundred; the youth of Rome are ardent cyclists, with a great taste for flashing about in more or less denuded or costumed athletic and romantic bands and guilds, and on our return cityward, toward evening, along the right bank of the river, the road swarmed with the patient wheels and bent backs of these budding *cives Romani* quite to the effect of its finer interest. Such at least, I felt, could only be one's acceptance of almost any feature of a scene bathed in that extraordinary august air that the waning Roman day is so insidiously capable of taking on when any other element of style happens at all to contribute. Were n't they present, these other elements, in the great classic lines and folds, the fine academic or historic attitudes of the darkening land itself as it hung about the old highway, varying its vague accidents, but achieving always perfect "composition"? I shamelessly add that cockneyfied impression, at all events, to what I have called my jumble; Rome, to which we all swept on together in the wondrous glowing medium, *saved* everything, spreading afar her wide wing and applying after all but her supposed grand gift of the secret of salvation. We kept on and on into the great dim rather sordidly papal streets that approach the quarter of St. Peter's; to the accompaniment, finally, of that markedly felt provocation of fond wonder which had never failed to lie in wait for me under any question of a renewed glimpse of the huge unvisited rear of the basilica. There was no renewed glimpse just then, in the gloaming; but the region I speak of had been for me, in fact, during the previous weeks, less unvisited than ever before, so that I had come to count an occasional walk round and about it as quite of the essence of the convenient small change with which the heterogeneous City may still keep paying you. These frequentations in the company of a sculptor friend had

---

dim rather sordidly papal streets. Until the Fascist period, the approach to the Vatican was as James described it, with Saint Peter's suddenly emerging out of the warrens of Rome, but in 1937 the Via della Conciliazione opened and transformed the *borgo*. A rather grim monumental avenue leading the long distance straight from the Tiber to the Piazza San Pietro, it obliterated two famous—and dim—streets that had dated from the Renaissance. Mussolini's urban planners had traded a sense of magnificent revelation for a frigid imperial cliché.

frequentations in the company of a sculptor friend. While in Rome in 1899 James had met Norwegian-born sculptor Hendrik Andersen (1872–1940) and had developed a strong affection for the young man; in *Henry James: The Treacherous Years* and *Henry James: The Master*, Edel explores the complex relationship that evolved.

been incidental to our reaching a small artistic foundry of fine metal, an odd and interesting little establishment placed, as who should say in the case of such a mere left-over scrap of a large loose margin, nowhere: it lurked so unsuspectedly, that is, among the various queer things that Rome comprehensively refers to as "behind St. Peter's."

We had passed then, on the occasion of our several pilgrimages, in beneath the great flying, or at least straddling buttresses to the left of the mighty façade, where you enter that great idle precinct of fine dense pavement and averted and sacrificed grandeur, the reverse of the monstrous medal of the front. Here the architectural monster rears its back and shoulders on an equal scale and this whole unregarded world of colossal consistent symmetry and hidden high finish gives you the measure of the vast total treasure of items and features. The outward face of all sorts of inward majesties of utility and ornament here above all correspondingly reproduces itself; the expanses of golden travertine—the freshness of tone, the cleanness of surface, in the sunny air, being extraordinary—climb and soar and spread under the crushing weight of a scheme carried out in every ponderous particular. Never was such a show of *wasted* art, of pomp for pomp's sake, as where all the chapels bulge and all the windows, each one a separate constructional masterpiece, tower above almost grass-grown vacancy; with the full and immediate effect, of course, of reading us a lesson on the value of lawful pride. The pride is the pride of indifference as to whether a greatness so founded be gaped at in all its features or not. My friend and I were alone to gape at them most often while, for the unfailing impression of them, on our way to watch the casting of our figure, we extended our circuit of the place. To which I may add, as another example of that tentative, that appealing twitch of the garment of Roman association of which one kept renewing one's consciousness, the half-hour at the little foundry itself was all charming—with its quite shabby and belittered and ramshackle recall of the old Roman "art-life" of one's early dreams. Everything was somehow in the picture, the rickety sheds, the loose paraphernalia, the sunny, grassy yard where a goat was browsing; then the queer interior gloom of the pits, frilled with little overlooking scaffoldings and bridges, for the sinking fireward of the image that was to take on hardness; and all the pleasantness and quickness, the beguiling refinement, of the three or four light fine "hands" of whom the staff consisted and into whose type and tone one liked to read, with whatever harmless extravagance, so many signs that a lively sense of stiff processes, even in humble life, could still leave untouched the traditional rare feeling for the artistic. How delightful such an occupation in such a general setting—those of my friend, I at such moments irrepressibly moralised; and how one might after such a fashion endlessly go and come and ask nothing better; or if better, only so to the extent of another impression I was to owe to him: that of an evening meal spread, in the warm still darkness that made no candle flicker, on the wide high space of an old loggia that overhung, in one quarter, the great obelisked Square preceding one of the Gates, and in the other the Tiber and the far Trastevere and more things than I can say—above all, as it were, the whole backward past, the mild confused romance of the Rome one had loved and of which one was exactly taking leave under protection of the friendly lanterned and garlanded feast and the commanding, all-embracing roof-garden. It was indeed a reconciling, it was an altogether penetrating, last hour.

1909.

A Chain of Cities

One day in midwinter, some years since, during a journey from Rome to Florence perforce too rapid to allow much wayside sacrifice to curiosity, I waited for the train at Narni. There was time to stroll far enough from the station to have a look at the famous old bridge of Augustus, broken short off in mid-Tiber. While I stood admiring the measure of impression was made to overflow by the gratuitous grace of a white-cowled monk who came trudging up the road that wound to the gate of the town. Narni stood, in its own presented felicity, on a hill a good space away, boxed in behind its perfect grey wall, and the monk, to oblige me, crept slowly along and disappeared within the aperture. Everything was distinct in the clear air, and the view exactly as like the bit of background by an Umbrian master as it ideally should have been. The winter is bare and brown enough in southern Italy and the earth reduced to more of a mere anatomy than among ourselves, for whom the very *crânerie* of its exposed state, naked and unashamed, gives it much of the robust serenity, not of a fleshless skeleton, but of a fine nude statue. In these regions at any rate, the tone of the air, for the eye, during the brief desolation, has often an extraordinary charm: nature still smiles as with the deputed and provisional charity of colour and light, the duty of not ceasing to cheer man's heart. Her whole

[Originally published as "A Chain of Italian Cities" in the *Atlantic Monthly*, XXXII (February 1874), 158–64; reprinted in *Transatlantic Sketches*, 1875; reprinted in *Foreign Parts*, 1883.]

famous old bridge of Augustus. Completely rebuilt after the 1944 bombing, the Ponte d'Augusto carried the Via Flaminia across the Nera river.

crânerie. Jauntiness.

behaviour, at the time, cast such a spell on the broken bridge, the little walled town and the trudging friar, that I turned away with the impatient vow and the fond vision of how I would take the journey again and pause to my heart's content at Narni, at Spoleto, at Assisi, at Perugia, at Cortona, at Arezzo. But we have generally to clip our vows a little when we come to fulfil them; and so it befell that when my blest springtime arrived I had to begin as resignedly as possible, yet with comparative meagreness, at Assisi.

I suppose enjoyment would have a simple zest which it often lacks if we always did things at the moment we want to, for it's mostly when we can't that we're thoroughly sure we *would,* and we can answer too little for moods in the future conditional. Winter at least seemed to me to have put something into these seats of antiquity that the May sun had more or less melted away—a desirable strength of tone, a depth upon depth of queerness and quaintness. Assisi had been in the January twilight, after my mere snatch at Narni, a vignette out of some brown old missal. But you'll have to be a fearless explorer now to find of a fine spring day any such cluster of curious objects as does n't seem made to match before anything else Mr. Baedeker's polyglot estimate of its chief recommendations. This great man was at Assisi in force, and a brand-new inn for his accommodation has just been opened cheek by jowl with the church of St. Francis. I don't know that even the dire discomfort of this harbourage makes it seem less impertinent; but I confess I sought its protection, and the great view seemed hardly less beautiful from my window than from the gallery of the convent. This view embraces the whole wide reach of Umbria, which becomes as twilight deepens a purple counterfeit of the misty sea. The visitor's first errand is with the church; and it's fair furthermore to admit that when he has crossed that threshold the position and quality of his hotel cease for the time to be matters of moment. This twofold temple of St. Francis is one of the very sacred places of Italy, and it would be hard to breathe anywhere an air more heavy with holiness. Such seems especially the case if you happen thus to have come from Rome, where everything ecclesiastical is, in aspect, so very much of this world—so florid, so elegant, so full of accommodations and excrescences. The mere site here makes for authority, and they were brave builders who laid the foundation-stones. The thing rises straight from a steep mountain-side and plunges forward on its great substructure of arches even as a crowned headland may frown over the main. Before it stretches a long, grassy piazza, at the end of which you look up a small grey street, to see it first climb a little way the rest of the hill and then pause and leave a broad green slope, crested, high in the air, with a ruined castle. When I say

Mr. Baedeker's. See note, page 90.

before it I mean before the upper church; for by way of doing something supremely handsome and impressive the sturdy architects of the thirteenth century piled temple upon temple and bequeathed a double version of their idea. One may imagine them to have intended perhaps an architectural image of the relation between heart and head. Entering the lower church at the bottom of the great flight of steps which leads from the upper door, you seem to push at least into the very heart of Catholicism.

For the first minutes after leaving the clearer gloom you catch nothing but a vista of low black columns closed by the great fantastic cage surrounding the altar, which is thus placed, by your impression, in a sort of gorgeous cavern. Gradually you distinguish details, become accustomed to the penetrating chill, and even manage to make out a few frescoes; but the general effect remains splendidly sombre and subterranean. The vaulted roof is very low and the pillars dwarfish, though immense in girth, as befits pillars supporting substantially a cathedral. The tone of the place is a triumph of mystery, the richest harmony of lurking shadows and dusky corners, all relieved by scattered images and scintillations. There was little light but what came through the windows of the choir over which the red curtains had been dropped and were beginning to glow with the downward sun. The choir was guarded by a screen behind which a dozen venerable voices droned vespers; but over the top of the screen came the heavy radiance and played among the ornaments of the high fence round the shrine, casting the shadow of the whole elaborate mass forward into the obscured nave. The darkness of vaults and side-chapels is overwrought with vague frescoes, most of them by Giotto and his school, out of which confused richness the terribly distinct little faces characteristic of these artists stare at you with a solemn formalism. Some are faded and injured, and many so ill-lighted and ill-placed that you can only glance at them with decent conjecture; the great group, however—four paintings by Giotto on the ceiling above the altar—may be examined with some success. Like everything of that grim and beautiful master they deserve examination; but with the effect ever of carrying one's appreciation in and in, as it were, rather than of carrying it out and out, off and off, as happens for us with those artists who have been helped by the process of "evolution" to grow wings. This one, "going in" for emphasis at any price, stamps hard, as who should say, on the very spot of his idea—thanks to which fact he has a concentration that has never been surpassed. He was in other words, in proportion to his means, a genius

---

four paintings by Giotto. On the vault, scenes from the life of Saint Francis, *The Marriage with the Lady Poverty, The Allegory of Obedience, The Vow of Chastity,* and *Saint Francis in Glory.*

supremely expressive; he makes the very shade of an intended meaning or a represented attitude so unmistakable that his figures affect us at moments as creatures all too suddenly, too alarmingly, too menacingly met. Meagre, primitive, undeveloped, he yet is immeasurably strong; he even suggests that if he had lived the due span of years later Michael Angelo might have found a rival. Not that he is given, however, to complicated postures or superhuman flights. The something strange that troubles and haunts us in his work springs rather from a kind of fierce familiarity.

It is part of the wealth of the lower church that it contains an admirable primitive fresco by an artist of genius rarely encountered, Pietro Cavallini, pupil of Giotto. This represents the Crucifixion; the three crosses rising into a sky spotted with the winged heads of angels while a dense crowd presses below. You will nowhere see anything more direfully lugubrious, or more approaching for direct force, though not of course for amplitude of style, Tintoretto's great renderings of the scene in Venice. The abject anguish of the crucified and the straddling authority and brutality of the mounted guards in the foreground are contrasted in a fashion worthy of a great dramatist. But the most poignant touch is the tragic grimaces of the little angelic heads that fall like hailstones through the dark air. It is genuine realistic weeping, the act of irrepressible "crying," that the painter has depicted, and the effect is pitiful at the same time as grotesque. There are many more frescoes besides; all the chapels on one side are lined with them, but these are chiefly interesting in their general impressiveness—as they people the dim recesses with startling presences, with apparitions out of scale. Before leaving the place I lingered long near the door, for I was sure I should n't soon again enjoy such a feast of scenic composition. The opposite end glowed with subdued colour; the middle portion was vague and thick and brown, with two or three scattered worshippers looming through the obscurity; while, all the way down, the polished pavement, its uneven slabs glittering dimly in the obstructed light, was of the very essence of expensive picture. It is certainly desirable, if one takes the lower church of St. Francis to represent the human heart, that one should find a few bright places there. But if the general effect is of brightness terrorised and smothered, is the symbol less valid? For the contracted, prejudiced, passionate heart let it stand.

One thing at all events we can say, that we should rejoice to boast as capacious, symmetrical and well-ordered a head as the upper sanctuary. Thanks to these merits, in spite of a brave array of Giottesque work which

---

Pietro Cavallini. Attributed to Cavallini throughout the nineteenth century but now given to Pietro Lorenzetti.

has the advantage of being easily seen, it lacks the great character of its counterpart. The frescoes, which are admirable, represent certain leading events in the life of St. Francis, and suddenly remind you, by one of those anomalies that are half the secret of the consummate *mise-en-scène* of Catholicism, that the apostle of beggary, the saint whose only tenement in life was the ragged robe which barely covered him, is the hero of this massive structure. Church upon church, nothing less will adequately shroud his consecrated clay. The great reality of Giotto's designs adds to the helpless wonderment with which we feel the passionate pluck of the Hero, the sense of being separated from it by an impassable gulf, the reflection on all that has come and gone to make morality at that vertiginous pitch impossible. There are no such high places of humility left to climb to. An observant friend who has lived long in Italy lately declared to me, however, that she detested the name of this moralist, deeming him chief propagator of the Italian vice most trying to the would-be lover of the people, the want of personal self-respect. There is a solidarity in the use of soap, and every cringing beggar, idler, liar and pilferer flourished for her under the shadow of the great Franciscan indifference to it. She was possibly right; at Rome, at Naples, I might have admitted she was right; but at Assisi, face to face with Giotto's vivid chronicle, we admire too much in its main subject the exquisite play of that subject's genius—we don't remit to him, and this for very envy, a single throb of his consciousness. It took in, that human, that divine embrace, everything *but* soap.

I should find it hard to give an orderly account of my next adventures or impressions at Assisi, which could n't well be anything more than mere romantic *flânerie*. One may easily plead as the final result of a meditation at the shrine of St. Francis a great and even an amused charity. This state of mind led me slowly up and down for a couple of hours through the steep little streets, and at last stretched itself on the grass with me in the shadow of the great ruined castle that decorates so grandly the eminence above the town. I remember edging along the sunless side of the small mouldy houses and pausing very often to look at nothing in particular. It was all very hot, very hushed, very resignedly but very persistently old. A wheeled vehicle in such a place is an event, and the *forestiero's* interrogative tread in the blank sonorous lanes has the privilege of bringing the inhabitants to their doorways. Some of the better houses, however, achieve a sombre stillness that protests against the least curiosity as to what may happen in any such century as this. You wonder, as you pass, what lingering old-world social

---

great ruined castle. The Rocca Maggiore, an old German fortress in which Frederick II spent several years of his youth.

types vegetate there, but you won't find out; albeit that in one very silent
little street I had a glimpse of an open door which I have not forgotten. A
long-haired peddler who must have been a Jew, and who yet carried without
prejudice a burden of mass-books and rosaries, was offering his wares to a
stout old priest. The priest had opened the door rather stingily and appeared
half-heartedly to dismiss him. But the peddler held up something I could n't
see; the priest wavered with a timorous concession to profane curiosity and
then furtively pulled the agent of sophistication, or whatever it might be,
into the house. I should have liked to enter with that worthy.

I saw later some gentlemen of Assisi who also seemed bored enough to
have found entertainment in his tray. They were at the door of the café on
the Piazza, and were so thankful to me for asking them the way to the
cathedral that, answering all in chorus, they lighted up with smiles as sympathetic as if I had done them a favour. Of that type were my mild, my delicate
adventures. The Piazza has a fine old portico of an ancient Temple of
Minerva—six fluted columns and a pediment, of beautiful proportions, but
sadly battered and decayed. Goethe, I believe, found it much more interesting than the mighty mediæval church, and Goethe, as a cicerone, doubtless
could have persuaded one that it was so; but in the humble society of
Murray we shall most of us find a richer sense in the later monument. I
found quaint old meanings enough in the dark yellow façade of the small
cathedral as I sat on a stone bench by the oblong green stretched before it.
This is a pleasing piece of Italian Gothic and, like several of its companions
at Assisi, has an elegant wheel window and a number of grotesque little
carvings of creatures human and bestial. If with Goethe I were to balance
anything against the attractions of the double church I should choose the
ruined castle on the hill above the town. I had been having glimpses of it all

---

Temple of Minerva . . . Goethe. "One could never tire of looking at the facade and admiring
the logical procedure of the architect. The order is Corinthian and the space between the
columns about two modules. The bases of the columns and the plinths below them appear to be
standing on pedestals, but this is only an illusion, for the stylobate has been cut through in five
places, and through each gap five steps lead up between the columns. By these one reaches the
platform on which the columns actually stand, and enters the temple. The bold idea of cutting
through the stylobate was a sensible one, given the site. Since the temple stands on a hill, the
stairs up to it would otherwise have jutted out too far into the square and made it too cramped.
How many steps there were originally is now impossible to determine, because, except for a
few, they lie buried under the earth and paved over. I tore myself away reluctantly. . . . There, in
the foreground, walked those rude fellows while, behind them, Minerva looked down on me
kindly, as if she wanted to console me. I turned to look at the dreary Duomo of St. Francis to
my left . . ." (Goethe, *Italian Journey*, 107–9).

Murray. Murray's *Handbook for Central Italy*, 1867 (404), judges the church one of the
most remarkable monuments of the Middle Ages and comments only in passing on the portico
of the Temple of Minerva, now the church of Santa Maria.

the afternoon at the end of steep street-vistas, and promising myself half-an-hour beside its grey walls at sunset. The sun was very late setting, and my half-hour became a long lounge in the lee of an abutment which arrested the gentle uproar of the wind. The castle is a splendid piece of ruin, perched on the summit of the mountain to whose slope Assisi clings and dropping a pair of stony arms to enclose the little town in its embrace. The city wall, in other words, straggles up the steep green hill and meets the crumbling skeleton of the fortress. On the side off from the town the mountain plunges into a deep ravine, the opposite face of which is formed by the powerful undraped shoulder of Monte Subasio, a fierce reflector of the sun. Gorge and mountain are wild enough, but their frown expires in the teeming softness of the great vale of Umbria. To lie aloft there on the grass, with silver-grey ramparts at one's back and the warm rushing wind in one's ears, and watch the beautiful plain mellow into the tones of twilight, was as exquisite a form of repose as ever fell to a tired tourist's lot.

Perugia too has an ancient stronghold, which one must speak of in earnest as that unconscious humourist the classic American traveller is supposed invariably to speak of the Colosseum: it will be a very handsome building when it's finished. Even Perugia is going the way of all Italy—straightening out her streets, preparing her ruins, laying her venerable ghosts. The castle is being completely *remis à neuf*—a Massachusetts schoolhouse couldn't cultivate a "smarter" ideal. There are shops in the basement and fresh putty on all the windows; so that the only thing proper to a castle it has kept is its magnificent position and range, which you may enjoy from the broad platform where the Perugini assemble at eventide. Perugia is chiefly known to fame as the city of Raphael's master; but it has a still higher claim to renown and ought to figure in the gazetteer of fond memory as the little City of the infinite View. The small dusky, crooked place tries by a hundred prompt pretensions, immediate contortions, rich mantling flushes and other ingenuities, to waylay your attention and keep it at home; but your consciousness, alert and uneasy from the first moment, is all abroad even when your back is turned to the vast alternative or when fifty house-walls conceal it, and you are for ever rushing up by-streets and peeping round corners in the hope of another glimpse or reach of it. As it stretches away before you in that eminent indifference to limits which is at the same time at every step an eminent homage to style, it is altogether too free and fair for compasses and terms. You can only say, and rest upon it, that you prefer it to any other visible fruit of position or claimed empire of the eye that you are anywhere likely to enjoy.

---

remis à neuf. The Palazzo dei Priori—made to look just like new—on the Corso Vannucci today is as accommodating to merchants as in James's time.

Raphael's master. Pietro Vannucci, called Perugino (c. 1445–1523).

For it is such a wondrous mixture of blooming plain and gleaming river and wavily-multitudinous mountain vaguely dotted with pale grey cities, that, placed as you are, roughly speaking, in the centre of Italy, you all but span the divine peninsula from sea to sea. Up the long vista of the Tiber you look—almost to Rome; past Assisi, Spello, Foligno, Spoleto, all perched on their respective heights and shining through the violet haze. To the north, to the east, to the west, you see a hundred variations of the prospect, of which I have kept no record. Two notes only I have made: one—though who has n't made it over and over again?—on the exquisite elegance of mountain forms in this endless play of the excrescence, it being exactly as if there were variation of sex in the upheaved mass, with the effect here mainly of contour and curve and complexion determined in the feminine sense. It further came home to me that the command of such an outlook on the world goes far, surely, to give authority and centrality and experience, those of the great seats of dominion, even to so scant a cluster of attesting objects as here. It must deepen the civic consciousness and take off the edge of ennui. It performs this kindly office, at any rate, for the traveller who may overstay his curiosity as to Perugino and the Etruscan relics. It continually solicits his wonder and praise—it reinforces the historic page. I spent a week in the place, and when it was gone I had had enough of Perugino, but had n't had enough of the View.

I should perhaps do the reader a service by telling him just how a week at Perugia may be spent. His first care must be to ignore the very dream of haste, walking everywhere very slowly and very much at random, and to impute an esoteric sense to almost anything his eye may happen to encounter. Almost everything in fact lends itself to the historic, the romantic, the æsthetic fallacy—almost everything has an antique queerness and richness that ekes out the reduced state; that of a grim and battered old adventuress, the heroine of many shames and scandals, surviving to an extraordinary age and a considerable penury, but with ancient gifts of princes and other forms of the wages of sin to show, and the most beautiful garden of all the world to sit and doze and count her beads in and remember. He must hang a great deal about the huge Palazzo Pubblico, which indeed is very well worth any acquaintance you may scrape with it. It masses itself gloomily above the narrow street to an immense elevation, and leads up the eye along a cliff-like surface of rugged wall, mottled with old scars and new repairs, to the loggia dizzily perched on its cornice. He must repeat his visit to the Etruscan Gate,

---

Etruscan Gate . . . immemorial composition. The Arco d'Augusto, the lower part of which was constructed from the third to the second centuries B.C., the upper part added after 40 B.C., and the loggia and the buttresses completed in the sixteenth century.

by whose immemorial composition he must indeed linger long to resolve it back into the elements originally attending it. He must uncap to the irrecoverable, the inimitable style of the statue of Pope Julius III before the cathedral, remembering that Hawthorne fabled his Miriam, in an air of romance from which we are well-nigh as far to-day as from the building of Etruscan gates, to have given rendezvous to Kenyon at its base. Its material is a vivid green bronze, and the mantle and tiara are covered with a delicate embroidery worthy of a silversmith.

Then our leisurely friend must bestow on Perugino's frescoes in the Exchange, and on his pictures in the University, all the placid contemplation they deserve. He must go to the theatre every evening, in an orchestra-chair at twenty-two soldi, and enjoy the curious didacticism of "Amore senza Stima," "Severità e Debolezza," "La Società Equivoca," and other popular specimens of contemporaneous Italian comedy—unless indeed the last-named be not the edifying title applied, for peninsular use, to "Le Demi-Monde" of the younger Dumas. I shall be very much surprised if, at the end of a week of this varied entertainment, he has n't learnt how to live, not exactly in, but with, Perugia. His strolls will abound in small accidents and mercies of vision, but of which a dozen pencil-strokes would be a better memento than this poor word-sketching. From the hill on which the town is

---

statue of Pope Julius . . . Hawthorne. By Vincenzio Danti, 1555, the statue figures prominently as part of the scenery of Hawthorne's *The Marble Faun*. It remained memorable to James for many years; for a personal reaction to this feature of Perugia see the letter of 15 May 1900 to Paul Bourget: "Yet it would be delightful to receive from you one echo of Perugia. Give my love, my tenderest, to the old green Pope in the old brown Piazza" (*Letters*, IV, 139–41).

"Amore senza Stima," "Severità e Debolezza," "La Società Equivoca." James refers to a derivative period during which the French theater exercised strong influence on the Italian comedies and sentimental dramas of the first half of the nineteenth century—and often beyond (Paolo Ferrari's [1822–89] popular *Amore senza Stima* [Love Without Respect], was produced in 1868). Although this play clearly owed much to Goldoni's *La Moglie Saggia* (The Wise Wife), his work was generally modeled on French theatrical methods. The editor is unable to find references to the other two works cited by James.

"Le Demi-Monde" of the younger Dumas. In the New York Edition preface (1908) to the "Lady Barbarina" volume, James records a particularly negative reaction to a performance of this 1855 work by Alexandre Dumas *fils* (1825–95); the play, about the milieu of women of easy virtue, brought "demi-monde" into the European vocabulary.

"The play had been 'Le Demi-Monde' of the younger Dumas, a masterpiece which I had not heard for the first time, but a particular feature of which on this occasion more than ever yet filled up the measure of my impatience. I could less than ever swallow it . . . [it] seemed to have made me present at something inhuman and odious. It was the old story—that from the positive, the prodigious *morality* of such a painter of the sophisticated life as Dumas, not from anything else or less edifying, one must pray to be delivered" (*Literary Criticism: French Writers*, 1218–19).

planted radiate a dozen ravines, down whose sides the houses slide and
scramble with an alarming indifference to the cohesion of their little rugged
blocks of flinty red stone. You ramble really nowhither without emerging on
some small court or terrace that throws your view across a gulf of tangled
gardens or vineyards and over to a cluster of serried black dwellings which
have to hollow in their backs to keep their balance on the opposite ledge. On
archways and street-staircases and dark alleys that bore through a density of
massive basements, and curve and climb and plunge as they go, all to the
truest mediæval tune, you may feast your fill. These are the local, the architectural, the compositional commonplaces. Some of the little streets in out-of-
the-way corners are so rugged and brown and silent that you may imagine
them passages long since hewn by the pick-axe in a deserted stone-quarry.
The battered black houses, of the colour of buried things—things buried,
that is, in accumulations of time, closer packed, even as such are, than
spadefuls of earth—resemble exposed sections of natural rock; none the less
so when, beyond some narrow gap, you catch the blue and silver of the
sublime circle of landscape.

But I ought n't to talk of mouldy alleys, or yet of azure distances, as if they
formed the main appeal to taste in this accomplished little city. In the Sala
del Cambio, where in ancient days the money-changers rattled their embossed coin and figured up their profits, you may enjoy one of the serenest
æsthetic pleasures that the golden age of art anywhere offers us. Bank
parlours, I believe, are always handsomely appointed, but are even those of
Messrs. Rothschild such models of mural bravery as this little counting-
house of a bygone fashion? The bravery is Perugino's own; for, invited
clearly to do his best, he left it as a lesson to the ages, covering the four low
walls and the vault with scriptural and mythological figures of extraordinary beauty. They are ranged in artless attitudes round the upper half of the
room— the sibyls, the prophets, the philosophers, the Greek and Roman
heroes—looking down with broad serene faces, with small mild eyes and
sweet mouths that commit them to nothing in particular unless to being
comfortably and charmingly alive, at the incongruous proceedings of a
Board of Brokers. Had finance a very high tone in those days, or were genius
and faith then simply as frequent as capital and enterprise are among ourselves? The great distinction of the Sala del Cambio is that it has a friendly
Yes for both these questions. There was a rigid transactional probity, it
seems to say; there was also a high tide of inspiration. About the artist
himself many things come up for us—more than I can attempt in their
order; for he was not, I think, to an attentive observer, the mere smooth and
entire and devout spirit we at first are inclined to take him for. He has that
about him which leads us to wonder if he may not, after all, play a proper
part enough here as the patron of the money-changers. He is the delight of a

million of young ladies; but who knows whether we should n't find in his works, might we "go into" them a little, a trifle more of manner than of conviction, and of system than of deep sincerity?

This, I allow, would put no great affront on them, and one speculates thus partly but because it's a pleasure to hang about him on any pretext, and partly because his immediate effect is to make us quite inordinately embrace the pretext of his lovely soul. His portrait, painted on the wall of the Sala (you may see it also in Rome and Florence) might at any rate serve for the likeness of Mr. Worldly-Wiseman in Bunyan's allegory. He was fond of his glass, I believe, and he made his art lucrative. This tradition is not refuted by his preserved face, and after some experience—or rather after a good deal, since you can't have a *little* of Perugino, who abounds wherever old masters congregate, so that one has constantly the sense of being "in" for all there is—you may find an echo of it in the uniform type of his creatures, their monotonous grace, their prodigious invariability. He may very well have wanted to produce figures of a substantial, yet at the same time of an impeccable innocence; but we feel that he had taught himself *how* even beyond his own belief in them, and had arrived at a process that acted at last mechanically. I confess at the same time that, so interpreted, the painter affects me as hardly less interesting, and one can't but become conscious of one's style when one's style has become, as it were, so conscious of one's, or at least of its own, fortune. If he was the inventor of a remarkably calculable *facture,* a calculation that never fails is in its way a grace of the first order, and there are things in this special appearance of perfection of practice that make him the forerunner of a mighty and more modern race. More than any of the early painters who strongly charm, you may take all his measure from a single specimen. The other samples infallibly match, reproduce unerringly the one type he had mastered, but which had the good fortune to be adorably fair, to seem to have dawned on a vision unsullied by the shadows of earth. Which truth, moreover, leaves Perugino all delightful as composer

---

His portrait . . . also in Rome and Florence. A self-portrait is painted on a pilaster in the Sala del Cambio, with an inscription in Latin ("Petrus Perusinus . . ."). The Florence portrait in the Uffizi today is recognized as a portrait of Francesco delle Opere but was identified as Perugino's self-portrait throughout the nineteenth century; in the Sistine Chapel fresco of Peter receiving the keys to heaven, Perugino represents himself looking straight out at the spectators, the fifth figure from the right (Scarpellini, 79, 88, 98).

Mr. Worldly-Wiseman . . . Bunyan's allegory. In John Bunyan's *Pilgrim's Progress* (1678; 1684), a resident of Carnal Policy who attempts to discourage Christian from making the pilgrimage.

facture. An artistic treatment.

and draughtsman; he has in each of these characters a sort of spacious neatness which suggests that the whole conception has been washed clean by some spiritual chemistry the last thing before reaching the canvas; after which it has been applied to that surface with a rare economy of time and means. Giotto and Fra Angelico, beside him, are full of interesting waste and irrelevant passion. In the sacristy of the charming church of San Pietro—a museum of pictures and carvings—is a row of small heads of saints formerly covering the frame of the artist's Ascension, carried off by the French. It is almost miniature work, and here at least Perugino triumphs in sincerity, in apparent candour, as well as in touch. Two of the holy men are reading their breviaries, but with an air of infantine innocence quite consistent with their holding the book upside down.

Between Perugia and Cortona lies the large weedy water of Lake Thrasymene, turned into a witching word for ever by Hannibal's recorded victory over Rome. Dim as such records have become to us and remote such realities, he is yet a passionless pilgrim who does n't, as he passes, of a heavy summer's day, feel the air and the light and the very faintness of the breeze all charged and haunted with them, all interfused as with the wasted ache of experience and with the vague historic gaze. Processions of indistinguishable ghosts bore me company to Cortona itself, most sturdily ancient of Italian towns. It must have been a seat of ancient knowledge even when Hannibal and Flaminius came to the shock of battle, and have looked down afar from its grey ramparts on the contending swarm with something of the philosophic composure suitable to a survivor of Pelasgic and Etruscan revolutions. These grey ramparts are in great part still visible, and form the chief attraction of Cortona. It is perched on the very pinnacle of a mountain, and I wound and doubled interminably over the face of the great hill, while the jumbled roofs and towers of the arrogant little city still seemed nearer to the sky than to the railway-station. "Rather rough," Murray pronounces the

---

San Pietro . . . Ascension, carried off by the French . . . holy men. The polytych that Perugino painted for the church of San Pietro Vincioli (also known as San Pietro dei Cassinensi). In 1797 a Napoleonic requisition caused the work to be dismantled and moved to France, with the central panel going to Lyon and other parts to Rouen, to Nantes, and to the church of Saint-Gervais in Paris; some of the panels were returned to Italy after the fall of Napoleon, but they went to the Vatican, not back to Perugia. The two holy men cited are San Costanzo and San Mauro.

Lake Thrasymene . . . Hannibal's recorded victory . . . indistinguishable ghosts . . . Cortona. Livy, *History of Rome*, xxi–xxx, provides the details of Hannibal's victory over the Roman troops on the northern shore of Lago Trasimeno, in 217 B.C. Hannibal also laid waste to Cortona, an ancient city, believed by Virgil to have been the burial place of Corythus, father of Dardanus, founder of Troy (*Aeneid*, vii, 209).

local inn; and rough indeed it was; there was scarce a square foot of it that you would have cared to stroke with your hand. The landlord himself, however, was all smoothness and the best fellow in the world; he took me up into a rickety old loggia on the tip-top of his establishment and played showman as to half the kingdoms of the earth. I was free to decide at the same time whether my loss or my gain was the greater for my seeing Cortona through the medium of a festa. On the one hand the museum was closed (and in a certain sense the smaller and obscurer the town the more I like the museum); the churches—an interesting note of manners and morals—were impenetrably crowded, though, for that matter, so was the café, where I found neither an empty stool nor the edge of a table. I missed a sight of the famous painted Muse, the art-treasure of Cortona and supposedly the most precious, as it falls little short of being the only, sample of the Greek painted picture that has come down to us. On the other hand, I saw—but this is what I saw.

A part of the mountain-top is occupied by the church of St. Margaret, and this was St. Margaret's day. The houses pause roundabout it and leave a grassy slope, planted here and there with lean black cypresses. The contadini from near and far had congregated in force and were crowding into the church or winding up the slope. When I arrived they were all kneeling or uncovered; a bedizened procession, with banners and censers, bearing abroad, I believe, the relics of the saint, was re-entering the church. The scene made one of those pictures that Italy still brushes in for you with an incomparable hand and from an inexhaustible palette when you find her in the mood. The day was superb—the sky blazed overhead like a vault of deepest sapphire. The grave brown peasantry, with no great accent of costume, but with sundry small ones—decked, that is, in cheap fineries of scarlet and yellow—made a mass of motley colour in the high wind-stirred light. The procession halted in the pious hush, and the lovely land around and beneath us melted away, almost to either sea, in tones of azure scarcely less intense than the sky. Behind the church was an empty crumbling citadel, with half-a-dozen old women keeping the gate for coppers. Here were views and breezes and sun and shade and grassy corners to the heart's content, together with one could n't say what huge seated mystic melancholy presence, the after-taste of everything the still open maw of time had consumed. I chose a spot that fairly

---

famous painted Muse. In the Museo dell'Accademia Etrusca of the Palazzo Pretorio, "La Musa Polimnia," formerly believed to have been a unique example of Greco-Roman painting of the first or second century A.D., today is judged the work of an unknown Renaissance artist of the sixteenth century; some attributions are to Dosso Dossi.

citadel. The Fortezza Medicea.

combined all these advantages, a spot from which I seemed to look, as who should say, straight down the throat of the monster, no dark passage now, but with all the glorious day playing into it, and spent a good part of my stay at Cortona lying there at my length and observing the situation over the top of a volume that I must have brought in my pocket just for that especial wanton luxury of the resource provided and slighted. In the afternoon I came down and hustled a while through the crowded little streets, and then strolled forth under the scorching sun and made the outer circuit of the wall. There I found tremendous uncemented blocks; they glared and twinkled in the powerful light, and I had to put on a blue eye-glass in order to throw into its proper perspective the vague Etruscan past, obtruded and magnified in such masses quite as with the effect of inadequately-withdrawn hands and feet in photographs.

I spent the next day at Arezzo, but I confess in very much the same uninvestigating fashion—taking in the "general impression," I dare say, at every pore, but rather systematically leaving the dust of the ages unfingered on the stored records: I should doubtless, in the poor time at my command, have fingered it to so little purpose. The seeker for the story of things has moreover, if he be worth his salt, a hundred insidious arts; and in that case indeed—by which I mean when his sensibility has come duly to adjust itself—the story assaults him but from too many sides. He even feels at moments that he must sneak along on tiptoe in order not to have too much of it. Besides which the case all depends on the kind of use, the range of application, his tangled consciousness, or his intelligible genius, say, may come to recognize for it. At Arezzo, however this might be, one was far from Rome, one was well within genial Tuscany, and the historic, the romantic decoction seemed to reach one's lips in less stiff doses. There at once was the "general impression"—the exquisite sense of the scarce expressible Tuscan quality, which makes immediately, for the whole pitch of one's perception, a grateful, a not at all strenuous difference, attaches to almost any coherent group of objects, to any happy aspect of the scene, for a main note, some mild recall, through pleasant friendly colour, through settled ample form,

---

Arezzo . . . uninvestigating fashion. James makes no mention of Piero della Francesca's fresco cycle "The Legend of the True Cross" at the church of San Francesco, largely because in 1873 Piero had almost no reputation; with the appearance of Roberto Longhi's *Piero della Francesca* (1927), the Arezzo frescoes finally began to receive the attention they deserve. In his 1951 monograph on the artist, Kenneth Clark remarks that although Piero has "taken his place as one of the greatest artists of the fifteenth century, and thus one of the greatest artists who have ever lived . . . few of our bewildering revolutions of taste would have been more incomprehensible to the aesthetes of the nineteenth century" (Clark, 9). Ruskin's thirty-nine volumes refer to the artist only in passing.

through something homely and economic too at the very heart of "style," of an identity of temperament and habit with those of the divine little Florence that one originally knew. Adorable Italy in which, for the constant renewal of interest, of attention, of affection, these refinements of variety, these so harmoniously-grouped and individually-seasoned fruits of the great garden of history, keep presenting themselves! It seemed to fall in with the cheerful Tuscan mildness for instance—sticking as I do to that ineffectual expression of the Tuscan charm, of the yellow-brown Tuscan dignity at large—that the ruined castle on the hill (with which agreeable feature Arezzo is no less furnished than Assisi and Cortona) had been converted into a great blooming, and I hope all profitable, podere or market-garden. I lounged away the half-hours there under a spell as potent as the "wildest" forecast of propriety—propriety to all the particular conditions—could have figured it. I had seen Santa Maria della Pieve and its campanile of quaint colonnades, the stately, dusky cathedral—grass-plotted and residenced about almost after the fashion of an English "close"—and John of Pisa's elaborate marble shrine; I had seen the museum and its Etruscan vases and majolica platters. These were very well, but the old pacified citadel somehow, through a day of soft saturation, placed me most in relation. Beautiful hills surrounded it, cypresses cast straight shadows at its corners, while in the middle grew a wondrous Italian tangle of wheat and corn, vines and figs, peaches and cabbages, memories and images, anything and everything.

1873.

John of Pisa's elaborate marble shrine. The intricate baptismal font to which James refers is by Giovanni di Agostino (c. 1311–c. 1347), not by Giovanni Pisano (c. 1248–c. 1314).

Siena Early and Late

I

Florence being oppressively hot and delivered over to the mos-
quitoes, the occasion seemed to favour that visit to Siena which I
had more than once planned and missed. I arrived late in the
evening, by the light of a magnificent moon, and while a couple of
benignantly-mumbling old crones were making up my bed at the inn strolled
forth in quest of a first impression. Five minutes brought me to where I might
gather it unhindered as it bloomed in the white moonshine. The great Piazza
of Siena is famous, and though in this day of multiplied photographs and
blunted surprises and profaned revelations none of the world's wonders can
pretend, like Wordsworth's phantom of delight, really to "startle and way-
lay," yet as I stepped upon the waiting scene from under a dark archway I was
conscious of no loss of the edge of a precious presented sensibility. The
waiting scene, as I have called it, was in the shape of a shallow horse-shoe—
as the untravelled reader who has turned over his travelled friends' portfolios
will respectfully remember; or, better, of a bow in which the high wide face of
the Palazzo Pubblico forms the cord and everything else the arc. It was void of
any human presence that could figure to me the current year; so that, the
moonshine assisting, I had half-an-hour's infinite vision of mediæval Italy.

[The first part was originally published as "Siena" in the *Atlantic Monthly,* XXXIII (June
1874), 664–69; reprinted in *Transatlantic Sketches,* 1875. The second part was published for
the first time in *Italian Hours*].

Wordsworth's phantom of delight. "She was a Phantom of delight" (1804; 1807)—"A
dancing Shape, an Image gay, / To haunt, to startle, and way-lay" (ll. 9–10).

The Piazza being built on the side of a hill—or rather, as I believe science affirms, in the cup of a volcanic crater—the vast pavement converges downwards in slanting radiations of stone, the spokes of a great wheel, to a point directly before the Palazzo, which may mark the hub, though it is nothing more ornamental than the mouth of a drain. The great monument stands on the lower side and might seem, in spite of its goodly mass and its embattled cornice, to be rather defiantly out-countenanced by vast private constructions occupying the opposite eminence. This *might* be, without the extraordinary dignity of the architectural gesture with which the huge high-shouldered pile asserts itself.

On the firm edge of the palace, from bracketed base to grey-capped summit against the sky, where grows a tall slim tower which soars and soars till it has given notice of the city's greatness over the blue mountains that mark the horizon. It rises as slender and straight as a pennoned lance planted on the steel-shod toe of a mounted knight, and keeps all to itself in the blue air, far above the changing fashions of the market, the proud consciousness or rare arrogance once built into it. This beautiful tower, the finest thing in Siena and, in its rigid fashion, as permanently fine thus as a really handsome nose on a face of no matter what accumulated age, figures there still as a Declaration of Independence beside which such an affair as ours, thrown off at Philadelphia, appears to have scarce done more than helplessly give way to time. Our Independence has become a dependence on a thousand such dreadful things as the incorrupt declaration of Siena strikes us as looking for ever straight over the level of. As it stood silvered by the moonlight, while my greeting lasted, it seemed to speak, all as from soul to soul, very much indeed as some ancient worthy of a lower order, but-tonholing one on the coveted chance and at the quiet hour, might have done, of a state of things long and vulgarly superseded, but to the pride and power, the once prodigious vitality, of which who could expect any one effect to testify more incomparably, more indestructibly, quite, as it were, more im-mortally? The gigantic houses enclosing the rest of the Piazza took up the tale and mingled with it their burden. "We are very old and a trifle weary, but we were built strong and piled high, and we shall last for many an age. The present is cold and heedless, but we keep ourselves in heart by brooding over our store of memories and traditions. We are haunted houses in every creaking timber and aching stone." Such were the gossiping connections I established with Siena before I went to bed.

Since that night I have had a week's daylight knowledge of the surface of the subject at least, and don't know how I can better present it than simply as another and a vivider page of the lesson that the ever-hungry artist has only to *trust* old Italy for her to feed him at every single step from her hand—and if not with one sort of sweetly-stale grain from that wondrous mill of history which during so many ages ground finer than any other on earth, why then always with something else. Siena has at any rate "preserved appearances"—kept the greatest number of them, that is, unaltered for the eye—about as consistently as one can imagine the thing done. Other places perhaps may treat you to as drowsy an odour of antiquity, but few exhale it from so large an area. Lying massed within her walls on a dozen clustered hill-tops, she shows you at every turn in how much greater a way she once lived; and if so much of the grand manner is extinct, the receptacle of the ashes still solidly rounds itself. This heavy general stress of all her emphasis on the past is what she constantly keeps in your eyes and your ears, and if you be but a casual observer and admirer the generalised response is mainly what you give her. The casual observer, however beguiled, is mostly not very learned, not over-equipped in advance with data; he has n't specialised, his notions are necessarily vague, the chords of his imagination, for all his good-will, are inevitably muffled and weak. But such as it is, his received, his welcome impression serves his turn so far as the life of sensibility goes, and reminds him from time to time that even the lore of German doctors is but the shadow of satisfied curiosity. I have been living at the inn, walking about the streets, sitting in the Piazza; these are the simple terms of my experience. But streets and inns in Italy are the vehicles of half one's knowledge; if one has no fancy for their lessons one may burn one's note-book. In Siena everything is Sienese. The inn has an English sign over the door—a little battered plate with a rusty representation of the lion and the unicorn; but advance hopefully into the mouldy stone alley which serves as vestibule and you will find local colour enough. The landlord, I was told, had been servant in an English family, and I was curious to see how he met the probable argument of the casual Anglo-Saxon after the latter's first twelve hours in his establishment. As he failed to appear I asked the waiter if he were n't at home. "Oh," said the latter, "he's a *piccolo grasso vecchiotto* who does n't like to move." I'm afraid this little fat old man has simply a bad conscience. It's no small burden for one who likes the Italians—as who does n't, under this restriction?—to have so much indifference even to rudimentary purify-ing processes to dispose of. What is the real philosophy of dirty habits, and are foul surfaces merely superficial? If unclean manners have in truth the moral meaning which I suspect in them we must love Italy better than consistency. This a number of us are prepared to do, but while we are making the sacrifice it is as well we should be aware.

We may plead moreover for these impecunious heirs of the past that even if it were easy to be clean in the midst of their mouldering heritage it would

---

piccolo grasso vecchiotto. A little fat old man, as James indicates in the next sentence.

be difficult to appear so. At the risk of seeming to flaunt the silly superstition of restless renovation for the sake of renovation, which is but the challenge of the infinitely precious principle of duration, one is still moved to say that the prime result of one's contemplative strolls in the dusky alleys of such a place is an ineffable sense of disrepair. Everything is cracking, peeling, fading, crumbling, rotting. No young Sienese eyes rest upon anything youthful; they open into a world battered and befouled with long use. Everything has passed its meridian except the brilliant façade of the cathedral, which is being diligently retouched and restored, and a few private palaces whose broad fronts seem to have been lately furbished and polished. Siena was long ago mellowed to the pictorial tone; the operation of time is now to deposit shabbiness upon shabbiness. But it's for the most part a patient, sturdy, sympathetic shabbiness, which soothes rather than irritates the nerves, and has in many cases doubtless as long a career to run as most of our pert and shallow freshnesses. It projects at all events a deeper shadow into the constant twilight of the narrow streets—that vague historic dusk, as I may call it, in which one walks and wonders. These streets are hardly more than sinuous flagged alleys, into which the huge black houses, between their almost meeting cornices, suffer a meagre light to filter down over rough-hewn stone, past windows often of graceful Gothic form, and great pendent iron rings and twisted sockets for torches. Scattered over their many-headed hill, they suffer the roadway often to incline to the perpendicular, becoming so impracticable for vehicles that the sound of wheels is only a trifle less anomalous than it would be in Venice. But all day long there comes up to my window an incessant shuffling of feet and clangour of voices. The weather is very warm for the season, all the world is out of doors and the Tuscan tongue (which in Siena is reputed to have a classic purity) wags in every imaginable key. It does n't rest even at night, and I am often an uninvited guest at concerts and *conversazioni* at two o'clock in the morning. The concerts are sometimes charming. I not only don't curse my wakefulness, but go to my window to listen. Three men come carolling by, trolling and quavering with voices of delightful sweetness, or a lonely troubadour in his shirt-sleeves draws such artful love-notes from his clear, fresh tenor, that I seem for the moment to be behind the scenes at the opera, watching some Rubini or Mario go "on" and waiting for the round of applause. In the intervals a couple of friends or enemies stop—Italians always make their points in conversation by pulling up, letting you walk on a few paces, to turn and find them standing with finger on nose and engaging your interrogative eye—they pause, by a happy instinct, directly under my window, and dispute their point or tell their story or make their confidence. One scarce is sure which it may be; everything has such an explosive promptness, such a redundancy of inflection and action. But everything for that matter takes on such dramatic life as *our* lame colloquies never know—so that almost any uttered communications here become an acted play, improvised, mimicked, proportioned and rounded, carried bravely to its *dénoûment.* The speaker seems actually to establish his stage and face his foot-lights, to create by a gesture a little scenic circumscription about him; he rushes to and fro and shouts and stamps and postures, he ranges through every phase of his inspiration. I noted the other evening a striking instance of the spontaneity of the Italian gesture, in the person of a small Sienese of I hardly know what exact age—the age of inarticulate sounds and the experimental use of a spoon. It was a Sunday evening, and this little man had accompanied his parents to the café. The Caffè Greco at Siena is a most delightful institution; you get a capital *demi-tasse* for three sous, and an excellent ice for eight, and while you consume these easy luxuries you may buy from a little hunchback the local weekly periodical, the *Vita Nuova,* for three centimes (the two centimes left from your sou, if you are under the spell of this magical frugality, will do to give the waiter). My young friend was sitting on his father's knee and helping himself to the half of a strawberry-ice with which his mamma had presented him. He had so many misadventures with his spoon that this lady at length confiscated it, there being nothing left of the ice but a little crimson liquid which he might dispose of by the common instinct of childhood. But he was no friend, it appeared, to such freedoms; he was a perfect little gentleman and he resented it being expected of him that he should drink down his remnant. He protested therefore, and it was the manner of his protest that struck me. He did n't cry audibly, though he made a very wry face. It was no stupid squall, and yet he was too young to speak. It was a penetrating concord of inarticulately pleading, accusing sounds, accompanied by gestures of the most exquisite propriety. These were perfectly mature; he did everything that a man of forty would have done if he had been pouring out a flood of sonorous eloquence. He shrugged his shoulders and wrinkled his eyebrows, tossed out his hands and folded his arms, obtruded his chin and bobbed about his head—and at last, I am happy to say, recovered his spoon. If I had had a solid little silver one I would have presented it to him as a testimonial to a perfect, though as yet unconscious, artist.

My actual tribute to him, however, has diverted me from what I had in mind—a much weightier matter—the great private palaces which are the massive majestic syllables, sentences, periods, of the strange message the place addresses to us. They are extraordinarily spacious and numerous, and one wonders what part they can play in the meagre economy of the actual city. The Siena of to-day is a mere shrunken semblance of the rabid little republic which in the thirteenth century waged triumphant war with Florence, cultivated the arts with splendour, planned a cathedral (though it had ultimately to curtail the design) of proportions almost unequalled, and contained a population of two hundred thousand souls. Many of these dusky piles still bear the names of the old mediæval magnates the vague mild occupancy of whose descendants has the effect of armour of proof worn over "pot" hats and tweed jackets and trousers. Half-a-dozen of them are as high as the Strozzi and Riccardi palaces in Florence; they could n't well be higher. The very essence of the romantic and the scenic is in the way these colossal dwellings are packed together in their steep streets, in the depths of their little enclosed, agglomerated city. When we, in our day and country, raise a structure of half the mass and dignity, we leave a great space about it in the manner of a pause after a showy speech. But when a Sienese countess, as things are here, is doing her hair near the window, she is a wonderfully near neighbour to the cavalier opposite, who is being shaved by his valet. Possibly the countess does n't object to a certain chosen publicity at her toilet; what does an Italian gentleman assure me but that the aristocracy make very free with each other? Some of the palaces are shown, but only when the occupants are at home, and now they are in *villeggiatura*. Their villeggiatura lasts eight months of the year, the waiter at the inn informs me, and they spend little more than the carnival in the city. The gossip of an inn-waiter ought perhaps to be beneath the dignity of even such thin history as this; but I confess that when, as a story-seeker always and ever, I have come in from my strolls with an irritated sense of the dumbness of stones and mortar, it has been to listen with avidity, over my dinner, to the proffered confidences of the worthy man who stands by with a napkin. His talk is really very fine, and he prides himself greatly on his cultivated tone, to which he calls my attention. He has very little good to say about the Sienese nobility. They are "proprio d'origine egoista"—whatever that may be—and there are many who can't write their names. This may be calumny; but I doubt whether the most blameless of them all could have spoken more delicately of a lady of peculiar personal appearance who had been dining near me. "She's too fat," I grossly said on her leaving the room. The waiter shook his head with a little sniff: "È troppo materiale." This lady and her companion were the party whom, thinking I might relish a little company—I had been dining alone for a week—he gleefully announced to me as newly arrived Americans. They were Americans, I found, who wore, pinned to their heads in permanence, the black lace veil or mantilla, conveyed their beans to their mouth with a knife, and spoke a strange raucous Spanish. They were in fine compatriots from Montevideo. The genius of old Siena, however, would make little of any stress

---

"**proprio d'origine egoista.**" Decidedly of a selfish nature.

"**È troppo materiale.**" She is too material, with the suggestion that she falls short of the commonly antithetical quality of spirit.

of such distinctions; one representative of a far-off social platitude being about as much in order as another as he stands before the great loggia of the Casino di Nobili, the club of the best society. The nobility, which is very numerous and very rich, is still, says the apparently competent native I began by quoting, perfectly feudal and uplifted and separate. Morally and intellectually, behind the walls of its palaces, the fourteenth century, it's thrilling to think, has n't ceased to hang on. There is no bourgeoisie to speak of; immediately after the aristocracy come the poor people, who are very poor indeed. My friend's account of these matters made me wish more than ever, as a lover of the preserved social specimen, of type at almost any price, that one were n't, a helpless victim of the historic sense, reduced simply to staring at black stones and peeping up stately staircases; and that when one had examined the street-face of the palace, Murray in hand, one might walk up to the great drawing-room, make one's bow to the master and mistress, the old abbé and the young count, and invite them to favour one with a sketch of their social philosophy or a few first-hand family anecdotes.

The dusky labyrinth of the streets, we must in default of such initiations content ourselves with noting, is interrupted by two great candid spaces: the fan-shaped piazza, of which I just now said a word, and the smaller square in which the cathedral erects its walls of many-coloured marble. Of course since paying the great piazza my compliments by moonlight I have strolled through it often at sunnier and shadier hours. The market is held there, and wherever Italians buy and sell, wherever they count and chaffer—as indeed you hear them do right and left, at almost any moment, as you take your way among them—the pulse of life beats fast. It has been doing so on the spot just named, I suppose, for the last five hundred years, and during that time the cost of eggs and earthen pots has been gradually but inexorably increasing. The buyers nevertheless wrestle over their purchases as lustily as so many fourteenth-century burghers suddenly waking up in horror to current prices. You have but to walk aside, however, into the Palazzo Pubblico really to feel yourself a thrifty old mediævalist. The state affairs of the Republic were formerly transacted here, but it now gives shelter to modern law-courts and other prosy business. I was marched through a number of vaulted halls and chambers, which, in the intervals of the administrative sessions held in them, are peopled only by the great mouldering archaic frescoes—anything but inanimate these even in their present ruin—that cover the walls and ceiling. The chief painters of the Sienese school lent a hand in producing the works I name, and you may complete there the connoisseurship in which, possibly, you will have embarked at the Academy.

Academy. The Galleria dell'Accademia, in Florence.

I say "possibly" to be very judicial, my own observation having led me no great length. I have rather than otherwise cherished the thought that the Sienese school suffers one's eagerness peacefully to slumber—benignantly abstains in fact from whipping up a languid curiosity and a tepid faith. "A formidable rival to the Florentine," says some book—I forget which—into which I recently glanced. Not a bit of it thereupon boldly say I; the Florentines may rest on their laurels and the lounger on his lounge. The early painters of the two groups have indeed much in common; but the Florentines had the good fortune to see their efforts gathered up and applied by a few pre-eminent spirits, such as never came to the rescue of the groping Sienese. Fra Angelico and Ghirlandaio said all their feebler *confrères* dreamt of and a great deal more beside, but the inspiration of Simone Memmi and Ambrogio Lorenzetti and Sano di Pietro has a painful air of never efflorescing into a maximum. Sodoma and Beccafumi are to my taste a rather abortive maximum. But one should speak of them all gently—and I do, from my soul; for their labour, by their lights, has wrought a precious heritage of still-living colour and rich figure-peopled shadow for the echoing chambers of their old civic fortress. The faded frescoes cover the walls like quaintly-storied tapestries; in one way or another they cast their spell. If one owes a large debt of pleasure to pictorial art one comes to think tenderly and easily of its whole evolution, as of the conscious experience of a single mysterious, striving spirit, and one shrinks from saying rude things about any particular phase of it, just as one would from referring without precautions to some error or lapse in the life of a person one esteemed. You don't care to remind a grizzled veteran of his defeats, and why should we linger in

---

"A formidable rival to the Florentine," says some book. The editor is unable to locate the reference.

Simone Memmi . . . Ambrogio Lorenzetti . . . Sano di Pietro. Sienese records indicate no painter named Simone Memmi, but a Lippo di Memmi was Simone Martini's brother-in-law and at times the two were confused. In 1855 Eastlake (156) had attempted to clear up the error, but as late as 1868 "Mrs. Jameson," whose work James read and admired, followed nineteenth-century habit and still referred to "Simone di Martino" as Simone Memmi; in 1877 John Addington Symonds blamed the confusion on an error in Vasari (Symonds, *The Renaissance in Italy*, III, 158n).

James omits mention of Duccio di Buoninsegna and other Sienese painters whose greatness is now appreciated; Berenson's preface to the second edition of *Central Italian Painters* (1908) comments on the drastic shift of the taste for certain painters toward the end of the nineteenth century. He noted that "twelve years and more have passed since this book first went to press. At that time the painters of Central Italy still lay under the ban of Academic judgement. . . . It is different now." Also see his discussion of "Why Taste Changes," 12–16. Duccio, it might be noted, received a slim two-page comment in Eastlake. See Kenneth Clark's related remarks on Piero della Francesca, above, note to page 218.

Siena to talk about Beccafumi? I by no means go so far as to say, with an amateur with whom I have just been discussing the matter, that "Sodoma is a precious poor painter and Beccafumi no painter at all"; but, opportunity being limited, I am willing to let the remark about Beccafumi pass for true. With regard to Sodoma, I remember seeing four years ago in the choir of the Cathedral of Pisa a certain small dusky specimen of the painter—an Abraham and Isaac, if I am not mistaken—which was charged with a gloomy grace. One rarely meets him in general collections, and I had never done so till the other day. He was not prolific, apparently; he had however his own elegance, and his rarity is a part of it.

"**Sodoma . . . Beccafumi no painter at all; . . . Abraham and Isaac . . . Descent from the Cross . . . first of the modern Christs.** Gianantonio Bazzi (1477–1549), called "Il Sodoma," a nickname that Vasari says he bore because of personal vices. Born at Vercelli, he was stylistically eclectic and not especially representative of the Sienese school, although during the nineteenth century he was often grouped among them; Berenson would discuss him as a northern and not central Italian painter. Sodoma's *Descent from the Cross,* painted for the church of San Francesco, is presently in the Pinacoteca, referred to by James as the Academy. The late (1541–42) *Sacrifice of Isaac* is in the Duomo at Pisa. (Illustrations of Sodoma are not always easily accessible, but reproductions of all the works James cites may be found in Hayum, *Giovanni Antonio Bazzi—"Il Sodoma."*)

Domenico Beccafumi (c. 1486–1551), "no painter at all" in the view of James's acquaintance, claims a considerably higher reputation today; Frederick Hartt ranks Beccafumi with Pontormo and calls him "the greatest Sienese painter since Sassetta" (Hartt, 510).

Motivating strong reactions throughout the nineteenth century, the so-called modern *Christ at the Column,* a fragment of a larger fresco, was the object of heartfelt appreciation in Hawthorne's *The Marble Faun:*

> Sodoma, beyond a question, both prayed and wept, while painting his fresco, at Siena, of Christ bound to the pillar.
>
> In her present need and hunger for a spiritual revelation, Hilda felt a vast and weary longing to see this last-mentioned picture once again. It is inexpressibly touching. So weary is the Saviour, and utterly worn out with agony, that his lips have fallen apart from mere exhaustion; his eyes seem to be set; he tries to lean his head against the pillar, but is kept from sinking down upon the ground only by the cords that bind him. One of the most striking effects produced, is the sense of loneliness. You behold Christ deserted both in Heaven and earth; that despair is in him, which wrung forth the saddest utterance man ever made—"Why hast Thou forsaken me?" Even in this extremity, however, he is still divine. The great and reverent painter has not suffered the Son of God to be merely an object of pity, though depicting him in a state so profoundly pitiful. He is rescued from it, we know not how—by nothing less than miracle—by a celestial majesty and beauty, and some quality of which these are the outward garniture. He is as much, and as visibly, our Redeemer, there bound, there fainting, and bleeding from the scourge, with the Cross in view, as if he sat on his throne of glory in the heavens! Sodoma, in this matchless picture, has done more towards reconciling the incongruity of Divine Omnipotence and outraged, suffering Humanity, combined in one person, than the theologians ever did. (339–40)

Here in Siena are a couple of dozen scattered frescoes and three or four canvases; his masterpiece, among others, an harmonious Descent from the Cross. I would n't give a fig for the equilibrium of the figures or the ladders; but while it lasts the scene is all intensely solemn and graceful and sweet—too sweet for so bitter a subject. Sodoma's women are strangely sweet; an imaginative sense of morbid appealing attitude—as notably in the sentimental, the pathetic, but the none the less pleasant, "Swooning of St. Catherine," the great Sienese heroine, at San Domenico—seems to me the author's finest accomplishment. His frescoes have all the same almost appealing evasion of difficulty, and a kind of mild melancholy which I am inclined to think the sincerest part of them, for it stikes me as practically the artist's depressed suspicion of his own want of force. Once he determined, however, that if he could n't be strong he would make capital of his weakness, and painted the Christ bound to the Column, of the Academy. Here he got much nearer and I have no doubt mixed his colours with his tears; but the result can't be better described than by saying that it is, pictorially, the first of the modern Christs. Unfortunately it has n't been the last.

The main strength of Sienese art went possibly into the erection of the Cathedral, and yet even here the strength is not of the greatest strain. If, however, there are more interesting temples in Italy, there are few more richly and variously scenic and splendid, the comparative meagreness of the architectural idea being overlaid by a marvellous wealth of ingenious detail. Opposite the church—with the dull old archbishop's palace on one side and a dismantled residence of the late Grand Duke of Tuscany on the other—is an ancient hospital with a big stone bench running all along its front. Here I have sat a while every morning for a week, like a philosophic convalescent, watching the florid façade of the cathedral glitter against the deep blue sky. It has been lavishly restored of late years, and the fresh white marble of the densely clustered pinnacles and statues and beasts and flowers flashes in the sunshine like a mosaic of jewels. There is more of this goldsmith's work in stone than I can remember or describe; it is piled up over three great doors with immense margins of exquisite decorative sculpture—still in the ancient cream-coloured marble—and beneath three sharp pediments embossed with images relieved against red marble and tipped with golden mosaics. It is in the highest degree fantastic and luxuriant—it is on the whole very lovely. As a triumph of the many-hued it prepares you for the interior, where the same parti-coloured splendour is endlessly at play—a confident complication of harmonies and contrasts and of the minor structural refinements and braveries. The internal surface is mainly wrought in alternate courses of black and white marble; but as the latter has been dimmed by the centuries to a fine mild brown the place is all a concert of relieved and dispersed glooms. Save for Pinturicchio's brilliant frescoes in the Sacristy there are no pictures to speak of; but the pavement is covered with many elaborate designs in black and white mosaic after cartoons by Beccafumi. The patient skill of these compositions makes them a rare piece of decoration; yet even here the friend whom I lately quoted rejects this over-ripe fruit of the Sienese school. The designs are nonsensical, he declares, and all his admiration is for the cunning artisans who have imitated the hatchings and shadings and hair-strokes of the pencil by the finest curves of inserted black stone. But the true romance of handiwork at Siena is to be seen in the wondrous stalls of the choir, under the coloured light of the great wheel-window. Wood-carving has ever been a cherished craft of the place, and the best masters of the art during the fifteenth century lavished themselves on this prodigious task. It is the frost-work on one's window-panes interpreted in polished oak. It would be hard to find, doubtless, a more moving illustration of the peculiar patience, the sacred candour, of the great time. Into such artistry as this the author seems to put more of his personal substance than into any other; he has to wrestle not only with his subject, but with his material. He is richly fortunate when his subject is charming—when his devices, inventions and fantasies spring lightly to his hand; for in the material itself, after age and use have ripened and polished and darkened it to the richness of ebony and to a greater warmth there is something surpassingly delectable and venerable. Wander behind the altar at Siena when the chanting is over and the incense has faded, and look well at the stalls of the Barili.

1873

II

I LEAVE the impression noted in the foregoing pages to tell its own small story, but have it on my conscience to wonder, in this connection, quite candidly and publicly and by way of due penance, at the scantness of such first-fruits of my

---

Pinturicchio's brilliant frescoes. The present sacristy of the Duomo contains no frescoes by Pinturicchio; the fresco cycle is in the Libreria Piccolomini.

cartoons by Beccafumi. Although more than forty artists contributed to the design of the pavement (now covered by protective boards, except during the period after Ferragosto, from 15 August to 15 September), the work was largely the responsibility of Beccafumi.

stalls of the Barili. Exceptionally detailed intaglio choir stalls worked on by several artists, among them Francesco del Toghio and Giovanni da Verona, although the highest achievement—particularly impressive in regard to tricks of perspective—is the work of Antonio and Giovanni di Neri Barili.

sensibility. I was to see Siena repeatedly in the years to follow, I was to know her better, and I would say that I was to do her an ampler justice did n't that remark seem to reflect a little on my earlier poor judgment. This judgment strikes me to-day as having fallen short—true as it may be that I find ever a value, or at least an interest, even in the moods and humours and lapses of any brooding, musing or fantasticating observer to whom the finer sense of things is *on the whole* not closed. If he has on a given occasion nodded or stumbled or strayed, this fact by itself speaks to me of him—speaks to me, that is, of his faculty and his idiosyncrasies, and I care nothing for the application of his faculty unless it be, first of all, in itself interesting. Which may serve as my reply to any objection here breaking out—on the ground that if a spectator's languors are evidence, of a sort, about that personage, they are scarce evident about the case before him, at least if the case be important. I let my perhaps rather weak expression of the sense of Siena stand, at any rate—for the sake of what I myself read into it; but I should like to amplify it by other memories, and would do so eagerly if I might here enjoy the space. The difficulty for these rectifications is that if the early vision has failed of competence or of full felicity, if initiation has thus been slow, so, with renewals and extensions, so, with the larger experience, one hindrance is exchanged for another. There is quite such a possibility as having lived into a relation too much to be able to make a statement of it.

I remember on one occasion arriving very late of a summer night, after an almost unbroken run from London, and the note of that approach—I was the only person alighting at the station below the great hill of the little fortress city, under whose at once frowning and gaping gate I must have passed, in the warm darkness and the absolute stillness, very much after the felt fashion of a person of importance about to be enormously incarcerated—gives me, for preservation thus belated, the pitch, as I may call it, at various times, though always at one season, of an almost systematised æsthetic use of the place. It was n't to be denied that the immensely better "accommodations" instituted by the multiplying, though alas more bustling, years had to be recognised as supplying a basis, comparatively prosaic if one would, to that luxury. No sooner have I written which words, however, than I find myself adding that one "would n't," that one does n't—does n't, that is, consent now to regard the then "new" hotel (pretty old indeed by this time) as anything but an aid to a free play of perception. The strong and rank old Arme d'Inghilterra, in the darker street, has passed away; but its ancient rival the Aquila Nera put forth claims to modernisation, and the Grand Hotel, the still fresher flower of modernity near the gate by which you enter from the station, takes on to my present remembrance a mellowness as of all sorts of comfort, cleanliness and kindness. The particular facts, those of the visit I began here by alluding to and those of still others, at all events, inveterately made in June or early in

July, enter together in a fusion as of hot golden-brown objects seen through the practicable crevices of shutters drawn upon high, cool, darkened rooms where the scheme of the scene involved longish days of quiet work, with late afternoon emergence and contemplation waiting on the better or the worse conscience. I thus associate the compact world of the admirable hill-top, the world of a predominant golden-brown, with a general invocation of sensibility and fancy, and think of myself as going forth into the lingering light of summer evenings all attuned to intensity of the idea of compositional beauty, or in other words, freely speaking, to the question of colour, to intensity of picture. To communicate with Siena in this charming way was thus, I admit, to have no great margin for the prosecution of inquiries, but I am not sure that it was n't, little by little, to feel the whole combination of elements better than by a more exemplary method, and this from beginning to end of the scale.

More of the elements indeed, for memory, hang about the days that were ushered in by that straight flight from the north than about any other series—if partly, doubtless, but because of my having then stayed longest. I specify it at all events for fond reminiscence as the year, the only year, at which I was present at the Palio, the earlier one, the series of furious horse-races between elected representatives of different quarters of the town taking place toward the end of June, as the second and still more characteristic exhibition of the same sort is appointed to the month of August; a spectacle that I am far from speaking of as the finest flower of my old and perhaps even a little faded cluster of impressions, but which smudges that special sojourn as with the big thumb-mark of a slightly soiled and decidedly ensanguined hand. For really, after all, the great loud gaudy romp or heated frolic, simulating ferocity if not achieving it, that is the annual pride of the town, was not intrinsically, to my view, extraordinarily impressive—in spite of its bristling with all due testimony to the passionate Italian clutch of any pretext for costume and attitude and utterance, for mumming and masquerading and raucously representing; the vast cheap vividness rather somehow refines itself, and the swarm and hubbub of the immense square melt, to the uplifted sense of a very high-placed balcony of the overhanging Chigi palace, where everything was superseded but the intenser passage, across the ages, of the great Renaissance tradition of architecture and the infinite sweetness of the waning golden day. The Palio, indubitably, was *criard*—and the more so for quite monopolising, at Siena, the note of crudity; and much of it demanded doubtless of one's patience a due respect for the long local continuity of such things; it drops into its humoured position, however, in any

---

criard. Loud, shrill, high-pitched.

retrospective command of the many brave aspects of the prodigious place. Not that I am pretending here, even for rectification, to take these at all in turn; I only go on a little with my rueful glance at the marked gaps left in my original report of sympathies entertained.

I bow my head for instance to the mystery of my not having mentioned that the coolest and freshest flower of the day was ever that of one's constant renewal of a charmed homage to Pinturicchio, coolest and freshest and signally youngest and most matutinal (as distinguished from merely primitive or crepuscular) of painters, in the library or sacristy of the Cathedral. Did I *always* find time before work to spend half-an-hour of immersion, under that splendid roof, in the clearest and tenderest, the very cleanest and "straightest," as it masters our envious credulity, of all storied frescoworlds? This wondrous apartment, a monument in itself to the ancient pride and power of the Church, and which contains an unsurpassed treasure of gloriously illuminated missals, psalters and other vast parchment folios, almost each of whose successive leaves gives the impression of rubies, sapphires and emeralds set in gold and practically embedded in the page, offers thus to view, after a fashion splendidly sustained, a pictorial record of the career of Pope Pius II, Æneas Sylvius of the Siena Piccolomini (who gave him for an immediate successor a second of their name), most profanely literary of Pontiffs and last of would-be Crusaders, whose adventures and achievements under Pinturicchio's brush smooth themselves out for us very much to the tune of the "stories" told by some fine old man of the world, at the restful end of his life, to the cluster of his grandchildren. The end of Æneas Sylvius was not restful; he died at Ancona in troublous times, preaching war, and attempting to make it, against the then terrific Turk; but over no great worldly personal legend, among those of men of arduous affairs, arches a fairer, lighter or more pacific memorial vault than the shining Libreria of Siena. I seem to remember having it and its unfrequented enclosing precinct so often all to myself that I must indeed mostly have resorted to it for a prompt benediction on the day. Like no other strong solicitation, among artistic appeals to which one may compare it up and down the whole wonderful country, is the felt neighbouring presence of the overwrought

---

career of Pope Pius II. Aeneas Silvius Piccolomini (1405–64), Pope Pius II, an ardent humanist, opportunist, and sensualist early in life, long resisted the church, wrote a bawdy novel, a play, and light poems, was made poet laureate of Germany, and displayed a general talent for wit, intrigue, and danger. He conspired against Pope Eugenius IV, was imprisoned, eventually escaped, and finally took holy orders at the age of forty-one, frankly stating that a clerical post offered more advantages than could be found outside the ecclesiastical establishment. As pope he was known both for his zeal in launching a crusade and for his attempt to create a united Europe.

Cathedral in its little proud possessive town: you may so often feel by the week at a time that it stands there really for your own personal enjoyment, your romantic convenience, your small wanton æsthetic use. In such a light shines for me, at all events, under such an accumulation and complication of tone flushes and darkens and richly recedes for me, across the years, the treasure-house of many-coloured marbles in the untrodden, the drowsy, empty Sienese square. One could positively do, in the free exercise of any responsible fancy or luxurious taste, what one would with it.

But that proposition holds true, after all, for almost any mild pastime of the incurable student of loose meanings and stray relics and odd references and dim analogies in an Italian hill-city bronzed and seasoned by the ages. I ought perhaps, for justification of the right to talk, to have plunged into the Siena archives of which, on one occasion, a kindly custodian gave me, in rather dusty and stuffy conditions, as the incident vaguely comes back to me, a glimpse that was like a moment's stand at the mouth of a deep, dark mine. I did n't descend into the pit; I did, instead of this, a much idler and easier thing: I simply went every afternoon, my stint of work over, I like to recall, for a musing stroll upon the Lizza—the Lizza which had its own unpretentious but quite insidious art of meeting the lover of old stories half-way. The great and subtle thing, if you are not a strenuous specialist, in places of a heavily charged historic consciousness, is to profit by the sense of that consciousness—or in other words to cultivate a relation with the oracle—after the fashion that suits yourself; so that if the general after-taste of experience, experience at large, the fine distilled essence of the matter, seems to breathe, in such a case, from the very stones and to make a thick strong liquor of the very air, you may thus gather as you pass what is most to your purpose; which is more the indestructible mixture of lived things, with its concentrated lingering odour, than any interminable list of num-bered chapters and verses. Chapters and verses, literally scanned, refuse coincidence, mostly, with the divisional proprieties of your own pile of manuscript—which is but another way of saying, in short, that if the Lizza is a mere fortified promontory of the great Sienese hill, serving at once as a

---

Lizza . . . lover of old stories. In modern times a public park to the northwest of the city, once the site of a fortress erected by order of Charles V to help intimidate a discordant—"this Italy, tranquillized in every part, you alone excepted"—people. The Sienese felt the force of the threat and asked the intervention of Pope Julius, whose mother's Sienese birth linked him to the city. The pope responded to the representative of Charles V—"if one castle was not enough to keep those hare-brained Sienese in order, his Imperial Majesty had better build two." In 1552, led by one of the Piccolomini kinsman, a revolt drove the Spanish from the city and the fortress was razed with pickaxes. Another fortress was built by the Medici, the Fortezza Medicea, or the Fortezza Santa Barbara (Heywood, 109–19; Gardner, 220–27).

stronghold for the present military garrison and as a planted and benched and band-standed walk and recreation-ground for the citizens, so I could never, toward close of day, either have enough of it or yet feel the vaguest saunterings there to be vain. They were vague with the qualification always of that finer massing, as one wandered off, of the bronzed and seasoned element, the huge rock pedestal, the bravery of walls and gates and towers and palaces and loudly asserted dominion; and then of that pervaded or mildly infested air in which one feels the experience of the ages, of which I just spoke, to be exquisitely in solution; and lastly of the wide, strange, sad, beautiful horizon, a rim of far mountains that always pictured, for the leaner on old rubbed and smoothed parapets at the sunset hour, a country not exactly blighted or deserted, but that had had its life, on an immense scale, and had gone, with all its memories and relics, into rather austere, in fact into almost grim and misanthropic, retirement. This was a manner and a mood, at any rate, in all the land, that favoured in the late afternoons the divinest landscape blues and purples—not to speak of its favouring still more my practical contention that the whole guarded headland in question, with the immense ramparts of golden brown and red that dropped into vineyards and orchards and cornfields and all the rustic elegance of the Tuscan *podere,* was knitting for me a chain of unforgettable hours; to the justice of which claim let these divagations testify.

It was n't, however, that one might n't without disloyalty to that scheme of profit seek impressions further afield—though indeed I may best say of such a matter as the long pilgrimage to the pictured convent of Monte Oliveto that it but played on the same fine chords as the overhanging, the far-gazing Lizza. What it came to was that one simply put to the friendly test, as it were, the mood and manner of the country. This remembrance is precious, but the demonstration of that sense as of a great heaving region stilled by some final shock and returning thoughtfully, in fact tragically, on itself, could n't have been more pointed. The long-drawn rural road I refer to, stretching over hill and dale and to which I devoted the whole of the longest day of the year—I was in a small single-horse conveyance, of which I had already made appreciative use, and with a driver as disposed as myself ever to sacrifice speed to contemplation—is doubtless familiar now with the rush of the motor-car; the thought of whose free dealings with the solitude of Monte Oliveto makes me a little ruefully reconsider, I confess, the spirit in

---

Monte Oliveto . . . lonely, bleak and stricken . . . secular State. Just south of Siena, the Benedictine monastery of Monte Oliveto Maggiore was founded in 1313, suppressed by Napoleon, and eventually made a national monument by the Italian government; only a few monks remained as caretakers, and in 1866 regular guest quarters were offered, as they are still.

which I have elsewhere in these pages, on behalf of the lust, the landscape lust, of the eyes, acknowledged our general increasing debt to that vehicle. For that we met nothing whatever, as I seem at this distance of time to recall, while we gently trotted and trotted through the splendid summer hours and a dry desolation that yet somehow smiled and smiled, was part of the charm and the intimacy of the whole impression—the impression that culminated at last, before the great cloistered square, lonely, bleak and stricken, in the almost aching vision, more frequent in the Italy of to-day than anywhere in the world, of the uncalculated waste of a myriad forms of piety, forces of labour, beautiful fruits of genius. However, one gaped above all things for the impression, and what one mainly asked was that it should be strong of its kind. That was the case, I think I could n't but feel, at every moment of the couple of hours I spent in the vast, cold, empty shell, out of which the Benedictine brotherhood sheltered there for ages had lately been turned by the strong arm of a secular State. There was but one good brother left, a very lean and tough survivor, a dusky, elderly, friendly Abbate, of an indescribable type and a perfect manner, of whom I think I felt immediately thereafter that I should have liked to say much, but as to whom I must have yielded to the fact that ingenious and vivid commemoration was even then in store for him. Literary portraiture had marked him for its own, and in the short story of *Un Saint,* one of the most finished of contemporary French *nouvelles,* the art and the sympathy of Monsieur Paul Bourget preserve his interesting image. He figures in the beautiful tale, the Abbate of the desolate cloister and of those comparatively quiet years, as a clean, clear type of sainthood; a circumstance this in itself to cause a fond analyst of other than "Latin" race (model and painter in this case having their Latinism so strongly in common) almost endlessly to meditate. Oh, the unutterable differences in any scheme or estimate of physiognomic values, in any range of sensibility to expressional association, among observers of different, of inevitably more or less opposed, traditional and "racial" points of view! One had heard convinced Latins—or at least I had!—speak of situations of trust and intimacy in which they could n't have endured near them a Protestant or, as who should say for instance, an Anglo-Saxon; but I was to remember my own

---

Un Saint... Paul Bourget. In 1884 James met French novelist and critic Paul Bourget (1852–1935). Eventually their sincere friendship would be strained by Bourget's increasingly reactionary views, but his travel book, *Sensations d'Italie* (chapter 7 on Monte Oliveto), and especially his 1891 "Un Saint," impressed James deeply. Bourget, increasingly a Roman Catholic apologist, had written something of a fable in the story of Gabriele Griffi, a reclusive Benedictine monk, whose act of extraordinary generosity begins the conversion of a cynical young writer who has stolen two of Dom Gabriele's rare Roman coins. In 1892 James met the Bourgets in Siena for a tour of Tuscany and Umbria.

private attempt to measure such a change of sensibility as might have permitted the prolonged close approach of the dear dingy, half-starved, very possibly all heroic, and quite ideally urbane Abbate. The depth upon depth of things, the cloud upon cloud of associations, on one side and the other, that would have had to change first!

To which I may add nevertheless that since one ever supremely invoked intensity of impression and abundance of character, I feasted my fill of it at Monte Oliveto, and that for that matter this would have constituted my sole refreshment in the vast icy void of the blighted refectory if I had n't bethought myself of bringing with me a scrap of food, too scantly apportioned, I recollect—very scantly indeed, since my *cocchiere* was to share with me— by my purveyor at Siena. Our tragic—even if so tenderly tragic— entertainer had nothing to give us; but the immemorial cold of the enormous monastic interior in which we smilingly fasted would doubtless not have had for me without that such a wealth of reference. I was to have "liked" the whole adventure, so I must somehow have liked that; by which remark I am recalled to the special treasure of the desecrated temple, those extraordinarily strong and brave frescoes of Luca Signorelli and Sodoma that adorn, in admirable condition, several stretches of cloister wall. These creations in a manner took care of themselves; aided by the blue of the sky above the cloister-court they glowed, they insistently lived; I remember the frigid prowl through all the rest of the bareness, including that of the big dishonoured church and that even of the Abbate's abysmally resigned testimony to his mere human and personal situation; and then, with such a force of contrast and effect of relief, the great sheltered sun-flares and colour-patches of scenic composition and design where a couple of hands centuries ago turned to dust had so wrought the defiant miracle of life and beauty that the effect is of a garden blooming among ruins. Discredited somehow, since they all would, the destroyers themselves, the ancient piety, the general spirit and intention, but still bright and assured and sublime—practically, enviably immortal—the other, the still subtler, the all æsthetic good faith.

1909.

---

cocchiere. Coachman.

frescoes of Luca Signorelli and Sodoma ... admirable condition. The fresco series in the Chiostro Grande illustrates the life of Saint Benedict; nine of the works are by Signorelli, thirty-two by Sodoma. James mentions the good condition of the rather poorly preserved frescoes; either the past century has been particularly hard on the painted surfaces, or, in 1873, James's standard of admirable preservation was considerably lower than that of the modern tourist accustomed to the restorer's intervening hand.

The Autumn in Florence

Florence too has its "season," not less than Rome, and I have been rejoicing for the past six weeks in the fact that this comparatively crowded parenthesis has n't yet been opened. Coming here in the first days of October I found the summer still in almost unmenaced possession, and ever since, till within a day or two, the weight of its hand has been sensible. Properly enough, as the city of flowers, Florence mingles the elements most artfully in the spring—during the divine crescendo of March and April, the weeks when six months of steady shiver have still not shaken New York and Boston free of the long Polar reach. But the very quality of the decline of the year as we at present here feel it suits peculiarly the mood in which an undiscourageable gatherer of the sense of things, or taster at least of "charm," moves through these many-memoried streets and galleries and churches. Old things, old places, old people, or at least old races, ever strike us as giving out their secrets most freely in such moist, grey, melancholy days as have formed the complexion of the past fortnight. With Christmas arrives the opera, the only opera worth speaking of—which indeed often means in Florence the only opera worth talking through; the gaiety, the gossip, the reminders in fine of the cosmopolite and watering-place character to which the city of the Medici long ago began to bend her antique temper. Meanwhile it is pleasant enough for the tasters of charm, as I say, and for the makers of invidious distinctions, that the Americans have n't all arrived, however many may be on their way, and that the weather has a monotonous overcast softness in which, apparently, aimless

[Originally published (unsigned) in the Nation, XVIII (January 1874), 6–7; reprinted in Transatlantic Sketches, 1875.]

contemplation grows less and less ashamed. There is no crush along the Cascine, as on the sunny days of winter, and the Arno, wandering away toward the mountains in the haze, seems as shy of being looked at as a good picture in a bad light. No light, to my eyes, nevertheless, could be better than this, which reaches us, all strained and filtered and refined, exquisitely coloured and even a bit conspicuously sophisticated, through the heavy air of the past that hangs about the place for ever.

I first knew Florence early enough, I am happy to say, to have heard the change for the worse, the taint of the modern order, bitterly lamented by old haunters, admirers, lovers—those qualified to present a picture of the conditions prevailing under the good old Grand-Dukes, the two last of their line in especial, that, for its blest reflection of sweetness and mildness and cheapness and ease, of every immediate boon in life to be enjoyed quite for nothing, could but draw tears from belated listeners. Some of these survivors from the golden age—just the beauty of which indeed was in the gold, of sorts, that it poured into your lap, and not in the least in its own importunity on that head—have needfully lingered on, have seen the ancient walls pulled down and the compact and belted mass of which the Piazza della Signoria was the immemorial centre expand, under the treatment of enterprising syndics, into an ungirdled organism of the type, as they viciously say, of Chicago; one of those places of which, as their grace of a circumference is nowhere, the dignity of a centre can no longer be predicated. Florence loses itself to-day in dusty boulevards and smart *beaux quartiers,* such as Napoleon III and Baron Haussmann were to set the fashion of to a too mediæval Europe—with the effect of some precious page of antique text swallowed up in a marginal commentary that smacks of the style of the newspaper. So much for what has happened on this side of that line of demarcation which, by an odd law, makes us, with our preference for what we are pleased to call the picturesque, object to such occurrences even *as* occurrences. The real truth is that objections are too vain, and that he would be too rude a critic here, just now, who should n't be in the humour to take the thick with the thin and to try at least to read something of the old soul into the new forms.

Cascine. The former Medici farms, the Cascine—"the great Bois de Boulogne of Florence" (*Letters,* I, 154)—forms a large public park that begins outside the Porta al Prato and runs along the Arno for about two miles.

Napoleon III and Baron Haussmann. George Eugène Haussmann became Prefect of the Seine in 1853, a year after Charles-Louis-Napoleon Bonaparte (1808–73) was proclaimed emperor; with the support of Napoleon III he set about to transform the physical aspect of Paris—for scenic reasons and also to allow for more efficient troop movement in the city—laying out the Bois de Boulogne, constructing new water systems, commissioning fountains, and building the present grand boulevards. See note, page 101.

There is something to be said moreover for your liking a city (once it's a question of your actively circulating) to pretend to comfort you more by its extent than by its limits; in addition to which Florence was anciently, was in her palmy days peculiarly, a daughter of change and movement and variety, of shifting moods, policies and régimes—just as the Florentine character, as we have it to-day, is a character that takes all things easily for having seen so many come and go. It saw the national capital, a few years since, arrive and sit down by the Arno, and took no further thought than sufficed for the day; then it saw the odd visitor depart and whistled her cheerfully on her way to Rome. The new boulevards of the Sindaco Peruzzi come, it may be said, but they don't go; which, after all, it is n't from the æsthetic point of view strictly necessary they should. A part of the essential amiability of Florence, of her genius for making you take to your favour on easy terms everything that in any way belongs to her, is that she has already flung an element of her grace over all their undried mortar and plaster. Such modern arrangements as the Piazza d'Azeglio and the *viale* or Avenue of the Princess Margaret please not a little, I think—for what they are!—and do so even in a degree, by some fine local privilege, just because they are Florentine. The afternoon lights rest on them as if to thank them for not being worse, and their vistas are liberal where they look toward the hills. They carry you close to these admirable elevations, which hang over Florence on all sides, and if in the foreground your sense is a trifle perplexed by the white pavements dotted here and there with a policeman or a nursemaid, you have only to reach beyond and see Fiesole turn to violet, on its ample eminence, from the effect of the opposite sunset.

Facing again then to Florence proper you have local colour enough and to spare—which you enjoy the more, doubtless, from standing off to get your

---

It saw the national capital. Although Cavour and many others had declared that the capital eventually would be at Rome, when the kingdom of Italy first was formed in 1860, the city was held by the Papal States, and therefore Turin—the site of the first Italian parliament—was settled on. In 1865, as part of a controversial "approach" to the goal of *Roma capitale*, more centrally located Florence was named temporary capital, a distinction it held until the Italian troops breached the Porta Pia in 1870 and claimed the Eternal City for the united Italy.

new boulevards of the Sindaco Peruzzi. Ubaldino Peruzzi, a descendant of the great Renaissance Peruzzi family, was mayor ("sindaco") of Florence during the year 1870; his attempt to modernize the city—as Paris was being "modernized"—led to the demolition of the old fourteenth-century city walls, and to the laying out of wide avenues or "viali."

modern arrangements . . . Piazza d'Azeglio . . . Avenue of the Princess Margaret. With many trees, the Piazza d'Azeglio seems more a modern English square than an Italian piazza; the Viale Principessa Margherita, a wide nineteenth-century boulevard, is at present known as the Viale Spartaco Lavagnini.

light and your point of view. The elder streets abutting on all this newness bore away into the heart of the city in narrow, dusky perspectives that quite refine, in certain places, by an art of their own, on the romantic appeal. There are temporal and other accidents thanks to which, as you pause to look down them and to penetrate the deepening shadows that accompany their retreat, they resemble little corridors leading out from the past, mystical like the ladder in Jacob's dream; so that when you see a single figure advance and draw nearer you are half afraid to wait till it arrives—it must be too much of the nature of a ghost, a messenger from an underworld. However this may be, a place paved with such great mosaics of slabs and lined with palaces of so massive a tradition, structures which, in their large dependence on pure proportion for interest and beauty, reproduce more than other modern styles the simple nobleness of Greek architecture, must ever have placed dignity first in the scale of invoked effect and laid up no great treasure of that ragged picturesqueness—the picturesqueness of large poverty—on which we feast our idle eyes at Rome and Naples. Except in the unfinished fronts of the churches, which, however, unfortunately, are mere ugly blankness, one finds less of the poetry of ancient over-use, or in other words less romantic southern shabbiness, than in most Italian cities. At two or three points, none the less, this sinister grace exists in perfection—just such perfection as so often proves that what is literally hideous may be constructively delightful and what is intrinsically tragic play on the finest chords of appreciation. On the north side of the Arno, between Ponte Vecchio and Ponte Santa Trinità, is a row of immemorial houses that back on the river, in whose yellow flood they bathe their sore old feet. Anything more battered and befouled, more cracked and disjointed, dirtier, drearier, poorer, it would be impossible to conceive. They look as if fifty years ago the liquid mud had risen over their chimneys and then subsided again and left them coated for ever with its unsightly slime. And yet forsooth, because the river is yellow, and the light is yellow, and here and there, elsewhere, some mellow mouldering surface, some hint of colour, some accident of atmosphere, takes up the foolish tale and repeats the note—because, in short, it is Florence, it is Italy, and the fond appraiser, the infatuated alien, may have had in his eyes, at birth and afterwards, the micaceous sparkle of brownstone fronts no more interesting than so much sand-paper, these miserable dwellings, instead of suggesting mental invocations to an enterprising board of health, simply create their own standard of felicity and shamelessly live in it. Lately, during the misty autumn nights, the moon has shone on them

---

a row of immemorial houses. The original houses, fronting the Arno on the Borgo San Jacopo, received heavy bombing during World War II and few of the structures survive.

faintly and refined their shabbiness away into something ineffably strange and spectral. The turbid stream sweeps along without a sound, and the pale tenements hang above it like a vague miasmatic exhalation. The dimmest back-scene at the opera, when the tenor is singing his sweetest, seems hardly to belong to a world more detached from responsibility

What it is that infuses so rich an interest into the general charm is difficult to say in a few words; yet as we wander hither and thither in quest of sacred canvas and immortal bronze and stone we still feel the genius of the place hang about. Two industrious English ladies, the Misses Horner, have lately published a couple of volumes of "Walks" by the Arno-side, and their work is a long enumeration of great artistic deeds. These things remain for the most part in sound preservation, and, as the weeks go by and you spend a constant portion of your days among them the sense of one of the happiest periods of human Taste—to put it only at that—settles upon your spirit. It was not long; it lasted, in its splendour, for less than a century; but it has stored away in the palaces and churches of Florence a heritage of beauty that these three enjoying centuries since have n't yet exhausted. This forms a clear intellectual atmosphere into which you may turn aside from the modern world and fill your lungs as with the breath of a forgotten creed. The memorials of the past here address us moreover with a friendliness, win us by we scarcely know what sociability, what equal amenity, that we scarce find matched in other great æsthetically endowed communities and periods. Venice, with her old palaces cracking under the weight of their treasures, is, in her influence, insupportably sad; Athens, with her maimed marbles and dishonoured memories, transmutes the consciousness of sensitive observers, I am told, into a chronic heartache; but in one's impression of old Florence the abiding felicity, the sense of saving sanity, of something sound and human, predominates, offering you a medium still conceivable for life. The reason of this is partly, no doubt, the "sympathetic" nature, the temperate joy, of Florentine art in general—putting the sole Dante, greatest of literary artists, aside; partly the tenderness of time, in its lapse, which, save in a few cases, has been as sparing of injury as if it knew that when it should have dimmed and corroded these charming things it would have nothing so sweet

---

Misses Horner. Susan and Joanna Horner, *Walks in Florence and Its Environs,* 1873.

Athens . . . her maimed marbles. From 1802 to 1812 Thomas Bruce, Earl of Elgin (1766–1841), had collected the sculptural figures from the Parthenon frieze during his term as ambassador to Constantinople; by 1810 he felt it necessary to publish a pamphlet defending his so-called act of vandalism. The figures today remain in the British Museum, but the controversy around the collection continues, as do the efforts of the Greek government to regain both the pieces and the honor of their heritage.

again for its tooth to feed on. If the beautiful Ghirlandaios and Lippis are fading, this generation will never know it. The large Fra Angelico in the Academy is as clear and keen as if the good old monk stood there wiping his brushes; the colours seem to *sing,* as it were, like new-fledged birds in June. Nothing is more characteristic of early Tuscan art than the high-reliefs of Luca della Robbia; yet there is n't one of them that, except for the unique mixture of freshness with its wisdom, of candour with its expertness, might n't have been modelled yesterday.

But perhaps the best image of the absence of stale melancholy or wasted splendour, of the positive presence of what I have called temperate joy, in the Florentine impression and genius, is the bell-tower of Giotto, which rises beside the cathedral. No beholder of it will have forgotten how straight and slender it stands there, how strangely rich in the common street, plated with coloured marble patterns, and yet so far from simple or severe in design that we easily wonder how its author, the painter of exclusively and portentously grave little pictures, should have fashioned a building which in the way of elaborate elegance, of the true play of taste, leaves a jealous modern criticism nothing to miss. Nothing can be imagined at once more lightly and more pointedly fanciful; it might have been handed over to the city, as it stands, by some Oriental genie tired of too much detail. Yet for all that suggestion it seems of no particular time—not grey and hoary like a Gothic steeple, not cracked and despoiled like a Greek temple; its marbles shining so little less freshly than when they were laid together, and the sunset lighting up its cornice with such a friendly radiance, that you come at last to regard it simply as the graceful, indestructible soul of the place made visible. The Cathedral, externally, for all its solemn hugeness, strikes the same note of would-be reasoned elegance and cheer; it has conventional grandeur, of course, but a grandeur so frank and ingenuous even in its *parti-pris*. It has seen so much, and outlived so much, and served so many sad purposes, and yet remains in aspect so full of the fine Tuscan geniality, the feeling for life, one may almost say the feeling for amusement, that inspired it. Its vast many-coloured marble walls become at any rate, with this, the friendliest note of all Florence; there is an unfailing charm in walking past them while they lift their great acres of geometrical mosaic higher in the air than you have time or other occasion to look. You greet them from the deep street as

---

large **Fra Angelico.** From 1918 to 1921 both the Galleria dell'Accademia and the Uffizi turned over many of their works by Fra Angelico to the Museo San Marco at the Dominican monastery where the monk lived. James almost certainly refers to *The Deposition of Christ,* now at San Marco.

parti-pris. Purposefulness.

you greet the side of a mountain when you move in the gorge—not twisting back your head to keep looking at the top, but content with the minor accidents, the nestling hollows and soft cloud-shadows, the general protection of the valley.

Florence is richer in pictures than we really know till we have begun to look for them in outlying corners. Then, here and there, one comes upon lurking values and hidden gems that it quite seems one might as a good New Yorker quietly "bag" for the so aspiring Museum of that city without their being missed. The Pitti Palace is of course a collection of masterpieces; they jostle each other in their splendour, they perhaps even, in their merciless multitude, rather fatigue our admiration. The Uffizi is almost as fine a show, and together with that long serpentine artery which crosses the Arno and connects them, making you ask yourself, whichever way you take it, what goal can be grand enough to crown such a journey, they form the great central treasure-chamber of the town. But I have been neglecting them of late for love of the Academy, where there are fewer copyists and tourists, above all fewer pictorial lions, those whose roar is heard from afar and who strike us as expecting overmuch to have it their own way in the jungle. The pictures at the Academy are all, rather, doves—the whole impression is less pompously tropical. Selection still leaves one too much to say, but I noted here, on my last occasion, an enchanting Botticelli so obscurely hung, in one of the smaller rooms, that I scarce knew whether most to enjoy or to resent its relegation. Placed, in a mean black frame, where you would n't have looked for a masterpiece, it yet gave out to a good glass every characteristic of one. Representing as it does the walk of Tobias with the angel, there are really parts of it that an angel might have painted; but I doubt whether it is observed by half-a-dozen persons a year. That was my excuse for my wanting to know, on the spot, though doubtless all sophistically, what dishonour, could the transfer be artfully accomplished, a strong American light and a brave gilded frame would, comparatively speaking, do it. There and then it would shine with the intense authority that we claim for the fairest things—would exhale its wondrous beauty as a sovereign example. What it comes to is that this master is the most interesting of a great band—the only Florentine save Leonardo and Michael in whom the impulse was original and the invention rare. His imagination is of things strange, subtle and complicated—things it at first strikes us that we moderns have reason to know, and that it has taken us all the ages to learn; so that we permit ourselves to wonder how a "primitive" could

---

Tobias with the angel. The work, later attributed to Francesco Botticini, one of Botticelli's imitators, now is identified as by Domenico di Michelino.

Michael. A common Victorian diminutive of Michelangelo.

come by them. We soon enough reflect, however, that we ourselves have
come by them almost only *through* him, exquisite spirit that he was, and that
when we enjoy, or at least when we encounter, in our William Morrises, in
our Rossettis and Burne-Joneses, the note of the haunted or over-charged
consciousness, we are but treated, with other matters, to repeated doses of
diluted Botticelli. He practically set with his own hand almost all the copies
to almost all our so-called pre-Raphaelites, earlier and later, near and remote.

Let us at the same time, none the less, never fail of response to the great
Florentine geniality at large. Fra Angelico, Filippo Lippi, Ghirlandaio, were
not "subtly" imaginative, were not even riotously so; but what other three
were ever more gladly observant, more vividly and richly true? If there
should some time be a weeding out of the world's possessions the best works
of the early Florentines will certainly be counted among the flowers. With
the ripest performances of the Venetians—by which I don't mean the over-
ripe—we can but take them for the most valuable things in the history of
art. Heaven forbid we should be narrowed down to a cruel choice; but if it
came to a question of keeping or losing between half-a-dozen Raphaels and
half-a-dozen things it would be a joy to pick out at the Academy, I fear that,
for myself, the memory of the Transfiguration, or indeed of the other Roman relics of the painter, would n't save the Raphaels. And yet this was so

---

**William Morrises . . . Rossettis and Burne-Joneses . . . haunted or over-charged conscious-
ness.** Morris (1834–96), poet, essayist, and revolutionary designer, Dante Gabriel Rossetti
(1828–82), painter and poet, and Sir Edward Coley Burne-Jones (1833–98), painter and
designer, were associated with the Pre-Raphaelite Brotherhood; in a discussion of the movement James cited Burne-Jones's *Days of Creation* as a supreme example of "that vague, morbid
pathos, that appealing desire for an indefinite object, which seems among these artists an
essential part of the conception of human loveliness" ("The Picture Season in London: 1877,"
Painter's Eye, 146).

Transfiguration . . . other Roman relics . . . would n't save the Raphaels. James's only mildly
appreciative estimate of Raphael was unusual during the nineteenth century (for a fully documented sense of the popularity, among American collectors, of anything by the painter, see
David Alan Brown, *Raphael and America*). Although James was to praise fully the force and
commitment of Michelangelo, in 1869 he found Raphael "undecided, slack and unconvinced"
(*Letters*, I, 181) and his works "vitiated by their affected classicism—their elegance and cold-
ness" (I, 166). In this letter to Alice James he reported that he "sat stupidly" before the Vatican
Pinacoteca Transfiguration (incomplete at Raphael's death in 1520 and finished by Giulio
Romano) and was "*surprised* by the thinness" of a work that had been held in the highest
esteem throughout the century; Hawthorne judged it as "worthy of its fame" (Woodson,
Nathaniel Hawthorne: The French and Italian Note-books, 186), and had an engraving of the
painting in his Concord home (Woodson, ed., *Nathaniel Hawthorne: Letters, 1843–1853*,
109). Other Roman "relics" of Raphael include the famous *stanze* in the Palazzo Vaticano, and
works at the Villa Farnesina and the churches of S. Agostino, Santa Maria della Pace, and Santa
Maria del Popolo.

far from the opinion of a patient artist whom I saw the other day copying
the finest of Ghirlandaios—a beautiful Adoration of the Kings at the Hospital of the Innocenti. Here was another sample of the buried art-wealth of
Florence. It hangs in an obscure chapel, far aloft, behind an altar, and
though now and then a stray tourist wanders in and puzzles a while over the
vaguely-glowing forms, the picture is never really seen and enjoyed. I found
an aged Frenchman of modest mien perched on a little platform beneath it,
behind a great hedge of altar-candlesticks, with an admirable copy all completed. The difficulties of his task had been well-nigh insuperable, and his
performance seemed to me a real feat of magic. He could scarcely move or
turn, and could find room for his canvas but by rolling it together and
painting a small piece at a time, so that he never enjoyed a view of his
ensemble. The original is gorgeous with colour and bewildering with decorative detail, but not a gleam of the painter's crimson was wanting, not a curl
in his gold arabesques. It seemed to me that if I had copied a Ghirlandaio in
such conditions I would at least maintain for my own credit that he was the
first painter in the world. "Very good of its kind," said the weary old man
with a shrug of reply for my raptures; "but oh, how far short of Raphael!"
However that may be, if the reader chances to observe this consummate
copy in the so commendable Museum devoted in Paris to such works, let
him stop before it with a due reverence; it is one of the patient things of art.
Seeing it wrought there, in its dusky nook, under such scant convenience, I
found no bar in the painter's foreignness to a thrilled sense that the old art-
life of Florence is n't yet extinct. It still at least works spells and almost
miracles.

1873.

Adoration of the Kings. No longer in a dim chapel, the painting now hangs in the Museo
dello Spedale degli Innocenti.

commendable Museum devoted in Paris. Along with a general collection of portraits, sculpture, and architectural fragments, the École Nationale Supérieure des Beaux-Arts, on the Rue
Bonaparte, holds fine student copies of major Italian Renaissance paintings and sculpture,
inherited from the old Academy of Painting and Sculpture. Many of the copies are still on
display, including an impressive reproduction of the Sistine Chapel *Last Judgment,* but today
the galleries are commonly used for special shows and the old copies are often hidden behind
temporary exhibit walls.

Florentine Notes

I

Yesterday that languid organism known as the Florentine Carnival put on a momentary semblance of vigour, and decreed a general *corso* through the town. The spectacle was not brilliant, but it suggested some natural reflections. I encountered the line of carriages in the square before Santa Croce, of which they were making the circuit. They rolled solemnly by, with their inmates frowning forth at each other in apparent wrath at not finding each other more worth while. There were no masks, no costumes, no decorations, no throwing of flowers or sweetmeats. It was as if each carriageful had privately and not very heroically resolved not to be at costs, and was rather discomfited at finding that it was getting no better entertainment than it gave. The middle of the piazza was filled with little tables, with shouting mountebanks, mostly disguised in battered bonnets and crinolines, offering chances in raffles for plucked fowls and kerosene lamps. I have never thought the huge marble statue of Dante, which overlooks the scene, a work of the last refinement; but, as it stood there on its high pedestal, chin in hand, frowning down on all this cheap foolery, it seemed to have a great moral intention. The carriages followed a prescribed course—through Via Ghibellina, Via del Proconsolo,

[Originally published in eight parts in the *Independent;* "Florentine Notes," 23 and 30 April, 21 May; "Florentine Gardens," 14 May; "Old Italian Art," 11 June; "Florentine Architecture," 18 June; and "An Italian Convent," 2 July; "The Churches of Florence," 9 July 1874. Reprinted in *Transatlantic Sketches,* 1875, as "Florentine Notes"; parts I, III, IV, and V reprinted in *Foreign Parts,* 1883.]

past the Badia and the Bargello, beneath the great tessellated cliffs of the Cathedral, through Via Tornabuoni and out into ten minutes' sunshine beside the Arno. Much of all this is the gravest and stateliest part of Florence, a quarter of supreme dignity, and there was an almost ludicrous incongruity in seeing Pleasure leading her train through these dusky historic streets. It was most uncomfortably cold, and in the absence of masks many a fair nose was fantastically tipped with purple. But as the carriages crept solemnly along they seemed to keep a funeral march—to follow an antique custom, an exploded faith, to its tomb. The Carnival is dead, and these good people who had come abroad to make merry were funeral mutes and grave-diggers. Last winter in Rome it showed but a galvanised life, yet compared with this humble exhibition it was operatic. At Rome indeed it was too operatic. The knights on horseback there were a bevy of circus-riders, and I'm sure half the mad revellers repaired every night to the Capitol for their twelve sous a day.

I have just been reading over the Letters of the Président de Brosses. A hundred years ago, in Venice, the Carnival lasted six months; and at Rome for many weeks each year one was free, under cover of a mask, to perpetrate the most fantastic follies and cultivate the most remunerative vices. It's very well to read the President's notes, which have indeed a singular interest; but they make us ask ourselves why we should expect the Italians to persist in manners and practices which we ourselves, if we had responsibilities in the matter, should find intolerable. The Florentines at any rate spend no more money nor faith on the carnivalesque. And yet this truth has a qualification; for what struck me in the whole spectacle yesterday, and prompted these observations, was not at all the more or less of costume of the occupants of the carriages, but the obstinate survival of the merry-making instinct in the people at large. There could be no better example of it than that so dim a shadow of entertainment should keep all Florence standing and strolling, densely packed for hours, in the cold streets. There was nothing to see that might n't be seen on the Cascine any fine day in the year—nothing but a name, a tradition, a pretext for sweet staring idleness. The faculty of making

Letters of the Président de Brosses . . . the Carnival. Scholar and magistrate, Charles de Brosses (1709–77) was first president of the Parliament of Burgundy. His letters on Italy—with many vigorous passages on the carnival as it was celebrated in the eighteenth century (see James on the decline of the Roman carnival, 122–29)—were found in manuscript and published in 1799, more than twenty years after his death; the 1858 edition, ed. R. Colomb, *Le Président de Brosses en Italie,* was widely circulated and relatively famous. Although de Brosses was particularly impressed by the Carnival, in *Letters,* IV, 265, James writes to Urbain Mengin that, compared to other travelers, de Brosses saw little beauty in Italy.

much of common things and converting small occasions into great pleasures is, to a son of communities strenuous as ours are strenuous, the most salient characteristic of the so-called Latin civilisations. It charms him and vexes him, according to his mood; and for the most part it represents a moral gulf between his own temperamental and indeed spiritual sense of race, and that of Frenchmen and Italians, far wider than the watery leagues that a steamer may annihilate. But I think his mood is wisest when he accepts the "foreign" easy surrender to *all* the senses as the sign of an unconscious philosophy of life, instilled by the experience of centuries—the philosophy of people who have lived long and much, who have discovered no short cuts to happiness and no effective circumvention of effort, and so have come to regard the average lot as a ponderous fact that absolutely calls for a certain amount of sitting on the lighter tray of the scales. Florence yesterday then took its holiday in a natural, placid fashion that seemed to make its own temper an affair quite independent of the splendour of the compensation decreed on a higher line to the weariness of its legs. That the *corso* was stupid or lively was the shame or the glory of the powers "above"—the fates, the gods, the *forestieri,* the town-councilmen, the rich or the stingy. Common Florence, on the narrow footways, pressed against the houses, obeyed a natural need in looking about complacently, patiently, gently, and never pushing, nor trampling, nor swearing, nor staggering. This liberal margin for festivals in Italy gives the masses a more than man-of-the-world urbanity in taking their pleasure.

Meanwhile it occurs to me that by a remote New England fireside an unsophisticated young person of either sex is reading in an old volume of travels or an old romantic tale some account of these anniversaries and appointed revels as old Catholic lands offer them to view. Across the page swims a vision of sculptured palace-fronts draped in crimson and gold and shining in a southern sun; of a motley train of maskers sweeping on in voluptuous confusion and pelting each other with nosegays and love-letters. Into the quiet room, quenching the rhythm of the Connecticut clock, floats an uproar of delighted voices, a medley of stirring foreign sounds, an echo of far-heard music of a strangely alien cadence. But the dusk is falling, and the unsophisticated young person closes the book wearily and wanders to the window. The dusk is falling on the beaten snow. Down the road is a white wooden meeting-house, looking grey among the drifts. The young person surveys the prospect a while, and then wanders back and stares at the fire. The Carnival of Venice, of Florence, of Rome; colour and costume, romance and rapture! The young person gazes in the firelight at the flickering chiaroscuro of the future, discerns at last the glowing phantasm of opportunity, and determines with a wild heart-beat to go and see it all—twenty years hence!

II

A COUPLE of days since, driving to Fiesole, we came back by the castle of Vincigliata. The afternoon was lovely; and, though there is as yet (February 10th) no visible revival of vegetation, the air was full of a vague vernal perfume, and the warm colours of the hills and the yellow western sunlight flooding the plain seemed to contain the promise of Nature's return to grace. It's true that above the distant pale blue gorge of Vallombrosa the mountain-line was tipped with snow; but the liberated soul of Spring was nevertheless at large. The view from Fiesole seems vaster and richer with each visit. The hollow in which Florence lies, and which from below seems deep and contracted, opens out into an immense and generous valley and leads away the eye into a hundred gradations of distance. The place itself showed, amid its chequered fields and gardens, with as many towers and spires as a chessboard half cleared. The domes and towers were washed over with a faint blue mist. The scattered columns of smoke, interfused with the sinking sunlight, hung over them like streamers and pennons of silver gauze; and the Arno, twisting and curling and glittering here and there, was a serpent crossstriped with silver.

Vincigliata is a product of the millions, the leisure and the eccentricity, I suppose people say, of an English gentleman—Mr. Temple Leader, whose name should be commemorated. You reach the castle from Fiesole by a narrow road, returning toward Florence by a romantic twist through the hills and passing nothing on its way save thin plantations of cypress and cedar. Upward of twenty years ago, I believe, this gentleman took a fancy to the crumbling shell of a mediæval fortress on a breezy hill-top overlooking the Val d'Arno and forthwith bought it and began to "restore" it. I know nothing of what the original ruin may have cost; but in the dusky courts and chambers of the present elaborate structure this impassioned archæologist must have buried a fortune. He has, however, the compensation of feeling that he has erected a monument which, if it is never to stand a feudal siege, may encounter at least some critical overhauling. It is a disinterested work of art and really a triumph of æsthetic culture. The author has reproduced with minute accuracy a sturdy home-fortress of the fourteenth century, and has kept throughout such rigid terms with his model that the result is literally

---

Vincigliata . . . Mr. Temple Leader. Dating from 1855–65, this mock medieval structure was built for the dilettante collector John Temple-Leader upon eleventh-century ruins, not far from the sixteenth-century Villa "I Tatti," bought and restored by Bernard Berenson in 1900. *Il Castello di Vincigliata e I Suoi Contorni,* an anonymous illustrated work, in Italian and Latin, appeared in 1871 and brought some publicity to the castle.

uninhabitable to degenerate moderns. It is simply a massive facsimile, an elegant museum of archaic images, mainly but most amusingly counterfeit, perched on a spur of the Apennines. The place is most politely shown. There is a charming cloister, painted with extremely clever "quaint" frescoes, celebrating the deeds of the founders of the castle—a cloister that is every-thing delightful a cloister should be except truly venerable and employable. There is a beautiful castle court, with the embattled tower climbing into the blue far above it, and a spacious loggia with rugged medallions and mild-hued Luca della Robbias fastened unevenly into the walls. But the apart-ments are the great success, and each of them as good a "reconstruction" as a tale of Walter Scott; or, to speak frankly, a much better one. They are all low-beamed and vaulted, stone-paved, decorated in grave colours and lighted, from narrow, deeply recessed windows, through small leaden-ringed plates of opaque glass.

The details are infinitely ingenious and elaborately grim, and the indoor atmosphere of mediævalism most forcibly revived. No compromising fact of domiciliary darkness and cold is spared us, no producing condition of mediæval manners not glanced at. There are oaken benches round the room, of about six inches in depth, and gaunt fauteuils of wrought leather, illustrat-ing the suppressed transitions which, as George Eliot says, unite all contrasts—offering a visible link between the modern conceptions of torture and of luxury. There are fireplaces nowhere but in the kitchen, where a couple of sentry-boxes are inserted on either side of the great hooded chimney-piece, into which people might creep and take their turn at being toasted and smoked. One may doubt whether this dearth of the hearth-stone could have raged on such a scale, but it's a happy stroke in the representa-tion of an Italian dwelling of any period. It shows how the graceful fiction that Italy is all "meridional" flourished for some time before being refuted by grumbling tourists. And yet amid this cold comfort you feel the incongru-ous presence of a constant intuitive regard for beauty. The shapely spring of the vaulted ceilings; the richly figured walls, coarse and hard in substance as

---

suppressed transitions which, as George Eliot says, unite all contrasts. "To those who have looked at Rome with the quickening power of a knowledge which breathes a growing soul into all historic shapes, and traces out the suppressed transitions which unite all contrasts, Rome may still be the spiritual centre and interpreter of the world. But let them conceive one more historical contrast: the gigantic broken revelations of that Imperial and Papal city thrust abruptly on the notions of a girl who had been brought up in English and Swiss Puritanism, fed on meagre Protestant histories and on art chiefly of the hand-screen sort." (*Middlemarch,* chapter 20).

graceful fiction that Italy is all "meridional." James alludes to the stereotype of Italy as uniformly a sunny, seductive, pleasure-seeking "southern" land.

they are; the charming shapes of the great platters and flagons in the deep recesses of the quaintly carved black dressers; the wandering hand of ornament, as it were, playing here and there for its own diversion in unlighted corners—such things redress, to our fond credulity, with all sorts of grace, the balance of the picture.

And yet, somehow, with what dim, unillumined vision one fancies even such inmates as those conscious of finer needs than the mere supply of blows and beef and beer would meet passing their heavy eyes over such slender household beguilements! These crepuscular chambers at Vincigliata are a mystery and a challenge; they seem the mere propounding of an answerless riddle. You long, as you wander through them, turning up your coat-collar and wondering whether ghosts can catch bronchitis, to answer it with some positive notion of what people so encaged and situated "did," how they looked and talked and carried themselves, how they took their pains and pleasures, how they counted off the hours. Deadly ennui seems to ooze out of the stones and hang in clouds in the brown corners. No wonder men relished a fight and panted for a fray. "Skull-smashers" were sweet, ears ringing with pain and ribs cracking in a tussle were soothing music, compared with the cruel quietude of the dim-windowed castle. When they came back they could only have slept a good deal and eased their dislocated bones on those meagre oaken ledges. Then they woke up and turned about to the table and ate their portion of roasted sheep. They shouted at each other across the board and flung the wooden plates at the serving-men. They jostled and hustled and hooted and bragged; and then, after gorging and boozing and easing their doublets, they squared their elbows one by one on the greasy table and buried their scarred foreheads and dreamed of a good gallop after flying foes. And the women? They must have been strangely simple—simpler far than any moral archæologist can show us in a learned restoration. Of course, their simplicity had its graces and devices; but one thinks with a sigh that, as the poor things turned away with patient looks from the viewless windows to the same, same looming figures on the dusky walls, they had n't even the consolation of knowing that just this attitude and movement, set off by their peaked coifs, their falling sleeves and heavily-twisted trains, would sow the seed of yearning envy—of sorts—on the part of later generations.

There are moods in which one feels the impulse to enter a tacit protest against too gross an appetite for pure æsthetics in this starving and sinning world. One turns half away, musingly, from certain beautiful useless things. But the healthier state of mind surely is to lay no tax on any really intelligent manifestation of the curious and exquisite. Intelligence hangs together essentially, all along the line; it only needs time to make, as we say, its connections. The massive *pastiche* of Vincigliata has no superficial use; but, even if it were less complete, less successful, less brilliant, I should feel a reflective kindness for it. So disinterested and expensive a toy is its own justification; it belongs to the heroics of dilettantism.

III

ONE grows to feel the collection of pictures at the Pitti Palace splendid rather than interesting. After walking through it once or twice you catch the key in which it is pitched—you know what you are likely not to find on closer examination; none of the works of the uncompromising period, nothing from the half-groping geniuses of the early time, those whose colouring was sometimes harsh and their outlines sometimes angular. Vague to me the principle on which the pictures were originally gathered and of the æsthetic creed of the princes who chiefly selected them. A princely creed I should roughly call it—the creed of people who believed in things presenting a fine face to society; who esteemed showy results rather than curious processes, and would have hardly cared more to admit into their collection a work by one of the laborious precursors of the full efflorescence than to see a bucket and broom left standing in a state saloon. The gallery contains in literal fact some eight or ten paintings of the early Tuscan School—notably two admirable specimens of Filippo Lippi and one of the frequent circular pictures of the great Botticelli—a Madonna, chilled with tragic prescience, laying a pale cheek against that of a blighted Infant. Such a melancholy mother as this of Botticelli would have strangled her baby in its cradle to rescue it from the future. But of Botticelli there is much to say. One of the Filippo Lippis is perhaps his masterpiece—a Madonna in a small rose-garden (such a "flowery close" as Mr. William Morris loves to haunt), leaning over an Infant who kicks his little human heels on the grass while half-a-dozen curly-pated angels gather about him, looking back over their shoulders with the candour

---

two admirable specimens of Filippo Lippi . . . circular pictures of the great Botticelli. Although the *Madonna with Child, with Scenes from the Life of Saint Anne* has been maintained as a work of Filippo Lippi (Marcini, 209), *The Madonna and Child, with Angels, in a Rose Garden* is now attributed to Francesco Botticini. In 1890 the tondo of the *Madonna and Child, with Archangels and the Young John the Baptist* was reattributed to the "school of Botticelli" (Lightbown, II, 128).

"flowery close" as Mr. William Morris. The "flowery close," from Morris's *The Earthly Paradise*—"Then a light wind arose / That shook the light stems of that flowery close, / And made men sigh for pleasure"—is also cited by James in a review essay on the poem in the *North American Review;* reprinted in *Literary Criticism: Essays on Literature,* 1186.

of children in *tableaux vivants,* and one of them drops an armful of gathered roses one by one upon the baby. The delightful earthly innocence of these winged youngsters is quite inexpressible. Their heads are twisted about toward the spectator as if they were playing at leap-frog and were expecting a companion to come and take a jump. Never did "young" art, never did subjective freshness, attempt with greater success to represent those phases. But these three fine works are hung over the tops of doors in a dark back room—the bucket and broom are thrust behind a curtain. It seems to me, nevertheless, that a fine Filippo Lippi is good enough company for an Allori or a Cigoli, and that that too deeply sentient Virgin of Botticelli might happily balance the flower-like irresponsibility of Raphael's "Madonna of the Chair."

Taking the Pitti collection, however, simply for what it pretends to be, it gives us the very flower of the sumptuous, the courtly, the grand-ducal. It is chiefly official art, as one may say, but it presents the fine side of the type— the brilliancy, the facility, the amplitude, the sovereignty of good taste. I agree on the whole with a nameless companion and with what he lately remarked about his own humour on these matters; that, having been on his first acquaintance with pictures nothing if not critical, and held the lesson incomplete and the opportunity slighted if he left a gallery without a head-ache, he had come, as he grew older, to regard them more as the grandest of all pleasantries and less as the most strenuous of all lessons, and to remind himself that, after all, it is the privilege of art to make us friendly to the human mind and not to make us suspicious of it. We do in fact as we grow older unstring the critical bow a little and strike a truce with invidious comparisons. We work off the juvenile impulse to heated partisanship and discover that one spontaneous producer is n't different enough from another to keep the all-knowing Fates from smiling over our loves and our aversions. We perceive a certain human solidarity in all cultivated effort, and are conscious of a growing accommodation of judgment—an easier disposition,

---

Allori or a Cigoli. Alessandro Allori (1535–1607), a painter of the Florentine school trained by Bronzino; in the Pitti Palace his most notable work is *Judith and Holofernes.* Lodovico Cardi di Cigoli (1559–1613), trained by Allori; his "Ecce Homo" at the Pitti won a prize in competition with Caravaggio.

too deeply sentient Virgin of Botticelli. Others doubted that the slightly exaggerated aspect of the virgin was the work of Botticelli; in 1890 it was reattributed to the "school of Botticelli."

Raphael's "Madonna of the Chair." The *Madonna della Seggiola,* believed by Hawthorne to be the "most beautiful picture in the world" (Woodson, ed., *Nathaniel Hawthorne: The French and Italian Note-books,* 305). Tintner argues that the title of James's 1873 "The Madonna of the Future" alludes to this work by Raphael (*The Museum World,* 27–30).

the fruit of experience, to take the joke for what it is worth as it passes. We have in short less of a quarrel with the masters we don't delight in, and less of an impulse to pin all our faith on those in whom, in more zealous days, we fancied that we made our peculiar meanings. The meanings no longer seem quite so peculiar. Since then we have arrived at a few in the depths of our own genius that are not sensibly less striking.

And yet it must be added that all this depends vastly on one's mood—as a traveller's impressions do, generally, to a degree which those who give them to the world would do well more explicitly to declare. We have our hours of expansion and those of contraction, and yet while we follow the traveller's trade we go about gazing and judging with unadjusted confidence. We can't suspend judgment; we must take our notes, and the notes are florid or crabbed, as the case may be. A short time ago I spent a week in an ancient city on a hill-top, in the humour, for which I was not to blame, which produces crabbed notes. I knew it at the time, but could n't help it. I went through all the motions of liberal appreciation; I uncapped in all the churches and on the massive ramparts stared all the views fairly out of countenance; but my imagination, which I suppose at bottom had very good reasons of its own and knew perfectly what it was about, refused to project into the dark old town and upon the yellow hills that sympathetic glow which forms half the substance of our genial impressions. So it is that in museums and palaces we are alternate radicals and conservatives. On some days we ask but to be somewhat sensibly affected; on others, Ruskin-haunted, to be spiritually steadied. After a long absence from the Pitti Palace I went back there the other morning and transferred myself from chair to chair in the great golden-roofed saloons—the chairs are all gilded and covered with faded silk—in the humour to be diverted at any price. I need n't mention the things that diverted me; I yawn now when I think of some of them. But an artist, for instance, to whom my kindlier judgment has made permanent concessions is that charming Andrea del Sarto. When I first knew him, in my cold youth, I used to say without mincing that I did n't like him. *Cet âge est sans pitié.* The fine sympathetic, melancholy, pleasing painter! He has a dozen faults, and if you insist pedantically on your rights the conclusive word you use about him will be the word weak. But if you are a generous soul you will utter it low—low as the mild grave tone of his own sought harmonies. He is monotonous, narrow, incomplete; he has but a

---

Andrea del Sarto . . . a dozen faults. With reference to Browning's "Andrea del Sarto: The Faultless Painter," the designation given first by Vasari.

Cet âge est sans pitié. La Fontaine, *Fables,* livre IX, 2, "Les deux Pigeons": "Mais un fripon d'enfant (cet âge est sans pitié)"—But a rascal child (that age is pitiless).

dozen different figures and but two or three ways of distributing them; he seems able to utter but half his thought, and his canvases lack apparently some final return on the whole matter—some process which his impulse failed him before he could bestow. And yet in spite of these limitations his genius is both itself of the great pattern and lighted by the air of a great period. Three gifts he had largely: an instinctive, unaffected, unerring grace; a large and rich, and yet a sort of withdrawn and indifferent sobriety; and best of all, as well as rarest of all, an indescribable property of relatedness as to the moral world. Whether he was aware of the connection or not, or in what measure, I cannot say; but he gives, so to speak, the taste of it. Before his handsome vague-browed Madonnas; the mild, robust young saints who kneel in his foregrounds and look round at you with a conscious anxiety which seems to say that, though in the picture, they are not of it, but of your own sentient life of commingled love and weariness; the stately apostles, with comely heads and harmonious draperies, who gaze up at the high-seated Virgin like early astronomers at a newly seen star—there comes to you the brush of the dark wing of an inward life. A shadow falls for the moment, and in it you feel the chill of moral suffering. Did the Lippis suffer, father or son? Did Raphael suffer? Did Titian? Did Rubens suffer? Perish the thought—it would n't be fair to *us* that they should have had everything. And I note in our poor second-rate Andrea an element of interest lacking to a number of stronger talents.

Interspersed with him at the Pitti hang the stronger and the weaker in splendid abundance. Raphael is there, strong in portraiture—easy, various, bountiful genius that he was—and (strong here is n't the word, but) happy beyond the common dream in his beautiful "Madonna of the Chair." The general instinct of posterity seems to have been to treat this lovely picture as a semi-sacred, an almost miraculous, manifestation. People stand in a worshipful silence before it, as they would before a taper-studded shrine. If we suspend in imagination on the right of it the solid, realistic, unidealised portrait of Leo the Tenth (which hangs in another room) and transport to the left the fresco of the School of Athens from the Vatican, and then reflect that these were three separate fancies of a single youthful, amiable genius we recognise that such a producing consciousness must have been a "treat." My companion already quoted has a phrase that he "does n't care for Raphael," but confesses, when pressed, that he was a most remarkable young man. Titian has a dozen portraits of unequal interest. I never particularly noticed till lately—it is very ill hung—that portentous image of the Emperor Charles

---

Leo the Tenth. The painting is generally known as the portrait of Cardinal Bibbiena (later Pope Leo X).

the Fifth. He was a burlier, more imposing personage than his usual legend figures, and in his great puffed sleeves and gold chains and full-skirted over-dress he seems to tell of a tread that might sometimes have been inconveniently resonant. But the *purpose* to have his way and work his will is there—the great stomach for divine right, the old monarchical temperament. The great Titian, in portraiture, however, remains that formidable young man in black, with the small compact head, the delicate nose and the irascible blue eye. Who was he? What was he? *"Ritratto virile"* is all the catalogue is able to call the picture. "Virile!" Rather! you vulgarly exclaim. You may weave what romance you please about it, but a romance your dream must be. Handsome, clever, defiant, passionate, dangerous, it was not his own fault if he had n't adventures and to spare. He was a gentleman and a warrior, and his adventures balanced between camp and court. I imagine him the young orphan of a noble house, about to come into mort-gaged estates. One would n't have cared to be his guardian, bound to paternal admonitions once a month over his precocious transactions with the Jews or his scandalous abduction from her convent of such and such a noble maiden.

The Pitti Gallery contains none of Titian's golden-toned groups; but it boasts a lovely composition by Paul Veronese, the dealer in silver hues—a Baptism of Christ. W—— named it to me the other day as the picture he most enjoyed, and surely painting seems here to have proposed to itself to discredit and annihilate—and even on the occasion of such a subject—everything but the loveliness of life. The picture bedims and enfeebles its neighbours. We ask ourselves whether painting as such can go further. It is simply that here at last the art stands complete. The early Tuscans, as well as Leonardo, as Raphael, as Michael, saw the great spectacle that surrounded them in beautiful sharp-edged elements and parts. The great Venetians felt its indissoluble unity and recognised that form and colour and earth and air

---

Charles the Fifth. He was a burlier, more imposing personage. Although no portrait of Charles V exists in the Pitti collection, this description fits the museum's *Pietro Aretino*, by Titian; depicted is, as noted in the catalogue, a figure of particularly "massive bulk" (Wethey, 75–76). The Misses Horner (see page 242 above) had mentioned that Charles V had given Aretino the gold chain he wears in the picture; the fact may have contributed to James's confusion.

"Ritratto virile." Portrait of a man; variously titled *Ritratto di gentiluomo in nero, L'inglese* (The Englishman), and *L'Uomo dagli occhi grigi* (Man with gray eyes).

W—— named it to me. After a difficult and depressing year, William James, the "inveterate companion" referred to throughout these Florentine essays, took a temporary leave from his position as physiology professor at Harvard, and in November 1873 made his first trip to Italy, where he joined his brother for a two-month visit.

were equal members of every possible subject; and beneath their magical touch the hard outlines melted together and the blank intervals bloomed with meaning. In this beautiful Paul Veronese of the Pitti everything is part of the charm—the atmosphere as well as the figures, the look of radiant morning in the white-streaked sky as well as the living human limbs, the cloth of Venetian purple about the loins of the Christ as well as the noble humility of his attitude. The relation to Nature of the other Italian schools differs from that of the Venetian as courtship—even ardent courtship—differs from marriage.

IV

I WENT the other day to the secularised Convent of San Marco, paid my franc at the profane little wicket which creaks away at the door—no less than six custodians, apparently, are needed to turn it, as if it may have a recusant conscience—passed along the bright, still cloister and paid my respects to Fra Angelico's Crucifixion, in that dusky chamber in the basement. I looked long; one can hardly do otherwise. The fresco deals with the pathetic on the grand scale, and after taking in its beauty you feel as little at liberty to go away abruptly as you would to leave church during the sermon. You may be as little of a formal Christian as Fra Angelico was much of one; you yet feel admonished by spiritual decency to let so yearning a view of the Christian story work its utmost will on you. The three crosses rise high against a strange completely crimson sky, which deepens mysteriously the tragic expression of the scene, though I remain perforce vague as to whether this lurid background be a fine intended piece of symbolism or an effective accident of time. In the first case the extravagance quite triumphs. Between the crosses, under no great rigour of composition, are scattered the most exemplary saints—kneeling, praying, weeping, pitying, worshipping. The swoon of the Madonna is depicted at the left, and this gives the holy presences, in respect to the case, the strangest historical or actual air. Everything is so real that you feel a vague impatience and almost ask yourself how it was that amid the army of his consecrated servants our Lord was permitted to suffer. On reflection you see that the painter's design, so far as coherent, has been simply to offer an immense representation of Pity, and all with such concentrated truth that his colours here seem dissolved in tears that drop and drop, however softly, through all time. Of this single yearning consciousness the figures are admirably expressive. No later painter learned to render with deeper force than Fra Angelico the one state of the spirit he could conceive—a passionate pious tenderness. Immured in his quiet convent, he apparently never received an intelligible impression of evil; and his conception of human life was a perpetual sense of sacredly loving and being loved. But how, immured in his quiet convent, away from the streets and the studios, did he become that genuine, finished, perfectly professional painter? No one is less of a mere mawkish amateur. His range was broad, from this really heroic fresco to the little trumpeting seraphs, in their opaline robes, enamelled, as it were, on the gold margins of his pictures.

I sat out the sermon and departed, I hope, with the gentle preacher's blessing. I went into the smaller refectory, near by, to refresh my memory of the beautiful Last Supper of Domenico Ghirlandaio. It would be putting things coarsely to say that I adjourned thus from a sermon to a comedy, though Ghirlandaio's theme, as contrasted with the blessed Angelico's, was the dramatic spectacular side of human life. How keenly he observed it and how richly he rendered it, the world about him of colour and costume, of handsome heads and pictorial groupings! In his admirable school there is no painter one enjoys—*pace* Ruskin—more sociably and irresponsibly. Lippo Lippi is simpler, quainter, more frankly expressive; but we retain before him a remnant of the sympathetic discomfort provoked by the masters whose conceptions were still a trifle too large for their means. The pictorial vision in their minds seems to stretch and strain their undeveloped skill almost to a sense of pain. In Ghirlandaio the skill and the imagination are equal, and he gives us a delightful impression of enjoying his own resources. Of all the painters of his time he affects us least as positively not of ours. He enjoyed a crimson mantle spreading and tumbling in curious folds and embroidered with needlework of gold, just as he enjoyed a handsome well-rounded head, with vigorous dusky locks, profiled in courteous adoration. He enjoyed in short the various reality of things, and had the good fortune to live in an age when reality flowered into a thousand amusing graces—to speak only of those. He was not especially addicted to giving spiritual hints; and yet how hard and meagre they seem, the professed and finished realists of our own day, with the spiritual *bonhomie* or candour that makes half Ghirlandaio's richness left out! The Last Supper at San Marco is an excellent example of the natural reverence of an artist of that time with whom reverence was not, as one may say, a specialty. The main idea with him has been the variety, the material bravery and positively social charm of the scene, which finds expression, with irrepressible generosity, in the accessories of the background. Instinctively he imagines an opulent garden—imagines it with a good faith which quite tides him over the reflection that Christ and his disciples were

pace **Ruskin.** For Ruskin's negative view of Ghirlandaio ("And it is all simply—good for nothing"), see *Mornings in Florence* (*Works*, XXIII, 313–14).

poor men and unused to sit at meat in palaces. Great full-fruited orange-trees peep over the wall before which the table is spread, strange birds fly through the air, while a peacock perches on the edge of the partition and looks down on the sacred repast. It is striking that, without any at all intense religious purpose, the figures, in their varied naturalness, have a dignity and sweetness of attitude that admits of numberless reverential constructions. I should call all this the happy tact of a robust faith.

On the staircase leading up to the little painted cells of the Beato Angelico, however, I suddenly faltered and paused. Somehow I had grown averse to the intenser zeal of the Monk of Fiesole. I wanted no more of him that day. I wanted no more macerated friars and spear-gashed sides. Ghirlandaio's elegant way of telling his story had put me in the humour for something more largely intelligent, more profanely pleasing. I departed, walked across the square, and found it in the Academy, standing in a particular spot and looking up at a particular high-hung picture. It is difficult to speak adequately, perhaps even intelligibly, of Sandro Botticelli. An accomplished critic—Mr. Pater, in his *Studies on the History of the Renaissance*—has lately paid him the tribute of an exquisite, a supreme, curiosity. He was rarity and distinction incarnate, and of all the multitudinous masters of his group incomparably the most interesting, the one who detains and perplexes and fascinates us most. Exquisitely fine his imagination—infinitely audacious and adventurous his fancy. Alone among the painters of his time he strikes us as having invention. The glow and thrill of expanding observation—this was the feeling that sent his comrades to their easels; but Botticelli's moved him to reactions and emotions of which they knew nothing, caused his faculty to sport and wander and explore on its own account. These impulses have fruits often so ingenious and so lovely that it would be easy to talk nonsense about them. I hope it is not nonsense, however, to say that the picture to which I just alluded (the "Coronation of the Virgin," with a group of life-sized saints below and a garland of miniature angels above) is one of the supremely beautiful productions of the human mind. It is hung so high that

---

Botticelli . . . Mr. Pater . . . *Studies on the History of the Renaissance* . . . an exquisite, a supreme, curiosity. In his chapter on "Sandro Botticelli" Pater attempts to answer the question, "What is the peculiar sensation, what is the peculiar quality of pleasure, which his work has the property of exciting in us, and which we cannot get elsewhere?"

"Coronation of the Virgin." James's ambiguous reference to "unprecedented delicacy" may be more a curatorial judgment than an aesthetic one; the painting has been off exhibition for many years because of the extremely precarious condition of the painted surface. See Lightbown, II, 71, and I, 113, for a description and illustration.

you need a good glass to see it; to say nothing of the unprecedented delicacy of the work. The lower half is of moderate interest; but the dance of hand-clasped angels round the heavenly couple above has a beauty newly exhaled from the deepest sources of inspiration. Their perfect little hands are locked with ineffable elegance; their blowing robes are tossed into folds of which each line is a study; their charming feet have the relief of the most delicate sculpture. But, as I have already noted, of Botticelli there is much, too much to say—besides which Mr. Pater has said all. Only add thus to his inimitable grace of design that the exquisite pictorial force driving him goes a-Maying not on wanton errands of its own, but on those of some mystic superstition which trembles for ever in his heart.

V

THE more I look at the old Florentine domestic architecture the more I like it—that of the great examples at least; and if I ever am able to build myself a lordly pleasure-house I don't see how in conscience I can build it different from these. They are sombre and frowning, and look a trifle more as if they were meant to keep people out than to let them in; but what equally "important" type—if there be an equally important—is more expressive of domiciliary dignity and security and yet attests them with a finer æsthetic economy? They are impressively "handsome," and yet contrive to be so by the simplest means. I don't say at the smallest pecuniary cost—that's another matter. There is money buried in the thick walls and diffused through the echoing excess of space. The merchant nobles of the fifteenth century had deep and full pockets, I suppose, though the present bearers of their names are glad to let out their palaces in suites of apartments which are occupied by the commercial aristocracy of another republic. One is told of fine old mouldering chambers of which possession is to be enjoyed for a sum not worth mentioning. I am afraid that behind these so gravely harmonious fronts there is a good deal of dusky discomfort, and I speak now simply of the large serious faces themselves as you can see them from the street; see them ranged cheek to cheek, in the grey historic light of Via dei Bardi, Via Maggio, Via degli Albizzi. The force of character, the familiar severity and majesty, depend on a few simple features: on the great iron-caged windows of the rough-hewn basement; on the noble stretch of space between the summit of one high, round-topped window and the bottom of that above; on the high-hung sculptured shield at the angle of the house; on the flat far-projecting roof; and, finally, on the magnificent tallness of the whole build-

ing, which so dwarfs our modern attempts at size. The finest of these Florentine palaces are, I imagine, the tallest habitations in Europe that are frankly
and amply habitations—not mere shafts for machinery of the American
grain-elevator pattern. Some of the creations of M. Haussmann in Paris may
climb very nearly as high; but there is all the difference in the world between
the impressiveness of a building which takes breath, as it were, some six or
seven times, from storey to storey, and of one that erects itself to an equal
height in three long-drawn pulsations. When a house is ten windows wide
and the drawing-room floor is as high as a chapel it can afford but three
floors. The spaciousness of some of those ancient drawing-rooms is that of a
Russian steppe. The "family circle," gathered anywhere within speaking
distance, must resemble a group of pilgrims encamped in the desert on a
little oasis of carpet. Madame Gryzanowska, living at the top of a house in
that dusky, tortuous old Borgo Pinti, initiated me the other evening most
good-naturedly, lamp in hand, into the far-spreading mysteries of her apartment. Such quarters seem a translation into space of the old-fashioned idea
of leisure. Leisure and "room" have been passing out of our manners together, but here and there, being of stouter structure, the latter lingers and
survives.

Here and there, indeed, in this blessed Italy, reluctantly modern in spite
alike of boasts and lamentations, it seems to have been preserved for curiosity's and fancy's sake, with a vague, sweet odour of the embalmer's spices
about it. I went the other morning to the Corsini Palace. The proprietors
obviously are great people. One of the ornaments of Rome is their great
white-faced palace in the dark Trastevere and its voluminous gallery, none
the less delectable for the poorness of the pictures. Here they have a palace

---

M. Haussmann. See note, page 239.

Madame Gryzanowska. The E. Gryzanowskas (Gryzanowski and Grisanowski in the correspondence), identified by Edel, *Henry James: The Conquest of London,* 164, and Edel and
Powers, *Complete Notebooks,* 17, as an expatriate of Polish extraction, in 1873 something of a
peripatetic medical professor but formerly a German diplomat ("manners formed in diplomacy,
brain formed in Koenigsberg"), and his English-born wife. In a letter to Lizzie Boott, James
wrote that in Florence, "We became intimate with Mrs. G., who showed us her apartment,
minutely and separately, lamp in hand and 'pride in her past.' It is very handsome, certainly, but
terrifically cold. The drawing-room is as big as Papanti's hall, and marble-paved; cosy on the
December nights!" (*Letters,* I, 416).

Corsini Palace . . . poorness of the pictures. The Palazzo Corsini in Florence (see note, page
71) today is considered the city's most important private art collection; twentieth-century
attribution gives some of the works to Giovanni Bellini, Luca Signorelli, Pontormo, Filippino
Lippo, and Raphael.

on the Arno, with another large, handsome, respectable and mainly uninteresting collection. It contains indeed three or four fine examples of early Florentines. It was not especially for the pictures that I went, however; and certainly not for the pictures that I stayed. I was under the same spell as the inveterate companion with whom I walked the other day through the beautiful private apartments of the Pitti Palace and who said: "I suppose I care for nature, and I know there have been times when I have thought it the greatest pleasure in life to lie under a tree and gaze away at blue hills. But just now I had rather lie on that faded sea-green satin sofa and gaze down through the open door at that retreating vista of gilded, deserted, haunted chambers. In other words I prefer a good 'interior' to a good landscape. The impression has a greater intensity—the thing itself a more complex animation. I like fine old rooms that have been occupied in a fine old way. I like the musty upholstery, the antiquated knick-knacks, the view out of the tall deep-embrasured windows at garden cypresses rocking against a grey sky. If you don't know why, I'm afraid I can't tell you." It seemed to me at the Palazzo Corsini that I did know why. In places that have been lived in so long and so much and in such a fine old way, as my friend said—that is under social conditions so multifold and to a comparatively starved and democratic sense so curious—the past seems to have left a sensible deposit, an aroma, an atmosphere. This ghostly presence tells you no secrets, but it prompts you to try and guess a few. What has been done and said here through so many years, what has been ventured or suffered, what has been dreamed or despaired of? Guess the riddle if you can, or if you think it worth your ingenuity. The rooms at Palazzo Corsini suggest indeed, and seem to recall, but a monotony of peace and plenty. One of them imaged such a noble perfection of a home-scene that I dawdled there until the old custodian came shuffling back to see whether possibly I was trying to conceal a Caravaggio about my person: a great crimson-draped drawing-room of the amplest and yet most charming proportions; walls hung with large dark pictures, a great concave ceiling frescoed and moulded with dusky richness, and half-a-dozen south windows looking out on the Arno, whose swift yellow tide sends up the light in a cheerful flicker. I fear that in my appreciation of the particular effect so achieved I uttered a monstrous folly—some momentary willingness to be maimed or crippled all my days if I might pass them in such a place. In fact half the pleasure of inhabiting this spacious saloon would be that of using one's legs, of strolling up and down past the windows, one by one, and making desultory journeys from station to station and corner to corner. Near by is a colossal ball-room, domed and pilastered like a Renaissance cathedral, and superabundantly decorated with marble effigies, all yellow and grey with the years.

VI

IN the Carthusian Monastery outside the Roman Gate, mutilated and profaned though it is, one may still snuff up a strong if stale redolence of old Catholicism and old Italy. The road to it is ugly, being encumbered with vulgar waggons and fringed with tenements suggestive of an Irish-American suburb. Your interest begins as you come in sight of the convent perched on its little mountain and lifting against the sky, around the bell-tower of its gorgeous chapel, a coronet of clustered cells. You make your way into the lower gate, through a clamouring press of deformed beggars who thrust at you their stumps of limbs, and you climb the steep hillside through a shabby plantation which it is proper to fancy was better tended in the monkish time. The monks are not totally abolished, the government having the grace to await the natural extinction of the half-dozen old brothers who remain, and who shuffle doggedly about the cloisters, looking, with their white robes and their pale blank old faces, quite anticipatory ghosts of their future selves. A prosaic, profane old man in a coat and trousers serves you, however, as custodian. The melancholy friars have not even the privilege of doing you the honours of their dishonour. One must imagine the pathetic effect of their former silent pointings to this and that conventual treasure under stress of the feeling that such pointings were narrowly numbered. The convent is vast and irregular—it bristles with those picture-making arts and accidents which one notes as one lingers and passes, but which in Italy the overburdened memory learns to resolve into broadly general images. I rather deplore its position at the gates of a bustling city—it ought rather to be lodged in some lonely fold of the Apennines. And yet to look out from the shady porch of one of the quiet cells upon the teeming vale of the Arno and the clustered towers of Florence must have deepened the sense of monastic quietude.

The chapel, or rather the church, which is of great proportions and designed by Andrea Orcagna, the primitive painter, refines upon the consecrated type or even quite glorifies it. The massive cincture of black sculptured stalls, the dusky Gothic roof, the high-hung, deep-toned pictures and the superb pavement of verd-antique and dark red marble, polished into glassy lights, must throw the white-robed figures of the gathered friars into the highest romantic relief. All this luxury of worship has nowhere such

---

Carthusian Monastery. The Certosa del Galluzzo or di Val d'Ema, three miles from the city, founded in 1341 by Niccolò Acciaiolli as a Carthusian order, but suspended by Napoleon in 1810 (Fantozzi, "Le soppressioni napoleoniche," 26–27); in 1958 the charterhouse was turned over to the Cistercians.

value as in the chapels of monasteries, where we find it contrasted with the otherwise so ascetic economy of the worshippers. The paintings and gildings of their church, the gem-bright marbles and fantastic carvings, are really but the monastic tribute to sensuous delight—an imperious need for which the fond imagination of Rome has officiously opened the door. One smiles when one thinks how largely a fine starved sense for the forbidden things of earth, if it makes the most of its opportunities, may gratify this need under cover of devotion. Nothing is too base, too hard, too sordid for real humility, but nothing too elegant, too amiable, too caressing, caressed, caressable, for the exaltation of faith. The meaner the convent cell the richer the convent chapel. Out of poverty and solitude, inanition and cold, your honest friar may rise at his will into a Mahomet's Paradise of luxurious analogies.

There are further various dusky subterranean oratories where a number of bad pictures contend faintly with the friendly gloom. Two or three of these funereal vaults, however, deserve mention. In one of them, side by side, sculptured by Donatello in low relief, lie the white marble effigies of the three members of the Accaiuoli family who founded the convent in the thirteenth century. In another, on his back, on the pavement, rests a grim old bishop of the same stout race by the same honest craftsman. Terribly grim he is, and scowling as if in his stony sleep he still dreamed of his hates and his hard ambitions. Last and best, in another low chapel, with the trodden pavement for its bed, shines dimly a grand image of a later bishop—Leonardo Buonafede, who, dying in 1545, owes his monument to Francesco di San Gallo. I have seen little from this artist's hand, but it was clearly of the cunningest. His model here was a very sturdy old prelate, though I should say a very genial old man. The sculptor has respected his monumental ugliness, but has suffused it with a singular homely charm—a look of confessed physical comfort in the privilege of paradise. All these figures have an inimitable reality, and their lifelike marble seems such an incorruptible incarnation of the genius of the place that you begin to think of it as even more reckless than cruel on the part of the present public powers to have begun to pull the establishment down, morally speaking, about their ears. They are lying quiet yet a while; but when the last old friar dies and the convent formally lapses, won't they rise on their stiff old legs and hobble out to the gates and thunder forth anathemas before which even a future and more enterprising régime may be disposed to pause?

Out of the great central cloister open the snug little detached dwellings of the absent fathers. When I said just now that the Certosa in Val d'Ema gives

---

Donatello . . . Francesco di San Gallo. The attribution to Donatello has not held; they are now also considered the works of Francesco da San Gallo.

you a glimpse of old Italy I was thinking of this great pillared quadrangle, lying half in sun and half in shade, of its tangled garden-growth in the centre, surrounding the ancient customary well, and of the intense blue sky bending above it, to say nothing of the indispensable old white-robed monk who pokes about among the lettuce and parsley. We have seen such places before; we have visited them in that divinatory glance which strays away into space for a moment over the top of a suggestive book. I don't quite know whether it's more or less as one's fancy would have it that the monk-ish cells are no cells at all, but very tidy little *appartements complets,* consist-ing of a couple of chambers, a sitting-room and a spacious loggia, projecting out into space from the cliff-like wall of the monastery and sweeping from pole to pole the loveliest view in the world. It's poor work, however, taking notes on views, and I will let this one pass. The little chambers are terribly cold and musty now. Their odour and atmosphere are such as one used, as a child, to imagine those of the school-room during Saturday and Sunday.

VII

IN the Roman streets, wherever you turn, the façade of a church in more or less degenerate flamboyance is the principal feature of the scene; and if, in the absence of purer motives, you are weary of æsthetic trudging over the corrugated surface of the Seven Hills, a system of pavement in which small cobble-stones anomalously endowed with angles and edges are alone em-ployed, you may turn aside at your pleasure and take a reviving sniff at the pungency of incense. In Florence, one soon observes, the churches are rela-tively few and the dusky house-fronts more rarely interrupted by specimens of that extraordinary architecture which in Rome passes for sacred. In Florence, in other words, ecclesiasticism is less cheap a commodity and not dispensed in the same abundance at the street-corners. Heaven forbid, at the same time, that I should undervalue the Roman churches, which are for the most part treasure-houses of history, of curiosity, of promiscuous and asso-ciational interest. It is a fact, nevertheless, that, after St. Peter's, I know but one really beautiful church by the Tiber, the enchanting basilica of St. Mary Major. Many have structural character, some a great *allure,* but as a rule they all lack the dignity of the best of the Florentine temples. Here, the list being immeasurably shorter and the seed less scattered, the principal

---

St. Mary Major. Santa Maria Maggiore, in Rome. See pages 132–33.

churches are all beautiful. And yet I went into the Annunziata the other day and sat there for half-an-hour because, forsooth, the gildings and the marbles and the frescoed dome and the great rococo shrine near the door, with its little black jewelled fetish, reminded me so poignantly of Rome. Such is the city properly styled eternal—since it is eternal, at least, as regards the consciousness of the individual. One loves it in its sophistications—though for that matter is n't it all rich and precious sophistication?—better than other places in their purity.

Coming out of the Annunziata you look past the bronze statue of the Grand Duke Ferdinand I (whom Mr. Browning's heroine used to watch for—in the poem of "The Statue and the Bust"—from the red palace near by), and down a street vista of enchanting picturesqueness. The street is narrow and dusky and filled with misty shadows, and at its opposite end rises the vast bright-coloured side of the Cathedral. It stands up in very much the same mountainous fashion as the far-shining mass of the bigger prodigy at Milan, of which your first glimpse as you leave your hotel is generally through another such dark avenue; only that, if we talk of mountains, the white walls of Milan must be likened to snow and ice from their base, while those of the Duomo of Florence may be the image of some mighty hillside enamelled with blooming flowers. The big bleak interior here has a naked majesty which, though it may fail of its effect at first, becomes after a while extraordinarily touching. Originally disconcerting, it soon inspired me with a passion. Externally, at any rate, it is one of the loveliest

---

Annunziata . . . little black jewelled fetish. In the Florentine church of the Santissima Annunziata, Michelozzo's highly wrought baroque "tempietto della madonna" holds a legendary fresco depicting the annunciation. According to tradition, the mysterious work is attributed to a Fra Bartolomeo, a thirteenth-century painter, who, after having finished all but the head of the virgin, went to sleep in despair of his ability to fulfill the glory of his conception; he awoke to find the fresco finished by the hand of an angel. The fragile image is generally covered by a dark curtain (a reproduction of a nineteenth-century engraving of the tempietto—as well as of the uncovered fresco—may be found in Taucci, 14, 113).

Grand Duke Ferdinand I (whom Mr. Browning's heroine . . .). In Browning's "The Statue and the Bust" (1855), just before her wedding a young bride-to-be views Ferdinand di Medici (1549–1608) pass before the window of her chamber in the Palazzo Riccardi, now the Palazzo Antinori; although her wedding takes place, the exchange of glances is sufficient to stir lifelong unrequited love between the pair. As age finally begins to silver her hair, she orders that her image in marble be placed in one of the niches of the palace—"Eyeing ever, with earnest eye / And quick-turned neck at its breathless stretch, / Some one who ever is passing by." The duke, on his part, has a statue of bronze erected in the piazza across from her image. A bronze equestrian figure does exist, but the statue of the lady is part of Browning's invention.

bigger prodigy at Milan. The Duomo at Milan is, after Saint Peter's in Rome and the cathedral of Seville, the third largest Catholic church in the world.

works of man's hands, and an overwhelming proof into the bargain that when elegance belittles grandeur you have simply had a bungling artist.

Santa Croce within not only triumphs here, but would triumph anywhere. "A trifle naked if you like," said my irrepressible companion, "but that's what I call architecture, just as I don't call bronze or marble clothes (save under urgent stress of portraiture) statuary." And indeed we are far enough away from the clustering odds and ends borrowed from every art and every province without which the ritually builded thing does n't trust its spell to work in Rome. The vastness, the lightness, the open spring of the arches at Santa Croce, the beautiful shape of the high and narrow choir, the impression made as of mass without weight and the gravity yet reigning without gloom—these are my frequent delight, and the interest grows with acquaintance. The place is the great Florentine Valhalla, the final home or memorial harbour of the native illustrious dead, but that consideration of it would take me far. It must be confessed moreover that, between his coarsely-imagined statue out in front and his horrible monument in one of the aisles, the author of *The Divine Comedy,* for instance, is just hereabouts rather an extravagant figure. "Ungrateful Florence," declaims Byron. Ungrateful indeed—would she were more so! the susceptible spirit of the great exile may be still aware enough to exclaim; in common, that is, with most of the other immortals sacrificed on so very large a scale to current Florentine "plastic" facility. In explanation of which remark, however, I must confine myself to noting that, as almost all the old monuments at Santa Croce are small, comparatively small, and interesting and exquisite, so the modern, well nigh without exception, are disproportionately vast and pompous, or in other words distressingly vague and vain. The aptitude of hand, the compositional assurance, with which such things are nevertheless turned out, constitutes an anomaly replete with suggestion for an observer of the present state of the arts on the soil and in the air that once befriended them, taking them all together, as even the soil and the air of Greece scarce availed to do. But on this head, I repeat, there would be too much to say; and I find myself

---

Florentine Valhalla ... "Ungrateful Florence." Somewhat like Valhalla, the abode into which Odin received the souls of the noble dead, Santa Croce is the resting place of the remains of some of Florence's most distinguished citizens, among them Michelangelo, Machiavelli, Galileo, and Ghiberti, but not those of Dante; his tomb is in Ravenna, where he died in exile from his native city. "Ungrateful Florence! Dante sleeps afar, / Like Scipio, buried by the upbraiding shore; / Thy factions, in their worse than civil war, / Proscribed the bard whose name for evermore / Their children's children would in vain adore / With the remorse of ages; and the crown / Which Petrarch's laureate brow supremely wore, / Upon a far and foreign soil had grown, / His life, his fame, his grave, though rifled—not thine own," Byron, *Childe Harold's Pilgrimage,* canto IV, lvii.

checked by the same warning at the threshold of the church in Florence really interesting beyond Santa Croce, beyond all others. Such, of course, easily, is Santa Maria Novella, where the chapels are lined and plated with wonderful figured and peopled fresco-work even as most of those in Rome with precious inanimate substances. These overscored retreats of devotion, as dusky, some of them, as eremitic caves swarming with importunate visions, have kept me divided all winter between the love of Ghirlandaio and the fear of those seeds of catarrh to which their mortal chill seems propitious till far on into the spring. So I pause here just on the praise of that delightful painter—as to the spirit of whose work the reflections I have already made are but confirmed by these examples. In the choir at Santa Maria Novella, where the incense swings and the great chants resound, between the gorgeous coloured window and the florid grand altar, he still "goes in," with all his might, for the wicked, the amusing world, the world of faces and forms and characters, of every sort of curious human and rare material thing.

VIII

I HAD always felt the Boboli Gardens charming enough for me to "haunt" them; and yet such is the interest of Florence in every quarter that it took another *corso* of the same cheap pattern as the last to cause me yesterday to flee the crowded streets, passing under that archway of the Pitti Palace which might almost be the gate of an Etruscan city, so that I might spend the afternoon among the mouldy statues that compose with their screens of cypress, looking down at our clustered towers and our background of pale blue hills vaguely freckled with white villas. These pleasure-grounds of the austere Pitti pile, with its inconsequent charm of being so rough-hewn and yet somehow so elegantly balanced, plead with a voice all their own the general cause of the ample enclosed, planted, cultivated private preserve— preserve of tranquillity and beauty and immunity—in the heart of a city; a cause, I allow, for that matter, easy to plead anywhere, once the pretext is found, the large, quiet, distributed town-garden, with the vague hum of big grudging boundaries all about it, but with everything worse excluded, being of course the most insolently-pleasant thing in the world. In addition to which, when the garden is in the Italian manner, with flowers rather remark-

---

Santa Maria Novella . . . fresco-work. Frescoes attributed to Nardo di Cione, Andrea Orcagna, Filippino Lippi, Botticelli, Masaccio, and Domenico Ghirlandaio assisted by both his brother Davide and by the young Michelangelo.

ably omitted, as too flimsy and easy and cheap, and without lawns that are too smart, paths that are too often swept and shrubs that are too closely trimmed, though with a fanciful formalism giving style to its shabbiness, and here and there a dusky ilex-walk, and here and there a dried-up fountain, and everywhere a piece of mildewed sculpture staring at you from a green alcove, and just in the right place, above all, a grassy amphitheatre curtained behind with black cypresses and sloping downward in mossy marble steps— when, I say, the place possesses these attractions, and you lounge there of a soft Sunday afternoon, the racier spectacle of the streets having made your fellow-loungers few and left you to the deep stillness and the shady vistas that lead you wonder where, left you to the insidious irresistible mixture of nature and art, nothing too much of either, only a supreme happy resultant, a divine *tertium quid:* under these conditions, it need scarce be said the revelation invoked descends upon you.

The Boboli Gardens are not large—you wonder how compact little Florence finds room for them within her walls. But they are scattered, to their extreme, their all-romantic advantage and felicity, over a group of steep undulations between the rugged and terraced palace and a still-surviving stretch of city wall, where the unevenness of the ground much adds to their apparent size. You may cultivate in them the fancy of their solemn and haunted character, of something faint and dim and even, if you like, tragic, in their prescribed, their functional smile; as if they borrowed from the huge monument that overhangs them certain of its ponderous memories and regrets. This course is open to you, I mention, but it is n't enjoined, and will doubtless indeed not come up for you at all if it is n't your habit, cherished beyond any other, to spin your impressions to the last tenuity of fineness. Now that I bethink myself I must always have happened to wander here on grey and melancholy days. It remains none the less true that the place contains, thank goodness—or at least thank the grave, the infinitely-distinguished traditional *taste* of Florence—no cheerful, trivial object, neither parterres, nor pagodas, nor peacocks, nor swans. They have their famous amphitheatre already referred to, with its degrees or stone benches of a thoroughly aged and mottled complexion and its circular wall of ever-greens behind, in which small cracked images and vases, things that, according to association, and with the law of the same quite indefinable, may make as much on one occasion for exquisite dignity as they may make on another for (to express it kindly) nothing at all. Something was once done in this charmed and forsaken circle—done or meant to be done; what was it, dumb statues, who saw it with your blank eyes? Opposite stands the huge flat-roofed palace, putting forward two great rectangular arms and looking, with its closed windows and its foundations of almost unreduced rock, like some ghost of a sample of a ruder Babylon. In the wide court-like space between the wings is a fine old white marble fountain that never plays. Its dusty idleness completes the general air of abandonment. Chancing on such a cluster of objects in Italy—glancing at them in a certain light and a certain mood—I get (perhaps on too easy terms, you may think) a sense of *history* that takes away my breath. Generations of Medici have stood at these closed windows, embroidered and brocaded according to their period, and held *fêtes champêtres* and floral games on the greensward, beneath the mouldering hemicycle. And the Medici were great people! But what remains of it all now is a mere tone in the air, a faint sigh in the breeze, a vague expression in things, a passive—or call it rather, perhaps, to be fair, a shyly, pathetically responsive—accessibility to the yearning guess. Call it much or call it little, the ineffaceability of this deep stain of experience, it is the interest of old places and the bribe to the brooding analyst. Time has devoured the doers and their doings, but there still hangs about some effect of their passage. We can "lay out" parks on virgin soil, and cause them to bristle with the most expensive importations, but we unfortunately can't scatter abroad again this seed of the eventual human soul of a place—that comes but in its time and takes too long to grow. There is nothing like it when it *has* come.

[1874.]

Tuscan Cities

The cities I refer to are Leghorn, Pisa, Lucca and Pistoia, among which I have been spending the last few days. The most striking fact as to Leghorn, it must be conceded at the outset, is that, being in Tuscany, it should be so scantily Tuscan. The traveller curious in local colour must content himself with the deep blue expanse of the Mediterranean. The streets, away from the docks, are modern, genteel and rectangular; Liverpool might acknowledge them if it were n't for their clean-coloured, sun-bleached stucco. They are the offspring of the new industry which is death to the old idleness. Of interesting architecture, fruit of the old idleness or at least of the old leisure, Leghorn is singularly destitute. It has neither a church worth one's attention, nor a municipal palace, nor a museum, and it may claim the distinction, unique in Italy, of being the city of no pictures. In a shabby corner near the docks stands a statue of one of the elder Grand Dukes of Tuscany, appealing to posterity on grounds now vague—chiefly that of having placed certain Moors under tribute. Four colossal negroes, in very bad bronze, are chained to the base of the monument, which forms with their assistance a sufficiently fantastic group; but to patronise

[Originally published (unsigned) in the *Nation*, xviii (21 May 1874), 329–30; reprinted in *Transatlantic Sketches*, 1875, where it was dated 1873.]

new industry which is death to the old idleness. Livorno, known to the English and American tourist as Leghorn, was a popular seaside resort—Shelley took a villa here in 1819, as did Byron in 1822—until the mid-nineteenth century, when the shipyard industries began to dominate and change the character of the city. By World War I Livorno had become known for an increasingly modern aspect; the heavy bombing of World War II wiped out almost all remaining traces of scenic interest.

the arts is not the line of the Livornese, and for want of the slender annuity which would keep its precinct sacred this curious memorial is buried in dockyard rubbish. I must add that on the other hand there is a very well-conditioned and, in attitude and gesture, extremely natural and familiar statue of Cavour in one of the city squares, and in another a couple of effigies of recent Grand Dukes, represented, that is dressed, or rather undressed, in the character of heroes of Plutarch. Leghorn is a city of magnificent spaces, and it was so long a journey from the sidewalk to the pedestal of these images that I never took the time to go and read the inscriptions. And in truth, vaguely, I bore the originals a grudge, and wished to know as little about them as possible; for it seemed to me that as *patres patriæ,* in their degree, they might have decreed that the great blank, ochre-faced piazza should be a trifle less ugly. There is a distinct amenity, however, in any experience of Italy almost anywhere, and I shall probably in the future not be above sparing a light regret to several of the hours of which the one I speak of was composed. I shall remember a large cool bourgeois villa in the garden of a noiseless suburb—a middle-aged Villa Franco (I owe it as a genial pleasant *pension* the tribute of recognition), roomy and stony, as an Italian villa should be. I shall remember that, as I sat in the garden, and, looking up from my book, saw through a gap in the shrubbery the red house-tiles against the deep blue sky and the grey underside of the ilex-leaves turned up by the Mediterranean breeze, it was all still quite Tuscany, if Tuscany in the minor key.

If you should naturally desire, in such conditions, a higher intensity, you have but to proceed, by a very short journey, to Pisa—where, for that matter, you will seem to yourself to have hung about a good deal already, and from an early age. Few of us can have had a childhood so unblessed by contact with the arts as that one of its occasional diversions shan't have been a puzzled scrutiny of some alabaster model of the Leaning Tower under a glass cover in a back-parlour. Pisa and its monuments have, in other words, been industriously vulgarised, but it is astonishing how well they have survived the process. The charm of the place is in fact of a high order and but partially foreshadowed by the famous crookedness of its campanile. I felt it irresistibly and yet almost inexpressibly the other afternoon, as I made my way to the classic corner of the city through the warm drowsy air which

---

Cavour . . . *patres patriæ.* Arturo Conti's 1871 statue of Camillo Benso di Cavour (1810–61), the great Italian statesman and premier, instrumental in bringing about the unification of Italy, and therefore something of a "father of his country." James's admiration of Cavour was to grow over the years; see his enthusiastic 1877 review of the recent English translation of Charles de Mazade, *The Life of Count Cavour,* reprinted in *Literary Criticism: Essays on Literature, French Writers,* 556–61.

nervous people come to inhale as a sedative. I was with an invalid companion who had had no sleep to speak of for a fortnight. "Ah! stop the carriage," she sighed, or yawned, as I could feel, deliciously, "in the shadow of
this old slumbering palazzo, and let me sit here and close my eyes, and taste
for an hour of oblivion." Once strolling over the grass, however, out of
which the quartette of marble monuments rises, we awaked responsively
enough to the present hour. Most people remember the happy remark of
tasteful, old-fashioned Forsyth (who touched a hundred other points in his
"Italy" scarce less happily) as to the fact that the four famous objects are
"fortunate alike in their society and their solitude." It must be admitted that
they are more fortunate in their society than we felt ourselves to be in ours;
for the scene presented the animated appearance for which, on any fine
spring day, all the choicest haunts of ancient quietude in Italy are becoming
yearly more remarkable. There were clamorous beggars at all the sculptured
portals, and bait for beggars, in abundance, trailing in and out of them
under convoy of loquacious ciceroni. I forget just how I apportioned the
responsibility of intrusion, for it was not long before fellow-tourists and
fellow-countrymen became a vague, deadened, muffled presence, that of the
dentist's last words when he is giving you ether. They suffered mystic disinte-
gration in the dense, bright, tranquil air, so charged with its own messages.
The Cathedral and its companions are fortunate indeed in everything—
fortunate in the spacious angle of the grey old city-wall which folds about
them in their sculptured elegance like a strong protecting arm; fortunate in
the broad greensward which stretches from the marble base of Cathedral
and cemetery to the rugged foot of the rampart; fortunate in the little
vagabonds who dot the grass, plucking daisies and exchanging Italian cries;
fortunate in the pale-gold tone to which time and the soft sea-damp have
mellowed and darkened their marble plates; fortunate, above all, in an
indescribable grace of grouping, half hazard, half design, which insures
them, in one's memory of things admired, very much the same isolated
corner that they occupy in the charming city.

Of the smaller cathedrals of Italy I know none I prefer to that of Pisa; none

---

invalid companion. A Mrs. Lombard, of Cambridge, Massachusetts; in 1874 James warned
a correspondent about her and her daughter Fanny: "They are both, I imagine, great invalids,
so avoid committing yourself farther than you can help with them" (Edel, *The Conquest of
London*, 163–64); in 1881 Mrs. Lombard, at San Remo, was discovered to be "very feeble and
very deaf," and, in Paris in 1884, "still seriously ill" (*Letters*, II, 348; III, 35). Edel recognizes
her as the model for several itinerant female invalids in James's fiction.

Forsyth . . . "fortunate alike. . . ." The duomo, the baptistry, the leaning tower, and the
walled cemetery, or *camposanto,* on the Piazza dei Miracoli, are "fortunate both in their society
and their solitude"—Joseph Forsyth, *Remarks on Antiquities*, 8.

that, on a moderate scale, produces more the impression of a great church. It has without so modest a measurability, represents so clean and compact a mass, that you are startled when you cross the threshold at the apparent space it encloses. An architect of genius, for all that he works with colossal blocks and cumbrous pillars, is certainly the most cunning of conjurors. The front of the Duomo is a small pyramidal screen, covered with delicate carvings and chasings, distributed over a series of short columns upholding narrow arches. It might be a sought imitation of goldsmith's work in stone, and the area covered is apparently so small that extreme fineness has been prescribed. How it is therefore that on the inner side of this façade the wall should appear to rise to a splendid height and to support one end of a ceiling as remote in its gilded grandeur, one could almost fancy, as that of St. Peter's; how it is that the nave should stretch away in such solemn vastness, the shallow transepts emphasise the grand impression and the apse of the choir hollow itself out like a dusky cavern fretted with golden stalactites, is all matter for exposition by a keener architectural analyst than I. To sit somewhere against a pillar where the vista is large and the incidents cluster richly, and vaguely revolve these mysteries without answering them, is the best of one's usual enjoyment of a great church. It takes no deep sounding to conclude indeed that a gigantic Byzantine Christ in mosaic, on the concave roof of the choir, contributes largely to the particular impression here as of very old and choice and original and individual things. It has even more of stiff solemnity than is common to works of its school, and prompts to more wonder than ever on the nature of the human mind at a time when such unlovely shapes could satisfy its conception of holiness. Truly pathetic is the fate of these huge mosaic idols, thanks to the change that has overtaken our manner of acceptance of them. Strong the contrast between the original sublimity of their pretensions and the way in which they flatter that free sense of the grotesque which the modern imagination has smuggled even into the appreciation of religious forms. They were meant to yield scarcely to the Deity itself in grandeur, but the only part they play now is to stare helplessly at our critical, or æsthetic patronage of them. The spiritual refinement marking the hither end of a progress had n't, however, to wait for *us* to signalise it; it found expression three centuries ago in the beautiful specimen of the painter Sodoma on the wall of the choir. This latter, a small Sacrifice of Isaac, is one of the best examples of its exquisite author, and perhaps, as chance has it, the most perfect opposition that could be found in the way of the range of taste to the effect of the great mosaic. There are many painters more powerful than Sodoma—painters who, like the author of the mosaic, attempted and compassed grandeur; but none has a more persuasive grace, none more than he was to sift and chasten a conception till it should affect one with the sweetness of a perfectly distilled perfume.

Of the patient successive efforts of painting to arrive at the supreme refinement of such a work as the Sodoma the Campo Santo hard by offers a most interesting memorial. It presents a long, blank marble wall to the relative profaneness of the Cathedral close, but within it is a perfect treasure-house of art. This quadrangular defence surrounds an open court where weeds and wild roses are tangled together and a sunny stillness seems to rest consentingly, as if Nature had been won to consciousness of the precious relics committed to her. Something in the quality of the place recalls the collegiate cloisters of Oxford, but it must be added that this is the handsomest compliment to that seat of learning. The open arches of the quadrangles of Magdalen and Christ Church are not of mellow Carrara marble, nor do they offer to sight columns, slim and elegant, that seem to frame the unglazed windows of a cathedral. To be buried in the Campo Santo of Pisa, I may however further qualify, you need only be, or to have more or less anciently been, illustrious, and there is a liberal allowance both as to the character and degree of your fame. The most obtrusive object in one of the long vistas is a most complicated monument to Madame Catalani, the singer, recently erected by her possibly too-appreciative heirs. The wide pavement is a mosaic of sepulchral slabs, and the walls, below the base of the paling frescoes, are incrusted with inscriptions and encumbered with urns and antique sarcophagi. The place is at once a cemetery and a museum, and its especial charm is its strange mixture of the active and the passive, of art and rest, of life and death. Originally its walls were one vast continuity of closely pressed frescoes; but now the great capricious scars and stains have come to outnumber the pictures, and the cemetery has grown to be a burial-place of pulverised masterpieces as well as of finished lives. The fragments of painting that remain are fortunately the best; for one is safe in believing that a host of undimmed neighbours would distract but little from the two great works of Orcagna. Most people know the "Triumph of Death" and the "Last Judgment" from descriptions and engravings; but to measure the possible good faith of imitative art one must stand there and see

perfect treasure-house of art. The Camposanto was heavily bombed during World War II. Lost were the frescoes of the eastern wing and particularly damaged, but subsequently some-what restored, were the twenty-three scenes by Benozzo Gozzoli (c. 1421–97), which James admired.

Madame Catalani. Angelica Catalani (1780–1849), an opera singer of only moderate fame; the monument, along with the monuments of many other lay people, have since been removed.

Orcagna. The attribution to Orcagna first appears in Vasari, but both frescoes are now labeled anonymous works by the *Master of the Triumph of Death;* some claims are made for Francesco Traini or Bonamico Buffalmacco (Binni, 444; Meiss, 77).

the painter's howling potentates dragged into hell in all the vividness of his bright hard colouring; see his feudal courtiers, on their palfreys, hold their noses at what they are so fast coming to; see his great Christ, in judgment, refuse forgiveness with a gesture commanding enough, really inhuman enough, to make virtue merciless for ever. The charge that Michael Angelo borrowed his cursing Saviour from this great figure of Orcagna is more valid than most accusations of plagiarism; but of the two figures one at least could be spared. For direct, triumphant expressiveness these two superb frescoes have probably never been surpassed. The painter aims at no very delicate meanings, but he drives certain gross ones home so effectively that for a parallel to his process one must look to the art of the actor, the emphasising "point"-making mime. Some of his female figures are superb—they represent creatures of a formidable temperament.

There are charming women, however, on the other side of the cloister—in the beautiful frescoes of Benozzo Gozzoli. If Orcagna's work was appointed to survive the ravage of time it is a happy chance that it should be balanced by a group of performances of such a different temper. The contrast is the more striking that in subject the inspiration of both painters is strictly, even though superficially, theological. But Benozzo cares, in his theology, for nothing but the story, the scene and the drama—the chance to pile up palaces and spires in his backgrounds against pale blue skies cross-barred with pearly, fleecy clouds, and to scatter sculptured arches and shady trellises over the front, with every incident of human life going forward lightly and gracefully beneath them. Lightness and grace are the painter's great qualities, marking the hithermost limit of unconscious elegance, after which "style" and science and the wisdom of the serpent set in. His charm is natural fineness; a little more and we should have refinement—which is a very different thing. Like all *les délicats* of this world, as M. Renan calls

---

Michael Angelo borrowed his cursing Saviour. A view offered in 1847 by Lord Lindsay, *Sketches of the History of Christian Art,* 139–41, a work Ruskin reviewed. In 1845, in correspondence James would not have known, Ruskin had written to his parents that in this fresco the "central angel is rising, looking back however towards Sodom with his hand raised in the attitude of condemnation, afterwards adopted by M. Angelo in the Judgment" (Shapiro, 65). See also Meiss, 76–77.

les délicats . . . **M. Renan.** In a lengthy 1883 *Atlantic Monthly* review of Ernest Renan's *Souvenir d'Enfance et de Jeunesse,* James calls Renan "the first writer in France," particularly distinguished in that he "proposed—or rather he was naturally disposed—to remain a model of delicacy. Mr. Renan is the great apostle of the delicate; he upholds the waning fashion on every occasion. His mission is to say delicate things, to plead the cause of intellectual good manners, and he is wonderfully competent to discharge it" (*Literary Criticism: French Writers,* 634). See also page 86 and note.

them, Benozzo has suffered greatly. The space on the walls he originally covered with his Old Testament stories is immense; but his exquisite handi-work has peeled off by the acre, as one may almost say, and the latter compartments of the series are swallowed up in huge white scars, out of which a helpless head or hand peeps forth like those of creatures sinking into a quicksand. As for Pisa at large, although it is not exactly what one would call a mouldering city—for it has a certain well-aired cleanness and bright-ness, even in its supreme tranquillity—it affects the imagination very much in the same way as the Campo Santo. And, in truth, a city so ancient and deeply historic as Pisa is at every step but the burial-ground of a larger life than its present one. The wide empty streets, the goodly Tuscan palaces— which look as if about all of them there were a genteel private understand-ing, independent of placards, that they are to be let extremely cheap—the delicious relaxing air, the full-flowing yellow river, the lounging Pisani, smelling, metaphorically, their poppy-flowers, seemed to me all so many admonitions to resignation and oblivion. And this is what I mean by saying that the charm of Pisa (apart from its cluster of monuments) is a charm of a high order. The architecture has but a modest dignity; the lions are few; there are no fixed points for stopping and gaping. And yet the impression is profound; the charm is a moral charm. If I were ever to be incurably disap-pointed in life, if I had lost my health, my money, or my friends, if I were resigned forevermore to pitching my expectations in a minor key, I should go and invoke the Pisan peace. Its quietude would seem something more than a stillness—a hush. Pisa may be a dull place to live in, but it's an ideal place to wait for death.

Nothing could be more charming than the country between Pisa and Lucca—unless possibly the country between Lucca and Pistoia. If Pisa is dead Tuscany, Lucca is Tuscany still living and enjoying, desiring and intend-ing. The town is a charming mixture of antique "character" and modern inconsequence; and not only the town, but the country—the blooming romantic country which you admire from the famous promenade on the city-wall. The wall is of superbly solid and intensely "toned" brickwork and of extraordinary breadth, and its summit, planted with goodly trees and swelling here and there into bastions and outworks and little open gardens, surrounds the city with a circular lounging-place of a splendid dignity. This well-kept, shady, ivy-grown rampart reminded me of certain mossy corners of England; but it looks away to a prospect of more than English loveliness—a broad green plain where the summer yields a double crop of grain, and a circle of bright blue mountains speckled with high-hung con-vents and profiled castles and nestling villas, and traversed by valleys of a deeper and duskier blue. In one of the deepest and shadiest of these recesses one of the most "sympathetic" of small watering-places is hidden away yet a while longer from easy invasion—the Baths to which Lucca has lent its name. Lucca is pre-eminently a city of churches; ecclesiastical architecture being indeed the only one of the arts to which it seems to have given attention. There are curious bits of domestic architecture, but no great palaces, and no importunate frequency of pictures. The Cathedral, however, sums up the merits of its companions and is a singularly noble and interesting church. Its peculiar boast is a wonderful inlaid front, on which horses and hounds and hunted beasts are lavishly figured in black marble over a white ground. What I chiefly appreciated in the grey solemnity of the nave and transepts was the superb effect of certain second-storey Gothic arches— those which rest on the pavement being Lombard. These arches are delicate and slender, like those of the cloister at Pisa, and they play their part in the dusky upper air with real sublimity.

At Pistoia there is of course a Cathedral, and there is nothing unexpected in its being, externally at least, highly impressive; in its having a grand campanile at its door, a gaudy baptistery, in alternate layers of black and white marble, across the way, and a stately civic palace on either side. But even had I the space to do otherwise I should prefer to speak less of the particular objects of interest in the place than of the pleasure I found it to lounge away in the empty streets the quiet hours of a warm afternoon. To say where I lingered longest would be to tell of a little square before the hospital, out of which you look up at the beautiful frieze in coloured earthenware by the brothers Della Robbia, which runs across the front of the building. It represents the seven orthodox offices of charity and, with its brilliant blues and yellows and its tender expressiveness, brightens up amazingly, to the sense and soul, this little grey corner of the mediæval city. Pistoia is still mediæval. How grass-grown it seemed, how drowsy, how full of idle vistas and melancholy nooks! If nothing was supremely wonderful, everything was delicious.

1874.

---

before the hospital . . . brothers Della Robbia. The terracotta depictions of the seven works of mercy on the frieze of the Ospedale del Ceppo are attributed to Santi Buglioni and Filippo di Lorenzo, not the della Robbia brothers; the representation of the cardinal virtues has been given to Giovanni della Robbia (1459–1529).

Other Tuscan Cities

I

I had scanted charming Pisa even as I had scanted great Siena in my original small report of it, my scarce more than stammering notes of years before; but even if there had been meagreness of mere gaping vision—which there in fact had n't been—as well as insufficiency of public tribute, the indignity would soon have ceased to weigh on my conscience. For to this affection I was to return again still oftener than to the strong call of Siena; my eventual frequentations of Pisa, all merely impressionistic and amateurish as they might be—and I pretended, up and down the length of the land, to none other—leave me at the hither end of time with little more than a confused consciousness of exquisite *quality* on the part of the small sweet scrap of a place of ancient glory; a consciousness so pleadingly content to be general and vague that I shrink from pulling it to pieces. The Republic of Pisa fought with the Republic of Florence, through the ages, so ferociously and all but invincibly that what is so pale and languid in her to-day may well be the aspect of any civil or, still more, military creature bled and bled and bled at the "critical" time of its life. She has verily a just languor and is touchingly anæmic; the past history, or at any rate the present perfect acceptedness, of which condition hangs about her with the last grace of weakness, making her state in this particular the very secret of her irresistible appeal. I was to find the appeal, again and again, one of the sweetest, tenderest, even if not one of the fullest and richest

[First published in *Italian Hours*.]

impressions possible; and if I went back whenever I could it was very much as one does n't indecently neglect a gentle invalid friend. The couch of the invalid friend, beautifully, appealingly resigned, has been wheeled, say, for the case, into the warm still garden, and your visit but consists of your sitting beside it with kind, discreet, testifying silences. Such is the figurative form under which the once rugged enemy of Florence, stretched at her length by the rarely troubled Arno, to-day presents herself; and I find my analogy complete even to my sense of the mere mild *séance,* the inevitably tacit communion or rather blank interchange, between motionless cripple and hardly more incurable admirer.

The terms of my enjoyment of Pisa scarce departed from that ideal—slow contemplative perambulations, rather late in the day and after work done mostly in the particular decent inn-room that was repeatedly my portion; where the sunny flicker of the river played up from below to the very ceiling, which, by the same sign, anciently and curiously raftered and hanging over my table at a great height, had been colour-pencilled into ornament as fine (for all practical purposes) as the page of a missal. I add to this, for remembrance, an inveteracy of evening idleness and of reiterated ices in front of one of the quiet cafés—quiet as everything at Pisa is quiet, or will certainly but in these latest days have ceased to be; one in especial so beautifully, so mysteriously void of bustle that almost always the neighbouring presence and admirable chatter of some group of the local University students would fall upon my ear, by the half-hour at a time, not less as a privilege, frankly, than as a clear-cut image of the young Italian mind and life, by which I lost nothing. I use such terms as "admirable" and "privilege," in this last most casual of connections—which was moreover no connection at all but what my attention made it—simply as an acknowledgment of the interest that might play there through some inevitable thoughts. These were, for that matter, intensely in keeping with the ancient scene and air: they dealt with the exquisite difference between that tone and type of ingenuous adolescence—in the mere relation of charmed *audition*—and other forms of juvenility of whose mental and material accent one had elsewhere met the assault. Civilised, charmingly civilised, were my loquacious neighbours—as how had n't they to be, one asked one's self, through the use of a medium of speech that is in itself a sovereign saturation? *There* was the beautiful congruity of the happily-caught impression; the fact of my young men's general Tuscanism of tongue, which related them so on the spot to the whole historic consensus of things. It was n't dialect—as it of course easily might have been elsewhere, at Milan, at Turin, at Bologna, at Naples; it was the clear Italian in which all the rest of the surrounding story was told, all the rest of the result of time recorded; and it made them delightful, prattling, unconscious men of the particular little constituted and bequeathed world which everything else that was charged with old meanings and old beauty referred to—all the more that their talk was never by any chance of romping games or deeds of violence, but kept flowering, charmingly and incredibly, into eager ideas and literary opinions and philosophic discussions and, upon my honour, vital questions.

They have taken me too far, for so light a reminiscence; but I claim for the loose web of my impressions at no point a heavier texture. Which comes back to what I was a moment ago saying—that just in proportion as you "feel" the morbid charm of Pisa you press on it gently, and this somehow even under stress of whatever respectful attention. I found this last impulse, at all events, so far as I was concerned, quite contentedly spend itself in a renewed sense of the simple large pacified felicity of such an afternoon aspect as that of the Lung' Arno, taken up or down its course; whether to within sight of small Santa Maria della Spina, the tiny, the delicate, the exquisite Gothic chapel perched where the quay drops straight, or, in the other direction, toward the melting perspective of the narrow local pleasure-ground, the rather thin and careless bosky grace of which recedes, beside the stream whose very turbidity pleases, to a middle distance of hot and tangled and exuberant rural industry and a proper blue horizon of Carrara mountains. The Pisan Lung' Arno is shorter and less featured and framed than the Florentine, but it has the fine accent of a marked curve and is quite as bravely Tuscan; witness the type of river-fronting palace which, in half-a-dozen massive specimens, the last word of the anciently "handsome," are of the essence of the physiognomy of the place. In the glow of which retrospective admission I ask myself how I came, under my first flush, reflected in other pages, to fail of justice to so much proud domestic architecture—in the very teeth moreover of the fact that I was for ever paying my compliments, in a wistful, wondering way, to the fine Palazzo Lanfranchi, occupied in 1822 by the migratory Byron, and whither Leigh Hunt, as commemorated in the latter's Autobiography, came out to join him in an odd journalistic scheme.

Of course, however, I need scarcely add, the centre of my daily revolution—quite thereby on the circumference—was the great Company of Four in their sequestered corner; objects of regularly recurrent pious pilgrimage,

Palazzo Lanfranchi ... Byron ... Leigh Hunt ... Autobiography ... odd journalistic scheme. Hunt's *Examiner* was beginning to fail in 1821, and Byron invited him to come to Italy to plan another liberal periodical publication in conjunction with him and Shelley; although both Hunt and his wife were quite ill, he left the *Examiner* in the hands of his brother John and went to Italy to start the venture. It was while Hunt was staying at the Casa Lanfranchi that Shelley drowned in the nearby Gulf of Spezia (Hunt, *The Autobiography of Leigh Hunt*, II, 59–60, 97–105).

if for no other purpose than to see whether each would each time again so inimitably carry itself as one of a group of wonderfully-worked old ivories. Their charm of relation to each other and to everything else that concerns them, that of the quartette of monuments, is more or less inexpressible all round; but not the least of it, ever, is in their beautiful secret for taking at different hours and seasons, in different states of the light, the sky, the wind, the weather—in different states, even, it used verily to seem to me, of an admirer's imagination or temper or nerves—different complexional appearances, different shades and pallors, different glows and chills. I have seen them look almost viciously black, and I have seen them as clear and fair as pale gold. And these things, for the most part, off on the large grassy carpet spread for them, and with the elbow of the old city-wall, not elsewhere erect, respectfully but protectingly crooked about, to the tune of a usual unanimity save perhaps in the case of the Leaning Tower—so abnormal a member of any respectable family this structure at best that I always somehow fancied its three companions, the Cathedral, the Baptistery and the Campo Santo, capable of quiet common understandings, for the major or the minor effect, into which their odd fellow, no hint thrown out to him, was left to enter as he might. If one haunted the place, one ended by yielding to the conceit that, beautifully though the others of the group may be said to behave about him, one sometimes caught them in the act of tacitly combining to ignore him— as if he had, after so long, begun to give on their nerves. Or is that absurdity but my shamefaced form of admission that, for all the wonder of him, he finally gave on mine? Frankly—I would put it at such moments—he becomes at last an optical bore or *bêtise*.

II

To Lucca I was not to return often—I was to return only once; when that compact and admirable little city, the very model of a small *pays de Cocagne*, overflowing with everything that makes for ease, for plenty, for beauty, for interest and good example, renewed for me, in the highest degree, its genial and robust appearance. The perfection of this renewal must indeed have been, at bottom, the ground of my rather hanging back from

---

bêtise. Nonsense.

pays de Cocagne. An imaginary utopia where idleness and luxury were supreme; in its satire on the monastic life, the thirteenth-century English poem *The Land of Cockaygne* referred to this medieval realm.

possible excess of acquaintance—with the instinct that so right and rich and
rounded a little impression had better be left than endangered. I remember
positively saying to myself the second time that no brown-and-gold Tuscan
city, even, could *be* as happy as Lucca looked—save always, exactly, Lucca;
so that, on the chance of any shade of human illusion in the case, I would
n't, as a brooding analyst, go within fifty miles of it again. Just so, I fear I
must confess, it was this mere face-value of the place that, when I went back,
formed my sufficiency; I spent all my scant time—or the greater part, for I
took a day to drive over to the Bagni—just gaping at its visible attitude. This
may be described as that of simply sitting there, through the centuries, at the
receipt of perfect felicity; on its splendid solid seat of russet masonry, that
is—for its great republican ramparts of long ago still lock it tight—with its
wide garden-land, its ancient appanage or hereditary domain, teeming and
blooming with everything that is good and pleasant for man, all about, and
with a ring of graceful and noble, yet comparatively unbeneficed uplands
and mountains watching it, for very envy, across the plain, as a circle of
bigger boys, in the playground, may watch a privileged or pampered smaller
one munch a particularly fine apple. Half smothered thus in oil and wine
and corn and all the fruits of the earth, Lucca seems fairly to laugh for good-
humour, and it's as if one can't say more for her than that, thanks to her
putting forward for you a temperament somehow still richer than her heritage, you forgive her at every turn her fortune. She smiles up at you her
greeting as you dip into her wide lap, out of which you may select almost
any rare morsel whatever. Looking back at my own choice indeed I see it
must have suffered a certain embarrassment—that of the sense of too many
things; for I scarce remember choosing at all, any more than I recall having
had to go hungry. I turned into all the churches—taking care, however, to
pause before one of them, though before which I now irrecoverably forget,
for verification of Ruskin's so characteristically magnified rapture over the

---

Ruskin's so characteristically magnified rapture.

In St. Michele of Lucca we have perhaps the noblest instance in Italy of the Lombard
spirit in its later refinement. . . . The entire arrangement is perfect beyond all praise, and
the morbid restlessness of the old designs is now appeased. Geometry seems to have
acted as a febrifuge, for beautiful geometrical designs are introduced amidst the tumult
of the hunt. . . . The fragments have come together: we are out of the Inferno with its
weeping down the spine. . . . My good friend Mr. Cockerell wonders, in one of his
lectures, why I give so much praise to this 'crazy front of Lucca.' But it is not crazy; not
by any means. Altogether sober, in comparison with the early Lombard work, or with
our Norman. Crazy in one sense it is: utterly neglected, to the breaking of its old stout
heart; the venomous nights and salt frosts of the Maremma winters have their way with
it—'Poor Tom's a cold!' The weeds that feed on the marsh air have twisted themselves
into its crannies; the polished fragments of serpentine are split and rent out of their cells,

high and rather narrow and obscure hunting-frieze on its front—and in the
Cathedral paid my respects at every turn to the greatest of Lucchesi, Matteo
Civitale, wisest, sanest, homeliest, kindest of *quattro-cento* sculptors, to
whose works the Duomo serves almost as a museum. But my nearest approach to anything so invidious as a discrimination or a preference, under
the spell of so felt an equilibrium, must have been the act of engaging a
carriage for the Baths.

That inconsequence once perpetrated, let me add, the impression was as
right as any other—the impression of the drive through the huge general
tangled and fruited *podere* of the countryside; that of the pair of jogging
hours that bring the visitor to where the wideish gate of the valley of the
Serchio opens. The question after this became quite other; the narrowing,
though always more or less smiling gorge that draws you on and on is a
different, a distinct proposition altogether, with its own individual grace of
appeal and association. It is the association, exactly, that would even now,
on this page, beckon me forward, or perhaps I should rather say backward—
were n't more than a glance at it out of the question—to a view of that easier
and not so inordinately remote past when "people spent the summer" in
these perhaps slightly stuffy shades. I speak of that age, I think of it at least,
as easier than ours, in spite of the fact that even as I made my pilgrimage the
mark of modern change, the railway in construction, had begun to be distinct, though the automobile was still pretty far in the future. The relations
and proportions of everything are of course now altered—I indeed, I confess,
wince at the vision of the cloud of motor-dust that must in the fine season
hang over the whole connection. That represents greater promptness of
approach to the bosky depths of Ponte-a-Serraglio and the Bagni Caldi, but it
throws back the other time, that of the old jogging relation, of the Tuscan
grand-ducal "season" and the small cosmopolite sociability, into quite Arca-

---

and lie in green ruins along its ledges; the salt sea winds have eaten away the fair shafting
of its star window into a skeleton of crumbling rays. It cannot stand much longer; may
heaven only, in its benignity, preserve it from restoration. (*The Stones of Venice,* vol. I,
"Appendix" [*Works,* IX, 429–30])

Yet the church was restored, badly, in 1862, and some later refabrication substituted the faces
of *risorgimento* heroes for the original Gothic figures on the facade; many nineteenth-century
tourists, James among them, saw a church far different from that which inspired Ruskin's
rapture.

Matteo Civitale . . . *quattro-cento.* In the cathedral the work of this quattrocento, or
fifteenth-century, artist includes the pulpit and the "Tempietto," a shrine for a cedar-wood
image of Christ supposed to have been carved by Nicodemus and finished by an angel. In the
right transept is his tomb of Pietro da Noceto, secretary of Pope Nicolas V; in the Cappella del
Sacramento are two of his angels and numerous altar figures.

dian air and the comparatively primitive scale. The "easier" Italy of our infatuated precursors there wears its glamour of facility not through any question of "the development of communications," but through the very absence of the dream of that boon, thanks to which every one (among the infatuated) lived on terms of so much closer intercourse with the general object of their passion. After we had crossed the Serchio that beautiful day we passed into the charming, the amiably tortuous, the thickly umbrageous, valley of the Lima, and then it was that I seemed fairly to remount the stream of time; figuring to myself wistfully, at the small scattered centres of entertainment—modest inns, pensions and other places of convenience clustered where the friendly torrent is bridged or the forested slopes adjust themselves—what the summer days and the summer rambles and the summer dreams must have been, in the blest place, when "people" (by which I mean the contingent of beguiled barbarians) did n't know better, as we say, than to content themselves with such a mild substitute, such a soft, sweet and essentially elegant apology, for adventure. One wanted not simply to hang about a little, but really to live back, as surely one might have done by staying on, into the so romantically strong, if mechanically weak, Italy of the associations of one's youth. It was a pang to have to revert to the present even in the form of Lucca—which says everything.

III

If undeveloped communications were to become enough for me at those retrospective moments, I might have felt myself supplied to my taste, let me go on to say, at the hour of my making, with great resolution, an attempt on high-seated and quite grandly out-of-the-way Volterra: a reminiscence associated with quite a different year and, I should perhaps sooner have bethought myself, with my fond experience of Pisa—inasmuch as it was during a pause under that bland and motionless wing that I seem to have had to organise in the darkness of a summer dawn my approach to the old Etruscan stronghold. The railway then existed, but I rose in the dim small hours to take my train; moreover, so far as that might too much savour of an incongruous facility, the fault was in due course quite adequately repaired by an apparent repudiation of any awareness of such false notes on the part of the town. I may not invite the reader to penetrate with me by so much as a step

---

Volterra: a reminiscence associated with quite a different year. The editor is unable to identify the reference.

the boundless backward reach of history to which the more massive of the Etruscan gates of Volterra, the Porta all'Arco, forms the solidest of thresholds; since I perforce take no step myself, and am even exceptionally condemned here to impressionism unashamed. My errand was to spend a Sunday with an Italian friend, a native in fact of the place, master of a house there in which he offered me hospitality; who, also arriving from Florence the night before, had obligingly come on with me from Pisa, and whose consciousness of a due urbanity, already rather overstrained, and still well before noon, by the accumulation of our matutinal vicissitudes and other grounds for patience, met all ruefully at the station the supreme shock of an apparently great desolate world of volcanic hills, of blank, though "engineered," undulations, as the emergence of a road testified, unmitigated by the smallest sign of a wheeled vehicle. The station, in other words, looked out at that time (and I daresay the case has n't strikingly altered) on a mere bare huge hill-country, by some remote mighty shoulder of which the goal of our pilgrimage, so questionably "served" by the railway, was hidden from view. Served as well by a belated omnibus, a four-in-hand of lame and lamentable quality, the place, I hasten to add, eventually put forth some show of being; after a complete practical recognition of which, let me at once further mention, all the other, the positive and sublime, connections of Volterra established themselves for me without my lifting a finger.

The small shrunken, but still lordly prehistoric city is perched, when once you have rather painfully zigzagged to within sight of it, very much as an eagle's eyrie, oversweeping the land and the sea; and to that type of position, the ideal of the airy peak of vantage, with all accessories and minor features a drop, a slide and a giddiness, its individual items and elements strike you at first as instinctively conforming. This impression was doubtless after a little modified for me; there were levels, there were small stony practicable streets, there were walks and strolls, outside the gates and roundabout the cyclopean wall, to the far end of downward-tending protrusions and promontories, natural buttresses and pleasant terrene headlands, friendly suburban spots (one would call them if the word had less detestable references) where games of bowls and overtrellised wine-tables could put in their note; in spite of which however my friend's little house of hospitality, clean and charming and oh, so immemorially Tuscan, was as perpendicular and ladder-like as so compact a residence could be; it kept up for me beautifully—as regards

---

small shrunken, but still lordly prehistoric city. Modern Volterra is about one-third the size of ancient Velathri, one of the most prominent of the twelve Etruscan confederacies. Although Volterra long had been noted for its antiquity, in 1898 its reputation as an ancient town was enhanced when a sixth-century B.C. tomb was excavated just outside the city walls.

posture and air, though humanly and socially it rather cooed like a dovecote—the illusion of the vertiginously "balanced" eagle's nest. The air, in truth, all the rest of that splendid day, must have been the key to the promptly-produced intensity of one's relation to every aspect of the charming episode; the light, cool, keen air of those delightful high places, in Italy, that tonically correct the ardours of July, and which at our actual altitude could but affect me as the very breath of the grand local legend. I might have "had" the little house, our particular eagle's nest, for the summer, and even on such touching terms; and I well remember the force of the temptation to take it, if only other complications had permitted; to spend the series of weeks with that admirable *interesting* freshness in my lungs: interesting, I especially note, as the strong appropriate medium in which a continuity with the irrecoverable but still effective past had been so robustly preserved. I could n't yield, alas, to the conceived felicity, which had half-a-dozen appealing aspects; I could only, while thus feeling how the atmospheric medium itself made for a positively initiative exhilaration, enjoy my illusion till the morrow. The exhilaration therefore supplies to memory the whole light in which, for the too brief time, I went about "seeing" Volterra; so that my glance at the seated splendour reduces itself, as I have said, to the merest impressionism; nothing more was to be looked for, on the stretched surface of consciousness, from one breezy wash of the brush. I find there the clean strong image simplified to the three or four unforgettable particulars of the vast rake of the view; with the Maremma, of evil fame, more or less immediately below, but with those islands of the sea, Corsica and Elba, the names of which are sharply associational beyond any others, dressing the far horizon in the grand manner, and the Ligurian coast-line melting northward into beauty and history galore; with colossal uncemented blocks of Etruscan

---

Maremma, of evil fame. A coastal region in Tuscany that, although drained and fertile in Etruscan and Roman times, became marshy again in the Middle Ages, a breeding ground for malaria, and a focus of much speculation. A curious report once came to a Sienese governor that the African sirocco wind wafted the poisonous breath of serpents to the Maremma, and, since in that irreverent region it met with so little pure Christian air to purge it, the serpents' breath brought death to the people (Lyall, 103). In Dante's *Purgatorio,* v, 133–34, Pia's lament contributes to the fame of Maremma (cf. Eliot's footnotes to *The Waste Land*)—"ricorditi di me, che son la Pia; / Siena mi fé, disfecemi Maremma"—remember me, I who am Pia; / Siena made me, Maremma unmade me. The intention of her complaint has long been considered ambiguous. Longfellow, in a note to his translation of *The Divine Comedy,* suggested that when Pia's husband discovered her sin, he shut her up in an isolated castle in the Maremma and watched as the pestilential air eventually killed her. In his recent translation of Dante, Allen Mandelbaum identified a wife hurled down from a balcony in the Maremma by her husband.

Corsica and Elba . . . sharply associational. Napoleon, born at Ajaccio, Corsica, in 1769, was exiled to Elba during 1814 and 1815.

gates and walls plunging you—and by their very interest—into a sweet surrender of any privilege of appreciation more crushing than your general synthetic stare; and with the rich and perfectly arranged museum, an unsurpassed exhibition of monumental treasure from Etruscan tombs, funereal urns mainly, reliquaries of an infinite power to move and charm us still, contributing to this same so resigned, but somehow at the same time so inspired, collapse of the historic imagination under too heavy a pressure, or abeyance of "private judgment" in too unequal a relation.

IV

I REMEMBER recovering private judgment indeed in the course of two or three days following the excursion I have just noted; which must have shaped themselves in some sort of consonance with the idea that as we were hereabouts in the very middle of dim Etruria a common self-respect prescribed our somehow profiting by the fact. This kindled in us the spirit of exploration, but with results of which I here attempt no record, so utterly does the whole impression swoon away, for present memory, into vagueness, confusion and intolerable heat. Our self-respect was of the common order, but the blaze of the July sun was, even for Tuscany, of the uncommon; so that the project of a trudging quest for Etruscan tombs in shadeless wastes yielded to its own temerity. There comes back to me nevertheless at the same time, from the mild misadventure, and quite as through this positive humility of failure, the sense of a supremely intimate revelation of Italy in undress, so to speak (the state, it seemed, in which one would most fondly, most ideally, enjoy her); Italy no longer in winter starch and sobriety, with winter manners and winter prices and winter excuses, all addressed to the *forestieri* and the philistines; but lolling at her length, with her graces all relaxed, and thereby only the more natural; the brilliant performer, in short, *en famille*, the curtain down and her salary stopped for the season—thanks to which she is by so much more the easy genius and the good creature as she is by so much less the advertised *prima donna*. She received us nowhere more sympathetically, that is with less ceremony or self-consciousness, I seem to recall, than at Montepulciano, for instance—where it was indeed that the recovery of private judgment I just referred to could n't help taking place. What we were doing, or what we expected to do, at Montepulciano I keep no other trace of than is bound up in a present quite tender consciousness that I would n't for the world not have been there. I think my reason must have been largely just in the beauty of the name (for could any beauty be greater?), reinforced no doubt by the fame of the local vintage and the sense of how we should quaff it on the spot. Perhaps we quaffed it too constantly; since the romantic picture reduces itself for me but to two definite appearances; that of the more priggish discrimination so far reasserting itself as to advise me that Montepulciano was dirty, even remarkably dirty; and that of her being not much else besides but perched and brown and queer and crooked, and noble withal (which is what almost any Tuscan city more easily than not acquits herself of; all the while she may on such occasions figure, when one looks off from her to the end of dark street-vistas or catches glimpses through high arcades, some big battered, blistered, over-laden, overmasted ship, swimming in a violet sea).

If I have lost the sense of what we were doing, that could at all suffer commemoration, at Montepulciano, so I sit helpless before the memory of small stewing Torrita, which we must somehow have expected to yield, under our confidence, a view of shy charms, but which did n't yield, to my recollection, even anything that could fairly be called a breakfast or a dinner. There may have been in the neighbourhood a rumour of Etruscan tombs; the neighbourhood, however, was vast, and that possibility not to be verified, in the conditions, save after due refreshment. Then it was, doubtless, that the question of refreshment so beckoned us, by a direct appeal, straight across country, from Perugia, that, casting consistency, if not to the winds, since alas there were none, but to the lifeless air, we made the sweltering best of our way (and it took, for the distance, a terrible time) to the Grand Hotel of that city. This course shines for me, in the retrospect, with a light even more shameless than that in which my rueful conscience then saw it; since we thus exchanged again, at a stroke, the tousled *bonne fille* of our vacational Tuscany for the formal and figged-out presence of Italy on her good behaviour. We had never seen her conform more to all the proprieties, we felt, than under this aspect of lavish hospitality to that now apparently quite inveterate swarm of pampered *forestieri,* English and Americans in especial, who, having had Roman palaces and villas deliciously to linger in, break the north-ward journey, when once they decide to take it, in the Umbrian paradise. They were, goodness knows, within their rights, and we profited, as any one may easily and cannily profit at that time, by the sophistications paraded for them; only I feel, as I pleasantly recover it all, that though we had arrived perhaps at the most poetical of watering-places we had lost our finer clue. (The difference from other days was immense, all the span of evolution from the ancient malodorous inn which somehow did n't matter, to that new type of polyglot caravanserai which everywhere insists on mattering—mattering, even in places where other interests abound, so much more than anything else.) That clue, the finer as I say, I would fain at any rate to-day pick up for its close attachment to another Tuscan city or two—for a felt pull from strange little San Gimignano delle belle Torre in especial; by which I mean from the memory of a summer Sunday spent there during a stay at Siena. But I have already superabounded, for mere love of my general present rubric— the real thickness of experience having a good deal evaporated, so that the Tiny Town of the Many Towers hangs before me, not to say, rather, far behind me, after the manner of an object directly meeting the wrong or diminishing lens of one's telescope.

It did everything, on the occasion of that pilgrimage, that it was expected to do, presenting itself more or less in the guise of some rare silvery shell, washed up by the sea of time, cracked and battered and dishonoured, with its mutilated marks of adjustment to the extinct type of creature it once harboured figuring against the sky as maimed gesticulating arms flourished in protest against fate. If the centuries, however, had pretty well cleaned out, vulgarly speaking, this amazing little fortress-town, it was n't that a mere aching void was bequeathed us, I recognise as I consult a somewhat faded impression; the whole scene and occasion come back to me as the exhibi- tion, on the contrary, of a stage rather crowded and agitated, of no small quantity of sound and fury, of concussions, discussions, vociferations, hurry- ings to and fro, that could scarce have reached a higher pitch in the old days of the siege and the sortie. San Gimignano affected me, to a certainty, as not dead, I mean, but as inspired with that strange and slightly sinister new life that is now, in case after case, up and down the peninsula, and even in presence of the dryest and most scattered bones, producing the miracle of resurrection. The effect is often—and I find it strikingly involved in this particular reminiscence—that of the buried hero himself positively waking up to show you his bones for a fee, and almost capering about in his appeal to your attention. What has become of the soul of San Gimignano who shall say?—but, of a genial modern Sunday, it is as if the heroic skeleton, risen from the dust, were in high activity, officious for your entertainment and your detention, clattering and changing plates at the informal friendly inn, personally conducting you to a sight of the admirable Santa Fina of Ghirlandaio, as I believe is supposed, in a dim chapel of the Collegiata church; the poor young saint, on her low bed, in a state of ecstatic vision

---

strange little San Gimignano delle belle Torre. Unique for the number and impressiveness of its extant medieval towers. Thirteen of approximately seventy survive.

Santa Fina of Ghirlandaio. A young woman from the San Gimignano countryside who was graced by ecstatic vision but plagued by sickness; she died after five years of lying on a board. The attribution to Ghirlandaio has been amended to "with P. F. Fiorentino and Bastiano Mainardo."

(the angelic apparition is given), accompanied by a few figures and accessories of the most beautiful and touching truth. This image is what has most vividly remained with me, of the day I thus so ineffectually recover; the precious ill-set gem or domestic treasure of Santa Fina, and then the wonderful drive, at eventide, back to Siena: the progress through the darkening land that was like a dense fragrant garden, all fireflies and warm emanations and dimly-seen motionless festoons, extravagant vines and elegant branches intertwisted for miles, with couples and companies of young countryfolk almost as fondly united and raising their voices to the night as if superfluously to sing out at you that they were happy, and above all were Tuscan. On reflection, and to be just, I connect the slightly incongruous loudness that hung about me under the Beautiful Towers with the really too coarse competition for my favour among the young vetturini who lay in wait for my approach, and with an eye to my subsequent departure, on my quitting, at some unremembered spot, the morning train from Siena, from which point there was then still a drive. That onset was of a fine mediæval violence, but the subsiding echoes of it alone must have afterwards borne me company; mingled, at the worst, with certain reverberations of the animated rather than concentrated presence of sundry young sketchers and copyists of my own nationality, which element in the picture conveyed beyond anything else how thoroughly it was all to sit again henceforth in the eye of day. My final vision perhaps was of a sacred reliquary not so much rudely as familiarly and "humorously" torn open. The note had, with all its references, its own interest; but I never went again.

[1909.]

Ravenna

I write these lines on a cold Swiss mountain-top, shut in by an intense white mist from any glimpse of the under-world of lovely Italy; but as I jotted down the other day in the ancient capital of Honorius and Theodoric the few notes of which they are composed, I let the original date stand for local colour's sake. Its mere look, as I transcribe it, emits a grateful glow in the midst of the Alpine rawness, and gives a depressed imagination something tangible to grasp while awaiting the return of fine weather. For Ravenna was glowing, less than a week since, as I edged along the narrow strip of shadow binding one side of the empty, white streets. After a long, chill spring the summer this year descended upon Italy with a sudden jump and an ominous hot breath. I stole away from Florence in the night, and even on top of the Apennines, under the dull starlight and in the rushing train, one could but sit and pant perspiringly.

At Bologna I found a festa, or rather two festas, a civil and a religious, going on in mutual mistrust and disparagement. The civil, that of the

[Dated here by James 1873; originally published in the *Nation*, xix (9 July 1874), 23–25; reprinted in *Transatlantic Sketches*, 1875.]

Honorius and Theodoric. The so-called "Emperor of the West" (see also page 144 and note), Honorius moved the imperial court to Ravenna after learning that Alaric, who was to capture Rome in 410 after three years of siege, had reentered Italy. His sister was Galla Placidia (see pages 295–96 and 300). It was said that Gothic king Theodoric ruled the Goths and the Romans as one people, and under him there was relative peace and security; he began many Arian churches, among them Sant'Apollinare Nuovo and San Vitale.

Statuto, was the one fully national Italian holiday as by law established—the day that signalises everywhere over the land at once its achieved and hard-won unification; the religious was a jubilee of certain local churches. The latter is observed by the Bolognese parishes in couples, and comes round for each couple but once in ten years—an arrangement by which the faithful at large insure themselves a liberal recurrence of expensive processions. It was n't my business to distinguish the sheep from the goats, the pious from the profane, the prayers from the scoffers; it was enough that, melting together under the scorching sun, they filled the admirably solid city with a flood of spectacular life. The combination at one point was really dramatic. While a long procession of priests and young virgins in white veils, bearing tapers, marshalled itself in one of the streets, a review of the King's troops went forward outside the town. On its return a large detachment of cavalry passed across the space where the incense was burning, the pictured banners swaying and the litany being droned, and checked the advance of the little ecclesiastical troop. The long vista of the street, between the porticoes, was festooned with garlands and scarlet and tinsel; the robes and crosses and canopies of the priests, the clouds of perfumed smoke and the white veils of the maidens, were resolved by the hot bright air into a gorgeous medley of colour, across which the mounted soldiers rattled and flashed as if it had been a conquering army trampling on an embassy of propitiation. It was, to tell the truth, the first time an Italian festa had really exhibited to my eyes the genial glow and the romantic particulars promised by song and story; and I confess that those eyes found more pleasure in it than they were to find an hour later in the picturesque on canvas as one observes it in the Pinacoteca. I found myself scowling most unmercifully at Guido and Domenichino.

Statuto. In 1861 the first Sunday in June was declared a national holiday, the "festa dello Statuto," to celebrate the 1848 "Statuto del Regno," the codification of which marked the formation of the kingdom of Italy.

scowling most unmercifully at Guido and Domenichino. Although at moments even Goethe had his doubts ("It is always the same, even with a genius like Guido. You find yourself in the dissecting room, at the foot of a gallows, on the edge of a corpse pit," *Italian Journey*, 96), generally during the seventeenth and eighteenth centuries the reputation of Guido Reni (1575–1642) was extremely high. It was crushed in large part by Ruskin's opinion that his work was "devoid alike of art and decency, as that Susannah of Guido, in our own gallery" (*Modern Painters, Works,* IV, 197). Although there has been a revival of the positive estimate of Guido (see Pepper, *Guido Reni,* 48–50), James's distaste and a 1911 article by William Michael Rossetti give a representative sense of the painter's general post-Ruskin reputation: "His best works have beauty, great amenity, artistic feeling and high accomplishment of manner, all alloyed by a certain core of commonplace; in the worst pictures the commonplace swamps everything, and Guido has flooded European galleries with trashy and empty pretentiousness, all the more noxious in that its apparent grace of sentiment and form misleads the unwary into

For Ravenna, however, I had nothing but smiles—grave, reflective, philo-sophic smiles, I hasten to add, such as accord with the historic dignity, not to say the mortal sunny sadness, of the place. I arrived there in the evening, before, even at drowsy Ravenna, the festa of the Statuto had altogether put itself to bed. I immediately strolled forth from the inn, and found it sitting up a while longer on the piazza, chiefly at the café door, listening to the band of the garrison by the light of a dozen or so of feeble tapers, fastened along the front of the palace of the Government. Before long, however, it had dispersed and departed, and I was left alone with the grey illumination and with an affable citizen whose testimony as to the manners and customs of Ravenna I had aspired to obtain. I had, borrowing confidence from prompt observation, suggested deferentially that it was n't the liveliest place in the world, and my friend admitted that it was in fact not a seat of ardent life. But had I seen the Corso? Without seeing the Corso one did n't exhaust the possibilities. The Corso of Ravenna, of a hot summer night, had an air of surprising seclusion and repose. Here and there in an upper closed window glimmered a light; my companion's footsteps and my own were the only sounds; not a creature was within sight. The suffocating air helped me to believe for a moment that I walked in the Italy of Boccaccio, hand-in-hand with the plague, through a city which had lost half its population by pesti-lence and the other half by flight. I turned back into my inn profoundly satisfied. This at last was the old-world dulness of a prime distillation; this at last was antiquity, history, repose.

The impression was largely confirmed and enriched on the following day; but it was obliged at an early stage of my visit to give precedence to another—the lively perception, namely, of the thinness of my saturation with Gibbon and the other sources of legend. At Ravenna the waiter at the

---

approval, and the dilettante dabbler into cheap raptures" (Rossetti, "Guido Reni," *Encyclope-dia Britannica*, eleventh edition, XII, 689). For James's related comments on Domenichino—referred to by Ruskin as "the Scum of Titian" (v, 400)—see pages 164–65 and notes. Many works by both artists are held by the Pinacoteca Nazionale in Bologna.

Italy of Boccaccio . . . a city which had lost half its population by pestilence. Giovanni Boccaccio's *Decameron* begins in Florence during the plague of 1348; a group of ten young people depart from the city, settle at a villa in the country, and provide entertainment by telling one-hundred tales, one of the more famous being set in Ravenna (see note on the "Pineta," page 296 below). The city's decline began in the eighth century, when growing silt deposits began to make the sea withdraw, finally to a distance of several miles. A pestilent lagoon was formed between the city and the Adriatic, frequent outbreaks of malaria began, and Ravenna's eco-nomic position changed dramatically.

Gibbon . . . Galla Placidia and Justinian as to any attractive topic. Daughter of Emperor Theodosius I, Galla Placidia (c. 390–450), noted by James for her "great adventures," was

café and the coachman who drives you to the Pine-Forest allude to Galla Placidia and Justinian as to any attractive topic of the hour; wherever you turn you encounter some fond appeal to your historic presence of mind. For myself I could only attune my spirit vaguely to so ponderous a challenge, could only feel I was breathing an air of prodigious records and relics. I conned my guide-book and looked up at the great mosaics, and then fumbled at poor Murray again for some intenser light on the court of Justinian; but I can imagine that to a visitor more intimate with the originals of the various great almond-eyed mosaic portraits in the vaults of the churches these extremely curious works of art may have a really formidable interest. I found in the place at large, by daylight, the look of a vast straggling depopulated village. The streets with hardly an exception are grass-grown, and though I walked about all day I failed to encounter a single wheeled vehicle. I remember no shop but the little establishment of an urbane photographer, whose views of the Pineta, the great legendary pine-forest just without the town, gave me an irresistible desire to seek that refuge. There was no architecture to speak of; and though there are a great many large domiciles with aristocratic names they stand cracking and baking in the sun in no very comfortable fashion. The houses have for the most part an all but rustic rudeness; they are low and featureless and shabby, as well as interspersed with high garden walls over which the long arms of tangled vines hang

---

captured during Alaric's Sack of Rome in 410. She married Ataulphus, King of the Goths, "without reluctance," according to Gibbon, in an attempt to help her brother Honorius bring peace to his empire. When Ataulphus was killed, Placidia soon married Constantius, a distinguished general who later was to reign as emperor only for seven months. Their son Valentinian III was named emperor at the age of six, but Placidia ruled in his name for twenty-five years and added much to the splendor of Ravenna (Gibbon, chapter 31).

Justinian I (483–565), or Justinian the Great, aimed at restoring the Roman Empire to its former stature by reconquering that territory lost to the German invaders. Successful in many military ventures, he is best remembered for the codification of Roman law in the Corpus Juris Civilis, or the Code of Justinian, developed from 529 to 565. Among splendid contributions to the glory of the empire, he rebuilt Hagia Sofia in Constantinople after the original structure was destroyed by fire (Gibbon, chapters 40–44).

Pineta, the great legendary pine-forest. The earthly paradise in Dante, *Purgatorio*, canto XXVIII, 19–20, is compared to the Pineta di Classe, or Pinetum—"tal qual di ramo in ramo si raccoglie / per la pineta in su 'l lito di Chiassi" (just like the wind that sounds from branch to branch / along the shore of Classe, through the pines; trans. Mandelbaum). In Boccaccio's *Decameron* the Pineta is the setting of much of Fiammetta's tale "Nastagio degli Onesti"; it provides a setting in Tasso, *Gerusalemme Liberata*, XVII, in Dryden, "Theodore and Honoria, From Boccace," and in Byron, *Don Juan*, canto III, cv–cvi, "Ravenna's immemorial wood . . . which Boccaccio's lore / And Dryden's lay made haunted ground to me." For many years the Pineta faded out of history and legend; then while fleeing the Austrian troops with her husband, Anita Garibaldi died there in 1849.

motionless into the stagnant streets. Here and there in all this dreariness, in some particularly silent and grassy corner, rises an old brick church with a front more or less spoiled by cheap modernisation, and a strange cylindrical campanile pierced with small arched windows and extremely suggestive of the fifth century. These churches constitute the palpable interest of Ravenna, and their own principal interest, after thirteen centuries of well-intentioned spoliation, resides in their unequalled collection of early Christian mosaics. It is an interest simple, as who should say, almost to harshness, and leads one's attention along a straight and narrow way. There are older churches in Rome, and churches which, looked at as museums, are more variously and richly informing; but in Rome you stumble at every step on some curious pagan memorial, often beautiful enough to make your thoughts wander far from the strange stiff primitive Christian forms.

Ravenna, on the other hand, began with the Church, and all her monuments and relics are harmoniously rigid. By the middle of the first century she possessed an exemplary saint, Apollinaris, a disciple of Peter, to whom her two finest places of worship are dedicated. It was to one of these, jocosely entitled the "new," that I first directed my steps. I lingered outside a while and looked at the great red, barrel-shaped bell-towers, so rusty, so crumbling, so archaic, and yet so resolute to ring in another century or two, and then went in to the coolness, the shining marble columns, the queer old sculptured slabs and sarcophagi and the long mosaics that scintillated, under the roof, along the wall of the nave. San Apollinare Nuovo, like most of its companions, is a magazine of early Christian odds and ends; fragments of yellow marble incrusted with quaint sculptured emblems of primitive dogma; great rough troughs, containing the bones of old bishops; episcopal chairs with the marble worn narrow by centuries of pressure from the solid episcopal person; slabs from the fronts of old pulpits, covered with carven hieroglyphics of an almost Egyptian abstruseness—lambs and stags and fishes and beasts of theological affinities even less apparent. Upon all these

---

exemplary saint, Apollinaris. Martyred during the reign of Vespasian, Apollinaris was a disciple of Saint Peter, who made him first bishop of Ravenna. In the mosaics at Classe, James viewed a winningly serene figure in an ecstatic landscape, not the tough combatant—he is sometimes represented as being beaten by a club, as standing on red-hot coals, or as holding a sword—who upon occasion shed blood for the early church.

jocosely entitled the "new." Sant'Apollinare "Nuovo" was built by Theodoric before 526, actually prior to Sant'Apollinare in Classe, which was consecrated in 649. The denomination "nuovo" refers not to its relative youth, but to the fact that until the ninth century the church was named for Saint Martin of Tours; it was renamed when a crypt for the body of Saint Apollinaris was donated to the church. The "joke" refers to the fact that both these churches are among the most ancient in Christendom.

strange things the strange figures in the great mosaic panorama look down, with coloured cheeks and staring eyes, lifelike enough to speak to you and answer your wonderment and tell you in bad Latin of the decadence that it was in such and such a fashion they believed and worshipped. First, on each side, near the door, are houses and ships and various old landmarks of Ravenna; then begins a long procession, on one side, of twenty-two white-robed virgins and three obsequious magi, terminating in a throne bearing the Madonna and Child, surrounded by four angels; on the other side, of an equal number of male saints (twenty-five, that is) holding crowns in their hands and leading to a Saviour enthroned between angels of singular expressiveness. What it is these long slim seraphs express I cannot quite say, but they have an odd, knowing, sidelong look out of the narrow ovals of their eyes which, though not without sweetness, would certainly make me murmur a defensive prayer or so were I to find myself alone in the church towards dusk. All this work is of the latter part of the sixth century and brilliantly preserved. The gold backgrounds twinkle as if they had been inserted yesterday, and here and there a figure is executed almost too much in the modern manner to be interesting; for the charm of mosaic work is, to my sense, confined altogether to the infancy of the art. The great Christ, in the series of which I speak, is quite an elaborate picture, and yet he retains enough of the orthodox stiffness to make him impressive in the simpler, elder sense. He is clad in a purple robe, even as an emperor, his hair and beard are artfully curled, his eyebrows arched, his complexion brilliant, his whole aspect such a one as the popular mind may have attributed to Honorius or Valentinian. It is all very Byzantine, and yet I found in it much of that interest which is inseparable, to a facile imagination, from all early representations of our Lord. Practically they are no more authentic than the more or less plausible inventions of Ary Scheffer and Holman Hunt; in spite of which they borrow a certain value, factitious perhaps but irresistible, from the mere fact that they are twelve or thirteen centuries less distant from the original. It is something that this was the way the people in the sixth century imagined Jesus to have looked; the image has suffered by so many

---

Valentinian. Valentinian III, son of Galla Placidia.

Ary Scheffer and Holman Hunt. Ary Scheffer (1795–1858), French painter of Dutch extraction. After a series dedicated to Goethe's "Margaret," he turned to religious subjects, *Christus Consolator* and *Christus Remunerator*, among many others. After his death his reputation fell and his work was generally seen as vapid.
English painter William Holman Hunt (1827–1910) helped inaugurate the Pre-Raphaelite Brotherhood; his allegorical *The Light of the World*, where Christ knocks at the door of the human soul, and *The Finding of Christ in the Temple* exerted great influence. In "The Picture Season in London: 1877" (*Painter's Eye*, 143), James finds him "prosaic."

the fewer accretions. The great purple-robed monarch on the wall of Ravenna is at least a very potent and positive Christ, and the only objection I have to make to him is that though in this character he must have had a full apportionment of divine foreknowledge he betrays no apprehension of Dr. Channing and M. Renan. If one's preference lies, for distinctness' sake, between the old plainness and the modern fantasy, one must admit that the plainness has here a very grand outline.

I spent the rest of the morning in charmed transition between the hot yellow streets and the cool grey interiors of the churches. The greyness everywhere was lighted up by the scintillation, on vault and entablature, of mosaics more or less archaic, but always brilliant and elaborate, and everywhere too by the same deep amaze of the fact that, while centuries had worn themselves away and empires risen and fallen, these little cubes of coloured glass had stuck in their allotted places and kept their freshness. I have no space for a list of the various shrines so distinguished, and, to tell the truth, my memory of them has already become a very generalised and undiscriminated record. The total aspect of the place, its sepulchral stillness, its absorbing perfume of evanescence and decay and mortality, confounds the distinctions and blurs the details. The Cathedral, which is vast and high, has been excessively modernised, and was being still more so by a lavish application of tinsel and cotton-velvet in preparation for the centenary feast of St. Apollinaris, which befalls next month. Things on this occasion are to be done handsomely, and a fair Ravennese informed me that a single family had contributed three thousand francs towards a month's vesper-music. It seemed to me hereupon that I should like in the August twilight to wander into the quiet nave of San Apollinare, and look up at the great mosaics through the resonance of some fine chanting. I remember distinctly enough, however, the tall basilica of San Vitale, of octagonal shape, like an exchange or custom-house—modelled, I believe, upon St. Sophia at Constantinople. It has a great span of height and a great solemnity, as well as a choir densely pictured over on arch and apse with mosaics of the time of Justinian. These are regular pictures, full of movement, gesture and perspective, and just enough sobered in hue by time to bring home their remoteness. In the middle of the church, under the great dome, sat an artist whom I envied, making at

---

Dr. Channing and M. Renan. William Ellery Channing (1780–1842), American Congregationalist clergyman, later a Unitarian minister; through scriptural reference, which he did not hold infallible, he viewed Jesus as inferior to God the father. He became known as the "apostle of Unitarianism" and the prophet of God in mankind. For Renan, see 86, 277, and notes.

modelled, I believe, upon St. Sophia. Modeled on the church of Saints Sergius and Bacchus at Constantinople, not on Hagia Sophia.

an effective angle a study of the choir and its broken lights, its decorated altar and its incrusted twinkling walls. The picture, when finished, will hang, I suppose, on the library wall of some person of taste; but even if it is much better than is probable—I did n't look at it—all his taste won't tell the owner, unless he has been there, in just what a soundless, mouldering, out-of-the-way corner of old Italy it was painted. An even better place for an artist fond of dusky architectural nooks, except that here the dusk is excessive and he would hardly be able to tell his green from his red, is the extraordinary little church of the Santi Nazaro e Celso, otherwise known as the mausoleum of Galla Placidia. This is perhaps on the whole the spot in Ravenna where the impression is of most sovereign authority and most thrilling force. It consists of a narrow low-browed cave, shaped like a Latin cross, every inch of which except the floor is covered with dense symbolic mosaics. Before you and on each side, through the thick brown light, loom three enormous barbaric sarcophagi, containing the remains of potentates of the Lower Empire. It is as if history had burrowed under ground to escape from research and you had fairly run it to earth. On the right lie the ashes of the Emperor Honorius, and in the middle those of his sister, Galla Placidia, a lady who, I believe, had great adventures. On the other side rest the bones of Constantius III. The place might be a small natural grotto lined with glimmering mineral substances, and there is something quite tremendous in being shut up so closely with these three imperial ghosts. The shadow of the great Roman name broods upon the huge sepulchres and abides for ever within the narrow walls.

But still other memories hang about than those of primitive bishops and degenerate emperors. Byron lived here and Dante died here, and the tomb of the one poet and the dwelling of the other are among the advertised appeals. The grave of Dante, it must be said, is anything but Dantesque, and the

---

mausoleum of Galla Placidia. Galla Placidia died in Rome; it is unlikely that her tomb is either in Ravenna or, as is also claimed, in the San Aquilino chapel of the basilica of San Lorenzo Maggiore in Milan.

Constantius III. Second husband of Galla Placidia.

Byron lived here. Byron had several residences in Ravenna, the Palazzo Rasponi, also called the Casa Rizzetti, which stood at the corner of the Piazza San Francesco and the Via Ricci, the house on the Strada di Porta Sisi, 225, and the Palazzo Guiccioli, the Via di Porta Adriana, 328, now the Via Cavour, 26; there with Teresa Guiccioli he stayed with the Count and Countess Guiccioli and finished *Don Juan*.

Dante . . . the tomb. The tomb of Dante was built in 1780 to enshrine the older mausoleum of 1483, which was built to enshrine the sarcophagus of 1321, the year of Dante's death; additions to the tomb have been made since 1921.

whole precinct is disposed with that odd vulgarity of taste which distinguishes most modern Italian tributes to greatness. The author of *The Divine Comedy* commemorated in stucco, even in a slumbering corner of Ravenna, is not "sympathetic." Fortunately of all poets he least needs a monument, as he was pre-eminently an architect in diction and built himself his temple of fame in verses more solid than Cyclopean blocks. If Dante's tomb is not Dantesque, so neither is Byron's house Byronic, being a homely, shabby, two-storied dwelling, directly on the street, with as little as possible of isolation and mystery. In Byron's time it was an inn, and it is rather a curious reflection that "Cain" and the "Vision of Judgment" should have been written at an hotel. The fact supplies a commanding precedent for self-abstraction to tourists at once sentimental and literary. I must declare indeed that my acquaintance with Ravenna considerably increased my esteem for Byron and helped to renew my faith in the sincerity of his inspiration. A man so much *de son temps* as the author of the above-named and other pieces can have spent two long years in this stagnant city only by the help of taking a great deal of disinterested pleasure in his own genius. He had indeed a notable pastime—the various churches are adorned with monuments of ancestral Guicciolis—but it is none the less obvious that Ravenna, fifty years ago, would have been an intolerably dull residence to a foreigner of distinction unequipped with intellectual resources. The hour one spends with Byron's memory then is almost compassionate. After all, one says to one's self as one turns away from the grandiloquent little slab in front of his house and looks down the deadly provincial vista of the empty, sunny street, the author of so many superb stanzas asked less from the world than he gave it. One of his diversions was to ride in the Pineta, which, beginning a couple of miles from the city, extends some twenty-five miles along the sands of the Adriatic. I drove out to it for Byron's sake, and Dante's, and Boccaccio's, all of whom have interwoven it with their fictions, and for that of a possible whiff of coolness from the sea. Between the city and the forest, in the midst of malarious rice-swamps, stands the finest of the Ravennese churches, the stately temple of San Apollinare in Classe. The Emperor Augustus constructed hereabouts a harbour for fleets, which the ages have choked up, and which survives only in the title of this ancient church. Its extreme loneliness

---

not "sympathetic." The quotation marks suggest the Italian *simpatico,* pleasant, pleasing, or gracious.

Emperor Augustus . . . harbour for fleets, which the ages have choked up. Augustus founded the imperial military port at Classis, which was connected to Ravenna by the Via Cesarea. Over the centuries silt deposits from the Po into the shallow Adriatic coastal region have caused the sea to retreat from Classe and Ravenna; today both lie about six miles inland.

makes it doubly impressive. They opened the great doors for me, and let a shaft of heated air go wander up the beautiful nave between the twenty-four lustrous, pearly columns of cipollino marble, and mount the wide staircase of the choir and spend itself beneath the mosaics of the vault. I passed a memorable half-hour sitting in this wave of tempered light, looking down the cool grey avenue of the nave, out of the open door, at the vivid green swamps, and listening to the melancholy stillness. I rambled for an hour in the Wood of Associations, between the tall smooth, silvery stems of the pines, and beside a creek which led me to the outer edge of the wood and a view of white sails, gleaming and gliding behind the sand-hills. It was infinitely, it was nobly "quaint," but, as the trees stand at wide intervals and bear far aloft in the blue air but a little parasol of foliage, I suppose that, of a glaring summer day, the forest itself was only the more characteristic of its clime and country for being perfectly shadeless.

1873.

The Saint's Afternoon
and Others

Before and above all was the sense that, with the narrow limits of past adventure, I had never yet had such an impression of what the summer could be in the south or the south in the summer; but I promptly found it, for the occasion, a good fortune that my terms of comparison were restricted. It was really something, at a time when the stride of the traveller had become as long as it was easy, when the seven-league boots positively hung, for frequent use, in the closet of the most sedentary, to have kept one's self so innocent of strange horizons that the Bay of Naples in June might still seem quite final. That picture struck me—a particular corner of it at least, and for many reasons—as the last word; and it is this last word that comes back to me, after a short interval, in a green, grey northern nook, and offers me again its warm, bright golden meaning before it also inevitably catches the chill. Too precious, surely, for us not to suffer it to help us as it may is the faculty of putting together again in an order the sharp minutes and hours that the wave of time has been as ready to pass over as the salt sea to wipe out the letters and words your stick has traced in the sand. Let me, at any rate, recover a sufficient number of such signs to make a sort of sense.

[Parts I–V were first published as "The Saint's Afternoon" in *The May Book*, compiled by Eliza Aria, 1901. Parts VI and VII were published for the first time in *Italian Hours*.]

I

FAR aloft on the great rock was pitched, as the first note, and indeed the highest, of the wondrous concert, the amazing creation of the friend who had offered me hospitality, and whom, more almost than I had ever envied any one anything, I envied the privilege of being able to reward a heated, artless pilgrim with a revelation of effects so incalculable. There was none but the loosest prefiguration as the creaking and puffing little boat, which had conveyed me only from Sorrento, drew closer beneath the prodigious island—beautiful, horrible and haunted—that does most, of all the happy elements and accidents, towards making the Bay of Naples, for the study of composition, a lesson in the grand style. There was only, above and below, through the blue of the air and sea, a great confused shining of hot cliffs and crags and buttresses, a loss, from nearness, of the splendid couchant outline and the more comprehensive mass, and an opportunity—oh, not lost, I assure you—to sit and meditate, even moralise, on the empty deck, while a happy brotherhood of American and German tourists, including, of course, many sisters, scrambled down into little waiting, rocking tubs and, after a few strokes, popped systematically into the small orifice of the Blue Grotto. There was an appreciable moment when they were all lost to view in that receptacle, the daily "psychological" moment during which it must so often befall the recalcitrant observer on the deserted deck to find himself aware of how delightful it might be if none of them should come out again. The

---

amazing creation of the friend. Arriving at Capri in 1876, Swedish physician Axel Munthe began transforming the ruins of the chapel of San Michele into the eclectic Villa San Michele, the construction of which was romantically documented in his interesting and enormously successful—it went through fifteen printings within fifteen months—*The Story of San Michele* (1929). In his preface Munthe reports that just before the outbreak of World War I Henry James

> reminded me that years ago [in 1899] when he was staying with me at San Michele he had encouraged me to write a book about my island home, which he had called the most beautiful place in the world. Why not write the Story of San Michele now if it came to the worst and my courage began to flag? Who could write about San Michele better than I who had built it with my own hands? Who could describe better than I all these priceless fragments of marbles strewn over the garden where the villa of Tiberius once stood? And the sombre old Emperor himself whose weary foot had trod the very mosaic floor I had brought to light under the vines, what a fascinating study for a man like me who was so interested in psychology! There was nothing like writing a book for a man who wanted to get away from his own misery, nothing like writing a book for a man who could not sleep. These were his last words, I never saw my friend again.

San Michele, accessible to few privileged guests until Munthe's death in 1949, today is open to the tourist.

charm, the fascination of the idea is not a little—though also not wholly—in the fact that, as the wave rises over the aperture, there is the most encouraging appearance that they perfectly may not. There it is. There is no more of them. It is a case to which nature has, by the neatest stroke and with the best taste in the world, just quietly attended.

Beautiful, horrible, haunted: that is the essence of what, about itself, Capri says to you—dip again into your Tacitus and see why; and yet, while you roast a little under the awning and in the vaster shadow, it is not because the trail of Tiberius is ineffaceable that you are most uneasy. The trail of Germanicus in Italy to-day ramifies further and bites perhaps even deeper; a proof of which is, precisely, that his eclipse in the Blue Grotto is inexorably brief, that here he is popping out again, bobbing enthusiastically back and scrambling triumphantly back. The spirit, in truth, of his effective appropriation of Capri has a broad-faced candour against which there is no standing up, supremely expressive as it is of the well-known "love that kills," of Germanicus's fatal susceptibility. If I were to let myself, however, incline to *that* aspect of the serious case of Capri I should embark on strange depths. The straightness and simplicity, the classic, synthetic directness of the German passion for Italy, make this passion probably the sentiment in the world that is in the act of supplying enjoyment in the largest, sweetest mouthfuls; and there is something unsurpassably marked in the way that on this irresistible shore it has seated itself to ruminate and digest. It keeps the record in its

---

Beautiful, horrible, haunted . . . Capri . . . Tacitus . . . Tiberius. Capri, or Capreae, was the home of the Emperor Tiberius (42 B.C.–A.D. 37) for the last ten years of his life, the period during which he communicated with the Roman Senate by letter. It was when he was at Capri that his reputation for depravity grew, as recorded particularly by Tacitus in the *Annals*, IV–VI, and by Suetonius in *The Twelve Caesars*. See page 312 below and note.

trail of Germanicus . . . eclipse in the Blue Grotto. Julius Caesar Germanicus (15 B.C.–A.D. 19) figures prominently in Tacitus's *Annals*, IV, as a great general who won many victories against the Germans, but who died mysteriously, perhaps by his uncle Tiberius's hand. Nonetheless, James's wordplay is more ironic than allusive; the Romans had once conquered Germany, but now the "Germanicus" tourist was in the process of peacefully reconquering Italy. After the discovery of the Blue Grotto in 1826, Capri entered the pages of German romantic literature and became an extremely popular tourist sight, one that inspired the poet August Von Platen (1796–1835) to compose "The Fisherman of Capri," and the great historian Ferdinand Gregorovius (1821–91) to write extensively on the history of the island. The "eclipse" of Germanicus refers to the inevitable seclusion and quiet of the grotto, a place offering difficult access to the visitor, German or otherwise. Gregorovius, *Figuren. Geschichte, Leben und Scenerie aus Italien*, 380–85, describes the eerie silence in the grotto as so moving that the tourists who confronted it stopped speaking. In "The Philosophy of the Blue Grotto," Norman Douglas discusses the discovery of the Blue Grotto "on the crest of an immense wave of cavern and ruin worship that overswept Northern Europe" (*Siren Land*, 94–95).

own loud accents; it breaks out in the folds of the hills and on the crests of the crags into every manner of symptom and warning. Huge advertisements and portents stare across the bay; the acclivities bristle with breweries and "restorations" and with great ugly Gothic names. I hasten, of course, to add that some such general consciousness as this may well oppress, under any sky, at the century's end, the brooding tourist who makes himself a prey by staying anywhere, when the gong sounds, "behind." It is behind, in the track and the reaction, that he least makes out the end of it all, perceives that to visit any one's country for any one's sake is more and more to find some one quite other in possession. No one, least of all the brooder himself, is in his own.

II

I CERTAINLY, at any rate, felt the force of this truth when, on scaling the general rock with the eye of apprehension, I made out at a point much nearer its summit than its base the gleam of a dizzily-perched white sea-gazing front which I knew for my particular landmark and which promised so much that it would have been welcome to keep even no more than half. Let me instantly say that it kept still more than it promised, and by no means least in the way of leaving far below it the worst of the outbreak of restorations and breweries. There is a road at present to the upper village, with which till recently communication was all by rude steps cut in the rock and diminutive donkeys scrambling on the flints; one of those fine flights of construction which the great road-making "Latin races" take, wherever they prevail, without advertisement or bombast; and even while I followed along the face of the cliff its climbing consolidated ledge, I asked myself how I could think so well of it without consistently thinking better still of the temples of beer so obviously destined to enrich its terminus. The perfect answer to that was of course that the brooding tourist is never bound to be consistent. What happier law for him than this very one, precisely, when on at last alighting, high up in the blue air, to stare and gasp and almost disbelieve, he embraced little by little the beautiful truth particularly, on this occasion, reserved for himself, and took in the stupendous picture? For here above all had the thought and the hand come from far away—even from *ultima Thule,* and yet were in possession triumphant and acclaimed. Well,

---

ultima Thule. The ancient world's name for the most northerly inhabitable land, located in the northern Atlantic, perhaps the Orkneys, the Shetlands, or Scandinavia, but generally employed with some latitude to indicate the farthest possible limit.

all one could say was that the way they had felt their opportunity, the divine conditions of the place, spoke of the advantage of some such intellectual perspective as a remote original standpoint alone perhaps can give. If what had finally, with infinite patience, passion, labour, taste, got itself done there, was like some supreme reward of an old dream of Italy, something perfect after long delays, was it not verily in *ultima Thule* that the vow would have been piously enough made and the germ tenderly enough nursed? For a certain art of asking of Italy all she can give, you must doubtless either be a rare *raffiné* or a rare genius, a sophisticated Norseman or just a Gabriele d'Annunzio.

All she can give appeared to me, assuredly, for that day and the following, gathered up and enrolled there: in the wondrous cluster and dispersal of chambers, corners, courts, galleries, arbours, arcades, long white ambulatories and vertiginous points of view. The greatest charm of all perhaps was that, thanks to the particular conditions, she seemed to abound, to overflow, in directions in which I had never yet enjoyed the chance to find her so free. The indispensable thing was therefore, in observation, in reflection, to press the opportunity hard, to recognise that as the abundance was splendid, so, by the same stroke, it was immensely suggestive. It dropped into one's lap, naturally, at the end of an hour or two, the little white flower of its formula: the brooding tourist, in other words, could only continue to brood till he had made out in a measure, as I may say, what was so wonderfully the matter with him. He was simply then in the presence, more than ever yet, of the possible poetry of the personal and social life of the south, and the fun would depend much—as occasions are fleeting—on his arriving in time, in the interest of that imagination which is his only field of sport, at adequate new notations of it. The sense of all this, his obscure and special fun in the general bravery, mixed, on the morrow, with the long, human hum of the bright, hot day and filled up the golden cup with questions and answers. The feast of St. Antony, the patron of the upper town, was the one thing in the air, and of the private beauty of the place, there on the narrow shelf, in the

---

sophisticated Norseman or just a Gabriele d'Annunzio. James's friend and host, Swedish physician Axel Munthe, would be the Norseman. Gabriele D'Annunzio (1863–1938), recognized even in relative youth for the sensuality and passion both of his writing and of his personal life (his love affair with the actress Eleonora Duse lasted from 1897 to 1902), was to achieve further notoriety for his dramatic actions as a patriot during World War I—he lost an eye during combat—and later for his extreme rightest politics. In 1904, in a lengthy, fundamentally appreciative but nonetheless troubled article on several recently translated novels of D'Annunzio, James wrote that "for the critic who simplifies a little to state clearly, the only ideas he urges upon us are the erotic and the plastic, which have for him about an equal intensity" (*Literary Criticism: French Writers,* 910).

shining, shaded loggias and above the blue gulfs, all comers were to be made free.

<h1 style="text-align:center">III</h1>

THE church-feast of its saint is of course for Anacapri, as for any self-respecting Italian town, the great day of the year, and the smaller the small "country," in native parlance, as well as the simpler, accordingly, the life, the less the chance for leakage, on other pretexts, of the stored wine of loyalty. This pure fluid, it was easy to feel overnight, had not sensibly lowered its level; so that nothing indeed, when the hour came, could well exceed the outpouring. All up and down the Sorrentine promontory the early summer happens to be the time of the saints, and I had just been witness there of a week on every day of which one might have travelled, through kicked-up clouds and other demonstrations, to a different hot holiday. There had been no bland evening that, somewhere or other, in the hills or by the sea, the white dust and the red glow did n't rise to the dim stars. Dust, perspiration, illumination, conversation—these were the regular elements. "They're very civilised," a friend who knows them as well as they can be known had said to me of the people in general; "plenty of fireworks and plenty of talk— that's all they ever want." That they were "civilised"—on the side on which they were most to show—was therefore to be the word of the whole business, and nothing could have, in fact, had more interest than the meaning that for the thirty-six hours I read into it.

Seen from below and diminished by distance, Anacapri makes scarce a sign, and the road that leads to it is not traceable over the rock; but it sits at its ease on its high, wide table, of which it covers—and with picturesque southern culture as well—as much as it finds convenient. As much of it as possible was squeezed all the morning, for St. Antony, into the piazzetta before the church, and as much more into that edifice as the robust odour mainly prevailing there allowed room for. It was the odour that was in prime occupation, and one could only wonder how so many men, women and children could cram themselves into so much smell. It was surely the smell, thick and resisting, that was least successfully to be elbowed. Mean-

---

small "country," in native parlance. It is a feature of the Italian language—and perhaps indicative of the degree of chauvinism and distinct traditions among regions—that the word *paese* may be translated as village, as well as native land or country.

while the good saint, before he could move into the air, had, among the
tapers and the tinsel, the opera-music and the pulpit poundings, bravely to
snuff it up. The shade outside was hot, and the sun was hot; but we waited
as densely for him to come out, or rather to come "on," as the pit at the
opera waits for the great tenor. There were people from below and people
from the mainland and people from Pomerania and a brass band from
Naples. There were other figures at the end of longer strings—strings that,
some of them indeed, had pretty well given way and were now but little
snippets trailing in the dust. Oh, the queer sense of the good old Capri of
artistic legend, of which the name itself was, in the more benighted years—
years of the contadina and the pifferaro—a bright evocation! Oh, the echo,
on the spot, of each romantic tale! Oh, the loafing painters, so bad and so
happy, the conscious models, the vague personalities! The "beautiful Capri
girl" was of course not missed, though not perhaps so beautiful as in her
ancient glamour, which none the less did n't at all exclude the probable
presence—with *his* legendary light quite undimmed—of the English lord in
disguise who will at no distant date marry her. The whole thing was there;
one held it in one's hand.

The saint comes out at last, borne aloft in long procession and under a
high canopy: a rejoicing, staring, smiling saint, openly delighted with the
one happy hour in the year on which he may take his own walk. Frocked
and tonsured, but not at all macerated, he holds in his hand a small wax
puppet of an infant Jesus and shows him to all their friends, to whom he
nods and bows: to whom, in the dazzle of the sun he literally seems to grin
and wink, while his litter sways and his banners flap and every one gaily
greets him. The ribbons and draperies flutter, and the white veils of the
marching maidens, the music blares and the guns go off and the chants
resound, and it is all as holy and merry and noisy as possible. The
procession—down to the delightful little tinselled and bare-bodied babies,
miniature St. Antonys irrespective of sex, led or carried by proud papas or
brown grandsires—includes so much of the population that you marvel
there is such a muster to look on—like the charades given in a family in
which every one wants to act. But it is all indeed in a manner one house, the
little high-niched island community, and nobody therefore, even in the presence of the head of it, puts on an air of solemnity. Singular and suggestive
before everything else is the absence of any approach to our notion of the
posture of respect, and this among people whose manners in general struck
one as so good and, in particular, as so cultivated. The office of the saint—
of which the festa is but the annual reaffirmation—involves not the faintest
attribute of remoteness or mystery.

While, with my friend, I waited for him, we went for coolness into the second church of the place, a considerable and bedizened structure, with the rare curiosity of a wondrous pictured pavement of majolica, the garden of Eden done in large coloured tiles or squares, with every beast, bird and river, and a brave *diminuendo,* in especial, from portal to altar, of perspective, so that the animals and objects of the foreground are big and those of the successive distances differ with much propriety. Here in the sacred shade the old women were knitting, gossipping, yawning, shuffling about; here the children were romping and "larking"; here, in a manner, were the open parlour, the nursery, the kindergarten and the *conversazione* of the poor. This is everywhere the case by the southern sea. I remember near Sorrento a wayside chapel that seemed the scene of every function of domestic life, including cookery and others. The odd thing is that it all appears to interfere so little with that special civilised note—the note of manners—which is so constantly touched. It is barbarous to expectorate in the temple of your faith, but that doubtless is an extreme case. Is civilisation really measured by the number of things people do respect? There would seem to be much evidence against it. The oldest societies, the societies with most traditions, are naturally not the least ironic, the least *blasées,* and the African tribes who take so many things into account that they fear to quit their huts at night are not the fine flower.

IV

WHERE, on the other hand, it was impossible not to feel to the full all the charming *riguardi*—to use their own good word—in which our friends *could* abound, was, that afternoon, in the extraordinary temple of art and hospitality that had been benignantly opened to me. Hither, from three o'clock to seven, all the world, from the small in particular to the smaller and the smallest, might freely flock, and here, from the first hour to the last, the huge straw-bellied flasks of purple wine were tilted for all the thirsty. They were many, the thirsty, they were three hundred, they were unending; but the draughts they drank were neither countable nor counted. This boon was dispensed in a long, pillared portico, where everything was white and

---

second church . . . majolica. After Santa Sofia the "second church" is the baroque S. Michele, or the "chiesa del Paradiso Terrestre," so-called because of Leonardo Chiaiese's extraordinary majolica pavement representing Adam and Eve abandoning an earthly paradise populated by exceedingly charming animals (illustrations in De Seta, 100–103, 269).

riguardi. Considerations.

light save the blue of the great bay as it played up from far below or as you took it in, between shining columns, with your elbows on the parapet. Sorrento and Vesuvius were over against you; Naples furthest off, melted, in the middle of the picture, into shimmering vagueness and innocence; and the long arm of Posilippo and the presence of the other islands, Procida, the stricken Ischia, made themselves felt to the left. The grand air of it all was in one's very nostrils and seemed to come from sources too numerous and too complex to name. It was antiquity in solution, with every brown, mild figure, every note of the old speech, every tilt of the great flask, every shadow cast by every classic fragment, adding its touch to the impression. What was the secret of the surprising amenity?—to the essence of which one got no nearer than simply by feeling afresh the old story of the deep interfusion of the present with the past. You had felt that often before, and all that could, at the most, help you now was that, more than ever yet, the present appeared to become again really classic, to sigh with strange elusive sounds of Virgil and Theocritus. Heaven only knows how little they would in truth have had to say to it, but we yield to these visions as we must, and when the imagination fairly turns in its pain almost any soft name is good enough to soothe it.

It threw such difficulties but a step back to say that the secret of the amenity was "style"; for what in the world was the secret of style, which you might have followed up and down the abysmal old Italy for so many a year only to be still vainly calling for it? Everything, at any rate, that happy afternoon, in that place of poetry, was bathed and blessed with it. The castle of Barbarossa had been on the height behind; the villa of black

---

stricken Ischia. Since the eleventh century B.C., Ischian colonies repeatedly had been struck by earthquakes, but two particularly terrible quakes hit the island in 1881 and in 1883 and left thousands dead, an event that was given some celebrity when in 1885 an illustrated monograph on the disaster was published in London (H. J. Johnson-Lavis, *The Earthquakes of Ischia*). These disasters, in addition to the cholera epidemics of 1837 and 1854, left the island in a near-devastated condition (Frenkel, *Ischia*, 31–33).

Virgil and Theocritus. Virgil died in 19 B.C. at Brundisium, the present-day Brindisi; his body was brought back to Naples—where he had written the *Eclogues*—and his remains were entombed near the grotto of Posillipo (as does Hare with "Posilipo," James provides a spelling variation common among travel writers). The pastoral idylls of Theocritus, however, can claim no direct association with this specific region; born in Sicily in the third century B.C., Theocritus traveled to Cos, to Alexandria, and to Asia Minor, but not to Naples.

castle of Barbarossa. Constructed during the ninth century and traditionally considered the work of Byzantine architects; the ruins are described inaccurately by Hare (*Cities of Southern Italy*, 190) as the remains of a sixteenth-century pirates' "castle."

Tiberius had overhung the immensity from the right; the white arcades and the cool chambers offered to every step some sweet old "piece" of the past, some rounded porphyry pillar supporting a bust, some shaft of pale alabaster upholding a trellis, some mutilated marble image, some bronze that had roughly resisted. Our host, if we came to that, had the secret; but he could only express it in grand practical ways. One of them was precisely this wonderful "afternoon tea," in which tea only—*that*, good as it is, has never the note of style—was not to be found. The beauty and the poetry, at all events, were clear enough, and the extraordinary uplifted distinction; but where, in all this, it may be asked, was the element of "horror" that I have spoken of as sensible?—what obsession that was not charming could find a place in that splendid light, out of which the long summer squeezes every secret and shadow? I'm afraid I'm driven to plead that these evils were exactly in one's imagination, a predestined victim always of the cruel, the fatal historic sense. To make so much distinction, how much history had been needed!—so that the whole air still throbbed and ached with it, as with an accumulation of ghosts to whom the very climate was pitiless, condemning them to blanch for ever in the general glare and grandeur, offering them no dusky northern nook, no place at the friendly fireside, no shelter of legend or song.

V

My friend had, among many original relics, in one of his white galleries—and how he understood the effect and the "value" of whiteness!—two or three reproductions of the finest bronzes of the Naples museum, the work of a small band of brothers whom he had found himself justified in trusting to deal with their problem honourably and to bring forth something as different as possible from the usual compromise of commerce. They had brought forth, in especial, for him, a copy of the young resting, slightly-panting Mercury which it was a pure delight to live with, and they had come over from Naples on St. Antony's eve, as they had done the year before, to report

---

villa of black Tiberius had overhung the immensity. The grim history of the Villa Jovis, standing one thousand feet above the sea, is mentioned in Suetonius: "In Capri they still show the place at the cliff top where Tiberius used to watch his victims being thrown into the sea after prolonged and exquisite tortures" ("Life of Tiberius," section 62, *The Twelve Caesars,* 140–41).

My friend. Axel Munthe.

themselves to their patron, to keep up good relations, to drink Capri wine and to join in the tarantella. They arrived late, while we were at supper; they received their welcome and their billet, and I am not sure it was not the conversation and the beautiful manners of these obscure young men that most fixed in my mind for the time the sense of the side of life that, all around, was to come out strongest. It would be artless, no doubt, to represent them as high types of innocence or even of energy—at the same time that, weighing them against *some* ruder folk of our own race, we might perhaps have made bold to place their share even of these qualities in the scale. It was an impression indeed never infrequent in Italy, of which I might, in these days, first have felt the force during a stay, just earlier, with a friend at Sorrento—a friend who had good-naturedly "had in," on his wondrous terrace, after dinner, for the pleasure of the gaping alien, the usual local quartette, violins, guitar and flute, the musical barber, the musical tailor, sadler, joiner, humblest sons of the people and exponents of Neapolitan song. Neapolitan song, as we know, has been blown well about the world, and it is late in the day to arrive with a ravished ear for it. That, however, was scarcely at all, for me, the question: the question, on the Sorrento terrace, so high up in the cool Capri night, was of the present outlook, in the world, for the races with whom it has been a tradition, in intercourse, positively to please.

The personal civilisation, for intercourse, of the musical barber and tailor, of the pleasant young craftsmen of my other friend's company, was something that could be trusted to make the brooding tourist brood afresh—to say more to him in fact, all the rest of the second occasion, than everything else put together. The happy address, the charming expression, the indistinctive discretion, the complete eclipse, in short, of vulgarity and brutality— these things easily became among these people the supremely suggestive note, begetting a hundred hopes and fears as to the place that, with the present general turn of affairs about the globe, is being kept for them. They are perhaps what the races politically feeble have still most to contribute— but what appears to be the happy prospect for the races politically feeble? And so the afternoon waned, among the mellow marbles and the pleasant folk—the purple wine flowed, the golden light faded, song and dance grew free and circulation slightly embarrassed. But the great impression remained and finally was exquisite. It was all purple wine, all art and song, and nobody a grain the worse. It was fireworks and conversation—the former, in the piazzetta, were to come later; it was civilisation and amenity. I took in the greater picture, but I lost nothing else; and I talked with the contadini about antique sculpture. No, nobody was a grain the worse; and I had plenty to think of. So it was I was quickened to remember that we others, we of my own country, as a race politically *not* weak, had—by what I had somewhere just heard—opened "three hundred 'saloons' " at Manila.

VI

THE "other" afternoons I here pass on to—and I may include in them, for that matter, various mornings scarce less charmingly sacred to memory— were occasions of another and a later year; a brief but all felicitous impression of Naples itself, and of the approach to it from Rome, as well as of the return to Rome by a different wonderful way, which I feel I shall be wise never to attempt to "improve on." Let me muster assurance to confess that this comparatively recent and superlatively rich reminiscence gives me for its first train of ineffable images those of a motor-run that, beginning betimes of a splendid June day, and seeing me, with my genial companions, blissfully out of Porta San Paolo, hung over us thus its benediction till the splendour had faded in the lamplit rest of the Chiaja. "We'll go by the mountains," my friend, of the chariot of fire, had said, "and we'll come back, after three days, by the sea"; which handsome promise flowered into such flawless performance that I could but feel it to have closed and rounded for me,

---

"three hundred 'saloons' " at Manila. In August 1898, during the last stages of the Spanish-American War's Pacific campaign, American troops captured Manila and the Philippines passed to the control of the United States. Within a year the total American forces in the city numbered approximately 60,000; their presence, and the general American economic presence, helped change the face of the city. James's point—suggesting an aspect of cultivation inherent in the Neapolitan sensibility but perhaps absent in the American—is emphasized by the inverted commas around "saloon," which suggest the ordinary American usage. Derived from *salon,* the word as used in Great Britain had a slightly archaic flavor in 1901 but still retained reference to the stately public rooms.

occasions of another and a later year. The visit to Naples and the short stay with Munthe took place in June 1899. James was to return one more time to Italy, from 20 May to 26 June 1907.

my friend, of the chariot of fire. With ironic allusion to the "chariot of fire" of Blake's "Jerusalem," James's admittedly lengthy aside on "monstrous" automobile transportation— "However, I wander wild"—does not express his usual opinion of motor touring. In 1907 Filippo de Filippi (1869–1938) and his American wife Caroline drove James, as he reported to Edith Wharton, "in their wondrous car" around Rome and down to Naples, and at least at first he was deeply impressed with this "most monstrous aid to motion," even if he recognized that "Italian driving is *crapulous*" (*Letters,* IV, 455–59). He later wrote to Wharton—"But your silver-sounding toot that invites me to the Car—the wondrous cushioned *general* Car of your so wondrously india-rubber-tyred and deep-cushioned fortune—echoes for me but too mockingly in the dim, if snug, cave of my permanent *retraîte*" (*Letters,* IV, 462).

beyond any further rehandling, the long-drawn rather indeed than thick-studded chaplet of my visitations of Naples—from the first, seasoned with the highest sensibility of youth, forty years ago, to this last the other day. I find myself noting with interest—and just to be able to emphasise it is what inspires me with these remarks—that, in spite of the milder and smoother and perhaps, pictorially speaking, considerably emptier, Neapolitan face of things, things in general, of our later time, I recognised in my final impression a grateful, a beguiling serenity. The place is at the best wild and weird and sinister, and yet seemed on this occasion to be seated more at her ease in her immense natural dignity. My disposition to feel that, I hasten to add, was doubtless my own secret; my three beautiful days, at any rate, filled themselves with the splendid harmony, several of the minor notes of which ask for a place, such as it may be, just here.

Wondrously, it was a clean and cool and, as who should say, quiet and amply interspaced Naples—in tune with itself, no harsh jangle of *forestieri* vulgarising the concert. I seemed in fact, under the blaze of summer, the only stranger—though the blaze of summer itself was, for that matter, everywhere but a higher pitch of light and colour and tradition, and a lower pitch of everything else; even, it struck me, of sound and fury. The appeal in short was genial, and, faring out to Pompeii of a Sunday afternoon, I enjoyed there, for the only time I can recall, the sweet chance of a late hour or two, the hour of the lengthening shadows, absolutely alone. The impression remains ineffaceable—it was to supersede half-a-dozen other mixed memories, the sense that had remained with me, from far back, of a pilgrimage

---

any further rehandling . . . my visitations of Naples . . . forty years ago . . . my final impression a grateful, a beguiling serenity. Years before, James had recorded an entirely different first impression of a city that, finally, at moments, he found serene. On 27 December 1869 he had written to his brother William that "I conceived at Naples a tenfold deeper loathing than ever of the hideous heritage of the past—and felt for a moment as if I should like to devote my life to laying rail-roads and erecting long blocks of stores on the most classic and romantic sites" (*Letters*, I, 182).

other mixed memories . . . thanks to a friendliest hospitality. In 1875 in Paris James met and formed a friendship with one of Turgenev's circle, the painter Paul Zhukovsky (also spelled Zhukovski, and by James in correspondence, Joukowsky). In 1880 Zhukovsky had taken a villa near Posilippo, where James was a guest for three days. It seems to be this visit to which James is referring, but see Edel, *Henry James: The Conquest of London*, 404–7, for James's general disillusionment with Zhukovsky, with the apparent homosexuality of his circle, and with the "fantastic immorality and aesthetics of the circle I had left in Naples" (*Letters*, II, 288). Edel reports that an unpublished letter from Zhukovsky, written late in life and preserved among James's papers, indicates that contact was reestablished. If the reference in "The Saint's Afternoon," is to the early visit with Zhukovsky, its tone may supply some evidence of renewed affection or at least of transformed nostalgia.

always here beset with traps and shocks and vulgar importunities, achieved under fatal discouragements. Even Pompeii, in fine, haunt of *all* the cockneys of creation, burned itself, in the warm still eventide, as clear as glass, or as the glow of a pale topaz, and the particular cockney who roamed without a plan and at his ease, but with his feet on Roman slabs, his hands on Roman stones, his eyes on the Roman void, his consciousness really at last of some good to him, could open himself as never before to the fond luxurious fallacy of a close communion, a direct revelation. With which there were other moments for him not less the fruit of the slow unfolding of time; the clearest of these again being those enjoyed on the terrace of a small island-villa—the island a rock and the villa a wondrous little rock-garden, unless a better term would be perhaps rock-salon, just off the extreme point of Posilippo and where, thanks to a friendliest hospitality, he was to hang ecstatic, through another sublime afternoon, on the wave of a magical wand. Here, as happened, were charming wise, original people even down to delightful amphibious American children, enamelled by the sun of the Bay as for figures of miniature Tritons and Nereids on a Renaissance plaque; and above all, on the part of the general prospect, a demonstration of the grand style of composition and effect that one was never to wish to see bettered. The way in which the Italian scene on such occasions as this seems to purify itself to the transcendent and perfect *idea* alone—idea of beauty, of dignity, of comprehensive grace, with all accidents merged, all defects disowned, all experience outlived, and to gather itself up into the mere mute eloquence of what has just incalculably *been,* remains for ever the secret and the lesson of the subtlest daughter of History. All one could do, at the heart of the overarching crystal, and in presence of the relegated City, the far-trailing Mount, the grand Sorrentine headland, the islands incomparably stationed and related, was to wonder what may well become of the so many other elements of any poor human and social complexus, what might become of any successfully working or only struggling and floundering civilisation at all, when high Natural Elegance proceeds to take such exclusive charge and recklessly assume, as it were, *all* the responsibilities.

VII

THIS indeed had been quite the thing I was asking myself all the wondrous way down from Rome, and was to ask myself afresh, on the return, largely within sight of the sea, as our earlier course had kept to the ineffably romantic inland valleys, the great decorated blue vistas in which the breasts of the mountains shine vaguely with strange high-lying city and castle and church and convent, even as shoulders of no diviner line might be hung about with dim old jewels. It was odd, at the end of time, long after those initiations, of comparative youth, that had then struck one as extending the very field itself of felt charm, as exhausting the possibilities of fond surrender, it was odd to have positively a new basis of enjoyment, a new gate of triumphant passage, thrust into one's consciousness and opening to one's use; just as I confess I have to brace myself a little to call by such fine names our latest, our ugliest and most monstrous aid to motion. It is true of the monster, as we have known him up to now, that one can neither quite praise him nor quite blame him without a blush—he reflects so the nature of the company he's condemned to keep. His splendid easy power addressed to noble aims makes him assuredly on occasion a purely beneficent creature. I parenthesise at any rate that I know him in no other light—counting out of course the acquaintance that consists of a dismayed arrest in the road, with back flattened against wall or hedge, for the dusty, smoky, stenchy shock of his passage. To no end is his easy power more blest than to that of ministering to the ramifications, as it were, of curiosity, or to that, in other words, of achieving for us, among the kingdoms of the earth, the grander and more genial, the comprehensive and *complete* introduction. Much as was ever to be said for our old forms of pilgrimage—and I am convinced that they are far from wholly superseded—they left, they had to leave, dreadful gaps in our yearning, dreadful lapses in our knowledge, dreadful failures in our energy; there were always things off and beyond, goals of delight and dreams of desire, that dropped as a matter of course into the unattainable, and over to which our wonder-working agent now flings the firm straight bridge. Curiosity has lost, under this amazing extension, its salutary renouncements perhaps; contemplation has become one with action and satisfaction one with desire—speaking always in the spirit of the inordinate lover of an enlightened use of our eyes. That may represent, for all I know, an insolence of advantage on which there will be eventual heavy charges, as yet obscure and incalculable, to pay, and I glance at the possibility only to avoid all thought of the lesson of the long run, and to insist that I utter this dithyramb but in the immediate flush and fever of the short. For such a beat of time as our fine courteous and contemplative advance upon Naples, and for such another as our retreat northward under the same fine law of observation and homage, the bribed consciousness could only decline to question its security. The sword of Damocles suspended over that presumption, the skeleton at the banquet of extravagant ease, would have been that even at our actual inordinate rate—leaving quite apart "improvements" to come—such savings of trouble begin to use up the world; some hard grain of difficulty being always a necessary part of the composition of pleasure. The hard grain in our old comparatively pedestrian mixture, before this business of our learning not so much even to fly (which might indeed involve trouble) as to be mechanically and prodigiously flown, quite another matter, was the element of uncertainty, effort and patience; the handful of silver nails which, I admit, drove many an impression home. The seated motorist misses the silver nails, I fully acknowledge, save in so far as his æsthetic (let alone his moral) conscience may supply him with some artful subjective substitute; in which case the thing becomes a precious secret of his own.

However, I wander wild—by which I mean I look too far ahead; my intention having been only to let my sense of the merciless June beauty of Naples Bay at the sunset hour and on the island terrace associate itself with the whole inexpressible taste of our two motor-days' feast of scenery. That queer question of the exquisite grand manner as the most emphasised *all* of things—of what it may, seated so predominant in nature, insidiously, through the centuries, let generations and populations "in for," had n't in the least waited for the special emphasis I speak of to hang about me. I must have found myself more or less consciously entertaining it by the way— since how could n't it be of the very essence of the truth, constantly and intensely before us, that Italy is really so much the most beautiful country in the world, taking all things together, that others must stand off and be hushed while she speaks? Seen thus in great comprehensive iridescent stretches, it is the incomparable wrought *fusion,* fusion of human history and mortal passion with the elements of earth and air, of colour, composition and form, that constitutes her appeal and gives it the supreme heroic grace. The chariot of fire favours fusion rather than promotes analysis, and leaves much of that first June picture for me, doubtless, a great accepted blur of violet and silver. The various hours and successive aspects, the different strong passages of our reverse process, on the other hand, still figure for me even as some series of sublime landscape-frescoes—if the great Claude, say, had ever used that medium—in the immense gallery of a palace; the home- ward run by Capua, Terracina, Gaeta and its storied headland fortress, across the deep, strong, indescribable Pontine Marshes, white-cattled, strangely pastoral, sleeping in the afternoon glow, yet stirred by the near sea- breath. Thick somehow to the imagination as some full-bodied sweetness of

---

Capua, Terracina, Gaeta . . . Pontine Marshes . . . thick with the sense of history. Hannibal's army wintered at ancient Capua (Casilinum) after the defeat of the Roman armies in 215 B.C. The Pontine Marshes, now largely drained, ran from Nettuno to the strategically important town of Terracina and were long famous for waves of malaria. Gaeta, the ancient Roman naval port of Caietai Portuo, was, according to Virgil, the burial place of Aeneas's nurse, Caieta (*Aeneid,* VII, 2), from whom the town took its name. After his 1848 flight in disguise from Rome, Pius IX found protection in Gaeta's great fortress, as did Francesco II of Naples in 1861, following an unsuccessful attempt to resist Garibaldi's forces.

syrup is thick to the palate the atmosphere of that region—thick with the sense of history and the very taste of time; as if the haunt and home (which indeed it is) of some great fair bovine aristocracy attended and guarded by halberdiers in the form of the mounted and long-lanced herdsmen, admirably congruous with the whole picture at every point, and never more so than in their manner of gaily taking up, as with bell-voices of golden bronze, the offered wayside greeting.

There had been this morning among the impressions of our first hour an unforgettable specimen of that general type—the image of one of those human figures on which our perception of the romantic so often pounces in Italy as on the genius of the scene personified; with this advantage, that as the scene there has, at its best, an unsurpassable distinction, so the physiognomic representative, standing for it all, and with an animation, a complexion, an expression, a fineness and fulness of humanity that appear to have gathered it in and to sum it up, becomes beautiful by the same simple process, very much, that makes the heir to a great capitalist rich. Our early start, our roundabout descent from Posilippo by shining Baiæ for avoidance of the city, had been an hour of enchantment beyond any notation I can here recover; all lustre and azure, yet all composition and classicism, the prospect developed and spread, till after extraordinary upper reaches of radiance and horizons of pearl we came at the turn of a descent upon a stalwart young gamekeeper, or perhaps substantial young farmer, who, well-appointed and blooming, had unslung his gun and, resting on it beside a hedge, just lived for us, in the rare felicity of his whole look, during that moment and while, in recognition, or almost, as we felt, in homage, we instinctively checked our speed. He pointed, as it were, the lesson, giving the supreme right accent or final exquisite turn to the immense magnificent phrase; which from those moments on, and on and on, resembled doubtless nothing so much as a page written, by a consummate verbal economist and master of style, in the noblest of all tongues. Our splendid human plant by the wayside had flowered thus into style—and there was n't to be, all day, a lapse of eloquence, a wasted word or a cadence missed.

These things are personal memories, however, with the logic of certain insistences of that sort often difficult to seize. Why should I have kept so sacredly uneffaced, for instance, our small afternoon wait at tea-time or, as we made it, coffee-time, in the little brown piazzetta of Velletri, just short of

---

from **Posilippo by shining Baiæ.** With allusion to Horace, *Epistles,* I, 84—"Nullus in orbe sinus Baiis praelucet amoenis"—nothing in the world outshines the lovely bay of Baiæ. But over the centuries volcanic activity has shifted the water level, and today the sea covers many of the ruins of an ancient town renowned for beauty, for luxury, and for episodes of excess.

the final push on through the flushed Castelli Romani and the drop and home-stretch across the darkening Campagna? We had been dropped into the very lap of the ancient civic family, after the inveterate fashion of one's sense of such stations in small Italian towns. There was a narrow raised terrace, with steps, in front of the best of the two or three local cafés, and in the soft enclosed, the warm waning light of June various benign contemplative worthies sat at disburdened tables and, while they smoked long black weeds, enjoyed us under those probable workings of subtlety with which we invest so many quite unimaginably blank (I dare say) Italian simplicities. The charm was, as always in Italy, in the tone and the air and the happy hazard of things, which made any positive pretension or claimed importance a comparatively trifling question. We slid, in the steep little place, more or less down hill; we wished, stomachically, we had rather addressed ourselves to a tea-basket; we suffered importunity from unchidden infants who swarmed about our chairs and romped about our feet; we stayed no long time, and "went to see" nothing; yet we communicated to intensity, we lay at our ease in the bosom of the past, we practised intimacy, in short, an intimacy so much greater than the mere accidental and ostensible: the difficulty for the right and grateful expression of which makes the old, the familiar tax on the luxury of loving Italy.

1900–1909.

Appendix I: Textual Variants

As indicated in A Note on the Text, because of the major revisions James made in the various incarnations of the *Italian Hours* essays, an overwhelmingly complex collation of all printings would require numerous, and almost entire, parallel texts. Such an unwieldly undertaking is fundamentally unnecessary since scholars can find all earlier such printings in the periodical collections of most research libraries. The ambition of this collation is modest: to provide the differences that exist in the relatively rare American and English first editions of *Italian Hours*—differences that often support the decision to use the American first edition as the copy text. Most are variants of punctuation and represent accommodation to editorial house style, although occasionally there are more important changes and corrections. Accidental differences, where a hyphen at the end of a line indicates the break of a word, are not listed. Where the editor has corrected errors, those corrections are indicated in this listing. Errors in Italian are noted in the text but not corrected.

American First Edition		*English First Edition*
3.21	[No date.]	1909.
9.2	thoroughgoing	thorough-going
9.31	St. Mark's,—abominable	St. Mark's—abominable
9.31	habit,—	habit—
10.25	antiquity mongers	antiquity-mongers
12.6	of injury.	of injury,
26.36	compartments;	compartments:
33.20	polygot [corrected]	polyglot
35.14	rhapsody of	rhapsody on
37.19	waterway	water-way
42.6	seventeenth century	seventeenth-century
52.21	star-light	starlight
55.2	a while	awhile
67.24	to continue, with a body of discussion, neither in itself and in its day	to continue attentive to an altercation neither in itself and in its day
72.n	February, 1902	February 1902
79.12	mor lise [corrected]	moralise
80.36	masterpieces:	masterpieces;
81.2	Feast of the House of Levi	Feast at the House of Levi
83.10	lines	line
84.heading	Chambéry	Chambery
87.15	for ever	forever
89.25	three miles	five miles
92.12	far as Bellinzona	far Bellinzona
95.15	Edward VI's	Edward VI.'s
96.5	*café au lait*	café au lait [Italicized elsewhere in same text.]
100.2	Autumn weather	Autumn-weather
100.18	Mont Cenis	Mont-Cenis
100.22	Mont Cenis	Mont-Cenis
112.3	a while	awhile
116.3	church, and,	church and,
120.21	consequence . . . In	consequence. . . . In
121.n	*Notes of Travel and Study in Italy.*	*Study and Travel in Italy.* [Incorrect title].
129.17	Carnival myself, his seemed	Carnival myself his seemed
130.2	a while	awhile
136.35	*trattoría* [corrected]	*trattoria*
145.13	Paul V	Paul V.
157.24	town on	town, on
158.21	lava,	lava

161.5	wild flowers	wild-flowers
161.14	James II)	James II.)
165.27	in the world.	in the world."
169.32	nippingly cool. [corrected]	nipplingly cool,
171.28	grander, smoother	grander smoother
178.12	think), which	think) which
184.8	café	cafe
184.12	cafés	cafe
184.30	for ever	forever
192.4	h's.	*h's.*
195.32	*Monastères Bénédictins*	*Monastères Benedictins*
196.22	ever, just	ever just
198.5	*guingettes* [corrected to *guinguettes*]	*guingettes*
199.20	for do [corrected]	do for
201.17	water-side	waterside
205.16	regions	regions,
208.8	springs	spring
209.18	Francisan [corrected]	Franciscan
211.17	humorist	humourist
213.3	Julius III	Julius III.
219.8	Tsucan charm [corrected]	Tuscan charm
222.7	hill-tops	hilltops
231.12	evident about	evidence about
232.5	hill-top	hilltop
233.19	Pius II,	Pius II.,
239.23	Napoleon III	Napoleon III.
243.2	fading, this	fading this
243.12	cathedral.	Cathedral.
245.20	painter,	painter
250.24	hill-top	hilltop
260.24	Botticelli's	Botticeili's
261.35	cheek to cheek, in	cheek to cheek in
263.16	why, I'm afraid	why I'm afraid
266.25	cobble-stones	cobblestones
267.10	Ferdinand I (whom	Ferdinand I. (whom
278.28	dead Tuscany, Lucca	dead Tuscany Lucca
279.22	earthernware [corrected.]	earthenware
283.19	place,	place
288.12	note, as	note as
290.5	her being	its being
297.18	a while	awhile
297.29	hierogylphics [corrected]	hieroglyphics
309.12	tale!	tale.
310.9	*conversazione*	conversazione

314.2	Manila.	Manilla.
314.18	my friend, of the chariot of fire, had said	my friend, of the winged chariot, had said
316.24	for ever	forever
318.23	constitutes	constitute

Appendix II: Henry James on Italian Travel Books

———

The appendix provides Henry James's reviews of Italian travel books or travel note-books by William Dean Howells, Hippolyte Taine, Nathaniel Hawthorne, Auguste Laugel, and Augustus J. C. Hare.

"Review of '*Italian Journeys*. By W. D. Howells, Author of *Venetian Life*. New York: Hurd and Houghton, 1867,' " *North American Review* 106 (January 1868): 336–39.

Under favor of his work on "Venetian Life," Mr. Howells took his place as one of the most charming of American writers and most satisfactory of American travellers. He is assuredly not one of those who journey from Dan to Beersheba only to cry out that all is barren. Thanks to the keenness of his observation and the vivacity of his sympathies, he treads afresh the most frequently trodden routes, without on the one hand growing cynical over his little or his great disappointments, or taking refuge on the other in the well-known alternative of the Baron Munchausen. Mr. Howells has an eye for the small things of nature, of art, and of human life, which enables him to extract sweetness and profit from adventures the most prosaic, and which prove him a very worthy successor of the author of the "Sentimental Journey."

Mr. Howells is in fact a sentimental traveller. He takes things as he finds them and as history has made them; he presses them into the service of no theory, nor scourges them into the following of his prejudices; he takes them as a man of the world, who is not a little a moralist—a gentle moralist, a good deal a humorist, and most of all a poet; and he leaves them,—he leaves them as the man of real literary power and the delicate artist alone know how to leave them, with new memories mingling, for our common delight, with the old memories that are the accumulation of ages, and with a fresh touch of color modestly gleaming amid the masses of local and historical coloring. It is for this solid literary merit that Mr. Howells's writing is valuable,— and the more valuable that it is so rarely found in books of travel in our own tongue. Nothing is more slipshod and slovenly than the style in which publications of this kind are habitually composed. Letters and diaries are simply strung into succession and transferred to print. If the writer is a clever person, an observer, an explorer, an intelligent devotee of the picturesque, his work will doubtless furnish a considerable amount of entertaining reading; but there will yet be something essentially common in its character. The book will be diffuse, overgrown, shapeless; it will not belong to literature. This charm of style Mr. Howells's two books on Italy possess in perfection; they belong to literature and to the centre and core of it,—the region where men think and feel, and one may almost say breathe, in good prose, and where the classics stand on guard. Mr. Howells is not an economist, a statistician, an historian, or a propagandist in any interest; he is simply an observer, responsible only to a kindly heart, a lively fancy, and a healthy conscience. It may therefore indeed be admitted that there was a smaller chance than in the opposite case of his book being ill written. He might notice what he pleased and mention what he pleased, and do it in just the manner that pleased him. He was under no necessity of sacrificing his style to facts; he might under strong provocation—provocation of which the sympathetic reader will feel the force—sacrifice facts to his style. But this privilege, of course, enforces a corresponding obligation, such as a man of so acute literary conscience as our author would be the first to admit and to discharge. He must have felt the importance of making his book, by so much as it was not to be a work of strict information, a work of generous and unalloyed entertainment.

These "Italian Journeys" are a record of some dozen excursions made to various parts of the peninsula during a long residence in Venice. They take the reader over roads much travelled, and conduct him to shrines worn by the feet—to say nothing of the knees—of thousands of pilgrims, no small number of whom, in these latter days, have imparted their impressions to the world. But it is plain that the world is no more weary of reading about Italy than it is of visiting it; and that so long as that deeply interesting country continues to stand in its actual relation, æsthetically and intellectually, to the rest of civilization, the topic will not grow threadbare. There befell a happy moment in history when Italy got the start of the rest of Christendom; and the ground gained, during that splendid advance, the other nations have never been able to recover. We go to Italy to gaze upon certain of the highest achievements of human power,—achievements, moreover, which, from their visible and tangible nature, are particularly well adapted to represent to the imagination the *maximum* of man's creative force. So wide is the interval between the great Italian monuments of art and the works of the colder genius of the neighboring nations, that we find ourselves willing to look upon the former as the ideal and the perfection of human effort, and to invest the country of their birth with a sort of half-sacred character. This is, indeed, but half the story. Through the more recent past of Italy there gleams the stupendous image of a remoter past; behind the splendid efflorescence of the Renaissance we detect the fulness of a prime which, for human effort and human will, is to the great æsthetic explosion of the sixteenth century very much what the latter is to the present time. And then, beside the glories of Italy, we think of her sufferings; and, beside the master-works of art, we think of the favors of Nature; and, along with these profane matters, we think of the Church,—until, betwixt admiration and longing and pity and reverence, it is little wonder that we are charmed and touched beyond healing.

In the simplest manner possible, and without declamation or rhetoric or affectation of any kind, but with an exquisite alternation of natural pathos and humor, Mr. Howells reflects this constant mute eloquence of Italian life. As to what estimate he finally formed of the Italian character he has left us uncertain; but one feels that he deals gently and tenderly with the foibles and vices of the land, for the sake of its rich and inexhaustible beauty, and of the pleasure which he absorbs with every breath. It is doubtless unfortunate for the Italians, and unfavorable to an exact appreciation of their intrinsic merits, that you cannot think of them or write of them in the same judicial manner as you do of other people,—as from equal to equal,—but that the imagination insists upon having a voice in the matter, and making you generous rather than just. Mr. Howells has perhaps not wholly resisted this temptation; and his tendency, like that of most sensitive spirits brought to know Italy, is to feel—even when he does not express it—that much is to be forgiven the people, because they are *so* picturesque. Mr. Howells is by no means indifferent, however, to the human element in all that he sees. Many of the best passages in his book, and the most delicate touches, bear upon the common roadside figures which he met, and upon the manners and morals of the populace. He observes on their behalf a vast number of small things; and he ignores, for their sake, a large number of great ones. He is not fond of generalizing, nor of offering views and opinions. A certain poetical inconclusiveness pervades his book. He relates what he saw with his own eyes, and what he thereupon felt and fancied; and his work has thus a thoroughly personal flavor. It is, in fact, a series of small personal adventures,—adventures so slight and rapid that nothing comes of them but the impression of the moment, and, as a final result, the pleasant chapter which records them. These chapters, of course, differ in interest and merit, according to their subject, but the charm of manner is never absent; and it is strongest when the author surrenders himself most completely to his faculty for composition, and works his matter over into the perfection of form, as in the episode entitled "Forza Maggiore," a real masterpiece of light writing. Things slight and simple and impermanent all put on a hasty comeliness at the approach of his pen.

Mr. Howells is, in short, a descriptive writer in a sense and with a perfection that, in our view, can be claimed for no American writer except Hawthorne. Hawthorne, indeed, was perfection, but he was only half descriptive. He kept an eye on an unseen world, and his points of contact with this actual sphere were few and slight. One feels through all his descriptions,—we speak especially of his book on England,— that he was not a man of the world,—of this world which we after all love so much better than any other. But Hawthorne cannot be disposed of in a paragraph, and we confine ourselves to our own author. Mr. Howells is the master of certain refinements of style, of certain exquisite intentions (intentions in which humor generally plays a large part), such as are but little practised in these days of crude and precipitate writing. At the close of a very forcible and living description of certain insufferable French *commis-voyageurs* on the steamer from Genoa to Naples, "They wore their hats at dinner," writes Mr. Howells; "but always went away, after soup, deadly pale." It would be difficult to give in three lines a better picture of unconscious vulgarity than is furnished by this conjunction of abject frailties with impertinent assumptions.

And so at Capri, "after we had inspected the ruins of the emperor's villa, a clownish imbecile of a woman, *professing to be the wife of the peasant who had made the excavations,* came forth out of a cleft in the rock and received tribute of us; why, I do not know." The sketch is as complete as it is rapid, and a hoary world of extortion and of stupefied sufferance is unveiled with a single gesture. In all things Mr. Howells's touch is light, but none the less sure for its lightness. It is the touch of a writer who is a master in his own line, and we have not so many writers and masters that we can afford not to recognize real excellence. It is our own loss when we look vacantly at those things which make life pleasant. Mr. Howells has the qualities which make literature a delightful element in life,—taste and culture and imagination, and the incapacity to be common. We cannot but feel that one for whom literature has done so much is destined to repay his benefactor with interest.

"Review of '*Italy: Rome and Naples.* Translated by John Durand. New York: Leypoldt & Holt, 1868,' " *Nation,* vol. 6, 7 May 1868, 373–75.

A few years since M. Taine, appointed to a professorial chair in the School of Fine Arts in Paris, made a journey to Italy to put himself in the humor for his office. The result, in the course of time, in addition to his lectures, was two large volumes of notes, letters, and journals. The first of these, "Rome and Naples," has just been translated for the American public. Whether it will be largely read in this country we are unable to say; but it is certain that M. Taine deserves well of English readers. He is the author of a really valuable history of English literature, and he has taken the trouble to arrive at a more intimate knowledge of the English mind than members of one race often care to possess of the idiosyncracies of another. Add to this that he is one of the most powerful writers of the day—to our own taste, indeed, the most powerful; the writer of all others who throws over the reader's faculties, for the time, the most irresistible spell, and against whose influence, consequently, the mental reaction is most violent and salutary—and you have an idea of his just claim on your attention. M. Taine's manner and style are extremely individual, and it is somewhat odd that being, as he is, a great stickler, in literary and historical problems, for the credit of national and local influences, he should personally be a signal example of their possible futility. He is scarcely a Frenchman. Not that he is anything else; but he is before all things the brilliant, dogmatic, sombre, and (from a reader's point of view) extremely heartless offspring of his own resolute will. His style, literally trans-lated (and Mr. Durand is very literal), makes very natural English. It has an energy, an impetus, a splendor to which no words of ours can do justice. It is not delicate, courteous, and persuasive like that of several of the most eminent French writers of the day—notably MM. Sainte-Beuve, Renan, and Cousin—it is vehement, impetu-ous, uncompromising, arrogant—insolent, if you will. The affirmative movement of M. Taine's mind is always a ringing hammer-blow. Every proposition is fastened down with a tenpenny nail. Finally, of course, this is very fatiguing; your head aches with the metallic resonance of the process. It is the climax of dogmatism. There was something ironical in M. Taine's being appointed professor; he was professor from the first, by natural right. His whole tone is didactic: every sentence comes *ex cathedra*. But with the essential energy and originality of his mind he invests the character with a new dignity, and reconciles it to the temperament of a man still young and audacious.

He has, intellectually, nothing of professorial dryness or prudery. Of all writers he is the most broadly picturesque. He throws into his language a wealth of color and a fulness of sound which would set up in trade a hundred minor poets and story-tellers. The secret of the power which he exerts on the mind, or on many minds, at least, we take to be the union of this vast current of imagery, of descriptive vigor and splendor, and of sensuous susceptibility with great logical precision and large erudi-tion. He describes a figure, a costume, a building, a picture, not only with all the richness of his imagination, but with the authority and *prestige* of his knowledge. The pictorial element in his style, its color and rhythm, is not the substance of his thought, as in so many charming second-class writers, but its mere vestment and gait. Nevertheless, we admit that, to our perception, in spite of his learning, his logic, and his merits as a metaphysician, or rather an anti-metaphysician (whatever they may be), he remains pre-eminently an artist, a *writer*. If we had doubted of the truth of this judgment, we should have been convinced by that singular work, recently pub-lished, "Notes sur Paris: Opinions de M. Thomas Graindorge." Of feeling in the work there is none; of ideas there are very few; but of images, pictures, description, style, a most overwhelming superabundance. The same relation between the two elements of his genius appears in the "History of English Literature." In his apprecia-tion of certain writers, the faculty of perception, apprehension, without being ab-sent, is quite lost to sight in the energy of the act of portraiture. There are a series of pages on Shakespeare which, although full of controvertible propositions and precipi-tate formulas, form to our mind a supremely valuable tribute to his genius, inasmuch as of all attempts to appreciate and measure it they are the most energetic, unre-served, and eloquent. They form a direct homage to the immensity of the theme; they are almost as vast as silence; they are, in short, on the Shakespearian scale. The nurse of *Juliet* is not assuredly distinguished on the immortal page by a more animated and furious loquacity than M. Taine exhibits on her behalf. But an example is more conclusive than our own logic, and we find one to our hand in a striking passage in the second volume (Florence and Venice) of the "Voyage en Italie." This passage is interesting as showing, as it seems to us, the thoroughly unreligious cast of the author's mind (for we know few writers who appear to find it more natural to speak of a religion—no matter which—from a distant external standpoint), and then its gravity, melancholy, and hopelessness, and then, finally, its supreme delight in the literary form. It begins, if we are not mistaken, in a moral key, and ends in an artistic one. It is tragical, but it is perfect, consciously perfect. We translate, premising that the author is speaking of the impression produced by certain primitive frescoes in various Italian churches, buried under the work of later painters, and restored to light by the excavation, as one may call it, of the subsequent applications of color:

> "You raise your eyes then and find before you the four edifices of old Pisa, lonely on a square where the grass grows, with the dead paleness of their marbles outlined against the blue divine. What a mass of ruins; what a cemetery is history! How many human palpitations, of which there remains no trace but a form imprinted on a block of stone! What a careless smile is that of the peaceful sky; and what a cruel beauty dwells in that luminous dome, stretched over the decease of successive generations like a canopy at a common burial! We have read these ideas in books, and with the pride of youth we have treated them as mere talk; but when a man has gone over half of his career, and, retiring within himself, he counts up all the ambitions he has strangled, all the hopes he has plucked up, all the dead things he carries in his heart; the magnificence and the hardness of nature appear to him at once, and the heavy sob of his inward obsequies suggests to him a deeper lamentation—that of the great human tragedy which unfolds itself from age to age to lay low so many strugglers in a single tomb. He stops, feeling upon his own head, as upon that of others, the hand of the fateful powers, and comprehends his condition. This humanity, of which he is a member, has its image in the 'Niobe' of Florence. Around her, her daughters and her sons, all her loved ones, fall unceasingly beneath the bolts of invisible archers. One of them is prostrate on his back, his bosom tremulous with a piercing wound; another, still living, lifts her useless hands toward the celestial murderers; the youngest hides her head in the robe of her mother. She, meanwhile, cold and still, erects herself hopeless, and, with her eyes raised to heaven, gazes with wonder and horror upon the dazzling, deathly nimbus, the outstretched arms, the inevitable arrows, and the implacable serenity of the gods."

M. Taine may certainly be said to belong to the materialist school of thinkers. He is no sentimentalist; in the way of sentiment he rarely treats us to anything lighter than the passage just quoted. To his perception man is extremely interesting as an object of study, but he is without sanctity or mystery of any sort. He takes a positive satisfaction in reminding the reader of the purely objective and finite character of his organization, and he uses for this purpose a special vocabulary. "La tragédie, la comédie humaine," "la colonie humaine," "la plante humaine," "la machine humaine," these expressions continually recur. M. Taine, in effect, studies man as a plant or as a machine. You obtain an intimate knowledge of the plant by a study of the soil and climate in which it grows, and of the machine by taking it apart and inspecting its component pieces. M. Taine applies this process to the human mind, to history, art, and literature, with the most fruitful results. The question remains, indeed, with each reader as to whether, as the author claims, the description covers all the facts; as to whether his famous theory of *la race, le milieu, le moment* is an adequate explanation of the various complications of any human organism—his own (the reader's) in particular. But he will be willing, at least, to admit that the theory makes incomparable observers, and that in choosing a travelling companion he cannot do better than take him from the school of M. Taine. For, in fact, you can do your own moralizing and sentimentalizing; you can draw your own inferences and arrange your own creed; what you wish in a companion, a guide, is to help you accumulate *data*, to call your attention to facts. The present writer observes everything, and selects and describes the best.

M. Taine rapidly traversed Italy, and began his journey at Naples upward. The early portion of his book is pervaded by that strong feeling of joy natural to an ardent dogmatist at the prospect of an unexplored field. He describes the city of Naples with singular vividness; its radiant, transparent, natural loveliness, the latent tokens of its pure Greek origin, the traces of the Spanish dominion, the splendor and squalor, the sensuality in manners and art and religion. Nothing grand, nothing Gothic (even remotely, as in Northern Italy), nothing impressive and mysterious. Parisian light and gorgeousness, and careless joyousness and superstition, form the substance of his impressions. Having described a church bedizened with a wilderness of florid ornament in the artificial Italian style of the seventeenth century, he opens a vista to thought at the close of the chapter by touching with eloquent brevity upon a passionate and sombre Spanish painting: "The breath of the great period still stirs the machine; it is Euripides, if it is no longer Sophocles. Some of the pieces are splendid; among others, 'A Descent from the Cross,' of Ribera. The sun struck upon the head of Christ through the half-drawn curtain of red silk. The darksome background seemed the more mournful beside this sudden radiance of luminous flash, and the dolorous Spanish coloring; the expression, here mystical, there violent, of the passionate figures in the shadow gave to the scene the aspect of a vision, such as used to people the monastic, chivalrous brain of a Calderon or a Lope." These few lines are assuredly picturesque writing; but it seems to us that they serve to illustrate the difference between the picturesque as practised by a writer with his facts in hand, and one who has nothing but fancies. At Naples, however, M. Taine found but few paintings, and these were to be his principal concern. *En revanche,* he gives us, *apropos* of the Greek and Roman relics of the neighborhood, some admirable pages on "Homeric Life and the City of Antiquity." It is not until he reaches Rome, Florence, and Venice that he really plunges into his subject. Here we are unable to follow him. We can only recommend him to the attentive perusal of all persons interested in the history of art, and gratified by the spectacle of an indefatigable critical *verve*. M. Taine is guilty, doubtless, of many errors of judgment; but we strongly suspect that the great masters—Michael Angelo, Raphael, Leonardo, and Titan—have never been more correctly, as well as more ardently, estimated. Several of the great painters of the second rank—notably, Veronese and Tintoretto—are celebrated with a splendor of coloring and a breadth of design which recall the aspect of their own immortal works. Finally, we cannot help laying down our conviction that M. Taine's two volumes form a truly great production; great not in a moral sense, and very possibly not in a philosophical, but appreciably great as a contribution to literature and history. One feels at moments as if, before this writer, there had been no critics, no travellers, observers, or æsthetic inquisitors. This is, of course, a mistake, and we shall like no genuine critic the less (we personally, on the contrary, from the character of our sympathies, feel that we shall like him the more) for giving

M. Taine has liberal dues. It is inexpressibly gratifying—fortifying, one may say—to see a writer, *armé en guerre,* fling himself into his subject with such energy, such fury. It is an admirable intellectual feat. M. Taine is a representative of pure intellect, and he exhibits the necessarily partial character of all purely intellectual estimates. But there are days when we resort instinctively to an intellectual standpoint. On such days our author is excellent reading.

"Review of '*Passages from the French and Italian Note-Books of Nathaniel Hawthorne.* Boston: J. R. Osgood & Co., 1872,' " *Nation,* vol. 14, 14 March 1872, 172–73.

Mr. Hawthorne is having a posthumous productivity almost as active as that of his lifetime. Six volumes have been compounded from his private journals, an unfinished romance is doing duty as a "serial," and a number of his letters, with other personal memorials, have been given to the world. These liberal excisions from the privacy of so reserved and shade-seeking a genius suggest forcibly the general question of the proper limits of curiosity as to that passive personality of an artist of which the elements are scattered in portfolios and table-drawers. It is becoming very plain, however, that whatever the proper limits may be, the actual limits will be fixed only by a total exhaustion of matter. There is much that is very worthy and signally serviceable to art itself in this curiosity, as well as much that is idle and grossly defiant of the artist's presumptive desire to limit and define the ground of his appeal to fame. The question is really brought to an open dispute between this instinct of self-conservatism and the general fondness for squeezing an orange dry. Artists, of course, as time goes on, will be likely to take the alarm, empty their table-drawers, and level the approaches to their privacy. The critics, psychologists, and gossip-mongers may then glean amid the stubble.

Our remarks are not provoked by any visible detriment conferred on Mr. Hawthorne's fame by these recent publications. He has very fairly withstood the ordeal; which, indeed, is as little as possible an ordeal in his case, owing to the superficial character of the documents. His journals throw but little light on his personal feelings, and even less on his genius *per se.* Their general effect is difficult to express. They deepen our sense of that genius, while they singularly diminish our impression of his general intellectual power. There can be no better proof of his genius than that these common daily scribblings should unite so irresistible a charm with so little distinctive force. They represent him, judged with any real critical rigor, as superficial, uninformed, incurious, inappreciative; but from beginning to end they cast no faintest shadow upon the purity of his peculiar gift. Our own sole complaint has been not that they should have been published, but that there are not a dozen volumes more. The truth is that Mr. Hawthorne belonged to the race of magicians, and that his genius took its nutriment as insensibly—to our vision—as the flowers take the dew. He was the last man to have attempted to explain himself, and these pages offer no adequate explanation of him. They show us one of the gentlest, lightest, and most leisurely of observers, strolling at his ease among foreign sights in blessed intellectual irresponsibility, and weaving his chance impressions into a tissue as smooth as fireside gossip. Mr. Hawthorne had what belongs to genius—a style individual and delightful; he seems to have written as well for himself as he did for others—to have written from the impulse to keep up a sort of literary tradition in a career singularly devoid of the air of professional authorship; but, as regards substance, his narrative flows along in a current as fitfully diffuse and shallow as a regular correspondence with a distant friend—a friend familiar but not intimate— sensitive but not exacting. With all allowance for suppressions, his entries are never confidential; the author seems to have been reserved even with himself. They are a record of things slight and usual. Some of the facts noted are incredibly minute; they imply a peculiar *leisure* of attention. How little his journal was the receptacle of Mr. Hawthorne's deeper feelings is indicated by the fact that during a long and dangerous illness of his daughter in Rome, which he speaks of later as "a trouble that pierced into his very vitals," he never touched his pen.

These volumes of Italian notes, charming as they are, are on the whole less rich and substantial than those on England. The theme, in this case, is evidently less congenial. "As I walked by the hedges yesterday," he writes at Siena, "I could have fancied that the olive trunks were those of apple-trees, and that I were in one or other of the two lands that I love better than Italy." There are in these volumes few sentences so deeply sympathetic as that in which he declares that "of all the lovely closes that I ever beheld, that of Peterborough Cathedral is to me the most delightful; so quiet is it, so solemnly and nobly cheerful, so verdant, so sweetly shadowed, and so presided over by the stately minister and surrounded by the ancient and comely habitations of Christian men." The book is full, nevertheless, of the same spirit of serene, detached contemplation; equally full of refined and gently suggestive description. Excessively detached Mr. Hawthorne remains, from the first, from Continental life, touching it throughout mistrustfully, shrinkingly, and at the rare points at which he had, for the time, unlearnt his nationality. The few pages describing his arrival in France betray the irreconcilable foreignness of his instincts with a frank simplicity which provokes a smile. "Nothing really thrives here," he says of Paris; "man and vegetables have but an artificial life, like flowers stuck in a little mould, but never taking root." The great city had said but little to him; he was deaf to the Parisian harmonies. Just so it is under protest, as it were, that he looks at things in Italy. The strangeness, the remoteness, the Italianism of manners and objects, seem to oppress and confound him. He walks about bending a puzzled, ineffective gaze at things, full of a mild, genial desire to apprehend and penetrate, but with the light wings of his fancy just touching the surface of the massive consistency of fact about him, and with an air of good-humored confession that he is too simply an idle Yankee *flâneur* to conclude on such matters. The main impression produced by his observations is that of his simplicity. They spring not only from an unsophisticated, but from an excessively natural mind. Never, surely, was a man of literary genius less a man of letters. He looks at things as little as possible in that composite historic light which forms the atmosphere of many imaginations. There is something extremely pleasing in this simplicity, within which the character of the man rounds itself so completely and so firmly. His judgments abound in common sense; touched as they often are by fancy, they are never distorted by it. His errors and illusions never impugn his fundamental wisdom; even when (as is almost the case in his appreciation of works of art) they provoke a respectful smile, they contain some saving particle of sagacity. Fantastic romancer as he was, he here refutes conclusively the common charge that he was either a melancholy or a morbid genius. He had a native relish for the picturesque greys and browns of life; but these pages betray a childlike evenness and clearness of intellectual temper. Melancholy lies deeper than the line on which his fancy moved. Toward the end of his life, we believe, his cheerfulness gave way; but was not this in some degree owing to a final sense of the inability of his fancy to grope with fact?— fact having then grown rather portentous and overshadowing.

It was in midwinter of 1858 that Mr. Hawthorne journeyed from England to Italy. He went by sea from Marseilles to Civita Vecchia, and arrived at Rome weary, homeless, dejected, and benumbed. "Ah! that was a dismal time!" he says with a shudder, alluding to it among the happier circumstances of his second visit. His imagination, dampened and stiffened by that Roman cold of which he declares himself unable to express the malignity, seems to have been slow to perceive its opportunities. He spent his first fortnight shivering over his fire, venturing out by snatches, and longing for an abode in the tepid, stagnant, constant climate—as one may call it—of St. Peter's. There seems from the first to have been nothing inflammable in his perception of things; there was a comfortable want of *eagerness* in his mind. Little by little, however, we see him thaw and relent, and in his desultory strolls project a ray of his gentle fancy, like a gleam of autumnal American sunshine, over the churches, statues, and ruins. From the first he is admirably honest. He never pretends to be interested unless he has been really touched; and he never attempts to work himself into a worshipful glow because it is expected of a man of fancy. He has the tone of expecting very little of himself in this line, and when by chance he is pleased and excited, he records it with modest surprise. He confesses to indifference, to ignorance and weariness, with a sturdy candor which has far more dignity, to our sense, than the merely mechanical heat of less sincere spirits. Mr. Hawthorne would assent to nothing that he could not understand; his understanding on the general æsthetic line was not comprehensive; and the attitude in which he figures to the mind's eye throughout the book is that of turning away from some dusky altar-piece with a good-humored shrug, which is not in the least a condemnation of the work, but simply an admission of personal incompetency. The pictures and statues of Italy were a heavy burden upon his conscience; though indeed, in a manner, his conscience bore them lightly—it being only at the end of three months of his Roman residence that he paid his respects to the "Transfiguration," and a month later that he repaired to the Sistine Chapel. He was not, we take it, without taste; but his taste was not robust. He is "willing to accept Raphael's violin-player as a good picture"; but he prefers "Mr. Brown," the American landscapist, to Claude. He comes to the singular conclusion that "the most delicate, if not the highest, charm of a picture is evanescent, and that we continue to admire pictures prescriptively and by tradition, after the qualities that first won them their fame have vanished." The "most delicate charm" to Mr. Hawthorne was apparently simply the primal freshness and brightness of paint and varnish, and—not to put too fine a point upon it—the new gilding of the frame. "Mr. Thompson," too, shares his admiration with Mr. Brown: "I do not think there is a better painter . . . living—among Americans at least; not one so earnest, faithful, and religious in his worship of art. I had rather look at his pictures than at any, except the very old masters; and taking into consideration only the comparative pleasure to be derived, I would not except more than one or two of those." From the statues, as a general thing, he derives little profit. Every now and then he utters a word which seems to explain his indifference by the Cis-Atlantic remoteness of his point of view. He remains unreconciled to the nudity of the marbles. "I do not altogether see the necessity of our sculpturing another nakedness. Man is no longer a naked animal; his clothes are as natural to him as his skin, and we have no more right to undress him than to flay him." This is the sentiment of a man to whom sculpture was a sealed book; though, indeed, in a momentary "burst of confidence," as Mr. Dickens says, he pronounces the Pompey of the Spada Palace "worth the whole sculpture gallery of the Vatican"; and when he gets to Florence, gallantly loses his heart to the Venus de' Medici and pays generous tribute to Michael Angelo's Medicean sepulchres. He has indeed, throughout, that mark of the man of genius that he may at any moment surprise you by some extremely happy "hit," as when he detects at a glance, apparently, the want of force in Andrea del Sarto, or declares in the Florentine cathedral that "any little Norman church in England would impress me as much and more. There is something, I do not know what, but it is in the region of the heart, rather than in the intellect, that Italian architecture, of whatever age or style, never seems to reach." It is in his occasional sketches of the persons—often notabilities—whom he meets that his perception seems finest and firmest. We lack space to quote, in especial, a notice of Miss Bremer and of a little tea-party of her giving, in a modest Roman chamber overhanging the Tarpeian Rock, in which in a few kindly touches the Swedish romancer is herself suffused with the atmosphere of romance, and relegated to quaint and shadowy sisterhood with the inmates of the "House of the Seven Gables."

Mr. Hawthorne left Rome late in the spring, and travelled slowly up to Florence in the blessed fashion of the days when, seen through the open front of a crawling *vettura,* with her clamorous beggars, her black-walled mountain-towns, the unfolding romance of her landscape, Italy was seen as she really needs and deserves to be seen. Mr. Hawthorne's minute and vivid record of this journey is the most delightful portion of these volumes, and, indeed, makes well-nigh as charming a story as that of the enchanted progress of the two friends in the Marble Faun from Monte Beni to Perugia. He spent the summer in Florence—first in town, where he records many talks with Mr. Powers, the sculptor, whom he invests, as he is apt to do the persons who impress him, with a sort of mellow vividness of portraiture which deepens what is gracious in his observations, and gains absolution for what is shrewd; and afterwards at a castellated suburban villa—the original of the dwelling of his Donatello. This last fact, by the way, is a little of a disenchantment, as we had fancied that gentle hero living signorial-wise in some deeper Tuscan rurality. Mr. Hawthorne took Florence quietly and soberly—as became the summer weather; and bids it farewell in the gravity of this sweet-sounding passage, which we quote as one of many:

> "This evening I have been on the tower-top star-gazing and looking at the comet which waves along the sky like an immense feather of flame. Over Florence there was an illuminated atmosphere, caused by the lights of the city gleaming upward into the mists which sleep and dream above that portion of the valley as well of the rest of it. I saw dimly, or fancied I saw, the Hill of

Fiesole, on the other side of Florence, and remembered how ghostly lights were seen passing thence to the Duomo on the night when Lorenzo the Magnificent died. From time to time the sweet bells of Florence rang out, and I was loath to come down into the lower world, knowing that I shall never again look heavenward from an old tower-top, in such a soft calm evening as this."

Mr. Hawthorne returned to Rome in the autumn, spending some time in Siena on his way. His pictures of the strange, dark little mountain-cities of Radicofani and Bolsena, on his downward journey, are masterpieces of literary etching. It is impossible to render better that impression as of a mild nightmare which such places make upon the American traveller. "Rome certainly draws itself into my heart," he writes on his return, "as I think even London, or even Concord itself, or even old sleepy Salem never did and never will." The result of this increased familiarity was the mature conception of the romance of his "Marble Faun." He journalizes again, but at rarer intervals, though his entries retain to the last a certain appealing charm which we find it hard to define. It lies partly perhaps in what we hinted at above—in the fascination of seeing so potent a sovereign in his own fair kingdom of fantasy so busily writing himself simple, during such a succession of months, as to the dense realities of the world. Mr. Hawthorne's, however, was a rich simplicity. These pages give a strong impression of moral integrity and elevation. And, more than in other ways, they are interesting from their strong national flavor. Exposed late in life to European influences, Mr. Hawthorne was but superficially affected by them—far less so than would be the case with a mind of the same temper growing up among us to-day. We seem to see him strolling through churches and galleries as the last pure American—attesting by his shy responses to dark canvas and cold marble his loyalty to a simpler and less encumbered civilization. This image deepens that tender personal regard which it is the constant effect of these volumes to produce.

"Review of '*Italie, Sicile, Bohême: Notes de Voyage*. Par Auguste Laugel. Paris: Henri Plon; New York: F. W. Christern, 1872,' " *Nation*, vol. 16, 27 February 1873, 152.

We have always considered the observations of an intelligent traveller worth recording, even when his experience is confined to the beaten track and repeats that of innumerable others. We find something eternally fresh and delightful in all first impressions of foreign scenes, and we confess that the outpourings of even the most ingenuous tourists always strike in us a sympathetic chord. Of course these productions are very likely to be diffuse and trivial—to neglect the essential for the accidental, and to hold the minute detail so close to the eye as to conceal the general view. These are common faults with literary tourists; but M. Auguste Laugel, in his charming little volume on Italy and Bohemia, seems to us to have completely escaped them. His book is a model for travellers inclined to publish their "impressions." Brief, compact, rapid in style, and yet expansive enough to be occasionally very vivid and pictorial, it is equally free from idle detail on the one hand and pretentious generalization on the other. In the art of putting literary material into form the French certainly excel us, and M. Laugel's volume is a capital example of this accomplishment. He has selected, condensed, retouched, and harmonized with extreme taste and discretion, and the result is one of those infrequent performances in which every sentence counts and there is not a sentence too much. M. Laugel is a general observer; he appreciates and describes the picturesque aspect of things with as much force and point as if they were his especial study, and yet he constantly strikes the moral note, the note of reflection, with a felicity unusual in the devotees of the picturesque— especially in France, where these gentlemen are fond of passing for unbridled Pagans. Of the deeper thoughts—not all cheerful—suggested in Italy at every turn, he is a particularly eloquent interpreter. We have rarely found the moral impression of Naples, for instance, as happily defined as in the few lines in which he resumes it:

> "Beneath this admirable sky, before this nature with its pure forms and solemn lines, this blue sea which nothing can pollute, lives a people without ideal, indifferent to the morrow, begging, crying, gesticulating, never still, whose religion is all in feasts and images, with no art, no country, debased by absolutism and servitude, with no gods but chance and force, vile, miserable, foul in its sensuality. Can liberty ever give back the least nobleness to this degenerate race? So long as the *frutti di mare* are cheap on the quay of Santa Lucia, so long as the *improvvisatori* are there to entertain them, as there are jugglers and tumblers to make them laugh, a sun to dry their rags, music, processions, and feasts to amuse them—do they need anything more? Their life is a long laugh, a perpetual grin. From the windows of the convent of San Martino, which overhangs the city from such a height, you hear the deafening hum of this shrill street life, tumultuous as the sound of a powerful tide. The great line stretches round the vast gulf; the houses are hung upon the rocks, among *cacti,* oranges, and aloes; you must raise your eyes to the summits of Vesuvius and to the highest crests of the Somma to find a space that man has respected. And yet, go down from these heights through the crooked streets which slope away in every direction, and in this large city you will not find a corner, an asylum, a church, a palace, a work to arrest your eyes—not one that reflects in its forms and lines the admirable splendor of this beautiful sky and of this nature eternally young and fair. . . . Naples is not, like Venice, Florence, and Rome, one of the cities of the soul. You are too constantly deafened; reverie and contemplation are perpetually interrupted; you must get out on the bay or shut yourself up with the silent company of the statues; you cannot live in the past; you are too much jostled; you are overcome by the continual fever, the sterile activity, the indefatigable and idle curiosity which stir so many thousand beings."

Of Venice, too, of which everything would seem to have been said, M. Laugel says excellent things, and at the close of his chapter some very pretty ones, for which we must refer the reader to his book. Of Rome his enjoyment is keen, and his notes have many happy descriptive touches. No reader who has stood in St. Peter's but will feel how exactly the author renders, in its finer points, the sensuous impression of the place:

> "I came in with my mind full of distrust of Bernini, on the defensive; I felt myself disarmed by so much spaciousness, by this unheard of luxury, which yet looks natural and does not weary you. Brutal size here acts as an æsthetic element; the immensity envelops details, melts them, drowns them; the light plays on the fine gilded cornices, on the multicolored marbles; it comes down through the azure, as it were, of the high dome, where the saints and angels are sitting in their motionless rings; it sparkles on the gold embroideries which twine about the bronze columns of the great altar; it flashes back from the immense glory which shines like a sun in the depth of the choir. The marble pavement, without a bench or chair to disturb its perspective, stretches away like a great lake. You take pleasure, without knowing why, in this vastness, in this order so obvious, in spite of the profusion of ornaments. Immensity produces here not the impression of terror, but a sort of contentment which makes you indulgent for all the pretentious tombs, the gigantic smirking attitudinizing saints of either sex, the white marble draperies twisted and blown by the impertinent wind that comes from nowhere, for the angels thrust into every corner—cupids of Christianity! The luxury is all so ample, so grandiose, so joyous! The sun comes in by the broad openings, and its rays, glancing back in every direction from polished angles, glittering mouldings, precious stones, and the gold of the mosaics, forms a sort of aureole which seems to lift and sustain the immense pillars and the colossal vaults. This formidable luxury, which exceeds all private or princely fortunes, has nothing which shocks or astonishes; you feel here none of the terrors and the sublime anxieties of Gothic art; you are far, too, from the robust and sombre simplicity of the basilicas; you assist at the definitive triumph of Catholicism—at its apotheosis."

The longest section is devoted to Sicily, where we are unable to compare impressions with the author. But this picture of the beauty and the misery of this once imperial island, its shrines and temples, its mountains and sea, its almost cruelly smiling nature, and its helpless and hopeless humanity, is forcible enough to beguile us into a half-sense of knowledge. His whole account of the ruined temples is admirable; it is that at once of an artist and a scholar. The author's errand in Bohemia was to visit the battlefields of the Seven Weeks' War—in distinguished company; that of the Orleans princes. We have sometimes fancied our intellect impenetrable to all allusions to military movements; but we have almost understood M. Laugel's. The tone of the whole book is grave, we might almost say melancholy. The reader may judge by the closing paragraph, suggested by a glance at some of the great Frederic's scenes of victory:

> "And yet for what strange heroes history works! Providence, the unknown God, has taken for his representative the old King of Prussia, and given a revolutionary task to a born enemy of the Revolution! What a jest is history, if

you look only at the outside—at the stage-setting! But there is a secret, terrible force which sets in motion all the gods and demi-gods of the earth; an unconscious force tending as a still more unconscious force drives it; history is an ordered succession of chances; it moves always towards something necessary; it uses everything, tribunes and kings, monarchies and republics, barbarism and civilization. Whither is it leading us? Whither is aged, worn-out Europe going? Whither our Latin races? Whither France, so vile and so charming, so cunning and so easy to cheat, so full of hatred and of sweetness, so brave and timid, so unjust to those who have loved her, so generous to those who have injured; insane nation, loved and hated, sole of her kind, who may be vanquished but not equalled, mastered but not subdued, who bids defiance to all measurement by the suppleness of her elusive and ungoverned genius? She is not only inconstant; she is tormented with a sort of perverse logic, which demonstrates to her the falsity of all things. Between all things and herself she places her mocking doubt and her incurable irony."

."Review of '*Days Near Rome*. By Augustus J. C. Hare. Two volumes. Philadelphia: Porter & Coates, 1875,' " *Nation,* vol. 20, 1 April 1875, 229.

Both Mr. Hare's subject, which is one of the most charming possible, and the great popularity of his 'Walks in Rome,' will assure his present work a general welcome. Ever since he had announced, in the preface to the 'Walks,' that it was in preparation, we had been eagerly impatient for it; and, on the whole, we have not been disappointed. He depends rather more than may seem desirable on other people to convey his impressions, and rather less upon himself; that is, he is a compiler rather than a describer. His own powers of description, though not brilliant, are always agreeable, and he might with advantage more frequently trust to them. His present work is, with modifications, fashioned in the same manner as the 'Walks'; the text constantly alternating with quotations from other writers. It was noticeable in the 'Walks' that almost every one who had written with any conspicuity about anything else in the world, had also written something about Rome that could be made to pass muster as an "extract." The extracts were sometimes rather trivial, but taken together they made an extremely entertaining book. The outlying towns and districts of the old Papal Dominion have lain less in the beaten track of literature, and the process of collecting pertinent anecdotes, allusions, descriptions, must have been a good deal more laborious. Mr. Hare has followed a very happy line. His book is meant for the average Anglo-Saxon tourist, who is usually not brimming with native erudition, and he reproduces a great many things which are probably familiar to the learned (though of which even the learned can afford to be reminded), but in which most people will find much of the freshness of unsuspected lore. He is abundant (as is quite right) in his quotations from the Latin poets—from Horace, Virgil, Ovid, and Juvenal. The smallest pretext for quoting from Horace—the most quotable of the ancients—should always be cultivated. For the rest, his tributaries have chiefly been the modern (English, German, and French) historians and antiquarians; to which it should be added, that his own share of the text is much more liberal than in the 'Walks.' In Mr. Hare's place, we should have treated the reader to rather less of Herr

Gregorovius, the German historian and tourist, for this writer possesses in excess the deplorable German habit of transforming, in description, the definite into the vague. Unfortunately, he seems to have penetrated into the most deliciously out-of-the-way nooks and corners, and his testimony about various charming places is the best that offers.

The author has thoroughly explored the field, and left no mossy stone unturned which might reveal some lurking treasure of picturesqueness. The volume represents in this way no small amount of good-natured submission to dire discomfort. It is true that the inspiration and the reward were great, and that there is no bed one would not lie down upon, no tavern fare he would not contrive to swallow, for the sake of a few hours in such places as Norma and Ninfa, Anagno or Sutri. The Alban and Sabine, the Ciminian and Volscian hills, the romantic Abruzzi, the Pontine Marshes, the Etruscan treasures of Cervetri and Corneto, the nearer towns along the railway to Florence, the direction of the Neapolitan railway as far as Monte Cassino—this great treasure-ground of antiquities and curiosities, of the picturesque in history, in scenery, in population, has been minutely inspected by Mr. Hare. Many of the places have long been among the regular excursions from Rome; others had to be discovered, to be reached in such scrambling fashion as might be, to be put into relation, after drowsy intervals, with the outer world. The author now tells us in detail the ways and means for following in his footsteps, and gives us valuable practical advice. He has made a great deal of delightful experience easier, but we hardly know whether to thank him. We see the mighty annual herd of tourists looming up behind him, and we sigh over the kindly obscurity that he has dispelled. It was thanks to their being down in no guide-book that he found many of the places he describes so charming; but he breaks the charm, even while he commemorates it, and he inaugurates the era of invasion. He has done a good work, but we should think that he must feel at times as if he had assumed a heavy responsibility. He makes in his opening pages a vivid and dismal statement of what the new régime means in Rome itself in the way of ruin of the old picturesqueness—a fact that had a perfectly substantial value which it is as culpable to underestimate as to exaggerate. But it is really a melancholy fact that he himself will have introduced a new régime into the strange, quaint places of the Volscians. The utmost that we can hope is that it will establish itself slowly.

"Review of '*Cities of Northern and Central Italy*. By Augustus J. C. Hare. In three volumes. New York: George Routledge & Sons, 1876,' " *Nation*, vol. 22, 10 May 1876, 325–26.

Mr. Hare has already earned the gratitude of tourists by his two elaborate compilations—the 'Walks in Rome' and the 'Days Near Rome,' and the work before us will add largely to the obligations felt by that numerous class of travellers who find their Murray and their Baedeker dry and meagre, and yet have not time or means for making researches. If the 'Cities of Italy' (like its immediate predecessor) is not such entertaining reading as the 'Walks in Rome,' this is not the fault of the author, who appears to have been equally zealous and careful; it is explained simply by the fact that no place in Italy, and no combination of places, is so interesting as

Rome, and that the fund of quotable matter which Mr. Hare had to draw from is in this case very much less rich. Every one who has written at all (and who at the same time has been a traveller) seemed, by the testimony of Mr. Hare's pages, to have recorded some impression or some memory of Rome, and the subject, for the moment at least, has always made the writers vivid and eloquent. It was therefore easy, comparatively speaking, to make up a book very largely of quotations. Mr. Hare still follows the same system—that of giving himself the mere facts and directions, and letting some one else speak for him in matters of opinion and description. He has had some trouble, we imagine, in drumming up his authorities in the present case, and he has admitted a few rather ragged recruits. It is rather a shock to the discriminating reader's faith in his guide to find him offering us the spurious rhapsodies of "Ouida" and the flimsy observations of Alexandre Dumas. The author might have trusted himself a little more. The 'Walks in Rome' was for all practical uses a guide-book, but it was also very possible to read it continuously at a distance from the localities. Few readers will be tempted to follow this course with the volumes before us—their guide-book quality is much less mitigated. The extracts from other books, though always sufficiently pertinent, are rarely very entertaining *per se,* and the author's own text consists mainly of enumerations and catalogues.

Mr. Hare's first volume treats of the Rivieras, Piedmont, and Lombardy; the second, of Venice, Bologna, the cities of the upper Adriatic, and those of Tuscany north of Florence; and the third, of Florence, the minor Tuscan cities, and those which lie along the road to Rome. All this is very complete and exhaustive, and the author has taken pains to acquaint himself with places that are rarely visited. We wish, indeed, that he had devoted to some of these obscurer lurking-places of the picturesque a portion of the large space he has allotted to Venice and Florence. Murray's hand-book for France contains no account of Paris, on the ground that it is so well described elsewhere; and on some such principle as this Mr. Hare might have neglected the cities we have mentioned in the interest of certain by-ways and unvisited nooks. Mr. Hare would be very sorry, however, to take example in any respect by Murray, for whom he appears to cherish a vigorous contempt. This sentiment is on some grounds well-deserved—chiefly on that of the antiquated tone and exploded instructions of the great father of guide-books; but a generous tourist, it seems to us, should remember that Murray was a precursor in days when the tourist's lot was not so easy a one as now, and that he has smoothed the path for those who, thanks in a measure to his exertions, are in a position to cavil at him. But, as we say, Mr. Hare is extremely thorough—his excursions to places so off the beaten track (and in one case indeed so inaccessible) as Bobbio and Canossa are good examples of his determination to be complete. His volumes have been to us an eloquent reminder of the inexhaustible charm and interest of Italy, and of her unequalled claims to our regard as the richest museum in the world. It may cost us some pangs to see her treated more and more as a museum simply, and overrun with troops of more or less idly-gazing foreigners—a state of things which such publications as Mr. Hare's do much to confirm and encourage; but we are obliged to make the best of what we cannot prevent, and confine ourselves to wishing that, since Italy is to be "vulgarized" beyond appeal, the thing may be done with as much good taste as possible. To this good taste Mr. Hare very successfully ministers. He has evidently a passionate affection for Italy, as regards which some of his readers will profess a strong fellow-feeling, and though he opens the gate wider still to the terrible tourist-brood, he recommends no ways of dealing with the country that are inconsistent with a delicate appreciation of it. He has in his Introduction some very good general remarks as to what the traveller is to expect, and the way in which he is to conduct himself. He says, very justly, that the great beauty of the country is beauty of detail. "Compare most of her buildings in their entirety with similar buildings in England, much more in France and Germany, and they will be found very inferior. There is no castle in Italy of the importance of Raby or Alnwick; and, with the sole exception of Caprarola, there is no private palace so fine as Hatfield, Burleigh, or Longleat. There is no ruin half so beautiful as Tintern or Rievaux. There is no cathedral so stately as Durham, Lincoln, or Salisbury," etc. (This last statement obviously requires modification.) But "in almost every alley of every quiet country town," Mr. Hare continues, "the past lives still in some lovely statuette, some exquisite wreath of sculptured foliage, or some slight but delicate fresco—a variety of beauty which no English architect or sculptor has ever dreamed of." On the other hand, we think that the author goes too far when he says that the beauty of Italy is almost exclusively the beauty of her towns—that fine scenery is rare. He enumerates a small number of "show" districts—the Rivieras, the Lakes, the line of the railroad from Florence to Rome (together with the neighborhood of the former city), and appears to think that he has exhausted the list. But the truth is that all the scenery of Italy is *fine,* in the literal sense of the word—it is all delicate and full of expression—all exquisite in quality. Even where the elements are tame, outline and color always make a picture—the eyes need never be idle. The towns in Italy certainly deserve every admiring thing that can be said about them, but the landscape in which they are set is at least worthy of them. Mr. Hare has the good taste to like the Italian character, and to deprecate the brutal manners, in dealing with it, inculcated by Murray—especially that "making your bargain beforehand" which appears to be the sum of Murray's practical wisdom. "Never make your bargain beforehand," says Mr. Hare; "it is only an offensive exhibition of mistrust by which you gain nothing from a people who are peculiarly sensitive to any expression of confidence." We do not hesitate to pronounce this sound advice, and to admire, with the author, that sweetness of disposition which is proof against the irritation so plentifully provoked by the usual conduct of tourists. "The horrible ill-breeding of our countrymen never struck me more than one day at Porlezza. A clean, pleasing Italian woman had arranged a pretty little café near the landing-place. The Venetian blinds kept out the burning sun; the deal tables were laid with snowy linen; the brick floor was scoured till not a speck of dust remained. The diligences arrived, and a crowd of English and American women rushed in while waiting for the boat, thought they would have some lemonade, then thought they would not, shook out the dust from their clothes, brushed themselves with the padrona's brushes, laid down their dirty travelling-bags on all the clean table-cloths, chattered and scolded for half an hour, declaimed upon the miseries of Italian travel, ordered nothing and paid for nothing, and, when the steamers arrived, flounced out without even a syllable of thanks or recognition. No wonder that the woman said her own pigs would have behaved better." We differ, however, from Mr. Hare in the estimation in which we hold Italian unity, and the triumph of what he never alludes to but as the "Sardinian Government." He deplores the departure of the little ducal courts, thinks Italy had no need to be united, and never mentions the new order of things without a sneer. His tone strikes us as very childish. Certainly the "Sardinians" have destroyed the picturesque old walls of Florence, and increased—very heavily—the taxes, but it is a very petty view of matters that cannot perceive that these are but regrettable incidents in a great general gain. It is certainly something that Italy has been made a nation, with a voice in the affairs of Europe (to say nothing of her own, for the first time), and able to offer her admirable people (if they will choose to take it) an opportunity to practise some of those responsible civic virtues which it can do no harm even to the gifted Italians to know something about. But on this subject Mr. Hare is really rabid; in a writer who loves Italy as much as he does, his state of mind is an incongruity. It is a small defect, however, in a very useful and valuable work.

General Bibliography

Ambrosetti, G., et al. *I Cattolici e il Risorgimento*. Rome: Editrice Studium, 1963.

Anderson, Charles R. *Person, Place, and Thing in Henry James's Novels*. Durham, N.C.: Duke University Press, 1977.

Andreae, Bernard. *The Art of Rome*. Translated by Robert Erich Wolf. New York: Harry N. Abrams, 1977.

Andreola, Amina. *Veio*. Florence: Istituto Geografia Militare, 1966.

[Anon.] *Il Castello di Vincigliata e I Suoi Contorni*. Florence: Tipografia del Vocabolario, 1871.

Aria, Mrs. [Eliza], compiler. *The May Book, in Aid of Charing Cross Hospital*. London: Macmillan, 1901.

Armellini, Mariano. *Le Chiese di Roma: Dal Secolo IV al XIX*. Rome: Edizioni del Pasquino, 1982. ["Ristampa della seconda edizione del 1891."]

Baedeker, Karl. *Central Italy and Rome*. Leipzig: Baedeker, 1909.

———. *Italy: Handbook for Travellers. Third Part. Southern Italy and Sicily*. Leipzig: Karl Baedeker, 1903.

———. *Italien: Handbuch für Reisende von Baedeker. Erster Theil: Ober-Italien*. Leipzig: Verlag Von Karl Baedeker, 1882.

————. *Paris and Its Environs,* 6th ed. Leipzig: Karl Baedeker, 1878.

————. *Paris and Northern France,* 2d ed. Koblenz: Karl Baedeker, 1867.

————. *Switzerland,* 6th ed. Koblenz: Karl Baedeker, 1873.

Baker, Paul R. *The Fortunate Pilgrims: Americans in Italy: 1800–1860.* Cambridge, Mass.: Harvard University Press, 1964.

Bandinelli, Ranuccio Bianchi. *Rome: The Center of Power, 500 B.C. to A.D. 200.* New York: George Braziller, 1970.

Barcham, William L. *The Imaginary View Scenes of Antonio Canaletto.* New York: Garland, 1977.

Barine, Arvède [Louise-Cécile Bouffé]. *Alfred de Musset.* Paris: Hachette, 1893.

Barroero, Liliana, ed. *Guide Rionali di Roma. Rione I—Monti.* 4 vols. Rome: [Fratelli Palombi], 1978–84.

Barzini, Luigi. *The Europeans.* New York: Simon and Schuster, 1983.

————. *The Italians.* New York: Bantam, 1964.

Bassi, Elena. *Palazzi di Venezia.* Venice: La Stamperia di Venezia Editrice, 1976.

Battilana, Marilla. *English Writers of Venice: Scrittori inglesi e Venezia, 1350–1950.* Venice: La Stamperia di Venezia Editrice, 1981.

————. "Sei personaggi in cerca di nome." *Ateneo Veneto,* X, 10 (1972): 217–30.

————. *Venezia: Sfondo e simbolo nella narrativa di Henry James.* Milan: Laboratorio delle Arti, 1987.

Becchetti, Piero, and Carlo Pietrangeli. *Un inglese fotografo a Roma: Robert Macpherson.* Rome: Edizioni Quasar, 1987.

Belli-Barsali, I. *Ville di Roma: Lazio I.* Milan: Edizioni Sisar, 1970.

Beny, Roloff, and Peter Gunn. *The Churches of Rome.* New York: Simon and Schuster, 1981.

Berenson, Bernard. *The Venetian Painters of the Renaissance.* New York: G. P. Putnam's Sons, 1894.

————. *The Central Italian Painters of the Renaissance,* 2d ed. New York: G. P. Putnam's Sons, 1897 [1908].

Bernardini, A., and A. Castri. *Cortona: Guida Turistica.* Arezzo: ENTE Provinciale Turismo, 1951.

Berti, Luciano, Bianca Bellardoni, and Eugenio Battisti. *Angelo a San Marco.* Rome: Armando Curcio Editore, 1965.

Binni, Lanfranco. *Arte in Italia: Guida ai Luoghi ed alle Opere dell'Italia Artistica.* Milan: Electa, 1983.

Blunt, Anthony. *Guide to Baroque Rome.* London: Granada, 1982.

Borsook, Eve. *The Companion Guide to Florence.* London: Collins, 1966.

Bortolotti, Landa. *Siena.* Rome and Bari: Editori Laterza, 1983.

Bourget, Paul. *Un Saint.* New York: Huibland et Meyer, 1893. Originally published in *Nouveaux Pastels,* Paris: Lemerre, 1891.

————. *A Saint.* Translated by Katherine Prescott Wormely. Boston: Roberts, 1895.

————. *Sensations d'Italie.* Paris: A. Lemerre, 1891.

Brooks, Van Wyck. *The Dream of Arcadia: American Writers and Artists in Italy, 1760–1915.* New York: Dutton, 1958.

Brown, David Alan. *Leonardo's "Last Supper": The Restoration.* Washington, D.C.: National Gallery of Art, 1983.

————. *Raphael and America.* Washington, D.C.: National Gallery of Art, 1983.

Brown, Horatio. *Venice: An Historical Sketch of the Republic.* London: Percival, 1893.

Callari, Luigi. *I Palazzi di Roma,* 3d ed. Rome: Apollon, 1944.

————. *Le Ville di Roma.* Rome: Libreria di Scienze e Lettere, 1934.

Carpeggiani, Paolo. *Itinerari per l'Emilia Romagna.* Rome: Editoriale l'Espresso, 1982.

Caterbi, Giuseppe. *La Chiesa di S. Onofrio in Roma.* N.p.: Tipografia Forense, 1858.

Chastel, André. *Studios and Styles of the Italian Renaissance.* Translated by Jonathan Griffin. New York: Odyssey, 1966.

Clark, Kenneth. *The Nude: A Study in Ideal Form.* Garden City, N.Y.: Doubleday Anchor, 1959.

————. *Piero della Francesca,* 2d ed., revised. London and New York: Phaidon, 1969 [1951].

Coccanari, Gustavo. *Tivoli: Itinerario storico, archeologico.* Tivoli: Aldo Chicca, 1951.

Coffin, David. *The Villa D'Este at Tivoli.* Princeton: Princeton University Press, 1960.

Constable, W. G. *Canaletto: Giovanni Antonio Canal: 1697–1768.* 2 vols. Oxford: Clarendon, 1976.

Coxe, Harvey. *Picture of Italy.* London: Sherwood, Neely, and Jones, 1815.

Crowe, J. A., and G. B. Cavalcaselle. *A New History of Painting in Italy.* 3 vols. London: John Murray, 1864; facsimile rpt., New York: Garland, 1980.

Dantier, Alphonse. *Monastères bénédictins d'Italie: Souvenirs d'un voyage littéraire au delà des Alpes.* Paris: Didier, 1866.

Davis, Richard Harding, et al. *The Great Streets of the World.* New York: Scribner's, 1892.

D'Azeglio, Massimo. *I Miei Ricordi,* 5th ed. 2 vols. Florence: G. Barbèra, 1871.

de Brosses, Charles. *Lettres Historiques et Critiques sur L'Italie.* 3 vols. Paris: Ponthieu an VII, 1799.

de Mazade, Charles. *The Life of Count Cavour.* New York: G. P. Putnam's, 1877.

De Seta, Cesare. *Capri: Con una guida ai monumenti.* Turin: ERI, 1983.

Douglas, Norman. *Capri: Materials for the Description of the Island.* Florence: G. Oriol, 1930. ["The Lost Literature of Capri," originally published in July 1906.]

————. *Siren Land.* London: Martin Secker, 1911.

————. *South Wind.* London: Martin Secker, 1917.

Dussler, Luitpold. *Raphael: A Critical Catalogue of His Pictures, Wall-paintings, and Tapestries.* London and New York: Phaidon, 1971.

Eastlake, Sir Charles L., ed. *[Murray's] Handbook of Painting: The Italian Schools,* 3d ed. From the German of [F.] Kugler, by a Lady. 2 vols. London: John Murray, 1855.

Edel, Leon. *Henry James: The Untried Years: 1843–1870, Henry James: The Conquest of London: 1870–1881, Henry James: The Middle Years: 1882–1895,*

Henry James: The Treacherous Years: 1895–1901, Henry James: The Master: 1901–1916. 5 vols. Philadelphia: J. B. Lippincott, 1953–72.

———. *Henry James: A Life.* New York: Harper & Row, 1985.

———, and Dan H. Laurence. Revised with the Assistance of James Rambeau. *A Bibliography of Henry James,* 3d ed. Oxford: Clarendon Press, 1982.

Enciclopedia Italiana. 35 vols. Milan: Istituto Giovanni Treccani, 1956.

Encyclopedia Britannica, 11th ed. 29 vols. New York: Encyclopedia Britannica, 1910.

Fantozzi, Micali and Piero Roselli. *Le Soppressioni dei Conventi a Firenze: Riuso e trasformazioni dal sec. XVIII in poi.* Florence: Libreria Editrice Fiorentina, 1980.

Feydeau, M. Ernest. *L'Allemagne en 1871, impressions de voyage.* Paris: M. Lévy, 1872.

Fiengo, Giuseppe. *Gaeta: Monumenti e Storia Urbanistica.* Naples: Edizioni Scientifiche Italiane, 1971.

Forlati, Ferdinando. *S. Giorgio Maggiore: Il complesso monumentale e i suoi restauri (1951–1956).* Padua: Antoniani, 1977.

Forsyth, Joseph. *Remarks on Antiquities, Arts, and Letters During an Excursion in Italy in the Years 1802 and 1803,* 2d ed. London: John Murray, 1816.

Francini Ciaranfi, Anna Maria. *Pitti: Firenze.* Novara: Istituto Geografico de Agostini, 1971.

Franzoi, Umberto e Dina Di Stefano. *Le Chiese di Venezia.* Venice: Alfieri, 1976.

Frenkel, Wladimiro. *Capri.* Torre del Greco: H. Bernard-Frenkel, 1928.

———. *Ischia: L'Isola e Le Sue Sorgenti Termali.* Torre del Greco: H. Bernard-Frenkel, 1924.

Fumagalli, G., ed. *Piccola Enciclopedia Hoepli,* 2d ed. 3 vols. Milan: Ulrico Hoepli, 1917–27.

Gale, Robert L. "Henry James and Italy." *Studi Americani* 3 (1957): 189–204.

Gardner, Edmund G. *The Story of Siena and San Gimignano.* London: J. M. Dent, 1902; Nendeln-Liechtenstein: Kraus Reprint, 1971.

Gautier, Théophile. *Italia.* Paris: Victor Lecou, 1852.

———. *Journeys in Italy.* Translated by Daniel B. Vermilye. New York: Brentanos, 1902.

Gibbon, Edward. *The History of the Decline and Fall of the Roman Empire.* Edited by J. B. Bury. 7 vols. London: Methuen, 1909.

Giorcelli, Cristina. *Henry James e l'Italia.* Rome: Edizioni di Storia e Letteratura, 1968.

Giuliano, Antonio, ed. *Museo Nazionale Romano: Le Sculture. I:5. I Marmi Ludovisi nel Museo Nazionale Romano.* Rome: De Luca Editore, 1983.

Goethe, J. W. *Italian Journey (1786–1788).* Translated by W. H. Auden and Elizabeth Mayer. San Francisco: North Point Press, 1982.

Gould, Cecil. *The Sixteenth-Century Venetian School.* London: National Gallery, 1959.

La Grande Encyclopédie. 16 vols. Paris: Lamirault, [n.d.].

Gregorovius, Ferdinand. *Diari Romani.* Milan, 1885.

————. *Figuren. Geschichte, Leben und Scenerie aus Italien* [*Wanderjahre in Italien.*]. Leipzig: Brodhaus, 1864.

Guida ai Misteri e Segreti del Lazio. Milan: SUGAR Editore, 1969.

Guida ai Misteri e Segreti di Roma. Milan: SUGAR Editore, 1968.

Guido, Margaret. *Southern Italy: An Archaeological Guide—the Main Prehistoric, Greek and Roman Sites.* London: Faber and Faber, 1972.

Halperin, S. William. *Italy and the Vatican at War: A Study of Their Relationships from the Outbreak of the Franco-Prussian War to the Death of Pius IX.* Chicago: University of Chicago Press, 1939.

Hare, Augustus J. C. *Cities of Northern and Central Italy.* 3 vols. London: Daldy, Isbister & Company, 1876.

————. *Cities of Southern Italy and Sicily.* London: George Routledge & Sons, [188–].

————. *Days Near Rome.* 2 vols. London: Daldy, Isbister & Company, 1875.

————. *Florence.* London: George Routledge, [1884].

————. *Walks in Rome,* 3d ed. London: Strahan & Co., 1872.

————. *Venice.* London: Smith, Elder, & Co., 1884.

Harrier, Richard C. " 'Very Modern Rome'—An Unpublished Essay of Henry James," *Harvard Library Bulletin* (Spring 1954): 125–40.

Hartt, Frederick. *History of Italian Renaissance Art.* Englewood Cliffs, N.J.: Prentice-Hall and New York: Harry N. Abrams, 1970.

Hawthorne, Nathaniel. *The Marble Faun: or, the Romance of Monte Beni.* Edited by William Charvat, Roy Harvey Pearce, and Claude M. Simpson. Columbus: Ohio State University Press, 1968.

————. *Nathaniel Hawthorne: The French and Italian Notebooks.* Edited by Thomas Woodson. Columbus: Ohio State University Press, 1980.

————. *Nathaniel Hawthorne: The Letters, 1843–1853.* Eds. Thomas Woodson, L. Neal Smith, and Norman Holmes Pearson. Columbus: Ohio State University Press, 1985.

Hayum, Andrée. *Giovanni Antonio Bazzi—"Il Sodoma."* New York: Garland Press, 1976.

Heywood, William, and Lucy Olcott. *Guide to Siena: History and Art,* 4th ed. Siena: Libreria Editrice Senese, 1924.

Honour, Hugh. *The Companion Guide to Venice.* London: Collins, 1965.

Horner, Susan, and Joanna Horner. *Walks in Florence and Its Environs.* 2 vols. London: Smith, Elder, & Co., 1873.

"How the Palazzo Dandolo became the Danieli Hotel." Milan: Grafiche Francesco Ghezzi, 1985. [Publicity brochure.]

Howells, William Dean. *Italian Journeys.* New York: Hurd & Houghton, 1867.

————. *Venetian Life.* London: N. Trübner & Co., 1866; New York: Hurd and Houghton, 1866.

Huelsen, Christian Carl Friedrich. *Le chiese di Roma nel medioevo, cataloghi et appunti.* Florence: L. S. Olschki, 1927.

Huetter, Luigi, and Emilio Lavagnino. *S. Onofrio al Gianicolo.* Rome: Marietta: 1934.

Humfrey, Peter. *Cima da Conegliano.* Cambridge: Cambridge University Press, 1983.

Hunt, Leigh. *The Autobiography of Leigh Hunt.* Edited by Roger Ingpen. 2 vols. Westminster: Archibald Constable, 1903.

Hutton, Edward. *Ravenna: A Study.* London: J. M. Dent & Sons, 1913.

James, Henry. *The American Scene.* With an Introduction by W. H. Auden. New York: Charles Scribner's Sons, 1946.

———. *The Art of the Novel.* Edited by R. P. Blackmur. New York: Charles Scribner's Sons, 1934.

———. *The Art of Travel.* Edited by Morton Dauwen Zabel. Garden City, N.Y.: Doubleday, 1958.

———. *Autobiography: A Small Boy and Others. Notes of a Son and Brother. The Middle Years.* Edited by Frederick Dupee. New York: Criterion Books, 1956.

———. *The Complete Notebooks of Henry James.* Edited with introductions and notes by Leon Edel and Lyall H. Powers. New York: Oxford University Press, 1987.

———. *Foreign Parts.* Leipzig: Bernard Tauchnitz, 1883.

———. *Hawthorne.* London: Macmillan, 1879.

———. *Henry James Letters.* 4 vols. Edited by Leon Edel. Cambridge, Mass.: Harvard University Press, 1974–84.

———. *Italian Hours.* London: William Heinemann, 1909.

———. *Italian Hours.* Boston and New York: Houghton Mifflin Company, 1909.

———. *Literary Criticism: Essays on Literature, American Writers, English Writers.* Edited by Leon Edel with Mark Wilson. New York: Library of America, 1984.

———. *Literary Criticism: Essays on Literature, French Writers, Other European Writers, The Prefaces to the New York Edition.* Edited by Leon Edel with Mark Wilson. New York: Library of America, 1984.

———. *The Painter's Eye: Notes and Essays on the Pictorial Arts.* Edited by John L. Sweeney. London: Rupert Hart Davis, 1956.

———. *Portraits of Places.* London: Macmillan, 1883.

———. *The Scenic Art: Notes on Acting and Drama, 1892–1901.* Edited by Allan Wade. New Brunswick, N.J.: Rutgers University Press, 1948.

———. "Swiss Notes," *Nation,* vol. 15, 12 September 1872, 183–84.

———. *Transatlantic Sketches.* Boston: James R. Osgood, 1875.

———. *William Wetmore Story and His Friends.* 2 vols. Boston: Houghton, Mifflin & Co., 1903.

Jameson, Mrs. [Anna Brownell Murphy]. *Legends of the Madonna, as Represented in the Fine Arts.* London: Longman, Brown, Green, and Longmans, 1852.

———. *Legends of the Monastic Orders, as Represented in the Fine Arts.* London: Longman, Brown, Green, and Longmans, 1850.

———. *Memoirs of Early Italian Painters, and the Progress of Painting in Italy: Cimabue to Bassano.* London: C. Knight and Co., 1845.

Johnston-Lavis, H. J. *The Earthquake of Ischia.* London: Dulau & Co., 1885.

Klaczko, Julian. *Rome and the Renaissance: The Pontificate of Julius II.* Translated by John Dennie. New York: G. P. Putnam's Sons, 1903.

Krautheimer, Richard. *The Rome of Alexander VII, 1655–1667.* Princeton: Princeton University Press, 1985.

Lanciani, Rodolfo. *Wandering in the Roman Campagna.* London: Constable, 1909.

Lauritzen, Peter, and Alexander Zielcke. *Palaces of Venice.* Oxford: Phaidon, 1978.

Lepschy, Anna Laura. *Tintoretto Observed: A Documentary Survey of Critical Reaction from the Sixteenth to the Twentieth Century.* Ravenna: Longo, 1983.

Leslie, Charles Robert. *Handbook for Young Painters.* London: John Murray, 1855.

Lightbown, Ronald. *Sandro Botticelli: Complete Catalogue.* London: Paul Elek, 1978.

Lindsay, Lord [Alexander William Crawford Lindsay]. *Sketches of the History of Christian Art.* London: J. Murray, 1847.

Longhi, Roberto. *Piero della Francesca (1927) con aggiunte fino al 1962,* new ed. Florence: Sansoni, 1975.

Lorenzetti, Guilio. *Venice and Its Lagoon.* Rome: Istituto Poligrafico dello Stato, 1961.

Lucas, John. "Manliest of Cities: The Image of Rome in Henry James." *Studi Americani* 11 (1965): 117–36.

Lugano, O.S.B., P. Placido. *S. Maria Nova (S. Francesca Romana).* Rome: Casa Editrice "Roma," 1923.

Luxoro, Maria. *Il Palazzo Vendramin-Calergi ("Non Nobis, Domine . . .").* Florence: Olschki, 1957.

Lyall, Archibald. *The Companion Guide to Tuscany.* London: Collins, 1973.

Macadam, Alta. *Florence (The Blue Guide).* London: Ernest Benn, 1982.

———. *Rome and Environs (The Blue Guide).* London: A. & C. Black, 1985.

MacDonald, Bonney. *Henry James's "Italian Hours": Revelatory and Resistant Impressions.* Ann Arbor and London: UMI Research Press, 1990.

Mancini, Gioacchino. *Hadrian's Villa and Villa D'Este,* 9th English ed. Rome: Istituto Poligrafico dello Stato, 1976.

Marchini, Giuseppe. *Filippo Lippi.* Milan: Electa Editrice, 1975.

Mariani, Umberto. "L'esperienza italiana di Henry James." *Studi Americani* 6 (1960): 221–52.

Mariéton, Paul. *Une Histoire d'Amour: Les Amants de Venise, George Sand et Musset.* Paris: Harvard fils, 1897.

Marmori, Franco. *Itinerari per la Liguria.* Rome: Editoriale L'Espresso, 1982.

Massé, Domenico. *Cattolici e Risorgimento.* Rome: Edizioni Paolini, 1961.

Matthiae, G. *Ss. Cosma e Damiano.* Rome: Marietti, 1960.

Maurois, André. *Lélia: The Life of George Sand.* Translated by Gerard Hopkins. New York: Harper and Bros., 1953.

Maves, Carl. *Sensuous Pessimism: Italy in the Work of Henry James.* Bloomington: Indiana University Press, 1973.

Meiss, Millard. *Painting in Florence and Siena after the Black Death.* Princeton: Princeton University Press, 1951.

Melchiori, Barbara e Giorgio. *Il Gusto di Henry James.* Turin: Giulio Einaudi, editore, 1974.

Menegazzi, Luigi. *Cima da Conegliano.* Treviso: Canova, 1981.

Minisci, Teodoro. *Santa Maria di Grottaferrata: La Chiesa e il Monastero.* Grottaferrata (Rome): Breve Monografia, 1976.

Monmarché, Marcel. *Savoie.* Paris: Librairie Hachette, 1934.

Moore, Rayburn S., ed. *Selected Letters of Henry James to Edmund Gosse: 1882–
1915. A Literary Friendship.* Baton Rouge: Louisiana State University Press,
1988.

Müller, Adalbert. *Venise: Ses Trésors Artistiques.* Venice: Ongania Münster, 1875.

Munthe, Axel. *The Story of San Michele.* New York: Dutton, 1929.

Murray, John [publisher]. *A Handbook for Travellers in Central Italy,* 7th ed. London: John Murray, 1867.

———. *A Handbook for Travellers in Central Italy,* 8th ed. London: John Murray,
1874.

———. *A Handbook for Travellers in Switzerland,* 12th ed. London: John Murray,
1867.

———. *A Handbook of Rome and Its Environs,* 8th ed. London: John Murray,
1867.

———. *A Handbook of Rome and Its Environs,* 11th ed. London: John Murray,
1873.

———. *A Handbook of Rome and Its Environs,* 12th ed. London: John Murray,
1875.

———. *A Handbook of Rome and Its Environs,* 13th ed. London: John Murray,
1881.

———. *A Handbook of Rome and Its Environs,* 15th ed. London: John Murray,
1894.

———. *A Handbook of Rome and the Campagna,* 16th ed. London: John Murray,
1899.

———. *A Handbook of Rome and the Campagna,* 17th ed. London: John Murray,
1908 [1909].

Napoli e Dintorni. Milan: Touring Club Italiano, 1970.

New Catholic Encyclopedia. New York: McGraw Hill, 1967.

Nibby, A. *Analisi Storico-Topografico-Antiquaria della Carta dei Dintorni di Roma,*
2d ed. 3 vols. Rome: Tipografia delle belle arti, 1848.

Niebuhr, Barthold Georg. *The History of Rome.* 3 vols. Translated by Julius Charles
Hare. Cambridge: J. Taylor, 1828–42. (First edition, *Römische Geschichte.*
Berlin, 1811–12).

Norton, Charles Eliot. *Notes of Travel and Study in Italy.* Boston: Ticknor and
Fields, 1859.

Osmaston, F. P. B. *The Paradise of Tintoretto.* Bognore, Sussex: Pear Tree, 1910.

Owen, Felicity, and David Blagney Brown. *Collector of Genius: A Life of Sir George
Beaumont.* New Haven and London: Yale University Press, 1988.

Pallucchini, Rodolfo, and Paola Rossi. *Tintoretto: Le opere sacre e profane.* 2 vols.
Milan: Alfieri, 1982.

Parenzo, Henri. *Nouveau Guide de Venise.* Venice: Gerli, 1870.

Parsi, Publio. *Chiese Romane.* 6 vols. Rome: Edizioni "Liber," 1970.

Pater, Walter. *Studies in the History of the Renaissance.* London: Macmillan, 1873.

Pepper, D. Stephen. *Guido Reni: A Complete Catalogue of His Works with an Introductory Text.* New York: New York University Press, 1981.

Perocco, Guido, and Antonio Salvadori. *Civiltà di Venezia.* Venice: La Stamperia di Venezia Editrice, 1976.

Piccarreta, F. *Genzano di Roma. La Città dell' Infiorata. Note Storiche—Tradizioni—Impressioni.* Foligno: R. Stab. Feliciano Campitelli, [1925].

Pignatti, Terisio. *Il Museo Correr di Venezia: Dipinti del XVII e XVIII Secolo.* Venice: Neri Pozzo Editore, 1960.

———. *Veronese: Testo e Cataloghi.* 2 vols. Venice: Alfieri, 1976.

Praz, Mario. "Impressioni italiane di americani dell'800." *Studi Americani* 4 (1958): 85–108.

Prezzolini, Giuseppe. *Come gli americani scoprirono l'Italia.* Bologna: Massimiliano Boni Editore, 1971.

Pullini, Giorgio. *Teatro Italiano fra due secoli: 1850–1950.* Florence: Parenti Editore, 1958.

Quadri, Antonio. *Otto Giorni a Venezia,* 16th ed. Venice: G. Grimaldo, 1866.

Quennell, Peter. *Byron in Italy.* London: St. James's Library, 1951.

Raggi, Oreste. *I Colli Albani e Tusculani,* 2d ed. Rome: Unione Tipografica—Editrice Torinese, 1879.

Ravaglioli, Armando. *The Heart of Rome.* Rome: Edizioni di Roma Centro Storico, 1984.

Reynolds, Sir Joshua. *Discourses on Art.* Edited by Robert R. Wark. San Marino, Calif.: Huntington Library, 1959.

Ricci, Corrado. *Guida di Ravenna.* Bologna: Nicola Zanichelli, 1923.

Roma e Dintorni. Milan: Touring Club Italiano, 1977.

Rosenberg, John. *The Darkening Glass: A Portrait of Ruskin's Genius.* New York: Columbia University Press, 1961.

Rousseau, Jean-Jacques. *The Confessions.* Translated by J. M. Cohen. Baltimore: Penguin Books, 1954.

Rossiter, Stuart. *Northern Italy from the Alps to Rome (The Blue Guide).* London: Ernest Benn, 1971.

———. *Rome and Environs (The Blue Guide).* London: Ernest Benn, 1971.

Röthlisberger, Marcel. *Claude Lorrain: The Paintings.* 2 vols. New Haven: Yale University Press, 1961.

Ruskin, John. *The Works of John Ruskin.* Edited by E. T. Cook and Alexander Wedderburn. 39 vols. London: George Allen, 1903.

———. *Mornings in Florence, Being Simple Studies of Christian Art for English Travellers.* New York: Lovell, [n.d.].

———. *St. Mark's Rest.* New York: Lovell, [n.d.].

———. *The Stones of Venice: Introductory Chapters and Local Indices. (Printed Separately) for the Use of Travellers while Staying in Venice and Verona.* 2 vols. Sunnyside, Orpington, Kent: George Allen, 1879; 1881.

Sand, George. *La Daniella,* new ed. 2 vols. Paris: Calmann Lévy, 1887.

———. "Lettres à Alfred de Musset," *La Revue de Paris,* vol. 3, 12 November 1896, 1–48.

Scarpellini, Pietro. *Perugino.* Milan: Electa, 1984.

Schudt, Ludwig, *Le Guide di Roma.* Vienna: [n.p.], 1930.

Shapiro, Harold I., ed. *Ruskin in Italy: Letters to His Parents.* Oxford: Clarendon, 1972.

Shearman, John. *Andrea del Sarto.* Oxford: Clarendon, 1965.

Spear, Richard E. *Domenichino.* 2 vols. New Haven: Yale University Press, 1982.

Stendhal [Henri Beyle]. *Oeuvres Complètes.* Edited by Victor Del Litto and Ernest Abravanel, new ed. 50 vols. Paris: Cercle du Bibliophile, 1972.

Street, George Edmund. *Brick and Marble in the Middle Ages: Notes of a Tour in the North of Italy.* London: J. Murray, 1855.

Symonds, John Addington. *Renaissance in Italy.* 5 vols. London: Smith and Elder, 1880–86.

Taine, Hippolyte. *Italy: Rome and Naples.* Translated by John Durand. New York: Leypoldt & Holt, 1868.

———. *Voyage en Italie.* Paris: Hachette, 1860.

Tamassia Mazzarotto, Bianca. *Le Feste Veneziane: I Giochi Popolari, le Cerimonie Religiose e di Governo.* Florence: Sansoni, 1961.

Tassini, Giuseppe. *Curiosità Veneziane, ovvero origini delle denominazioni stradali di Venezia,* 8th ed. Venice: Filippi Editore, 1970.

Taucci, Raffaele. *Un Santuario e la sua Citta: La SS. Annunziata di Firenze.* Florence: Edizione Convento SS. Annunziata, 1976.

Thynne, Roger. *The Churches of Rome.* London: Kegan Paul, Trench, Trubner, & Co., 1924.

Tinter, Adeline R. *The Book World of Henry James: Appropriating the Classics.* Ann Arbor, Mich.: UMI Research, 1987.

———. *The Museum World of Henry James.* Ann Arbor, Mich.: UMI Research, 1986.

Tuttleton, James W., and Agostino Lombardo, eds. *The Sweetest Impression of Life: The James Family and Italy.* New York: New York University Press, and Rome: Istituto della Enciclopedia Italiana, 1990.

Vance, William L. *America's Rome.* 2 vols. New Haven and London: Yale University Press, 1989.

Vasari, Giorgio. *Vasari on Technique.* Translated by Louisa S. Maclehose; edited by G. Baldwin Brown. London: J. M. Dent, 1907 (rpt. New York: Dover, 1960).

Weinberg, G. S. "Ruskin, Pater, and the Rediscovery of Botticelli," *Burlington Magazine* 129 (January 87): 25–27.

Wethey, Harold E. *The Paintings of Titian: Vol II, The Portraits.* London: Phaidon, 1971.

Wharton, Edith. *Italian Backgrounds.* New York: C. Scribner's Sons, 1905.

Winckelmann, Johann. *History of Ancient Art.* 4 vols. Translated by G. Henry Lodge. Boston: J. R. Osgood, 1949–73; New York: Ungar, 1968 [rpt.].

Winner, Viola Hopkins. *Henry James and the Visual Arts.* Charlottesville: University Press of Virginia, 1970.

Wright, Nathalia. *American Novelists in Italy. The Discoverers: Allston to James.* Philadelphia: University of Pennsylvania Press, 1965.

Bibliography of Period Photography

═══

Alinari, Fratelli. *Gli Alinari fotografi a Firenze, 1852–1920.* Florence: Alinari, 1977.
————. *Alinari, Photographers of Florence: 1852–1920.* London: Idea Books, 1978.
————. *Firenze: Cinquanta fotografie dell'Ottocento tratte dagli archivi Alinari.* Florence: Alinari, 1981.
————. *Fotografie degli archivi Alinari in Emilia e in Romagna: L'immagine della Regione.* Florence: Alinari, 1980.
————. *Napoli e il suo golfo.* Florence: Alinari, 1984.
————. *Perugia: Immagini del XIX secolo dagli archivi Alinari.* Florence, 1985.
————. *Roma: Cinquanta fotografie dell'Ottocento tratte dagli archivi Alinari.* Florence: Alinari, 1985.
————. *Siena e il suo territorio: Immagini del XIX secolo dagli archivi Alinari.* Florence: Alinari, 1985.
————. *La Valle d'Aosta: Immagini del XIX secolo dagli archivi Alinari.* Florence: Alinari, 1985.
————. *Verona nelle immagini degli archivi Alinari.* Edited by Nino Cenni. Florence: Alinari, 1978.

————. *Verona: Immagini del XIX secolo dagli archivi Alinari.* Florence: Alinari, 1985.

Amici, Domenico. *Die Ansichten Roms.* Dortmund: Harenberg, 1983.

Asmus, Gesine, ed. *Rom in frühen Photographien, 1846–1878.* Munich: Schirmer/ Mosel, 1978.

Becchetti, Piero. *La fotografia a Roma: Dalle origini al 1915.* Rome: Colombo, 1983.

————. *Fotografi e fotografia in Italia, 1839–1880.* Rome: Quasar, 1978.

————. *Immagini della campagna romana: 1853–1915.* Rome: Quasar, 1983.

————. *Roma in dagherrotipia.* Rome: Edizione Quasar, 1979.

————. *Roma tra storia e cronaca dalle fotografie di Giuseppe Primoli.* Preface by Mario Praz. Rome: Edizione Quasar, 1981.

Brizzi, Bruno. *Album di Roma: 1880.* Rome: Editori Romani Associati, 1980.

————. *Lazio scomparso.* Rome: Quasar, 1977.

————. *Roma cento anni fa nelle fotografie della raccolta Parker.* Rome: Edizione Quasar, 1978.

————. *Roma fine secolo nelle fotografie di Ettore Roesler Franz.* Rome: Edizione Quasar, 1978.

————. *Roma italiana, 1870–1895: Emma Perodi.* Rome: Edizione Quasar, 1980.

Cenni, Nino, ed. *Verona fra Ottocento e Novecento.* Milan: Rusconi, 1981.

————. *Verona nelle immagini degli Archivi Alinari.* Florence: Alinari, 1983.

Clarke, Sir Ashley. *Immagini di Venezia e della laguna nelle fotografie degli archivi Alinari e della Fondazione Querini Stampalia.* Florence: Edizioni Alinari, 1979.

Coffey, John. *Twilight of Arcadia: American Landscape Painters in Rome, 1830– 1880.* Brunswick, Maine: Bowdoin College Museum of Art, 1987. [An exhibit catalogue of oil paintings.]

Colombo, Cesare. *Italia: Cento anni di fotografia.* Florence: Alinari, 1984.

Crispolti, Francesco Carlo, ed. *Scene di vita quotidiana a Roma dalle fotografie di Giuseppe Primoli.* Rome: Quasar, 1980.

Detta, Edoardo. *Firenze Scomparsa.* Florence: Vallecchi editore, 1970.

Fotografia pittorica, 1889–1911: Venezia. Milan: Electa, 1979.

Galasso, Giuseppe, Mariantonietta Picone Petrusa, and Daniela del Pesco. *Napoli nelle collezioni Alinari e nei fotografi napoletani fra ottocento e novecento.* Naples: Gaetano Macchiaroli editore, 1981.

Manodori, Alberto. *Roma mai più Roma: Attraverso le fotografie di Alessandro Vasari.* [Rome]: Golden Series, 1983.

Moretti, Lino. *Vecchie Immagini di Venezia.* Venice: Filippo Editore, 1966.

Negro, Silvio. *Nuovo Album Romano: Fotografie di un secolo.* Venice: Neri Pozzo Editore, 1964.

Portoghesi, Paolo. *Roma: Un'altra città: Eccezionali fotografie d'epoca rivelano immagini segrete di luoghi, monumenti e ambienti di una vita urbana sparita.* Rome: Newton Compton, 1981.

Primoli, Giuseppe. *Roma tra storia e cronaca dalle fotografie di Giuseppe Primoli.* Edited by Piero Becchetti. Rome: Quasar, 1981.

————. *Tevere e Agro romano dalle fotografie di Giuseppe Primoli.* Edited by Piero Becchetti and Carlo Pietrangeli. Rome: Quasar, 1982.

Pucci, Eugenio. *Com'era Firenze.* Florence: Bonechi, 1969.

Ravaglioli, Armando. *Roma 1870–1970, immagini a confronto.* Milan: Periodici Scientifici, 1970.

————. *Vecchia Roma: 1850–1900.* Aosta: Musemeci Editore, 1981.

————. *Vecchia Roma: 1900–1950.* Aosta: Musemeci Editore, 1982.

————. *Vedere e Capire Roma.* Rome: Roma Centro Storico, 1980.

Roma cento anni fa nelle fotografie del tempo. Rome: Palazzo Braschi, 1971.

Roma dei fotografi al tempo di Pio IX, 1846–1878: Fotografie da collezioni danesi e romane. Rome: Multigrafica, 1978

Roma Sparita in Serie Prima, Seconda, Terza. 3 vols. Rome: Danesi Editori, 1931–36.

Rome in Early Photographs: The Age of Pius IX, Photographs 1846–1878, from Roman and Danish Collections. Copenhagen: Thorvaldsen Museum, 1977.

Siegert, Dietmar. *Rom: Vor hundert Jahren, Photographien, 1846–1890.* Ebersberg: Achteinhalb Lothar Just, 1985.

————. *Venedig in frühen Photographien, 1848–1905.* Ebersberg: Edition Achteinhalb Lothar Just, 1984.

Zannier, Italo. *70 Anni di fotografia in Italia.* Modena: Punto e virgola, 1978.

Zorzi, Alvise. *Venezia Scomparsa. Storia di una secolare degradazione,* vol 1. Milan: Electa, 1972.

————. *Venezia Scomparsa: Repertorio degli edifici distrutti, alterati o manomessi,* vol 2. Milan: Electa, 1972

————. *Venezia Scomparsa.* Milan: Electa, 1984.

Index

Since many of the foreign expressions used in *Italian Hours* have entered general usage or offer apparent cognates, not all have been annotated in this edition. Annotated foreign terms that appear only once in the text and need no cross-reference (e.g., *étalage*) are not indexed below. When, however, James repeats a foreign term that has been annotated (e.g., *vetturini**), this index supplies the page number of the annotation.

abbate, abbati,* 80n
Abruzzi, 340
Académie de France (French Academy), xvii, 169, 185, 185n
Accaiuoli family, 265
Achmett III, 41n
Acqua Paola (Rome), 145n
Acta Sanctorum, xxiii
Addison, Joseph, xxi
Aeneas Silvius. *See* Pius II

Agostino, Giovanni di, 219n
Alban Hills, 132, 145–46, 152, 157–60, 162n, 181, 188, 192, 340
Alban Lake (Lago Albano), 157–60
  legends concerning, 158, 158n
Albano, 145, 152, 161
Allori, Alessandro, 254, 254n
Ambrosian Library (Milan), 86
Amore senza Stima, 213, 213n
Anacapri, 307–10

Anagno, 340
Andermatt, 94–95
Andersen, Hendrik, 202, 202n
Andrea del Sarto, 119, 255–56, 255n
  Hawthorne's estimate, 335
  and suffering, 256
  John the Baptist, 104n
Angelico, Fra, 119, 121, 121n, 216, 227,
    245, 258–60
  Crucifixion, 258
  Deposition of Christ, 243
Anio waterfalls, 198, 198n
Antinuous (at Villa Albani), 188, 188n
Apollo Belvedere (at the Vatican), xiv
Apollo theater (Rome), 190, 190n
Appian Way, 132
Arco d'Augusto (Perugia), 212, 212n
Arezzo, 218, 218n, 219
Aria, Eliza,
  The May Book, 303n
Ariosto, Ludovico, 150, 150n, 182
  Orlando Furioso, 150n
Arno, the, 70, 110–12, 119, 239–42, 248,
    250, 263, 281–82
Arnolfo di Cambio, 118n
Arricia, 152–57
Ascham, Roger, xxi
Asolo, 75, 75n, 76
Assisi, 206–10, 219
Athens, 242
Atlantic Monthly, xxxiv, 99n, 122n, 139n,
    152n, 205n, 220n
Attila, 53n
Auber, Daniel,
  Masaniello, 108, 108n
  La Muette de Portici, 108n
Auden, W. H., xxv, xxxvi
Augustus III (Poland), 41n
Augustus, Emperor, 301n
Austen, Jane, xxix

Baedeker, Karl, xxiii, 20n, 69, 90n, 118,
    122n, 169, 206, 341
Bagni di Lucca, 284
Baiæ, 319, 319n
Balzac, Honoré de, 67n
Baptistry (Pisa), 274, 274n, 283
Barbarossa, castle of, 311, 311n
Barcham, William L., 50n
Barcilon, Brambilla Pinin, 84n
Barili, Antonio and Giovanni, 230, 230n
Barzini, Luigi, xxix
Bassano, 76
Bathurst, Rosa, monument to, 173n

Battilana, Marilla, xxxii, 64n, 66n
Beaumont, Sir George, 182, 182n
Beccafumi, Domenico, 228, 228n, 229, 230,
    230n
  Abraham and Isaac, 228, 228n
  floor of Siena Cathedral, 230, 230n
Bellini, Giovanni, 20–21, 26–27, 27n, 55,
    262n
  Madonna Enthroned, with Child and
    Saints, 26–27, 26n, 27n
  Madonna of San Zaccaria, 27, 27n
  Saint Jerome, 27, 27n
Bellinzona, 94, 96, 98
Bembo, Pietro, 75n
  Gli Asolani, 75n
Benedict, Clare, xxii
Benedict, St. (Benedetto da Norcia), 195,
    195n, 196n, 199, 199n
Berenson, Bernard, xxii, 162n, 228n, 250n
Berg Collection, New York Public Library,
    xxxix
Berne, 88, 90
Bernini, Giovanni Lorenzo, xxv, 153n, 181,
    182, 338
Bibliotheca Hertziana (Rome), 176n
Blake, William, 314n
Blue Grotto (Capri), 305, 305n
Blum, A. Whitney, xxxvi
Bobbio, 341
Boboli Gardens (Florence), 269–71
Boccaccio, Giovanni, 182, 295–96, 301
  The Decameron, 295n, 296n
Bologna, 293–94
Bolsena, 336
Boltraffio, Giovanni, 183n
Bolzano. See Botzen
Boncompagni family, xvii
Boott, Elizabeth, xxxiv, 111n, 177n, 181n,
    190n
Boott, Francis, xv, xxxiv, 111n, 177n, 181n
Borgia family, 199n
Borromeus, Charles (Carlo Borromeo), 83–
    84, 83n
Botticelli, Sandro, 119, 244n, 253–54, 260
  "too deeply sentient Virgin," 254, 254n
  Coronation of the Virgin, 260, 260n
  Tobias with the Angel, 244, 244n
Botticelli, School of,
  Madonna and Child, with Archangels,
    253, 253n
Botticini, Francesco, 244n, 253n
Botzen (Bolzano), 58, 58n, 59
Bourget, Paul,
  James's friendship with, 236n
  and Perugia, 213n

Un Saint, 236, 236n
Sensations d'Italie, 236n
Bradshaw, George. *See* travel guides
Bremer, Frederika, 335
Brescia, 51
Brignole-Sale family, 108, 108n
British Museum (London), 69
Bronson, Katharine De Kay (Mrs. Arthur),
    xv, 35, 35n, 43, 43n, 72–76, 72n,
    75n
    Casa Alvisi, 35, 35n, 72–76
    Browning in Venice, 72n
Brooks, Van Wyck, xxxii
Brosses, Charles de (Président de Brosses),
    on the carnival, xviii, 248, 248n
    Letters on Italy, 248n
Brown, David Alan, 84n, 245n
Brown, George Loring, 334
Brown, Rawdon, 44n
Browning, Robert, 67, 72n
    at Ca' Rezzonico, 42, 42n
    with Mrs. Bronson in Venice, 74
    with Mrs. Bronson in Asolo, 75, 75n
    "Andrea del Sarto," 255n
    Asolando, 75n
    Pippa Passes, 75n
    The Ring and the Book, 186, 186–87n
    "The Statue and the Bust," 267, 267n
    "A Toccata of Galuppi's," xviii, 74
    "Two in a Gondola," 74
Browning, Robert "Pen," xx, 42n
Brunelleschi, Filippo, 115
Buffalmacco, Bonamico, 276n
Bunyan, John,
    Pilgrim's Progress, 215, 215n
Buonafede, Francesco da (di Buonafede),
    265
Burano (Venice), 30–31, 30n
Burne-Jones, Sir Edward Coley, 245n
    James on *Days of Creation,* 245n
Busati, Andrea, 23n
Byron, George Gordon, sixth baron, xxi,
    109, 109n
    on Dante and Florence, 268, 268n
    at Leghorn (Livorno), 272n
    in Pisa, 282, 282n
    in Ravenna, 300–301, 300n
    in Venice, 46, 46n
    "Cain," 301
    Childe Harold's Pilgrimage, 146n, 198,
    198n, 268n
    The Corsair, 109n
    Don Juan, 296n, 300n
    "Vision of Judgment," 301
Byron's Grotto (Tivoli), 109n

Ca' Foscari (Venice), 42, 42n
Ca' d'Oro (Venice), 48
Ca' Rezzonico (Venice), xx, 42, 42n
Caffè Greco (Siena), 224
Caius Cestius pyramid (Rome), 172, 178,
    178n
*calle,** 17n
Cambridge University, xxi
campagna (Roman), xxix, 53, 139–43, 145–
    49, 152–53
*campo,** 22n
Campo (Siena), 220–21
Camposanto (Pisa), 274, 274n, 276–78,
    276n, 283
Canalazzo. *See* Grand Canal
Canaletto (Antonio Canal), 50
    as perfidious painter, 50, 50n
    view of San Simeone profeta (Venice), 50,
    50n
Canareggio (Venice), 49, 49n
Candide (Voltaire), 41, 41n
Canossa, 341
La Capitale, 123, 123n, 137, 137n
Capitol (Rome), 126–27
    disparagement of Michelangelo's architec-
    ture, 126n
Capri, 304–12, 304n, 305n, 312n
    Howells on, 328
Capua, 318
Capuchin convent (Arricia), 157–59, 157n
Caravaggio, 154, 263
Cardinal of York (Henry Stuart), 161, 161n
carnival, xxi, 248–49, 248n
    Baedeker on, 122n
    carnevale dei preti, 137, 137n
    coriandoli, 129, 129n
    decline of, 40, 40n, 74, 122, 122n, 125,
    248n
    Florentine carnival, 247–49
    Goethe on, 122n, 129n, 137n
    moccoletti, 137, 137n
    Président de Brosses on, xviii, 248, 248n
    Roman carnival, xv, 122–38, 129n, 249
    Venetian carnival, xviii, 40, 40n, 74, 249
Carpaccio, Vittore, 20–21, 27, 28–29, 28n,
    29n, 48–49, 48n, 54
    Ruskin on, 29, 29n
    The Courtesans, 29, 29n
    St. Jerome, 28
    St. Ursula, 28, 28n
    Two Venetian Ladies with their Pets, 29,
    29n
Carthusian Monastery (Florence), 264–66
Casa Alvisi (Venice), 35, 35n, 72–76
Casa Correr (Venice), 48, 48n

Cascine (Florence), 239, 239n, 248
Casino dell'Aurora (Rome), xvii, 191
Casino di Nobili (Siena), 226
Castel Fusano, 200
Castel Gandolfo, 159, 163
Castelli Romani, 319
Il Castello di Vincigliata e I Suoi Contorni,
    250n
Castello Farnese, 141n
Castiglione, Baldassare,
    The Courtier (*Il Libro del Cortegiano*), 75n
Castlefranco, 76
Catalani, Angelica, 276, 276n
Catena, Vincenzo,
    Warrior Adoring the Infant Christ and the
    Virgin, 69n
Caterina Cornaro (Queen of Cyprus), 75n
Catholicism, Catholic Church (*see also* pa-
    pacy), xv–xvi, 83–84, 207, 209
    after 1870, 123, 154, 177, 177n, 180,
    180n
    "cross-fire of influences," 181
    financial condition, 84
    Gregorovius on government divesting
        church groups, 174n
    Jesuits, 167, 167n
    last pompous effort, 178
    lapsing of authority, 133
    Law of Convents, 174, 174n
    Norton on corruption, 121n
    as part of Italian charm, 327
    power of the church, 233
    property seized by government, 174, 174n
    Religious Corporations Bill, 174, 174n
    rich possessions, 84
    St. Peter's as the apotheosis of, 135, 338
    in Santa Sabina, 179
    secularization, xv, 236, 258, 264n
    shrunken proportions, 154
Cavalcaselle, G. B., xxiii
Cavallini, Pietro, 208, 208n
Cavour, Camillo Benso di, 240n
    James's admiration of, 273, 273n
    statue in Leghorn (Livorno), 273, 273n
cemetery. *See* Camposanto and Protestant
    Cemetery
Century Magazine, xxxvi, xxxix, 7n
Certosa del Galluzzo. *See* Carthusian Monas-
    tery
Certosa di Val d'Ema. *See* Carthusian Monas-
    tery
Cervantes, Miguel de,
    Don Quixote, 164n
Cervetri, 340
Cesarini, Duke of, 155, 155n, 159, 160

Chambéry, 77
Chambord, Comte de, 41n, 49, 49n, 99, 99n
Channing, William Ellery, 299, 299n
Charles, "Bonnie" Prince, 41n
Les Charmettes, 78–79, 78n
Chiaiese, Leonardo, 310n
Chigi Palace (Genzano), 154–55
Chioggia (Venice), 30–31, 30n
churches (for *Duomo,* see Cathedral)
    Ara Coeli (Rome), 126, 126n
    Cathedral (Assisi), 206–10, 210n
    Cathedral (Florence), 82n, 115, 118,
        118n, 243, 247, 267, 336
        exterior views, 267
        Hawthorne's estimate, 335
        as incomplete structure, 118
        neo-gothic facade, 118n
        Ruskin's estimate, 118, 118n
    Cathedral (Lucca), 279, 285
    Cathedral (Milan), 82–84, 82n, 267, 267n
    Cathedral (Orvieto), 121
    Cathedral (Pisa), 228, 274–76, 274n, 283
    Cathedral (Pistoia), 279
    Cathedral (Ravenna), 299
    Cathedral (San Gimignano). *See* Collegiata
    Cathedral (Siena), 224, 229–30, 230n,
        233, 234
    Cathedral (Torcello), 54, 54n
    Collegiata (San Gimignano), 291
    Frari. *See* Santa Maria Gloriosa dei Frari
    Il Gesù (Rome), 180, 180n
    Madonna dell'Orto (Venice), 23, 23n
    Redentore (Venice), 39–40, 39–40n
    St. Agnes (Rome), 54
    Sant'Agostino (Rome), 245n
    St. Ambrose (Milan), 86
    Santa Anastasia (Verona), 60
    Ss. Annunziata (Florence), 267, 267n
    Sant'Apollinare in Classe (Ravenna), 297,
        297n, 301
    Sant'Apollinare Nuovo (Ravenna), 293n,
        297–99, 297n
    S. Bonaventura (Rome), 128n
    San Cassano (Venice), 55, 55n
    St. Clement (Rome), 54
    SS. Cosma e Damiano, 138n
    Santa Croce (Florence), 115, 118, 247,
        268–69, 268n
        as Florentine Valhalla, 268, 268n
        Ruskin's estimate, 118n
    Santa Croce in Gerusalemme (Rome), 132,
        192
    San Fermo (Verona), 60
    Santa Francesca Romana (Rome), 138,
        138n

St. Francis. *See* Cathedral, Assisi
San Geremia (Venice), 49
San Giorgio Maggiore (Venice), 16, 16n
San Giorgio Schiavoni (Venice), 28, 28n, 29
San Giovanni in Bragora (Venice), 23
San Giovanni in Laterano. *See* St. John Lateran
San Gregorio Magno (Rome), 130, 130n
St. John Lateran (Rome), 131–32, 192–93
  Scala Santa, 193, 193n
San Marco. *See* St. Mark's
St. Margaret (Cortona), 217
Santa Maria degli Scalzi (Venice), 50, 50n, 179
Santa Maria Assunta (Torcello), 54, 54n
Santa Maria del Popolo (Rome), 245n
Santa Maria dell'Assunzione (Arriccia), 153, 153n
Santa Maria dell'Orto (Venice), 22n
Santa Maria della Pace (Rome), 245n
Santa Maria della Pieve (Arezzo), 219
Santa Maria della Salute (Venice), 34–35, 34–35n, 73
Santa Maria della Spina (Pisa), 282
Santa Maria di Nazareth (Venice), 50, 50n
Santa Maria Gloriosa dei Frari (Venice), 26
Santa Maria Maggiore (Rome), xvi, 132–33, 266, 266n
Santa Maria Nova (Rome), 138n
Santa Maria Novella (Florence), 115, 269, 269n
Santa Maria Zobenigo (Venice), 41
St. Mark's (Venice), 9, 12–15, 14n, 34, 53–54
  restoration controversy, 13, 13n, 14
St. Mary Major. *See* Santa Maria Maggiore, Rome
San Michele (Anacapri), 310, 310n
San Michele (Lucca), 284–85
  Ruskin on, 284–85n
Ss. Nazaro e Celso (Ravenna), 300
San Nicola in Carcere (Rome), xxiv
San Onofrio (Rome), 182–83, 182–83n
St. Paul's without the Walls, San Paolo fuori le Mura (Rome), 135, 135n, 178–79, 178n
St. Peter's (Rome), xxiv, 82n, 131, 134–35, 140, 152, 192, 203, 266, 334, 338
St. Peter's, Old (Rome), xxvi
San Pietro Vincioli (Perugia), 216n
San Paolo fuori le Mura. *See* St. Paul's without the Walls

Santa Sabina (Rome), 179, 179n
San Simeone Grande (Venice), 50n
San Simeone piccolo e Giuda (Venice), 50n
San Simeone Profeta (Venice), 50, 50n
Santa Sofia (Anacapri), 310n
St. Sophia (Constantinople), 299, 299n
San Stefano (Rome), 181, 181n
San Vitale (Ravenna), 293n, 299
San Zenone (Verona), 60
Scalzi. *See* Santa Maria degli Scalzi
Cigoli, Lodovico Cardi di, 254, 254n
Cima da Conegliano, Giovanni Battista,
  Baptism of Christ, 23, 23n
  Saint John the Baptist with Saints Peter, Mark, Jerome, and Paul, 23, 23n
Ciminian Hills, 340
Civico Museo Correr (Venice), 48, 48n
civilization, xxiv–xxvi, xxix, 9, 249, 308–10, 312–14, 336
  as aspect of common people, 313
  as aspect of speech, 281
  Italy in forefront of, 326
  and vulgarity, xxviii
Civitale, Matteo, 120, 285, 285n
Clark, Kenneth, 218n, 227n
Classe, 297, 297n, 301, 301n
Claude Lorraine (Claude Gellée), 96, 96n, 141, 149–50, 198, 198n
  Hawthorne prefers George Loring Brown, 334
  Landscape with Cephalus and Procris, 149n
  Landscape with Dancing Figures, 149n
Claudian aqueduct, 132, 146
Colonna gardens (Rome), 177–78, 177n
Colosseum (Rome), xiv, 129–30, 211
  in "Daisy Miller," xi, xii
  in *Roderick Hudson*, 129–30n
  restoration of, 59, 59n
Colvin, Sidney, xxi
commercialism (*see also* modernization), xv, xxii
  of Venice, 12–15, 13n, 33, 38
  and Italy of the past, 104
Como, Lake, 86–87, 87n, 96, 98
  in Stendhal, 87, 87n
Coney Island, 201, 201n
Constantine, Arch of (Rome), 130, 130n
Constantine, Emperor, 128, 128n
Constantinople, 299, 299n
Constantius III, 300, 300n
contadino,* 198n
Contarini family, 69n
Cook, Thomas, travel agency, 88–89, 88n
Coppet, 79, 79n

coriandoli,* 129n
Corneto, 340
Cornhill Magazine, 72n
Correggio, Antonio, 54
Corsica, 288, 288n
Cortona, 216–19
  Muse (Cortona's Musa Polimnia), 217, 217n
costume, 156, 164, 232
Cousin, Victor, 329
Cox, Harvey,
  Picture of Italy, x
Crawford, F. Marion, xv
Critic, 72n
Croce, Benedetto, xxix
Crowe, J. A., xxiii
Curtis, Mr. and Mrs. Daniel, xv
  Palazzo Barbaro (Venice), 38, 38n, 63–64, 64n

D'Annunzio, Gabriele, 307
  James's estimate, xiii
  Il Piacere, 177n
  The Triumph of Death, xiii
D'Azeglio, Massimo,
  I Miei Ricordi, 161, 161n
d'Enzemberg, Conte Rodolfo, 64n
Danei, Paul Francis, 130n
Danieli, Hotel (Venice), 67, 67n
Dante (Alighieri), 242
  exile from Florence, 268, 268n
  Pia in the Purgatorio, 288n
  tomb in Ravenna, 300–301, 300n
  The Divine Comedy, 266, 268, 301
Dantier, Alphonse,
  Monastères Bénédictins d'Italie, xvi, 195–96, 195n
Darwin, Mrs. William, xxxvii
Davidson, H., xxxvi
Davis, Richard Harding,
  The Great Streets of the World, 32n
de Berry, Duchess, 43n
de Staël, Madame, 79n
death,
  as metaphor, xi, xvii, xviii
  in Pisa, 278
  in Venice, xviii, xx, xxi, xxv, 62
Defoe, Daniel, xxi
Depretis, Agostino, 107n
Devil's Bridge, 94, 94n
di Berry, Duchessa Maria Carolina, 64n
dialect. *See* language
Dickens, Charles, 67n, 335
disease, xi
  in "Daisy Miller," xii

malaria, 54, 54n, 201, 201n, 295, 295n, 318n
  Ostia, 201
  plague in Boccaccio, 295
  Roman air, xii, 148–49
  Torcello, 54, 54n, 201n
Dogana da Mar (Venice), 34, 34n
Domenichino (Domenico Zampieri), 164–66
  Goethe on, 294n
  The Chase of Diana, 165–66, 165n
  Communion of St. Jerome, 165, 165n
  Persian Sibyl, 165–66, 165n
  Triumph of David, 165–66; 165n
Domenico di Michelino, 244n
Donatello (Donato di Niccolò Bardi), 120, 265
Dosso Dossi, 217n
Douglas, Norman, xi
  Siren Land, 305n
Dryden, John,
  "Theodore and Honoria," 296n
Duccio (Duccio di Buoninsegna), 227n
Dumas, Alexandre *fils,* 20n, 341
  Le Demi-Monde, 213, 213n
Duse, Eleonora, 307n

Eastlake, Sir Charles, 227n
Edel, Leon, xv, xxi, xxii, 49n, 64n
  on dowager Empress Victoria, 64n
  on Hendrik Andersen, 202n
  on James friendship with Paul Zhukovsky, 315n
  on Mrs. Lombard, 274n
  Henry James (1952–73), xxxi
  Henry James: A Life (1985), xxxi
  Henry James: Letters, xxxi
Elba, Isola di, 288, 288n
Elgin Marbles, 188, 242, 242n
Elgin, Lord (Thomas Bruce), 242, 242n
Eliot, George,
  Middlemarch, xxxix, 140, 140n, 251n
Eliot, T. S., xxiv
  The Waste Land, 288n
Emerson, Ralph Waldo, 189, 189n
Etruria, 289
Etruscan gate (Perugia), 212–13, 212n
Euripides, 331
The Examiner, 282n
Exchange (Perugia), 213

*facchino,** 98n
Faido, 96
Fanfulla, 123
Farnese, Margaret (Margherita di Parma), 187, 187n

feasts, festivals, saint days (*see also* carnival), 249, 293
  Annunziata (Frascati), 163, 163n
  Palio (Siena), 232
  Pork Fair (Frascati), 163, 163n
  Redentore (Venice), 39–41, 39n, 40n
  St. Anthony (Anacapri), 307–9, 312
  St. Apollinaris (Ravenna), 299
  San Giovanni Decollato (Venice), 49n
  St. John (Venice), 49
  St. John the Baptist (Florence), 70
  St. Margaret's (Cortona), 217
  Statuto del Regno (Bologna), 293–94, 294n
*felze,** 63n
Fenice theater (Venice), 16
Fenway Court (Boston), 64n
Ferdinand, Grand Duke, statue (Florence), in Browning's "The Statue and the Bust," 267, 267n
Ferney, 79, 79n
Ferrari, Paolo,
  Amore senza Stima, 213, 213n
Feydeau, Ernest, 58
  L'Allemagne en 1871, 58n
  Fanny, 58n
Fiesole, 112, 240, 250
Filippi, Filippo de, 314n
Fiumincino, 200–201, 201n
Flaminius, Gaius, 216
Flavius Honorius, 144
Florence (*see also* churches, palaces, villas, and individual names), xxi, 100, 110–20, 220, 238–46, 247–71
  decay of, xvii, 241, 241n
  domestic architecture, 261, 263
  feast of St. John the Baptist, 69, 70
  "Florentine question," 71, 71n
  modernization of, 71, 239–40, 239n, 240n
  opera season, 238
  Republic of, 280
  Taine on, 330
  as temporary capital of Italy, 240n
  tourist season, 239
Florian's café (Venice), 52, 52n
Flüelen, 93
Fondaco dei Turchi (Venice), 48n
*fondamenta,** 47n
La Fontaine,
  Fables, 255n
Forsyth, Joseph, 274
  Remarks on Antiquities, 274n
Fortezza Medicea (Siena), 234n
Fortezza Santa Barbara (Siena), 234n

Forum (Rome), 128
Foxhall, 40n
franc (currency), 83, 83n
France, 77, 77n, 99–100, 99n, 339
Frascati, 163, 166–67, 166n, 167n
Frederick II (Prussia), 339
Frederick III (Prussia), 64n
Frederick, Empress (Empress Victoria), 64n
French, Frank, xxxvi
Fullerton, W. Morton, xxii

Gaeta, 318, 318n
Galaxy, xxxiv, 88n, 176n
Gale, Robert L., xxxii
Galileo (Galileo Galilei), 268n
Galla Placidia, 293n, 295, 295n, 296, 298n, 300n
  tomb in Ravenna, 300, 300n
Galliera, Duchess of, 108, 108n
Galliera, Duke of, 105
gardens, 177, 269–71
  Boboli (Florence), 269–70
  Colonna (Rome), 177–78, 177n
  Papadopoli or Communale (Venice), 50, 50n
Gardner, Isabella Stewart, xv
  Fenway Court (Boston), 64n
Garibaldi, Anita, 296n
Garibaldi, Giuseppe, 144, 296n
Gautier, Théophile, xxi, xxiv, 55, 55n
  "de turquoise malade," 81, 81n
  on Tintoretto, 55, 55n
  on Venetian patronage, 43
  on Venetian vitality, xix
  on Veronese, 25, 25n
  Constantinople, xxiv
  Italia, xvii, xix, xxiv, 14
  Journeys in Italy, 43
  Voyage en Espagne, xxiv
  Voyage en Russie, xxiv
Genoa, 105–8
Genzano, 154–55, 154n, 160–61
Germanicus, 305, 305n
Germany, German manners, 58–59, 58n
ghetto (Venice), 49n
Ghiberti, Lorenzo, 268n
Ghirlandaio, Domenico, 115, 227, 245–46, 269n
  deterioration of pictures, 243
  Ruskin's negative view, 259, 259n
  The Adoration of the Kings, 246
  Last Supper, 259
  Santa Fina, 291–92, 291n
Giardino Communale (Venice), 50
Gibbon, Edward, xv, xxv, 295–96, 295–96n

Giorcelli, Cristina, xxxii
Giorgione, 55, 76
Giottino, 114n
Giotto (Giotto di Bondone), 116, 208–9,
    216
  campanile in Florence, 114, 118n, 243
  St. Francis frescoes (Assisi), 207–9, 207n
Giudecca (Venice), 39, 41
Goethe, Johann Wolfgang von, xxiii
  on the Acqua Paola (Rome), 145n
  on Domenichino, 294n
  on Guido Reni, 294n
  on the Ludovisi Juno, 191n
  on the Roman carnival, 122n, 129n, 137n
  and Sicily, xii
  Temple of Minerva (Assisi), 210, 210n
  Italian Journey, xii, xxiii, 122n, 129n,
      137n, 145n, 191n, 210, 210n, 294n
Golden Legend, xxiii
Goldoni, Carlo,
  I Quattro Rusteghi, 189, 189n
  La Moglie Saggia, 213n
gondola, 18–19, 62–63
Gosse, Edmund, xxxviii
Gozzoli, Benozzo, 276–78, 276n
Grand Canal (Venice), 16, 32–50
Grand Dukes of Tuscany, statue at Leghorn
    (Livorno), 272
Grand Tour, xxi
Gravesend, 201, 201n
Gregorovius, Ferdinand, 340n
  on Capri, 305n
  on government divesting religious groups,
      174n
Grotta Ferrata, 163, 163n
Gryzanowska, Dr. and Mrs. E., 262, 262n
Guercino (Giovanni Francesco Barbieri),
    191–92
  Aurora, 191, 191n
Guiccioli, Teresa, 46n, 300–301, 300n

Hagia Sophia. *See* St. Sophia
Hamburg (Homburg), 58
Hannibal, 216n
Hare, Augustus J. C., xxiii, 23n, 141n, 146n,
    155n, 158n, 161n, 178n, 311n, 339–
    43
  compares Italy to England, 342
  James differs with political conservatism,
      xxvi
  James's estimate, 339, 341
  may have confused James, 198n
  on Italian character, 342
  on Naples, xxvii
  on political advances, 343
  on Veii, 141n
  on Soracte, 146n
  Cities of Northern and Central Italy, 340
  Days Near Rome, xxiii, 141n, 146n, 339–
      40
  Walks in Rome, xxiii, 339, 340
Harrier, Richard, xxxix
Hartt, Frederick, 228n
Haussmann, George Eugène, Baron, 71n,
    262
  modernization of Paris, 239, 239n
Hawthorne, Nathaniel, 32, 126
  compared to Howells, 327, 328
  detachment of, 333
  estimate of Raphael, 254n
  Italian and English travel writings com-
      pared, 333
  on Marcus Aurelius statue (Rome), 127,
      127n
  on Raphael, 245n
  on Roman Capitol, 126, 126n
  on Sodoma, 228n
  French and Italian Note-books, xiii, 126n,
      245n, 254n, 332–36
  The House of the Seven Gables, 335
  The Marble Faun, 127n, 213n, 228n, 335,
      336
  "Rappaccini's Daughter," xiii
Hérbert, Ernest, 169n, 185, 185n, 186, 186n
Heidelberg, 58
Holbein, Hans, 91, 91n, 95
Homburg (Hamburg), 58
Homer, 94, 94n
Honorius, 293, 293n, 298
Horace, xxiv, 94, 94n, 319n
Horner, Susan and Joanna,
  Walks in Florence and Its Environs, 242,
      242n, 257, 257n
Hospenthal, 95
Hospital of the Innocenti (Florence), 246,
    246n
Hotel Europa-Regina (Casa Alvisi), 73n
Howells, William Dean,
  compared to Hawthorne, 327, 328
  Italian Journeys, 32, 32n, 325–28
  Venetian Life, 32, 32n, 325
Humbert I (Umberto I), 125n, 184
Hunt, Leigh, 172n
  Autobiography, 282, 282n
Hunt, William Holman, 298, 298n

Independent, 247n
industrialization. *See* modernization
Innsbruck, 58

Ischia, 311
  disasters of, 311n
Italian language. *See* language
Ivan IV (Russia), 41n

James, Alice,
  letters to, xvi, xxxi, 169n, 185n
James, Henry:
  NOVELS:
  The Europeans, 171n
  The Portrait of a Lady, xiv, 10n, 11n,
    111n, 177n
  Roderick Hudson, xxix, 129n, 191n
  The Tragic Muse, 24n
  The Wings of the Dove, xiv, xviii, xxix,
    52n, 64n
  REVIEWS:
  "An English Critic of French Painting,"
    xxiii
  Gabriele D'Annunzio, *The Triumph of
    Death,* xiii
  de Mazade, *Life of Count Cavour,* 273n
  Théophile Gautier, *Mystères, Comédies, et
    Ballets,* xix
    Théatre de Théophile Gautier, xxiv
  Augustus Hare, *Cities of Northern and
    Central Italy,* xxvi, 340
    Days Near Rome, xxiii, 339–40
  Nathaniel Hawthorne, *French and Italian
    Note-books,* xiii, 332–36
  William Dean Howells, *Italian Journeys,*
    32n, 325
  Auguste Laugel, *Italie, Sicile, Bohême,*
    336–39
  William Morris, *The Earthly Paradise,*
    253n
  Francis Parkman, *The Jesuits in North
    America,* 167n
  "The Picture Season in London," 245n
  Ernest Renan, *Souvenir d'Enfance et de
    Jeunesse,* 277n
  "Matilde Serao," xxix
  Hippolyte Taine, *Italy: Rome and Naples,*
    327–32
  TALES:
  "The Aspern Papers," xiv, xviii
  "At Isella," xxiii, 91n
  "Daisy Miller," xi, 172n
  "The Last of the Valerii," 181n
  "The Madonna of the Future," 254n
  "The Solution," 167n
  "Travelling Companions," xxiii, 55n, 85n,
    87n
  TRAVEL WRITING:
  The American Scene, xxxvi

English Hours, x, xxxviii
Foreign Parts, xxxiv, 51n, 77n, 88n, 139n,
  152n, 176n, 205n, 247n
Italian Hours, cover design related to temporal concerns, x; judged pornographic,
  xxxviii; original illustrations, xxxiii;
  original index, xxxvii–xxxiii; publica-
  tion history, xxxiii–xxxix, revisions,
  xxxiii–xxxvii, textual issues, xxx–
  xxxix; use of initials in the text, 177n
Portraits of Places, xxxiii, xxxv, 7n, 99n
  "Swiss Notes," 88n
Transatlantic Sketches, xxxiii, 51n, 77n,
  88n, 122n, 139n, 152n, 168n, 176n,
  205n, 210n, 238n, 247n, 272n, 293n
"Very Modern Rome," xxxix
OTHER WORKS:
  "The Late Mrs. Arthur Bronson," 72n
  New York Edition preface to "Lady
    Barbarina" volume, 213n
  Notes of a Son and Brother, 177n
  "The Novel in *The Ring and the Book,*"
    187n
James, Henry, Sr.,
  letters to, xxxi
James, Mary Walsh,
  letters to, xxxi
James, William,
  letters to, xxxi, 14n, 20n, 25n
  trip to Italy, 257, 257n
Jameson, Anna Brownell (Mrs. Jameson),
  xxiii, 227n
Jesuits, 167
  review of Francis Parkman on, 167n
Jewish quarter (Venice), 49, 49n
John of Pisa (Giovanni Pisano), 219, 219n
Jonson, Ben, xxi
Joshua Reynolds,
  Discourses on Art, xxiii
Julius II, xxvi, 234n
Julius III, statue of (Perugia), 213, 213n
  Hawthorne's *The Marble Faun,* 213, 213n
Juno at Villa Ludovisi (Rome), 190–91,
  190–91n
Justinian, 295–96, 299
Juvarra, Filippo, 80n

Keats, John,
  grave in Rome, 172, 172n
Kemble, Fanny, 185n
Klaczko, Julian,
  Rome and the Renaissance, xiv

Lake Thrasymeno (Lago Trasimeno), 216,
  216n

Lampedusa, Giuseppe di,
  The Leopard, xiii
Land of Cockaygne, 283, 283n
language,
  aspects of dialect, 281
  "dreadful Ticinese French," 98, 98n
  James's knowledge of Italian, 189n
  "languages without style," 168
  Latin, 179
  Roman dialect, 179n
  Romanesco, 179n
  Tuscan dialect, 281
  Tuscan purity in Siena, 223
  Venetian dialect, 31, 39, 189n
Lateran Pacts, xv, 123n, 180n
Latin Monetary Union, 83n
Laugel, Auguste,
  Italie, Sicile, Bohême: Notes de Voyage,
    336–39, 336
Law of Convents, 174, 174n
Leader, Temple, 250, 250n
Leaning Tower (Pisa), 273, 283
Lechzinski, Stanislas, 41n
Leghorn (Livorno), 272–73, 272n
Leonardo Da Vinci, 84, 84n, 182–83n, 183,
    244, 257
  in James's fiction, 85n
  restoration, 84n
  Taine's estimate, 331
  Last Supper, 84–85, 84n
Lerici, 109–10
Leslie, Charles,
  Handbook for Young Painters, xxiii
Lewis, Monk, xxi
Libertà, 123, 123n
Lido (Venice), 10, 29n
Lima valley, 286
Lindsay, Lord (Alexander Lindsay), 277,
    277n
Lippi, Filippino, 262n, 269n
Lippi, Fra Filippo (Fra Lippo), 119, 245,
    253–54, 253n, 259
  and suffering, 259
  deterioration of pictures, 243
  Madonna with Child, 253n, 119
lira (currency), 83, 83n
Liverpool, 272
Livorno. *See* Leghorn
Livy (Titus Livius),
  History of Rome, 216n
Lizza (Siena), 234–35, 234n
Lombard, Mrs. ("invalid companion"), 274
  Edel recognizes in fiction, 274n
Lombardo, Agostino, xxxii
Longfellow, Henry Wadsworth,
  translation of *The Divine Comedy,* 288n

Longhena, Baldassare, 35, 35n
Longhi, Alessandro, 48n
Longhi, Pietro, xviii, 48n
Longhi, Roberto, 218n
Lorenzetti, Ambrogio, 227, 227n
Lorenzetti, Pietro, 208n
Lorenzo di Credi, 119
Lucca, 272, 278, 279, 283–86, 284–85n
Lucchesi-Palli, Enrico, 49n
Lucchesi-Palli, Maria Carolina, 64n
Lucerne, 90–92
Lung'Arno (Pisa), 282
Luther, Martin, 145

MacDonald, Bonney, xxxi
Machiavelli, Niccolò, 268n
MacMahon, Marshal, 99, 99n
madonnina, madonnetta, 43n, 75
Malamocco (Venice), 30, 30n, 51–53
malaria. *See* disease
Mandelbaum, Alan, 288n
Mandeville, Bernard, xxi
Manila (Philippines), 314, 314n
Mann, Thomas, xxi
  Death in Venice, xii
Mantegna, Andrea,
  Madonna and Child, 60, 60n
Mantua, 51
Manzoni, Alessandro, 83n
Marcus Aurelius Antoninus, 144, 144n
  statue in Rome, xvi, 127–28, 127n,
    128n
Maremma, 288, 288n
Margaret, Princess (Margherita di Savoia),
    125, 125n, 190, 190n
Mariéton, Paul,
  Une Histoire d'Amour, 67n
Mars, statue at Villa Ludovisi (Rome), 191,
    190–91n
Martini, Simone, 227n
Masaccio (Tommaso Guidi), 269n
"Masaniello," 108, 108n
Masaniello, Tommaso Aniello, 108n
Massé, Domenico, 174n
Il Mattino, xxviii
Maves, Carl, xxxii
Medici family, 271
Melinger, Caspar,
  Dance of Death, 91n
Melville, Herman, xviii
Memmi, Lippo di, 227n
Memmi, Simone, 227, 227n
Menegazzi, Luigi, 23n
Meng, Raphael, 177n
Mengin, Urbain, 248n

Mestre, 51
Michelangelo (Buonarroti), 126, 208, 244–45, 257, 269, 335
  borrowing from Orcagna, 277, 277n
  Hawthorne's estimate, 335
  Taine's estimate, 331
  tomb in Santa Croce (Florence), 268, 268n
  David, xiv
  Last Judgment, 56n, 246n, 277n
  Pietà, 135
Michelozzo di Bartolommeo, 267n
Milan, xv, 51, 81–86
  Austrian occupation, 82, 82n
  Spanish occupation, 82n
Milton, John,
  "Lycidas," 188
Mina da Fiesole, 120
moccoletti, 137, 137n, 138
Mocenigo family, 66, 66n, 69
modernization (*see also* vulgarization, vulgarity; restoration), ix, xi, xiv, 79n, 104, 105, 201, 239, 239n;
  Florence, 71, 71n, 114, 114n, 239–40, 239n, 240n
  Leghorn (Livorno), 272, 272n
  Lerici, 109, 109n
  Paris, 101, 239, 239n
  Rome, xiv–xv, 132n, 202n
  Venice, 51, 51n
Moerae, 66n
Molière (Jean-Baptiste Poquelin),
  Le Malade Imaginaire, 189n
Mondane, 100
Mont Cenis, 86, 100
  Mont Cenis tunnel, 79, 79n
Montagu, Mary Wortley, xxi
Montaigne, xvii
Montalba, Clara, xxxvi
Monte Cassino, xvi, 196, 196n, 340
Monte Mario (Rome), 150
Monte Oliveto Maggiore, xiv, 235–37
Montepulciano, 289–90
Monte Subasio, 211
Moore, Rayburn S., xxxviii
Moravia, Alberto, xiv
morganatic marriage, 125n, 171, 171n, 190, 190n
Morris, William, 13n, 245, 245n
  The Earthly Paradise, 253, 253n
Munich, 58
Munthe, Axel, xv, 307n, 312n, 314n
  The Story of San Michele, 304n
Murray, John, xxiii, 132, 132–33n, 161n, 163, 163n, 164, 190n, 210, 210n, 216–17, 226, 296, 341

museums,
  Academy (Florence), 119, 226–28, 226n, 243–45, 243n, 260
  Academy (Venice), 12, 20–22, 20n, 23n, 27–28, 44, 57
  Bargello (Florence), 119
  British Museum (London), 69
  Civico Correr (Venice), 29, 48, 48n
  Corsini Palace (Florence), 262–63
  École Nationale Supérieure des Beaux-Arts (Paris), 246n
  Galleria Sabauda (Turin), 80–81, 80n
  Lateran (Rome), 169, 169n
  Louvre (Paris), 55n, 57, 58
  Metropolitan Museum of Art (New York), 244
  Museo dell'Accademia Etrusca (Cortona), 217n
  Museo dello Spedale degli Innocenti (Florence), 246, 246n
  Museo Archeologico Nazionale (Naples), 312
  National Gallery (London), 21, 21n, 69
  Paolino (Vatican), 169n
  Pinacoteca (Bologna), 294
  Pitti Palace (Florence), 119, 244, 253, 254, 256, 257, 263
  Uffizi (Florence), 118–19, 244
Musset, Alfred de, 67, 67n
Mussolini, Benito, 202n

Naples, xv, xxv, xxvii, xxviii, 311, 314–15, 314n, 315n
  Bay of, 303, 318
  early and late impressions, 314–16, 315n
  Hare's estimate, xxvii
  Laugel on, 337, 338
  Symon's estimate, xxvii, xxviii
  Taine on, 331
Napoleon I, xviii, 49n, 235n, 288n
Napoleon III, 71n, 174n
  modernization of Paris, 239, 239n
Nardo di Cione, 269n
Narni, 205–6
Nashe, Thomas, xxi
Nation, xxxiv, 51n, 77n, 168n, 238n, 272n, 293n
Necker, Jacques, 79n
Negroponte, battle of, 49n
Nemi, 160–61
Nemi Lake (Lago di Nemi), 159
nero, 153, 153n
Nero (Roman Emperor), 178, 178n, 186, 186n
New York, 101, 119, 244
New York Public Library, xxxix

newspapers, 123
  La Capitale, 123, 123n, 137, 137n, 174,
    174n
  Fanfulla, 123, 123n
  La Gazzetta del Popolo, 123, 123n
  La Libertà, 123, 123n
  Il Mattino, xxviii
  The New York Times, 13n
  The New York Tribune, 92
  Osservatore Romano, 123, 123n
  Swiss Times, 91
  The Times (London), 13n
  La Vita Nuova, 224
  Voce della Verità, 123
Ninfa, 340
Norfolk, Thomas Mowbray, 1st duke of,
    44n
Norma, 340
Norton, Charles Eliot, xxi
  on Catholic corruption, 121, 121n
  Notes of Travel and Study in Italy, 121,
    121n
Norton, Grace, xxviii
Notre Dame (Paris), 135
Nuremberg, 58

Opere, Francesco delle, 215n
Orcagna, Andrea, 264, 269n, 276
  incorrect attribution, 276n
  and Michelangelo, 277, 277n
  Last Judgment, 276
  Triumph of Death, 276, 276n
Orvieto, 120–21, 120n
Osmond, Gilbert, 111n, 177n
Ospedale del Ceppo (Pistoia), 279n
Osservatore Romano, 123, 123n
Ostia, 200, 200n
Otway, Thomas, xxi
"Ouida" (Maria Louise de la Ramée), 341
Oxford, 171

Padua, 51
Pagello, Pietro, 67n
Paine, Thomas, 83n
palaces, palazzi, xv, 38, 101
  Angarem (Venice), 41n
  Barbaro (Venice), 38n, 64n
  Cesarini (Genzano), 155, 155n
  Chiericata (Vicenza), 80n
  Chigi (Arricia), 153, 153n
  Chigi (Siena), 232
  Contarini da Zaffo (Venice), 41n
  Contarini S. Vito (Venice), 41n
  Cornaro a San Maurizio (Venice), 45n
  Cornaro della Ca' Grande (Venice), 46n
  Corner della Ca' Grande (Venice), 45n
  Corner-Spinelli (Venice), 45n
  Corsini (Florence), 71, 71n, 262, 262n,
    263
  Dario (Venice), 44, 44n
  Doria Pamphilj (Rôme), 149, 149n
  Ducal (Venice), 12, 24, 54
  Facanon (Venice), 45
  Farnese (Rome), xvii
  Foscari (Venice), 37
  Giustianiani (Venice), 74
  Grimani a San Luca (Venice), 45
  Lanfranchi (Pisa), 282, 282n
  Lateran (Rome), 193n
  Loredan (Venice), 46
  Madama (Turin), 80n
  Menzoni (Venice), 41n
  Mocenigo (Venice), 46, 46n
  Montecuculi (Venice), 41, 41n
  Pesaro (Venice), 46, 46n, 49
  Pitti (Florence) (see also under museums),
    263, 269–70
  Polignac-Decazes (Venice), 41n
  della Prefettura (Venice), 45,45n
  dei Priori (Perugia), 211, 211n
  Pubblico (Perugia), 212
  Pubblico (Siena), 220–21, 226
  Quirinale (Rome), 124, 174–75, 174–
    75n, 178, 184, 184n
  Riccardi (Florence), 225
  Rosso (Genoa), 108n
  Ruzzini (Venice), 41n
  Strozzi (Florence), 225
  Vaticano (Rome), 245n
  Vendramin Calergi (Venice), 49, 49n
  Zuccari (Rome), 176n
Palazzuola (Franciscan monastery), 159,
    161, 161–62n
Palio (Siena), 232
Palladio, Andrea, 80, 80n
palo,* 43n
Pancratii burial societies, 181, 181n
Pantheon (Rome), xxiv–xxv
papacy (see also Catholicism, Catholic
    Church), xv
  decline of, 152–54, 177, 180, 180n
  James's estimate, xvi, xxxvi, 153, 153n
  Lateran Pacts, xv, 123n, 180n
  loss of papal Rome, 122–23, 122–23n
  nostalgia for papal Rome, xvi, 169, 177,
    177n
  part of Roman society, 145, 185
  residences, 174–75, 174–75n
Papadopoli gardens (Venice), 50, 50n

Paris, 176, 333
  modernization of, 239n
  redesigning of, 101n
  scenic tradition, 101, 101n
passeggiata,* 109n
Passionists, 130, 130n
  Passionist convent (Rocca di Papa), 161, 161n
Pater, Walter, xxi
  art for art's sake, 82n
  on Botticelli, 260, 260n
  Studies in the History of the Renaissance, 82n, 260, 260n
Paul V, 145, 145n
Pelham, Henry, 142, 142n
Pepys, Samuel, 40n
Perugia, 211–16, 290
  restoration at, 211, 211n
Perugino (Pietro Vannucci), 211–12, 211n, 216, 216n
  frescoes in Perugia, 213
  imitators of, 162, 162n
  in Sala del Cambio (Perugia), 214
  self-portraits, 215, 215n
  Ascension, 216, 216n
Peruzzi, Ulbaldino (Mayor of Florence), 240, 240n
Philadelphia, 221
photography, 34
Piazza dei Miracoli (Pisa), 274, 274n
Piazza Navona (Rome), xiv
Piazza of Siena. *See* Campo
Piazza San Marco, St. Mark's Square (Venice), 32–34
Picasso, Pablo, xxv
Piccolomini, Aeneas Silvius. *See* Pius II
Piero della Francesca, 227n
  The Legend of True Cross, 218n
Pincio (Rome), 132, 140, 169, 183–85
Pineta (Ravenna), 296, 296n, 302
Pinturicchio, Bernardino,
  Pius II (Piccolomini) series, 230, 230n, 233, 233n
Pisa, 272, 273–78, 280–83, 286
  as enemy of Florence, 281
  Leaning Tower, 273
  Taine on, 330
  University of, 280
Pisano, Giovanni (John of Pisa), 219, 219n
Pistoia, 272, 278–79
Pius II (Aeneas Silvius), 233n
  Pinturicchio fresco series, 230, 230n, 233, 233n
Pius VII, 139n
Pius IX, xvi, 137n, 139n, 152–54, 153n, 318

illness, 173–74, 173–74n
Platen, August Von, 305n
Plutarch, 273
podere,* 104n
political issues,
  communists, 107, 107n
  conservatism, xxvi
  elections, 107, 107n
  government as a new order, 343
  Italian government, xxvi, 13n, 107, 107n, 343
  political fervor in Rome, 123n
  political future of Italy, 103
  political unrest, 107, 107n, 174, 174n, 175, 175n
  "Sardinian Government," xxvi, 343
Pompeii, 128, 200n, 201, 315–16
Ponte Carraja, Ponte Carraia (Florence), 69–70, 69n
Ponte Molle, 139, 139n
Ponte Santa Trinità (Florence), 241
Ponte Vecchio (Florence), 241
Pontine Marshes, 318, 318n, 340
Pontormo, Jacopo, 262n
Porta Pia (Rome), 144, 144n
porto di mare,* 35n
Porto Venere, 109, 109n
Posillipo (Posilipo, Posilippo), 311, 311n, 316, 319
Powers, Hiram, 335
Pre-Raphaelites, 245, 245n, 298n
Prefect (Venice), 45, 45n
Prévost, Abbé,
  Manon Lescaut, xv
Primoli, Giuseppe, xxviii
Procida, 311
Prohibition Party, 92n
Propaganda Fide, Collegio di (Rome), 151, 151n, 171
Protestant Cemetery (Rome), 172–73, 178
  Bathurst monument, 173, 173n
  Shelley's "Adonais," 178, 178n
Proust, Marcel, xxi, 67n

Quadri, Caffè (Venice), 12

Racine, Jean, 189n
  Les Plaideurs, 189, 189n
Radcliffe, Ann, 167n
  Mysteries of Udolpho, 180n
Radicofani, 336
Raggi, Antonio, 154, 154n
Raphael (Raffaello Sanzio), 245, 245n, 254–57, 262n
  James finds fault with, 245

"other Roman relics," 245n
popularity among collectors, 245n
and suffering, 256
Taine's estimate, 331
Leo the Tenth (Cardinal Bibbiena), 256, 256n
Madonna of the Chair, 254, 254n, 256
Marriage of the Virgin, 86
School of Athens, 256
Transfiguration, 188, 245, 245n, 334
Ravenna, 293–302
Dante's tomb, 268, 268n
decadence, 298
mosaics, 297–99, 297n, 302
retreat of sea, 301, 301n
"Regno Italico," xviii
Religious Corporations Bill, 174, 174n
Renan, Ernest, xxiv, 86, 86n, 299, 299n, 329
les délicats, 277, 277n
Souvenirs d'Enfance et de Jeunesse, 86n
La Vie de Jésus, 86n
Reni, Guido, 154, 294, 294–95n
Goethe's estimate, 294n
Ruskin's estimate, 294n
Susannah, 294n
restoration, xi, xiv, 178, 178n, 181n
of Ca' Foscari, 42, 42n
of Cima da Conegliano, 23, 23n
of Da Vinci's *Last Supper,* 84n
James's doubts concerning, xiv, 59n, 104, 104n, 119, 129n
newspaper controversy over St. Mark's, 13, 13n
of Pisa's Camposanto, 276n
in Perugia, 211, 211n
of Roman Colosseum, 59, 59n
Ruskin's fear concerning, 285n
of St. Paul's without the Walls, 178n
of San Michele in Pisa, 285n
of Siena cathedral, 223
of Signorelli, 237n
of Tintoretto at Scuola di San Rocco, 57n
in Venice, 13, 14, 16n
of Verona arena, 59n
and Vincigliata counterfeit, 251
of Villa d'Este, 196n
of Villa Madama, 186n
Reuss River (Switzerland), 91
Reynolds, Sir Joshua, 177n
Rialto Bridge (Venice), 46–47
Richard II (England), 44n
Rico, D. Martin, xxxvi
*ricordi,** 33n
risorgimento, xi, 126n, 127, 127n, 273n, 285n

Riva degli Schiavoni (Venice), , 10–11, 10–11n, 15
Robbia, Giovanni della, 279, 279n
Robbia, Luca della, 120, 243, 251, 279n
Rocca di Papa, 161
Massimo d'Azeglio on, 161, 161n
Rocca Maggiore (Assisi), 209n
Roman Catholicism. *See* Catholicism
Romanesco. *See* language
Romano, Antoniazzo, 162n
Romano, Giulio, 186n, 187
Rome (*see also* churches, palaces, villas, and individual names and sites), xxi, 122–38, 139–51, 152–67, 168–75, 176, 193, 194–204
as described by Hare, 339
behind St. Peter's, 148
carnival, 122–38, 248
compared to Babylon, 137
compared to Ravenna, 297
first impression, ix
Hawthorne on, 336
the King as a presence, 171, 184
Auguste Laugel on, 338
memories of the city, 176, 176n, 194, 203
newspapers, 123, 123n
papal city, xv, xvi, 123, 169, 173, 177, 177n, 184
political discord, 174, 174n
Roman air, 148
secularization, xv
society life, 171, 183–84
theater, 189–90
tourism, xvii, 168–70
transformation after 1870, xiv–xvii, 177, 177n, 180, 180n, 184
Rosa, Salvator, 198, 198n
Rosenberg, John, 8n
"Rosina" (Rosa Vercellone), 171, 171n
Rossetti, Dante Gabriel, 245n
Rossi, Ernesto, 190, 190n
Rossini theater (Venice), 16
Rothschild banking firm, 214
Rousseau, Jean-Jacques, 78–79, 78n
Confessions, 78n, 79
Rubens, Peter Paul, 256
Ruskin, John, xxi–xxvi, 9, 44, 48, 55–56, 67
on Ca' Foscari restoration, 42, 42n
on Carpaccio, 29, 29n
critical of Florentine architecture, 118, 118n
defense of Veronese, 55–56, 55–56n
disregard of Piero della Francesca, 218n
on duomo of Florence, 82, 82n, 118, 118n

on Ghirlandaio, 114n
on Giotto, 114n
James's estimate, xxi, 8, 8n, 55, 56, 114–17, 114n
magnified rapture in Lucca, 284–85, 284–285n
negative view of Ghirlandaio, 259, 259n
on old and new approaches to Venice, 51–52, 51n
on Palazzo Pesaro, 46n
on St. Peter's (Rome), 82n
on Tiepolo, 20, 20n
on Titian, 20, 20n
on Tintoretto, 36, 36n
on the wreck of Florence, 114, 114n
Mornings in Florence, xxii, 114–17, 114n, 118n
St. Mark's Rest, 8, 8n, 20, 20n, 29, 29n
"The Shrine of the Slaves," 29, 29n
The Stones of Venice, xxi, xxvi, xxxvii, 8, 14, 51, 53, 54

Sabine Hills, 146, 146n, 340
Saint-Gothard, 86
    tunnel, 94
Sainte-Beuve, Charles Augustin, 329
St. Mark's Square. *See* Piazza San Marco
St. Paul of the Cross, 130n
St. Theodore, 33, 33n
Sala del Cambio (Perugia), 214, 215n
Salvini, Tommaso, 190, 190n
San Gimignano, 291–92, 291n
San Marco, convent (Florence), 258–61
San Michele (Capri), 304, 304n
Sand, George, xxi, xxiv, 20n, 67, 67n, 78, 78n
    La Daniella, 167, 167n
Sano di Pietro, 227, 227n
Sansovino (Jacopo Tatti), 45
Santa Maria di Galloro, santuario di (Arriccia), 157–59, 157n
Santa Scolastica, convent of (Subiaco), 199n
Scala Santa (Rome), 132, 193, 193n
Scheffer, Ary, 298, 298n
Scott, Walter, 251
Scribner's Magazine, 32n
Scuola di San Rocco (Venice), 23–24, 23n, 26, 57, 57n
Sebastiano del Piombo,
    Saint John Crisostomo, 27–28, 27n
Serao, Matilde, xxviii
Serchio river, 286
Servius Tullus, 144, 144n
Seven Weeks' War (Austro-Prussian War), 338

Severità e Debolezza, 213, 213n
Shakespeare, William, xxi, 24n, 57, 329
    Hamlet, 188
    King Lear, 130n
    Macbeth, 190n
    Measure for Measure, 143n
    Othello, 190, 190n
Shelley, Percy Bysshe, 109n, 110
    drowned near Spezia, 110, 282n
    grave in Protestant Cemetery at Rome, 172, 172n
    at Leghorn (Livorno), 272n
    "Adonais," 178, 178n
    "Julian and Maddalo," 41n
Shylock, race of, 49, 49n
Sicily, xii
    Laugel on, 338
Siena, 220–37, 333, 336
    Palio, 232
    Republic of, 280
    shabbiness of, xiv, 223
    Sienese painters, 226–27
Signorelli, Luca, 262
    St. Benedict frescoes, 237, 237n
    "theological frescoes," 121, 121n
Sistine Chapel, 177
La Società Equivoca, 213, 213n
Sodoma (Giovanni Antonio Bazzi), 228, 237
    Hawthorne on, 228n
    Christ at the Column, 228–29, 228n
    Descent from the Cross, 228–29, 228n
    Sacrifice of Isaac, 275
    St. Benedict, 237, 237n
    Swooning of St. Catherine, 229
Sonzongno, Raffaele, 123n
Sophocles, 331
Soracte, 146, 146n, 149, 149n
Sorrento, 304, 308, 310, 311, 316
Spanish-American War, 314n
Spenser, Edmund, xxxvi
La Spezia, 108–9
Spillman Frères, 200, 200n
States of Church, 174n
Statuto del Regno, 294, 294n
Stendhal (Henri Beyle), xxiii, 103n, 188
    anecdotal method, 180, 180n
    on Milan, 82n
    The Charterhouse of Parma, xv, 82n, 87, 87n
Sterne, Laurence,
    A Sentimental Journey through France and Italy, 97, 97n, 326
Story, William Wetmore, xv
Strauss, David Friedrich, 86, 86n
    Das Leben Jesu, 86n

Street, Edmund,
  Brick and Marble in the Middle Ages, 82n
Stuart, Henry (Cardinal of York), 161, 161n
Subiaco, xvi, 195–96, 195n, 198
Suetonius (Gaius Suetonius Tranquillus),
  The Twelve Caesars, 305n, 312n
Suseler, T., xxxvi
Sutri, 340
Sweeney, John L., xxxii
The Swiss Times, 91
Switzerland, 88–89, 293
Symonds, John Addington, 227n
  on Veronese, 25n, 56n
  Renaissance in Italy, xxiii, 25n
Symons, Arthur, xxvii, xxviii
  Cities of Italy, xxviii

"Table of Italian Hours," x
Tacitus (Cornelius Tacitus),
  on Capri, 305
  Annals, 305n
Taine, Hippolyte,
  "History of English Literature," 329
  "Homeric Life and the City of Antiquity,"
    331
  Italy: Rome and Naples, 327–332
  *Notes sur Paris: Opinions of M. Thomas
    Graindorge,* 329
Tassini, Giuseppe, 43n
Tasso, Torquato, 182–83, 182–83n
  Gerusalemme Liberata, 296n
Te Deum service in Rome, 180, 180n
Temple of Minerva (Assisi), 210, 210n
Temple of Peace, Templum et Forum Pacis
  (Rome), 138, 138n
Teniers, David, 164, 164n
Tennyson, Alfred Lord,
  "Mariana," 143, 143n
Terracina, 318
Terry, Luther, xv
Tessein river (Switzerland), 97, 97n
Thackeray, William Makepeace, 103
  The Newcomes, 103n
theater, 189–90, 189–90n, 213, 213n
Theater of Marcellus (Rome), xxiv
Theocritus, 150, 150n, 311, 311n
Theodoric, 293, 293n
Thiers, Louis Adolphe, 77, 77n, 99n
Tiber, the, 139, 145, 146, 173, 173n, 176,
  187, 200, 204, 205, 212, 266
Tiberius, 312, 312n
Ticino canton (Switzerland), 97, 97n
Tiepolo, Giambattista, 20, 20n
time (standard time),
  and cover design of *Italian Hours,* x

as local phenomenon, x
Greenwich mean time, x
Tintner, Adeline, xxxii, 254n
Tintoretto (Jacopo Robusti), xxi, 9, 20–23,
  20n, 23, 26–27, 52–56
  compared to Veronese, 57
  Gautier on *le roi de fougueux,* 55, 55n
  James decries condition of pictures, 57,
    57n
  self-portrait, 58
  Taine's estimate, 331
  Bearing of the Cross, 57
  Crucifixion, 24, 55–57, 55n, 208
  Last Supper, 57
  Marriage Feast of Cana, 35–36, 35n, 57
  Pallas Chasing Away Mars, 26
  Paradise, 26, 26n, 55n,
  Presentation of the Virgin, 22, 22n, 57
  St. Mark Freeing a Slave, 20n
Titian (Tiziano Vecelli), 9, 20n, 52, 54–57,
  85, 166
  Ruskin's estimate, 20, 20n
  and suffering, 256
  Taine's estimate, 331
  Annunciation, 21
  Assumption, 20, 20n, 27
  Emperor Charles V, 256–57, 256n
  Man with the Grey Eyes, 257, 257n
  Pietro Aretino, 257n
  Presentation of the Virgin, 20n, 57
Titus, arch of (Rome), 128
Tivoli, 196–98, 196n, 198n
Tor di Quinto Road (Rome), 141, 141n
Torcello (Venice), xx, 30, 53, 53n, 54
  depopulated by malaria, 54n
Torre di Nerone (Rome), 178, 178n
Torre delle Milizie (Rome), 178, 178n
Torrita, 290
tourism, xi, xxii
  automobile travel, 314, 314n, 316–18
  Capri, 304–6, 304n, 305
  Cook's package tours, 88–89, 88n
  in Florence, xviii, 238–39
  Grand Tour, xi
  at La Spezia, 109, 109n
  in Pisa, 274
  in Pompeii, 316
  railroad travel, 120
  in Rome, 168–69
  in Switzerland, 88–90, 93, 95
  threat of disease, xii
  tourist season, xi, xii, 168, 238–39
  in Umbria, 290
  in Venice, xviii, xxii, 12, 25, 33
  at the Venice Lido, 29–30, 29–30n

*traghetto, traghetti,** 18n
Traini, Francesco, 276n
Trastevere, 262
travel writing, travel guides (*see also* primary
    headings for individual authors),
    xxiii, 141
  distinguished from letters and diaries, 326
  as literature, 326
  slipshod production of, 326
  Karl Baedeker, xxiii
  George Bradshaw, 86
  Harvey Coxe, x
  Théophile Gautier, xxiii–xxiv
  Augustus Hare, xxiii
  Nathaniel Hawthorne, 332–36
  Susan and Joanna Horner, 242
  William Dean Howells, 325–328
  Auguste Laugel, 336–39
  John Murray, xxiii
  John Ruskin, xxi–xxii, xxvi, xxxvii
  Stendhal (Henri Beyle), 180
  Laurence Sterne, 326
  Hippolyte Taine, 327–32
La Tremenda Giustizia di Dio, 59
Trevi fountain (Rome), 176, 193
The Triumph of Death (Pisa), 276
Turin, 80–81, 100–102, 105
  scenic tradition, 101, 101n
  as temporary capital of Italy, 240n
Tuttleton, James W., xxxii
Tweedy, Edward and Mary, 176n

Umberto I. *See* Humbert I
Unitarianism, 299n
University of Pisa, 281
University of Venice, 42n

Valentinian III, 298, 298n
Valerii, tomb of, 181, 181n
Valhalla, 268, 268n
Vallombrosa, 250
Van Dyck, Anthony, 81
  Sons and Daughters of Charles I, 81
Vance, William L., xxxii
Vandyck family (Genoa), 108
*vaporetto, vaporetti,** 47n
Vasari, Giorgio, 84n, 227n, 228n, 255n
  Lives, xxiii
Vatican City,
  formally established, xv
  newspaper, 123, 123n
Vauxhall Gardens (London), 40, 39–40n
Veii (Veio), 141, 141n
Velathri, 287n
"Venetian Outrages," 13n

Venice (*see also* churches, palaces, and indi-
    vidual names), xvii–xxii, xxv–xxix,
    7–31, 32–50, 51–58, 61–69
  death in, xviii, xxi, xxvii, 62
  decay of, xx, 47, 61, 62, 68, 242
  decline of, xviii, 61, 68–69
  Howell's residence in, 326
  Laugel on, 338
  melancholy of, 18, 24
  metaphor of, xviii
  as a museum, 10
  quality of light in, 53–54
  silence of, 18–19
  society, 73
  tourism in, 10
  transformation of, xvii
  vitality of, xix, xx, 19
  vulgarization of, xxii
Venus de Medici, statue of,
  Hawthorne's estimate, 335
Vercellone, Rosa, 171, 171n
Verona, 51, 58–60
Veronese, Paolo, 20, 20n, 21, 21n, 27, 52,
    57
  compared to Tintoretto, 57
  Ruskin's defense, 55–56, 55–56n
  Symonds on, 25n
  Taine's estimate, 331
  Baptism of Christ, 257–58
  Family of Darius, 21, 21n
  Feast in the House of Levi, 56n, 81
  Marriage of Cana, 57
  Pilgrims of Emmaus, 81n
  Queen of Sheba, 81
  Rape of Europa, 14n, 25n, 56
Vesuvius, 311
*vetturini,** 90n
Via Appia Nuova, 132
Via della Conciliazione (Rome), xiv, 202n
Via Gregoriana (Rome), 176, 176n
Victor Emmanuel II (Vittorio Emanuele),
    124, 124n, 178, 184n
  income and expenses, 184n
  mistress, 171n, 190n
  monument in Rome, xiv, 126n
Victoria, Empress (Empress Frederick), 64n
villas, xv, 112, 170, 188
  rental of by foreigners, 112–13
  as "subject," 188
  variety in Rome, xvii, 170, 170n
  Albani (Rome), xvii, 170, 188, 188n
  Aldobrandini (Frascati), 166, 166n
  Borghese (Rome), 151, 170–71, 170n
  Castellani (Florence), 111n
  Chigi (Rome), xvii, 170

Doria (Rome), xvii, 151
d'Este (Tivoli), 196–97, 196
Farnesina (Rome), 245n
Franco (Leghorn/Livorno), 273
Jovis (Capri), 312n
Ludovisi (Rome), xvii, 170–71, 170n,
     190–92
Madama (Rome), 186, 186n
Massimo (Rome), xvii, 170
Medici (Rome), xvii, 170–71, 185–86,
     185n
Mellini (Rome), xvii, 170, 182, 182n
Mondragone (Frascati), 167, 167n
Phaon's villa (Rome), 186, 186n
San Michele (Capri), 304n
I Tatti (near Florence), 250n
Torlonia. *See* Albani
Wolkonski (Rome), xvii, 170
*villeggiatura,** 162n
Vincigliata, castle of, 250–53, 250n
Virgil (Publius Vergilius Maro), 150, 311,
     318
   Aeneid, 216
   Eclogues, 150
"Vita di Gesù Cristo" (*La Capitale*), 137
Vita Nuova (periodical), 224
Vittorio Emanuele II. *See* Victor Emmanuel
Volscian Hills, 340
Volstead Act, 92n
Voltaire (François-Marie Arouet de), xxi,
     79n
   Candide, 41, 41n
Volterra, 286–89, 286n, 287n
von Neuhof, Theodore, 41n
vulgarization, vulgarity (*see also* moderniza-
     tion), ix, xii, xxviii
   Howells on, 328
   of modern Italy, 102, 116, 343

and Naples, xxviii
of Pisa, 273
of Rome, 201
of Venice, xi, xxii

Wagner, Richard, 67
   death in Venice, xx, 49n
War of Spanish Succession, 82n
Warens, Madame de, 78, 78n
Westminster Abbey (London), 135
Wharton, Edith,
   automobile travel with James, 314n
William of Prussia, King, 67n
Winckelmann, Johann Joachim, 177n, 188,
     188n
Winner, Viola Hopkins, xxxii
Wister, Owen, 185n
Wister, Sarah Butler, xxxiv, 185, 185n, 188
wolf of Rome, 127, 127n
Woman's Christian Temperance Union, 92n
Woolson, Constance Fenimore, 27n
   death in Venice, xx, 172n
   grave in Rome, 172n, 173n
Wordsworth, William,
   "On the Extinction of the Venetian Repub-
       lic," xvii, 68–69, 69n
   "The Pine of Monte Mario at Rome,"
       182, 182n
   "She was a Phantom of delight," 220,
       220n
World War II bombing, 108n, 152n, 205n,
     241n
Worth of Paris, 142, 142n
Wright, Nathalia, xxxii

Zhukovsky, Paul, 315n
Zola, Émile, xxviii